Practical Guide to Land Registration Proceedings

First Edition

Practical Guide to Land Registration Proceedings

First Edition

Simon Brilliant LLB (Manchester) BCL (Oxon)
of the Middle Temple, Barrister
Judge of the First-tier Tribunal

Michael Michell MA (Oxon)
A Bencher of Lincoln's Inn
Judge of the First-tier Tribunal

LexisNexis®

Members of the LexisNexis Group worldwide

United Kingdom	LexisNexis, a Division of Reed Elsevier (UK) Ltd, Lexis House, 30 Farringdon Street, London, EC4A 4HH,, and London House, 20-22 East London Street, Edinburgh EH7 4BQ
United Kingdom	LexisNexis, a Division of Reed Elsevier (UK) Ltd, London House, 20-22 East London Street, Edinburgh EH7 4BQ and Lexis House, 30 Farringdon Street, London, EC4A 4HH
Australia	LexisNexis Butterworths, Chatswood, New South Wales
Austria	LexisNexis Verlag ARD Orac GmbH & Co KG, Vienna
Benelux	LexisNexis Benelux, Amsterdam
Canada	LexisNexis Canada, Markham, Ontario
China	LexisNexis China, Beijing and Shanghai
France	LexisNexis SA, Paris
Germany	LexisNexis GmbH, Dusseldorf
Hong Kong	LexisNexis Hong Kong, Hong Kong
India	LexisNexis India, New Delhi
Italy	Giuffrè Editore, Milan
Japan	LexisNexis Japan, Tokyo
Malaysia	Malayan Law Journal Sdn Bhd, Kuala Lumpur
New Zealand	LexisNexis NZ Ltd, Wellington
Singapore	LexisNexis Singapore, Singapore
South Africa	LexisNexis Butterworths, Durban
USA	LexisNexis, Dayton, Ohio

Published by LexisNexis

This is a Butterworths title

A CIP Catalogue record for this book is available from the British Library.

ISBN for this volume: 9781405795753

Printed and bound by Hobbs the Printers Ltd, Totton, Hampshire SO40 2WX.

Visit LexisNexis Butterworths at www.lexisnexis.co.uk

Dedication

To Edward Cousins, the Adjudicator to HM Land Registry and the Deputy Adjudicators who developed from the very beginning the jurisdiction in Land Registration disputes now vested in the Property Chamber

About the Authors

Simon Brilliant is a barrister and mediator in practice at Lamb Chambers, Temple, London. He specialises in property law. Having been a part-time Deputy Adjudicator to HM Land Registry since 2004, he became a fee-paid Judge of the Property Chamber of the First-tier Tribunal on 1 July 2013. He is editor of *Law of Limitation* published by Bloomsbury Professional and has contributed to titles in *Atkin's Court Forms*, also published by LexisNexis.

Michael Michell is a salaried judge of the Property Chamber of the First-tier Tribunal, sitting in the Land Registration division. From 1985 until 2009, he practiced at the Chancery Bar, specialising in property law. He was a part-time Deputy Adjudicator to HM Land Registry from 2005 to 2009 and a full-time Deputy Adjudicator from 2009, becoming a judge of the First-tier Tribunal on 1 July 2013. He is an experienced writer and lecturer on property law and a sometime contributing editor to *The Encyclopaedia of Financial Provision in Family Matters*.

Foreword by Lord Neuberger

In 2011, Simon Brilliant and Michael Michell published a book called 'A Practical Guide to Land Registry Adjudication', to which they kindly asked me to write a Foreword. In that Foreword, I referred to the great changes which had happened since 2002, when the Land Registration Act had been passed, and in particular how the newly created Adjudicators had been called on to decide a wholly unanticipated number of disputes, many of them raising points of fact and/or law of considerable difficulty. I also said that the Adjudicators (technically speaking, the Adjudicator and the Deputy Adjudicators) were performing their task with conspicuous ability.

The pace of change continues unabated. In July 2013, pursuant to regulations made under the Tribunals, Courts and Enforcement Act 2007, the post of Adjudicator was abolished and their functions were transferred to the newly created Property Chamber of the First-tier Tribunal, and the Adjudicator and the Deputy Adjudicators became judges of that Chamber and that Tribunal, with the Adjudicator also becoming a deputy judge of the Lands Chamber of the Upper Tribunal (which hears appeals from the First-tier Tribunal). While it may seem a shame that the post of Land Registry Adjudicator has been abolished and merged into the wider Courts and Tribunal Service after the Adjudicators had built up so much expertise and such a strong reputation in just a few years, it is an inevitable consequence of the rationalisation of the courts and tribunals system, and it has been accomplished in such a way as to ensure the advantage of a cadre of specialised and renowned experts in maintained at the same time as giving them the possibility of wider experience and of being able to draw from tribunal members with different experiences.

It is by no means only because of this important procedural change that this new book by Simon Brilliant and Michael Michell, 'A Practical Guide to Land Registry Proceedings' is to be welcomed. There have been a number of developments since 2011 in the procedural and substantive law which more than justify this new book. One only has to look through the Table of Cases to see how many significant decisions have been taken by the Adjudicators, the Chancery Judges and the Court of Appeal to appreciate how the 2002 Act and its consequences have resulted in legal principles and procedural rules being established and refined.

The authors have also taken the opportunity to cast their net rather wider than in their previous book, in that they deal with the substantive law relating to land registration more fully, which must be of real benefit to those involved in land registry proceedings, whether lawyers or lay people. Like its predecessor, the authors of this book have always had in mind the need for comprehensive, clear and practical advice, and both the structure of the book and its contents are user-friendly as well as being authoritative. It also seems to me to be a good idea, for instance, to have a chapter which gives 'tips' on particularly difficult types of case (Chapter 22), to include 'procedural table and check lists' at the end of the very full and helpful appendices.

This is a worthy successor to the authors' previous book, and it is a book which anyone who wishes to know about, or is involved with, land registration, and in particular disputes or potential disputes involving registered land, would be very well advised to consult.

David Neuberger

Supreme Court of the United Kingdom
November 2014

Foreword by Siobhan McGrath

I am pleased to have been asked to write a foreword for this second edition of the Practical Guide to Land Registration Proceedings. Issues of property ownership and rights in and over property engender strong feelings. Disputes can be hard fought and hard felt.

The Guide provides a timely and practical overview of land registration and dispute resolution. In July 2013 the First-tier Tribunal (Property Chamber) was created. Its jurisdictions include those previously conducted by the Adjudicator to the Land Registry. We are now eighteen months into the new regime and this is a good point at which to reflect on and to explain the Chamber's procedures. The authors are both judges in the jurisdiction and therefore very familiar with the day to day workings of the Tribunal. This brings an important perspective to the work.

The style of the book is very attractive. Propositions are explained by reference to practical examples which give context and substance to sometimes heady concepts. In particular Chapter 22 very helpfully gives tips on particular cases. The approach assists to make law and procedure accessible. For parties, ultimately it is the end result of litigation that is important and comprehensive coverage is given not only to decisions, appeals and the new power to review but also to settlements, withdrawal and mediation.

The strength of this work lies both in its clarity and in the attention to detail. I have not doubt that for all those involved in disputes or appeal before the Land Registration division of the Property Chamber, the guide will be an invaluable source of essential knowledge and information.

Siobhan McGrath

President – First-tier Tribunal (Property Chamber)
November 2014

Preface

On 1 July 2013 the Adjudicator to HM Land Registry was abolished and his functions were transferred to the newly created, Property Chamber of the First-tier Tribunal. The Property Chamber comprises three divisions, Residential Property, Agricultural Land and Drainage and Land Registration. The Adjudicator and his Deputies were transferred into the First-tier Tribunal as judges assigned to the Property Chamber, where they formed the judicial element of the Land Registration division. Though the judiciary is the same, the practice and procedure in the Land Registration division is somewhat different from that of the Adjudicator. The Tribunal Procedure (First-tier Tribunal) (Property Chamber) Rules 2013 contain some rules applicable to all divisions of the Property Chamber and some applicable to only one division. The Rules are supplemented by practice directions applicable to Land Registration division proceedings. We have attempted to provide a clear guide to practice and procedure in the Land Registration division, providing a route map through the relevant rules and practice directions while also exploring the extent and limitations of the jurisdiction. Our aim is to assist all those who may find themselves involved in proceedings concerning land registration or registered land, whether involving a disputed application, a claim to rectify or set aside a document connected with land registration or a challenge to a decision of Land Registry. We have sought to state the law as at 1 October 2014.

We are indebted to the staff of LexisNexis who are responsible for guiding the production of this book to a successful conclusion.

We are also indebted to the many colleagues, both judicial and administrative, who have advised us in the course of producing this book and contributed many ideas.

Simon Brilliant

Michael Michell
London
November 2014

Contents

Key to abbreviations and defined terms

For ease of reference some terms and acronyms have been adopted throughout to assist the reader. These are explained at the first reference in the text and as per the table below:

Adjudicator to HM Land Registry	the Adjudicator
Adjudicator to HM Land Registry (Practice and Procedure) Rules 2003	AR 2003
Chief Land Registrar	the Registrar
Civil Procedure Rules	CPR
HM Courts and Tribunals Service	HMCTS
HM Land Registry	Land Registry
Land Registration Act 2002	LRA 2002
Land Registration Rules 2003	LRR 2003
Network Access Appeal Rules 2008	NAAR 2008
Practice Directions for the Land Registration division of the Tribunal	PDLR
Tribunals, Courts and Enforcement Act 2007	TCEA 2007
Tribunal Procedure (First-tier Tribunal) (Property Chamber) Rules 2013	the Rules
The Tribunal Procedure (Upper Tribunal) Rules 2008	UTR 2008

Table of Statutes

Table of Statutory Instruments

Table of Cases

A

B

C

D

F

G

H

I

J

S

T

W

Y

Z

Chapter 1

INTRODUCTION

Key topics in this chapter

The origin of a specialist land registration jurisdiction
The Adjudicator
The demise of the Adjudicator
The Land Registration division of the Property Chamber of the First-tier Tribunal
Transitional cases
Appeals from Land Registry concerning network access agreements
Free-Standing applications for the rectification or setting aside of certain documents relating to registered land
The types of cases heard by the Adjudicator
The types of cases heard by the Tribunal
The advantages of using the Tribunal

THE ORIGIN OF A SPECIALIST LAND REGISTRATION JURISDICTION

1.1 In 2003 the whole law of land registration was reformed and modernised by the coming into force of the Land Registration Act 2002 ('LRA 2002'). This Act was the result of six years' work by the Law Commission and HM Land Registry ('Land Registry').

Prior to the coming into force of LRA 2002 the Solicitor to HM Land Registry had jurisdiction to determine contested applications to the Chief Land Registrar ('the Registrar'). Since issues could arise which involved decisions of Land Registry officials, or which might lead Land Registry open to pay an indemnity, it was felt by the Law Commission and Land Registry that he might be perceived not to be independent. Accordingly, his judicial role was abolished and there was created a new judicial office known as the Adjudicator to HM Land Registry ('the Adjudicator').

The Adjudicator's office was in existence between 13 October 2003 and 1 July 2013 when his functions were transferred to the Property Chamber of the First-tier Tribunal.

THE ADJUDICATOR

1.2 The title of the Adjudicator was an unfortunate one for two reasons. In the first place it suggested that he had some connection with, or was part of, Land Registry, whereas he was entirely independent of Land Registry. Secondly, the term 'adjudication' has become associated with the informal dispute resolution procedure in place since 1996 in the construction industry, whereas the Adjudicator conducted a full scale hearing in a manner similar to a County Court case.

The jurisdiction of the Adjudicator was considerably wider than that of the Solicitor to HM Land Registry and the Adjudicator's caseload was significantly heavier. It soon became recognised that the part played by the Adjudicator in the determination of property disputes was greater than had been anticipated by the Law Commission and Land Registry when proposing the setting up of the office. In many cases the Adjudicator became used as an alternative to the courts.

The Adjudicator operated under his own procedural rules known as the Adjudicator to HM Land Registry (Practice and Procedure) Rules 2003 ('AR 2003'). These have now been revoked. But they may still apply, particularly on the question of costs, in transitional cases which commenced before 1 July 2013. For this reason they have been included in this book at **APPENDIX 6**.

The Adjudicator during the entirety of the office was Mr Edward Cousins. There were appointed by him three full time deputies and 29 part time ones. They were members of his staff, but had complete judicial independence. AR 2003, r 61 provided that when undertaking a non-administrative function of the Adjudicator on the Adjudicator's authorisation, a member of the Adjudicator' staff was not subject to the direction of the Lord Chancellor or any other person or body.

For the sake of convenience references to the Adjudicator in this work include references to the deputies as well, save where the context indicates otherwise.

THE DEMISE OF THE ADJUDICATOR

1.3 In 2006 the Tribunals Service was created. This followed Sir Andrew Leggatt's review of the tribunal system, entitled 'Tribunals for Users: One System, One Service', which was published in 2001. The report criticised the existing system. Some tribunals were not independent of the administrative bodies over which they were supposed to exert control. There was no uniformity of administration between the different tribunals.

The Tribunals, Courts and Enforcement Act 2007 ('TCEA 2007') created the First-tier Tribunal and the Upper Tribunal. Numerous decision-making bodies which were formerly entirely separate have been brought together within either the Upper Tribunal or the First-tier Tribunal.

Each Tribunal is divided into a number of separate Chambers. Within the Upper Tribunal is the Lands Chamber which has superseded the old Lands Tribunal.

Prior to 1 July 2013 there were six Chambers in the First-tier Tribunal, namely (1) the General Regulatory Chamber, (2) the Health, Education and Social Care Chamber, (3) the Immigration and Asylum Chamber, (4) the Social Entitlement Chamber, (5) the Tax Chamber and (6) the War Pensions and Armed Forces Compensation Chamber.

On 1 July 2013 the Property Chamber was brought into being. By the First-tier Tribunal and Upper Tribunal (Chambers) (Amendment) Order 2013, which is set out in APPENDIX 7, the Property Chamber was added to the list of First-tier Tribunal Chambers in the First-tier Tribunal and Upper Tribunal (Chambers) Order 2010.

At the same time, the Transfer of Tribunal Functions Order 2013, which is set out, where relevant, in **APPENDIX 8**:

- amended LRA 2002, so that the references in it to the Adjudicator were replaced by references to the First-tier Tribunal;
- transferred the functions of the Adjudicator to the First-tier Tribunal;
- abolished the Adjudicator;
- revoked AR 2003;
- conferred on the Adjudicator himself the office of a transferred-in judge of the First-tier Tribunal and deputy judge of the Upper Tribunal;
- conferred on each deputy Adjudicator the office of a transferred-in judge of the First-tier Tribunal;
- made transitional arrangements in respect of proceedings before the Adjudicator which were pending immediately before 1 July 2013.

THE LAND REGISTRATION DIVISION OF THE PROPERTY CHAMBER OF THE FIRST-TIER TRIBUNAL

1.4 The First-tier Tribunal and Upper Tribunal (Chambers) (Amendment) Order 2013 allocates all functions relating to land registration matters conferred on the First-tier Tribunal under LRA 2002 to the Property Chamber, and provides that an appeal in any such case is to be a function of the Tax and Chancery Chamber of the Upper Tribunal.

The Property Chamber is administered by the merged HM Courts and Tribunals Service ('HMCTS'). HMCTS is an executive agency of the Ministry of Justice, and its mission statement is to provide for a fair, efficient and effective justice system delivered by an independent judiciary.

The work of the staff involves opening a file for each new case, dealing with correspondence with the parties and the directions issued by the Tribunal, all of which are retained on the appropriate file, and making arrangements for the convenient listing of hearings.

The Transfer of Tribunal Functions Order 2013 did not just transfer the functions of the Adjudicator to the First-tier Tribunal. It also transferred to the First-tier Tribunal the functions of:

- The Residential Property Tribunal Service, which included:
  - Rent Tribunals;
  - Rent Assessment Committees;
  - Leasehold Valuation Tribunals;
  - Residential Property Tribunals.
- Agricultural Lands Tribunals.

The Order also abolished Rent Assessment Committees and Agricultural Lands Tribunals.

The First-tier Tribunal and Upper Tribunal (Chambers) (Amendment) Order 2013 also allocates all functions relating to the Residential Property Tribunal Service and Agricultural Lands Tribunals conferred on the First-tier Tribunal to the Property Chamber, and provides that an appeal in any such case is to be a function of the Lands Chamber of the Upper Tribunal.

For administrative purposes the Property Chamber of the First-tier Tribunal is divided into three separate divisions to reflect these three different jurisdictions:

- Land Registration;
- Residential Property;
- Agricultural Land and Drainage.

Each division has a Principal Judge. The first Principal Judge of the Land Registration division was Mr Cousins, who had been the Adjudicator. The deputy Adjudicators each became a transferred-in judge of the First-tier Tribunal.

This book is principally concerned with the Land Registration division, although CHAPTER 5 looks at the Chamber as a whole. Save where the context indicates otherwise, all references in this book to "the Tribunal" are references to the Land Registration division of the Property Chamber of the First-tier Tribunal.

The rules which govern the procedure of the Tribunal are the Tribunal Procedure (First-tier Tribunal) (Property Chamber) Rules 2013 ('the Rules 2013'). They are generic rules for the whole of the Property Chamber and therefore cover the Residential Property and Agricultural Land and Drainage divisions as well as the Land Registration division. However, Rules 37-40 are specific only to land registration cases. The Rules 2013 will be found in **APPENDIX 9**.

The Senior President of Tribunals, Sir Jeremy Sullivan, has issued Practice Directions for the Land Registration division of the Tribunal ('PDLR'), which will be found in **APPENDIX 11**.

Since the Tribunal has, in respect of its statutory jurisdiction, stepped into the shoes of the Adjudicator, decisions about the statutory jurisdiction of the Adjudicator are still of direct relevance to the powers and function of the Tribunal and several decisions about the statutory jurisdiction of the Adjudicator will be cited in this book. Decisions about the procedural powers of the Adjudicator under AR 2003 are of less significance now as the Rules 2013 are in some respects very different to the earlier rules, but where the rules are similar such decisions will again be cited.

Although the Tribunal deals exclusively with land registration matters, the Tribunal is entirely independent of Land Registry: this was the whole point of the Adjudicator's office being created. Practitioners should be astute to advise their clients of this fact. Neighbour disputes give rise to strong passions, and often a client who has corresponded at length with Land Registry prior to taking legal advice will have developed a sense of grievance with officialdom. Justice is more likely to be seen to be done if it is appreciated that the body which will determine the matter is truly independent.

The passions which a boundary dispute can arise are illustrated by *Pius v Fearnley* [2013] EWHC 2216 (Ch). Dr Pius applied to Land Registry to alter the register by having a small piece of disputed land removed from his neighbours' title. The dispute was referred to the Adjudicator, and those proceedings were then stayed pending parallel court proceedings. Dr Pius lost the court proceedings and the Adjudicator consequently directed the Registrar to cancel his application to Land Registry. Subsequently, Dr Pius sued the Registrar, Mr Fearnley (who as well as being a distinguished contributor to Atkins' Encyclopaedia of Forms and Precedents dealt with the application at Land Registry), the Adjudicator, Lambeth County Court, Central London County Court, the Court of Appeal, six individual judges who had dealt with the case and his neighbours.

Not entirely surprisingly, Roth J struck the actions out. As far as the Adjudicator was concerned the judge said that he did not have sufficient evidence before him about the Adjudicator's procedures to determine whether he was entitled to absolute immunity at common law on the same basis as a judge. It is submitted that had he been provided with a fuller explanation of the Adjudicator's procedures the judge would undoubtedly have found that the Adjudicator was entitled to absolute immunity. As it was, the judge determined that the process of challenging a decision of the Adjudicator was by way of an appeal pursuant to LRA 2002, s 111, so that it was an abuse of process to bring a personal claim against the Adjudicator.

The independence of the Tribunal from Land Registry also means that the Tribunal will not have seen many documents or items of correspondence which will have been before the Registrar prior to a dispute being referred to it. Parties wishing to rely on such documents or items of correspondence will need to send further copies directly to the Tribunal. It cannot be assumed that the Tribunal will have been provided with them by Land Registry.

Although the Tribunal is entirely independent of Land Registry, LRA 2002, s 108(5), as amended empowers the Lord Chancellor to require the Registrar to make payments towards the Lord Chancellor's expenses in support of the functions conferred on the Tribunal in respect of land registration matters.

The Tribunal is a listed tribunal for the purposes of TCEA 2007. By virtue of this, the Tribunal falls within the definition of a court for the purposes of the Courts and Legal Services Act 1990 and the Legal Services Act 2007. This means that rights of audience and the conduct of litigation before the Tribunal fall within the scope of the Legal Services Act 2007. The Litigants in Person (Costs and Expenses) Act 1975 applies to proceedings before the Tribunal.

As we shall see, most of the work of the Land Registration division of the Tribunal is referred to it directly by Land Registry. It is not begun by the parties themselves. This aspect of procedure does not, therefore, fit easily into a generic model which presupposes cases are being begun by the parties themselves, which is the norm in the Residential Property and Agricultural Land and Drainage divisions. So the start of the procedure in land registration cases is rather clumsy, as we shall see when we look at Rules 26-30 in more detail in due course. Apart from this, the Rules 2013 provide a satisfactory and sensible framework and the rules are similar, but by no means identical, to the Civil Procedure Rules 1998 ('CPR 1998'), with which practitioners will be familiar.

One distinction is that the overriding objective in Rule 3, and the rule about what is to happen if a party has failed to comply with a requirement of a rule or a direction in Rule 8(2), differ from the post Jackson amendments to CPR 1998. In *Leeds City Council v Revenue and Customs Comrs* [2014] UKUT 0350 (TCC) it was held that as the overriding objective applicable in the Upper Tribunal (which is worded identically to the overriding objective applicable in the Tribunal) differs from the post Jackson overriding objective in CPR 1998, the Upper Tribunal is not to take the same approach to a failure to comply with a requirement of a rule or direction as the courts are now required to do by the decision of the Court of Appeal in *Mitchell v News Group Newspapers* [2013] EWCA Civ 1537, [2014] 2 All ER 430, [2014] 1 WLR 795 and the cases following it.

Accordingly, the Tribunal has not been beset with the problems arising from *Mitchell*. Many practitioners will regard this distinction as being a fortunate one.

One matter to regret is that the Tribunal Procedure Committee did not include any provision akin to CPR 1998, Part 21 for the appointment of a litigation friend for a protected party, that is to say a party who lacks the capacity to conduct the proceedings. This means that if the Tribunal is concerned that a party lacks capacity, it will be driven to direct that court proceedings be commenced pursuant to its powers under LRA 2002, s 110, as amended, or direct the proceedings to be transferred pursuant to its powers under Rule r 6(3)(n).

The Tribunal should not be confused with the separate specialist property tribunal, formerly known as the Lands Tribunal, whose functions were transferred to the Lands Chamber of the Upper Tribunal in 2009.

TRANSITIONAL CASES

1.5 The Rules 2013 replace AR 2003 which have been revoked, but are to be found in APPENDIX 6, because they are still relevant in transitional cases where proceedings were already before the Adjudicator on 1 July 2013. Such proceedings automatically continued as proceedings before the Tribunal: see the Transfer of Tribunal Functions Order 2013, Art 6(3) para 1.

Art 6(3) para 3 provides that in respect of such proceedings, the Tribunal may give any direction to ensure that they are dealt with fairly. In particular, the Tribunal may:

- apply any provision in AR 2003;
- dis-apply provisions in the Rules 2013.

Costs apart, it is unlikely with the passage of time that any current transitional cases will be dealt with other than in accordance with the Rules 2013.

As far as costs are concerned, it is expressly provided by Art 6(3) para 7 that in a transitional case an order for costs may only be made if, and to the extent that, an order could have been made before 1 July 2013. Accordingly, costs in transitional cases will be governed by AR 2003, rr 42 and 43 and not by Rule 13 and PDLR para 9.

DISPUTED APPLICATIONS REFERRED BY LAND REGISTRY

1.6 The Tribunal has three quite separate jurisdictions. The first jurisdiction is to determine disputed applications referred by Land Registry. This forms the vast bulk of the work before the Tribunal. There are over 1,000 of such references annually. Note that a party cannot bring a dispute directly to the Tribunal under this jurisdiction.

There are many circumstances in which a person may make an application to Land Registry. Procedures exist whereby someone who is affected by such an application may object to the application. We consider this in more detail in CHAPTER 3, but the following are typical examples:

EXAMPLE 1

A and B live together as partners in a house of which B is the sole registered proprietor. The relationship breaks down and the parties separate. A claims a beneficial interest in the house on the basis of a common intention constructive trust: see *Oxley v Hiscock* [2004] EWCA Civ 546, [2005] Fam 211, [2004] 3 All ER 703, CA, *Stack v Dowden* [2007] UKHL 17, [2007] 2 AC 432, [2007] 2 All ER 929, HL and *Jones v Kernott* [2011] UKSC 53, SC, [2012] 1 AC 776, [2012] 1 All ER 1265. A applies to the Registrar to enter a restriction in the register of B's title to protect her beneficial interest. B disputes that A has any such interest and objects to the application.

EXAMPLE 2

A and B are neighbours. A claims to have acquired a right of way on foot by prescription over B's back garden to reach a road the other side of B's house. A applies to the Registrar to be registered as the proprietor of an easement acquired otherwise than by express grant or reservation: see the Land Registration Rules 2003 ('LRR 2003'), r 73A(1)(b). B accepts that the route has been used for the time alleged, but claims he has always given permission for it to be used and objects to the application.

EXAMPLE 3

A is a property developer. B is the registered proprietor of a disused factory. A enters into a contract to purchase the factory and enters a unilateral notice on the register of B's title to protect his interest. B claims to rescind the contract under the conditions of sale and applies to the Registrar to cancel the unilateral notice: see LRA 2002, s 36. A denies that the contract has been rescinded and objects to the application.

In each of these cases, provided the objection is not groundless, the Registrar may not determine the application until the objection has been disposed of: see LRA 2002, s 73(5), (6). If the parties are unable to dispose of the objection by agreement, then the Registrar must refer the matter to the Tribunal: see LRA 2002, s 73(7), as amended. It is the function of the Tribunal to determine matters referred to it under s 73(7): see LRA 2002, s 108(1)(a), as amended.

The Tribunal usually carries out its function – after coming to its decision – by directing the Registrar either:

- to give effect to the application made to the Registrar, which is known as the 'original application', as if the objection had not been made,
- or to cancel the original application.

The Tribunal does not make any other kind of order, such as an injunction, an order for specific performance, a declaration or an award of damages.

The Court of Appeal has confirmed that, in performing this function, the Tribunal has jurisdiction to determine the underlying merits of the substantive dispute between the parties in a judicial capacity: *Chief Land Registrar v Silkstone* [2011] EWCA Civ 801, [37],CA, [2012] 1 WLR 400, [2011] 2 P & CR 258, approving *Jayasinghe v Liyanage* [2010] EWHC 265 (Ch), [2010] 1 WLR 2106, [2010] 1 EGLR 61. It is not the function of the Tribunal just to act administratively and give temporary relief to an Applicant who can show an apparently arguable, or non-fanciful, claim prior to the matter being determined judicially in court.

In *Garwood (trustee of the estate in bankruptcy of Adekunbi Ibrahim Fabumni-Stone) v Bank of Scotland plc* [2013] EWHC 415 (Ch), [2013] All ER (D) 14 (Mar) the court rejected an argument that the Adjudicator's jurisdiction in respect of references given by LRA s 108(1) was in any way limited by the wholly separate free standing jurisdiction to rectify or set aside documents given by LRA s 108(2).

In example 1 given above the Tribunal will conduct a full hearing to decide whether or not A can demonstrate that she has a beneficial interest in the house. The Tribunal will search to ascertain the parties' shared intentions, actual, inferred or imputed, with respect to the property in the light of their whole course of conduct in relation to it. This is the same task as the judge would embark on if A brought an application in court under the Trusts of Land and Appointment of Trustees Act 1996, s 14. The same evidence will be needed.

We shall see in CHAPTER 8 that the Tribunal may, instead of deciding a matter itself, direct a party to commence court proceedings. We shall also see in CHAPTER 11 that the Tribunal may itself transfer the proceedings before it to a court. Although the Tribunal in a beneficial interest case may quantify the respective interest of each party if the Applicant succeeds, there is no power given to the Tribunal to order a sale of the property. This is to be contrasted with the powers of the court where an application has been brought under the Trusts of Land and Appointment of Trustees Act 1996, s 14. For this reason the Tribunal will in a beneficial interest case sometimes direct court proceedings to be commenced instead, or might use its power to order a transfer of the proceedings to a court.

In example 2 above the Tribunal will be concerned with the substantive law of prescription, including the Prescription Act 1832 and the doctrine of lost modern grant. In example 3 above the Tribunal will be concerned with the contract law relating to the sale and purchase of commercial property.

In some cases the power of the Registrar and that of the court under LRA 2002 are expressed to be different. The Tribunal's role on a reference is to consider how the Registrar should exercise his powers. So in the case of proceedings before the Tribunal it is the Registrar's powers and not those of the court which are relevant.

> **EXAMPLE 4**
>
> A is the registered proprietor of a house. B forges A's signature to a transfer of the house to C. C is registered as sole proprietor of the house. A applies to the Registrar to alter the register by removing C as proprietor and restoring herself as the proprietor.
>
> Both the Registrar and the court have jurisdiction to alter the register for a mistake. If C objects to A's application and the matter is referred to the Tribunal, the jurisdiction of the Tribunal is to be found in LRA 2002, s 65, Sch 4 para 5 (alteration otherwise than pursuant to a court order) rather than in Sch 4 para 4 (alteration pursuant to a court order).
>
> There is no reason why the Tribunal should not hear a forgery case such as in this example, and frequently it does do so. There is no need for such an issue to be determined in court. The Tribunal will give directions for expert handwriting evidence.

A party cannot unilaterally bring a reference to an end. Rules 22(1) enables a party to give notice of the withdrawal of its case, but Rule 22(3) provides that the withdrawal will not be effective unless the Tribunal consents to it. If, following a reference, a party wishes to withdraw the original application or the objection to it the Tribunal has a discretion. It can permit the withdrawal, make an appropriate direction to the Registrar and deal with costs. Alternatively, it can proceed to a substantive hearing, rule upon the merits of the dispute and then make such orders as are appropriate: *The Chief Land Registrar v Silkstone* [2011] EWCA Civ 801, [48]-[50],CA.

We describe how a reference to the Tribunal is made in CHAPTER **6**. In CHAPTERS **7-21** we consider in detail the various stages of the procedure before the Tribunal following a reference, starting from what happens when a reference is received through to appeals and stays of execution. In CHAPTER **22** we consider particularly popular types of cases, such adverse possession, alteration of the register, beneficial interests, boundary disputes, charging orders, forgeries and prescriptive easements.

It should be noted that the Tribunal has no jurisdiction in a dispute between one party only and the Registrar. If the Registrar refuses to entertain an application at all or decides that an objection is groundless there is no dispute between the parties to be referred to the Tribunal, and the only remedy of the party is by way of judicial review: see Law Commission Report 271 (July 2001) paras 16.7, 16.14.

For an early example, see *R v Vice-Registrar of Land Registry Office* (1889) 24 QBD 178, where the court refused to issue a writ of mandamus compelling Land Registry to register certain expenses incurred by a local authority under the Public Health Act 1875, s 257 as 'land charges' within the meaning of the Land Charges Registration and Searches Act 1888, as such charges were not intended to be registered.

For modern examples, see:

- *R (on the application of Smith) v Land Registry*, [2010] EWCA (Civ) 200, [2011] QB 413, [2010] 3 All ER 113, where a party unsuccessfully challenged by way of judicial review Land Registry's refusal to grant a title by adverse possession to part of the public highway.
- *R (on the application of Baker) v Land Registry* [2009] EWHC 3880 (Admin), where in the course of an unsuccessful challenge to a decision of the Adjudicator directing the Applicant to commence court proceedings (an appeal should have been sought instead) the Applicant was refused disclosure of the tape from which the transcript of the hearing before the Adjudicator was made. For the eventual court proceedings, see *Line v Baker* [2014] EWHC 1368 (Ch), [2014] All ER (D) 42 (May).
- *R (on the application of Diep) v Land Registry* [2010] EWHC 3315 (Admin), (2011) Times, 09 March, where a party who was dissatisfied with the class of title granted to him unsuccessfully applied for judicial review.
- *R (on the application of Kornhauser) v Land Registry* [2012] EWHC 751 (Admin), where an assured tenant of a flat unsuccessfully challenged by way of judicial review Land Registry's refusal to register him as the freehold proprietor of the entire building. The tenant had relied upon the doctrine of 'interversion of possession' as explained in the 'American Law Register' of December 1861. The judge thought any land lawyer in this country would be astonished to hear of the doctrine and courteously remarked that he did not find anything in this learned article to change his views.
- *R (on the application of Palmer) v Land Registry* [2013] EWHC 1531 (Admin), where a party unsuccessfully challenged by way of judicial review Land Registry's refusal to cancel a registered charge over her house because the grounds put forward for cancelling the charge were hopeless. The application was also an abuse as the County Court had already made a possession order against her.
- *R (on the application of Heaton) v Land Registry* [2013] EWHC 2449 (Admin), where a grandson unsuccessfully challenged by way of judicial review Land Registry's refusal to close the title of the purchaser of his grandfather's house. The secondary evidence pointed inexorably to the purchaser having acquired a good title to the house and the grandson had never been in adverse possession of it, as he always lived there with consent.
- *R (on the application of DeVere) v Land Registry* [2013] EWHC 2477 (Admin), where a party unsuccessfully challenged by way of judicial review Land Registry's decision to give effect to a decision of the Adjudicator. The only remedy if the Adjudicator's decision was based on a legal error was for the party to appeal, but permission had already been refused because the proposed appeal had no prospect of success.
- *R (on the application of Best) v Chief Land Registrar (Secretary of State for Justice, interested party)* [2014] EWHC 1370 (Admin), [2014] 3 All ER 637, [2014] PLSCS 141, where the court held that the criminalising of trespass by 'living in' a residential building, pursuant

to Legal Aid, Sentencing and Punishment of Offenders Act 2012, s 144(1) did not prevent time running for applications for registration of title by adverse possession.

Judicial review of the Registrar's decisions is dealt with in CHAPTER 4.

APPEALS FROM LAND REGISTRY CONCERNING NETWORK ACCESS AGREEMENTS

1.7 The Tribunal's second jurisdiction is an appellate one. The Tribunal hears appeals from Land Registry concerning network access agreements, which are an essential part of e-conveyancing.

A person who is not a member of Land Registry only has access to a land registry network under authority conferred by means of an agreement with the Registrar. Such an agreement is known as a 'network access agreement': see LRA 2002, s 92, Sch 5 para 1.

An e-conveyancer will require a full network access agreement, which is a network access agreement which permits the subscriber to carry out network transactions. If the applicant meets the criteria set out in the Land Registration (Network Access) Rules 2008, the Registrar must enter into a network access agreement with him. The Registrar can only terminate a full network access agreement on one of several specified grounds.

The refusal to enter into a network access agreement or the termination of a network access agreement will be an extremely serious matter for the person concerned, who will not be able to carry out conveyancing work. A person who is aggrieved by a decision of the Registrar with respect to entry into, or termination of, a network access agreement may appeal against the decision to the Tribunal: see LRA 2002, s 108 (1)(b), as amended, Sch 5 para 4(1), as amended.

Procedure on network access agreement appeals to the Tribunal is also governed by the Rules 2013. We consider network access agreement appeals in CHAPTER 23.

FREE-STANDING APPLICATIONS FOR THE RECTIFICATION OR SETTING ASIDE OF CERTAIN DOCUMENTS RELATING TO REGISTERED LAND

1.8 The Tribunal's third jurisdiction is a free-standing independent jurisdiction, wholly separate from its jurisdiction to determine matters referred to it by the Registrar, to rectify or set aside certain documents connected with land registration: see LRA 2002, s 108(2), as amended. This is the only original jurisdiction of the Tribunal. An application can be made directly to the Tribunal. No prior application to Land Registry is needed. Indeed, the Registrar has no jurisdiction to rectify documents. Rectification of documents is not to be confused with alteration or rectification of the register, although the rectification of a document may be the prelude to a subsequent alteration or rectification of the register.

The jurisdiction is restricted to a document which:

- effects a qualifying disposition of a registered estate or charge;
- is a contract to make such a disposition; or
- effects the transfer of an interest which is the subject of a notice in the register.

A qualifying disposition is either a registrable disposition (for example, a transfer of the freehold) or a disposition which creates an interest which may be the subject of a notice in the register (for example, a right of way): see LRA 2002, s 108(3).

EXAMPLE 5

A contracts to sell his flat to B (Guernsey) Ltd. By mistake the transferee in panel 5 of the transfer form TR1 is named as B (Jersey) Ltd. Land Registry registers B (Jersey) Ltd as that is the entity named in the transfer, and correctly refuses to alter the register as no mistake in registration has been made. A's solicitor writes to B (Jersey) Ltd asking for a transfer back, but receives no reply. What should B (Guernsey) Ltd's solicitor do?

B (Guernsey) Ltd can apply directly to the Tribunal for rectification of panel 5 of the transfer in order to substitute B (Guernsey) Ltd for B (Jersey) Ltd. Notice of the application will be given by the Tribunal to B (Jersey) Ltd which is entitled to object. If it does, the matter will be determined judicially by the Tribunal. For these purposes the Tribunal has the powers of the High Court and the Tribunal's order has the same effect as an order of the High Court. If rectified, the transfer can then be sent to Land Registry and the register corrected.

The procedure in the hearing of a rectification or setting aside case before the Tribunal is broadly similar to the procedure in a reference, and the Rules 2013 apply. We consider rectification and setting aside cases in CHAPTER **24**.

THE TYPES OF CASES HEARD BY THE TRIBUNAL

1.9 Because registration impinges on so many aspects of property law, a wide range of issues fall within the Tribunal's workload. The Tribunal routinely deals with adverse possession, beneficial interests, boundary disputes, charging orders, easements, forgeries, mortgages, alteration and rectification of the register, trustees in bankruptcy and undue influence. More esoteric areas such as lordships of the manor, riparian rights or public international law arise from time to time.

The value of the cases varies considerably. An easement can involve the right to place a dustbin in the back yard of a neighbour's terraced house or the right to walk across one of London's most valuable private squares. The amount of property in dispute can vary from an area the size of a broom cupboard to several hundred acres. Parties might appear by leading counsel or act as litigants in person. A hearing can last an hour to several days. The Tribunal is unlikely to decline jurisdiction and direct court proceedings just because of the value of the land or the complexity of the arguments.

THE ADVANTAGES OF USING THE TRIBUNAL

1.10 The Tribunal has become an important specialist property tribunal resolving a large number of disputes which would previously have gone to court.

Provided a dispute involves some change to the register, such as the addition, removal or alteration of an entry, an Applicant has no need to start court proceedings but can make an appropriate application to the Registrar. If there is an objection to the application the matter will be referred to the Tribunal for determination. But this route will not be so attractive if a party also wishes to claim damages or an injunction because these are matters outside the jurisdiction of the Tribunal.

Practitioners and the judiciary have welcomed the role of the Tribunal as a specialist property tribunal. All those who sit as judges in it are experienced practitioners in the areas of law covered by the jurisdiction. They enjoy the work, understand the care to detail that is often required and are appreciative of the highly charged emotional atmosphere that property litigation, particularly a boundary dispute, can engender. Cases are individually listed, trial bundles and skeletons are read in advance and a site view will be held in all cases where the layout of the land and what has happened on it is relevant.

The Court of Appeal has recognised the relevant expertise of those sitting in the Tribunal and has said that a measure of weighed deference should be accorded to the findings and conclusions in their reasoned decisions: *Wilkinson v Farmer* [2010] EWCA Civ 1148, [2010] All ER (D) 217 (Oct). This approach has been followed on a number of occasions, including *Drake v Fripp* [2011] EWCA Civ 1279, [2012] 1 P & CR 69, *Prashar v Tunbridge Wells Borough Council* [2012] EWHC 1734 (Ch), [2012] All ER (D) 230 (Jul) and *Orme v Lyons* [2012] EWHC 3308 (Ch).

There are no fees to be paid to the Tribunal in the course of a reference from Land Registry, a network access agreement appeal or an application to rectify or set aside a document. So court fees can be avoided. But clients should be warned from the outset that, unlike the Residential Property and Agricultural Land and Drainage divisions of the Tribunal, the Land Registration division is a costs jurisdiction and the loser will be expected to pay the winner's costs. We look at the question of costs in CHAPTER **19**. Although the parties are informed in the first letters sent out following a reference that it is a costs jurisdiction, many litigants do not appreciate that the costs of a contested hearing may amount to a five figure sum.

A final advantage is that there is, subject to permission, a statutory right of appeal to the Upper Tribunal: see LRA 2002, s 111(1), as amended, and TCEA 2007, s 11(1), (2). In respect of references by Land Registry and applications to rectify or set aside documents, the right of appeal is on the facts as well as the law.

Chapter 2

AN OVERVIEW OF THE LAND REGISTRATION SYSTEM IN ENGLAND AND WALES

Key topics in this Chapter

History of Land Registration
HM Land Registry
Fundamental principles of registration
The Register
What interests may be registered
First Registration
Classes of title
Dealings with a registered estate
Interests protected by entry on the Register
Overriding interests
Alteration of the Register
Indemnity

HISTORY

2.1 A register of title to property in the county of Middlesex (but excluding the City of London) operated from 1709. In 1857 the Royal Commission on Registration of Title proposed a system of registration administered by a central registry in London with district offices. This proposal led to the enactment of the Land Registration Act 1862, the first attempt to introduce a national system of land registration in England and Wales. The 1862 Act created HM Land Registry and introduced a voluntary national system of registration of freehold and long leasehold estates. Brent Spencer Follett, the first Chief Land Registrar, opened the Land Registry's first offices, at 34 Lincoln's Inn Fields, London, on 15 October 1862. Mr Follett had a staff of just six people and was paid £2,500 a year, at a time when the average labourer's wage was £40.

There were serious flaws with the system introduced by the 1862 Act, not least that once property was registered it was not compulsory to register any subsequent transactions, including a conveyance of the property. Thus it was possible for the person registered as the owner of a property to cease to be the owner while remaining on the register.

Attempts to improve the voluntary system were made in 1875 by the enactment of the Land Transfer Act 1875. An element of compulsory registration was first introduced in 1897 by the enactment of the Land Transfer Act 1897. However, it was left up to each county council to decide whether to introduce compulsory registration into its county.

London County Council voted in favour of compulsory registration and it was introduced in stages within the London County Council area between 1899 and 1902. This led to the expansion of the Land Registry. At this time the first female staff were employed and new technology, in the form of typewriters, was introduced. From 1905 to 1913 new Land Registry headquarters were built in Lincoln's Inn Fields.

The present system was enacted by the Land Registration Act 1925 but the designation of areas as areas of compulsory registration proceeded slowly. Eastbourne and Hastings voluntarily decided to become areas of compulsory registration in 1926 and 1929 respectively. Compulsory registration was extended to Middlesex in 1937 and to the County Borough of Croydon in 1939. Compulsory registration was extended to the remainder of England and Wales in stages after the end of the Second World War. The last order designating an area as an area of compulsory registration was made in 1990. Initially under the 1925 Act land became compulsorily registrable only when it was the subject of certain transactions for value. In April 1998 unregistered land became registrable when it changed ownership after death and in the same year, it became compulsory to register land when a mortgage of it was created.

The Land Registration Act 2002 leaves the 1925 system substantially in place but enables the future compulsory introduction of electronic conveyancing using electronic signatures to transfer and charge property and to register property and charges.

HM LAND REGISTRY

2.2 The registration of property under the Land Registration Act 2002 is carried out by HM Land Registry. Land Registry is a non-ministerial government department, an executive agency and a government trading fund. It used to report to the Lord Chancellor's Department, then the Ministry of Justice but since 18 July 2011 it has reported to the Department for Business, Innovation and Skills.

Land Registry receives no government funding and finances itself from registration and search fees. Land Registry is required to ensure that its income covers its expenditure.

The organisation is led by the Chief Land Registrar and Chief Executive (both one role). The Chief Land Registrar is assisted by the Land Registry Board and Executive Board. The Land Registry Board sets the overall strategy for the department. The Executive Board delivers the annual business plan and is responsible for day to day management

Land Registry's Head Office has been based in Croydon since 2011. The purpose-built headquarters building erected in Lincoln's Inn Fields between 1905 and 1913 was sold to the London School of Economics.

Land Registry has 14 offices at: Birkenhead, Coventry, Croydon, Durham, Fylde (Warton), Gloucester, Kingston upon Hull, Leicester, Nottingham, Peterborough, Plymouth, Swansea, Telford and Weymouth. The in-house IT department (Information Systems) and Land Charges Departments are based in Plymouth

Each local office has an Area Manager (sometimes shared between offices), a Land Registrar who is the senior lawyer in the office, an Operations Manager, and an Integrity Manager. Each office also has staff responsible for processing applications lodged by members of the legal profession and the public.

Each office traditionally deals with applications concerning land located in a distinct geographical area. However, since 2009 teams have been set up to deal with applications from particular applicants, such as banks and building societies, regardless of where the property to which the application relates is located.

As of August 2012, there were over 23 million registered titles representing 80 per cent of the land mass of England and Wales. Much of the remaining unregistered land is rural property in the hands of large institutional landowners such as the Church of England, educational institutions and the Crown.

During the peak of the property boom in 2007, £1 million worth of property was processed every minute in England and Wales

Since December 1990, the Land Register has been open to the public to inspect for a fee.

FUNDAMENTAL PRINCIPLES OF LAND REGISTRATION

2.3 Theodore Ruoff, who was appointed Chief Land Registrar in 1963, laid down what he considered to be the three fundamental principles of Land Registration:

- The Mirror principle — the register of title should reflect, accurately and completely, and beyond all argument, the facts that are material to the title
- The Curtain principle — the register should be the sole and definitive source of information for proposing purchasers, but should not reveal sensitive information
- The Insurance principle — if, as a result of human error, the title is proved to be defective in any way, then the person or persons suffering loss as a result must be able to claim compensation

It will be apparent from the outline of the system set out below that it does not completely satisfy the principles. In particular, the curtain principle is not wholly satisfied because a proposing purchaser may be bound by certain matters not appearing on the register. There are serious limitations on the application of the insurance principle because of the restricted circumstances in which an indemnity is payable where the title proves to be defective.

THE REGISTER

2.4 The register is made up of individual registers of registered estates. The vast majority of registered estates are estates in land but there are also registered rent charges, manors, franchises and profits a prendre in gross. Each registered estate is given its own title number.

Each individual register is made up of three parts; the property register, the proprietorship register and the charges register.

The Property Register contains a description of the registered estate by reference to the title plan. The title plan is based on an Ordnance Survey map. Unless a boundary has been determined under LRA 2002 s 60(3), the title plan will show only general boundaries and not the exact position of the boundaries.

The Property Register will also include reference to rights benefiting the registered estate, such as easements and covenants. It will also include details of any defect in title discovered by the Registrar.

The Proprietorship Register contains the name of the registered proprietor and an address for service. It will also include details of the quality of title with which the property is registered.

The Charges Register records interests adverse to the registered estate, such as charges, restrictive covenants, and leases and easements to which the registered land is subject.

WHAT INTERESTS MAY BE REGISTERED

2.5 All freehold estates may be registered.

All leases which at the date of the transfer or grant have a term remaining to run of more than 7 years must be registered – see LRA 2002 s 3(3).

Some shorter leases are required to be registered. These are:

- leases which take effect in possession more than three months after the date of the grant; and
- leases in which the right to possession is discontinuous eg timeshare leases – see LRA 2002 s 3(3) and (4).

Other legal interests that may be registered are:

- rentcharges,
- franchises
- profits a prendre in gross
- charges by way of legal mortgage
- easements and
- other interests or charges which benefit or burden any registered estate or interest.

COMPULSORY FIRST REGISTRATION

2.6 First registration is required when the following dealings with an unregistered estate occur, namely

- the transfer of an unregistered freehold estate;
- the transfer, whether or not for value, of an unregistered leasehold estate with more than 7 years to run at the date of transfer;
- the grant out of an unregistered estate of a lease which is for a term of more than 7 years;
- the grant out of an unregistered estate of a lease which is for a term to take effect more than three months from the date of the grant;

- the grant out of an unregistered estate of a lease in which the right to possession is discontinuous;
- the creation of a first legal mortgage protected by deposit of title deeds over an unregistered freehold estate;
- the creation of a first legal mortgage protected by deposit of title deeds over an unregistered leasehold estate having more than 7 years to run at the date when the mortgage is created.

VOLUNTARY FIRST REGISTRATION

2.7 Any freehold estate and any registrable leasehold estate may be registered at the election of the estate owner.

CLASSES OF TITLE

2.8 A freehold estate may be registered with absolute title, qualified title, or possessory title. A leasehold estate may be registered with absolute title, good leasehold title, qualified title or possessory title.

Absolute title

2.9 Title to an estate will be registered with absolute title where the title to the estate is such as a willing buyer could properly be advised by a competent professional adviser to accept.

The effect of registering title to a property with absolute title is to vest the freehold estate in the registered proprietor with all interests which benefit the estate and subject only to

- interests noted on the register;
- overriding interests;
- squatter's rights of which the proprietor has notice; and
- rights of beneficiaries under any trust where the proprietor holds as trustee.

Qualified title

2.10 Title to an estate will be registered with qualified title where the Registrar is of opinion that the person's title has been established only for a limited period or subject to certain reservations which cannot be disregarded – s 9(4).

Details of the defect in title will be entered on the register.

Registration with qualified title has the same effect as registration with absolute title except that it does not affect the enforcement of any estate right or interest which it appears from the register to be excepted from the effect of registration.

Qualified titles are very rare. The editors of *Ruoff and Roper; Registered Conveyancing*, para 5-08, say that perhaps only one in one hundred thousand registered titles is qualified.

Possessory title

2.11 The Registrar may register an estate with possessory title where he is of the opinion that the person applying for registration is in actual possession of the land or in receipt of the rents and profits of the land and that there is no other class of title with which he may be registered.

There is no requirement in the rules that the person in possession seeking to be registered with possessory title must have been in possession for any particular length of time. However, the Registrar will normally refuse to register unless the applicant has been in possession for a period of 12 years or more.

The effect of registration with possessory title has the same effect as registration with absolute title except that it does not affect the enforcement of any estate, right or interest adverse to or in derogation of the proprietor's title subsisting at the time of registration.

Good Leasehold Title

2.12 If there is some uncertainty as to the lessor's title to grant the lease, the lease may be registered with good leasehold title. Registration with good leasehold title does not affect the enforcement of any estate, right or interest affecting or in derogation of the title of the lessor to grant the lease – LRA 2002 s 12(6).

Upgrading Title

2.13 Qualified title and possessory title may be upgraded to absolute title at any time if the Registrar is 'satisfied as to title to the estate' – LRA 2002 s 62(1).

In determining whether he is satisfied as to the title, the Registrar is to apply the same standards as apply when an estate is first registered with absolute title – LRA 2002 s 62(8)-(10).

Possessory title may be upgraded to absolute title after 12 years if the Registrar is satisfied that the proprietor is in possession of the land – LRA 2002 s 62(4).

DEALINGS WITH A REGISTERED ESTATE

2.14 Certain dealings with a registered estate are required to be registered. These are referred to as 'registrable dispositions' and are listed in LRA s 27(2).

They include:

- a transfer of a registered estate;
- the grant of a lease for more than 7 years;
- the grant of certain other leases;
- the grant of a legal easement or profit;
- the creation of a legal rent charge;
- the creation of a right of entry in respect of a legal lease or a legal rent charge; and

- the grant of a legal charge.

INTERESTS PROTECTED BY ENTRY ON THE REGISTER

2.15 Interests may be protected by notice or by restriction.

Notices may be used to protect any interest affecting a registered estate or charge except for

- an interest under a trust of land or a strict settlement;
- a lease for not more than 3 years; or
- a restrictive covenant between lessor and lessee.

Entry of a notice does not make valid an interest which is invalid but it will have the effect of ensuring that the interest binds a purchaser for valuable consideration – see LRA 2002 s 32(3).

A restriction regulates the circumstances in which a disposition of a registered estate may be entered on the register – see LRA 2002 s 41(1). A restriction may impose a complete ban on any dealing or it may impose conditions that must be met before a dealing is registered.

The Registrar must enter a restriction where two or more persons are registered as joint proprietors – see LRA 2002 s 44(1).

The Registrar may enter a restriction on the application of the proprietor or of any person with a sufficient interest.

A restriction cannot be used to protect an interest which is capable of being protected by notice.

OVERRIDING INTERESTS

2.16 Overriding interests are interests which bind anyone taking under a registered disposition, although not appearing on the register.

Some interests override first registration. These interests are listed in LRA 2002 Schedule 1. They are:

- leasehold estates for terms not exceeding 7 years;
- the interests of persons in actual occupation relating to the land of which he is in actual occupation, except for
  - (i) an interest under a strict settlement;
  - (ii) an interest of a person of whom inquiry was made before the disposition and who failed to disclose the right when he could reasonably have been expected to do so;
  - (iii) an interest belonging to a person whose occupation would not have been obvious on a reasonably careful inspection of the land at the time of the disposition and of which the person to whom the disposition is made does not have actual knowledge at that time; and
- legal easements and profits
  - (i) registered under the Commons Act 2006; or
  - (ii) of which the person to whom the disposition is made had actual knowledge; or

(iii) the existence of which would have been obvious on a reasonably careful inspection of the servient land; or

(iv) which have been exercised within the period of one year ending with the date of the disposition in question.

ALTERATION OF THE REGISTER

2.17 The register may be altered on an order of the court or by the Registrar for the purpose of

- correcting a mistake on the register;
- bringing the register up to date; or
- giving effect to any estate, right or interest excepted from the effect of registration – LRA 2002 s 65 and Schedule 4, paras 2 and 5.

An alteration which involves the correction of a mistake and prejudicially affects the title of the registered proprietor is termed 'rectification' – LRA 2002 Schedule 4 para 1.

The register cannot be rectified where the registered proprietor is in possession without his consent unless

- the registered proprietor caused or contributed to the mistake by fraud or lack of proper care; or
- it would for any other reason be unjust for the rectification not to be made – LRA 2002 Schedule 4 paras 3 and 6.

An application to the court or to the Registrar to alter the register must be approved, if the court or Registrar has power to alter, unless there are exceptional circumstances which justify not making the alteration – LRA 2002 Schedule 4 paras 3(3) and 6(3).

Note that alteration of the register to give effect to an overriding interest is not 'rectification' because it does not involve the correction of a mistake.

Alteration of the register to close a possessory title where another person has established a better pre-registration title is not 'rectification' because it does not prejudicially affect the title of the proprietor with possessory title since his title is subject to the enforcement of any adverse estate existing at the date of registration with possessory title.

INDEMNITY

2.18 Compensation is payable in respect of loss caused by rectification of the register to correct a mistake or by refusal to rectify the register where there is a mistake on the register – LRA 2002 Schedule 8 para 1(1).

There are two important instances where an alteration to the register will not lead to an entitlement to an indemnity, namely

- where a possessory title is closed on the application of a person who establishes that at the date of the registration of the possessory title, he had a better title. This will not amount to rectification since the title of the proprietor with possessory title is subject to the enforcement of any adverse estate existing at the date of registration; and

- where the register is altered to give effect to an overriding interest. Such alteration is not rectification.

Loss consisting of costs and expenses incurred in relation to the matter is not recoverable under the indemnity unless the costs and expenses have been reasonably incurred and with the consent of the Registrar – LRA 2002 Schedule 8 para 3(1). The prior consent of the Registrar is not required if the costs and expenses have to be incurred urgently and it is not reasonably practicable to apply for the Registrar's consent – LRA 2002 Schedule 8 para 3(2). The Registrar may give his consent after the costs and expenses have been incurred – LRA 2002 Schedule 8 para 3(3).

No indemnity is payable in respect of loss suffered by a claimant wholly or partly as a result of his fraud or wholly as a result of his lack of proper care – LRA 2002 Schedule 8 para 5(1). Negligence on the part of the claimant which contributes to his loss (but does not cause it wholly) will reduce the amount of the indemnity payable – LRA 2002 Schedule 8 para 5(2).

Where the loss is the loss of an estate, right or interest, the value of the estate, right or interest for the purposes of the indemnity is

- where the claim for indemnity arises from rectification of the register, the value immediately before rectification (but as if there were to be no rectification) and
- where the claim arises from a mistake on the register which is not rectified, the value at the time the mistake which caused the loss was made – LRA 2002 Schedule 8 para 6.

A person may apply to the court to determine whether he is entitled to an indemnity or as to the amount of the indemnity and need not obtain the prior consent of the Registrar – see LRA Schedule 8 para 7.

The limitation period for bringing a claim for an indemnity is 6 years from the date when the person entitled to the indemnity knows or ought to have known of the existence of his claim for an indemnity – LRA 2002 Schedule 8 para 8.

Chapter 3

APPLICATIONS AND OBJECTIONS TO THE REGISTRAR

Key topics in this Chapter

Applications generally
Applications concerning notices and restrictions
Applications concerning adverse possession
Applications concerning legal easements
Applications to alter the Register
Objections generally
Objections concerning notices and restrictions
Objections concerning adverse possession
Replies
Production of documents
Disposal of objections
Costs
Appeals

APPLICATIONS GENERALLY

3.1 There are many circumstances in which a person may make an application to the Registrar. The Registrar has power to raise requisitions if an application is not in order: see LRR 2003, r 16(1). If the Registrar at any time considers that the production of any further documents or evidence or the giving of any notice is necessary or desirable, he may refuse to complete or proceed with an application, or to do any act or make any entry, until such documents, evidence or notices have been supplied or given: see LRR 2003, r 17. The Registrar can correct mistakes in applications: see LRR 2003, r 130.

The general rule is that all applications must be made in one of the prescribed forms and, where no particular form is prescribed, Form AP1 (application to change the register) must be used: see LRR 2003, r 13. For the detailed provision as to the use and content of forms, see LRR 2003, rr 206, 207A and 208-212, as amended. The prescribed forms are in LRR 2003, Sch 1 as substituted and amended. A number of prescribed forms are in APPENDIX **13**. For prescribed Form AP1, see Form 12 in APPENDIX **13**.

An entry in the register pursuant to an application has effect from the time of making the application: see LRR 2003, r 20(1). This is an important provision. If a dispute causes a prolonged delay between the date of the application and the date of entry, the Applicant is protected during the delay as the entry will be backdated to the date of the application. For the time at which applications are taken to be made, see LRR 2003, r 15, as amended. The time an application is made is recorded in the day list.

The following are examples of applications to the Registrar in the first column, showing the appropriate prescribed form in the second column:

3.1 *Applications and objections to the registrar*

First registration.	FR1 (see Form 1 in APPENDIX 13)
Lodging a caution against first registration.	CT1
Withdrawing a caution against first registration.	WCT
Cancelling a caution against first registration.	CCT
Registering a registrable disposition.	TP1, TP2, TR1, TR2, TR5, AS1 or AS3 as appropriate.
Registering the benefit of a legal easement or profit à prendre expressly granted over an unregistered legal estate.	AP1 (see Form 12 in APPENDIX 13)
Registering the benefit of a legal easement or profit à prendre acquired by implication or prescription.	AP1 (see Form 12 in APPENDIX 13)
Entering an agreed notice.	AN1
Cancelling an agreed notice.	CN1
Entering a home rights notice.	HR1
Entering a unilateral notice.	UN1 (see Forms 15 and 16 in APPENDIX 13)
Removing a unilateral notice.	UN2
Cancelling a unilateral notice.	UN4 (see Form 17 in APPENDIX 13)
Cancelling a caution against dealings.	CCD (see Form 20 in APPENDIX 13)
Entering a restriction.	RX1 (see Forms 23 and 24 in APPENDIX 13)
Disapplying or modifying a restriction.	RX2
Cancelling a restriction.	RX3
Withdrawing a restriction.	RX4
Registering the priority of registered charges as between themselves.	AP1 (see Form 12 in APPENDIX 13) and SC
Determining the exact line of a boundary.	DB
Upgrading title.	UT1
Altering the register.	AP1 (see Form 12 in APPENDIX 13)
Inspecting and making copies of, or any part of, the register of title, relevant documents kept by the Registrar and the register of cautions against first registration.	PIC
Obtaining an official copy.	OC1
Obtaining an official search with priority by a purchaser.	OS1 or OS2
Entering into a network access agreement.	–
Registering as proprietor of a registered estate in land on the grounds of adverse possession.	ADV1 (see Form 6 in APPENDIX 13)
Registering as a person entitled to be notified of an application for adverse possession of registered land.	ADV2

APPLICATIONS CONCERNING NOTICES AND RESTRICTIONS

The distinction between notices and restrictions

3.2 Two types of application which frequently give rise to disputes referred by Land Registry to the Tribunal for determination are applications to cancel a unilateral notice and applications to enter a restriction. Before we look in more detail at notices and restrictions, it is important to distinguish between them. The critical distinction between notices and restrictions is based on the difference between specific and non-specific burdens (for an explanation see *Gray and Gray, Elements of Land Law* (5th edn, 2008) paras 1.7.31-1.7.34).

EXAMPLE 1

A and B are neighbours in Penzance. B covenants with A that B will not develop the back garden of his house. This restrictive covenant is a burden which necessarily affects one particular parcel of land, namely B's house. If B moved to Newcastle, A would not have a right to prevent development of B's new back garden. A restrictive covenant is therefore a specific burden.

EXAMPLE 2

A and B live together as partners in a house of which B is the sole registered proprietor. A has a beneficial interest in the house on the basis of a common intention constructive trust: see *Oxley v Hiscock* [2004] EWCA Civ 546, [2005] Fam 211, [2004] 3 All ER 703, CA, *Stack v Dowden* [2007] UKHL 17, [2007] 2 AC 432, [2007] 2 All ER 929, HL and *Jones v Kernott* [2011] UKSC 53, SC, [2012] 1 AC 776, [2012] 1 All ER 1265. A's right to a share in the proceeds of sale of the house is a burden which can be transferred to a share in some other asset, such as the cash proceeds of sale or another property bought with the proceeds of sale. It is therefore a non-specific burden.

Occasionally, a notice and a restriction can be entered in respect of the same right.

> **EXAMPLE 3**
>
> A agrees with B that he will not sell his house without offering it for sale to B first. B can protect the priority of his right of pre-emption by a notice. However, a restriction can be entered as well as a notice, to ensure that A first offers to sell the house to B.

Notices

3.3 Specific burdens are protected by notices. Provision for notices is made in LRA 2002, ss 32-39 and LRR 2003, rr 80-90, as amended. A notice is an entry in the register in respect of the burden of an interest affecting a registered estate or charge: see LRA 2002, s 32(1). By interest affecting an estate or charge is meant an adverse right affecting the title to the registered estate or charge: see LRA 2002, s 132(3)(b).

A notice is used to bestow priority, so that it binds a person acquiring the land. But the fact that an interest is the subject of a notice does not necessarily mean that the interest is valid: see LRA 2002, s 32(3). A notice has replaced the caution against dealings available under the Land Registration Act 1925 ('LRA 1925'). Transitional provisions enable applications to be made to remove cautions.

A notice is entered in the charges register of the title affected. A person who applies to enter a notice without reasonable cause commits a breach of statutory duty owed to any person who suffers damage in consequence of its breach: see LRA 2002, s 77(1)(b). A director of a company which entered a notice without reasonable cause has been held personally liable: see *Anderson Antiques (UK) Ltd v Anderson Wharf (Hull) Ltd* [2007] All ER (D) 409 (May).

In a case involving unilateral notices entered to protect an estate contract, the judge said that although he ultimately found against the buyer, he considered that the buyer had a reasonably arguable case to the effect that the contract remained in being. The existence of a reasonably arguable case was sufficient to show that the buyer had reasonable cause to continue to have the benefit of the unilateral notices against the seller's registered title: see *Fitzroy Development Ltd v Fitzrovia Properties Ltd* [2011] EWHC 1849 (Ch), [2011] All ER (D) 195 (Jul).

A number of interests are excluded from protection by notice: see LRA 2002, s 33. The most important interest excluded is an interest under a trust of land or a strict settlement, as it is properly protected by a restriction.

The specific burdens which can be protected by the entry of a notice include:

- a restrictive covenant;
- an easement;
- a charging order against a legal estate;

- an estate contract;
- an option;
- a right of pre-emption;
- an equitable mortgage;
- an unpaid vendor's lien.

Sometimes a statute will provide for a right to be protected by a notice, for example:

- a right of access ordered under the Access to Neighbouring Land Act;
- the initial notice served under the Leasehold Reform, Housing and Urban Development Act 1993: see *Wiggins v Regent Wealth Ltd* [2014] EWCA Civ 1078;
- a request for an overriding lease under the Landlord and Tenant (Covenants) Act 1995.

Applications to enter notices

3.4 An application can be made either for an agreed notice or a unilateral notice: see LRA 2002, s 32(2). In addition, the Registrar may enter one of his own accord. An application to enter an agreed notice or a unilateral notice can be made to the Registrar by a person who claims to be entitled to the benefit of an interest affecting a registered estate or charge, provided it is not an excluded interest: see LRA 2002, s 34.

An agreed notice is usually a consensual entry and is not subject to the same cancellation procedure as applies to a unilateral notice. A person who applies to enter a home rights notice and certain other notices must apply to enter an agreed notice, and not a unilateral notice: see the list in LRR 2003, r 80.

A unilateral notice is a unilateral hostile entry, as was the caution against dealings available under LRA 1925. Importantly, it will be entered on the register without investigation, or notice to the registered proprietor, and it is subject to a cancellation procedure. A person in whose favour a unilateral notice has been entered is known as the beneficiary of the notice: see LRA 2002, 36(4). If the Registrar enters a unilateral notice in the register, he must give notice of the entry to the registered proprietor of the estate or charge to which it relates: see LRA 2002, 35(1).

> **EXAMPLE 4**
>
> A and B are neighbours. B covenants with A that B will not develop the back garden of his house. A wishes to protect the benefit of the restrictive covenant against a disponee of B's house. A must apply in prescribed Form UN1 to enter a unilateral notice in the charges register of B's title (see Forms 15 and 16 in APPENDIX 13). The Registrar will enter the unilateral notice without consulting B, but will give B notice of its entry. A becomes the beneficiary of the notice.

Applications to cancel unilateral notices

3.5 A person may apply to the Registrar to cancel a unilateral notice if he is the registered proprietor of the estate or charge to which the notice relates or is the person entitled to be so registered: see LRA 2002, s 36(1). The beneficiary of the notice must be given notice of the application, and if he does not object to the application within the prescribed period, the Registrar must cancel the unilateral notice: see LRA 2002, s 36(3).

> **EXAMPLE 5**
>
> B disputes the validity of the restrictive covenant given to his neighbour A. He says that A has released him from it for a payment. B must apply in prescribed Form UN4 to cancel the unilateral notice (see FORM 17 in APPENDIX 13). Notice will be served on A who will have an opportunity to object. The procedure for objecting is explained below.

The Tribunal has a wide power under Rule 40(3)(a), on hearing an application to cancel a unilateral notice, to direct the Registrar to amend it, or replace it with an agreed notice, better reflecting the correct nature of the interest the Tribunal finds the beneficiary of the unilateral notice to have: see *Bank of Scotland plc v Joseph* [2014] EWCA Civ 28, [30], [2014] 1 P & CR 302. This was a decision under the comparable rule in AR 2003, where a unilateral notice protecting a legal charge said to be forged was sufficient to protect an alternative subrogated security.

As an alternative to making an application to the Registrar, the registered proprietor may apply directly to the High Court for the removal of a unilateral notice. In *Nugent v Nugent* [2013] EWHC 4095 (Ch), [49], [2014] 2 All ER 313, [2014] 3 WLR 59, it was held that the jurisdiction, recognised and developed by the courts, in relation to the vacation of cautions registered under LRA 1925, applies also in relation to unilateral notices registered under LRA 2002. That jurisdiction is to be applied in different ways in relation to notices to protect claims which were unsustainable (which should be removed summarily) and in relation to notices to protect claims which were well arguable (which should attract a more balanced and nuanced order protecting the rights of both parties).

Applications to remove unilateral notices

3.6 The hostile cancellation of a unilateral notice must be distinguished from its voluntary removal. The latter permits the beneficiary, his personal representative or trustee in bankruptcy to remove the unilateral notice: see LRA 2002, s 35(3), LRR 2003, r 85(2). The application must be made in prescribed Form UN2.

The beneficiary of a unilateral notice can remove it voluntarily even after the dispute as to whether or not it should be cancelled has been referred to the Tribunal. But this will not automatically bring the reference to an end: see *Chief Land Registrar v Silkstone* [2011] EWCA Civ 801, [53], CA, [2012] 1 WLR 400, [2011] 2 P & CR 258. However, as the unilateral notice has been removed, there will be nothing to be cancelled pursuant to the application referred to the Tribunal. It seems likely that all the Tribunal could do is to make an order as to costs. It remains to be decided whether the Tribunal could direct the Registrar to reject any future application to enter the unilateral notice under Rule 40(3)(b) in these circumstances.

Restrictions

3.7 Non-specific burdens are protected by restrictions. Provision for restrictions is made in LRA 2002, ss 40-47 and LRR 2003, rr 91-100, as amended.

A restriction is an entry in the register regulating the circumstances in which a disposition of a registered estate or charge may be the subject of an entry in the register: see LRA 2002, 40(1). The entry restrains or limits the otherwise wide and unfettered powers of a proprietor.

A restriction may prohibit:

- the making of an entry in respect of any disposition or a disposition of a specified kind;
- the making of an entry indefinitely, for a particular period or until the occurrence of a specified event, such as:
  - the giving of notice,
  - the obtaining of consent, or
  - the making of an order by the court or the Registrar.

Where a restriction is entered in the register, no entry in respect of a disposition to which the restriction applies may be made in the register otherwise than in accordance with the terms of the restriction: see LRA 2002, s 41(1). This is subject to the power of the Registrar to disapply or modify a restriction on the application of a person with sufficient interest. Such an application may be necessary if, for example, a restriction requires the consent of a person who cannot be found or will not respond.

A restriction is used to regulate the manner in which a registered estate or charge is dealt with; it does not bestow priority. No restriction can be entered for the purpose of protecting the priority of an interest which is or could be the subject of a notice: see LRA 2002, s 42(2). A restriction is commonly used to ensure that, where appropriate, any beneficial rights are overreached. It can also be used as a mechanism to pass on the burden of a positive freehold covenant.

In the case of a registered estate a restriction is entered in the proprietorship register of the title affected. A person who applies to enter a restriction without reasonable cause commits a breach of statutory duty owed to any person who suffers damage in consequence of its breach: see LRA 2002, s 77(1)(b).

In *Red River UK Ltd v Sheikh* [2007] EWHC 1038 (Ch), [2007] 2 P & CR D44, it was assumed that the High Court still had an inherent jurisdiction to make orders, including summary orders, vacating the entry of a restriction in the register. This can now be taken to be correct, in the light of the careful judgment in *Nugent v Nugent* [2013] EWHC 4095 (Ch), [2014] 2 All ER 313, [2014] 3 WLR 59 dealing with the inherent jurisdiction in so far as it related to unilateral notices.

The rights which can be protected by the entry of a restriction include:

- an interest under a trust of land;
- a charging order against a co-owner's interest under a trust of land;
- a freezing order;
- a bankruptcy order;
- the rights of a trustee in bankruptcy against a bankrupt's beneficial interest under a trust of land;
- an order appointing a receiver or sequestrator;
- a deed of arrangement.

Provision is made for a substantial number of standard form restrictions. There are now 42 standard form restrictions, consisting of Forms A to Y and AA to QQ, to be found in LRR 2003, Sch 4, as amended.

A person *may* apply to enter a restriction if:

- he is the proprietor of the registered estate or charge to which the application relates, or a person entitled to be so registered: see LRA 2002, s 43(1)(a);
- the proprietor of the registered estate or charge to which the application relates, or a person entitled to be so registered, consents to the application: see LRA 2002, s 43(1)(b);
- he otherwise has *a sufficient interest* in the making of the entry: see LRA 2002, s 43(1)(c) and the substantial, but non-exhaustive, list of those who are regarded as having *a sufficient interest* as set out in LRR 2003, r 93, as amended.

In certain circumstances a person *must* apply to enter a restriction: see LRA 2002, s 43(2)(a) and LRR 2003, r 94, as amended. A common example is where land is jointly owned and the beneficiaries are tenants in common.

Except where the application is by consent, is compulsory or is made pursuant to an order of the court or the Registrar or an undertaking given in place of such an order, the Registrar must give notice of the application, and of the right to object to it, to the proprietor of the registered estate or charge to which it relates: see LRA 2002, s 45(1). The Registrar may not determine such an application before the end of the prescribed period unless the person notified has either made an objection or consented to the application: see LRA 2002, s 45(2). So the procedure is quite different to that which applies when a unilateral notice is entered.

> EXAMPLE 6
>
> A and B used to live together as partners in a house of which B is the sole registered proprietor. A has a beneficial interest in the house on the basis of a common intention constructive trust. A is no longer living at B's house. She is concerned that B will sell it and disappear with the proceeds of sale. She must apply in prescribed Form RX1 to enter restrictions in Form A and II (see **FORM 23** and **FORM 24** in **APPENDIX 13**). Notice will be served on B who will have an opportunity to object. The procedure for objecting is explained below.

APPLICATIONS CONCERNING ADVERSE POSSESSION

3.8 Care must be taken when dealing with adverse possession as there are now three separate regimes:

- where the land is unregistered and an application is made for first registration by a person in adverse possession;
- where the land is registered and the person in adverse possession had acquired title prior to 13 October 2003;
- where the land is registered and the person in adverse possession had not acquired title prior to 13 October 2003.

Where the land is unregistered, an application for first registration by a person who has obtained title by adverse possession must be made in prescribed Form FR1 (see **FORM 1** in **APPENDIX 13**). The application must be supported by evidence, which may consist of or include a statement of truth in prescribed Form ST1 (see Forms 2 and 3 in **APPENDIX 13**).The law as to adverse possession and extinguishment of title continues to be that in force prior to the commencement of LRA 2002 on 13 October 2003.

Where land is registered but, prior to 13 October 2003, the land was held in trust by the registered proprietor for a person who had obtained title by adverse possession, the person in adverse possession still remains entitled to be registered as proprietor of the estate: see LRA 2002, s 134, Sch 12 para 18. An application for registration must be made in prescribed Form AP1 (see Form 12 in **APPENDIX 13**). The application must be supported by evidence, which may consist of or include a statement of truth in prescribed Form ST1 (see Forms 2 and 13 in **APPENDIX 13**).

Where the land is registered and the person in adverse possession had not acquired title prior to 13 October 2003, an entirely new system of adverse possession is introduced by LRA 2002: see LRA 2002, ss 96-98, Sch 6. Adverse possession in itself will not bar the paper title owner's title however long such adverse possession lasts.

After being in adverse possession for 10 (not 12) years, the person in adverse possession will become entitled to apply to be registered as the proprietor: see LRA 2002, s 97, Sch 6 para 1(1). The application for registration must be made in prescribed Form ADV1 (see **FORM 6** in **APPENDIX 13**). The application must be accompanied by a statutory declaration (see FORM 7 in APPENDIX 13) or a statement of truth. The paper title owner, any registered chargee and, in some cases, certain others will have to be notified of the application by the Registrar: see LRA 2002, s 97, Sch 6 para 2(1). The procedure on the registered proprietor being notified of the application is dealt with below.

Under the new system of adverse possession it is no longer possible for the paper title owner to lose his title without an application being made to Land Registry by the squatter. The squatter can no longer simply commence proceedings: see *Swan Housing Association Ltd v Gill* [2012] EWHC 3129 (QB), [2013] 1 WLR 1253, [2013] 1 EGLR 69, where it was held that it is not for the court to arrogate to itself the functions to be discharged, in the first instance, by Land Registry (and, if there is a dispute, by the Tribunal).

There is further discussion of adverse possession in CHAPTER 22.

APPLICATIONS CONCERNING LEGAL EASEMENTS

3.9 Only the express grant of an easement requires to be completed by registration before it will operate at law. Implied easements (including those granted as a result of the operation of the Law of Property Act 1925, ('LPA 1925'), s 62) and prescriptive easements become legal interests without the need for registration.

Provision is made for registered proprietors claiming the benefit of an implied easement (including an easement granted as a result of the operation of LPA 1925, s 62) or a prescriptive easement to apply for it to be registered as appurtenant to the estate: see LRR 2003, r 73A(1)(b) and (3), as inserted.

Provision is also made for registered proprietors claiming the benefit of an express easement (but not one granted as a result of the operation of LPA 1925, s 62) over an unregistered estate to apply for it to be registered as appurtenant to the estate: see LRR 2003, r 73A(1)(a) and (3), as inserted.

The application must be made in prescribed Form AP1 (see Form 12 in APPENDIX 13). The application must be supported by evidence, which may consist of or include a statement of truth in prescribed Form ST4 (see FORM 27 and FORM 28 in APPENDIX 13).

APPLICATIONS TO ALTER THE REGISTER

3.10 The question has arisen as to whether a party applying to alter the register by removing land from another party's title needs to show an interest in the land being removed.

EXAMPLE 7

A is the first registered proprietor of Whiteacre. B claims that A cannot show a good paper title to the rear garden and applies for the title plan to be altered accordingly. B does not claim to have any title to the rear garden himself. Is he entitled to make the application?

In *Wells v Pilling Parish Council* [2008] EWHC 556 (Ch), [2008] 2 EGLR 29, [2008] 22 EG 174, it was conceded that if the application to alter the register was properly categorised as a matter of private law, the common law required the Applicant to have standing. The judge, on appeal from the Adjudicator, held that the application only raised a question of a private right. In the light of the concession, he held that standing was required so the application must fail. The position of an Applicant is to be contrasted with that of an Objector, as the general rule is that anyone can object to an application to alter the register: see LRA 2002, s 73(1).

But in a preliminary ruling in *Burton v Walker* (Reference/2007/1124), (2009), unreported, the Adjudicator held that, because of the concession, *Wells v Pilling Parish Council* was not binding on him, and that it was not necessary for an Applicant seeking to rectify the register to demonstrate standing. The High Court has held that the preliminary ruling in *Burton v Walker* was correctly decided: *Mann v Dingley* [2011] EWLandRA 2010_0582. This approach has also been taken to be correct in *Paton v Todd* [2012] EWHC 1248 (Ch), [51] and *Balevents Ltd v Sartori* [2014] EWHC 1164 (Ch), [165], [2014] All ER (D) 152 (Apr).

For a statutory declaration in support of an application to alter the register to correct a mistake where land has been incorrectly registered, see **FORM 31** in **APPENDIX 13**. For a statutory declaration in the case of a forgery, see **FORM 34** in **APPENDIX 13**.

There is further discussion of alteration of the register in **CHAPTER 22**.

OBJECTIONS GENERALLY

3.11 There is a procedure whereby applications come to the attention of other interested parties. For example, in the case of an application for first registration the Registrar may give notices to other persons and advertise the application: see LRR 2003, r 30. In the case of an application to cancel a caution against first registration, the Registrar must give notice of the application to the cautioner: see LRA 2002, s 18(3).

Disputes arise from objections made to applications. The general rule is that anyone may object to an application to the Registrar: see LRA 2002, s 73(1).

> EXAMPLE 8
>
> A applies to register a prescriptive right of way on foot over a private lane owned by B. B knows A has only used the route for 15 and not the necessary 20 years. But he is not troubled by A's use, does not wish to incur costs and does not oppose the application. C owns land next to the lane and is afraid his privacy would be disturbed if A established a right of way. He is entitled to object and call evidence that A has not used the right of way for 20 years.

There are two important exceptions to the general rule that anyone may object. The first exception relates to an application to cancel a caution against first registration. The only persons who may object are:

- the person who lodged the caution to which the application relates: see LRA 2002, s 73(2);
- the person for the time being shown as cautioner in the cautioner's register, where that person is not the person who lodged the caution against first registration: see LRR 2003, r 52(1), as amended;
- where the cautioner shown in the cautioner's register comprises more than one person, then each such person has a separate right to object to the application: see LRR 2003, r 52(2), as amended.

The second exception relates to an application to cancel a unilateral notice and is dealt with below.

An objection must be made by delivering to the Registrar at the appropriate office a written statement signed by the objector or his conveyancer: see LRR 2003, r 19. The statement must:

- state that the Objector objects to the application;
- state the grounds for the objection;
- give the full name of the Objector and an address for service;
- be delivered in paper form or to the electronic address or the fax number of the appropriate office.

Following the coming into force of the Land Registration (Proper Office) Order 2013 on 1 October 2013 all 14 Land Registry local offices can receive any application. Land Registry's Office Finder, available online, contains advice as to the recommended office in any particular case.

There is no prescribed form for the objection, which should set out the salient points in a clear, logical and chronological order. For examples, see the following Forms in APPENDIX 13:

Form 4	Adverse possession: unregistered land.
Form 10	Adverse possession: registered land.
Form 14	Adverse possession: transitional provisions.
Form 18	Cancellation of a unilateral notice protecting a restrictive covenant.
Form 25	Entry of a restriction protecting a beneficial interest.
Form 29	Prescriptive easement.

Form 32	Alteration of the register to correct a mistake where land has been incorrectly registered.
Form 35	Alteration of the register to correct a mistake in the case of a forgery.

A party showing cause why a caution against dealings lodged under LRA 1925 should not be cancelled (see **FORM 21** in **APPENDIX 13**) is treated as objecting to the application to cancel the caution.

A person who objects to an application to the Registrar without reasonable cause commits a breach of statutory duty owed to any person who suffers damage in consequence of its breach: see LRA 2002, s 77(1)(c). For a case where at first instance the judge found that the duty had been broken by an unreasonable objection to an application for first registration by the Claimants, but no recoverable loss had been proven and the damages claim was dismissed, see *Hudson Industrial Services Ltd v Wood* [2012] EWCA Civ 599, 142 ConLR 48, [2012] 2 P & CR D33. However, on appeal, the Court of Appeal found that the Claimants had not been entitled to register the land: [2012] EWCA Civ 599.

OBJECTIONS CONCERNING NOTICES AND RESTRICTIONS

Notices

3.12 In the case of an application to cancel a unilateral notice, the Registrar must give notice of the application to the beneficiary of the unilateral notice: see LRA 2002, s 36(2). If the beneficiary (the person in whose favour the unilateral notice has been entered) does not object to the application within the prescribed period, the Registrar must cancel the unilateral notice: see LRA 2002, s 36(3).

The only persons who can object to an application to cancel a unilateral notice are:

- the person shown in the register as the beneficiary of the notice to which the application relates: see LRA 2002, s 73(3);
- a person entitled to be registered as the beneficiary of a notice under the LRR 2003, r 88: see LRR 2003, r 86(7);
- where there are two or more persons shown in the register as the beneficiary of the notice, or who are entitled to object in accordance with LRR 2003, r 86(7), each such person is deemed to be a beneficiary of the notice for the purpose of objecting: see LRR 2003, r 86(8), as inserted.

EXAMPLE 9

A and B are neighbours. B covenants with A that B will not develop the back garden of his house. A protects the benefit of the restrictive covenant by the entry of a unilateral notice in the charges register of B's title. B subsequently disputes the validity of the restrictive covenant. He says that A has released him from it for a payment. B applies in prescribed Form UN4 to cancel the unilateral notice. A receives notice of B's application to cancel the unilateral notice. A is entitled to object to the application as he is the beneficiary of the unilateral notice. Unless he does so (see **FORM 18** in **APPENDIX 13**), it will be cancelled.

Restrictions

3.13 Except where the application is by consent, is compulsory or is made pursuant to an order of the court or the Registrar or an undertaking given in place of such an order, the Registrar must give notice of the application, and of the right to object to it, to the proprietor of the registered estate or charge to which it relates: see LRA 2002, s 45(1). The Registrar may not determine such an application before the end of the prescribed period unless the person notified has either made an objection or consented to the application: see LRA 2002, s 45(2).

Any person may object to an application to enter a restriction.

EXAMPLE 10

A and B used to live together as partners in a house of which B is the sole registered proprietor. A claims a beneficial interest in the house on the basis of a common intention constructive trust, and applies to enter a restriction. B is given notice of the application to enter a restriction as he is the proprietor of the registered estate to which it relates. He is entitled to object. Unless he does so (see **FORM 25** in **APPENDIX 13**), it will be entered on the register.

OBJECTIONS CONCERNING ADVERSE POSSESSION

Counter notice

3.14 Care is required in responding on behalf of the paper title owner to an application made in prescribed Form ADV1 for registration as proprietor on the grounds of adverse possession under LRA 2002, s 97, Sch 6 para 1. Such an application faces a formidable barrier, but only if the paper title owner, or any other of those notified of the application by the Registrar, gives a counter notice in prescribed Form NAP (see **FORM 9** in **APPENDIX 13**) requiring the application to be dealt with in accordance with LRA 2002, s 97, Sch 6 para 5.

Giving this notice is done by ticking the second box in panel 5 of the Form NAP. However, the procedural rules are not mandatory and the correct approach is to consider whether the Form NAP, together with any accompanying documents, would have indicated to a reasonable Registrar that the Applicant sought to invoke the procedure under LRA 2002, s 97, Sch 6 para 5: *Hopkins v Beacon* [2011] EWHC 2899 (Ch).

If this notice is given the squatter will have to bring himself within one of three exceptional conditions, or the application will be refused: see LRA 2002, s 97, Sch 6 para 5(1). The conditions are that the squatter can show:

- proprietary estoppel, or
- an entitlement otherwise to the land (as under the deceased owner's will), or
- that he is the owner of adjacent property and has been in adverse possession under a mistaken but reasonable belief that he was the owner.

If a counter notice is given and the squatter is relying on one of the conditions, Land Registry will contact anyone who gave the counter notice. If any one of them disputes that the condition has been met, that will be treated as an objection to the application: see Land Registry Practice Guide 4 (2013) para 8. For an objection, see **FORM 10** in **APPENDIX 13**.

Objection

3.15 Any person may object to an application for registration as proprietor where the Applicant is relying on adverse possession. Such an objection will usually be on the basis that the squatter has been in possession for less than 10 years or that permission has been given. This right to object is quite separate to, and independent of, the right to give a counter notice as explained above. An objection may be made in the normal way by delivering to the Registrar at the appropriate office a written statement signed by the Objector or his conveyancer (see **FORM 10** in **APPENDIX 13**). Alternatively, where a counter notice is being given, the objection can be made by ticking the third box in panel 5 and filling in panel 6 (see Form 11 in **APPENDIX 13**).

There is no reason why a party cannot both require the application to be dealt with in accordance with LRA 2002, s 97, Sch 6 para 5 and object on the grounds that the squatter has not satisfied any of the conditions in LRA 2002, s 97, Sch 6 para 5 and/or been in adverse possession for the required period.

If, after a counter notice has been served, the application is refused but the person in adverse possession remains in adverse possession for a further two years, he will be entitled to apply to be registered as the proprietor once again, but this time he will be registered as proprietor whether or not there is an objection. The application for registration must be made in prescribed Form ADV1 (see **FORM 6** in **APPENDIX 13**). The application must be accompanied by a statutory declaration (see **FORM 8** in **APPENDIX 13**) or a statement of truth.

There is further discussion of adverse possession in **CHAPTER 22**.

REPLIES

3.16 If the Registrar considers the objection to be groundless, he does not need to give notice of it to the Applicant and he can give effect to the application: see LRA 2002, s 73(6). In *Silkstone v Tatnall* [2010] EWHC 1627 (Ch) [17], [2010] 3 EGLR 25, [2010] 28 EG 84 (CS), Floyd J described the groundless test as a very low threshold. There is no requirement for the Objector to provide evidence when he objects. There may be extensive correspondence between the Registrar and the Objector before the Registrar is able to decide whether or not there are any grounds to the objection. An Objector whose objection is considered to be groundless no longer has a statutory right of appeal to the Chancery Division against such a decision and his only remedy is to seek judicial review, if appropriate.

If the objection is not groundless, the Registrar must give notice of the objection to the Applicant and he may not determine the application until the objection has been disposed of: see LRA 2002, s 73(5). Accordingly, the Applicant has the opportunity to reply to the objection, and in some cases will take that opportunity.

Again, there is no there is no prescribed form for a reply, which should set out the salient points in a clear, logical and chronological order. For examples, see the following Forms in **APPENDIX 13**:

Form 5	Adverse possession: unregistered land.
Form 19	Cancellation of a unilateral notice protecting a restrictive covenant.
Form 22	Cancellation of a caution relating to a claim of proprietary estoppel.
Form 26	Entry of a restriction protecting a beneficial interest.
Form 30	Prescriptive easement.
Form 33	Alteration of the register to correct a mistake where land has been incorrectly registered.

PRODUCTION OF DOCUMENTS

3.17 Where an application has been made to the Registrar, he may require any person to produce a document: see LRA 2002, s 75(1). This power may only be exercised where the Registrar has received a request from one party that the document should be produced by the person who is alleged to have control of it: see LRR 2003, r 201(1). Where the Registrar makes such a requirement, it is enforceable as an order of the court: see LRA 2002, s 75(3). This does not mean that the Registrar has the power to enforce the direction or order personally but it can be enforced by an application to the court under CPR 1998, Part 70.5.

There is a right to appeal to the County Court the Registrar's requirement to produce a document. The County Court may make any order which appears appropriate.

DISPOSAL OF OBJECTIONS

3.18 As explained in Land Registry Practice Guide 37: Objections and Disputes (February 2014) para 3, there are five courses open to the parties once the Registrar has decided the objection is not groundless:

- the application is withdrawn;
- the objection is withdrawn;
- the objection is disposed of by agreement;
- one of the parties commences court proceedings;
- there is no prospect of agreement and the Registrar refers the matter to the Tribunal.

The parties will be asked if they wish to have time in which to negotiate. There may be correspondence between the Registrar and the parties in the course of which the issues are addressed and an attempt made to dispose of the dispute by agreement. The Registrar may express his views on the merits of each party's case in an impartial and independent manner. These views are not, of course, binding on the Tribunal (or judge if there are court proceedings) and the Registrar will not send such correspondence to the Tribunal. But it may be produced in evidence at the hearing (and therefore any such correspondence will not be confidential).

If there is an agreement, the Registrar will take into account the terms of the agreement so far as they affect the application.

Where an objection remains to an application, the Registrar must refer the matter to the Tribunal in the absence of an agreement: see LRA 2002, s 73(7), as amended.

The Registrar no longer has the power to determine the matter himself or to direct the parties to commence proceedings in the Chancery Division. The parties, however, are free at any time to institute court proceedings to determine the dispute. This will not in itself stop a reference being made to the Tribunal. But the existence of such court proceedings will be relevant to the manner in which the Tribunal disposes of the reference to it. This is discussed further in CHAPTER 8.

However, the withdrawal, prior to the reference, of the application or of the objection to it would stop a reference being made to the Tribunal, as there would then be no dispute to refer to the Tribunal. Neither the application, nor the objection, can be withdrawn following the reference, unless the Tribunal consents: see Rule 22(3). The Tribunal will only consent if it considers it just: see *Chief Land Registrar v Silkstone* [2011] EWCA Civ 801, [37],CA, [2012] 1 WLR 400, [2011] 2 P & CR 258. The principles of that decision still apply although it was a decision under AR 2003 which contained no express power to permit a withdrawal.

COSTS

3.19 The Registrar has a limited power to award costs: See LRA 2002, s 76 and Land Registry Practice Guide 38: Costs (July 2013). A person who has incurred costs in relation to proceedings before the Registrar may request the Registrar to make an order requiring a party to those proceedings to pay the whole or part of those costs: see LRR 2003, r 202. Since the Registrar no longer conducts judicial proceedings, this reference to proceedings must be a reference to making or opposing an application to the Registrar. However, the Registrar may only order a party to proceedings before him to pay costs where those costs have been occasioned by the unreasonable conduct of that party in relation to the proceedings.

A request for the payment of costs must be made in accordance with the prescribed manner and the party against whom the order is sought is then given an opportunity to respond. The Registrar must determine the matter on the basis of the written request and any response submitted to him, all the circumstances including the conduct of the parties, and the result of any enquiries he considers it necessary to make.

Where the Registrar makes a costs order, it is enforceable as an order of the court. This does not mean that the Registrar has the power to enforce the direction or order personally. It means that it can be enforced by an application to the court under CPR 1998, Part 70.5.

There is a right to appeal the Registrar's costs order to the County Court, which may make any order which appears appropriate.

The Registrar has no jurisdiction to make any order in respect of costs incurred after a dispute has been referred to the Tribunal. Equally, the Tribunal has no jurisdiction to make any order in respect of costs incurred before a dispute has been referred to it.

APPEALS

3.20 There is a right of appeal from the Registrar to the County Court but only in relation to a requirement to produce a document or a costs order. Since such an appeal is from the decision of a person who did not hold a hearing to come to that decision, the appeal will presumably be a rehearing rather than a review.

Chapter 4

JUDICIAL REVIEW

Key topics in this Chapter

INTRODUCTION

4.1 The staff of Land Registry make hundreds of decisions every year directly affecting the property rights and economic interests of individuals and companies. They may by accepting or rejecting an application for first registration or to register a disposition of registered land confer or refuse a registered title. They may protect or weaken a security interest by registering or refusing to register a charge. They may protect or deny protection to derivative interests. In making these decisions, Land Registry carries out a public function. Each local Land Registry office has a land Registrar who has delegated authority from the Registrar to make registration decisions under the Land Registration Acts and Rules, affecting land/properties dealt with by the local office. Any registration decision made by a land Registrar is final; the only way to challenge an administrative decision of the land Registrar is by judicial review in the courts.

A very small proportion of the decisions are in fact the subject of an application to the High Court for judicial review. Information provided by the Ministry of Justice in March 2014 in response to a freedom of information request revealed that between 1st January 1996 and March 2014, there were only 46 applications for judicial review to which Land Registry was a party, either as a defendant or as an interested party. Of those applications, none had been allowed at a substantive hearing.

The Ministry of Justice provided a table giving a breakdown of the progress of each of the 46 cases. The table appears below.

Number of Cases	Stage of Progression in Case
21	Refused permission at the paper and oral permission stage
8	Refused permission at the paper application stage and did not request an oral hearing

Number of Cases	Stage of Progression in Case
5	Cases are currently still live and awaiting decisions from Judges on permission
4	Settled by agreement with the other parties
2	Discontinued by the Claimants
1	Closed before any decision was made – non-compliance with CPR 54
1	Transferred to Chancery Division
4	Granted permission

Of the four cases that were granted permission to proceed, three cases were dismissed at the substantive hearing and one case did not continue to the substantive hearing because the continuation fee was not paid.

Since those figures were provided, there has been one case in which the application for judicial review has succeeded in the High Court. In *R (on the application of Best) v Chief Land Registrar (Secretary of State for Justice, interested party)* [2014] EWHC 1370 Admin, [2014] 3 All ER 637, [2014] PLSCS 141, Mr Best challenged the refusal of Land Registry to grant his application for a possessory title of a house based on adverse possession. Mr Best went into possession of the house in 2002. He spent the next 10 years working on the property. In 2012, he took up occupation. On 1 September 2012 after he had taken up occupation but before he made his application to Land Registry, the Legal Aid, Sentencing, and Punishment of Offenders Act 2012 s 144(1) came into force. That section made it a criminal offence to live in a residential building as a trespasser, having entered as a trespasser. In November 2012, Mr Best applied to be registered as proprietor of the house under Land Registration Act 2002 Schedule 6 paragraph 1 on the basis that he had been in adverse possession of the house for the period of 10 years ending on the date of the application. The Registrar refused Mr Best's application on the grounds that his adverse possession between 1st September 2012 and the date of his application involved a criminal offence under s 144 and that he could not rely on any period which involved a criminal offence to support his claim. The High Court allowed Mr Best's application for judicial review, holding that Parliament had not intended by passing s 144(1) to alter the law of adverse possession as it affected registered land and that Mr Best could rely on a period of adverse possession, notwithstanding that his possession involved a criminal offence.

STATUTORY REGULATION OF JUDICIAL REVIEW

4.2 The power of the High Court to judicially review the lawfulness of a decision, action or failure to act in relation to the exercise of a public function is regulated by Supreme Court Act 1981, s 31. That section requires an application for a mandatory, prohibiting or quashing order to be made by the judicial review procedure in accordance with the rules of court.

The section gives the High Court power to make a declaration or injunction in judicial review proceedings where

> the High Court considers that, having regard to—

(a) the nature of the matters in respect of which relief may be granted by prohibiting or quashing orders;
(b) the nature of the persons and bodies against whom relief may be granted by such orders; and
(c) all the circumstances of the case,

it would be just and convenient for the declaration to be made or the injunction to be granted, as the case may be.

REQUIREMENT FOR PERMISSION

4.3 Supreme Court Act 1981 s 31(3) provides that no application may be made for judicial review unless the permission of the High Court has been obtained in accordance with the rules of court.

It also provides that the court may not grant permission to make a judicial review application unless it considers that the applicant has a sufficient interest in the matter to which the application relates.

POWERS OF THE HIGH COURT

4.4 On an application for judicial review, the High Court may

- make an order requiring the public body to do something (a mandatory order);
- make an order quashing the public body's decision (a quashing order)
- make an order prohibiting a public body from doing something (a prohibiting order)
- award the applicant damages, restitution or the recovery of a sum due, under Supreme Court Act 1981, s 31(4) if
  - a claim for such an award is included in the application; and
  - such an award would have been made if an action claiming such an award had been begun at the time of the making of the judicial review application;
- if it makes an order quashing the decision to which the application relates, it may in addition remit the matter to the court, tribunal or authority which made the decision, with a direction to reconsider the matter and reach a decision in accordance with the findings of the High Court.

PRE-ACTION PROTOCOL

4.5 There is a Pre-Action Protocol for Judicial Review. Annexed to the Protocol are standard form letters of claim and response which it is suggested should be used.

The Protocol states that the letter of claim should contain the date and details of the decision, act or omission being challenged and a clear summary of the facts on which the claim is based. It should also contain the details of any relevant information that the claimant is seeking and an explanation of why this is considered relevant.

The letter should normally contain the details of any interested parties known to the claimant. They should be sent a copy of the letter before claim for information.

A claim should not normally be made until the proposed reply date given in the letter before claim has passed, unless the circumstances of the case require more immediate action to be taken.

The Protocol provides that defendants should normally respond within 14 days. Failure to do so may be taken into account by the court and sanctions may be imposed unless there are good reasons.

Where it is not possible to reply within the proposed time limit the Protocol states that the defendant should send an interim reply and propose a reasonable extension. Where an extension is sought, reasons should be given and, where required, additional information requested. The request for an extension of time to respond will not affect the time limit for making a claim for judicial review nor will it bind the claimant where he or she considers this to be unreasonable. However, where the court considers that a subsequent claim is made prematurely it may impose sanctions.

If the claim is being conceded in full, the reply should say so in clear and unambiguous terms.

If the claim is being conceded in part or not being conceded at all, the reply should say so in clear and unambiguous terms, and:

- where appropriate, contain a new decision, clearly identifying what aspects of the claim are being conceded and what are not, or, give a clear timescale within which the new decision will be issued;
- provide a fuller explanation for the decision, if considered appropriate to do so;
- address any points of dispute, or explain why they cannot be addressed;
- enclose any relevant documentation requested by the claimant, or explain why the documents are not being enclosed; and
- where appropriate, confirm whether or not they will oppose any application for an interim remedy.

The response should be sent to all interested parties identified by the claimant and contain details of any other parties who the defendant considers also have an interest.

Use of the protocol will not be appropriate in all cases. It will not be appropriate where the defendant does not have the legal power to change the decision being challenged. It also may not be appropriate in circumstances where the application is urgent.

PROCEDURE FOR APPLYING FOR JUDICIAL REVIEW

4.6 The procedure for judicial review is set out in CPR Part 54 and the Part 54 Practice Direction. The judicial review procedure **must** be used in a claim for judicial review where the claimant is seeking a mandatory order, a prohibitory order or a quashing order, with or without a claim for a declaration or an injunction. If the claimant is seeking a declaration or an injunction and not a mandatory, prohibitory or quashing order then the judicial review procedure **may** be used.

The claimant may include in a claim for judicial review a claim for damages, restitution or the recovery of a sum due but a claimant may not in judicial review proceedings make only a monetary claim.

MAKING THE CLAIM

4.7 The claim for judicial review must be brought promptly and in any event within three months after the grounds to make the claim first arose.

The claim is brought by claim form under Part 8. In addition to the matters required by CPR Part 8 to be in the claim form, it must also include the name and address of any person considered by the applicant to be an interested party, a claim for permission to seek judicial review, and the remedy claimed. Form N461 is the published form of judicial review claim form. For Claim Form see **Appendix 12.**

Part 54 Practice Direction lists in paragraph 5.6 what must be included in and accompany the claim form. Included in the claim form or accompanying it there must be:

- (1) a detailed statement of the claimant's grounds for bringing the claim for judicial review;
- (2) a statement of the facts relied on;
- (3) any application to extend the time limit for filing the claim form; and
- (4) any application for directions.

For a precedent example of Details of Claim see **Appendix 12.**

In addition, the Practice Direction provides so far as is relevant to a claim for judicial review of a decision of HM Land Registry that the claim form must be accompanied by:

- (1) any written evidence in support of the claim or application to extend time;
- (2) a copy of any order that the claimant seeks to have quashed;
- (3) . . . .;
- (4) copies of any documents on which the claimant proposes to rely;
- (5) copies of any relevant statutory material; and
- (6) a list of essential documents for advance reading by the court (with page references to the passages relied on).

If the claimant cannot for any reasons file all the documents with the claim form, he must include with his claim form a document indicating which documents have not been filed and the reasons why they are not currently available.

The claimant must file two copies of a paginated and indexed bundle containing all the documents accompanying the claim form.

Claims for judicial review are dealt with in the Administrative Court. Claims may be issued at the District Registry of the High Court at Birmingham, Cardiff, Leeds or Manchester as well as at the Royal Courts of Justice in London. Cases started in Birmingham will normally be determined at a court in the Midland region; in Cardiff in Wales; in Leeds in the North-Eastern

Region; in London at the Royal Courts of Justice and in Manchester, in the North-Western Region.

The sealed claim form must be served within seven days of the date of issue. The claimant should lodge with the Administrative Court a certificate of service in Form N215 within seven days of service.

For Certificate of Service see **Appendix 12.**

RESPONDING TO A CLAIM FORM

4.8 A person served with the claim form must acknowledge service within 21 days or will be unable to take part in the hearing of the application for permission to seek judicial review without the permission of the court. Form N462 is the published form of acknowledgement of service of a judicial review claim. For Form N462 see **Appendix 12.** The acknowledgement of service must set out a summary of grounds for contesting the claim and give the name and address of any person considered by the defendant to be an interested party.

CONSIDERING APPLICATION FOR PERMISSION

4.9 The court will generally, in the first instance, consider the question of permission without a hearing.

On consideration of the application for permission, the court may either grant permission, refuse permission or refuse permission on the grounds that the application is totally without merit.

If permission is granted without a hearing, neither the defendant nor any interested party may apply to set aside the decision granting permission.

If permission is refused without a hearing, the claimant may seek reconsideration of the decision at a hearing.

If permission is refused without a hearing on the grounds that the application is totally without merit, then the claimant may not seek reconsideration at an oral hearing and the court is required to consider whether to make a civil restraint order – see CPR 23.12

An application for reconsideration at an oral hearing must be made using Form 86b which will be sent with the notification of refusal on paper of permission. For Form 86b see **Appendix 12.** The application must be made within seven days of service of notification of the refusal.

The Practice Direction provides that on an oral hearing of an application for permission, neither the defendant nor any other interested party need attend the hearing unless the court directs otherwise. A defendant or other interested party may be tempted to attend if he thinks he can persuade the court to refuse permission and thereby secure an earlier and possibly cheaper disposal of the proceedings. However, if the defendant or other party does attend the hearing, he is not likely to be awarded his costs. The Practice Direction provides that where the defendant or any party does attend a hearing of the application for permission, the court will not generally make an order for costs against the claimant.

PROCEDURE AFTER GRANT OF PERMISSION

4.10 Within 35 days of the order granting permission, the defendant or any person interested may file grounds for contesting the application or alternative grounds for supporting it and any written evidence.

Any person may apply under CPR 54.17 for permission to file evidence or make representations at the judicial review hearing. An application for permission should be made by letter to the Administrative Court office, identifying the claim, explaining who the applicant is and indicating why and in what form the applicant wants to participate in the hearing.

If permission is granted then the court may impose conditions and it may make case management directions.

THE HEARING

4.11 The judicial review application will be heard at an oral hearing. The court may only decide a judicial review application without a hearing where all parties agree.

The claim may be heard by a single judge of the Administrative Court or by a Divisional Court, comprising two judges. The court may sit in London, Birmingham, Cardiff, Leeds, Manchester or if appropriate, in other locations.

Chapter 5

THE PROPERTY CHAMBER OF THE FIRST-TIER TRIBUNAL

Key topics in this chapter

Background
Creation of the Property Chamber
Transfer of cases
Organisation of the Property Chamber
Land Registration division
Residential property division
Agricultural lands and drainage division
Costs
Appeals

BACKGROUND

5.1 On 16 August 2001, the report of a review of tribunals by Sir Andrew Legatt entitled '*Tribunals for Users – One System, One Service*' was published. Its main recommendations were:

- the citizen should be presented with a single, overarching structure, giving access to all tribunals;
- tribunals should have the separate rules and procedures they need;
- both citizen and state tribunals and party and party tribunals should form part of the tribunals system;
- there should be a Tribunals Service committed to producing a service and approach of the highest quality and responsive to the user;
- the tribunals system should be divided by subject-matter into divisions in a structure which was readily apparent to the user;
- divisions should be composed by creating sensibly coherent areas of work, and by bringing together as far as possible the tribunals for which each Government department then had overall responsibility; and
- there should be a single route of appeal for all tribunals, to a single appellate Division.

In the context of land, property and housing tribunals, the report noted that 'there are confusing overlaps of jurisdiction between courts and tribunals, as well as between tribunals' and that 'an expert decision-making forum, without overlapping jurisdictions, is a precondition of effective procedural reform'. Sir Andrew Leggatt recommended that the Law Commission should be asked to work out 'a comprehensive solution' for land, property and housing tribunals, with a view in particular to removing any jurisdictional overlaps and any scope for forum shopping. In accordance with this recommendation, the Law Commission was asked to consider a group of tribunals concerned with land, valuation and housing. The group of tribunals the Law Commission looked at were:

- The Adjudicator to HM Land Registry
- The Agricultural Lands Tribunal
- The Commons Commissioners
- The Lands Tribunal
- The Leasehold Valuation Tribunal
- The Rent Assessment Committees
- The Rent Tribunal
- The Valuation Service

The Law Commission held a consultation in December 2002. Its report, '*Land, Valuation and Housing Tribunals: The Future (Law Com 281)* was published in September 2003. The Law Commission recommended that the tribunals should be grouped together into a generic Property and Valuation Tribunal and a reformed Lands Tribunal. The former would be composed of all of the tribunals except for the Commons Commissioners and the Adjudicator, who would be absorbed into the Lands Tribunal. The latter would retain its existing first instance jurisdiction and also act as an appellate tribunal to the new Property and Valuation Tribunal. The reformed Lands Tribunal should have the same range of powers on appeal as the civil courts. In addition to its appellate jurisdictions, the reformed Lands Tribunal should have jurisdiction to adjudicate on disputes then within the first instance jurisdiction of the Lands Tribunal and disputes then within the jurisdictions of the Commons Commissioners and the Adjudicator to HM Land Registry. Appeals from the reformed Lands Tribunal should be to the Court of Appeal on a point of law only. Judicial review of decisions of the Property and Valuation Tribunal should be barred by statute where other remedies had not been exhausted. Judicial review of the reformed Lands Tribunal should be barred by statute.

The government did not accept The Law Commission's recommendations. The government's own proposals were set out in its Consultation Paper on Part 1 of the Tribunals Courts and Enforcement Act, *Transforming Tribunals: Implementing Part 1 of the Tribunals Courts and Enforcement Act 2007* (CP 30/07, Ministry of Justice, 2007.

That paper stated that in the new Tribunals Service, there was to be both a specialist Lands Chamber in the Upper Tribunal, and a specialist Land, Property and Housing chamber in the First-tier Tribunal. The First-tier Tribunal was to include the Adjudicator to HM Land Registry, the Agriculture Lands Tribunals and the tribunals coming under the umbrella of the Residential Tribunal Service, namely the Leasehold Valuation Tribunal, the Rent Assessment Committees and the Rent Tribunal. It was also proposed that it should include the Valuation Tribunal. The Lands Chamber in the Upper Tribunal was to consist only of the Lands Tribunal, retaining both its first-instance and appellate jurisdictions.

The Leasehold Valuation Tribunal, Rent Assessment Committees and Residential Property Tribunals had previously been administered by the Department for Communities and Local Government. These tribunals were brought together within the Residential Property Tribunal Service. On Friday 1 July 2011 the Residential Property Tribunal Service transferred to Her Majesty's Courts and Tribunals Service.

After consultation, the government produced the proposals which were subsequently brought into effect. There was to be a new, seventh, first-tier chamber, called the Property Chamber. The Property Chamber was to consist of the Residential Property Service, the Agricultural Lands Tribunal and the Adjudicator to HM Land Registry. The Valuation Tribunal was to be left out of the chamber for the time being, although it was intended that it should be brought in at some future date.

The government's expressed aim was to create 'cohesion within the system and allow more flexible deployment of judges and panel members across jurisdictions'. One example of cohesion was to be the creation of a common set of procedural rules,

CREATION OF THE PROPERTY CHAMBER

5.2 The Property Chamber of the First-tier Tribunal came into being on the 1st July 2013 pursuant to the Transfer of Tribunal Functions Order 2013. The Transfer of Tribunal Functions Order was made under Tribunals Courts and Enforcement Act 2007, s 30. It provided for the functions of tribunals to be transferred to the First–tier Tribunal or the Upper Tribunal and for the 'old tribunals' to be abolished. The Transfer Order includes in its first and second schedules consequential provisions amending very many provisions in primary and secondary legislation. The Order has amended every statutory reference to the old tribunals. For this reason, the Transfer Order itself runs to over 50 pages. The task was made even more complex by the fact that the equivalent Welsh tribunals in Wales of the Agricultural Lands Tribunal and the Residential Property Tribunals, were not brought into the Property Chamber and are not administered by HM Courts and Tribunals Service.

The Transfer Order also made provision for salaried and fee-paid judiciary and members to be transferred into the First-tier Tribunal as judges and other members. The orders were made on 29 April 2013 and came into force on 1 July 2013.

TRANSFER OF CASES

5.3 Schedule 3 to the Transfer Order made provision as to what was to happen in respect of proceedings started before 1st July 2013. The Schedule provided that all cases started on or after the 1 July 2013 would be proceedings before the First-tier Tribunal and that all proceedings started before 1 July 2013 and pending on that date, would continue as proceedings before the First-tier Tribunal.

The new rules would apply to cases whether started before or after 1 July 2013, although the Tribunal had power to disapply a provision of the new rules in particular cases.

ORGANISATION OF THE PROPERTY CHAMBER

5.4 Overall responsibility for tribunals within the Upper and First-tier Tribunals lies with the Senior President of Tribunals, Lord Justice Sullivan. Each Chamber has its own President. The President of the Property Chamber is Siobhan McGrath, the former President of the Residential Property Tribunal Service.

5.4 *The Property Chamber of the First-tier Tribunal*

The Property Chamber is divided into three divisions reflecting the grouping of the source jurisdictions: Land Registration; Residential Property; and Agricultural Land and Drainage. Each division is led by a Principal Judge, the Chamber President being the current Principal Judge of the Residential Property division. Each division has its own administrative and judicial staff.

LAND REGISTRATION DIVISION

5.5 The functions of the Adjudicator to HM Land Registry to determine matters referred to him under Land Registration Act 2002 s 73(7), to determine network access appeals under Land Registration Act 2002 Schedule 5 paragraph 4 and to make orders for the rectification or setting aside of documents under Land Registration Act 2002 s 108(2) were transferred to the Tribunal. Those functions are performed by the Land Registration division.

The Adjudicator to HM Land Registry, Mr Edward Cousins became the first Principal Judge of the Land Registration Division, providing judicial leadership. The three salaried and 29 fee-paid Deputy Adjudicators to HM Land Registry, who had been members of the Adjudicator's staff to whom he was authorised by Land Registration Act 2002 Schedule 9 paragraph 4 to delegate his judicial functions, became transferred-in salaried and fee-paid judges respectively of the First-tier Tribunal. They were assigned to the Property Chamber and they now sit in the Land Registration division.

The Land Registration division is based at Alfred Place in London, although it sits at hearing centres around England and Wales to hear cases.

The Land Registration division deals with about 1200 cases a year. Of those which are determined by a hearing, most require a hearing of at least one full day and often two, three or four days. Longer hearings are also sometimes required. Hearings of cases in the Land Registration division are conducted by a single judge sitting without lay or expert members.

RESIDENTIAL PROPERTY DIVISION

Origins

5.6 By of the Rent Act 1965 Schedule 2, Rent Assessment Committees were created to consider appeals against fair rent registrations. The Housing Act 1980 extended their jurisdiction by granting them jurisdiction to determine certain matters relating to the enfranchisement of leasehold houses, previously dealt with in the County Court. The Rent Assessment Committees when exercising the new jurisdiction relating to enfranchisement were known as the Leasehold Valuation Tribunal.

The Leasehold Reform Housing and Urban Development Act 1993 extended the Leasehold Valuation Tribunal's enfranchisement jurisdiction to leasehold flats. Jurisdiction was further widened by the Commonhold and Leasehold Reform Act 2002 which granted the Leasehold Valuation Tribunal powers to determine liability to pay both service and administrative charges, as well as the new 'Right to Manage' applications.

The work expanded, as wider jurisdiction over residential property matters was granted to the Residential Property Tribunal Service; including appeals against refusals of the Right to Buy, Housing Act 2004 enforcement provisions, and even cases involving park homes.

Structure

5.7 The Chamber President, Siobhan McGrath is also the Principal Judge of the Residential Property division. The Residential Property division has about 100 judges and valuers, 100 surveyor members and 100 lay members. Most are part-time and fee-paid, though they are supported by a dozen or so salaried judges and valuers.

On the coming into existence of the Property Chamber, the Presidents of each region of the Residential Property Tribunal Service became Regional Judges; the Vice-Presidents became Deputy Regional Judges; Valuer Vice-Presidents became Deputy Regional Valuers; Lawyer Chairmen became Tribunal Judges and Valuer Chairmen remained Valuer Chairmen.

The Residential Property division continues the regional structure of the former Residential Property Service. It has London, Southern, Eastern, Midland and Northern regions with regional offices in London, Chichester, Cambridge, Birmingham, and Manchester.

The Residential Property division carries out in England (but not in Wales) the functions of the former Residential Property Tribunal, the Leasehold Valuation Tribunal, the Rent Tribunal and the Rent Assessment Committees.

Work

5.8 The work of the Residential Property division includes some disputes about private sector rents, some disputes about residential leasehold management, including the payability of service charges, valuation for enfranchisement and lease extension, disputes about the right to buy where a property is considered to be particularly suitable for the elderly, disputes about park homes and appeals against local authority notices about the condition of a property and appeals about Houses in Multiple Occupation

The Residential Property division deals with about 10,500 cases per year, the average hearing length being much shorter than the length of hearings in the Land Registration division. About half of the cases are in London and the rest in the Southern, Eastern, Midland, and Northern Regions.

In the Residential Property division, cases are frequently heard by a panel made up of a judge and one or two members. The members may be valuers, other experts or lay people. Procedural hearings are frequently heard by a single judge.

AGRICULTURAL LAND AND DRAINAGE DIVISION

5.9 The Agricultural Land and Drainage division carries out the functions formerly carried out by the Agricultural Lands Tribunal. These are functions arising under the Agricultural Holdings Act 1986 and Land Drainage Act 1991, ss 28 and 30, in respect of certain drainage disputes between neighbours

The main issues dealt with by the Agricultural Land and Drainage division are:

- applications by close relatives of a deceased or retiring tenant to succeed to the tenancy
- applications by landlords for consent to a notice to quit served on the tenant
- applications for a direction to tend ditches or carry out drainage work on neighbouring land
- applications by landlords for a certificate of bad husbandry on the ground that the tenant is not farming in accordance with the rules of good husbandry
- applications by tenants for approval to carry out long-term improvements on the holding
- applications for a direction to provide fixed equipment

The Principal Judge of the Agricultural Land and Drainage division is Mr Nigel Thomas.

In the Agricultural Land and Drainage division, hearings are usually conducted by a judge sitting with two lay members. The members may have experience of farming, representing land owners or land drainage.

COSTS

5.10 The rules recognised and maintained the difference between the Adjudicator to HM Land Registry and the Residential Property Tribunal Service and the Agricultural Lands Tribunal as regards costs. In Land Registration division cases, cost recovery is provided for on a costs-follow-the-event basis, whereas for the latter two tribunals it is only allowable in prescribed circumstances: generally either for non-compliance, wasted costs or unreasonably bringing, defending or conducting proceedings.

The cost provisions in the Rules are wider and more extensive than the former rules governing the recovery of costs in the Residential Property Tribunal Service and the Agricultural Lands Tribunal. Formerly the Residential Property Tribunal Service could at best award costs limited to £500 when one party had acted in a way which was 'frivolous, vexatious or an abuse of process' in connection with the proceedings. Such orders were not commonly made in connection with the proceedings. Under the Rules, in agricultural land and residential property cases, the tribunal may make an order in respect of costs

- under section 29(4) of the 2007 Act (wasted costs); or
- if a person has acted unreasonably in bringing, defending or conducting proceedings.

There is no limit on the amount of costs which may be awarded. However, these provisions do not apply in rents cases.

The Residential Property division is working out in practice how frequently and in what circumstances it will use its power to award costs. Parties should certainly be aware of the risk of adverse costs orders being made against them.

APPEALS

5.11 All appeals from decisions of the Property Chamber lie to the Upper Tribunal. However, the Chamber of the Upper Tribunal hearing the appeals differs. All appeals from decisions of the Residential Property division and the Agricultural Lands and Drainage division lie to the Lands Chamber of the Upper Tribunal. All appeals from the Land Registration division go to the Tax and Chancery Chamber of the Upper Tribunal.

Chapter 6

REFERRALS BY LAND REGISTRY

Key topics in this chapter

Case summary
Notice of referral

CASE SUMMARY

6.1 The Land Registration (Referral to the Adjudicator to HM Land Registry) Rules 2003 as amended lay down what is to happen once the Registrar has decided the matter must be referred to the Tribunal. They are set out in APPENDIX 5.

The Registrar will, as soon as practicable, prepare a case summary. The case summary will contain:

- the names and addresses of the parties;
- details of their legal or other representation (if any);
- a summary of the core facts;
- details of the disputed application;
- details of the objection to that application;
- a list of any documents that will be copied to the Tribunal;
- anything else that the Registrar may consider to be appropriate.

If the address given of a party is not a postal address in England and Wales of that party or his representative, that party must provide the Registrar with such an address.

For an example of a case summary, see **FORM 36** in APPENDIX **14**.

In the case summary, the Registrar refers to the party making the disputed application as 'the applicant' and to the party objecting as 'the objector'. Usually it will be the party making the disputed application who will be making the underlying claim. But, in the case of a unilateral notice, it is the objector rather than the applicant who is making the underlying claim. This is because the objection is to an application to cancel a hostile entry already made in favour of the objector.

The Registrar will:

- send a copy of the case summary to the parties;
- give the parties an opportunity to make comments on the contents of the case summary within the time specified by him;
- inform the parties in writing that the case summary together with copies of the documents listed in it will be sent to the Tribunal with the notice of referral.

The Registrar may amend the case summary as he considers appropriate, having considered any written comments made to him by the parties.

Although the Tribunal sees the case summary, it is no more than a brief introduction to the matter. It enables the Tribunal to ascertain if there are any current or proposed court proceedings arising out of the dispute, and whether it ought to exercise his power to direct one of the parties to commence court proceedings.

The case summary does not form any part of the pleadings before the Tribunal and therefore does not contain full arguments or the evidence. Given the limited role of the case summary before the Tribunal, undue time and effort should not be spent trying to persuade the Registrar to alter the draft case summary.

Nevertheless, the case summary is an extremely concise and useful introduction to the dispute and the Tribunal when hearing a case will find it very useful when reading the papers before the hearing. It should therefore always be included in the trial bundle.

NOTICE OF REFERRAL

6.2 After the Registrar has considered the written comments, if any, made by the parties on the contents of the case summary and made any appropriate amendment to it, he will, as soon as practicable, send to the Tribunal a notice of referral (see **FORM 37** in **APPENDIX 14**).

This document informs the Tribunal that the matter has been referred to it and will be accompanied by a copy of the case summary and the documents listed in the case summary. The Registrar will at the same time inform the parties in writing that the matter has been referred to the Tribunal and send to the parties a copy of the case summary.

Chapter 7

PROCEDURE ON RECEIPT OF A REFERENCE

Key topics in this Chapter

Notice of receipt
Designating the applicant and the respondent
Deciding on whether to retain jurisdiction or to direct a party to commence court proceedings
The function of the Tribunal under LRA 2002, s 108(1)(a) (as amended)

NOTICE OF RECEIPT

7.1 Following receipt by the Tribunal of a reference, the Tribunal will serve written notice on the parties. This notice will:

- state that the reference has been received;
- give the date when the Tribunal received the reference;
- give the matter number allocated to the reference;
- give the name and any known address for service of the parties to the proceedings; and
- state which party or parties will be the Applicant for the purposes of the proceedings and which party or parties will be the Respondent.

The date of receipt of the reference may be important to the parties, because the Tribunal has power to award only costs incurred after the reference of the matter to him.

For such a notice see **Form 37** in **Appendix 14**.

Parties should check that the any address for service given for them in the notice is an accurate and complete postal address and is the address at which the party wishes to be served with documents by the Tribunal and by the other party.

A party will also wish to take note of the address for service of the other party.

DESIGNATING THE APPLICANT AND THE RESPONDENT

7.2 The Tribunal will consider the nature of the matter before it based on the information set out in the case summary and then decide who is to be the Applicant for the purposes of the proceedings and who is to be the Respondent. It is not the case that the party who has made the application to Land Registry is always named as the Applicant and that the party who has objected to the application is always named the Respondent. The principal point of relevance in deciding who is to be the Applicant for the purposes of the proceedings and who is to be the Respondent is where the burden of proof lies. There are cases where the burden of proof lies on the person who has objected to the application. The Tribunal will normally name as Applicant the party on whom the burden of proof lies and will name the other party as Respondent.

EXAMPLE 1

X applies to register the benefit of a prescriptive easement over land of which Y is the registered proprietor. Y objects, stating that there has been no user sufficient to give rise to an easement. The burden of proof of the existence of the easement is on X. The Tribunal will name X as Applicant and Y as Respondent.

EXAMPLE 2

X applies to alter the register to cancel a unilateral notice registered by Y on the title to land of which X is the registered proprietor. Y objects to the application to cancel the notice on the grounds that he is entitled to a charge over the land. Y will have stated in the prescribed Form UN1 used to apply for registration of the unilateral notice, the nature of the interest protected. This statement will be in the form of a statement or a certificate (Form UN1, panels 11 and 12) but in order to obtain registration of the unilateral notice, Y will not have had to satisfy the Registrar that the charge is valid.

The burden of proof is on Y to establish in the proceedings before the Tribunal that he has a valid charge. If he cannot establish this then the unilateral notice should be cancelled. The Tribunal will name Y as the Applicant and X as the Respondent.

EXAMPLE 3

X applies to register a transfer to him of land of which Y is the registered proprietor. Y objects, alleging that the execution of the transfer by him was obtained by fraud.

Although it is for X to establish that the transfer was validly executed, the burden is on Y to prove that he executed the transfer because of fraud. The Tribunal will name Y as Applicant and X as Respondent.

DECIDING ON WHETHER TO RETAIN JURISDICTION OR TO DIRECT A PARTY TO COMMENCE COURT PROCEEDINGS

Introduction

7.3 Where a dispute has been referred by the Registrar to the Tribunal for determination under LRA 2002, s 73(7) (as amended), the Tribunal has wide power, instead of deciding the matter for itself, to direct a party to the proceedings to commence court proceedings within a specified time for the purpose of obtaining the court's decision on the matter: see LRA 2002, s 110(1). The court proceedings can be commenced in the High Court or the County Court.

Following receipt of a reference, the Tribunal will consider whether:

- to retain jurisdiction to determine the matter itself; or
- to direct a party to commence court proceedings; or
- to adjourn the proceedings before it pending the outcome of existing or proposed court proceedings.

The Tribunal will consider first the information set out in the case summary provided by Land Registry. The case summary will state in a summary form the nature of the application and of the objection made to it. It will also usually state whether there are any existing court proceedings concerning the dispute or whether any party has indicated an intention to commence court proceedings to determine the dispute or a related matter.

Although the Law Commission suggested in its 2001 report 'Land Registration for the Twenty-First Century: A Conveyancing Revolution' that the Tribunal might direct court proceedings if the application raised an important or difficult point of law, or there were substantial or complex disputes of fact, in practice the Tribunal retains cases of significant weight. It often decides important and difficult points of law and complex disputes of fact.

The Tribunal may decide to direct the commencement of court proceedings if it has insufficient powers to deal justly or efficiently with the underlying dispute between the parties.

EXAMPLE 4

A applies to register a restriction on the title to a house of which B is the registered proprietor. A alleges that he formerly cohabited with B in the house, that the relationship has now broken down and that he is entitled to a beneficial interest under a resulting or constructive trust. In correspondence sent to Land Registry A states in passing that he needs to realise his share of the house. B acknowledges that she and A cohabited and that their relationship broke down, but denies that B is entitled to a beneficial interest. B has stated that she does not want to sell the house regardless of whether A has a beneficial interest.

The Tribunal is likely to direct A to commence court proceedings to determine whether he is entitled to a beneficial interest in the house. It is apparent that A will want to obtain an order for sale if he succeeds in establishing his beneficial interest. The Tribunal has no power to direct a sale of the house and does not have the other powers given to the court by the Trusts of Land and Appointment of Trustees Act 1996.

The Tribunal will not direct a party to commence court proceedings simply because an allegation of fraud has been made (such as a forged transfer). The Tribunal is accustomed to dealing with such cases, invariably with the assistance of expert handwriting evidence.

The Tribunal need not direct a party to commence court proceedings because an allegation has been made that a document is voidable in equity. The Tribunal has all the power of the High Court to set aside a document which effects a qualifying disposition of a registered estate or charge or is a contract to make such a disposition or effects a transfer of an interest which is subject to a notice in the register: see LRA 2002, s 108(2) (as amended).

A party to a reference who wishes to set aside a document can make a free standing application to the Tribunal to set aside the document. This jurisdiction is considered in **Chapter 24**. Such an application can be heard at the same time as the dispute referred by the Registrar.

Even if a separate application to the Tribunal to set aside the document has not been made, if on a reference an argument is advanced that the register should be rectified because a document is voidable, the Tribunal may treat that as an informal application to the Tribunal to exercise his power under LRA 2002, s 108(2) (as amended) to set aside the document. The Tribunal might dispense with the formal requirements of Rule 26 and Practice Direction 2 requiring a separate application. This would be on the basis that the rule is directory and not mandatory, in the light of the overriding objective to be found in Rule 3.

Where the Tribunal intends to direct a party to commence court proceedings it will invite representations or objections from the parties and make its decision in the light of any such representations or objections.

Rule 37 provides that the parties may make representations before the Tribunal decides to direct a party to commence proceedings. The rule provides that these representations or objections must be concerned with:

- whether the Tribunal should make a direction;
- which party should be directed to commence court proceedings;
- the time within which court proceedings should commence;
- the questions the court should determine.

Even though it intends to make such a direction the Tribunal will nevertheless name one party as the Applicant, and the other as the Respondent, on receipt of the reference. It needs to do so because the matter referred to the Tribunal where it directs court proceedings, will nevertheless remain with the Tribunal, albeit stayed, until an order is made following the determination of the court proceedings.

For a notice inviting such representations or objections in the case of an Applicant in a beneficial interest case, see **Form 38** in **Appendix 14**. For a similar direction in the case of an Applicant in a non-beneficial interest case, see **Form 39** in **Appendix 14**. A suitably modified version of the direction is sent to the Respondent.

Where the Tribunal does make a direction directing a party to commence court proceedings (see **Form 44** in **Appendix 14**), it will order the party bearing the burden of proof on the underlying issue to commence the court proceedings. That party will not necessarily have been the Applicant before the Registrar. In the case of a unilateral notice, it is the objector before the Registrar, rather than the Applicant before the Registrar, who is making the underlying claim. This is because the objection is to an application to cancel an entry already made in favour of the Objector.

The Tribunal can direct a party to commence court proceedings in respect of the whole of the matter referred to him or on just part of it, such as a single issue.

THE FUNCTION OF THE TRIBUNAL

7.4 The reference to the Tribunal opens a new chapter in the dispute between the parties and there is a new terminology. The application to the Registrar resulting in the reference is referred to as the "original application", the subject of the reference is the 'matter', whilst the proceedings of the matter before the Tribunal, following the reference, are referred to as the 'proceedings'.

If the Tribunal retains jurisdiction, it is its function to determine matters referred to it under LRA 2002, s 73(7): see LRA 2002, s 108(1)(a). The Court of Appeal has confirmed that, in performing this function, the Tribunal must determine the underlying merits of the substantive dispute between the parties in a judicial capacity: *Chief Land Registrar v Silkstone* [2011] EWCA Civ 801, [37], CA, [2012] 1 WLR 400, [2011] 2 P & CR 258, approving *Jayasinghe v Liyanage* [2010] EWHC 265 (Ch), [2010] 1 WLR 2106, [2010] 1 EGLR 61. It is not the function of the Tribunal to act administratively and give temporary relief to an Applicant who can show an apparently arguable, or non-fanciful, claim prior to the matter being determined judicially in court.

Moreover, in presenting the case on the underlying dispute, the parties are not restricted to the arguments previously put forward to the Registrar in respect of the application or objection, as the case may be. That there is such a restriction has been argued on more than one occasion, but there is no authority for such a proposition. So where an application for the entry of notice of an implied easement has been made to Land Registry based on the rule in *Wheeldon v Burrows* (1879) 12 Ch D 31, CA, the case could be argued, instead or additionally, on the basis of the LPA 1925, s 62.

A further example is *Quigley v Masterson* [2011] EWHC 2529 (Ch), [2012] 1 All ER 1224, [2012] 1 FCR 541. The dispute was whether, at the date of his death, Mrs Quigley's father had severed the joint tenancy of the house he owned jointly with Mrs Masterson. Mrs Quigley objected to an application to remove a restriction on the basis that the joint tenancy had been severed in her father's lifetime. She relied on a notice of severance sent by her father's solicitors and on a mutual course of conduct in Court of Protection proceedings commenced by Mrs Quigley. Both these arguments failed before the Adjudicator and on appeal to the High Court. But in the High Court a new argument was raised, namely that Mrs Masterson's own application to the Court of Protection, which had been given to Mrs Quigley but not to her father, constituted a notice of severance. Henderson J held that it was a notice of severance, and was to be treated as having been given to Mrs Quigley's father when the Court of Protection ordered Mrs Quigley should become her father's deputy.

In *Wakefield City Council v Symonds* (Reference/2006/0931) (2007), unreported, the Applicant claimed a paper title to the unregistered disputed land, and the Respondent claimed title to it by adverse possession. The Adjudicator found that the Respondent could not establish a title by adverse possession but that he had acquired prescriptive rights of way and parking on the disputed land. He directed the Registrar to register the Applicant as first proprietor, but subject to the Respondent's prescriptive rights. This was even though the Respondent had not made any application to Land Registry in respect of such prescriptive rights. For the power of the Tribunal to require the Registrar to make a specified entry such as this on the register, see CHAPTER **15**.

But if on a reference concerning an implied easement the Applicant raised the issue of an express grant of an easement over registered land, the Tribunal could not make a direction to the Registrar based on an express grant as that would be outside the scope of the original application. Such a grant does not have effect until completed by registration: see LRA 2002, s 27(1), (2)(d). However, the parties might agree that the Tribunal should determine any issues of fact and law relating to an express grant so as to bind them on any future application to Land Registry to register the grant.

This focused but limited jurisdiction of the Tribunal is reflected in the relief it gives. At the conclusion of the proceedings, the Tribunal will usually order the Registrar either to give effect to the original application in whole or in part, as if the objection to that original application had not been made, or to cancel the original application in whole or in part: see Rule 40

The Tribunal has no power by statute to award damages, grant an injunction or specific performance or accept an undertaking. In a beneficial interest case, there is as yet no authority on whether or not he may quantify any interest he does find established, but he cannot order a sale of the property. However, with regard to adverse possession, the Tribunal is expressly given wider powers: see LRA 2002, s 110(4) and CHAPTER 22 below.

The procedure before the Tribunal is governed by the Tribunal Procedure (First-tier Tribunal) (Property Chamber) Rules 2013, which are made pursuant to the Tribunals Courts and Enforcement Act 2007. They are set out in APPENDIX 2.

The CPR 1998 do not apply to proceedings before the Tribunal.

Rule 3 sets out the overriding objective of the Rules. The overriding objective is to enable the Tribunal to deal with cases fairly and justly. The authors are unaware of any authority as to the difference (if any) between dealing with a case 'fairly' and dealing with a case 'justly'. The Rule provides that dealing with a case fairly and justly includes:

- dealing with the case in ways which are proportionate to the importance of the case, the complexity of the issues, the anticipated costs and the resources of the parties and of the Tribunal;
- avoiding unnecessary formality and seeking flexibility in the proceedings;
- ensuring so far as practicable that the parties are able to participate fully in the proceedings;
- using any special expertise of the Tribunal effectively; and
- avoiding delay, so far as compatible with proper consideration of the issues.

The express inclusion of the need to avoid unnecessary formality and to seek flexibility in the proceedings is noteworthy. It is not something which was reflected in the overriding objective of the former Adjudicator to HM Land Registry (Practice and Procedure) Rules 2003. It represents an important way in which the Rules differ from the CPR 1998.

Attention to this distinction was drawn by Judge Hansen in *Singh v Ensaf* (Reference/2013/631), unreported where the learned judge refused to strike out a claim or debar the Applicant from calling evidence where the Applicant served witness statements on the Respondent very late, being only three weeks before the trial. No specific prejudice was alleged by the Respondent, the parties were ready for trial and the judge was satisfied that it would have been contrary to the overriding objective to accede to the Respondent's application.

The reference to using any special expertise of the Tribunal may not be appropriate to proceedings in the Land Registration division since the proceedings are invariably heard by a single judge sitting alone. It would appear to be directed to proceedings in the Residential Property and Agriculture and Drainage divisions where expert members can and frequently do sit on the Tribunal.

The procedure on a reference before the Tribunal is considered in more detail in Chapters 9 to 21.

Chapter 8

COURT PROCEEDINGS

Key topics in this Chapter

JURISDICTION TO DIRECT COURT PROCEEDINGS

8.1 Where a dispute has been referred by the Registrar to the Tribunal for determination under LRA 2002, s 73(7)) (as amended), the Tribunal has wide power, instead of deciding the matter for itself, to direct a party to the proceedings to commence court proceedings within a specified time for the purpose of obtaining the court's decision on the matter: see LRA 2002, s 110(1) (as amended). The court proceedings can be commenced in the High Court or the County Court.

The Tribunal will first consider whether or not to direct court proceedings when it receives the reference from Land Registry. This is dealt with in CHAPTER 7. If the Tribunal initially accepts jurisdiction but considers during the course of the reference that court proceedings ought to be commenced by one of the parties, similar considerations and procedure will apply.

PROCEDURE BEFORE THE TRIBUNAL WHEN COURT PROCEEDINGS ARE DIRECTED

8.2 A party who has been directed to commence court proceedings must serve on the Tribunal within 14 days of the commencement of the proceedings a written notice: see Rule 38(2). The notice must state:

- that the court proceedings have been issued;
- the date of issue;
- the names and any known addresses of the parties to the court proceedings;
- the name of the court at which the proceedings will be heard;
- the case number allocated to the court proceedings; and
- the way and extent to which the court proceedings concern or relate to the matter before the Tribunal.

The Tribunal will in directing a party to commence court proceedings, give a direction as to the nature of the proceedings to be commenced eg proceedings under Trusts of Land and Appointment of Trustees Act 1996, proceedings for a declaration that the Applicant is entitled to a right of way over specified land of the Respondent, etc. The notice should indicate to the Tribunal that the court proceedings commenced concern the matters which the Tribunal intended should be the subject of the proceedings before the court.

8.2 *Court proceedings*

A party who has been directed to commence court proceedings must also:

- within 14 days of the court making a decision on any application for an extension of time, serve a copy of that decision on the Tribunal: see Rule 38(2);
- within 14 days of the date that the matter before the court is finally disposed of, serve a copy of the final order on the Tribunal: see Rule 38(2).

Where the Tribunal has directed a party to commence court proceedings for the court's decision on the whole of the matter and has received the notice that court proceedings have been issued, the proceedings before the Tribunal are automatically stayed pending the final court order: see Rule 39(2). For a letter informing the parties of a stay see **Form 45** in **appendix 14.**

Once the Tribunal has received a copy of the final court order then, subject to one exception and unless the court otherwise directs, the proceedings before the Tribunal are to be regarded as stayed.

The exception applies if a further order, in addition to the final court order, is necessary to implement the decision of the court. In these circumstances, the Tribunal may make an order, either with or without giving notice to the parties, if it would have had the power to make such an order if it had made a substantive decision in relation to the proceedings: see Rule 39(4).

EXAMPLE 1

The Tribunal has referred a dispute as to whether or not A has a beneficial interest in a house to the County Court. The parties settle at the door of court and the district judge approves an order declaring that A has a 35% interest in the house and that it should be sold in 6 months' time. Nothing is said in the order about the restriction that A applied to Land Registry to have entered on the register. She needs the protection of the restriction pending sale. The Tribunal will direct the Registrar to enter the restriction (see **Form 47** in **appendix 14**).

Similarly, where the Tribunal has directed a party to commence court proceedings for the court's decision on only part of the matter and has received the notice that court proceedings have been issued in relation to that part, the relevant part of the proceedings before the Tribunal are automatically stayed pending the outcome of the court proceedings: see Rule 39(5).

Once the Tribunal has received a copy of the final court order then, the Rule provides that subject to the same exception where a further order, in addition to the final court order, is necessary to implement the decision of the court and unless the court otherwise directs, the Tribunal proceedings are, subject to any question of costs, to be regarded as stayed.

The reference to the proceedings be regarded as 'stayed' would seldom seem appropriate in the case of a referred case because the Tribunal will usually make an order directing the Chief Land Registrar to give effect to or cancel the application the subject of the reference. The making of such an order, subject to questions of costs, will usually finally determine the proceedings before the Tribunal.

The Tribunal has a discretion to adjourn the proceedings before him in relation to any other part pending the outcome of the court proceedings – see Rule 39(5).

While the court proceedings are still ongoing, the party directed to commence court proceedings must notify the court of any decision made by the Tribunal within 14 days of receipt by on that party of the decision.

It is yet to be determined on appeal what is to happen if the party directed to commence court proceedings does so, but thereafter fails to obtain a decision on the merits of the issue directed to be determined.

EXAMPLE 2

The Tribunal has required A to commence court proceedings to determine an issue arising in the matter referred to him. A repeatedly fails to serve her list of documents and the district judge eventually makes an unless order. After failing to comply with the unless order, the district judge strikes the claim out.

Although on the face of it this looks like a victory for B, it presents the Tribunal with a dilemma. It has no answer, decided on the merits, to the issue it has asked to be determined by the court. The choices are:

- to direct further court proceedings;
- to issue directions to decide the matter himself;
- to treat the party whose claim has been struck out as having failed to succeed on the issue the court was supposed to have determined.

The Adjudicator held that the better approach, giving effect to the overriding objective as required under AR 2003 r 3(3), was to say that there is discretion when court proceedings have ended in a striking out prior to a determination of the real issue. There may be cases where the more just course is to allow the proceedings to carry on before the Tribunal, and for the Tribunal to give case management directions. In other cases the failure of a party in the court proceedings to obtain a determination on the merits should be taken as a failure to establish that party's case before the Tribunal: see *Khan v Khan* [2011] EWLandRA 2008_0837.

There may be other cases in which the Tribunal would treat a party who has by his inaction allowed court proceedings to be struck out as being in default of the direction of the Tribunal to commence court proceedings. Such a direction may include an implied direction to take proper steps to pursue those proceedings to a substantive conclusion. If the party is in default, the Tribunal may impose a sanction under Rule 8(2) or (3), including a direction to the Registrar to cancel or give effect to the original application.

COURT PROCEDURE WHEN COURT PROCEEDINGS ARE DIRECTED

8.3 Proceedings in the High Court involving registered land are likely to be assigned to the Chancery Division: see Senior Courts Act 1981 Sch 1 para 1. Similarly, proceedings in the County Court are likely to be 'Chancery Business': see CPR PD 7A para 2.5.

There is no longer a requirement that proceedings by which an application is to be made to the court under any Act must be begun by a particular process. Therefore, where a party is directed by the Tribunal to commence proceedings, there is no reason why those proceedings should not be begun under CPR 1998 Part 7. Where there is likely to be a dispute of fact, they must be brought under CPR 1998 Part 7.

PARTY COMMENCING COURT PROCEEDINGS OF OWN ACCORD

8.4 Sometimes a party commences or has commenced court proceedings which concern or relate to the matter before the Tribunal, although not directed to do so by the Tribunal. In such circumstances, the party concerned must serve on the Tribunal a written notice relating to the commencement of the court proceedings: see Rule 38(1) and (2).

Such a notice must be served within 14 days of the commencement of the court proceedings or, if later, within seven days of service on that party of notification of the reference by the Tribunal. The notice must state:

- that court proceedings have been issued;
- the date of issue;
- the names and any known addresses of the parties to the court proceedings;
- the name of the court at which the proceedings will be heard;
- the case number allocated to the court proceedings;
- the way and the extent to which the court proceedings concern or relate to the matter before the Tribunal.

Such a party must:

- within 14 days after the date of any decision on any application for an extension of time, serve on the Tribunal and on all parties a copy of the decision; see rule 38(2)
- within 14 days of the date that the matter before the court is finally disposed of, serve a copy of the final order on the Tribunal: see rule 38(2)
- while proceedings are still pending, within 14 days of receipt by that party of any decision by the Tribunal on the matter, notify the court of the decision: see Rule 39(6).

Where court proceedings are commenced otherwise than following a direction by the Tribunal, the Tribunal has a discretion whether or not to adjourn the whole or part of the proceedings before it pending the outcome of the court proceedings. This would be an exercise of the general power to adjourn set out in Rule 6. The automatic stay of proceedings before the Tribunal applies only where proceedings are commenced pursuant to a direction of the Tribunal.

If, on receiving the reference, it is apparent that court proceedings have already been commenced, the Tribunal will send out a direction proposing to adjourn the proceedings before it and asking for the information required under Rule 38 (see **Form 40** and **Form 41** in **appendix 14**). A suitably modified direction will be sent out if, on receiving the reference, it is apparent that court proceedings are being contemplated by the parties of their own accord (see **Form 42** and **Form 43** in **appendix 14**) or it only becomes apparent at a later date that court proceedings have been commenced by the parties of their own accord.

For a direction adjourning the proceedings after the commencement of court proceedings otherwise than following a direction by the Tribunal, see **Form 46** in **appendix 14.**

POWER TO TRANSFER PROCEEDINGS TO COURT

8.5 Rule 6(3)(n) provides that the Tribunal may transfer proceedings to another court or tribunal if that other court of Tribunal has jurisdiction "in relation to the proceedings" and

- the Tribunal no longer has jurisdiction because of a change of circumstances since the proceedings were started; or
- the Tribunal considers that the other court or tribunal is a more appropriate forum for the determination of the case.

There is as yet no authority as to the meaning of this rule.

It is the view of the authors that the reference to the other court or tribunal having jurisdiction in relation to the proceedings is to be read as requiring the other court or tribunal to have jurisdiction to determine the underlying dispute between the parties. Thus, for example

- in a case of a disputed application to enter a restriction to protect a beneficial interest, where the objector disputes that the Applicant has a beneficial interest, the Tribunal could under Rule 6(3), if it thought it appropriate, transfer the proceedings to the county court having jurisdiction under the Trusts of Land and Appointment of Trustees Act 1996; or
- in a case where the Applicant had applied to register a right of way and the Respondent objected to the registration on the grounds that the right of way did not exist, the Tribunal could, if it thought it appropriate, transfer the matter to the High Court Chancery Division or to the County Court.

An alternative view has been expressed, namely that Rule 6(3)(n) has no application to reference cases before the Land Registration division because only the First-tier Tribunal has jurisdiction to determine references under LRA 2002, s 77. On this view, the reference to 'jurisdiction in relation to the proceedings' must be read as meaning jurisdiction to determine the reference.

This would seem to the authors to be an unduly restrictive interpretation but the matter has still to be fully argued and determined.

Chapter 9

STATEMENTS OF CASE

Key topics in this chapter

STATEMENTS OF CASE GENERALLY

9.1 On receiving a reference, if the Tribunal decides to retain jurisdiction, it will send out a direction to the parties informing them who is the Applicant and who is the Respondent, and directing the applicant to serve his statement of case within 28 days and the Respondent to serve his 28 days thereafter: see Rule 28(3) and (4) and Rule 30. The Respondent's statement of case is referred to in the rules as a response. For a direction to the Applicant, see **Form 60** in **appendix** 5. For a direction to the Respondent, see **Form 61** in **appendix** 5.

A statement of case will be similar to but not identical with a particulars of claim or a defence, as the case may be, in civil proceedings. It should be set out in clear and short numbered paragraphs, and be doubled spaced in at least size 12 font. Events should be set out in chronological order.

A statement of case must be verified by a statement of truth – PD3.

APPLICANT'S STATEMENT OF CASE

9.2 An Applicant's statement of case must include (see Rule 28(4) and PD3):

- the name and address of the Applicant;
- the name and address of the Applicant's representative (if any)
- an address in England and Wales where documents for the Applicant may be delivered;
- the Applicant's reasons for supporting or objecting to the original application, identifying all relevant facts and matters relied upon;
- a list of all copy documents provided with the statement of case

The reference to the Applicant's reasons for objecting to the original application arises because the 'original application' means the application to Land Registry referred to the Tribunal under section 73(7) of the 2002 Act. The party designated as Applicant for the purpose of the proceedings before the Tribunal may not be the party who made the original application but may be the party who objected to it.

The statement of case must be accompanied by copies of any documents available to the Applicant which –

- are important to the Applicant's case; or

- the Tribunal or any other party to the proceedings will require in order properly to understand the Applicant's case – see Rule 28(4)(c).

There is no authority as to the meaning of 'available to the Applicant' within Rule 28(4). It is to be noted that the requirement under Rule 28(4)(c) is different from the obligation to give disclosure. The documents to be served with the statement of case are only the documents important to the Applicant's case or required in order properly to understand the Applicant's case. They need not include documents important to the case of anyone who opposes the Applicant's case or required by the Tribunal to determine the matter before it.

In a change from the position under the ALR(PP)R 2003, there is no requirement that the party's address for service must be a postal address in England and Wales. However, the Practice Direction requires the Applicant to provide an address in England and Wales where documents for the Applicant can be delivered.

The representative need not be legally qualified – Rule 14(1).

For examples of an Applicant's statement of case, see the following Forms in APPENDIX **14**:

- FORM **50** (Adverse Possession: Unregistered Land);
- FORM **53** (Adverse Possession: Registered Land);
- FORM **55** (Adverse Possession: Transitional Provisions);
- FORM **57** (Cancellation Of A Unilateral Notice Relating To A Restrictive Covenant);
- FORM **59** (Cancellation Of A Caution Relating To A Claim Of Proprietary Estoppel);
- FORM **61** (Entry Of A Restriction Protecting A Beneficial Interest);
- FORM **63** (Prescriptive Easement);
- FORM **65** (Alteration Of The Register To Correct A Mistake).

RESPONDENT'S RESPONSE OR STATEMENT OF CASE

9.3 The requirements as to a Respondent's statement of case or 'response' are set out in Rule 30 and Practice Direction 4.

Rule 30(1) requires the Respondent's statement of case to state the Respondent's reasons for supporting or objecting to the original application.

The response must be accompanied by copies of any documents available to the Respondent which

- are important to the Respondent's case; or
- the Tribunal or any other party will require in order properly to understand the Respondent's case.

Practice Direction 4 requires a response served under Rule 30 to contain

- the name and address of the Respondent
- the name and address of the Respondent's representative (if any);
- an address in England and Wales where documents for the Respondent may be delivered;

- all relevant facts and matters relied upon by the Respondent in support of his case;
- a list of all copy documents provided under Rule 30(1)(b).

For examples of a Respondent's statement of case, see the following Forms in APPENDIX **14**:

- FORM **51** (Adverse Possession: Unregistered Land);
- FORM **54** (Adverse Possession: Registered Land);
- FORM **56** (Adverse Possession: Transitional Provisions);
- FORM **58** (Cancellation Of A Unilateral Notice Relating To A Restrictive Covenant);
- FORM **60** (Cancellation Of A Caution Relating To A Claim Of Proprietary Estoppel);
- FORM **62** (Entry Of A Restriction Protecting A Beneficial Interest);
- FORM **64** (Prescriptive Easement);
- FORM **66** (Alteration Of The Register To Correct A Mistake).

AMENDING A STATEMENT OF CASE

9.4 The Tribunal has an express power under Rule 6(3) to permit or require a party to amend a document. This power would permit the giving of permission to a party or the making of a requirement on a party to amend a statement of case.

Nevertheless care should be taken to ensure that a statement of case accurately and fully sets out a party's case as there is a risk that the case will fail if it is not properly particularised. In *Oakfinch v Hall* (Reference 2008/1088) (2009), unreported the Applicant claimed a right of way by necessity. The Adjudicator found that the Applicant had failed to plead a sufficient case to show, amongst other things, that at the relevant date there was no other means of access to the dominant tenement. There is also a risk that the Tribunal will not allow a party to rely upon facts which have not been pleaded but are only brought forward shortly before the hearing: see *Gordon v Chatfield* (Reference 005/1543) (2007), unreported and CHAPTER **17**.

An application to amend a statement of case should be made as soon as possible after the need to amend is discovered. Permission to amend may be given on terms as to costs. If amendment will mean that costs previously incurred by the other party have been needlessly incurred or that the other party will have to incur additional costs following the amendment, it may be that the party given permission to amend is required to pay costs of the other party.

Although there is not provision in the Rules as to how amendments to a statement of case should be made or shown, it is helpful to the parties and to the Tribunal if any words in a statement of case deleted by amendment are shown in the amended document struck through (rather than being removed from it) and if any words added by amendment are shown underlined.

Chapter 10

DISCLOSURE, WITNESS STATEMENTS AND EVIDENCE

Key topics in this Chapter

- Disclosure
- Inspection
- Witness statements
- Oath and affirmation
- Previous statements of witnesses
- Expert evidence
- Proof of documents
- Proof of contents of Register
- Photographic evidence

DISCLOSURE

Pre-disclosure – Documents with Statements of Case

10.1 With the statement of case there must be served, on both the Tribunal and all other parties, copies of any documents in the party's possession or control which are important to that party's case, or which the Tribunal or any other party to the proceedings will require in order properly to understand the party's case: see Rule 28(4)(c) and Rule 30(1)(b).

The requirement to serve these documents with the statement of case is designed to speed up the determination of the proceedings. If this requirement is overlooked (as unfortunately is often the case), the statement of case may not treated as served until the documents are also served.

Disclosure

10.2 The standard directions made by the Tribunal require that within 28 days after service of the Respondent's statement of case, each party must serve on the Tribunal and each of the other parties a list of all documents in that party's possession or control which that party intends to rely upon in the proceedings, or adversely affects that party's own case, or adversely affects another party's case, or supports another party's case. The power of the Tribunal to make such a direction arises from the general case management powers given to the Tribunal by Rule 6(1) and (2) and the specific power given by Rule 18 for the Tribunal to direct the exchange between the parties of lists of documents.

The standard directions provide that at the same time each party must send to the other party and to the Tribunal copies of all documents in the list. For a list of documents, see **Form 52** in **appendix 14**.

The list of documents should give, in respect of each document:

- a brief description of its nature;
- state whether it is an original, a copy certified to be a true copy, an office copy or another type of copy
- the date of the document,
- the parties to or the original author and recipient of the document;
- the version number or similar identification number or code of the document].

If a large number of documents fall into a particular class, that class of documents may be listed as if it were an individual document. In such a case, the description of the class of documents must be sufficiently clear and precise to enable any party receiving the list to identify the nature of the contents of each document included within that class of documents and whether any particular document which exists is included within that class of documents.

Care must be taken that coloured documents are accurately copied in colour. The list may be rejected if it fails to contain the required information.

The Tribunal also routinely requires the category of documents upon which a party intends to rely in the proceedings to be listed separately from the other documents in that party's possession or control, and only requires to be sent to it copies of those documents upon which the party intends to rely in the proceedings, rather than all the documents in the list.

The Tribunal routinely gives a direction subsequent to the service of the statements of case that each party must serve all other documents that party wishes the Tribunal to take into account in reaching his decision on the Tribunal and the other party.

Rule 18(3) provides that a party to whom a document has been disclosed may use it only for the purpose of the proceedings in which it is disclosed except where

- the document has been read to or by the Tribunal, or referred to, at a public hearing;
- the Tribunal gives permission; or
- the parties agree.

Hearings held by the Tribunal are almost invariably held in public and the Tribunal will read all documents included in the hearing bundle. It is probable therefore that Rule 18(3) does not restrict in practice the use of the documents included in the hearing bundle to use only for the purposes of the proceedings.

INSPECTION

10.3 As the standard directions made by the Tribunal provide for the provision to each party of copies of all documents disclosed by list, it is not normally necessary for an order for inspection to be made.

The Tribunal has a wide power to give directions or otherwise provide for the disclosure and inspection of documents to any extent which it considers relevant to the issues in dispute – see Rule 18. In an appropriate case therefore an order for inspection may be made in addition to or in place of the standard direction for disclosure by list and provision of copies. This would be appropriate for example in a case where a party needed to see the original of a disclosed document and not only a copy.

The provisions made by the Tribunal may include taking reasonable steps to ensure each party is given a copy of any document which has been received from any party or former party – see Rule 18(2).

On occasions the Tribunal might make its own enquiries eg of Land Registry as to the state of the register at a particular time. In this event, the Tribunal may and usually will provide a copy of any document which embodies the results of such enquiries e.g. an official copy of the register.

WITNESS STATEMENTS

10.4 In most cases before the Tribunal involving disputes of fact the parties will have to call witness evidence to prove their case.

The standard directions made by the Tribunal include a direction for the parties to serve the original witness statements of all their witnesses of fact on the Tribunal within 28 days, and to exchange copies of the witness statements with each other within 28 days.

By including a requirement for witness statements to be exchanged in the standard directions, the Tribunal ensures that the invariable practice is for witness evidence to be disclosed in advance.

The Rules do not contain any provisions as to the form or content of witness statements. However, the standard directions provide that a witness statement must contain a statement of truth to be made by the witness: 'I believe that the facts stated in this witness statement are true'.

If no witness other than the party himself is to be called, it will be sufficient if the party verifies his statement of case with a statement of truth: 'I believe that the facts and matters contained in this statement of case are true'. This should be done in any event in respect of all statements of case: see Practice Direction 3 and 4.

The parties are informed in advance in the standard directions that where a witness is called to give oral evidence his or her witness statement shall stand as his or her evidence, subject to any cross-examination unless the Tribunal orders otherwise. The practice at the hearing in this respect is considered in CHAPTER 17.

The parties are also warned in advance that they may not call witnesses other than those listed in their statement of case without the permission of the Tribunal. The better course is for a party, when serving witness statements of witnesses not already identified in the statement of case, to identify those witnesses and ask for permission to call them. As explained above, the party should inform all other parties of this application in advance to see if agreement can be reached. The Tribunal is likely to grant permission as the final hearing is still several months away at this stage.

OATH AND AFFIRMATION

10.5 Although there is generally no provision allowing an adult witness to give evidence in court without taking the oath or affirming, it would seem to be inherent in the Rules that the Tribunal may take evidence from a witness who has not taken the oath or affirmed. Rule 18(7) states that the Tribunal 'may consent' to a witness giving evidence on oath. The language of the Rule suggests that in the normal case witnesses will not take an oath or affirm before giving evidence. However, it is the practice of the Land Registration division in all cases of which the editors are aware to require all witnesses to take the oath or to affirm.

The terms of the oath and affirmation are set out in the Oaths Act 1978, s 1 and have the same legal effect as regards subsequent prosecutions for perjury. The oath is:

> 'I swear by Almighty God that the evidence I shall give shall be the truth, the whole truth and nothing but the truth.'

There are variations for members of religious faiths other than Christianity. The terms of the affirmation are:

> 'I do solemnly and sincerely and truly declare and affirm that the evidence I shall give shall be the truth, the whole truth and nothing but the truth.'

HEARSAY

10.6 The Tribunal may admit evidence whether or not it would be admissible in a civil trial in England and Wales. Hearsay evidence may therefore be admitted. The provisions of the Civil Evidence Act 1995 do not apply to proceedings before the Tribunal since that Act applies only to proceedings before any tribunal, in relation to which the strict rules of evidence apply: see the Civil Evidence Act 1995, s 11.

Although hearsay evidence is admissible, the Tribunal will have to consider the weight to be given to it in reaching its decision. Although the Civil Evidence Act 1995 does not apply to proceedings before the Tribunal, the matters set out in the Civil Evidence Act 1995, s 4(2), are likely to be of relevance when the Tribunal is considering the weight to be given to hearsay evidence. They are:

- whether it would have been reasonable and practicable for the party by whom the evidence was adduced to have produced the maker of the original statement as a witness;
- whether the original statement was made contemporaneously with the occurrence or existence of the matters stated;
- whether the evidence involves multiple hearsay;
- whether any person involved had any motive to conceal or misrepresent matters;
- whether the original statement was an edited account, or was made in collaboration with another or for a particular purpose;

- whether the circumstances in which the evidence is adduced as hearsay are such as to suggest an attempt to prevent proper evaluation of its weight.

PREVIOUS STATEMENTS OF WITNESSES

10.7 Although Rule 18(6) provides that the Tribunal may admit evidence whether or not it would be admissible in a civil trial, it is considered that the Tribunal remains bound by the restrictions on the use of previous statements of witnesses imposed by sections 3, 4 and 5 of the Criminal Procedure Act 1865.

Criminal Procedure Act 1865 s 1 provides that the provisions of sections 3 to 8 (inclusive) of the Act apply to 'all persons having, by law or by consent of parties, authority to hear, receive and examine evidence'. The Tribunal has such authority by law.

The Tribunal may give the party calling or intending to call a person as a witness permission to adduce a previous statement if in the opinion of the Tribunal, the witness is adverse. If a party calling a person as a witness wishes to adduce evidence of a previous statement, he must mention the circumstances in which the statement was made to the witness and ask the witness whether or not he made the statement: see the Criminal Procedure Act 1865, s 3.

A party cross-examining a witness may cross-examine him on relevant previous statements made by him in writing or reduced to writing. However, if the purpose of cross-examining him on a previous statement is to contradict his evidence given at the hearing then he must be taken to the parts of the statement which are to be used to contradict him: see the Criminal Procedure Act 1865, s 5. The Tribunal may itself call for production of the previous statement for his inspection and may make what use of it for the purposes of the hearing he thinks fit: see the Criminal Procedure Act 1865, s 5.

If a witness in cross-examination does not admit that he made the previous statement, proof can be given that he made the statement, but only after the witness has been told of the circumstances in which the statement was made and after he has been asked expressly whether or not he made the statement: see the Criminal Procedure Act 1865, s 4.

EXPERT EVIDENCE

10.8 Rule 19(2) provides that no party may adduce expert evidence without the permission of the Tribunal. Therefore, any party who wishes to call expert evidence should apply to the Tribunal for permission. The application can be made in writing. The application should include details of the issue in the case to which the expert evidence will relate and of the ability of the expert to deal with that issue.

A party should not instruct an expert before obtaining permission from the Tribunal to call the expert because he will be at risk of not recovering his costs if the Tribunal decides that expert evidence is not necessary.

An expert should possess:

- a high degree of skill and knowledge in a particular subject;
- relevant and up to date expertise with regard to issues in the case;
- the ability to produce a clear written report; and
- the communication skills to provide helpful oral evidence to the court.

Surveyors and handwriting experts are frequently called to give expert evidence in proceedings before the Tribunal.

The Tribunal is unlikely to give permission for a conveyancer to be called to give expert evidence.

The Tribunal may give permission for one or more party or parties to call expert evidence or he may make a direction for evidence to be given by a witness instructed by the parties jointly. A set of directions for expert evidence can be found in **Form 78** in **Appendix 14**. It is the practice of the Tribunal to require the expert's evidence to be given in a written report and to require the expert to attend for cross-examination upon his report.

The fundamental duty of an expert to help the Tribunal on matters within his expertise is set out clearly in Rule 19(1). The duty to help the Tribunal overrides any obligation to the person instructing or paying the expert.

The presumption is that the expert evidence will be given in a written report. Rule 19(2) provides that the evidence is to be given in a written report unless the Tribunal otherwise directs. The Tribunal has power under Rule 19(6) to direct that the expert attends the hearing to give oral evidence.

Where permission is given for expert evidence, the expert's report must be in the form and contain the contents set out in Rule 19(5). It should be addressed to the Tribunal and not to the party from whom the Tribunal received his instructions. It should:

- contain a statement that the expert understands his duty to the court, and has complied and will continue to comply with that duty;
- contain a statement of truth;
- give details of the expert's qualifications and relevant experience; and
- contain a summary of the instructions the expert received for the making of the report

The report ought also to

- give details of any literature or other material which the expert has relied on in making the report;
- make clear which of the facts stated in the report are within the expert's own knowledge;
- say who carried out any examination, measurement, test or experiment which the expert has used for the report, give the qualifications of that person, and say whether or not the test or experiment has been carried out under the expert's supervision;
- where there is a range of opinion on the matters dealt with in the report –
  - (i) summarise the range of opinion; and
  - (ii) give reasons for his own opinion;
- contain a summary of the conclusions reached; and
- if the expert is not able to give his opinion without qualification, state the qualification..

This list of additional matters derives from the summary of the duties and responsibilities of an expert witness given by Cresswell J in *National Justice Compania Naviera SA v Prudential Assurance Co Ltd* (The 'Ikarian Reefer') [1993] 2 Lloyds Rep. 68 at 81-82. An expert must be independent, objective on matters within his expertise and consider all material facts.

PROOF OF DOCUMENTS

10.9 There is a substantial quantity of detailed law, both common law and statute, concerning the proof of documents. For a detailed treatment of this subject, the reader is referred to the standard works on the law of evidence. What follows is a brief statement of the main points, with an emphasis on those points most likely to be of relevance in proceedings before the Tribunal.

An unattested document may be proved by

- calling the writer;
- by a witness who saw the document written or signed;
- by evidence from a handwriting expert;
- by comparison of the document with another document proved to be genuine: see the Criminal Procedure Act 1865 s 8; or
- by the admissions of the party against whom the document is tendered.

The sealing of a document may be proved by evidence of a witness who saw the seal affixed or, in the case of a corporation seal, anyone familiar with the seal may give evidence that the seal is the seal of the corporation. There is a general presumption in favour of a purchaser that a seal was affixed in compliance with requisite formalities and, if no formalities are required, with proper authority.

Wills and other testamentary documents must be proved by evidence from one of the attesting witnesses or, if none is available, by a person present when the will was executed.

Documents proved or purporting to be not less than 20 years old, which are produced from proper custody, are presumed to have been duly signed, sealed, attested and/or delivered – see Halsbury's Laws of England Vol. 11 para 869. The period of 20 years is reckoned from the time of signature or execution until the time of production at the hearing. Documents are produced from proper custody when they have been in the keeping of some person who might reasonably and naturally be expected to have possession of them.

Documents which are certified by an officer of the business or public authority to be part of the records of the business or public authority are admissible in evidence without further proof. The definition of 'business' is very wide; it includes any activity regularly carried on over a period of time, whether for profit or not, by anybody (whether corporate or not) or by an individual. 'Public authority' includes any public or statutory undertaking, any government department and any person holding office under HM The Queen: see the Civil Evidence Act 1995 s 9.

The contents of a document which has been lost or destroyed and which cannot be found after a diligent search can be proved by secondary evidence.

If a party is served with a notice to produce a document at the hearing and does not do so, the contents of the document may be proved by the party serving the notice, by secondary evidence.

PROOF OF CONTENTS OF THE REGISTER

10.10 An official copy of a register, title or caution plan or document kept by HM Land Registry is admissible in evidence to the same extent as the original: see LRA 2002, s 67(1).

PHOTOGRAPHIC EVIDENCE

10.11 Photographic evidence is frequently produced in proceedings before the Tribunal. Photographs are usually produced as evidence of the physical features of the land the subject of the proceedings, existing at the date the photograph was taken. The person who took the photograph may be called to give evidence of the date and time the photograph was taken and what location was photographed. It is usually also helpful for the photographer to state where he was standing when the photograph was taken and what type of lens he used, for example whether he used a wide angle or telephoto lens.

Aerial photographs are widely available, but will often need expert evidence to help interpret them. In particular they often require to be shown stereoscopically through special equipment.

If the photographer is not called, the photograph may be admitted as hearsay evidence.

Care should be taken to produce clear photographic copies of any photographs to be produced in evidence. If the original photograph is in colour then coloured copies should be produced. Black and white or colour copies produced on photocopying machines are frequently too poor to be of much assistance at a hearing.

Chapter 11

CASE MANAGEMENT

Key topics in this Chapter

INTRODUCTION

11.1 The procedure before the Tribunal following the service by the parties of their respective statements of case, and prior to the hearing, is governed by Part 2 of the Rules 2003, which is to be found in APPENDIX **9**. These are generic rules applicable to all three divisions of the Property Chamber.

CPR 1998 do not apply except where specifically mentioned, such as in the Rules 2003, r 12(4)(a) relating to security for costs, but many of the powers and provisions are similar in nature.

THE OVERRIDING OBJECTIVE

11.2 The overriding objective is to be found in Rule 3(1). It is not in precisely the same terms as the overriding objective to be found in either the original or the amended CPR 1998, r 1, but it is broadly similar in many respects. It provides that the overriding objective is to enable the Tribunal to deal with cases fairly and justly.

Rule 3(2) provides that dealing with a case fairly and justly includes the following matters:

- dealing with the case in ways which are proportionate to:
  - the importance of the case,
  - the anticipated costs,
  - the resources of the parties, and
  - the resources of the Tribunal;
- avoiding unnecessary formality and seeking flexibility in the proceedings;

- ensuring, so far as practicable, that the parties are able to participate fully in the proceedings;
- using any special expertise of the Tribunal effectively; and
- avoiding delay, so far as compatible with proper consideration of the issues.

Rule 3(3) provides that the Tribunal must seek to give effect to the overriding objective when it:

- exercises any power under the Rules 2013; or
- interprets any rule or practice direction.

Rule 3(4) places a duty on the parties:

- to help the Tribunal to further the overriding objective; and
- to co-operate with the Tribunal generally.

However, in one respect there is an important difference between, on the one hand, the overriding objective in Rule 3, and the rule about what is to happen if a party has failed to comply with a requirement of a rule or a direction in Rule 8(2), and, on the other hand, the post Jackson amendments to CPR 1998. In *Leeds City Council v Revenue and Customs Comrs* [2014] UKUT 0350 (TCC) it was held that as the overriding objective applicable in the Upper Tribunal (which is worded identically to the overriding objective applicable in the Tribunal) differs from the post Jackson overriding objective in CPR 1998, the Upper Tribunal is not to take the same approach to a failure to comply with a requirement of a rule or direction as the courts are now required to do by the decision of the Court of Appeal in *Mitchell v News Group Newspapers Ltd* [2013] EWCA Civ 1537, [2014] 2 All ER 430, [2014] 1 WLR 795 and the cases following it. The judge held that *Revenue and Customs Comrs v McCarthy & Stone (Developments) Ltd* [2014] UKUT 0196 (TCC), which had held that the Upper Tribunal should follow *Mitchell* had been wrongly decided.

Accordingly, the Tribunal has not been beset with the problems arising from *Mitchell*. Many practitioners will regard this distinction as being a fortunate one.

OVERVIEW

11.3 It may be helpful at this stage to have a brief overview of the procedure between the service of the statements of case (considered in CHAPTER **9**) and the decision at the final hearing (considered in CHAPTER **17**). The parties may make applications and the Tribunal will give directions as appropriate. This will normally be done in writing and not at a hearing. Generally, after both parties have served their statements of case, the Tribunal will give a direction (see FORM **89** in APPENDIX **14**) relating to:

- disclosure;
- the exchange of witness statements; and
- the preparation of hearing bundles, a list of issues, a chronology and skeleton arguments for the hearing.

At the same time, a further direction (see **FORM 90** in **APPENDIX 14**) is given to assist with the listing of the hearing, notice of which will duly be given to the parties.

The standard directions are considered further below.

APPLICATIONS FOR DIRECTIONS: GENERALLY

11.4 The Tribunal judges act as procedural judges during the course of the reference as well as conducting the final hearing. References are not normally assigned to any particular judge prior to the final hearing, but a substantial case may be reserved to a particular judge so that continuity of case management can be preserved.

Applications for directions during the course of the proceedings arise in relation to a wide range of issues, such as extensions of time and disclosure of documents. Subject to the provisions of TCEA 2007, the Tribunal may regulate its own procedure: see Rule 6(1).

Rule 6(2) provides that the Tribunal may give a direction in relation to the conduct or disposal of proceedings at any time. This includes a direction to:

- amend,
- suspend, or
- set aside

an earlier direction.

The procedure for applying for and giving directions is governed by Rule 7.

Rule 7(1) provides that the Tribunal may give a direction:

- on the application of one or more of the parties, or
- on its own initiative.

There are two ways for a party to make an application for a direction:

- by sending or delivering a written application to the Tribunal: Rule 7(2)(a); or
- orally during the course of a hearing: Rule 7(2)(b).

Clearly, an application for a direction should only be made orally during the course of a hearing in limited circumstances. These might include:

- matters arising urgently (such as an application to adjourn where a party or witness has fallen sick on the morning of the hearing); or
- matters arising during the heat of the battle (such as a witness referring for the first time to a previously undisclosed critical document which is then produced and an adjournment is required to consider it).

As far as written applications for directions are concerned, there is no prescribed application notice, but the application must include the reason for making the application: see Rule 7(3).

Applications for directions during the course of the proceedings are usually dealt with on paper, although in an appropriate case a hearing will be arranged to determine the application or for general case management. Rule 6(3)(h) provides that the Tribunal may hold a hearing to consider any matter, including a case management issue.

Where all the parties are represented, case management hearings are often conducted over the telephone. Indeed, the definition of a hearing' in Rule 1 includes a hearing conducted in whole or in part by video link, telephone or other means of instantaneous two-way electronic communication.

If the parties are agreed on the application direction, the Tribunal should be so informed. It does not necessarily follow in such circumstances that the Tribunal will give the direction sought. The Tribunal might consider that the application is premature or inappropriate.

Rule 7(4) states that, except with the permission of the Tribunal, where the application for a direction is made without the consent of every party, the applicant must provide:

- a copy of the proposed application to every other party before it is made; and
- confirm to the Tribunal that the other parties have been notified that any objection they wish to make to the application must be sent in writing to the Tribunal and to the party applying for the direction in accordance with Rule 7(5).

Rule 7(5), in turn, provides that a party who wishes to object to a written application for a direction must send written notice of the objection to the Tribunal and the applicant for the direction.

These are important provisions. Far too often one party writes to the Tribunal asking, say, for an extension of time to serve its statement of case or for permission to serve a witness statement out of time, without informing the other party that the application has been made. In such circumstances the Tribunal will not entertain the application unless and until confirmation has been given by the party making it that the other party has been served with the application and has been informed of the right to object to it.

Unless the Tribunal considers that there is a good reason not to do so, the Tribunal will send written notice of any direction which is made to every party and any other person affected by it: see Rule 7(6).

If a party or any other person sent such a written notice wishes to challenge that direction, they may do so by applying for another direction, which amends, suspends or set aside the first direction: see Rule 7(7). Such a challenge may be appropriate where a party overlooked making an objection to the application in the first place, or was not in fact given notice of it, or some new matter has emerged which now makes the direction inappropriate.

Where the Tribunal is minded to make a direction of its own initiative, it will send out the proposed direction in advance inviting representations from the parties. Alternatively, it will make the direction but give the parties a period of time in which to make an application to set it aside.

Directions commonly given are considered below in this chapter, and in CHAPTER 13.

STANDARD DIRECTIONS

Introduction

11.5 In order to ensure a tight timetable, after both parties have served their statements of case a Tribunal judge will consider them and undertake a case review. A decision will be taken as to whether the case is a suitable one in which to propose mediation (for mediation, see CHAPTER **14**). If mediation is not considered a suitable option, general directions will be sent out (see FORM **89** in APPENDIX **14**) relating to:

- disclosure;
- the exchange of witness statements; and
- the preparation of hearing bundles, a list of issues, a chronology and skeleton arguments for the hearing;
- any other direction considered necessary for the specific case, such as a direction permitting the calling of expert evidence in a particular field.

At the same time, a further direction (see FORM **90** in APPENDIX **14**) is given to assist with the listing of the hearing, notice of which will duly be given to the parties.

In some cases, the statements of case may disclose that the case of one party may not succeed and the standard directions will not be sent out.

EXAMPLE 1

A obtains a money judgment against B in the county court. A obtains a charging order against B's property to enforce the judgment, and enters a unilateral notice in the charges register of B's title to protect the charging order. B applies to cancel the unilateral notice as he disputes the debt. But, unless and until the judgment is set aside or satisfied, the Tribunal cannot go behind it. The Tribunal will not send out the standard directions but will send out a notice that it intends to strike out the proceedings summarily, as it considers there is no reasonable prospect of the Applicant's case succeeding. The Applicant will be given an opportunity to make representations in relation to the proposed strike out.

For summary disposals, see CHAPTER **12**.

Disclosure of documents

11.6 Rule 28(4)(c) provides that when a party whom the Tribunal has directed to act as an Applicant serves a statement of case, it must be accompanied by copies of any documents available to the Applicant which:

- are important to the Applicant's case; or
- the Tribunal or any other party to the proceedings will require in order properly to understand the Applicant's case.

PDLR para 3.2(f) provides that the Applicant must also serve a list of all the documents so provided.

Similarly, Rule 30(1)(b) provides that when a party whom the Tribunal has directed to act as a Respondent serves a statement of case, it must be accompanied by copies of any documents available to the Respondent which:

- are important to the Respondent's case; or
- the Tribunal or any other party to the proceedings will require in order properly to understand the Respondent's case.

PDLR para 4.1(e) provides that the Respondent must also serve a list of all the documents so provided.

In addition, Rule 18(1)(a) provides that the Tribunal may give directions as to the exchange between parties of list of documents which are relevant to the application, or relevant to particular issues, and the inspection of such documents.

Pursuant to this, the standard directions provide that each party must, within 21 days, serve on the Tribunal and the other parties:

- a list of all relevant documents in that party's possession or control which:
  - that party intends to rely on in the proceedings; or
  - adversely affects that party's own case; or
  - adversely affects another party's case; or
  - supports another party's case; and
- copies of documents in that list.

Further directions are given that:

- the parties must bring the original documents to the hearing; and
- documents not submitted within 21 days as directed will only be admitted with the permission of the Tribunal and following consultation with the other parties.

Witness statements

11.7 Rule 18(1)(g) provides that the Tribunal may give directions as to the manner in which any evidence is to be provided, which may include a direction for evidence to be given:

- orally at a hearing; or
- by witness statement.

Further, r 18(1)(h) provides that the Tribunal may give directions as to the time at which any evidence is to be provided.

Pursuant to this, the standard directions include a direction for the parties to file with the Tribunal, and exchange with the other parties, the witness statements of any witness of fact upon whose evidence they propose to rely within 42 days.

Each witness statement must contain a statement of truth. If a party intends to rely on a statement of case as evidence, that statement of case must itself contain a statement of truth. In any event, PDLR para 3.2(d) requires a statement of case to contain a statement of truth.

A direction will also be given that where a witness is called to give oral evidence, his or her witness statement will stand as his or her evidence, subject to cross-examination, unless the Tribunal orders otherwise. As in ordinary civil litigation, judges vary in the extent to which they permit a range of supplementary questions to be asked of a witness in his or her evidence in chief.

It will also be directed that the parties may not call any witness other than those in respect of whom a statement has been served, without the prior permission of the Tribunal.

Many of the applications for directions made to the Tribunal as the hearing date approaches are in respect of calling further witnesses. It is important that a copy of the proposed witnesses' witness statement is served on the Tribunal and the other parties when such an application is made. It is unlikely that the Tribunal will want to give permission without seeing the full contents of the witness statement.

Hearing bundles

11.8 Rule 6(3)(k) provides that the Tribunal may require a party to produce a bundle for a hearing. Pursuant to this the standard directions require a hearing bundle to be prepared.

Responsibility for the preparation of the hearing bundle normally lies with the Applicant. If only the Respondent is legally represented, then the Respondent will be directed to prepare the hearing bundle.

The standard directions direct the parties to cooperate in the preparation of the hearing bundles, and give other useful advice which should be followed.

The preparation of bundles is extremely important, and should be carried out carefully and conscientiously. Whilst it might seem time-consuming to do properly, in the long run thoughtful preparation saves time as a poorly prepared bundle wastes a considerable amount of time and can lead to serious costs consequences to the party at fault.

The standard directions remind the parties that only relevant documents should be included, and that it is wasteful for unnecessary documents be put in the bundle. In particular:

- Swathes of historic, bad tempered and contentious correspondence between the parties' solicitors should not be included.
- All the pages should be hole punched at the same level, and exactly in the middle of the page.
- No document should appear more than once.
- Coloured documents, such as plans, should be copied in colour.
- Copies of photographs should be clear and of a high quality, not an endless photocopy of a photocopy.

Each page of the bundle should be paginated separately like a book. Many litigants in person (and even some solicitors) number each document separately, but do not give individual numbers to the pages within the document. This is not acceptable.

Separate documents within the bundle should not be stapled together. Large documents, such as historic conveyances and deeds, which cannot be reduced to an A4 size, should be carefully folded so they fit neatly into the ring binder and are not hole punched in a way that prevents them from being opened.

These matters are considered further in CHAPTER **15**.

List of issues, chronology and skeleton argument

11.9 Rule 6(3)(d) provides that the Tribunal may require a party to provide information or submissions to the Tribunal or a party.

Pursuant to this, the standard directions direct the parties to send to the Tribunal and to each other party at least 7 days before the hearing:

- a list of issues to be decided by the Tribunal;
- a chronology of material events relating to the case;
- a brief statement of the arguments in support of their case, including details of any relevant parts of any authorities they intend to rely upon in support of those arguments and;
- copies of any authorities relied upon.

Again, these matters are considered further in CHAPTER **15**.

Original deeds

11.10 The parties are directed to bring to the hearing the originals of documents included in the hearing bundle if in their possession, custody and control.

LISTING QUESTIONNAIRES

11.11 At the same time, a further direction is given to assist with the listing of the hearing. Notice of the hearing will in due course be given to the parties.

Rule 6(3)(f) provides that the Tribunal may require a party to state whether that party intends at the hearing to:

- attend,
- be represented, or
- call witnesses.

Rule 6(3)(l) provides that the Tribunal may require a party to provide an estimate of the length of the hearing.

In accordance with these powers the Tribunal requires the parties, within 42 days, to fill in and return Form LRHRG: see FORM **90** in APPENDIX **14**.

The Form LRHRG requires the parties to:

- list the name of counsel (if any), the name of the solicitor, and the names, addresses and occupations of all witnesses to be called;
- give a time estimate for the hearing;

- give dates to avoid within a specified hearing window (currently 3 months);
- provide contact details if not legally represented;
- state whether the case can be conveniently heard in London, and, if not, what venue would be most convenient;
- state whether a site view is required;
- state if the party, a representative or a witness has any special needs and requires a venue with suitable access or facilities;
- state if any witness requires an interpreter and, if so, to identify the language required.

Once all parties have returned the Forms LRHRG, the Tribunal will consider:

- where the hearing should be listed,
- how long it should be listed for, and
- whether or not there should be a site view.

The Tribunal considers a site view important in a wide range of cases, particularly adverse possession and boundary disputes, and the judge considering the listing arrangements will apply his or her own judgment as to whether or not one is required. Site visits are discussed in detail in **CHAPTER 16**.

The Tribunal judge will then refer the file to administrative staff to arrange the listing at an appropriate venue on a date convenient to all the parties. If a party fails to return the **FORM LRHRG** the matter may be listed for hearing without consideration being given to any dates that party wishes to avoid.

Once the case is listed for hearing the date will only be moved to a different one in the most exceptional of circumstances. The unavailability of counsel or solicitor or the fact that a party or a witness has chosen to book a holiday will not suffice, if the Tribunal was not warned the date was one to avoid when **FORM LRHRG** was returned.

DELEGATION TO STAFF

11.12 Rule 5(1) provides that Tribunal staff may, with the approval of the Senior President of Tribunals, carry out functions of a judicial nature permitted or required to be done by the Tribunal.

Any party sent a decision made by a member of staff in this way is entitled to apply, within 14 days, to the Tribunal for that decision to be considered afresh by a judge: see Rule 5(2).

The purpose of this provision is to enable the administrative staff to assist with routine matters, such as the issuing of standard directions, thereby saving judicial time in the first instance, and for legally qualified staff to exercise case management powers akin to that of a registrar. The Senior President has so far issued practice statements delegating functions to administrative staff in the Social Entitlement Chamber and to administrative and legally qualified staff in the Health, Education & Social Care Chamber.

We now turn to specific directions which the Tribunal can give, either with or separately to the standard directions.

CONSOLIDATION, HEARING TOGETHER AND LEAD CASES

11.13 The Tribunal has the power to consolidate or hear together two or more sets of proceedings or parts of proceedings raising common issues, or treat a case as a lead case: see Rule 6(3)(b).

Consolidation is appropriate where the Applicant in one set of proceedings is also the Applicant in another. Otherwise the various sets of proceedings can simply be case managed and heard together.

> EXAMPLE 2
>
> A applies to Land Registry for first registration of land on the basis of a paper title. B opposes the application as he contends that he has acquired title to the land by adverse possession. The dispute is referred to the Tribunal. Subsequently, B makes his own application to Land Registry to be registered as proprietor. A objects as he disputes that B has been in possession for 12 years. The dispute is referred to the Tribunal, who directs that the two references be case managed and heard together.

Where there are a large number of proceedings, all involving the same issue, it is convenient to treat one of them as a lead case. The decision in the lead case can then determine result of all the others.

> EXAMPLE 3
>
> There are 25 adjacent houses built along a private road. A applies to Land Registry for a prescriptive right to drive a heavy goods vehicle over the private road to his factory at the end of it. All 25 house owners object to the original application and Land Registry refers 25 separate references to the Tribunal. The one issue in dispute is common to all 25 cases: has A driven his heavy goods vehicle over the private road for the full period of 20 years? Each of the house owners has instructed a different solicitor. The Tribunal selects one reference as a lead case which will bind all the others.
>
> Rules 23 and 24 make specific provisions about the procedure to be followed when there is a lead case.

There is no power for a difficult case land registration case to be transferred up to the Upper Tribunal for hearing. Such a power does exist, however, in respect of a difficult leasehold or residential property case: see Rule 25.

ADDITION AND SUBSTITUTION OF PARTIES

11.14 The Tribunal has power to add, substitute, or remove parties: see Rule 10(1). This power is wide and unfettered, and applies to both an Applicant and a Respondent. The power to add or substitute a party will be useful where ownership of the land in dispute passes to another person after the reference of the dispute to the Tribunal but before the hearing, for example where a party sells the land or a party dies.

> **EXAMPLE 4**
>
> A and B are neighbours. A enters a unilateral notice in the charges register of B's title to protect the benefit of a restrictive covenant. B applies to Land Registry to cancel the unilateral notice on the basis that the restrictive covenant has been released. A objects to the application and the dispute is referred to the Tribunal. Prior to the hearing B sells his property to C. B no longer has any interest in the dispute, whilst C now does. The Tribunal will substitute C for B as a party.

> **EXAMPLE 5**
>
> A applies to register a possessory title to land. B objects. Prior to the hearing A dies. A's interest passes to his executor, C. The Tribunal will substitute C for A.

Where the Tribunal gives a direction adding, substituted or removing a person as an Applicant or a Respondent, it may give such consequential directions as it considers appropriate: see Rule 10(2). For example, it might direct one of the existing parties to serve all the statements of case served so far, together with copies of all the orders from the Tribunal, on the new party.

A person who is not a party may apply to the Tribunal to be added or substituted as a party: see Rule 10(3). So, in example 5 above, C can apply to the Tribunal to be substituted in the place of A on his own initiative.

The position of the Crown (or, where appropriate, the Duchy of Cornwall or the Duchy of Lancaster) as a potential party to be joined (or at least notified of the proceedings) should not be overlooked where, as sometimes happens, no one knows the identity of the true owner of the land in dispute, or the last known owner was a company which has been wound up and its assets vested in the Crown. These problems usually, but not invariably, occur in adverse possession cases.

This was a difficulty which arose in *Walker v Burton* [2013] EWCA Civ 1228, [2013] 1 P & CR 116, [2013] 3 EGLR 129 where the Applicants had mistakenly been registered as the owners of 362 acres of moorland in the erroneous belief that they were the Lords of the Manor. Apart from the Applicants, no one else claimed a title to the moorland. It was unregistered land, and the Lordship of the Manor, having become extinct by the 17th-century, had become vested in the Crown either as royal desmesne land or in right of the Duchy of Lancaster by escheat. The Respondents were local villagers who did not claim a title to the land themselves, but wanted to close the Applicants' title.

The Crown and the Duchy had no interest in the outcome and reserved their position. But their position was only clarified after the hearing, and prior to the first appeal. In the end the Court of Appeal said that in the light of the Crown and the Duchy's position, no complaint could be made that no significant weight had been attached to the Crown title in deciding whether the Applicants should remain the registered proprietors of the moorland.

However, in the course of the first appeal, the judge gave some useful guidance. He said at [2012] EWHC 978 (Ch), [136]:

> For the future, I consider that it would be appropriate in any case of this kind which comes before [the Tribunal] or the court, in which a potential interest of the Crown, or a similar body, might be affected, for the Crown or that body to be given timely express prior notice of an application, so that proper consideration can be given at any stage of the dispute to any representations which may be made.

PROVIDING INFORMATION

11.15 Rule 6(3)(d) provides that the Tribunal may require a party to provide information to the Tribunal or a party. This provision enables the Tribunal to give directions, akin to those referred to in CPR 1998 Part 18, requiring a party to provide further information:

- clarifying any matter which is in dispute in the proceedings, or
- giving additional information in relation to such a matter,

whether or not the matter is contained or referred to in the statement of case.

TRANSFERS

11.16 Rule 6(3)(n) provides that the Tribunal may transfer proceedings to another court or tribunal:

- if that other court or tribunal has jurisdiction in relation to the proceedings, and
- because of a change of circumstances since the proceedings were started, the Tribunal no longer has jurisdiction in relation to the proceedings; or
- the Tribunal considers that the other court or tribunal is a more appropriate forum for the determination of the case.

This is a very important provision which had no parallel in AR 2003. It will not be often in a land registration case that the Tribunal ceases to have jurisdiction in relation to the proceedings. It is arguable that if a party ceases to have the mental capacity to act, and as there is no power to appoint a litigation friend in proceedings before the Tribunal, the Tribunal could transfer the proceedings to the County Court or the High Court under this rule.

On the other hand, there will be many occasions on which the Tribunal will consider that the County Court or the High Court is a more appropriate forum for the determination of the case. Examples are as follows:

- a beneficial interest case where one of the parties urgently requires an order for sale.
- a dispute over the ownership of land which is, in reality, a partnership dispute.

- a dispute over the ownership of land which is part of a wider dispute involving company law, probate law and the administration of estates: see *Line v Baker* [2014] EWHC 1368 (Ch), [2014] All ER (D) 42 (May) in which the dispute began as a reference to the Adjudicator.
- a case, as mentioned above, where a party ceases to have the mental capacity to act, as there is no power to appoint a litigation friend in proceedings before the Tribunal.

In any of these or similar cases we consider that the Tribunal now has power to direct a transfer directly to the County Court or to the High Court.

It has been suggested that in respect of references there is no power to direct a transfer to the County Court or to the High Court, as the County Court and the High Court do not have jurisdiction to receive references in the first place from the Registrar. We do not agree with this suggestion. All that the transferee court needs to have is jurisdiction to deal with the subject matter of the proceedings. The County Court has jurisdiction to deal with a beneficial interest case. What the Tribunal cannot do is transfer proceedings before it to courts or tribunals such as the Westminster Magistrates' Court, the Privy Council or the War Pensions and Armed Forces Compensation Chamber of the First-tier Tribunal. None of those bodies has jurisdiction to deal with land registration cases in England and Wales.

It is therefore suggested that, if during the course of the proceedings, the Tribunal decides it would be better for court proceedings to be started it no longer needs to direct one of the parties to commence court proceedings pursuant to its powers under Land Registration Act 2002, s 110(1) as amended, but can itself direct a transfer.

SECURITY FOR COSTS

11.17 Rule 12(1) provides that in a land registration case, a Respondent may apply for security for the Respondent's costs of the proceedings in the Tribunal.

Again, this is a very important provision which had no parallel in AR 2003.

However, the power to order security for costs does not apply where the Tribunal has directed a party to commence court proceedings pursuant to Land Registration Act 2002, s 110(1): see Rule 12(2).

In order to make an application for security for costs, the Respondent must support it by written evidence, and copies of the application and supporting evidence must be provided by the Respondent to the Applicant: see Rule 12(3).

For an application for security for costs, see **Form 74** in **appendix 14**. For a witness statement in support of an application for security for costs, see **Form 75** in **appendix 14**.

Rule 12(4) provides that the Tribunal may make an order for security for costs if it is satisfied that:

- one or more of the conditions subject to which security for costs might be ordered in proceedings in a court to which CPR 1998 apply exists;
- it is just to make such an order; and

- the Applicant in the proceedings has the ability to comply with the order.

The relevant conditions in CPR 1998, Part 25.13(2) (with suggested modifications for land registration cases in the Tribunal) are:

- the Applicant is:
    - resident out of the jurisdiction; but
    - not resident in a Brussels Contracting State, a State bound by the Lugano Convention or a Regulation State, as defined in Civil Jurisdiction and Judgments Act 1982, s 1(3);
- the Applicant is a company or other body (whether incorporated inside or outside Great Britain) and there is reason to believe that it will be unable to pay the Respondent's costs if ordered to do so;
- the Applicant has changed his address since the original application was made to Land Registry with a view to evading the consequences of the proceedings;
- the Applicant failed to give his address in the statement of case, or gave an incorrect address in that document;
- the Applicant is acting as a nominal Applicant, other than as a representative Applicant appointed as such by the Tribunal, and there is reason to believe that he will be unable to pay the Respondent's costs if ordered to do so;
- the Applicant has taken steps in relation to his assets that would make it difficult to enforce an order for costs against him.

Rule 12 does not limit the Respondent to making an application for security costs against the Applicant. CPR 1998, Part 25.14, as modified for land registration cases in the Tribunal, entitles the Respondent to seek an order against someone other than the Applicant if:

- the Tribunal is satisfied, having regard to all of the circumstances of the case, that it is just to make such an order; and
- one or more of the following conditions applies:
    - the person has assigned the right to make the original application to Land Registry with a view to avoiding the possibility of a costs order being made against him; or
    - has contributed or agreed to contribute to the Applicant's costs in return for a share of any property which the Applicant may establish title to in the proceedings; and

is a person against whom a costs order may be made.

As this is a new jurisdiction, the Tribunal will need time in which to develop its approach to ordering security for costs. No doubt it will pay regard to the overriding objective and the principles developed by the courts when applying the relevant provisions to be found in CPR 1998, Part 25.

Rule 12(4) provides that where the Tribunal decides to order security for costs, it must:

- determine the amount of the security; and
- direct the manner in which, and the time within which, the security must be given.

For an order for security of costs, see FORM 76 in APPENDIX 14.

SUMMONING WITNESSES

11.18 There are occasions when a party wishes to call a witness who will not give evidence voluntarily. The witness may be unwilling to assist the party who wishes to call him or may consider that, for professional reasons, he must be seen to be independent. Accordingly, a local government employee, a solicitor in certain circumstances, or a police officer will decline to be called as a witness, unless a summons is first obtained.

Rule 20(1)(a) provides that on the application of a party, or on its own initiative, the Tribunal may by summons require any person to attend as a witness at a hearing at the time and place specified in the summons.

For an application for a summons to require a person to attend as a witness, see **FORM 79** in **APPENDIX 14**.

Such a summons must give the person required to attend not less than 14 days' notice of the hearing or such shorter period as the Tribunal directs: see Rule 20(2)(a).

Where the person summonsed is not a party to the proceedings, the summons must also make provision for the person's necessary expenses of attendance to be paid, and state who is to pay them: see Rule 20(2)(b).

For a summons to require a person to attend as a witness, see **FORM 80** in **APPENDIX 14**.

For the avoidance of doubt, it is provided that no person may be compelled to give any evidence that the person could not be compelled to give on a trial of an action in the court of law: see Rule 20(3). In a beneficial interest case the Applicant may wish to call the conveyancing solicitor of the Respondent purchaser to give oral evidence, as well as to produce the conveyancing file (if still available). The solicitor cannot be compelled to give any oral evidence about matters which would attract privilege.

A person on whom a summons is served is entitled to vary or set it aside if he has not already had an opportunity to object to it. The person summonsed may be able to persuade the Tribunal that the oral evidence the party wishes him to give is in fact irrelevant to any issue in the proceedings. Rule 20(4)(a) provides that the summons must inform the person on whom the notice is served of this entitlement.

The summons must also state the consequences of a failure to comply with the summons: see Rule 20(4)(b). The consequences can be serious. Rule 8(5)(a) provides that the Tribunal may refer to the Upper Tribunal, and ask the Upper Tribunal to exercise its power under TCEA 2007, s 25 in relation to any failure by a person to comply with a requirement imposed by the Tribunal to attend at any place for the purpose of giving evidence. By TCEA 2007, s 25(1)(a) and (2)(a) the Upper Tribunal has the same powers, rights, privileges and authority as the High Court in relation to the attendance and examination of witnesses. This means that disobedience of a witness summons may be punished as a contempt of court by the Upper Tribunal.

ORDERS TO ANSWER QUESTIONS OR PRODUCE DOCUMENTS

11.19 There are occasions when a party wishes to make use of a document in someone else's possession or control which is relevant to an issue in the proceedings, but the person with possession or control of the document will not supply it to the party voluntarily. The person with possession or control of the document may be unwilling to assist the party who wishes to have sight of it or may consider that, for professional reasons, he must be seen to be independent. Accordingly, a local government employee, a solicitor in certain circumstances, a bank or building society employee or a police officer will decline to produce a document, unless a summons is first obtained.

Rule 20(1)(b) provides that on the application of a party, or on its own initiative, the Tribunal may order any person to answer any questions or produce any documents in that person's possession or control which relate to any issue in the proceedings.

For an application for an order to produce documents, see **Form 81** in **Appendix 14**.

For an order to produce documents, see **Form 82** in **Appendix 14**.

For the avoidance of doubt, it is provided that no person may be compelled to produce any document that the person could not be compelled to produce on a trial of an action in a court of law: see Rule 20(3).

EXAMPLE 6

A and B used to live together as partners in a house of which B is the sole registered proprietor. A applies to enter a restriction on the basis that she has a beneficial interest in the house. B objects and the dispute is referred to the Tribunal. A believes that the conveyancing file at the time of B's purchase contains evidence helpful to her. The solicitor refuses to release the file. The Tribunal will make an order requiring the solicitor to produce the file. This may be at a hearing listed prior to the final hearing so that all parties have time to consider the contents of the file in advance of the final hearing. The solicitor cannot be compelled to produce any document which would attract privilege.

A person on whom an order to produce a document is served is entitled to vary or set it aside if he has not already had an opportunity to object to it. The person ordered to produce a document may be able to persuade the Tribunal that the document in question is in fact irrelevant to any issue in the proceedings. Rule 20(4)(a) provides that the summons must inform the person on whom the notice is served of this entitlement.

The order must also state the consequences of a failure to comply with order: see Rule 20(4)(b). The consequences can be serious. Rule 8(5)(e) provides that the Tribunal may refer to the Upper Tribunal, and ask the Upper Tribunal to exercise its power under TCEA 2007, s 25 in relation to any failure by a person to comply with a requirement imposed by the Tribunal to produce a document. By TCEA 2007, s 25(1)(a) and (2)(b) the Upper Tribunal has the same powers, rights, privileges and authority as the

High Court in relation to the production and inspection of documents. This means that disobedience of the order may be punished as a contempt of court by the Upper Tribunal.

SANCTIONS AND ENFORCEMENT OF ORDERS

11.20 Rule 8(2) sets out what the Tribunal may do when a party has failed to comply with a direction.

The Tribunal may take such action as it considers just, which may include:

- waving the requirement;
- requiring the failure to be remedied;
- striking out a party's case;
- referring the failure to the Upper Tribunal; or
- barring or restricting a party's participation in the proceedings.

Striking out a party's case for failing to comply with a direction

11.21 Striking out a party's case for failing to comply with a direction may be either mandatory or discretionary.

The proceedings or case, or the appropriate part of them, will automatically be struck out if the Applicant has failed to comply with a direction that stated that failure by the Applicant to comply with the direction by a stated date would lead to the striking out of the proceedings or that part of them: see Rule 9(1).

For an order with sanctions where breach *will* lead to the striking out of the proceedings, see **FORM 87** in **APPENDIX 14**.

The Tribunal may strike out the whole or a part of the proceedings or case if the Applicant has failed to comply with a direction which stated that failure by the Applicant to comply with the direction could lead to the striking out of the proceedings or case or that part of it: see Rule 9(3)(a).

For an order with sanctions where breach *may* lead to the striking out of the proceedings, see **FORM 88** in **APPENDIX 14**.

In neither case is there a need for the Tribunal to hold a hearing before making the striking out order: see Rule 31(4).

Moreover, where the Tribunal has a discretion, the Tribunal does not have to give the parties an opportunity to make representations in relation to the proposed striking out before making the striking out order: see Rule 9(4) which does not include a discretionary striking out for failing to comply with a direction within the list of striking out cases where such an opportunity must be given.

However, in either case the Applicant may apply for the proceedings or case, or part of it, to be reinstated: see Rule 9(5). Such an application must be made in writing and received by the Tribunal within 28 days after the date on which the Tribunal sent notification of the striking out to that party: see Rule 9(6).

These provisions apply to a Respondent as much as they apply to an Applicant except that:

- a reference to the striking out of the proceedings or case or part of them is to be read as a reference to the barring of the Respondent from taking further part in the proceedings or part of them: see Rule 9(7)(a); and
- a reference to an application for the reinstatement of proceedings or case or part of them which have been struck out is to be read as a reference to an application for the lifting of the bar on the Respondent from taking further part in the proceedings, or part of them: see Rule 9(7)(b).

If a Respondent has been barred from taking further part in the proceedings in this way and that bar has not been lifted, the Tribunal need not consider any response or other submission made by that Respondent and may summarily determine any or all issues against that Respondent: see Rule 9(8).

Directions to the registrar

11.22 Where a dispute has been referred to the Tribunal by Land Registry, the proceedings cannot be disposed of simply by striking them out in the case of an Applicant, and by summarily determining them against a Respondent after he has been barred from taking further part in the proceedings. This is because the original application to Land Registry still has to be determined.

Accordingly, Rule 8(3) provides that, in land registration strike out cases, the Tribunal may:

- where the party who failed to comply was a person who made (or has been substituted for or added to the party who made) the original application, direct the Registrar to cancel the original application in whole or in part;
- where the party who failed to comply was an Objector to (or was substituted for or added as an Objector to) the original application, direct the Registrar to give effect to the original application in whole or in part as if that objection had not been made.

For an order including a direction to the Registrar, see **Form 91** in **appendix 14**.

If the Tribunal imposes a less draconian sanction not involving such a direction to the Registrar, it must send written notice to the parties of the Tribunal's decision as to what action is taken (if any) and give any consequential directions.

Chapter 12

PRELIMINARY ISSUES AND SUMMARY DISPOSAL

Key topics in this chapter

Preliminary issues
Lead cases
Summary disposal
Decisions without a hearing

PRELIMINARY ISSUES

12.1 Rule 6(3)(g) provides that the Tribunal may deal with an issue in the proceedings as a preliminary issue. A direction for the hearing of a preliminary issue may be made on the application of one or more parties or by the Tribunal on its own initiative.

If the decision on the preliminary issue will dispose of the whole of the matter (the subject of the reference) then the Tribunal must hold a hearing before making the decision unless each party and any other person sent notification of being entitled, invited or permitted to attend the hearing consents – Rule 31(1).

As soon as reasonably practicable after making a decision finally disposing of a preliminary issue dealt with following a direction under Rule 6(2)(g), the Tribunal must provide to each party

- a decision notice;
- written reasons for the decision; and
- notification of any right of appeal against the decision and the time within which, and the manner in which, the right of appeal must be exercised.

EXAMPLE 1

A is the first registered proprietor of Whiteacre. B claims that A cannot show a good paper title to the rear garden and applies to Land Registry for the title plan to be altered accordingly. B does not claim to have any title to the rear garden himself. A objects to the original application and the dispute is referred to the Tribunal. B is made the Applicant before the Tribunal as he bears the burden of showing that the register is wrong: *Baxter v Mannion* [2010] EWHC 573 (Ch) [52], [2010] 1 WLR 1965, [2011] 1 P & CR 133. A argues, on the authority of *Wells v Pilling Parish Council* [2008] EWHC 556 (Ch), [2008] 2 EGLR 29, [2008] 22 EG 174 that B had no standing to make the original application, and that the Tribunal should direct the Registrar to cancel it, without the need to determine the underlying merits.

The Tribunal decides that, rather than waiting to the final hearing, the question as to whether or not B requires standing should be dealt with as a preliminary issue. In this way the parties will not incur the expense of arguing the underlying dispute if B had no standing to make the original application.

As we saw in CHAPTER 3, the Adjudicator ruled in *Burton v Walker* (2009) Reference 2007/1124 that, because of a concession, *Wells v Pilling Parish Council* was not binding on him, and that it was not necessary for an Applicant seeking to rectify the register to demonstrate standing. This ruling was made on a preliminary issue, so the dispute in that case, which concerned title to a manor, proceeded to a final hearing. The High Court has since held that the preliminary ruling in *Burton v Walker* was correctly decided: *Mann v Dingley* [2011] EWLandRA 2010 0582.

LEAD CASES

12.2 Rule 23 makes provisions designed to enable the Tribunal to decide an issue or issues common to more than one case by a lead case. Where there are two or more cases before the Tribunal which have yet to be determined and which give rise to common or related cases, the Tribunal may specify that one or more of those cases be specified as a lead case and stay the other cases.

Within 28 days of receiving notice from the Tribunal that a case has been specified as a lead case, a party in a related case may apply to have that related case substituted as lead case.

The decision made by the Tribunal in the lead case in respect of the common or related issues will be sent to each party in each of the related cases. The decision will be binding on each of the parties in the related cases to whom the decision is sent unless the Tribunal orders otherwise.

A party in a related case may apply within 28 days after the date on which the Tribunal sent a copy of the decision to him for a direction that the decision is not binding on the parties to the related case. It will then be for the Tribunal to determine whether the decision should be binding on the parties in that related case.

Following the making of the decision in the lead case, the Tribunal will make directions in respect of the cases stayed pending the determination of the lead case.

If the common or related issues determined by a lead case arise in a later case, the Tribunal may record a decision on the common or related issues in the latter case in identical terms to the decision in the lead case – see Rule 24. Before it may do so, the Tribunal must send written notice to the parties to the latter case and must specify in that notice a date not less than 21 days after the notice was sent by which any objection to the proposal must be received by the Tribunal.

If no objection is received, the Tribunal need not determine the common or related issues in the latter case and must record its decision on those common or related issues in the lead case as its decision on those issues in the latter case.

If a party to the latter case objects on or before the specified date, the Tribunal must determine the latter case in accordance with the Rules. Thus if a party wishes to argue the issue determined in an earlier lead case afresh, he may do so provided that he makes objection in time.

SUMMARY DISPOSAL

12.3 Rule 9 provides for three different types of strike out

- automatic strike out;
- mandatory strike out; and
- discretionary strike out.

The reference to striking out is to striking out the proceedings or the Applicant's case. However, there is a similar provision for barring a Respondent from taking any further part in the proceedings.

Automatic and mandatory strike out are considered in CHAPTER **21** below.

Rule 9(3) (e) gives the Tribunal discretion to strike out the whole or part of proceedings where it considers that there is no reasonable prospect of the Applicant's case, or part of it, succeeding. Rule 9(7) provides for barring a Respondent from taking further part in the proceedings or part of them where the Tribunal considers there is no reasonable prospect of the Respondent succeeding in whole, or in part, on his case.

Rules 9(3) and 9(7) thus provide a mechanism for summary disposal of proceedings in an appropriate case.

Practice Direction 8.1 provides that an Applicant may not apply for summary disposal under Rule 9 (7) until the Respondent has served a response, except:

- with the permission of the Tribunal, or where
- the Respondent's time to serve a statement of case has expired.

A Respondent may apply for summary disposal under Rule 9(3) at any time after:

- the Applicant has served a notice of application (in a rectification or setting aside case under s 108(2) of Land Registration Act 2002; or
- the Applicant has served a statement of case in a referral case; or

- the Applicant's time for service of a statement of case has expired.

Where a Respondent applies for summary disposal before serving a statement of case and before the time to do so has expired, but that application does not result in the disposal of the entire proceedings, the Respondent's time for serving a statement of case will be extended to 28 days after service on the Respondent of the Tribunal's decision in relation to the application for summary disposal, or such other time as the Tribunal directs – see Practice Direction 8.5.

An application for summary disposal must be supported by a witness statement included with the application – Rule 8.6. That witness statement must state that the party making the application believes that the other party has no real prospect of succeeding on the proceedings or on the issue to which the application relates.

For a witness statement in support of an application for summary disposal, see FORM 72 in APPENDIX **14**.

When notice is given to the parties of an application which relates, in whole or in part, to summary disposal, the Tribunal will give directions for the service of evidence by the parties and for the determination of the issue of summary disposal.

When the Tribunal determines the issue of summary disposal it will either make an order:

- disposing of the proceedings or of any issue; or
- dismissing the application for or intention to consider summary disposal.

The order made striking out the proceedings under Rule 9(3) will take the form of an order either directing the Registrar to cancel the application or to give effect to the application or part thereof, as the case may be, with any other appropriate order.

Where such an order does not dispose of the entire proceedings, the Tribunal will give case management directions as to the future conduct of the proceedings.

DECISIONS WITHOUT A HEARING

12.4 Rule 31(1) provides that the Tribunal must hold a hearing before making a decision which disposes of proceedings.

However, Rule 31(2) provides that the Tribunal need not hold a hearing if consent to it's making a decision without holding a hearing is given by each party to the proceedings and also by anyone who has been sent a notification as being entitled, invited or permitted to attend the hearing.

A party or other person sent such a notification is to be deemed to have consented to the making of a decision without a hearing if the Tribunal has given them notice of the Tribunal's intention to make a decision without a hearing and they have not objected within the period specified in the notice.

The notice period should be not less than 28 days but may be shorter in urgent or exceptional circumstances – see Rule 31(3).

Where on reviewing the reference the Tribunal is of the view that it is suitable for determination on paper, it must seek the consent of the parties.

The Tribunal will consider it appropriate to make a decision without a hearing only if the nature of the dispute is such that a decision can properly be made on paper without oral evidence. A decision without a hearing is appropriate where the dispute turns on the construction of a document or a point of law. Written submissions can be submitted with the trial bundle and the Tribunal can come to a decision on the written material before it.

Even if one or more parties ask for a decision to be made without a hearing, the Tribunal will not accede to the application if the nature of the dispute is such that a decision cannot properly be made on paper. If there is a dispute of fact it will be necessary for witnesses to be called to give evidence and be cross-examined. This is often overlooked by parties who, in their understandable anxiety to save both time and costs, are prepared to dispense with a hearing in circumstances where it is simply not possible to reach a conclusion on the written material.

Where the dispute turns on the construction of a document or on a point of law, the Tribunal is not bound to make a decision on paper, even where all parties ask it to do so. The nature of the dispute may be such that the Tribunal requires oral submissions to be made. This is especially likely where the dispute involves a particularly complex dispute on a point of law.

HEARINGS FOLLOWING A RULE 31 NOTICE

12.5 Even though the Tribunal is satisfied that a substantive decision could be made without a hearing and has served a rule 31 notice, one party may still elect to have a hearing by objecting to a determination on paper.

The hearing will then be listed and proceed. However, the Tribunal might direct that no further evidence is to be called at the hearing, if it appears that he could properly reach a decision on the material already supplied. The hearing might then proceed in a similar manner to a strike out application in the County Court or the High Court.

Chapter 13

GENERAL POINTS OF PROCEDURE

Key topics in this Chapter

INTRODUCTION

13.1 This chapter deals with certain aspects of procedure of relevance throughout all the stages of the reference. Some particular topics are covered in detail in separate chapters:

- statements of case: see CHAPTER 9;
- disclosure: see CHAPTER 10;
- witness statements: see CHAPTER 10;
- evidence: see CHAPTER 10;
- case management: see CHAPTER 11;
- preliminary issues and summary disposal: see CHAPTER 12;
- mediation: see CHAPTER 14;
- settlement: see CHAPTER 14;
- preparing for hearings, see CHAPTER 15;
- site views: see CHAPTER 16;
- hearings: see CHAPTER 17;
- decisions and orders: see CHAPTER 18;
- costs and assessment: see CHAPTER 19;
- setting aside, reviews and appeals (including stays of execution): see CHAPTER 20;
- enforcement of orders: see CHAPTER 21.

AMENDMENT

13.2 AR 2003 contained no express power permitting a party to amend a document. But an Adjudicator held that a statement of case could be amended by permission of the Adjudicator, notwithstanding the absence of an express rule giving power to amend: see *Bush v Seymour* [2011] EWLandRA 2010_0593.

The position is now clearer. PCR 2013, r 6(3)(c) provides that the Tribunal may permit or require a party to amend a document. No specific guidance is given as to the principles upon which the Tribunal should act when deciding whether or not to permit an amendment. No doubt the Tribunal will take into account the overriding objective and seek broad guidance from, but not slavishly follow, the principles developed by the courts in applying CPR 1998, Part 17.

An application for permission to amend a statement of case should be made in writing to the Tribunal. The proposed amendment should be formulated and enclosed with the application. In accordance with PCR 2013, r 7(4), a copy of the proposed application and proposed amendment should be provided to every other party in advance. The other party should be notified that any objection they wish to make to the application must be sent in writing to the Tribunal and to the party making the application.

SERVICE OF DOCUMENTS

13.3 The law as to the service of documents in civil litigation has become increasingly complex in recent years, as demonstrated by CPR 1998, Part 6 which now contains 52 rules. Modern means of communication have added to the ways in which service can be effected, particularly email. The Tribunal's rules on service are not to be found within CPR 1998, Part 6, but in PCR 2013, r 16, which is entitled not 'service' of documents, but 'provision' of documents.

PCR 2013, r 16 applies to any document to be provided under:

- PCR 2013; or
- a practice direction; or
- a direction.

PCR 2013, r 16(1) provides for four methods of service.

The first method makes use of what, for the sake of convenience, will be called an "address for service", although this phrase is not used in the rules. Before we look at the rule itself, we need to consider what this address for service is. This address is set out in PCR 2013, r 16(5), and is as follows:

- In the case of the Tribunal, it is the address of the office of the Tribunal. This is 3rd Floor, 10 Alfred Place, London WC1E 7LR.
- In the case of an incorporated company or other body registered in the United Kingdom, it is the address of the registered or principal office of the company or body or any alternative address notified by that company or body to the Tribunal and all other parties for the purposes of provision of documents.
- In the case of any other person, body or authority, it is the usual or last known address of that person, body or authority.

This address for service is subject to the provisions of PCR 2013, r 16(6), which provides that the Tribunal and each party may assume that the address provided by a party or its representative or by the Registrar is and remains the address to which documents should be sent or delivered until receiving written notification to the contrary and an alternative address for communications.

The first method of service is set out in PCR 2013, r 16(1)(a) and consists of:

- sending the document by prepaid post or by document exchange to the address for service; or
- delivering the document by hand to the address for service.

The second method of service is set out in PCR 2013, r 16(1)(b) and consists of sending the document by fax to the number specified for the proceedings.

The third method of service is set out in PCR 2013, r 16(1)(c) and relates only to documents to be sent or delivered to or by the Tribunal. This method consists of any other method to those already mentioned as the Tribunal may permit. This includes email.

The fourth method of service is set out in PCR 2013, r 16(1)(d) and is, in effect, a sweeping up method of service. It provides that a document can be served in any method other than one provided for anywhere in the rules, as long as the recipient permits it.

Where it is the Tribunal that is serving the document, it has a choice:

- it can itself send or deliver the document: see PCR 2013, r 16(2)(a); or
- it can require a party to do so: see PCR 2013, r 16(2)(b).

Where any document is properly sent to the Tribunal by email, any requirement in the rules that it be signed may be satisfied by a typed instead of a handwritten signature: see PCR 2013, r 16(4).

The general rule is that if a party provides:

- a fax number,
- an email address, or
- other details for the electronic transmission of documents to that party,

then that party must accept delivery of documents by that method: see PCR 2013, r 16(7).

But a party is entitled to veto any particular form of service on that party, other than by pre-paid post or by delivery by hand, so long as that party informs the Tribunal and all other parties accordingly: see PCR 2013, r 16(8).

PCR 2013, r 16(9) provides that if the Tribunal or a party sends a document to another party or to the Tribunal by email or any other electronic means of communication, the recipient may request that the sender provide a hard copy of the document to the recipient. The recipient must make such a request as soon as reasonably practicable after receiving the document electronically.

A very important provision in land registration cases is that, unless the Tribunal otherwise permits, where the document is or contains:

- a map,
- plan,
- drawing, or
- photograph,

any copy provided of that map, plan, drawing or photograph must be in the same colours as the map, plan, drawing or photograph of which it is a copy: see PCR 2013, r 16(10). Where a parcels clause in a conveyance or transfer refers to an area edged in a particular colour on a plan, and the plan is copied in black and white, the plan is often useless to the reader. Faint and unreadable copies are equally useless.

PCR 2013, r 16(11) provides that the Tribunal has a discretion to:

- waive service, or
- provide for substituted service (whether by advertisement in a newspaper or otherwise)
  if the person to be served:
  - cannot be found after all diligent enquiries have been made;
  - has died and has no personal representative;
  - is out of the United Kingdom; or
  - for any other reason a notice or other document cannot readily be sent or delivered to that person in accordance with the rules.

Where an enactment requires evidence that a party has supplied any person with a document, that party may satisfy the requirement by providing a certificate signed by the party confirming that the document was provided in accordance with the requirements of PCR 2013, r 16: see PCR 2013, r 16(12).

STAY OF PROCEEDINGS

13.4 In PCR 2013 a distinction is drawn between the power to stay proceedings in r 6(3)(m), and the power to adjourn or postpone a hearing in r 6(3)(j). In AR 2003 the terminology was less clear. Sometimes what was, in effect, a stay was referred to as an adjournment: see AR 2003, r 8(2).

In certain circumstances the Tribunal is given a specific duty to stay the proceedings.

Where the Tribunal has directed a party under LRA 2002, s 110(1), as amended, to commence court proceedings for the court's decision on the whole or part of a matter and those court proceedings have been issued, the Tribunal proceedings, or the relevant part of those proceedings, are automatically stayed pending the final court order: see PCR 2013, r 39(2). The stay takes place when the Tribunal receives the notice that court proceedings have been issued, which the party directed to commence the court proceedings is required to provide by PCR 2013, r 38(2)(a).

But where the stay relates only to part of the matter, the Tribunal may stay the proceedings in relation to any other part pending the final court order: see PCR 2013, r 39(5).

The final court order means the order made by the court that records the court's final determination, whether on appeal or otherwise: see PCR 2013, r 38(6).

The party directed to commence the court proceedings is required to provide a copy of the final court order within 14 days after the date on which the matter before the court is finally disposed of: see PCR 2013, r 38(2)(c).

The date on which the matter before the court is finally disposed of means the earliest date on which the court proceedings, including any appeal, have been determined and any time for appealing or further appealing has expired: see PCR 2013, r 38(5).

When the Tribunal receives a copy of the final court order in accordance with r 38(2)(c), the Tribunal proceedings, or part of the matter, are to be regarded as stayed: see r 39(3).

There are two exceptions to this:

- The Tribunal retains the jurisdiction to decide any question of costs arising before the Tribunal prior to the commencement of court proceedings.
- The Tribunal may make a decision, including lifting a stay, either with or without a hearing and either with or without giving prior notice to the parties if:
  - such a decision is necessary, in addition to the final court order, to implement the final court order; and
  - the Tribunal would have had the power to make such a decision if the Tribunal had made a decision in relation to proceedings: see PCR 2013, r 39(4).

EXAMPLE 1

A applies to Land Registry to enter a restriction in the register of B's property on the grounds that she has a beneficial interest in it. The Tribunal directs A to commence court proceedings under Land Registration Act 2013, s 110(1), as amended. The court declares that A has a beneficial interest in the property, but says nothing about the restriction. On the basis of the court order, the Tribunal will direct the Registrar to give effect to A's original application so that the restriction is entered in the register.

For a direction see **FORM 47** in **APPENDIX 14**.

Where a party voluntarily commences court proceedings, and not as a result of a direction by the Tribunal pursuant to Land Registration Act 2013, s 110(1), as amended, there is no automatic stay of the Tribunal proceedings. The Tribunal has a discretion to decide whether or not to stay the proceedings before it pursuant to PCR 2013, r 6(3)(m).

If the Tribunal regards the commencement of court proceedings as being unnecessary and motivated by a desire to cause delay or injustice, it will not stay the proceedings before it, but will insist they go ahead. If a party commences court proceedings very shortly before the date set for the hearing of the Tribunal proceedings, the Tribunal is unlikely to stay the proceedings before it unless very good reason can be shown as to why the court proceedings should go ahead instead.

On the other hand, if a party voluntarily commences court proceedings very soon after the dispute has been referred to the Tribunal and before statements of case have been served, it is more than likely that the Tribunal will stay the proceedings before it. But each case will be considered on its individual merits.

For a direction see **FORM 46** in **APPENDIX 14**.

The Tribunal will also stay the proceedings before it if the parties want time to negotiate or to go to mediation. In deciding whether or not to allow a stay, and how long any stay should be, the Tribunal will have regard to the overriding objective. It will not allow the dispute to be left undecided for an inordinate amount of time. In particular, it will not allow a matter referred to it to be stayed generally. It is important to remember that while an application made to Land Registry has not been acted upon, it will remain on the day list and dealings with the land may thus be frozen in practice and priorities of interests in the land will be affected. If the parties wish to have time in which to negotiate or go to mediation, a stay will be granted for a specific period of time. At the end of that period the parties will be expected to bring the Tribunal up to date as to how the attempt to settle is proceeding. If the Tribunal is of the opinion that there is no reasonable prospect of a settlement or that the parties are not acting reasonably, no further stay will be granted.

A stay will also be granted if the some procedural reason the proceedings before the Tribunal cannot be carried on for the time being. When a party dies a stay will be granted pending a grant of representation to that person's estate.

ADJOURNMENT

13.5 The Tribunal has power to adjourn or postpone a hearing: see PCR 2013, r 6(3)(j).

PCR 2013, r 34 provides that if a party fails to attend a hearing the Tribunal may proceed with the hearing if the Tribunal:

- is satisfied that the party:
  - has been notified the hearing, or
  - that reasonable steps have been taken to notify the party of the hearing; and
- considers that it is in the interest of justice to proceed with the hearing.

If these tests are not met, the Tribunal will use its powers to adjourn the hearing.

One of the conditions which, if satisfied, entitles the Tribunal to set aside its decision, when it is in the interests of justice to do so, is that a party was not present at the hearing: see PCR 2013, r 51(2)(c). Setting aside a decision is discussed further in CHAPTER 20.

From time to time a party asks for a hearing to be adjourned shortly before it is due to be heard. The Tribunal will take into account the overriding objective, and will be unlikely to grant an adjournment where one party has simply failed to arrange adequate representation or notify his witnesses, or has booked a late holiday. Applications for an adjournment on medical grounds will be scrutinised carefully. Such applications must be supported by medical evidence, and a letter couched in non-specific terms from a general practitioner will carry little weight. A specific diagnosis genuinely preventing attendance will be required.

In deciding whether or not to allow an adjournment, and how long any adjournment which is allowed should be, the Tribunal will have regard to the overriding objective. It will not allow the dispute to be left undecided for an inordinate amount of time. In particular, it will not allow a matter referred to it to be adjourned generally, in the same way that it will not allow a matter referred to it to be stayed generally for the reasons given above.

ERRORS OF PROCEDURE

13.6 PCR 2013, r 8(1) provides that an irregularity resulting from a failure to comply with:

- any provision of the PCR 2013,
- a practice direction, or
- a direction,

does not of itself render void the proceedings or any step taken in the proceedings.

PCR 2013, r 8(2) sets out what the Tribunal may do when a party has failed to comply with:

- a requirement in the PCR 2013;
- a practice direction; or
- a direction.

The Tribunal may take such action as it considers just, which may include:

- waving the requirement;
- requiring the failure to be remedied;
- striking out a party's case;
- referring the failure to the Upper Tribunal; or
- barring or restricting a party's participation in the proceedings.

These matters are considered fully in CHAPTER **21**.

ACCIDENTAL SLIPS AND OMISSIONS

13.7 PCR 2013, r 50, which is similar to the slip rule in CPR 1998, Part 40.12, provides that the Tribunal may at any time correct any clerical mistake or other accidental slip or omission in a decision, direction or any document produced by it, by –

- sending notification of the amended decision or direction, or a copy of the amended document, to each party; and.
- making any necessary amendment to any information published in relation to the decision, directional document.

EXTENSIONS OF TIME

13.8 PCR 2013, r 6(3)(a) provides that the Tribunal may extend or shorten the time for complying with any rule, practice direction or direction, even if the application for an extension is not made until after the time limit has expired.

An application for an extension of time should not be made to the Tribunal without first seeking the consent of the other parties and notifying the other parties of their right to object to the application in writing, otherwise the Tribunal will have to refer the application to the other parties for their comments and time will be wasted: see PCR 2013, r 7(4).

For an application for an extension of time, see **Form 69** in **appendix 14**. For an order granting an extension of time, see **Form 70** in **appendix 14**.

CALCULATION OF TIME

13.9 Where something is required to be done by:

- PCR 2013,
- a practice direction, or
- a direction

on or by a particular day, it must be done before 5 pm on that day: see PCR 2013, r 15(1).

Where the time specified by:

- PCR 2013,
- a practice direction, or
- a direction

for doing any act ends on a day other than a working day, the act is done in time if it is done on the next working day: see PCR 2013, r 15(2).

For these purposes, a working day means any day except a Saturday, Sunday, Christmas Day, Good Friday or a bank holiday: see PCR 2013, r 15(3).

The practice of the Tribunal, when making directions requiring a party to do something, is to specify a date and time by which the thing is to be done.

REPRESENTATION

13.10 A party may appoint a representative who is legally qualified, or one who is not, to represent him in the proceedings: see PCR 2013, r 14(1).

When a representative is appointed, the name and address of the representative must be sent in writing to the Tribunal and each other party: see PCR 2013, r 14(2).

PCR 2013, r 14(3) provides that the appointed representative can act in all respects on behalf of the party who has appointed him, except:

- signing a witness statement; or
- giving the required written notice of his appointment, if he is not an authorised person in relation to exercising a right of audience or conducting litigation.

A person who has been given due notice of the appointment of a representative:

- must subsequently send the representative any document which has to be sent to the represented party, although he may also, but need not, send a copy of the document to the represented party: see PCR 2013, r 14(4)(a);
- may assume that the representative is and continues to be authorised until such time as he receives, from the representative or the represented party, written notification to the contrary, and an alternative address for communications: see PCR 2013, r 14(4)(b).

As far as the hearing itself is concerned, the party may:

- conduct the case himself; or
- be represented by the representative duly appointed by notice in the manner described above; or
- be represented or otherwise assisted, with the permission of the Tribunal, by an accompanying person who is not a representative duly appointed by notice in the manner described above: see PCR 2013, r 14(5).

PCR 2013, r 14(6) provides that a person accompanying a party at a hearing, who is not a representative duly appointed by notice in the manner described above:

- does not need to send written notice of his name and address to the Tribunal or any other party;
- does not have to be provided with documents required to be sent to the represented party; and
- is not to be assumed to be the representative of the represented party until written notice is given to the contrary.

PREVENTION OF DISCLOSURE

13.11 PCR 2013, r 17(1) provides that the Tribunal may make an order prohibiting the disclosure or publication of:

- specified documents or information relating to the proceedings; or
- any matter likely to lead members of the public to identify any person whom the Tribunal considers should not be identified.

PCR 2013, r 17(2) provides that the Tribunal may give a direction prohibiting the disclosure of a document or information to a person if the Tribunal is satisfied that:

- such disclosure would be likely to cause that person or some other person serious harm; and
- it is proportionate to give such a direction, having regard to the interest of justice.

PCR 2013, r 17(3)-(8) set out the machinery for obtaining a direction preventing disclosure from the Tribunal.

Chapter 14

MEDIATION, WITHDRAWAL AND SETTLEMENT

Key topics in this Chapter

Mediation
Withdrawal
Settlement
Consent orders

MEDIATION

The advantages of mediation and what will happen at a mediation

14.1 Practitioners will be well aware of the important part that alternative dispute resolution now plays in civil litigation. Mediation is one of the most useful and popular tools used by parties in attempting to settle a dispute out of court. The growth of mediation in England and Wales in recent times is well documented and has been exponential. Its use is encouraged by the senior judiciary and the government.

Rule 4(1) strikingly provides that the Tribunal should seek, where appropriate:

- to bring to the attention of the parties the availability of any appropriate alternative procedure for the resolution of the dispute; and
- if the parties wish, and provided that it is compatible with the overriding objective, to facilitate the use of the procedure.

As far as land registration cases are concerned, this rule has been taken very much to heart and mediation is promoted with enthusiasm. Importantly, the Tribunal offers its own in-house mediation service, free of charge, to the parties. They do not have to pay for the mediator's services in any circumstances nor for the use of the rooms, unless in exceptional circumstances where there are no court or tribunal facilities in the proximity of the land in dispute.

All the mediators provided by the Tribunal are Tribunal judges who are also accredited mediators. If the mediation is unsuccessful the mediator will play no part whatsoever in the further conduct of the proceedings. The success rate has been good with well over half of the cases going to mediation settling. Usually the mediation will begin with a short joint session, during which each side is asked to make a brief statement about what it is hoped the day will bring, and the remainder of the time is spent with the parties in separate rooms and the mediator shuttling between them.

Whilst many mediations will take place at a court or tribunal building, disputes involving adverse possession or boundaries lend themselves to a mediation on site. Where the parties have adjoining properties, be it suburban semi-detached houses or adjoining farms in rural Wales or Northumberland, the mediator will travel to, and shuttle between, the properties.

One of the great advantages of a mediation is that it is informal, and the relationship between the parties and a mediator is entirely different to the relationship between the parties and a judge, even though the mediator also happens to be a judge. Critically, the mediator is able to discuss matters before and during the mediation in complete confidence with one party without the other party being present, which could never happen in the course of a hearing. The mediator might even hold separate site views, if one party would rather explain his or her case and point out features in the absence of the other party.

Although the overriding objective seeks to avoid unnecessary formality at Tribunal hearings, the hearing judge, quite properly, has to adopt a coldly objective and somewhat remote position. Mediation, on the other hand, allows for a much more relaxed and informal method of dispute resolution, with everyone being on first name terms and the mediator simply being a facilitator rather than someone in charge.

The essential aspects of mediation are:

- it is a voluntary process;
- it is non-binding to the point of agreement;
- it is without prejudice;
- it is confidential;
- the parties come up with the solution.

The role of the mediator is to guide the discussion, and facilitate. Very often the real reason for, say, a boundary dispute is nothing to do with the legal merits of the case, but some wholly extraneous matter. The skill of the mediator is to tease out what is really driving and motivating the parties and to see if the real dispute can be sorted out in a sensible way, which is satisfactory to both sides.

The mediator might well ask probing questions of the parties, but this is done to clarify the issues and to enable him or her to understand, and not in order to make a judgment, form a view or impose a decision.

The parties might be told at the beginning of the mediation that one of its great advantages is that as time goes by the parties' control decreases and the costs and delay increase. Mediation puts the parties back in control. Another advantage is that everyone can think outside the box. The most sensible and desirable solution may well be one which no Tribunal could impose at a hearing.

EXAMPLE 1

A owns a farm consisting of several fields. B claims a prescriptive right of way for vehicles across one of those fields, field X, to reach his farm which also consists of several fields. A is adamantly opposed to B using field X for vehicles for sound agricultural reasons. But without access over A's farm, B's use of his property is seriously restricted. If the dispute went to a hearing, one side would win entirely and the other side would lose entirely. Either A or B would suffer a business disaster and have to pay the other party a five figure sum in costs on top. At the mediation A agrees to swap field X with field Y, which is part of B's farm adjoining A's farm. A loses nothing commercially by doing this, and B achieves the access he wants.

The procedure for starting and concluding a mediation

14.2 After all the parties' statements of case have been served, a Tribunal judge will conduct a case review. During the course of that review the judge will decide whether or not the case is one which is suitable for mediation. If it is considered to be suitable for mediation, the parties will be sent a letter proposing mediation to them: see **FORM 83** in **APPENDIX 14**.

The parties cannot be compelled to mediate, although there is always the possibility of an adverse costs order being made if mediation has been refused. If the parties to agree to mediate, then the Tribunal will send them a mediation agreement: see **FORM 84** in **APPENDIX 14**.

In addition, the parties are free at any time to suggest to the Tribunal that mediation might be appropriate.

A successful mediation will not necessarily lead to the final agreement being drafted on the day. If the parties agree to settle a dispute about, for example, the existence of a prescriptive right of way they may agree that the best solution is for a deed granting a right of way to be executed by one party in favour of the other. That deed may need to be drafted and approved by their respective conveyancing solicitors and, depending on the facts, may be a detailed and sophisticated document several pages long. At the mediation the parties will agree in writing to enter into such a deed. The Tribunal proceedings will be stayed pending the execution of the deed.

It is important to remember that any settlement reached at the mediation will need to dispose of the underlying dispute between the parties. In other words, the Tribunal will still need to make an order directing the Registrar, either to give effect to the original application, as if the objection had not been made, or to cancel the original application. It may be appropriate for the parties to agree that, upon the execution of the deed in question, the appropriate agreed direction will then be given to the Registrar.

WITHDRAWAL

14.3 Withdrawal must be distinguished from settlement, which is discussed below. When a settlement is reached, the dispute between the parties is resolved and that is the end of the litigation. If one party withdraws, the dispute is not resolved and the party is free, in the absence of any direction by the Tribunal, to make an application to Land Registry or to commence court proceedings in respect of the same issue in the future.

AR 2003 did not contain any express provision for withdrawal. Rule 22, on the other hand, does provide for withdrawal. By Rule 22(1) a party may give notice of the withdrawal of its case, or any part of it:

- orally at a hearing; or
- by sending or delivering to the Tribunal a written notice of withdrawal.

Rule 22(2) provides that a notice of withdrawal must:

- be signed and dated;
- identify the case or part of the case which is withdrawn;
- state whether any part of the case, and if so what, remains to be determined;
- confirm that a copy of the notice of the withdrawal has been provided to all other parties and state the date on which this was done;
- include the written consent of any of the other parties who have consented to the withdrawal.

For a notice of withdrawal, see **Form 85** in **appendix 14**.

A party has no absolute right to withdraw its case. Notice of withdrawal will not take effect unless the Tribunal consents to the withdrawal: see Rule 22(3).

In order to understand the basis upon which the Tribunal will decide whether or not to permit a party to withdraw its case, it is necessary to examine the decision of the Court of Appeal in *Chief Land Registrar v Silkstone* [2011] EWCA Civ 801, CA, [2012] 1 WLR 400, [2011] 2 P & CR 258. It is this decision which decided that the Adjudicator had discretion whether or not to allow a party to withdraw its case, and gave guidance as to when it would be appropriate for withdrawal to be permitted.

Paradoxically, the conventional wisdom at the time that the Adjudicator's office was established, robustly supported by Land Registry, was that the Adjudicator had no power to prevent a withdrawal. There was an attractive logic to this view.

Proceedings before the Adjudicator (and, similarly, proceedings before the Tribunal) are not like ordinary civil proceedings where one party brings a claim against another. The dispute which is the subject matter of the proceedings has been referred by Land Registry. After the reference, the argument runs, Land Registry still retains control of the original application and the objection to it. If either the original application or the objection to it is withdrawn, this brings the dispute and the reference to an end, save for the question of costs. One of the parties is always free on his own accord to give notice to Land Registry withdrawing from the underlying dispute and bringing the Adjudicator's (and, similarly, the Tribunal's) jurisdiction to an end.

This was the publicly adopted position of Land Registry. In *Blackraven Developments Ltd v Sapphire (Harlow) Nominee Ltd* (2007) Reference 2007/0274, the Adjudicator decided that once an application or objection is withdrawn, the Adjudicator's jurisdiction on the reference (save in respect of costs) comes to an end as there is no longer a dispute upon which to adjudicate.

The alternative approach is that, after the reference, Land Registry no longer has control of the original application and the objection to it. Control passed to the Adjudicator (now to the Tribunal).

In *Silkstone* the Court of Appeal authoritatively determined that the alternative approach is the correct one. After the reference Land Registry no longer has any control of the original application and the objection to it.

The facts of the case were as follows. The S brothers and T were neighbours. S claimed to have a right of way across the back garden of T's house and through a covered passage to the street. S entered a unilateral notice in the charges register of T's house in respect of the right of way. T did not accept the right of way existed and applied to cancel the unilateral notice. S objected to the application and the dispute was referred to the Adjudicator.

Four days before the hearing, S asked for permission to withdraw their objection as they were in difficulty in obtaining evidence supporting their claim to have acquired a right of way. A withdrawal would have led to the unilateral notice being cancelled without a determination of the underlying dispute. S indicated that they might commence court proceedings to establish the right of way at a later date.

The Adjudicator refused the request to withdraw. He did not consider it fair that after a dispute had been proceeding for a year it could be withdrawn just before the hearing, on the basis that it could subsequently be resurrected.

The parties attended a site view arranged for the day before the hearing. Following it S confirmed to the Adjudicator that they were withdrawing their objection to the cancellation of the unilateral notice for lack of evidence. Nevertheless the Adjudicator went ahead with the hearing the next day at which T was present but S were not. He held that he had a discretion whether or not to permit S to withdraw and decided that in the present case it would be wrong to permit a withdrawal and that the litigation between the parties needed to be brought to a conclusion.

S appealed on the grounds that the Adjudicator had no power to refuse to accept their withdrawal from the proceedings and he had no jurisdiction to deliver a decision on the merits. The Registrar was joined as a party to the appeal as Land Registry supported this approach. The appeal was heard by Floyd J in the High Court: *Silkstone v Tatnall* [2010] EWHC 1627 (Ch) [17], [2010] 3 EGLR 25, [2010] 28 EG 84 (CS). He agreed with the Adjudicator that, after the reference, Land Registry no longer has any control of the original application and the objection to it. He took a more extreme view than the Adjudicator and held that after the reference the Adjudicator had no discretion but was bound to decide the underlying dispute if the parties were unable to reach a settlement on the merits.

Land Registry appealed to the Court of Appeal who agreed with the Adjudicator and Floyd J that, after the reference, Land Registry no longer has any control of the original application and the objection to it. The Court of Appeal agreed with the view of the Adjudicator that he has a discretion whether or not to permit a party to withdraw.

The following principles, modified to reflect the transfer of functions from the Adjudicator to the Tribunal, emerge from the judgment of Rimer LJ:

- A party can always apply to withdraw his case, which will necessarily ordinarily include the withdrawal of the original application or the objection.
- No court or tribunal can require a party to advance a case he no longer wishes to advance. The real question is what, upon being given notice of such a withdrawal, the Tribunal is required or entitled to do.
- It does not make any difference whether the withdrawal is done by the Applicant or the Respondent.
- Neither party can by his unilateral act (including by his expressed withdrawal of his application, objection or case) bring the reference to an end.
- Equally, neither party can be compelled to advance a case to the Tribunal that he no longer wishes to advance. A party can apply to withdraw his application, objection or case but it is then for the Tribunal to rule in its discretion as to how to deal with any such withdrawal.
- That will require a consideration of all the circumstances. It may perhaps, particularly at the early stage of a reference, be regarded by the Tribunal as just simply to permit the withdrawal and to make an order terminating the reference, making any appropriate direction to the Registrar and dealing with costs. If the order says no more, it would no doubt leave the party free to revive the same claim. That may not necessarily be unjust.
- In other cases, particularly when the reference is significantly advanced, to deal with a withdrawal on terms like that may be unjust.
- It may still be appropriate in such cases for the Tribunal to terminate the reference but it may consider it just to do so not only on terms as to costs, but also on the basis of a direction to the Registrar requiring him to reject any future application of a specified kind from the withdrawing party: see Rule 40(3)(b).
- The imposition of such a direction is not a matter that requires the consent of the withdrawing party.
- It may in other cases, particularly those in which the reference is far advanced, be appropriate for the Tribunal to proceed to the substantive hearing, rule upon the merits of the issue and then make such order as is appropriate.

Silkstone concerned an attempt by S to withdraw his objection to T's application to cancel a unilateral notice. S had struck first by entering a unilateral notice in the charges register of T's house. The court was not prepared to let S walk away from the reference by withdrawing his objection and allowing the notice to be cancelled. It was argued on his behalf that he could outflank this refusal to bring the reference to an end by himself applying voluntarily to remove the unilateral notice: see LRA 2002, s 35(3).

Rimer LJ expressed the view that whilst S could remove the unilateral notice voluntarily in this way, he would not regard any removal of the notice by an exercise of the s 35(3) right as automatically bringing the reference to an end, any more than does the expressed wish of the Objector to withdraw his objection and case. The proceedings will still remain alive until he has made a decision disposing of them.

Silkstone remains directly relevant in so far as it sets out the principles upon which the grant of permission to withdraw should be governed. The implied right to withdraw, articulated by Rimer LJ, is now an express one in Rule 22.

The Tribunal itself has no direct power to interfere with the register. It cannot itself give effect to, or cancel, an original application when giving permission to a party to withdraw. Accordingly, Rule 22(4) provides that the Tribunal may make such directions or impose such conditions on withdrawal as it considers appropriate.

EXAMPLE 2

A makes an application to have the benefit and burden of a prescriptive right of way entered on the registers of the titles of his and his neighbour's land. As soon as the reference is received by the Tribunal, A applies to withdraw his original application and the proceedings. The Tribunal gives him permission to withdraw and directs the Registrar to cancel the original application. A is, in theory, at liberty at any time in the future to make another application to Land Registry or to commence court proceedings in which he alleges that he has the benefit of the prescriptive right of way.

EXAMPLE 3

A makes an application to have the benefit and burden of a prescriptive right of way entered on the registers of the titles of his and his neighbour's land. One year after the reference, after statements of case have been served, disclosure given, witness statements and expert evidence exchanged, and two days before the hearing is to begin, A applies to withdraw his original application and the proceedings. The Tribunal gives him permission to withdraw and directs the Registrar to cancel the original application, but directs the Registrar pursuant to Rule 40(3)(b) that the Registrar is to reject any further application from A in which he alleges that he has the benefit of the prescriptive right of way.

A party which has withdrawn its case may apply for it to be reinstated: see Rule 22(5). Such an application must be made in writing and be received within 28 days after:

- the date of the hearing at which the case was withdrawn orally: see Rule 22(6)(a); or
- the date on which the Tribunal received the notice of withdrawal: see Rule 22(6)(b).

Where there has been a withdrawal, the Tribunal must give notice of it to each party in writing: see Rule 22(7). Within 28 days of receiving this notification, any party may apply for a case, or part of a case, which has been withdrawn to be reinstated: see Rule 22(8).

SETTLEMENT

14.4 As in any form of litigation, settlement is to be encouraged. However, care needs to be taken as to the way in which the settlement is put into effect. There is no equivalent of CPR Part 36, although offers made without prejudice as to costs will be taken into account on the question of costs. Costs are dealt with in CHAPTER **19**.

The Tribunal will not make an order to adjourn generally the proceedings before it. The original application will have been entered on the day list kept by Land Registry and while it remains on the day list, the Registrar cannot give effect to subsequent applications. It is therefore necessary if a settlement is reached for the Tribunal to make an order to the Registrar for the giving effect to the original application as if the objection had not been made, or for the cancellation of the original application: see Rule 40(2) and CHAPTER **18**.

The Tribunal cannot make an order in *Tomlin* form because it does not have power to enforce the terms contained in the schedule to the order. There is no reason, however, why the parties cannot enter into an agreement containing the terms of settlement (such as the grant of a right of way or a land swap) and at the same time consent to an appropriate direction to the Registrar.

EXAMPLE 4

A is the paper title owner of Whiteacre, which is unregistered land. B, who is the registered proprietor of neighbouring land, makes an application to Land Registry to be registered as the first proprietor of Whiteacre on the grounds that he has acquired title to it by adverse possession. A objects and the dispute is referred to the tribunal under LRA 2002, s 73(7), as amended. The Tribunal directs B to be the Applicant and A to be the Respondent in the proceedings before it. Before the hearing A offers B a right of way over Whiteacre, in return for B giving up the claim to adverse possession and paying £5,000 towards his costs. B decides to accept this offer, and the parties execute a deed granting the right of way.

Both parties write to the Tribunal informing it of this agreement, enclosing a copy of the deed and a draft order in the terms of FORM **92** in APPENDIX **14**. The Tribunal having considered it an appropriate form of wording, the order is sealed and the reference is concluded.

Where the parties settle shortly before the hearing but have not yet had sufficient time in which to execute any necessary conveyancing document, the Tribunal may order the hearing to be vacated on terms that the parties file the completed document within a certain period of time. When that document is duly filed the consent order will be made and sent out to the parties and Land Registry.

Parties wishing to settle are encouraged to send a draft order to the Tribunal who will consider it and advise on any necessary changes.

Parties who wish to settle should reach agreement as to the costs of the proceedings. It is highly undesirable for the parties to reach agreement on terms other than as to costs and then to seek the Tribunal's decision as to who should pay the costs. A just determination of what order to make as to costs could involve a full consideration of the merits of the substantive dispute. In such circumstances, it is considered that the Tribunal is entitled to treat the matter as not having been settled.

CONSENT ORDERS

14.5 The jurisdiction of the Tribunal to make a consent order is derived from Rule 35(1), which provides that the Tribunal may, at the request of the parties but only if it considers it appropriate, make a consent order disposing of the proceedings and making such other appropriate provisions as the parties have agreed.

The Tribunal, when making such a consent order, need not hold a hearing or provide reasons: see Rule 35(2).

For a consent order, see **Form 92** in **appendix 14**.

Chapter 15

PREPARING FOR THE HEARINGS

Key topics in this chapter

Preparation of trial bundles
Lists of Issues
Skeleton arguments
Chronologies
Use of plans and photographs

PREPARATION OF TRIAL BUNDLES

15.1 The Tribunal will make a direction for the preparation of the trial bundles. Usually, the Applicant will be given responsibility for preparing the bundles. However, if the Applicant is not legally represented and the Respondent is represented then the Tribunal is likely to direct that the Respondent prepare the bundle.

The authors cannot stress too much the importance of proper care and attention being paid to the preparation of bundles for use at the hearing. All too frequently time at the hearing is wasted, with resultant increase in costs for the parties because:

- important documents are omitted or are illegible because of poor copying
- plans are not coloured
- the bundle is not paginated
- multiple copies of the same documents are included in the bundle in different places
- faulty ring binders are used

The Tribunal may not allow the cost of preparation of bundles where this has not been done properly.

Generally the bundles should contain clear legible copies of:

- The statements of case served by each of the parties;
- witness statements served by each of the parties;
- documents attached to or referred to in the statements of case or witness statements;
- any other relevant documents served by a party and which they wish to refer to at the hearing.

An index of key documents should be placed at the front of the bundle.

It will often be most convenient to place the documents in the following order:

- Applicant's statement of case; Respondent's statement of case; Applicant's statement of case in reply (if any);
- Witness statements of witnesses intended to be called by the Applicant;

- Witness statements of witnesses intended to be called by the Respondent;
- Documents of title intended to be referred to, in date order;
- Plans;
- Photographs;
- Correspondence in date order;
- Any other relevant documents.

Care should be taken to avoid including more than one copy of each document.

Where documents are attached to or referred to in the statements of case or witness statements, it will be convenient not to place the document after the relevant statement of case or witness statement but to place a sheet after each statement of case or witness statement stating the page numbers in the bundle where the documents referred to in the statement of case or witness statement can be found.

The documents should be presented in a ring binder and each page should be separately page numbered in black ink in the bottom right hand corner.

The standard directions made by the Tribunal provide for the party who does not have responsibility for preparation of the trial bundle at least 28 days prior to the hearing date to notify the party who is to prepare the trial bundle what documents he or she wishes to be included. The party preparing the bundle should then add the documents which the other party wishes to be included.

The Tribunal will direct the parties to co-operate in the preparation of the trial bundle. If the parties are unable to agree the contents of the trial bundle then the party preparing the bundle should include all the documents notified by the other party with a note stating what documents are objected to and a brief explanation as to why he objects. At the hearing the Tribunal will determine what documents should or should not be included.

At least 14 days before the hearing date the party preparing the trial bundle should deliver one copy to the other party (and to each of them if more than one party) and one copy to the Tribunal. The party preparing the trial bundle should bring an extra copy to the hearing for the use of witnesses.

The standard directions made by the Tribunal provide that the party preparing the bundle shall deliver the copy to each of the other parties free of charge. However, if the party who prepares the trial bundle is awarded costs then the award will usually include the costs of preparing the trial bundle, including the costs of delivering a copy to another party.

LIST OF ISSUES

15.2 The Tribunal will direct that all parties prepare a list of issues to be decided by the Tribunal. This list should set out briefly the issues of fact and of law that the Tribunal will have to decide. The list of issues should be agreed, if possible.

SKELETON ARGUMENTS

15.3 The Tribunal will direct that all parties prepare a skeleton argument. This should be a brief statement of the arguments in support of the case of the person preparing the skeleton. It should include details of any relevant parts of any authorities intended to be relied upon in support of the arguments.

CHRONOLOGY OF MATERIAL EVENTS

15.4 The standard directions made by the Tribunal provide that all parties must prepare a chronology of material events relating to the case. The directions provide that the chronology should be agreed, if possible. It should always be possible to agree a single chronology of material events and the parties ought to attempt to do so. In the event that there is disagreement between the parties as to whether an event is material the event can be included in the chronology together with a note that there is a dispute as to whether the event is material. If there is a dispute as to the date of a material event, both dates can be entered together with a note that the date is in dispute.

In certain cases, such as a prescriptive easement, it can be helpful to show both properties side by side in the chronology:

PROPERTY	15 HIGH STREET	17 HIGH STREET
TITLE NO	ABC111647	ABC183357
PARTIES	MR AND MRS [A]	MR AND MRS [B]
	Applicants	Respondents
	Dominant tenement	Servient tenement
16.08.1969	First registered [p.x].	
03.09.1974		First registered [p.x].
05.08.1986	Mr and Mrs [A] registered as proprietors [p.x].	
16.02.1987	Mr and Mrs [A] start to walk over side path belonging to No 17.	
20.01.1990		Transfer to Mr and Mrs [B] [p.x].
22.02.1990		Mr and Mrs [B] registered as proprietors [p.x].
06.12.2010	The original application [p.x]	
05.01.2011		Objection [p.x]

SERVICE OF LISTS OF ISSUES, CHRONOLOGIES AND SKELETON ARGUMENTS

15.5 The lists of issues, chronologies, and skeleton arguments should be sent to the Tribunal and to each of the other parties so that they arrive no later than seven days before the hearing date. Copies of authorities referred to in the skeleton arguments should be sent with the skeleton arguments to the Tribunal and to the other parties.

USE OF PLANS AND PHOTOGRAPHS

15.6 Although some disputes before the Tribunal do not turn on the geography or topography of a particular site (such as beneficial interest or forgery cases), in other disputes (such as adverse possession or a disputed boundary) the lay of the land is of paramount importance. In the latter type of case the use of plans and photographs is essential.

It is worth quoting in full what Arden LJ has had to say about the use of plans and photographs in bundles and skeleton arguments *in Hunte v Bottomley & Sons Ltd* [2007] EWCA Civ 1168 [30], [2007] All ER (D) 220 (Oct):

> The problem is this: there are a significant number of cases which involve this court using plans, maps, diagrams and photographs, and more importantly, understanding them. These cases usually concern land. Many cases of this kind, however, and I am sorry to say that this was one of them, are prepared in a way which makes it very difficult for members of this court, when reading the papers in preparation for the appeal hearing, to read the plan, map, diagram or photograph correctly, or to follow fully the submissions of the parties about those documents or the property which is the subject of the dispute. In these circumstances, the court cannot be certain about what the plan, diagram, map or photograph shows until the appeal is opened and they are fully explained. Those who prepare bundles or skeleton arguments would do well to remember that a plan, map, diagram or photograph which is clear to people who are fully familiar with the case may well not be wholly clear to a judge coming to the case for the first time. The problem is often exacerbated when the case comes to this court, and the parties very properly put into the appeal bundle some only of the maps, plans, diagrams or photographs. When that happens, this court does not have all the information which the court below had. In my judgment, it is absolutely essential in any case of this kind, where the court is going to have to grapple with plans, maps, diagrams or photographs, that there is at least one plan, photograph or map which leaves the court in no real doubt about the location of all the relevant features. The skeleton arguments should also identify that photograph, map, plan or diagram at an early point, so this court is left in no doubt when it is rereading its papers for the hearing. Very often, in my experience, this court is (for example) either given some only of the plans, or photocopies which do not have the colouring referred to in the original documents or by the judge in his judgment, or copies with parts cut off, or without compass points, or where appropriate, a statement of the scale. Those who prepare skeleton arguments for cases in this court or appeal bundles should please bear in mind that the court has properly and easily to understand any map, plan, diagram or photograph which is material in the appeal.

Where a plan is used it should be clear and simple and identify the various parcels of land which are relevant. It is often helpful to refer to a particular parcel of land by a colour, for example "the red land" and to identify it by red edging on the plan.

A helpful guide to plans and mapping is Land Registry's Practice Guide 40, which can be downloaded free of charge from Land Registry's website.

Where the value of the land in an adverse possession case makes it proportionate, it is useful for a joint surveyor to prepare an agreed 1:200 plan plotting the relevant boundaries and showing the various physical features the parties rely upon. The use of overlays can be very helpful.

Copies of photographs should be of good quality; faded photocopies of photographs are of no use. Coloured photographs should not be copied in black and white. Photographs can be confusing or misleading if the reader does not know where they are taken from. It is often helpful to enclose a plan showing the positions from which the photographs were taken.

In adverse possession cases Land Registry will often have conducted its own survey when the original application was made. A report is prepared for Land Registry's use accompanied by photographs. The positions from which the photographs were taken are shown on a plan. These photographs can be extremely helpful to the Tribunal and should be included in the trial bundle where appropriate.

In some disputes it is important to know how the land looked historically. In an adverse possession case it may be necessary to determine exactly when it was that the Applicant turned his neighbour's unused field into a well-manicured lawn and fenced it off to form part of his garden. If the field is unregistered land the Applicant will succeed if this happened 12 years or more before the original application. However many witnesses of fact are called, the best evidence is photographic. In the case of boundary features, aerial photographs can be illuminating and decisive.

Aerial photographs are widely available, but will often need expert evidence to help interpret them. In particular they often require to be shown stereoscopically through special equipment.

The significance of boundaries on maps and plans is considered further in CHAPTER 22 which includes reference to boundary disputes.

Chapter 16

SITE VIEWS

Key topics in this chapter

When a site view is appropriate
Power to conduct a site view
Practical arrangement for the site view
Conduct at the site view
Site view as evidence

WHEN A SITE VIEW IS APPROPRIATE

16.1 The Tribunal may wish to inspect land or premises for the purposes of determining the whole or part of the matter referred to it. It will usually be appropriate for it to do so where the physical characteristics of the land or premises to which the matter relates are relevant to determination of the matter. Thus the Tribunal will usually wish to inspect the land or premises in cases involving allegations of adverse possession, easements, or boundaries. It will not usually wish to inspect the land or premises where the extent or other physical characteristics of the land or premises are not in dispute, such as cases involving the beneficial ownership of land, or the validity or effectiveness of transactions.

POWER TO CONDUCT SITE VIEWS

16.2 If the Tribunal wishes to inspect land or premises for the purposes of determining the matter, it may serve a request for entry on the party who is in occupation or has ownership or control of the property.

The request for entry must be in writing. It will request permission for the Tribunal to enter onto and inspect the property. It may also request permission for the Tribunal to be accompanied by one or more of

- another party;
- a member or members of the Tribunal's staff;
- any other person, if the Tribunal considers it appropriate – Rule 21.

The Tribunal cannot demand to be allowed onto the property if the person in occupation or who owns or controls it refuses the request.

The service of a copy of the notice of entry on the other party is an important matter. In the different context of the trial of a personal injury action in the county court, it has been held that the view by a judge of the site of an accident in the absence of the plaintiff who had not been notified of the date of the view was an 'inadmissible view': see *Goold v Evans & Co* [1951] 2 TLR 1189, CA.

If a request for entry is refused without reasonable excuse, the Tribunal may take such refusal into account when making any decision or deciding any application for costs – Practice Direction 6.5.

The editors are unaware of any occasion on which a request for entry has been refused. It is difficult to see how it would be in the interests of a party to refuse entry where the Tribunal has requested entry to view the property.

PRACTICAL ARRANGEMENTS FOR THE SITE INSPECTION

16.3 The request for entry is usually made by a letter to the parties, which also informs them of the time and date of the hearing and the address of the hearing venue.

In a case concerning a boundary, the Tribunal will usually wish to inspect land on both sides of the alleged boundary and will make a request for entry of more than one party.

The parties are asked to complete risk assessment forms, giving details of any physical hazards on the land to be inspected.

The Tribunal usually conducts the site inspection prior to the start of the hearing. Typically, the site view will take place during the afternoon of the day prior to the commencement of the hearing or in the morning of the day on which the hearing is to commence. The timing of the view will be set so as to ensure that it can be conducted in adequate daylight.

The Tribunal will make his own arrangements for travelling to the site.

CONDUCT AT THE SITE VIEW

16.4 The site view should be treated by the parties as if it were part of the hearing. It is a formal occasion, the purpose of which is to enable the Tribunal to see the physical features existing at the time of the view.

If the parties are legally represented, they may wish the persons who will be conducting the hearing on their behalf to be present.

All parties wishing to be present at the site view should assemble on site a little time in advance of the time set for the view. The Tribunal Judge will not wish to commence his inspection until all parties or their representatives are present.

The judge will usually invite the parties or their representatives to point out to him any relevant features of which they wish him to take note.

The judge may conduct a site inspection in the absence of a party or representative but is highly desirable for both parties to be present or represented.

Practice Direction 6 provides that no-one should attempt to communicate with the Judge except in the hearing of the parties or their representatives. This is to avoid the risk of any subsequent accusation of bias or procedural irregularity.

The judge will usually have read the skeleton arguments and relevant documents in the hearing bundle prior to the site view.

The judge will not wish to be informed at the site view of the history of the dispute or to hear the respective arguments of the parties. Evidence should be given only at the hearing. The judge cannot take evidence at the site view without ensuring that the questions asked and the answers given are accurately recorded. He will also need to ensure that neither party is disadvantaged by evidence being taken at a site inspection. For this reason, the judge will almost invariably refuse to hear evidence on the site inspection and therefore, it is seldom helpful for the parties to bring their witnesses to the site inspection.

Where a judge sitting in the County Court held a site inspection with the experts for both sides, allowed them to explain their positions, did not take a note or recording of what was said and then dispensed with the experts attending the hearing for cross-examination, the Court of Appeal held there had been a serious procedural irregularity. The Court of Appeal said that a judge in taking evidence at a site inspection must be careful to ensure neither party is disadvantaged and do so only in the presence of the other party and after ensuring an accurate note is taken of the questions and answers – *Hatton v Connew* [2013] EWCA Civ 1560, [2013] All ER (D) 119 (Dec).

The judge attends the site view as part of the conduct of his judicial function. For this reason, he will not be able to accept any form of hospitality from any party, witness or representative. He will be careful to avoid acting in any way which might be thought to cast doubt on his impartiality.

SITE VIEW AND EVIDENCE

16.5 What the judge sees of the land or premises on a site view is part of the evidence; it is 'real evidence': see per Lord Denning LJ in *Goold v Evans* [1951] 2 TLR 1189, CA.

Chapter 17

HEARINGS

Key topics in this chapter

Definitions
Notice of hearing
Representation
Absence of parties
Venue and administration
Conducting the hearing
Substantive decisions
Consequential directions

DEFINITIONS

17.1 Rule 1 defines a 'hearing' as follows:

> 'hearing' means an oral hearing and includes a hearing conducted in whole or in part by video link, telephone or other means of instantaneous two-way electronic communication.

It is wider than the restrictive definition of 'hearing' in AR 2003.

The terms 'matter', 'substantive decision' and 'substantive order' which appeared in the AR 2003 have found no place in the Rules of the Property Chamber.

There are four types of hearing which could lead to the Tribunal making a decision which disposes of proceedings:

- a hearing of a preliminary issue;
- a summary disposal hearing;
- a hearing following a rule 31 notice;
- a final hearing.

For the particular procedure relating to the hearing of a preliminary issue, a summary disposal hearing and a hearing following a rule 31 notice, see CHAPTER 12.

A decision which disposes of proceedings can also be made without a hearing, but only in certain circumstances. This is also dealt with in CHAPTER 12.

NOTICE OF HEARING

17.2 The Tribunal will send out to the parties written notice of the date, time and location of the hearing. At least 28 days' notice will be given, unless the parties agree to a shorter period or the circumstances are urgent or exceptional: see Rule 31.

REPRESENTATION

17.3 It is expressly provided that a party may appoint a representative (whether legally qualified or not) to represent him in the proceedings: see Rule 14(1). Additionally, a party may be accompanied to a hearing by a person who, with the permission of the Tribunal, may act as a representative or otherwise help the party in presenting his case – see Rule 14(5)

If a party appoints a representative, he must give written notice to the Tribunal and to each other party of the representative's name and address – see Rule 14(2). If (and only if) the representative is a lawyer or other person authorised for the purposes of the Legal Services Act 2007 to exercise a right of audience or conduct litigation, the representative may give notice of the appointment of a representative under Rule 14(2).

An appointed representative of a party can do anything the party could do in the proceedings except sign a witness statement.

Once a person receives notice of appointment of a representative, he must supply any document required to be sent to the other party to the representative and need not send it to the party.

Having received notice of appointment of a representative, the recipient is entitled to assume the representative is the authorised representative until he receives both written notice to the contrary and an alternative address for communication with the party. The notice of that the representative is no longer authorised to act as representative might come from either the representative or from the party.

A sometimes useful provision can be found in Rule 6(3)(f) which permits the Tribunal to require a party to state whether he intends to attend or be represented at the hearing.

Unlike the Adjudicator, the Tribunal has no express power to refuse to permit a particular person to represent a party in the proceedings. However, where notice is not given under Rule 14(2), the Tribunal's permission is required before a person acts as representative or helps a party at the hearing.

The effect of Rule 14(1) is that a non-legally qualified representative can exercise a right of audience before the Tribunal, notwithstanding that a right of audience is a reserved legal activity within the meaning of the Legal Services Act 2007 s. 12(1)(a). – see Legal Services Act 2007, s 19, Schd 3 para 1(3)(b) and s 12(1)(a) and s 13(2)(b).

In practice, in a substantial proportion of the hearings before the Tribunal, the parties are represented by counsel or a solicitor. But at many hearings at least one of the parties is not represented. The cases that come before the Tribunal very often involve complex issues of law and for this reason parties are well advised to consider obtaining legal representation for the hearing. However, where a party is not legally represented, the Tribunal will endeavour to ensure that the hearing is a fair one to all the parties, whether represented or not.

ABSENCE OF PARTIES

17.4 If a party fails to attend the hearing after notice of the hearing has been served on him or reasonable steps have been taken to notify him of the hearing, the Tribunal may proceed with the hearing if the Tribunal considers it in the interests of justice to proceed – see Rule 34.

If a party is not present at a hearing and the Tribunal proceeds to make a decision disposing of the proceedings in his absence, the party may apply to set aside the decision under Rule 51. The application must be made in writing so that it is received within 28 days of the Tribunal sending notice of the decision or within 28 days of the Tribunal sending reasons for the decision, whichever is the later. The practice of the Land Registration division is for the decision and reasons for it to be sent out in writing at the same time.

The Tribunal may only set aside the decision in such circumstances if it considers it is in the interests of justice to do so.

VENUE AND ADMINISTRATION

17.5 Hearings are held either at the Property Chamber's hearing rooms at 10 Alfred Place, London WC1E 7LR or at courts or tribunal hearing centres in cities and towns around the country.

Hearings are in public, except where the Tribunal directs that the hearing or part of it be held in private – Rule 33.

If the Tribunal directs that the hearing be held in private, the Tribunal will determine who can be present at the hearing and the terms and conditions on which a person is admitted to the hearing.

If the hearing is in public, the Tribunal may exclude any person falling into the categories set out in Rule 33(5). These include

- a person disrupting or likely to disrupt the hearing;
- a person likely to intimidate a witness or a party; and
- a person whose exclusion the Tribunal considers necessary to prevent disclosure or publication of documents and information where the Tribunal has made an order prohibiting disclosure or publication under Rule 17

If medical evidence shows that a particular witness is unable to attend the hearing but the witness is able to give evidence at home, the Tribunal will consider taking that evidence in the witness's home or some other suitable place.

If there has been a site view directed, this will either before the hearing or during the course of the hearing. Site views are considered in CHAPTER **16**.

The hearing rooms are laid out in a formal fashion, with a dais for the judge and a witness box. The hearings are usually conducted in a formal manner; parties may be expected to stand to address the judge and should address the judge as 'sir' or 'madam'.

A clerk will be present to take the names of the parties and the witnesses, ensure the parties are seated correctly, bring the judge in and out of the hearing room, administer the oath and affirmation when a witness gives evidence and assist the judge generally in the conduct of the hearing.

The hearings are recorded and the clerk will oversee the recording equipment. A transcript will only be provided at public expense if required by the Upper

Tribunal for the purposes of an appeal or if permission is expressly given. Otherwise a party wanting a transcript will have to pay for it. The recordings can only be released to an approved transcriber, not to the parties or their solicitors.

The party responsible for preparing the trial bundle will have been asked to bring a set to the hearing for use in the witness box.

CONDUCTING THE HEARING

17.6 A summary disposal hearing will be conducted on the basis of the statements of case and witness statements.

A hearing of a preliminary issue requiring the determination of an issue of fact will be conducted with oral evidence.

A hearing following a rule 31 notice will be conducted on the basis of the statements of case and witness statements unless there is a dispute of fact which needs to be resolved by the calling of oral evidence. The evidence at a hearing following a rule 31 notice may be restricted, if it appears to the Tribunal that it could reach a decision on the material already supplied when the rule 31 notice is served.

A final hearing will almost invariably be conducted with oral evidence. There are a few cases, however, where the facts are not in dispute and the hearing will be conducted on the basis of the statements of case and witness statements and oral submissions of the parties. This might occur where the dispute turns on the construction of documents.

Where oral evidence is being called, the course of the hearing will normally be the same as that usually followed in the courts. The judge will invite the Applicant to open the case. The judge will have read the skeleton arguments (if any) prior to the commencement of the hearing and is likely to have looked at what appear to be the most important documents in the hearing bundle. However, the Applicant may use his opening to summarize what his case will be and to draw the attention of the judge to the crucial parts of important documents.

Following the opening, the Applicant will give evidence and call his witnesses to give evidence. Evidence before the Land Registration division is always given on oath or by affirmation. In this respect the procedure differs from other tribunals where evidence is given unsworn.

As witness statements will have been exchanged, it is the normal practice for a witness to give his evidence by confirming the contents of his statement of case (if it has been verified by a statement of truth) and his witness statement, and then to be cross-examined. A witness will have an opportunity when called to give evidence to correct any errors which may appear in his witness statement. Witnesses should be asked to read their witness statements over again shortly before the hearing so they can familiarise themselves again with the contents. Witnesses who are not used to working with documents should also be reminded to bring their reading glasses to the hearing: it is surprising the number of occasions on which a witness is unable to give evidence satisfactorily about where a feature is located on a plan because he has not brought his reading glasses to the hearing

The judge may in his discretion allow some supplementary questions to be asked of the witness by the party calling the witness. Supplementary questions might usefully be used to permit the witness to give evidence of relevant facts that have occurred since his witness statement was made and exchanged. However, supplementary questions ought not to be asked on matters of real substance since the substance of the witness's evidence should be set out in his witness statement. Moreover, the parties were informed in advance in the standard directions that where a witness is called to give oral evidence his or her witness statement shall stand as his or her evidence, subject to any cross-examination unless the Tribunal orders otherwise.

The extent to which the judge will permit supplementary questions in chief will vary from case to case, in the same way that the extent to which a judge in a civil court will permit such questions will vary from case to case. There is margin of discretion. Sometimes supplementary questions are permitted provided the further information is set out in a witness statement provided at the hearing following a short break, or on stringent terms as to costs. The safer course is to assume supplementary questions will be restricted and for witness statements to be drafted in the first place as fully, and in as much detail, as possible.

Evidence may be given in a language other than English or Welsh with the permission of the Tribunal. In a suitable case, the Tribunal will direct that evidence be given through an interpreter and that an interpreter be provided by HM Courts and Tribunals Service.

Evidence may be given by a person with hearing difficulties in British Sign Language and with the assistance of a BSL interpreter provided by HM Courts and Tribunals Service.

Following the evidence in chief the witness will be cross-examined by the other party or parties. The witness will then be re-examined by his own advocate, and finally the judge may ask some questions.

Where the Applicant is unrepresented the judge may require him to take the oath or affirmation at the outset and then the opening submissions and the evidence will be rolled into one. The judge may properly take on a more inquisitorial role in order to elucidate the evidence from the unrepresented Applicant.

After the Applicant has called all his witnesses, his case will be closed. The judge will not normally expect the respondent to make any submissions at the outset of his case. Occasionally, however, clarification of some or all of the Respondent's case may be helpful before the Respondent calls his witnesses.

The Respondent will then give evidence and call his witnesses to give evidence in the same way as the Applicant and his witnesses have done.

Normally a party will give his evidence before calling his witnesses, but the judge will be flexible and try to assist if a particular witness needs to be interposed. If a spouse or partner of a party has provided a witness statement corroborating that of the party and the party has been cross-examined at length, the judge may not insist the spouse or partner is cross-examined if the opposing party does not chose to do so. The judge may treat the evidence of the spouse or partner as having been challenged in the same way that the evidence of the party was.

Following the evidence, the judge will hear closing submissions from the parties. Normally the Respondent will go first, the Applicant will reply and the Respondent will have an opportunity to reply, but only on a point of law arising in the Applicant's submissions. Where the Respondent is unrepresented, but the Applicant is represented, the judge may prefer the Applicant to go first. This allows the Respondent to have the last word on the facts.

If time runs short or other circumstances render it appropriate, the judge may invite the parties to make their final submissions in writing.

DECISIONS

17.7 Following a hearing the judge will give his decision and that decision will be recorded in an order or direction. Decisions which dispose of proceedings made following a hearing are dealt with in CHAPTER **18**. Decisions without a hearing are dealt with in CHAPTER **12**.

The judge may give his decision orally at the end of the hearing or the decision may be reserved – see Rule 36. However, the Tribunal is required to give written reasons for a decision which finally disposes of all issues in the proceedings or of a preliminary issue: see Rule 36(2). For this reason, the judge usually reserves his decision rather than giving it orally at the end of the hearing. Where the decision is reserved, a written decision will be sent out to the parties and Land Registry in the post.

The practice is for the decisions to be as thorough and detailed as would be expected in a reserved judgment of the High Court or County Court. They may have a plan annexed showing the various parcels of land in dispute. The decision will set out the facts as found by the judge and his conclusion will be based on his application of the law, as he understands it, to those facts. The aim is that every losing party should know and understand precisely why he has lost.

Decisions of legal interest or importance are to be found on HM Courts and Tribunals Service website. Decisions of the Adjudicator and of the Tribunal can also to be found on the British and Irish Legal Information Institute (BAILLI) website.

CONSEQUENTIAL APPLICATIONS

17.8 Where the decision is reserved, it will not usually be possible for the parties to make oral submissions as to what order should be made as to costs. What is the appropriate order to be made as to costs will usually depend on what the substantive decision is and the reasons for that decision. The usual practice of the judges of the Land Registration division is to give the parties an opportunity to make submissions as to costs in writing following receipt by them of the Tribunal's decision. Often the judge will state in his decision what order as to liability costs he is minded to make (ie what order as to who, if anyone, is to be ordered to pay the costs) and invite the parties' to make written submissions within a specified time period if one or more of the parties objects to the making of such an order. Following the expiry of the time period and on consideration of any written submissions, the judge will then make an order as to costs, including directions for preparation for an assessment of the amount of costs payable, if appropriate.

Costs are considered in more detail in CHAPTER **19**.

Similarly, where the decision is reserved, it will not usually be possible for the parties to make oral submissions as to whether or not permission to appeal should be given. Whether permission to appeal should be given will usually depend on what the substantive decision is, the reasons for that decision and the grounds of appeal put forward. If either party wishes to apply for permission to appeal, the usual practice is for an application to be made in writing following receipt by the parties of the Tribunal's decision.

Appeals are considered in more detail in CHAPTER **20**.

Chapter 18

DECISIONS AND ORDERS

Key topics in this Chapter

What orders disposing of the proceedings the Tribunal can make
The form of the order
What orders disposing of the proceedings the Tribunal cannot make
Consent Orders
How effect is given to orders disposing of the proceeding
Orders requiring the Registrar to reject future applications

WHAT ORDERS DISPOSING OF THE PROCEEDINGS THE TRIBUNAL CAN MAKE

18.1 This chapter is concerned with decisions and orders which finally dispose of all issues in the proceedings. Directions given during the course of the proceedings are dealt with in CHAPTER **11**. Preliminary issues and summary disposal are dealt with in CHAPTER **12**.

The Tribunal may give a decision orally at the hearing: see Rule 36(1). This rarely happens in a land registration case.

The Tribunal must provide to each party as soon as reasonably practicable after making a decision which finally disposes of all issues in the proceedings:

- a decision notice stating the Tribunal's decision: see Rule 36(2)(a);
- written reasons for the decision: see Rule 36(2)(b); and
- notification of any right of appeal against the decision and the time within which, and manner in which, such right of appeal may be exercised: see Rule 36(2)(c).

This is subject to Rule 17(8) which prevents disclosure or publication of documents and information in certain circumstances where serious harm would be caused or it would be contrary to the interests of national security.

This requirement for written reasons also does not apply to decisions made under the Rules 2013 Part 6 correcting clerical mistakes, setting aside a decision for procedural irregularity, reviewing a decision, granting permission to appeal or granting a stay: see Rule 36(2).

In the decision notice, the Tribunal will either:

- make an order requiring the Registrar to give effect to the original application in whole or in part as if the objection to the original application had not been made: see Rule 40(2)(a); or
- make an order requiring the Registrar to cancel the original application in whole or in part: see Rule 40(2)(b).

The words 'as if the objection had not been made' are added to an order requiring the Registrar to give effect to an application in whole or in part to take account of the fact that there may be a reason, apart from the objection which has been considered by the Tribunal, why the Registrar cannot give effect to the original application. For example, there may have been a further objection to the original application that has not yet been referred to the Tribunal or determined by him.

Land Registry may take the view that a form of order requiring the Registrar to give effect to the application "as if the objection had not been made" will preserve any discretion the Registrar may have to refuse an application notwithstanding the Tribunal's decision.

EXAMPLE 1

A applies for registration with possessory title of unregistered land based on his allegation that he has been in possession for 12 years. R objects and Land Registry refers the matter to the Tribunal. The Tribunal finds on the facts that A has been in possession for a period of 10 years. It may direct that the Registrar to give effect to the application as if the objection of R had not been made. Land Registry may nevertheless refuse registration on the grounds that it has a discretion under LRA 2002, ss 9(5) and 10 (6). This is a point which needs to be authoritatively determined either by the Upper Tribunal or by way of judicial review: see *Dunn v Harrison West Ltd* (Reference/2011/0558) (2012), unreported.

The Tribunal has power to include in its order a condition that a specified entry be made on the register of the title affected: see Rule 40(3)(a).

EXAMPLE 2

A applies for first registration of Whiteacre on the grounds of adverse possession. B objects. At the hearing it becomes apparent that B has no real grounds for objecting to the original application, but is concerned to protect the benefit of a right of way he has acquired over Whiteacre by prescription. The Tribunal has power to direct the Registrar to give effect to the original application as if the objection had not been made, but to direct that the burden of the right of way is entered appropriately on the register of the new title: see *Wakefield City Council v Symonds* (2007) Reference 2006/0931.

It will be apparent that the examples given above of orders all require the Registrar to do something, as does an order requiring the Registrar to reject future applications, dealt with later in this chapter.

THE FORM OF THE ORDER

18.2 The decision notice stating the Tribunal's decision must be a written one, and must be sent to the Registrar as well as to the parties: see Rule 36(2)(a) and Rule 40(1).

For an order, see FORM **91** and FORM **92** in APPENDIX **14**.

It was noted in CHAPTER 8 that where the Tribunal has directed a party to commence court proceedings for the court's decision on the whole or part of a matter and has received notice that court proceedings have been issued, the Tribunal proceedings, or the relevant part of those proceedings, are automatically stayed pending the final court order: see Rule 39(2).

Once the Tribunal has received a copy of the final court order then, subject to one exception and any question of costs, unless the court directs otherwise, the Tribunal proceedings, or the part of the matter, are to be regarded as stayed: see Rule 39(3).

The exception applies if a further order, in addition to the final court order, is necessary to implement the final decision of the court. In these circumstances, the Tribunal may make an order, either with or without giving notice to the parties, if it would have had the power to make such an order if it had made a decision in relation to the proceedings: see Rule 39(4). For such an order, see FORM **47** in APPENDIX **14**.

WHAT ORDERS DISPOSING OF THE PROCEEDINGS THE TRIBUNAL CANNOT MAKE

18.3 It was explained in CHAPTER **7** that the Tribunal has no power by statute to award damages, grant an injunction or specific performance or accept an undertaking. In a beneficial interest case, it is considered that it may quantify any interest it does find established although this is never been authoritatively determined on appeal, but it cannot order a sale of the property.

CONSENT ORDERS

18.4 Before the hearing the parties may wish to settle, or one of the parties may wish to withdraw the original application or the objection. The Tribunal has a discretion whether or not to allow a party to withdraw the original application or the objection. Withdrawal and settlement is considered in CHAPTER **14**.

Rule 35(1) provides that the Tribunal may, at the request of the parties but only if it considers it appropriate, make a consent order disposing of the proceedings and making such other appropriate provisions as the parties have agreed.

The Tribunal, when making such a consent order, need not hold a hearing or provide reasons: see Rule 35(2).

Care has to be taken in respect of orders made on a settlement. The Tribunal cannot make an order in *Tomlin* form because it does not have power to enforce the terms contained in the schedule to the order.

The Tribunal will not make an order to adjourn generally the proceedings before it. The original application will have been entered on the day list kept by Land Registry and while it remains on the day list, the Registrar cannot give effect to subsequent applications. It is therefore necessary, if a settlement is reached or one party is allowed to withdraw the original application or the objection, for the Tribunal to make an order to the Registrar for the giving effect to the original application as if the objection had not been made, or for the cancellation of the original application.

For a consent order, see FORM 92 in APPENDIX 14.

HOW EFFECT IS GIVEN TO ORDERS DISPOSING OF THE PROCEEDING

18.5 The Tribunal will send a copy of its order to Land Registry and Land Registry will usually implement the order as soon as it is received. It is therefore important for a party who wishes to appeal an order of the Tribunal to seek a stay of the order as soon as possible, and in a really urgent case to notify Land Registry in writing that the party is proposing to appeal and will be applying for a stay.

ORDERS REQUIRING THE REGISTRAR TO REJECT FUTURE APPLICATIONS

18.6 The Tribunal has power to include in its direction a requirement on the Registrar to reject any future application of a specified kind by a named party to the proceedings either (1) unconditionally or (2) unless that party satisfies specified conditions: see Rule 40(3)(b). This power will enable the Tribunal to prevent applications which are frivolous and vexatious.

EXAMPLE 3

A lends B money. The debt in not repaid and A obtains judgment. A obtains a charging order over B's property to enforce the judgment and protects it by the entry of a unilateral notice on the register of B's property. B convinces himself that the debt was repaid before judgment was entered. No application has been made to set aside the judgment or the charging order. B applies to cancel the unilateral notice.

The Tribunal directs the Registrar to cancel the original application as the Tribunal cannot go behind the judgment. It makes a direction that the Registrar is to reject any future application to cancel the unilateral notice without the permission of the court. This will prevent B making a further original application without first applying to the court to set aside the judgment and the charging order.

Chapter 19

COSTS AND ASSESSMENT

Key topics in this Chapter

Jurisdiction to make a costs order
Circumstances to be taken into account in making a costs order
Types of order
Litigants in person
Non-legally qualified representatives
Procedure for and basis of assessment
Conditional fee agreements
Wasted costs orders

JURISDICTION TO MAKE A COSTS ORDER

19.1 In some jurisdictions costs are only payable by the losing party where that party is found to have acted unreasonably. For example, it was explained in CHAPTER 3 that the Registrar may only order a party to proceedings before him to pay costs where those costs have been occasioned by the unreasonable conduct of that party in relation to the proceedings: see LRR 2003, r 202 (2).

Similarly, the Tribunal can only make an order in respect of costs in agricultural land and drainage cases and in residential property and leasehold cases if a person has acted unreasonably in bringing, defending or conducting the proceedings: see Rule 13(1)(b).

The Tribunal can also make wasted costs orders in any type of case: see Rule 13(1)(a). This is discussed below.

However, in a land registration case the Tribunal does have jurisdiction to make costs orders: see Rule 13(1)(c).

It is important for the parties and their advisors to bear in mind that, whilst no fees are payable to the Tribunal in the course of a reference, it is a jurisdiction in which costs are normally awarded. The Tribunal may make an order as to costs either on the application of a party or on its own initiative: see Rule 13(3).

The Tribunal is concerned that parties, particularly unrepresented parties, are aware of the risks of costs following a reference by the Registrar. For this reason the direction sent out by the Tribunal to the parties on receipt of a reference, naming who is to be the Applicant and who is to be the Respondent and directing service of statements of case, contains a stark 'health warning' about costs in the following terms:

> The Tribunal's services are free of charge. However, there is power to decide whether to make orders for costs in Tribunal proceedings. The general rule is that the losing party will pay the successful party's costs, as well as his own.

For the direction, see **FORM 48** and **FORM 49** in **APPENDIX 14**.

In disputed cases which go to a hearing the total of both sides' costs is likely to run into five figures. In very substantial cases, particularly where expert evidence is involved, the costs can run into six figures. For example, see the costs decision of HH Judge David Cooke, sitting on appeal, in *Walker v Burton* [2013] EWHC 811 (Ch), [2013] NLJR 18, [2013] 3 Costs LR 469.

The costs of the proceedings before the Tribunal do not include the costs incurred prior to the reference of the matter to the Tribunal by Land Registry. Costs incurred prior to the date of the reference may be recoverable in an appropriate case as costs of proceedings before the Registrar, but it will be for the Registrar and not the Tribunal to make any order as to costs incurred prior to the date of the reference.

It is important, therefore, that the receiving party does not include any of the costs incurred prior to the date of the reference in any schedule of costs submitted to the Tribunal. Otherwise, the schedule will be returned with a direction that such costs be removed.

A person making an application for an order for costs must, unless the application is made orally at a hearing, send or deliver an application to the Tribunal and to the person against whom the order is sought to be made: see Rule 13(4)(a).

A person making an application for an order for costs may send or deliver together with the application a schedule of the costs claimed in sufficient detail to allow summary assessment of such costs by the Tribunal: see Rule 13(4)(b). A form similar to **Form N260** used in the County Court would be suitable.

Rule 13(5) provides that an application for an order for costs may be made at any time during the proceedings but must be made within 28 days after the date on which the Tribunal sends:

- a decision notice recording the decision which finally disposes of all issues in the proceedings; or
- notice of consent to a withdrawal which ends the proceedings.

It has not generally been the practice to make orders for costs in land registration cases except at the conclusion of the proceedings. However, there is power to do so in a suitable case. What usually happens is that at the end of the written decision the judge will invite submissions on costs to be served in writing by the parties.

The Tribunal is not entitled to make an order for costs without first giving the paying party an opportunity to make representations: see Rule 13(6). So the judge should not say at the end of the written decision that costs will follow the event and the losing party will pay. But he or she is entitled to state a preliminary view (eg that the losing party should pay the costs to be assessed on the standard basis) and to give the parties an opportunity to make written submissions within a specified time if they wish to submit that some different order ought to be made.

Once it has been determined which party should pay the costs, the paying party must, of course, be given an opportunity to make objections or representations as to the amount of costs to be paid.

CIRCUMSTANCES TO BE TAKEN INTO ACCOUNT IN MAKING A COSTS ORDER

19.2 In deciding what order, if any, to make as to costs the Tribunal is guided by PDLR para 9.1 rather than by the Rules r 13 itself.

PDLR para 9.1(a) emphasises that the Tribunal has discretion as to

- whether costs are payable by one party to another;
- the amount of those costs;
- when they are to be paid.

However, PDLR para 9.1(b) provides that if the Tribunal decides to make an order about costs:

- ordinarily the unsuccessful party will be ordered to pay the costs of the successful party; but
- the Tribunal may make a different order.

It will only be in a quite exceptional case that the successful party will be ordered to pay the unsuccessful party's costs. Such an order might be made where one party only disclosed a vital historic photograph or document which supported that party's case at the very last minute, up until which time the other party had a genuine reason to believe that the claim would succeed.

PDLR para 9.1(c) provides that in deciding what order (if any) to make about costs, the Tribunal will have regard to all the circumstances including:

- the conduct of all the parties;
- whether a party has succeeded on part of its case, even if that party has not been wholly successful; and
- any admissible offer to settle made by a party which is drawn to the Tribunal's attention.

PDLR para 9.1(d) provides that the conduct of the parties includes:

- conduct before, as well as during the proceedings;
- whether it was reasonable for a party to raise, pursue or contest a particular allegation or issue;
- the manner in which a party has pursued or defended its case or a particular allegation or issue; and
- whether a party who has succeeded in the case, in whole or in part exaggerated its case.

It will be noted that although the Tribunal cannot make an order in respect of costs incurred before the proceedings commenced (which is the date when the dispute was referred by Land Registry to the Tribunal), it can take into account the conduct of the parties prior to the proceedings.

In this respect the PDLR differs significantly from the AR 2003 which did not permit the Adjudicator to take into account conduct before the proceedings.

The following are examples of conduct occurring before the proceedings commenced which would be taken into account on the question of costs.

EXAMPLE 1

A makes an open offer or a Calderbank offer to B to settle the dispute subject to its being accepted within a reasonable period. B does not accept the offer. The decision of the Tribunal leaves A in as good a position as, or in a better position than, if the offer had been accepted. The offer will be taken into account whether made before or after the commencement of the proceedings before the Tribunal.

EXAMPLE 2

A is asked prior to the reference to the Tribunal to produce documents that would establish his case, but unreasonably refuses to do so. The dispute is referred to the Tribunal. A then produces them with, or after, his statement of case. B then concedes and A claims his costs. A's unreasonable refusal to produce the documents prior to the reference will be taken into account on the question of costs.

EXAMPLE 3

A presents his case to Land Registry on one basis, which is seriously flawed, but Land Registry does not consider it groundless and refers it to the Tribunal. A then puts his case very differently, on different evidence, to the Tribunal. Once B is aware of the new case and the basis on which it is put, he concedes. The Tribunal will take into account the fact that A only pleaded the winning case after the reference and that B immediately conceded it.

TYPES OF ORDER

19.3 PDLR para 9.1(e) provides that the orders which the Tribunal may make include that the party must pay:

- a proportion of another party's costs;
- a specified amount in respect of another party's costs;
- costs from or until a certain date only;
- costs relating to particular steps taken in the proceedings;
- costs relating only to a distinct part of the proceedings.

For a costs order following a summary assessment, see **Form 93** in **Appendix 14**.

The Tribunal has jurisdiction to make an order for a payment on account of costs prior to the costs being assessed: see Rule 13(9). This is a very useful tool where a detailed assessment has been ordered. If the paying party is ordered to pay, say, 65% of the costs it is seeking, this may facilitate the reaching of an agreement with the receiving party in respect of the balance being claimed.

LITIGANTS IN PERSON

19.4 The Litigants in Person (Costs and Expenses) Act 1975 applies to the courts and has been extended by TCEA 2007, Sch 8 para 6 to the Tribunal. The position is now different to that appertaining before 1 July 2013 as the scope of 1975 Act was never extended to proceedings before the Adjudicator.

The costs of litigants in person in court proceedings are governed by CPR 1998, Part 46.5, supplemented by PD 46, para 3.

The costs of a litigant in person cannot exceed, except in the case of a disbursement, two-thirds of the amount which would have been allowed if the litigant in person had been represented by a legal representative: see CPR 1998, r 46.5(2).

A litigant in person is allowed costs for the same categories of work and disbursements which would have been allowed if the work had been done or the disbursements had been made by a legal representative on the litigant in person's behalf: see CPR 1998, r 46.5(3)(a).

A litigant in person is also allowed the payments reasonably made by him for legal services relating to the conduct of the proceedings and the costs of obtaining expert assistance in assessing the costs claim: see CPR 1998, r 46.5(3)(b) and (c).

The amount of costs to be allowed to the litigant in person for any item of work claimed will be:

- where the litigant can prove financial loss, the amount that the litigant can prove to have been lost for time reasonably spent on doing the work: see CPR 1998, r 46.5(4)(a); or
- where the litigant cannot prove financial loss, an amount for the time reasonably spent on doing the work at £18 per hour: see CPR 1998, r 46.5(4)(b) and PD 46 para 3.4.

For the purpose of these provisions, a litigant in person includes a company or other corporation acting without a legal representative and persons such as barristers or solicitors when acting in person: see CPR 1998, r 46.5(6).

The effect of the Rules r 13(8) is to apply CPR 1998, r 46.5 to a detailed assessment of the costs of a litigant in person before the Tribunal so that the litigant in person will be awarded the same costs as if the proceedings were court proceedings. CPR 1998, r 46.5 is not expressly imported by the Rules for the purposes of a summary assessment but the authors consider that it is unlikely the Tribunal would allow differing amounts to a litigant in person depending only on the manner of assessment.

NON-LEGALLY QUALIFIED REPRESENTATIVES

19.5 The reasonable charges of a representative who is not legally qualified, including those of a professional person such as a surveyor, for acting in the proceedings before the Tribunal, including the hearing, are recoverable provided they have been reasonably incurred: see the decisions of the Adjudicator in *Weeks v Neophitou* (References/2008/0551 & 2009/0783)

(2010), unreported. Non-legally qualified representatives are discussed in CHAPTER 17.

Whether the representative is legally qualified or not, the indemnity principle applies. A party may only recover costs which he has paid or which he is contractually liable to pay. A representative submitting a schedule or bill of costs to be assessed by the Tribunal is required to certify that the schedule or bill complies with the indemnity principle.

PROCEDURE FOR AND BASIS OF ASSESSMENT

19.6 Rule 13(7) provides that the amount of costs paid may be determined by:

- a summary assessment by the Tribunal;
- the agreement of a specified sum made by the paying party and the receiving party;
- a detailed assessment by the Tribunal, or, if so directed, by the County Court.

Where there is to be a detailed assessment, the CPR 1998, the County Courts Act 1984, s 74 (interest on judgment debts) and the County Court (Interest on Judgment Debts) Order 1991 apply with necessary modifications. The provisions in the CPR 1998 relating to a detailed assessment are modified to the extent set out in the PDLR: see PDLR para 9.4.

As a rule of thumb, the Tribunal is only likely to order a detailed assessment when the receiving party is claiming costs in the region of £30,000 or more.

A summary assessment is almost invariably made on paper following receipt of written submissions after the decision has been handed down. It therefore differs from a summary assessment in court where the assessment is done by the judge in the presence of the parties at the end of the hearing.

The basis on which an assessment is carried out is regulated by PDLR para 9.2.

PDLR para 9.2(a) provides that where the Tribunal is to assess the amount of costs (whether by summary or detailed assessment) it will assess those costs:

- on the standard basis; or
- on the indemnity basis

but the Tribunal will in neither case allow costs which had been unreasonably incurred or are unreasonable in amount.

Where the Tribunal makes an order about costs without stating the basis on which the costs are to be assessed, the costs will be assessed on the standard basis: see PDLR para 9.2(d).

The Tribunal is likely to make an order for indemnity costs only in the same circumstances as a court would: see the White Book 2014 para 44x.4.3 for a commentary on when indemnity costs might be ordered.

PDLR para 9.2(b) provides that where the Tribunal assesses the amount of costs on the standard basis, it will:

- only allow costs which are proportionate to the matters in issue;

- costs which are disproportionate in amount may be disallowed or reduced even if they were reasonably or necessarily incurred;
- resolve any doubt which it may have as to whether costs were reasonably and proportionately incurred or were reasonable and proportionate in amount in favour of the paying party.

In order to determine what costs are proportionate, it is necessary to turn to PDLR para 9.2(e) which provides that costs are proportionate if they bear a reasonable relationship to:

- the value of any asset in issue in the proceedings;
- the complexity of the proceedings;
- any additional work caused by the conduct of the paying party; and
- any wider factors involved in the proceedings, such as reputation or public importance.

PDLR para 9.2(c) provides that where the Tribunal assesses the amount of costs on the indemnity basis, it will resolve any doubt which it may have as to whether costs were reasonably incurred or were reasonable in amount in favour of the receiving party.

The factors to be taken into account in deciding the amount of costs are set out in PDLR para 9.3.

The Tribunal will give effect to any orders which have already been made: see PDLR para 9.3(c).

PDLR para 9.3(a) provides that where the Tribunal assesses costs on the standard basis it will have regard to all the circumstances in deciding whether costs were:

- proportionately and reasonably incurred; or
- proportionate and reasonable in amount.

PDLR para 9.3(b) provides that where the Tribunal assesses costs on the indemnity basis it will have regard to all the circumstances in deciding whether costs were:

- unreasonably incurred; or
- unreasonable in amount.

PDLR para 9.3(d) provides that the Tribunal will also have regard to the:

- conduct of all the parties including, in particular,
  - conduct before, as well as during, the proceedings; and
  - the efforts made, if any, before and during the proceedings in order to try and resolve the dispute;
- amount or value of any money or property involved;
- importance of the matter to all the parties;
- particular complexity of the matter or the difficulty or novelty of the questions raised;
- skill, effort, specialised knowledge and responsibility involved;
- time spent on the case;
- place where and the circumstances in which work or any part of it was done.

If there is to be a detailed assessment it may be carried out by one of the several past or present Senior Courts deputy costs judges appointed as Tribunal judges for this purpose. For directions for a detailed assessment, see **Form 94** in **appendix 14**.

CONDITIONAL FEE AGREEMENTS

19.7 In principle, a successful party is entitled to recover a success fee under a conditional fee agreement: see *Abbott v Keeley* (Reference/2008/0305) (2009), unreported and *Walker v Burton* [2013] EWHC 811 (Ch), [2013] NLJR 18, [2013] 3 Costs LR 469.

WASTED COSTS ORDERS

19.8 The Tribunal also has a jurisdiction in respect of wasted costs.

TCEA 2007, s 29(4) provides that the Tribunal may:

- disallow, or
- (as the case may be) order the legal or other representative concerned to meet, the whole or part of any wasted costs.

TCEA 2007, s 29(5) provides that "wasted costs" means any costs incurred by a party:

- as a result of any improper, unreasonable or negligent act or omission on the part of any legal or other representative or any employee of such a representative, or
- which, in the light of any such act or omission occurring after they were incurred, the relevant Tribunal considers it is unreasonable to expect that party to pay.

For these purposes 'legal or other representative', in relation to a party to proceedings, means any person exercising a right of audience or right to conduct the proceedings on his behalf: see TCEA 2007, s 29(6).

Chapter 20

SETTING ASIDE, REVIEWS AND APPEALS

Key topics in this Chapter

SETTING ASIDE

20.1 Rule 51(1) provides that the Tribunal may set aside a decision which disposes of proceedings, or part of such a decision, and re-make the decision or the relevant part of it, if:

- the Tribunal considers that it is in the interests of justice to do so; and
- one or more of certain conditions are satisfied.

It is to be emphasised that this power of setting aside only relates to decisions which dispose of proceedings. Decisions which are made during the course of proceedings can be amended, suspended or set aside by a subsequent direction as part of the wide case management powers given to the Tribunal: see Rule 6(2).

Setting aside comes into play when a perceived procedural injustice has arisen. It is not concerned with substantive mistakes in the decision. Setting aside is not to be confused with a review, dealt with below, even though on a review the Tribunal has the power to set aside the decision. Setting aside on a review is setting aside for a different reason.

The Tribunal may treat an application for a decision to be set aside as an application for permission to appeal, triggering a consideration of whether or not to review the decision: see Rule 56.

The Tribunal's power to set aside a decision when a perceived procedural injustice has arisen derives from TCEA 2007, Sch 5 para 15.

The conditions which need to be satisfied to enable the Tribunal to set aside a decision for a procedural injustice are set out in Rule 51(2), and are as follows:

- a document relating to the proceedings was not sent to, or was not received at an appropriate time by, a party or a party's representative;

- a document relating to the proceedings was not sent to or was not received by the Tribunal at an appropriate time;
- a party, or a party's representative, was not present at the hearing related to the proceedings; or
- there has been some other procedural irregularity in the proceedings.

Rule 51(3) provides that a party applying for a decision, or part of a decision, to be set aside when one or more of these conditions are satisfied must make a written application to the Tribunal so that it is received:

- within 28 days after the date on which the Tribunal sent notice of the decision to the party; or
- if later, within 28 days after the date on which the Tribunal sent notice of the reasons for the decision to the party.

For an application to set aside a decision, see **Form 95** in **appendix 14**. For an order setting aside a decision, see **Form 96** in **appendix 14**.

Unless it would be impractical or would cause undue delay, the same judge should consider the application to set aside the decision as originally made the decision: see The Composition of Tribunals in the Property Chamber Practice Direction, paras 11 and 12.

REVIEWS

20.2 TCEA 2007, s 9 gives the Tribunal a power to review its own decisions. This is a new power in land registration cases. The Adjudicator had no such power.

The power to review is inextricably linked to an application for permission to appeal. Rule 55(1)(a) provides that the Tribunal may <u>only</u> undertake a review of a decision pursuant to Rule 53.

Rule 53(1), in turn, provides that on receiving an application for permission to appeal the Tribunal must first consider, taking into account the overriding objective, whether to review the decision in accordance with r 55. The Tribunal must do this of its own initiative, whether invited to do so by the appellant or not.

Rule 55(1)(b), in turn, provides that the Tribunal may <u>only</u> undertake a review of a decision if it is satisfied that the ground of appeal is likely to be successful.

It will be appreciated that the review is a useful procedure, which will save both time and expense, when the Tribunal accepts that it has fallen into a clear error. But, as we shall see below, the power to review should be used with care and only in appropriate cases.

The Tribunal may not review the following decisions of the Tribunal:

- a decision to review, or not to review, an earlier decision of the Tribunal: see TCEA 2007, ss 9 (1), 11(1) and (5)(d)(i);
- a decision to to take no action, or not to take any particular action, in the light of a review of an earlier decision of the Tribunal: see TCEA 2007, ss 9(1), 11(1) and (5)(d)(ii);

Similarly, the Tribunal may not review a decision of the Tribunal which has been set aside following a review, including a decision set aside after proceedings on an appeal on a point of law have been begun: see TCEA 2007, ss 9(1), 11(1) and (5)(e).

But the Tribunal does have the power to review a decision to set aside, made on a review. However, the Tribunal's only power in the light of a review of such a decision is to correct accidental errors in the decision or in a record of the decision: see TCEA 2007, s 9(9).

For an application to review a decision, see **FORM 97** in **APPENDIX 14**.

Unless it would be impractical or would cause undue delay, the same judge should consider the application to review the decision as originally made the decision: see The Composition of Tribunals in the Property Chamber Practice Direction, paras 11 and 12.

Where the Tribunal has reviewed a decision, it has the following powers:

- It may correct accidental errors in the decision or in the record of the decision: see TCEA 2007, s 9(4)(a).
- It may amend the reasons given for the decision: see TCEA 2007, s 9(4)(b).
- It may set the decision aside: see TCEA 2007, s 9(4)(c).

The decision whether or not to exercise any of these powers is a discretionary one. Care must be taken not to undermine the appeal process. The proper function of the Upper Tribunal should not be bypassed: see *JS v Secretary of State for Work and Pensions* [2013] UKUT 100 (ACC) and *R (RB) v First-tier Tribunal* [2013] UKUT 160 (ACC).

An example of when it may be appropriate to review a decision, rather than to give permission to appeal, would be where the Tribunal has overlooked a statutory provision or binding authority which would lead to a different decision being made.

In *Scriven v Calthorpe Estates* [2013] UKUT 0469 (LC) the Deputy President of the Lands Chamber (Martin Rogers QC) dealt with an appeal in a leasehold case in which there was no jurisdiction to review the decision as permission to appeal to the Upper Tribunal was granted before the power to review had come into force. The Tribunal had overlooked the reversing of a precedent it had purported to follow. This would, accordingly, have been an ideal case in which to carry out a review if the power had been available.

The Deputy President said that the power to review is important and valuable, and its exercise in appropriate cases has the potential to achieve significant savings for parties and tribunals by avoiding expensive and time-consuming appeals. The power should only be used in cases where a decision is clearly wrong. It was not intended to enable the Tribunal to take a different view of the law from that previously reached, when both views were tenable.

The Deputy President also said that before exercising any of the powers conferred on it on a review the Tribunal should consider whether it is appropriate to give notice to every other party to the proceedings that an application requesting a review has been received or that it proposes to carry out the review on its own initiative.

Rule 55(3) provides that if the Tribunal takes any action in relation to a decision following a review without first giving every party an opportunity to make representations, the notice sent to the parties must state that any party that did not have an opportunity to make representations may apply for such action to be set aside and the decision to be reviewed again.

It was suggested by the Deputy President at [41] that although r 55(3) provides safeguards for parties who are not heard at this stage, where the consequence of a review may be to deprive a successful party of the benefit of a decision in his favour, the fairer and more efficient course is likely to be to allow representations to be made at the outset.

When the Tribunal has set a decision aside it must either re-decide the matter concerned, or refer that matter to the Upper Tribunal: see TCEA 2007, s 9(5).

In a land registration cases the matter will not be referred to the Upper Tribunal following a review. There is power for any residential property or leasehold case to be transferred up to the Upper Tribunal for hearing if they are lengthy, complex, important or involve a large financial sum: see Rule 25. But this rule does not apply to land registration case. It would not therefore be logical to refer the matter up to the Upper Tribunal following a review.

Where the Tribunal re-decides the matter concerned it may make such findings of fact as it considers appropriate: see TCEA 2007, s 9(8).

The power to amend the reasons given for the decision is also to be used with care. The purpose of the power is not to correct defective reasoning or to provide a commentary on the grounds of appeal, but to show how the Tribunal made its decision: see *JS v Secretary of State for Work and Pensions* [2013] UKUT 100 (ACC), [36], [40].

The Tribunal must notify the parties in writing of the outcome of any review, and of any right of appeal in relation to the outcome: see Rule 55(2).

A decision of the Tribunal may not be reviewed more than once. Once the Tribunal has decided that an earlier decision should not be reviewed, it may not then subsequently review it: see TCEA 2007, s 9(10).

TCEA 2007, s 11(1) and (5)(d) prevents an appeal on a point of law from a decision of the Tribunal when conducting a review:

- to review, or not to review, an earlier decision of the Tribunal;
- to take no action, or not to take any particular action, in the light of a review of an earlier decision of the Tribunal;
- to set aside an earlier decision of the Tribunal.

Similarly, an appeal may not be brought on a point of law in respect of a decision of the Tribunal which has been set aside following a review, including a decision set aside after proceedings on the appeal on a point of law have been begun: see TCEA 2007, s 11(1) and (5)(e).

THE RIGHT TO APPEAL TO THE UPPER TRIBUNAL

20.3 An appeal lies to the Upper Tribunal from the Tribunal's decision on a reference from Land Registry to the Tribunal, either on the facts or on a point of law.

A 'decision' of the Tribunal means any decision, and the right to appeal is not restricted to decisions which dispose of the proceedings. Accordingly, an appeal may be brought in respect of interim (what used to be called 'interlocutory') decisions made by way of case management in the course of the proceedings, just as an appeal may be brought against a final decision.

The right to appeal on the facts is given by LRA 2002, s 111(1), as amended. An appeal on the facts may only be brought if, on an application made by the person concerned, the Tribunal or Upper Tribunal has given its permission for the appeal to be brought: see LRA 2002, s 111(2C), as amended.

But an appeal may not be brought on the facts if the decision is set aside on a review: see LRA 2002, s 111(2B), as amended.

The right to appeal on a point of law is given by TCEA 2007, s 11(1) and (2). An appeal on a point of law may only be brought if, on an application made by the person concerned, the Tribunal or Upper Tribunal has given its permission for the appeal to be brought: see TCEA 2007, s 11(3) and (4).

But an appeal may not be brought on a point of law in respect of the following decisions of the Tribunal:

- to review, or not to review, an earlier decision of the Tribunal: see TCEA 2007, s 11(1) and (5)(d)(i);
- to take no action, or not to take any particular action, in the light of a review of an earlier decision of the Tribunal: see TCEA 2007, s 11(1) and (5)(d)(ii);
- to set aside an earlier decision of the Tribunal: see TCEA 2007, s 11(1) and (5)(d)(iii).

Similarly, an appeal may not be brought on a point of law in respect of a decision of the Tribunal which has been set aside following a review, including a decision set aside after proceedings on the appeal on a point of law have been begun: see TCEA 2007, s 11(1) and (5)(e).

An appeal from the Tribunal to the Upper Tribunal is governed by:

- TCEA 2007, s 12;
- Rules 52-54; and
- The Tribunal Procedure (Upper Tribunal) Rules 2008, as amended ('UTR 2008'), rr 21-25.

Such an appeal is not governed by CPR 1998, Part 52. The position was different in respect of an appeal from the Adjudicator to the High Court, as such an appeal was a statutory appeal within the meaning of CPR PD 52 para 17.1.

An appeal lies to the Upper Tribunal, subject to permission being granted to appeal, in respect of any decision issued on or after 1 July 2013 even though the proceedings began before the Adjudicator prior to that date: see The Transfer of Tribunal Functions Order 2013, Sch 3 art 4.

A very important point to take note of is that an appeal from the Tribunal in respect of land registration cases lies not to the Lands Chamber of the Upper Tribunal (the old Lands Tribunal) — as might be thought logical – but to the Tax and Chancery Chamber of the Upper Tribunal: see The First-tier Tribunal and Upper Tribunal (Chambers) Order 2010, art 13(h) as inserted by The First-tier Tribunal and Upper Tribunal (Chambers) (Amendment) Order 2013, art 7.

Therefore, appeals in references from Land Registry to the Tribunal, in network access agreement appeals and in rectification applications all lie to the Tax and Chancery Chamber of the Upper Tribunal.

However, an appeal from the Tribunal in respect of agricultural land and drainage cases and leasehold and residential property cases lies to the Lands Chamber of the Upper Tribunal: see The First-tier Tribunal and Upper Tribunal (Chambers) Order 2010, art 12(ii)(aa) as inserted by The First-tier Tribunal and Upper Tribunal (Chambers) (Amendment) Order 2013, art 6(a).

A possible reason for this distinction is that all appeals from the Adjudicator in land registration cases went to the High Court: see Land Registration Act 2002, s 111(1), as originally enacted. As a matter of practice High Court judges are more frequently deployed to sit in the Tax and Chancery Chamber than they are to sit in the Lands Chamber. Accordingly, there is a better chance of a High Court judge sitting on an appeal in a land registration case under this arrangement.

The Court of Appeal has expressed the view that a measure of weighed deference should be accorded to the findings and conclusions in the reasoned decisions of the Adjudicator. In *Wilkinson v Farmer* [2010] EWCA Civ 1148, [2010] All ER (D) 217 (Oct) at [25], Mummery LJ said,

> The Deputy Adjudicator was the fact-finding tribunal. [The Adjudicator] and the Deputies have relevant experience. Although they might sometimes get things wrong, they are usually more experienced and expert at deciding this kind of question than appellate courts are.

This approach should apply equally to the decisions of the Tribunal in land registration cases.

APPLICATIONS FOR PERMISSSION TO APPEAL MADE TO THE TRIBUNAL

20.4 As we have seen, a person who wishes to appeal from a decision of the Tribunal must obtain permission to appeal: see LRA 2002, s 111(2C), as amended, in respect of appeals on the facts, and see TCEA 2007, s 11(3) and (4) in respect of appeals on a point of law.

A person seeking permission to appeal must make a written application to the Tribunal for permission to appeal: see Rule 52(1). Accordingly, a person is not permitted to make an application for permission to appeal direct to the Upper Tribunal without first making an application to the Tribunal.

The application must:

- identify the decision of the Tribunal to which it relates: see Rule 52(5)(a);
- state the grounds of appeal: see Rule 52(5)(b);
- state the result the party making the application is seeking: see Rule 52(5)(c).

For an application to the Tribunal for permission to appeal, see **Form 98** in **appendix 14**.

Rule 52(2) provides that an application for permission to appeal must be sent or delivered to the Tribunal so that it is received within 28 days after the latest of the dates that the Tribunal sends to the person making the application:

- written reasons for the decision;
- notification of amended reasons for, or correction of, the decision following a review; or
- notification that an application for the decision to be set aside has been unsuccessful.

If a party requires additional time in which to make an application for permission to appeal, an application should be made to the Tribunal for an extension of time. The Tribunal has a general power to extend the time for complying with any rule, even if the application for an extension is not made until after the time limit has expired: see Rule 6(3)(a).

Rule 52(4) provides that if the person seeking permission to appeal sends or delivers the application to the Tribunal later than the time required as set out above, or by any extension of time under Rule 6(3)(a):

- the application must include a request for an extension of time and the reason why the application was not received in time; and
- unless the Tribunal extends time for the application under r 6(3)(a) the Tribunal must not admit the application.

On receiving an application for permission to appeal the Tribunal must first consider, taking into account the overriding objective, whether to review the decision in accordance with Rule 55: see Rule 53(1). Reviews are considered above.

If the Tribunal decides not to review the decision, or reviews the decision and decides to take no action in relation to the decision, or part of it, the Tribunal must consider whether to give permission to appeal in relation to the decision or that part of it: see Rule 53(2).

Before reaching a decision as to whether to grant permission to appeal, the Tribunal will usually allow the respondent to the appeal an opportunity to make representations or objections. But if the view is taken that the application is without merit the Tribunal may consider it unnecessary to do this and will simply refuse the application.

Curiously, the test to be applied in deciding whether or not to grant permission is not laid down in the rules. It might be thought that the appropriate test as to whether or not to grant permission to appeal should be the familiar one set out in CPR 1998, Part 52.3(6) namely that:

- the court considers that the appeal would have a real prospect of success; or
- there is some other compelling reason why the appeal should be heard.

In *Fairhold Mercury Ltd v HQ (Block 1) Action Management Co Ltd* [2013] UKUT 0487 (LC), [2014] 1 P & CR D21 the Deputy President of the Lands Chamber (Martin Rogers QC) in dealing with an appeal from the Tribunal in a leasehold case said that permission to appeal to the Upper Tribunal should be given in any case where there was a reasonable prospect of the Applicant demonstrating that the Tribunal had wrongly interpreted or applied the relevant law.

The Tribunal should ask itself whether the appeal has a real or realistic prospect of success, as opposed to only a fanciful prospect. If the Tribunal, having heard the argument and made its own decision, is satisfied that there is no real prospect of the Upper Tribunal coming to a different conclusion, it should refuse permission. If it considers the point in issue remains fairly arguable, it should grant permission. If the point on which permission is sought is a purely technical one the Tribunal should be slower to grant permission that in cases of more substance.

The Tribunal must send a record of its decision on whether or not to grant permission to appeal to the parties as soon as practicable: see Rule 53(3).

Rule 53(4) provides that if the Tribunal refuses permission to appeal it must send with the record of its decision:

- a statement of its reasons for such refusal; and
- notification of the right to make an application to the Upper Tribunal for permission to appeal and the time within which, and the method by which, such application must be made.

The Tribunal may give permission to appeal on limited grounds, but must comply with the requirement to send a statement of its reasons and notification of the right to make a further application for permission to appeal in relation to any grounds on which it has refused permission: see Rule 53(5).

The Tribunal may treat an application for permission to appeal as an application for a decision to be set aside: Rule 56.

APPLICATIONS FOR PERMISSSION TO APPEAL MADE TO THE UPPER TRIBUNAL

20.5 A person may apply to the Upper Tribunal for permission to appeal to the Upper Tribunal against a decision of another Tribunal only if:

- they have made an application for permission to appeal to the Tribunal: see UTR 2008, r 21(2)(a);
- that application has been refused or has not been admitted or has been granted only on limited grounds: see UTR 2008, r 21(2)(b).

An application for permission to appeal must be made in writing and received by the Upper Tribunal no later than a month after the date on which the Tribunal sent notice of its refusal of permission to appeal, or refusal to admit the application for permission to appeal, to the appellant: see UTR 2008, r 21(3)(b).

If a party requires additional time in which to make an application for permission to appeal, an application should be made to the Upper Tribunal for an extension of time. The Upper Tribunal has a general power to extend the time for complying with any rule, even if the application for an extension is not made until after the time limit has expired: see UTR 2008, r 5(3)(a).

UTR 2008, r 21(6) provides that if the appellant provides the application to the Upper Tribunal later than the time required as set out above, or by any extension of time under r 5(3)(a):

- the application must include a request for an extension of time and the reason why the application was not received in time; and
- unless the Upper Tribunal extends time for the application under r 5(3)(a) the Upper Tribunal must not admit the application.

UTR 2008, r 21(4) provides that the application must state:

- the name and address of the appellant;
- the name and address of the representative (if any) of the appellant;
- an address where documents for the appellant may be sent or delivered;
- details (including the full reference) of the decision challenged;
- grounds on which the appellant relies; and
- whether the appellant wants the application to be dealt with at a hearing.

UTR 2008, r 21(5) provides that the applicant must provide with the application a copy of:

- any written record of the decision being challenged;
- any separate written statement of reasons for that decision;
- a copy of the notice of refusal of permission to appeal, or notice of refusal to admit the application for permission to appeal, from the Tribunal.

If the appellant makes an application to the Upper Tribunal for permission to appeal against the decision of the Tribunal, and the Tribunal refused to admit the appellant's application for permission to appeal because the application was not made in time:

- the application to the Upper Tribunal for permission to appeal must include the reason why the application to the Tribunal for permission to appeal was not made in time: see UTR 2008, r 21(7)(a);
- the Upper Tribunal must only admit the application if the Upper Tribunal considers that it is in the interest of justice for it to do so: see UTR 2008, r 21(7)(b).

Again, it is suggested that the appropriate test as to whether or not to grant permission to appeal is the familiar one set out in CPR 1998, Part 52.3(6) namely that:

- the court considers that the appeal would have a real prospect of success; or
- there is some other compelling reason why the appeal should be heard.

If the Upper Tribunal refuses permission to appeal, or refuses to admit a late application for permission, it must send written notice of refusal and of the reasons for refusal to the appellant: see UTR 2008, r 22(1).

If the Upper Tribunal gives permission to appeal:

- the Upper Tribunal must send written notice of the permission, and of the reasons for any limitations or conditions on such permission, to each party: see UTR 2008, r 22(2)(a);

- subject to any direction by the Upper Tribunal, the application for permission to appeal stands as the notice of appeal and the Upper Tribunal must send to each respondent a copy of the application for permission to appeal: see UTR 2008, r 22(2)(b);
- the Upper Tribunal may, with the consent of the appellant and each respondent, determine the appeal without obtaining any further response: see UTR 2008, r 22(2)(c).

Where the Upper Tribunal, without a hearing:

- refuses permission to appeal,
- refuses to admit a late application for permission, or
- gives permission to appeal on limited grounds or subject to conditions,

the appellant may apply for the decision to be reconsidered at a hearing: see UTR 2008, r 22(3) and (4). This power is similar to that provided by CPR 1998, Part 52.3(4).

Such an application must be made in writing and be received by the Upper Tribunal within 14 days after the date on which the Upper Tribunal sent written notice of its decision to the appellant: see UTR 2008, r 22(5).

NOTICE OF APPEAL, RESPONSE AND REPLY

Notice of appeal

20.6 We have seen above that, subject to any direction to the contrary, the application for permission to appeal will stand as the notice of appeal if the Upper Tribunal grants permission to appeal.

UTR 2008, r 23 applies where:

- the Tribunal, rather than the Upper Tribunal, has given permission for a party to appeal; or
- the Upper Tribunal has given permission to appeal but has directed that the application for permission to appeal should not stand as the notice of appeal.

In such circumstances, the appellant must provide a notice of appeal to the Upper Tribunal so that it is received within one month after the date that the tribunal that gave permission to appeal sent notice of such permission to the appellant: see UTR 2008, r 23(2).

If a party requires additional time in which to provide the notice of appeal, an application should be made to the Upper Tribunal for an extension of time. The Upper Tribunal has a general power to extend the time for complying with any rule, even if the application for an extension is not made until after the time limit has expired: see UTR 2008, r 5(3)(a).

UTR 2008, r 23(5) provides that if the appellant provides the notice of appeal to the Upper Tribunal later than the time required as set out above, or by any extension of time under r 5(3)(a):

- the notice of appeal must include a request for an extension of time and the reason why the notice was not provided in time; and

- unless the Upper Tribunal extends time for the notice of appeal under r 5(3)(a) the Upper Tribunal must not admit the notice of appeal.

UTR 2008, r 23(3) provides that the notice of appeal must include:

- the name and address of the appellant;
- the name and address of the representative (if any) of the appellant;
- an address where documents for the appellant may be sent or delivered;
- details (including the full reference) of the decision challenged;
- grounds on which the appellant relies; and
- (where the Upper Tribunal has given permission to appeal) the Upper Tribunal's case reference.

If the Tribunal has granted permission to appeal, UTR 2008, r 23(4) provides that the appellant must provide with the notice of appeal:

- any written record of the decision being challenged;
- any separate written statement of reasons for that decision; and
- the notice of permission to appeal.

When the Upper Tribunal receives the notice of appeal it must send a copy of the notice and any accompanying documents to each respondent: see UTR 2008, r 23(6).

Response

20.7 A respondent may provide a response to a notice of appeal, subject to any direction given by the Upper Tribunal: see UTR 2008, r 24(1A).

UTR 2008, r 24(2) provides that any response must be in writing and must be sent or delivered to the Upper Tribunal so that is received:

- if an application for permission to appeal stands as the notice of appeal, no later than one month after the date on which the respondent was sent notice that permission to appeal had been granted;
- in any other case, no later than one month after the date on which a Upper Tribunal sent a copy of the notice of appeal to the respondent.

If a party requires additional time in which to provide the response, an application should be made to the Upper Tribunal for an extension of time. The Upper Tribunal has a general power to extend the time for complying with any rule, even if the application for an extension is not made until after the time limit has expired: see UTR 2008, r 5(3)(a).

If the respondent provides the response to the Upper Tribunal later than the time required as set out above, or by any extension of time under r 5(3)(a), the response must include a request for an extension of time and the reason why the response was not provided in time: see UTR 2008, r 24(4).

UTR 2008, r 24(3) provides that the response must state:

- the name and address of the respondent;
- the name and address of the representative (if any) of the respondent;
- an address where documents for the respondent may be sent or delivered;
- whether the respondent opposes the appeal;

- the grounds on which the respondent relies;
- and, in particular, any grounds on which the respondent was unsuccessful in the proceedings before the Tribunal, but intends to rely in the appeal: this is the equivalent of a respondent's notice under CPR 1998, r 52.5(2)(b) asking the appeal court to uphold the order of the lower court for reasons different from or additional to those given by the lower court.

When the Upper Tribunal receives the response it must send a copy of the response and any accompanying documents to the appellant and each other party: see UTR 2008, r 24(5).

Reply

20.8 The appellant may provide a reply to a response, subject to any direction given by the Upper Tribunal: see UTR 2008, r 25(1).

Any reply must be in writing and must be sent or delivered to the Upper Tribunal so that is received within one month after the date on which the Upper Tribunal sent a copy of the response to the appellant: see UTR 2008, r 25(2).

When the Upper Tribunal receives the reply it must send a copy of the reply and any accompanying documents to each respondent: see UTR 2008, r 25(3).

TRANSCRIPTS

20.9 Hearings are usually recorded. A transcript will only be provided at public expense if required by an Upper Tribunal judge for the purposes of an appeal or permission is expressly given by the Tribunal. Otherwise a party wanting a transcript will have to pay for it. The recordings can only be released to an approved transcriber, not to the parties or their solicitors.

THE HEARING OF THE APPEAL BY THE UPPER TRIBUNAL

20.10 Where the appeal is on a point of law TCEA 2007, s 12 sets out the powers of the Upper Tribunal.

If the Upper Tribunal finds that the making of the decision concerned involved the making of an error on a point of law it may (but need not) set aside the decision of the Tribunal: see TCEA 2007, s 12(1) and (2)(a). Presumably, it would not set aside the decision where the losing party had two separate points of law on the appeal but was only successful on one of them.

If the Upper Tribunal does set aside the decision of the Tribunal it must either:

- remit the case to the Tribunal with directions for its reconsideration: see TCEA 2007, s 12(2)(b)(i); or
- re-make the decision: see TCEA 2007, s 12(2)(b)(ii).

Where the Upper Tribunal remits the case to the Tribunal with directions for its reconsideration it may also:

- direct that the Tribunal judge who is chosen to reconsider the case is not to be the same as the one who made the decision that has been set aside: see TCEA 2007, s 12(3)(a);
- give procedural directions in connection with the reconsideration of the case by the Tribunal: see TCEA 2007, s 12(3)(b).

Where the Upper Tribunal re-makes the decision, it may:

- make any decision which the Tribunal could make if the Tribunal were re-making the decision: see TCEA 2007, s 12(4)(a); and
- make such findings of fact as it considers appropriate: see TCEA 2007, s 12(4)(b).

Where the appeal is on the facts, LRA 2002, s 111(4), as amended, provides that the provisions of TCEA 2007, s 12(2)-(4), which are set out above, are to apply.

These provisions, however, offer no guidance as to whether the appeal is to be a rehearing or a review. It is suggested that an appeal on the facts will generally be limited to a review, as opposed to a re-hearing, of the decision of the Tribunal unless the Upper Tribunal considers that in the circumstances of an individual appeal it would be in the interests of justice to hold a re-hearing. This is by analogy with CPR 1998, r 52.11(1).

An extreme example of a review (rather than a re-hearing) is *SS Global Ltd v Sava* [2008] EWCA Civ 1308, [2008] 48 EG 101 (CS), 152 Sol Jo (no 46) 32 where the Adjudicator had determined, after a five day hearing, that the Applicant had obtained adverse possession of a substantial area of green belt land. The judge, on appeal, read all the transcripts but did not see any of the witnesses. He came to an opposite conclusion on the facts. His decision was upheld in the Court of Appeal.

There is a specific provision relating to certain adverse possession appeals. In the case of an application by a squatter under LRA 2002, s 97, Sch 6 para 1 to be registered as a proprietor on the basis of adverse possession, the registered proprietor can require the application to be dealt with under Sch 6 para 5. If so, the Applicant will only be entitled to be registered as the new proprietor if one of three conditions is met. The first condition, set out in Sch 6 para 5(2) is that:

- it would be unconscionable because of an equity by estoppel for the registered proprietor to seek to dispossess the Applicant, and
- the circumstances are such that the Applicant ought to be registered as the proprietor.

The reason that there are two limbs to the condition is that where a party establishes an equity by estoppel, it is an inchoate right. The court has a discretion as to how to give effect to that equity, and it will ascertain what constitutes 'the minimum equity' to do justice to that party. There is a wide range of relief ranging from ordering the paper title owner to transfer the freehold to ordering the paper title owner to make financial compensation.

When dealing with a reference relating to an application under Sch 6 para 1 the Tribunal determines that:

- it would be unconscionable because of an equity by estoppel for the registered proprietor to seek to dispossess the Applicant, but that
- the circumstances are not such that the Applicant ought to be registered as the proprietor,

the Tribunal:

- must determine how the equity due to the Applicant is to be satisfied, and
- may for that purpose make any order the High Court could make in the exercise of its equitable jurisdiction: see LRA 2002, s 110(4), as amended.

If, on an appeal, the Upper Tribunal determines that:

- it would be unconscionable because of an equity by estoppel for the registered proprietor to seek to dispossess the Applicant, but that
- the circumstances are not such that the Applicant ought to be registered as the proprietor,

the Upper Tribunal must determine how the equity due to the Applicant is to be satisfied: see LRA 2002, s 111(3), as amended.

Presumably, the Upper Tribunal may for that purpose make any order the High Court could make in the exercise of its equitable jurisdiction.

It has not been determined whether this power would permit the Upper Tribunal to substitute its own decision as to how the equity should be satisfied in a case where the registered proprietor appealed unsuccessfully on the grounds that no equity by estoppel arose.

STAYS OF EXECUTION

20.11 The Tribunal has the power to stay the implementation of the whole or part of a decision pending the outcome of the appeal: see Rule 6(3)(o).

The power to grant a stay is discretionary. It must be exercised judicially and in accordance with the overriding objective. In *Downs (R on the application of) v Secretary of State for the Environment, Food & Rural* [2009] EWCA Civ 257 Sullivan LJ said, 'A stay is the exception rather than the rule, solid grounds have to be put forward by the party seeking the stay, and, if such grounds are established, a balancing exercise weighing the risks of injustice to each side if a stay is or is not granted . . . '.

Where a party wishes to apply for a stay, the party must make such an application to the Tribunal at the same time as the party applies to the Tribunal for permission to appeal: see Rule 54(1).

The party applying for a stay must provide reasons for the application, and must provide notice of the application to the other parties: see Rule 54(2).

Before reaching a decision to stay implementation of the whole or part of a decision, the Tribunal must allow the parties the opportunity to make representations or objections: see Rule 54(3).

There is no express power to grant an interim stay pending receipt and consideration of representations or objections to the application for a stay. In a land registration case this could cause a real risk of prejudice. A successful party might become registered as the proprietor of a property as a result of the Tribunal's order. The property could then be sold and the proceeds dissipated before a stay is granted. In an appropriate case the Tribunal might want to delay sending out an order disposing of proceedings to Land Registry to allow time for the making of an application to appeal and for a stay. Alternatively, the losing party might wish to alert Land Registry to the possibility of an appeal and invite it not to implement the Tribunal's order pending an application for a stay.

The Tribunal must notify the parties and the Registrar in writing of any decision made as to the granting of a stay, specifying the decision and including the reasons for the decision: see Rule 54(4)-(6).

For an application for a stay, see **Form 100** in **Appendix 14**.

RESTORATION OF AN ORIGINAL APPLICATION CANCELLED BY THE REGISTRAR

20.12 If the Tribunal finds that the Applicant's case has not succeeded, it will direct the Registrar to cancel the original application. A problem has arisen where the Applicant wishes to pursue an appeal but, before a stay has been obtained, the Registrar has acted upon the direction and cancelled the original application.

Land Registry's view has been that once an application has been cancelled it cannot be restored with retrospective effect, because it would damage the integrity of the day list as a real time record. The disappointed Applicant was free to make a fresh application, but it would be subject to interests taking priority to it arising since the earlier application had been made.

In *Franks v Land Registrar* [2011] EWCA Civ 772, [2012] 1 All ER 326, [2012] 1 WLR 2418, the Court of Appeal, by a majority, rejected this approach. Although there was no power in the AR 2003 for the Adjudicator to make an order restoring the original application once it has been cancelled, the powers of the High Court on appeal were those set out in CPR 1998, Part 52.

CPR 1998, r 52.10(2)(a) provides that the appeal court has power to affirm, set aside or vary any order or judgment made or given by the lower court. That rule is wide enough to enable the High Court to make an order restoring the original application with retrospective effect.

The Court of Appeal considered that where no third party would be prejudiced by an order restoring the original application with retrospective effect, the High Court plainly had jurisdiction to do so.

The Court of Appeal held that the High Court also had jurisdiction to restore the original application with retrospective effect when a third party might be prejudiced. However, the jurisdiction should not ordinarily be exercised in a third party interest case since it cannot ordinarily be a proper exercise of the court's discretion to make an order whose effect is to re-arrange the priorities provided for by LRA 2002.

However, as we have seen above, the powers of the Upper Tribunal on an appeal are not to be found in CPR 1998, Part 52. By TCEA 2007, s 12(4) the Upper Tribunal may make any decision on an appeal which the Tribunal could make if the Tribunal were re-making the decision. Therefore, the Upper Tribunal does not have the wider powers the High Court does. It must follow therefore that the reasoning in *Franks v Land Registrar* no longer applies.

If this is correct, there is even more reason for the losing party to invite Land Registry not to cancel the original application pending the hearing of the application for a stay.

SECOND APPEALS TO THE COURT OF APPEAL

20.13 An appeal lies from the Upper Tribunal to the Court of Appeal on a point of law: see TCEA 2007, s 13(1), (2), (11) and (12).

The right of appeal may be exercised only with permission given by the Upper Tribunal or the Court of Appeal on an application by the party: see TCEA 2007, s 13(3), (4). Permission has to be sought from the Upper Tribunal first: see TCEA 2007, s 13(5).

The Appeals from the Upper Tribunal to the Court of Appeal Order 2008, art 2, provides that permission to appeal to the Court of Appeal must not be granted unless the Upper Tribunal or, where the Upper Tribunal refuses permission, the Court of Appeal, considers that:

- the proposed appeal would raise some important point of principle or practice; or
- there is some other compelling reason for the relevant appellate court to hear the appeal.

This is the same test for permitting a second appeal as is provided for in CPR 1998, r 52.13(2).

But an appeal may not be brought on a point of law in respect of the following decisions of the Upper Tribunal:

- any decision on an application for permission to appeal: see TCEA 2007, s 13(1) and (8)(c);
- to review, or not to review, an earlier decision of the Tribunal: see TCEA 2007, s 13(1) and (8)(d)(i);
- to take no action, or not to take any particular action, in the light of a review of an earlier decision of the Upper Tribunal: see TCEA 2007, s 13(1) and (8)(d)(ii);
- to set aside an earlier decision of the Upper Tribunal: see TCEA 2007, s 13(1) and (8)(d)(iii).

Similarly, an appeal may not be brought on a point of law in respect of a decision of the Upper Tribunal which has been set aside following a review, including a decision set aside after proceedings on the appeal on a point of law have been begun: see TCEA 2007, s 13(1) and (8)(e).

Chapter 21

ENFORCEMENT OF ORDERS

Key topics in this Chapter

Failure to comply with rules, practice directions or Tribunal directions: generally
Striking out a party's case for failing to comply with a direction
Directions to the Registrar
Requirements directed to the Registrar
Referrals to the Upper Tribunal
Requirements enforceable as orders of the court

FAILURE TO COMPLY WITH RULES, PRACTICE DIRECTIONS OR TRIBUNAL DIRECTIONS: GENERALLY

21.1 As is invariably the case in modern procedural codes, Rule 8(1) provides that an irregularity resulting from a failure to comply with:

- any provision of the Rules 2013;
- a practice direction, or
- a direction,

does not of itself render void the proceedings or any step taken in the proceedings.

Rule 8(2) sets out what the Tribunal may do when a party has failed to comply with:

- a requirement in the Rules 2013;
- a practice direction; or
- a direction.

The Tribunal may take such action as it considers just, which may include:

- waving the requirement;
- requiring the failure to be remedied;
- striking out a party's case;
- referring the failure to the Upper Tribunal; or
- barring or restricting a party's participation in the proceedings.

STRIKING OUT A PARTY'S CASE FOR FAILING TO COMPLY WITH A DIRECTION

21.2 Striking out a party's case for failing to comply with a direction may be either mandatory or discretionary.

The proceedings or case, or the appropriate part of them, will automatically be struck out if the Applicant has failed to comply with a direction that stated that failure by the Applicant to comply with the direction by a stated date would lead to the striking out of the proceedings or that part of them: see Rule 9(1).

For an order with sanctions where breach *will* lead to the striking out of the proceedings, see **Form 87** in **appendix 14.**

The Tribunal may strike out the whole or a part of the proceedings or case if the Applicant has failed to comply with a direction which stated that failure by the Applicant to comply with the direction could lead to the striking out of the proceedings or case or that part of it: see Rule 9(3)(a).

For an order with sanctions where breach *may* lead to the striking out of the proceedings, see **Form 88** in **appendix 14.**

In *Leeds City Council v Revenue and Customs Comrs* [2014] UKUT 0350 (TCC) it was held that as the overriding objective applicable in the Upper Tribunal (which is worded identically to the overriding objective applicable in the Tribunal) differs from the post Jackson overriding objective in CPR 1998, the Upper Tribunal is not to take the same approach to a failure to comply with a requirement of a rule or direction as the courts are now required to do by the decision of the Court of Appeal in *Mitchell v News Group Newspapers Ltd* [2013] EWCA Civ 1537, [2014] 2 All ER 430, [2014] 1 WLR 795 and the cases following it.

In neither case is there a need for the Tribunal to hold a hearing before making the striking out order: see Rule 31(4).

Moreover, where the Tribunal has a discretion, the Tribunal does not have to give the parties an opportunity to make representations in relation to the proposed striking out before making the striking out order: see Rule 9(4) which does not include a discretionary striking out for failing to comply with a direction within the list of striking out cases where such an opportunity must be given.

However, in either case the Applicant may apply for the proceedings or case, or part of it, to be reinstated: see Rule 9(5). Such an application must be made in writing and received by the Tribunal within 28 days after the date on which the Tribunal sent notification of the striking out to that party: see Rule 9(6).

These provisions apply to a Respondent as much as they apply to an Applicant except that:

- a reference to the striking out of the proceedings or case or part of them is to be read as a reference to the barring of the Respondent from taking further part in the proceedings or part of them: see Rule 9(7)(a); and
- a reference to an application for the reinstatement of proceedings or case or part of them which have been struck out is to be read as a reference to an application for the lifting of the bar on the Respondent from taking further part in the proceedings, or part of them: see Rule 9(7)(b).

If a Respondent has been barred from taking further part in the proceedings in this way and that bar has not been lifted, the Tribunal need not consider any response or other submission made by that Respondent and may summarily determine any or all issues against that Respondent: see Rule 9(8).

DIRECTIONS TO THE REGISTRAR

21.3 Where a dispute has been referred to the Tribunal by Land Registry, the proceedings cannot be disposed of simply by striking them out in the case of an Applicant, and summarily determining them against a Respondent after he has been barred from taking further part in the proceedings. This is because the original application to Land Registry still has to be determined.

Accordingly, Rule 8(3) provides that, in land registration strike out cases, the Tribunal may:

- where the party who failed to comply was a person who made (or has been substituted for or added to the party who made) the original application, direct the Registrar to cancel the original application in whole or in part;
- where the party who failed to comply was an Objector to (or was substituted for or added as an Objector to) the original application, direct the Registrar to give effect to the original application in whole or in part as if that objection had not been made.

If the Tribunal imposes a less draconian sanction not involving such a direction to the Registrar, it must send written notice to the parties of the Tribunal's decision as to what action is taken (if any) and give any consequential directions.

REQUIREMENTS DIRECTED TO THE REGISTRAR

21.4 We looked above at directions given to the Registrar when one party has his case struck out. We now consider the order which is made after a determination at a hearing on the merits of the case.

When a dispute has been referred by Land Registry to the Tribunal, the order that the Tribunal makes to Land Registry is of a binary nature.

If the party making the original application is successful, the Tribunal will direct the Registrar to give effect to the original application in whole or in part as if the objection to that original application had not been made: see Rule 40(2)(a).

The reason that the wording 'as if the objection to that original application had not been made' is included in rule is because there may well be other objections to the original application which are not before the Tribunal, and the Registrar will still have to deal with those other objections appropriately.

It is also arguable that in the case of adverse possession of unregistered land it gives the Registrar the power to refuse, in accordance with his usual practice, the grant of a possessory title where less than 12 years' adverse possession has been shown, even though the Tribunal has directed him to give effect to the original application having found, say, 8 years' adverse possession. This is a point which needs to be authoritatively determined either by the Upper Tribunal or by way of judicial review: see *Dunn v Harrison West Ltd* (Reference/2011/0558) (2012), unreported.

If the party making the original application is unsuccessful, the Tribunal will direct the Registrar to cancel the original application in whole or in part: see Rule 40(2)(b).

The Tribunal is required to send or deliver the appropriate direction to the Registrar in writing: see Rule 40(3). For an order including a direction to the Registrar, see **Form 91** in **appendix 14.**

The direction may include a condition that a specified entry be made on the register of any title affected: see Rule 40(3)(a). This is an important provision which should not be overlooked and which gives the Tribunal a considerable degree of flexibility in dealing with cases justly.

EXAMPLE 1

A litigant in person has opposed an application for first registration of unregistered land by a squatter claiming adverse possession. At the hearing it turns out that the Respondent accepts that the Applicant has been in adverse possession for 12 years, but is concerned that the Respondent's prescriptive right of way over the land might be prejudiced by the Applicant being granted a possessory title. The Applicant accepts that the Respondent has the prescriptive right of way claimed. In these circumstances the Registrar can be directed to give effect to the original application but to enter the benefit and burden of the prescriptive right of way on the register in the appropriate way.

Rule 40(3)(b) provides that the direction may also include a direction to reject any future application of a specified kind by a named party to the proceedings:

- unconditionally; or
- unless that party satisfies specified conditions.

This is a useful tool to prevent a vexatious or over enthusiastic litigant from making further applications to Land Registry in respect of the same land as the decision is concerned with. A conditional direction might be that he requires the permission of the court before making a further application. In that way he is not shut out from making an application but will need to persuade a judge that there is at least some merit in it.

REFERRALS TO THE UPPER TRIBUNAL

21.5 The Upper Tribunal has the same powers, rights, privileges and authority as the High Court in relation to:

- the attendance and examination of witnesses, and
- the production and inspection of documents.

These powers are conferred by TCEA 2007, s 25(1) and (2).

Rule 8(5) provides that the Tribunal may refer to the Upper Tribunal, and ask the Upper Tribunal to exercise its power under TCEA 2007, s 25 in relation to any failure by a person to comply with certain specified requirements imposed by the Tribunal.

The specified requirements and their source in the the Rules 2013 are set out in the table below:

(a) To attend at any place for the purpose of giving evidence.	The Tribunal made by summons require any person to attend as a witness at a hearing at the time and place specified in the summons: see Rules 20(1)(a).
(b) Otherwise to make themselves available to give evidence.	The Tribunal may order any person to answer any questions which relate to any issue in the proceedings: see Rule 20(1)(b).
(c) To swear an oath in connection with the giving of evidence.	The Tribunal may require any witness to give evidence on oath, and may administer an oath for that purpose: see Rule 18(7).
(d) To give evidence as a witness.	The Tribunal may require any witness to give evidence on oath, and may administer an oath for that purpose: see Rule 18(7).
(e) To produce a document.	The Tribunal may order any person to produce any documents in that person's possession or control which relate to any issue in the proceedings: see Rule 20(1)(b).
(f) To facilitate the inspection of the document or any other thing (including any premises).	The Tribunal may provide for the disclosure and inspection of documents, including taking all reasonable steps to ensure that each of the parties is given a copy of any document which has been received from any other party or former party: see Rule 18(2).

In High Court proceedings, disobedience of a witness summons either to attend court to give oral evidence or to produce documents may be punished as a contempt of court. For the procedure, see CPR 1998, Part 81.

REQUIREMENTS ENFORCEABLE AS ORDERS OF THE COURT

21.6 LRA 2002, s 112, as amended, states tersely that a requirement of the Tribunal shall be enforceable as an order of the court. Although the choice of the word 'requirement' is perplexing, it should be construed as including:

- a summons to attend as a witness;
- an order to produce documents;
- a costs order.

This does not mean that the Tribunal has the power to enforce the summons or order itself. It means that it can be enforced by an application made by one of the parties to the court under CPR 1998, Part 70.5. This rule applies where an enactment provides that a decision of a tribunal may be enforced as if it were a court order.

By CPR 1998, Part 70.5(2A) a party may enforce the decision by applying for a specific method of enforcement under Parts 71 to 73, 81, 83 and 84, and Schedule 2 CCR Orders 27 and 28, and must:

- file with the court a copy of the decision being enforced; and
- provide the court with the information required by PD 70.

By PD 70, para 4.1 the information referred to must:

- be included in practice FORM **N322B**;
- specify the statutory provision under which enforcement or the recovery of a sum of money is sought;
- state the name and address of the person against whom enforcement or recovery is sought;
- where the decision requires that person to pay a sum of money, state the amount which remains unpaid.

Now that the Tribunal can refer a failure to comply with a witness summons or an order to produce documents to the Upper Tribunal, it would seem that using CPR 1998, Part 70.5 will be most appropriate when it comes to enforcing an order for costs.

Many receiving parties who have not been paid the costs awarded to them by the Tribunal subsequently apply to the Tribunal for enforcement. The Tribunal has no powers of its own to enforce a costs order and will refer the receiving party to the provisions of CPR 1998, Part 70.5.

Chapter 22

TIPS ON PARTICULAR CASES

Key topics in this Chapter

Adverse possession
Alteration of the register
Beneficial interests
Boundary disputes
Charging orders and statutory charges
Forgeries
Prescriptive easements

ADVERSE POSSESSION

Introduction

22.1 Care must be taken when dealing with adverse possession as there are now three separate regimes:

- where the land is unregistered and an application is made for first registration by a person in adverse possession;
- where the land is registered and the person in adverse possession had acquired title prior to 13 October 2003;
- where the land is registered and the person in adverse possession had not acquired title prior to 13 October 2003.

The physical and mental components of adverse possession are set out in the seminal decision of the House of Lords in *JA Pye (Oxford) Ltd v Graham* [2002] UKHL 30, [2003] 1 AC 419, [2002] 3 All ER 865. This book is not a detailed study of the law of adverse possession and readers are recommended to a work such as Adverse Possession second edition by Stephen Jourdan QC and Oliver Radley-Gardner. The purpose of this part of this chapter is to give a general introduction to the three regimes, and to highlight some particular points relating to proceedings before the Tribunal.

Unregistered land

22.2 Where the land is unregistered, an application for first registration by a person who has obtained title by adverse possession must be made in prescribed **Form FR1** (see **Form 1** in **Appendix 13**). The application must be supported by evidence, which may consist of or include a statement of truth in prescribed Form ST1 (see **Form 2** and **Form 3** in **Appendix 13**). For an objection and reply, see **Form 4** and **Form 5** in **Appendix 13**. For statements of case where the dispute has been referred to the Tribunal, see **Form 50** and **Form 51** in **Appendix 14**. The law as to adverse possession and extinguishment of title continues to be that in force prior to the commencement of LRA 2002 on 13 October 2003.

There is no human rights point to be taken by the paper title owner of unregistered land. The law of adverse possession as it relates to unregistered land does not infringe the human rights legislation: see *JA Pye (Oxford) Ltd v United Kingdom* (Application 44302/02) (2007) 46 EHRR 1083, [2008] 1 EGLR 111; *Ofulue v Bossert* [2008] EWCA Civ 7, [2009] Ch 1, CA, [2008] 3 WLR 1253. Although both these cases concerned registered land, the reasoning of the majority of the European Court of Human Rights applies even more strongly to unregistered land, as title depends on possession not registration.

LRA 2002, s 9 (5) provides that a person may be registered with a possessory title if the Registrar is of the opinion:

- that the person is in actual possession of the land, or in receipt of the rents and profits of the land, by virtue of the estate, and
- that there is no other class of title with which he may be registered.

It will be noted that there is no requirement in the statute that the person has been in actual possession of the land for 12 years, although this is the length of possession required to extinguish the paper title owner's title under the Limitation Act 1980, s 15. As a matter of policy Land Registry no longer registers a possessory title unless the Applicant can show 12 years' possession.

There have been cases where the Adjudicator has directed the Registrar to grant a possessory title even though the Applicant was in possession for a lesser period of time: see *Crescent Farming Company Ltd v Bellway (Builders) Ltd* (Reference 2007/0978) (2009), unreported, *Bezkorowajny v Dawson* (Reference 2010/1203/2011/0521) (2011), unreported and *Investorin Ltd v Jacques* (Reference/2011/1070/1071) (2013), unreported.

In *Dunn v Harrison West Ltd* (Reference/2011/0558) (2012), unreported, the Adjudicator found that the Applicants had been in adverse possession of the disputed land for a number of years but for less than 12 years. He directed the Registrar to give effect to the original application as if the objection had not been made, in accordance with AR 2003, r 41(1)(a) (now TR 2013, r 40(2)(a)). He expressed the view that is was a matter for the Registrar to decide whether or not the wording 'as if the objection had not been made' entitled the Registrar to refuse to register a possessory title because the Applicant could not show 12 years' possession.

In the event the Registrar decided to maintain his usual policy and refused to give effect to the original application. The Applicant was given permission to appeal to the High Court and the Registrar was given permission to appear on the appeal to support his policy. The parties then reached a settlement, so, unfortunately, no guidance was given whether the Adjudicator was correct in leaving the last word to the Registrar. This is a point which still awaits a determination by an appeal court.

Registered land: the person in adverse possession had acquired title prior to 13 October 2003

22.3 Where land is registered but, prior to 13 October 2003, the land was held in trust by the registered proprietor for a person who had obtained title by adverse possession, the person in adverse possession still remains entitled to be registered as proprietor of the estate: see the transitional provisions in LRA 2002, s 134, Sch 12 para 18. An application for registration must be made in prescribed Form AP1 (see **Form 12** in **appendix 13**). The application must be supported by evidence, which may consist of or include a statement of truth in prescribed Form ST1 (see **Form 2** and **Form 13** in **appendix 13**). For an objection see **Form 14** in **appendix 13**. For statements of case where the dispute has been referred to the Tribunal, see **Form 55** and **Form 56** in **appendix 14**.

Despite an initial indication to the contrary, there is no human rights point to be taken by the paper title owner of registered land in a transitional case. It has been held at first instance that adverse possession of registered land, as applied prior to the reforms introduced by the LRA 2002, does infringe the human rights legislation: see *Beaulane Properties Ltd v Palmer* [2005] EWHC 1071 (Ch), [2006] Ch 79, [2005] 4 All ER 461.

However, it has subsequently been held in *JA Pye (Oxford) Ltd v United Kingdom* (Application 44302/02) (2007) 46 EHRR 1083, [2008] 1 EGLR 111 by the 17 judge Grand Chamber of the European Court of Human Rights, by a 10:7 majority, that adverse possession, as applied prior to the reforms introduced by the LRA 2002, does not infringe Article 1 of the First Protocol of the Convention. The Court of Appeal has since declined to depart from the Strasbourg jurisprudence: see *Ofulue v Bossert*. Although the latter case went to the House of Lords, the appeal was not on this point: *Ofulue v Bossert* [2009] UKHL 16, [2009] AC 990, [2009] 3 All ER 93.

Beaulane Properties Ltd v Palmer can no longer be regarded as good law. However, out of an abundance of caution, where in a transitional case the period of adverse possession has ended after the date of the coming into force of the Human Rights Act 1998 on 2 October 2000, the Registrar will not regard an objection based on the reasoning in *Beaulane Properties Ltd v Palmer* as groundless. It is unlikely that such an argument would meet with any success if the dispute were to be referred to the Tribunal.

Where, at the time of first registration, the paper title owner's title has already been extinguished by adverse possession, the squatter is entitled to apply to alter the register to correct the mistake.

Registered land: the person in adverse possession had not acquired title prior to 13 October 2003

22.4 Where the land is registered and the person in adverse possession had not acquired title prior to 13 October 2003, an entirely new system of adverse possession is introduced by LRA 2002: see LRA 2002, ss 96-98, Sch 6. Adverse possession in itself will not bar the paper title owner's title however long such adverse possession lasts. For this reason no human rights issue arises.

After being in adverse possession for 10 (not 12) years, the person in adverse possession will become entitled to apply to be registered as the proprietor: see LRA 2002, s 97, Sch 6 para 1(1). The application for registration must be made in prescribed Form ADV1 (see **Form 6** in **appendix 13**). The application must be accompanied by a statutory declaration (see **Form 7** in **appendix 13**) or a statement of truth. The paper title owner, any registered chargee and, in some cases, certain others will have to be notified of the application by the Registrar: see LRA 2002, s 97, Sch 6 para 2(1).

Care is required in responding on behalf of the paper title owner to an application made in prescribed Form ADV1 for registration as proprietor on the grounds of adverse possession under LRA 2002, s 97, Sch 6 para 1. Such an application faces a formidable barrier, but only if the paper title owner, or any other of those notified of the application by the Registrar, gives a counter notice in prescribed Form NAP (see **Form 9** in **appendix 13**) requiring the application to be dealt with in accordance with LRA 2002, s 97, Sch 6 para 5.

Giving this notice is done by ticking the second box in panel 5 of the Form NAP. However, the procedural rules are not mandatory and the correct approach is to consider whether the Form NAP, together with any accompanying documents, would have indicated to a reasonable Registrar that the Applicant sought to invoke the procedure under LRA 2002, s 97, Sch 6 para 5: *Hopkins v Beacon* [2011] EWHC 2899 (Ch).

If this notice is given the squatter will have to bring himself within one of three exceptional conditions, or the application will be refused: see LRA 2002, s 97, Sch 6 para 5(1).

The first condition is that it would be unconscionable because of an equity by estoppel for the registered proprietor to seek to dispossess the Applicant, and the circumstances are such that the Applicant ought to be registered as the proprietor.

If the Tribunal determines that it would be unconscionable because of an equity by estoppel for the registered proprietor to seek to dispossess the Applicant, but that the circumstances are not such that the Applicant ought to be registered as proprietor, the Tribunal must determine how the equity due to the Applicant is to be satisfied, and may for that purpose make any order that the High Court could make in the exercise of its equitable jurisdiction: see LRA 2002, s 110(4), as amended.

The second condition is that the Applicant is for some other reason entitled to be registered as the proprietor of the estate.

It sometimes happens that although a party has applied to be registered as the proprietor in prescribed Form ADV1, he already had title to the disputed land by adverse possession prior to 13 October 2003. This brings the party within the second condition: see *Balevents Ltd v Sartori* [2014] EWHC 1164 (Ch), [165], [2014] All ER (D) 152 (Apr). Even though he has not made an application to alter the register in prescribed Form AP1 in reliance on the transitional provisions contained in LRA 2002, s 134, Sch 12 para 18, the Tribunal can deal with the application on that basis, not least because the second condition will be satisfied

The third condition is that:

- the land to which the application relates is adjacent to land belonging to the Applicant,
- the exact line of the boundary between the two has not been determined under rules under s 60,

- for at least 10 years of the period of adverse possession ending on the date of the application, the Applicant (or any predecessor in title) reasonably believed that the land to which the application relates belonged to him, and
- the estate to which the application relates was registered more than one year prior to the date of the application.

Although an Adjudicator has held it is not necessary for the 10 years' belief to persist up to the date of the original application: see *Davies v John Wood Property plc* (Reference/2008/0528) (2010), unreported, the Court of Appeal without argument on the point decided otherwise in *Zarb v Parry* [2011] EWCA Civ 1306, [17], [2012] 2 All ER 320, [2012] 1 WLR 1240.

Any person may object to an application for registration as proprietor where the Applicant is relying on adverse possession. Such an objection will usually be on the basis that the squatter has been in possession for less than 10 years or that permission has been given.

This right to object is quite separate to, and independent of, the right to give a counter notice as explained above. An objection may be made in the normal way by delivering to the Registrar at the appropriate office a written statement signed by the Objector or his conveyancer (see **Form 10** in **appendix 13**). Alternatively, where a counter notice is being given, the objection can be made by ticking the third box in panel 5 and filling in panel 6 (see **Form 11** in **appendix 13**).

There is no reason why a party cannot both require the application to be dealt with in accordance with LRA 2002, s 97, Sch 6 para 5 and object on the grounds that the squatter has not satisfied any of the conditions in LRA 2002, s 97, Sch 6 para 5 and/or been in adverse possession for the required period.

For statements of case where the Applicant relies upon the third condition and the dispute has been referred to the Tribunal, see **Form 53** and **Form 54** in **appendix 14**.

Where a squatter was registered with an absolute title after the paper title owner had failed to object to the application for registration, the paper title owner succeeded in rectifying the register, and removing the squatter's registration as proprietor, when it emerged that the squatter had not been in adverse possession for the necessary ten years: *Baxter v Mannion* [2010] EWHC 573 (Ch) [52], [2010] 1 WLR 1965, [2011] 1 P & CR 133. This was on the basis that a mistake had been made in the register.

Although the issue has yet to be determined on appeal, the Adjudicator has held that the provision in the Limitation Act 1980, s 29, whereby a written acknowledgment of title causes the right of action to be treated as accruing on the date of acknowledgement, does not apply where the application is made under LRA 2002, s 97, Sch 6: see *Walton v Kerguelen* (Reference/2008/0321) (2008), unreported.

If, after a counter notice has been served, the application is refused but the person in adverse possession remains in adverse possession for a further two years, he will be entitled to apply to be registered as the proprietor once again, but this time he will be registered as proprietor whether or not there is an objection. The application for registration must be made in prescribed Form

ADV1 (see Form 6 in appendix 13). The application must be accompanied by a statutory declaration (see Form 8 in appendix 13) or a statement of truth.

Where a squatter is successful in an application brought under LRA 2002, s 97, Sch 6 in respect of land held under an absolute title, he will obtain an absolute title not merely a possessory one.

Miscellaneous issues

22.5 It sometimes happens that the court or the Tribunal determines that a party claiming a title on the grounds of adverse possession actually has a paper title to the disputed land. In one case a party applied to Land Registry on these grounds for title to part of a quay along the River Thames. The dispute before the Tribunal was stayed pending parallel court proceedings: *Couper v Albion Properties Ltd* [2013] EWHC 2293 (Ch), [2013] All ER (D) 113 (Oct). Arnold J held in those proceedings at [494] that the defendant (the Applicant to Land Registry) actually had a paper title to the quay. Following the judge's decision the Tribunal ordered Land Registry to cancel the application based on adverse possession on the understanding that the defendant would apply to Land Registry to have the relevant title plan altered to show the defendant's ownership.

Can a party be in adverse possession of the highway? In *R (on the application of Smith) v Land Registry (Cambridgeshire County Council, interested party)* [2010] EWCA Civ 200, [2011] QB 413, [2010] 3 All ER 113 the Court of Appeal held that a party could not. The reason given was that the public rights over a highway could not be extinguished by adverse possession; they would survive the acts necessary to found what would otherwise be acts of adverse possession. The trial judge had also relied upon a second reason, which the Court of Appeal did not consider. This reason was that it was an offence under the Highways Act 1980, s 137 to obstruct the highway and adverse possession could not be founded on an illegal act.

In *R (on the application of Best) v Chief Land Registrar (Secretary of State for Justice, interested party)* [2014] EWHC 1370 (Admin), [2014] 3 All ER 637, [2014] PLSCS 141 the court had to decide whether the criminalising of trespass by living in a residential building, pursuant to the Legal Aid, Sentencing and Punishment of Offenders Act 2012, s 144(1) prevents time running for applications for the registration of title by adverse possession. Ouseley J held that it did not. In the course of his decision he declined to follow the reasoning of the trial judge in *Smith* regarding illegality and adverse possession.

In *Parshall v Hackney* [2013] EWCA Civ 240, [2013] Ch 568, [2013] 3 All ER 224, the Court of Appeal held that a registered proprietor of land whose title is subject to a claim for rectification (because he has been mistakenly registered as the proprietor) cannot be in adverse possession of that land. This is because the possession of the registered proprietor was lawful, so long as he was the registered proprietor, so the possession could not be adverse to anyone else. This is a controversial decision, described as surprising by Ruoff & Roper Registered Conveyancing.

Presenting the case

22.6 Clarity of presentation is of prime importance in an adverse possession case. In particular, the disputed land must be clearly identified on a plan. The use of plans and photographs is discussed in CHAPTER 15. Historic aerial photography can play an important part in the evidence when the issue is how long the disputed land has been cultivated.

Where the value of the land makes it proportionate, it is useful for a joint surveyor to prepare an agreed 1:200 plan plotting the relevant boundaries and showing the various physical features the parties rely upon. The use of overlays can be very helpful. There will be no need for the surveyor to attend the hearing, but all those participating will have the benefit of working from a common document.

Land Registry will usually have carried out a survey, and have taken photographs, following the application and before the referral of the dispute to the Tribunal. The locations from which the photographs have been taken will be marked on a plan. Land Registry does not send the survey to the Tribunal, but it is often extremely useful for the Applicant to provide his copy for the trial bundle.

ALTERATION OF THE REGISTER

Circumstances in which the register can be altered

22.7 Alteration of the register is governed by LRA 2002, s 65, Sch 4. Provision is made for alteration pursuant to a court order (para 2) and alteration by the Registrar (para 5). When a disputed application to alter the register is referred by the Registrar to the Tribunal, then the Tribunal's role on the reference is to consider how the Registrar should exercise his powers. It is the Registrar's powers and not those of the court which are relevant.

The question has arisen as to whether a party applying to alter the register by removing land from another party's title needs to show an interest in the land being removed.

EXAMPLE 1

A is the first registered proprietor of Whiteacre. B claims that A cannot show a good paper title to the rear garden and applies for the title plan to be altered accordingly. B does not claim to have any title to the rear garden himself. Is he entitled to make the application?

In *Wells v Pilling Parish Council* [2008] EWHC 556 (Ch), [2008] 2 EGLR 29, [2008] 22 EG 174, it was conceded that if the application to alter the register was properly categorised as a matter of private law, the common law required the Applicant to have standing. The judge, on appeal from the Adjudicator, held that the application only raised a question of a private right. In the light of the concession, he held that standing was required so the application must fail. The position of an Applicant is to be contrasted with that of an Objector, as anyone can object to an application to alter the register.

But in a preliminary ruling in *Burton v Walker* (Reference/2007/1124), (2009), unreported, the Adjudicator held that, because of the concession, *Wells v Pilling Parish Council* was not binding on him, and that it was not necessary for an Applicant seeking to rectify the register to demonstrate standing. The High Court has held that the preliminary ruling in *Burton v Walker* was correctly decided: *Mann v Dingley* [2011] EWLandRA 2010_0582. This approach has also been taken to be correct in *Paton v Todd* [2012] EWHC 1248 (Ch), [51] and *Balevents Ltd v Sartori* [2014] EWHC 1164 (Ch), [165], [2014] All ER (D) 152 (Apr).

The Registrar may alter the register for the purpose of:

- correcting a mistake;
- bringing the register up to date;
- giving effect to any estate, right or interest excepted from the effect of registration; or
- removing a superfluous entry.

Examples of mistake are as follows:

- A forges a transfer of Whiteacre to himself and is registered as proprietor.
- A is registered as the first proprietor of Whiteacre, but his title had already been barred by a squatter.
- Both A and B are registered separately as the proprietors of Whiteacre.

There can be a mistake even though the correct procedure has been followed. We saw above that where a squatter was registered with an absolute title after the paper title owner had failed to object to the application for registration, the paper title owner succeeded in rectifying the register, and removing the squatter's registration as proprietor, when it emerged that the squatter had not been in adverse possession for the necessary ten years: *Baxter v Mannion* [2011] EWCA Civ 120, CA, [2011] 2 All ER 574, [2011] 20 EG 114.

The court rejected the argument that no mistake had been simply because the squatter had been registered as proprietor of the disputed land in accordance with the statutory procedure. But it clarified that the burden of proof in a case such as this lay on the party asserting that the register contained the mistake.

A controversial issue is whether a disposition by a registered proprietor, whose own title has been mistakenly registered, is also a mistake?

EXAMPLE 2

B owns Whiteacre. A forges a transfer of Whiteacre to himself and is registered as freehold proprietor. It is argued that the effect of registration is that the freehold is deemed to be vested in him: see LRA 2002, s 58(1). Subsequently, A charges Whiteacre as security for a £1M loan from the C Bank Ltd. B applies to alter the register by removing A as proprietor and restoring his name as proprietor. This he can do. But can he remove C Bank Ltd's charge? C Bank Ltd argues that because the freehold was deemed to be vested in A at the time of the charge, there has been no mistake.

Land Registry no longer accepts that argument and will now accept an application by A to remove C Bank's Ltd charge on the basis that either:

- the registration of the charge directly flows from the original mistake;
- the charge needs to be removed in order fully to correct the mistake.

In *Knights Construction (March) Ltd v Roberto Mac Ltd* [2011] 2 EGLR 123, the Adjudicator carried out a detailed review of several recent conflicting authorities and adopted the same approach. This can now be taken to be the correct view.

This passage was cited with approval by the Court of Appeal in *Gold Harp Properties Ltd v MacLeod* [2014] EWCA Civ 1084, [81].

Equally controversial is the effect of the registration of A as the registered proprietor in the first place in the above example. The High Court has held that in the case of a forged transfer the victim of the forgery remains the beneficial owner of the property concerned: see *Fitzwilliam v Richall Holdings Services Ltd* [2013] EWHC 86 (Ch), [2013] 1 P & CR 318, [2013] 2 EGLR 183, following *Malory Enterprises Ltd v Cheshire Homes (UK) Ltd* [2002] EWCA Civ 151, [2002] Ch 216, [2002] 3 WLR 1 which was a decision under the LRA 1925. As the beneficial owner, the victim is entitled to call for a transfer back of the property.

By way of contrast, where A is registered as the proprietor of Whiteacre following a transfer induced by undue influence, his registration as proprietor is not a mistake. This is because the question as to what is a mistake is decided at the time of registration. The transfer, being voidable rather than void, remains valid unless and until set aside. As explained in CHAPTER 24 the Tribunal has a free standing jurisdiction to set aside documents.

Where a squatter has obtained a possessory title (as opposed to an absolute title as happened in *Baxter v Mannion*) and the paper title owner seeks to close it on the basis that his title had not been extinguished, he will not be correcting a mistake but giving effect to any estate, right or interest excepted from the effect of registration: LRA 2002, s 11(7).

Rectification

22.8 There is a critical distinction between those cases of alteration which involve:

- the correction of a mistake, and
- prejudicially affect the title of the registered proprietor

and all other case of alteration.

Those cases of alteration which fall within the above category amount to rectification; see LRA 2002, s 65, Sch 4 para 1.

Where the Tribunal is dealing with a rectification case special protection is given to a proprietor in possession. LRA 2002, s 65, Sch 4 para 6(2) provides that no alteration affecting the title of the proprietor of a registered estate in land may be made without the proprietor's consent in relation to land in his possession unless:

- he has by fraud or lack of proper care caused or substantially contributed to the mistake, or
- it would for any other reason be unjust for the alteration not to be made.

When does the proprietor have to be in possession if he is to benefit from this special protection? In *Ghaus v Gateway Homes UK Ltd* (Reference 2010/1096/1098) (2011), unreported the Adjudicator concluded that the relevant time in respect of applications to the Registrar was the date of the application to Land Registry to alter the register. This decision was approved by the High Court in *Fitzwilliam v Richall Holdings Services Ltd* [2013] EWHC 86 (Ch), [101].

However, the court considered at [102] that in relation to applications made to court the relevant date might well be the date on which the issue fell to be determined.

It is important to consider in any given case whether or not the correction of a mistake prejudicially affects the title of the registered proprietor and thus amounts to rectification.

EXAMPLE 3

A and B are neighbours. A applies to alter the register by removing a strip of land (36 metres long and between 2 and 4 metres wide) from B's registered title plan as it is part of A's unregistered title. The Adjudicator finds that A owns the strip of land. The general boundary as shown on B's title plan is in the wrong place. This was a mistake that might be corrected. The High Court holds that this is not a rectification case. Since B only ever had a general boundary, altering the register by redrawing the boundary would not prejudicially affect B's title: see *Drake v Fripp* [2011] EWCA Civ 1279, [2012] 1 P & CR 69 and *Derbyshire County Council v Fallon* [2007] EWHC 1326 (Ch), [2007] 3 EGLR 44, [2007] 45 EG 164. For a similar decision see also *Barwell v Skinner* (Reference/2010/0982) (2011), unreported.

Similarly, on the basis of the decision of the High Court in *Fitzwilliam v Richall Holdings Services Ltd* referred to above, no question of rectification arises as the victim of the forgery has remained the beneficial owner of the property. Accordingly, the mistakenly registered proprietor suffers no prejudice by having the register altered in favour of victim. On the other hand, where a mistaken registration arose not from a forgery, but from a mistaken belief that the proprietors owned the land because they were the Lords of the Manor, and the true owner, the Crown, had shown no interest in the proceedings, the Court of Appeal did not interfere with the Adjudicator's decision allowing the registered proprietors to keep the land: *Walker v Burton* [2013] EWCA Civ 1228, [2013] 1 P & CR 116, [2013] 3 EGLR 129.

If in a rectification case the Registrar has power to make the alteration, the application must be approved, unless there are exceptional circumstances which justify not making the alteration: see LRA 2002, s 65, Sch 4 para 6(3). The same approach should be applied where the alteration does not involve rectification: see *Derbyshire County Council v Fallon*.

For a discussion of what constitutes exceptional circumstances, see *Paton v Todd* [2012] EWHC 1248 (Ch) [63]-[100], and *Balevents Ltd v Sartori* [2014] EWHC 1164 (Ch), [165], [2014] All ER (D) 152 (Apr). Delay in advancing a claim for rectification cannot constitute an exceptional circumstance, unless the delay has given rise to some substantial identifiable prejudice: see *Gold Harp Properties Ltd v MacLeod* [2014] EWCA Civ 1084, [104].

LRA 2002, s 65, Sch 4 para 8 states that the powers to rectify the register extend to changing for the future the priority of any interest affecting a registered estate concerned.

EXAMPLE 4

A, the freeholder, grant a long lease of a flat to B. A purports to forfeit the long lease, but does not lawfully do so. A applies to Land Registry to close B's title and as a result B's title is closed. This is a mistake as B's lease was not lawfully forfeited. A grants a new long lease of the flat to C. B applies to the County Court to have his title reinstated as if it had not been closed. The County Court orders B's title to be reinstated and re-opened as if it had not been closed. It also orders B's title to rank in priority to C's title.

The Court of Appeal in *Gold Harp Properties Ltd v MacLeod* [2014] EWCA Civ 532, [91]-[99], holds this to be correct, contrary to widely held views that the power to rectify is not retrospective. The effect of the decision is that henceforward B can occupy the property to the exclusion of C. But B cannot claim mesne profits from C up to that date.

For a statutory declaration in support of an application to alter the register to correct a mistake, see **Form 31** in **appendix 13**. For an objection and reply see **Form 32** and **Form 33** in **appendix 13**. For statements of case where the dispute has been referred to the Tribunal, see **Form 65** and **Form 66** in **appendix 14**.

Rectification is also relevant to whether or not a party can obtain an indemnity from Land Registry under LRA 2002, s 103, Sch 8. An indemnity will be payable if loss is suffered by reason of:

- rectification (not mere alteration) of the register; and
- a mistake whose correction would involve the rectification (not mere alteration) of the register.

The Tribunal has no jurisdiction in respect of indemnities.

LRA 2002, Sch 8 para 1(2) provides that the proprietor of a registered estate or charge claiming in good faith, under a forged disposition is, where the register is rectified, to be regarded as having suffered loss by reason of such rectification as if the disposition had not been forged. It has been held in the High Court that this provision entitles the victim of a forged disposition to an indemnity because the alteration to the register is deemed to prejudicially affect the victim's title: see *Swift 1st Ltd v Chief Land Registrar* [2014] Lexis Citation 6, [2014] All ER (D) 12 (Feb). As we have seen above, were it not for this deeming, *Fitzwilliam v Richall Holdings Services Ltd* would lead to a finding that rectification does not arise as the victim of the forgery has remained the beneficial owner of the property.

BENEFICIAL INTERESTS

22.9 The law relating to property owned by unmarried couples is governed by the law of trusts. It is quite common for the parties to have lived together in a property of which only one of them is the registered proprietor. Both may have contributed to the costs of purchase or of the household without there being any express declaration of trust.

After the relationship has broken down the party who is not the registered proprietor will often claim a beneficial interest in the property on the basis of a constructive trust: see *Oxley v Hiscock* [2004] EWCA Civ 546, [2005] Fam 211, [2004] 3 All ER 703, CA, *Stack v Dowden* [2007] UKHL 17, [2007] 2 AC 432, [2007] 2 All ER 929, HL and *Jones v Kernott* [2011] UKSC 53, SC, [2012] 1 AC 776, [2012] 1 All ER 1265. In order to protect that claim an application will be made to Land Registry for the entry of a restriction on the title of the property.

In a beneficial interest case, the application must be in prescribed Form RX1 for the entry of restrictions in Form A and II (see **FORM 23** and **FORM 24** in **APPENDIX 13**). Notice will be served on the registered proprietor who will have an opportunity to object. For an objection and reply, see **FORM 25** and **FORM 26** in **APPENDIX 13**. For statements of case where the dispute has been referred to the Tribunal, see **FORM 61** and **FORM 62** in **APPENDIX 14**.

In a beneficial interest case, there is as yet no authority on whether or not the Tribunal may quantify any interest it does find established. Generally, as a matter of practice if the evidence is there and the parties wish it to do so, the Tribunal will quantify the parties' respective interests. The Tribunal cannot order a sale of the property. The Tribunal does not have the powers given to the court by the Trusts of Land and Appointment of Trustees Act 1996.

If it is apparent that one party wants an order for sale or an order for equitable accounting, the Tribunal may consider this a good reason for directing the party seeking to establish the beneficial interest to commence court proceedings to determine that issue. The procedure when the Tribunal has to consider this is discussed in **CHAPTER 7**. The procedure after the Tribunal has directed court proceedings in discussed in **CHAPTER 8**.

A large number of beneficial interest cases do remain with the Tribunal for its determination. Any finding that the Applicant does have an interest in the property will be binding on the parties if the Applicant subsequently applies to the court for an order for sale.

A beneficial interest case before the Adjudicator will be conducted in a manner similar to such a case in the County Court. Disclosure of financial records, such as bank accounts and mortgage statements, will be important. These documents should be carefully sorted, properly paginated and included in the trial bundles.

Evidence of the amount and costs of any improvements carried out by parties will often need to be included as well. In this respect practitioners should not overlook the extension of the Matrimonial Proceedings and Property Act 1970, s 37 (contributions to improvements to be treated as giving or enlarging a beneficial interest in the property concerned) to engaged couples by the Law Reform (Miscellaneous Provisions) Act 1970, s 2: see *Wing v Eades* (Reference/2011/1178) (2014), unreported and *Hansford v Dawson* (Reference/2013/388) (2014), unreported.

The Tribunal will not allow an application for a restriction to be left in limbo as a form of interim injunction restraining the registered proprietor from disposing of the property until the dispute is heard in court. It is the tribunal's function to decide the underlying dispute: see *Jayasinghe v Liyanage* [2010] EWHC 265 (Ch), [2010] 1 WLR 2106, [2010] 1 EGLR 61.

BOUNDARY DISPUTES

22.10 Boundary disputes may come before the Tribunal in a number of different ways, including on the reference of an application:

- to alter the register;
- for first registration;
- to be registered as proprietor on the grounds of adverse possession, where the Applicant has indicated an intention to rely on the third condition set out in LRA 2002, s 97, Sch 6 para 5;
- to determine the exact line of the boundary.

The boundary of a registered estate as shown on the title plan is a general boundary, unless the boundary is determined under LRA 2003, s 60. A general boundary does not determine the exact line of the boundary. It is possible for an application to be made to alter the title plan to show the boundary more accurately. However, the altered boundary will still be only a general boundary: see *Derbyshire County Council v Fallon* [2007] EWHC 1326 (Ch), [2007] 3 EGLR 44, [2007] 45 EG 164, *Drake v Fripp* [2011] EWCA Civ 1279, CA, [2012] 1 P & CR 69 and *Barwell v Skinner* (Reference/2010/0982) (2011), unreported. Alteration of the general boundary is not rectification because it does not prejudicially affect the title of the registered proprietor.

For the distinction between a boundary dispute and a property dispute, see *Lee v Barrey* [1957] Ch 251, [1957] 1 All ER 191, CA and *Strachey v Ramage* [2008] EWCA Civ 384 [44], CA, [2008] 2 P & CR 154 at [44].

The procedure on an application for the exact line of the boundary to be determined is set out in Part 10 of LRR 2003. An application can be brought only by a proprietor of a registered estate and in respect of a boundary of that registered estate. The procedure cannot be used by the owner of unregistered land adjoining registered land to have the common boundary determined.

The application must be made in Form DB and be accompanied by:

- a plan or a plan and verbal description, identifying the exact line of the boundary and showing sufficient surrounding physical features to allow the general position of the boundary to be drawn on the Ordnance Survey map: see LRR 2003, r 118(2)(a); and
- evidence to establish the exact line of the boundary: see LRR 2003, r 118(2)(b).

Measurements shown on the plan need to be accurate to 10mm. For guidance generally see Land Registry Practice Guide 40: Supplements 3 (Boundaries) and 4 (Boundary Agreements and Determined Boundaries).

If the Registrar is satisfied that the exact line of the boundary is identified in the application and the Applicant has shown an arguable case that the exact line of the boundary is in the position claimed, he will give notice to the owners of land adjoining the boundary: see LRR 2003, r 119.

It is often the case that at a hearing of a disputed determined boundary application, the Applicant will establish that the exact line of the boundary is along the line shown on the application plan at some points, but not at others. In such a case the Tribunal may direct the Registrar to give effect to the application in part only.

If the Tribunal determines that the exact line of the boundary is in some different position from that shown on the application plan, the better view is that it may not order Land Registry to determine the exact line of the boundary in the position determined by the Tribunal. It must order the Registrar to cancel the application. However, in reaching its decision the Tribunal will probably have decided where the exact line of the boundary does lie. That decision will bind the parties, and can form the basis for a future application for a determined boundary so long as sufficient evidence and technical details are produced to satisfy Land Registry: see *Matson v Maynard* (Reference/2006/0261) (2006), unreported.

In *Cato v Murphy* [2011] EWLandR 2011_0053, an application for a determined boundary before the Adjudicator was struck out as an abuse of process when the Applicant had earlier applied in the County Court for a declaration as to the position of the boundary in exactly the same position. Those proceedings had been struck out for failure to comply with a costs order.

The resolution of boundary disputes usually involves the construction of old title deeds. The extrinsic evidence admissible on construction of the deeds will include evidence of the background facts reasonably available to the parties: see *Chadwick v Abbotswood Properties Ltd* [2004] EWHC 1058 (Ch), [2004] All ER (D) 213 (May). It will also include evidence of subsequent conveyances and subsequent conduct if the conveyances or conduct are probative of the intentions of the parties to the original conveyance: see *Ali v Lane* [2006] EWCA Civ 1532, [2007] 1 EGLR 71, (2006) Times, 4 December.

If the title documents and plans are not sufficiently clear to the reasonable layman with the plan in his hand to determine the position of the boundary, the court is entitled to seek assistance on the construction of the plan and title documents by taking account of the topographical features at the relevant date: see *Haycocks v Neville* [2007] EWCA Civ 78, CA, [2007] All ER (D) 96 (Jan), *Piper v Wakeford* [2008] EWCA Civ 1378, CA, [2009] 1 P & CR D38, *Pennock v Hodgson* [2010] EWCA Civ 873, CA, 154 Sol Jo (no 30) 33, *Dixon v Hodgson* [2011] EWCA Civ 1612, CA, [2012] 1 P & CR 317, *Akhtar v Brewster* [2012] EWHC 3521 Ch, [2012] All ER (D) 112 (Dec) and *Cameron v Boggiano* [2012] EWCA Civ 157, CA, [2012] 1 EGLR 127, [2012] 09 EG 151 (CS).

The determination of a boundary dispute may turn on whether or not the parties or their predecessors in title entered into a boundary agreement. A distinction has to be drawn between a boundary agreement, which resolves a dispute about the location of the boundary by giving certainty as to the location of the boundary, and an agreement to resolve a dispute between neighbouring landowners by the conveyance by one to the other of an area of land the title of which was in dispute. A boundary agreement does not need to satisfy any formalities, whereas an agreement of the second type will need to satisfy the requirements of the Law of Property (Miscellaneous Provisions) Act 1989, s 2 and will need to be put into effect by a conveyance or a transfer.

In *Yeates v Line* [2012] EWHC 3085 (Ch), [2013] Ch 363, [2013] 2 All ER 84 the judge, on an appeal from the Adjudicator, held that an oral compromise agreement did not infringe s 2 because, although it had a disposing effect, it did not have a disposing purpose.

CHARGING ORDERS AND STATUTORY CHARGES

22.11 The Charging Orders Act 1979, s 1 provides that where, under a judgment or order of the High Court or a county court, a debtor is required to pay a sum of money to the creditor then, for the purpose of enforcing that judgment or order, the court may make a charging order imposing on any such property of the debtor as may be specified in the order a charge for securing the payment of any money due or to become due under the judgment or order.

By s 3(4) a charge imposed by a charging order shall have the like effect and shall be enforceable in the same courts and in the same manner as an equitable charge created by the debtor by writing under his hand.

CPR 1998, Part 73 governs charging orders. An interim order, imposing a charge on the debtor's interest in the relevant asset and fixing a final hearing, will be made without a hearing: see CPR 73.4. If any person objects to the court making a final charging order, he must file and serve on the applicant written evidence stating the grounds of the objection, not less than 7 days before the final hearing: CPR 73.8.

An interim and final charging order on land should be protected by registration. Strictly, only the interim order needs to be registered but Land Registry accepts separate registration.

A charging order against the legal estate of registered land is protected by the entry of an agreed or unilateral notice. The application must be made in prescribed Form AN1 or UN1 respectively. For prescribed Form UN1, see **FORM 15** in **APPENDIX 13**.

If however the debtor only has a beneficial interest in registered land, the charging order is protected by a restriction: see LRA 2002, s 42 (4). The appropriate restriction is in Form K which simply requires that notice of the disposition has been given to the creditor. This is widely regarded as insufficient protection, and the creditor may apply to the court for the entry of a non-standard restriction.

Sometimes a debtor will object to the entry of a restriction protecting a charging order, or apply to cancel a notice or restriction protecting a charging order. This may be on the grounds that:

- the judgment debt is not owed or has been paid off;
- he has no beneficial interest in the land charged.

If the application is disputed, the matter will be referred to the Tribunal under LRA 2002, s 73 (7).

The Tribunal will not entertain an argument that the judgment debt is not owed or has been paid off. If the debtor alleges the judgment was wrong, he must appeal or seek to set it aside. The Tribunal cannot go behind the judgment. If the debtor alleges the judgment debt has been paid off, he must seek to set aside charging order.

Although it might be said that the court has already determined that the debtor has an interest in the land subject to the charging order, there are cases in which the Tribunal has entertained an argument that the debtor has no interest in the land subject to the charging order. The debtor might, for example, allege that he transferred all his interest in the land to someone else prior to the judgment.

Compare *Yorkshire Bank plc v Elliott* (Reference/2005/0256) (2007), unreported, where the Adjudicator found that the debtor no longer had any interest in the land subject to the charging order, with *Commercial First Business Ltd v Choudhry* (Reference/2011/0713/0716) (2012), unreported where a different Adjudicator declined to go behind the charging order. In *F&H (Didsbury) Ltd v Plant* (Reference/2012/0614) (2013), unreported, a third Adjudicator followed the former approach, but was encouraged to do so by the District Judge. He had expressly said when making the final charging order that he was not going to determine whether or not the judgment debtor any longer had any beneficial interest in the property, but that it was up to Land Registry to decide whether the charging order should be registered.

Many public bodies have a statutory right to charge land to secure payments due to it from individuals. Disputes arising in respect of the registration of these charges are also dealt with by the Tribunal. For a case in which the Adjudicator held he had jurisdiction to decide public law points where a local authority had registered a charge under the Health and Social Services and Social Security Act 1983, see *Kent County Council v Fremlin* [2011] EWLandRA 2010_0756.

FORGERIES

22.12 The Tribunal is accustomed to determining disputes in which the principle issue is whether or not the signature of a party to a document has been forged. As has been shown, the procedures of the Tribunal are wholly adequate for determining such disputes. There will be no need for parties to a reference to bring court proceedings where such an issue arises.

It may be the case that a party seeking to attack the validity of a document may be able to rely, as an alternative to an argument that a signature was forged, on an argument that the signature was procured by the exercise of undue influence or by misrepresentation. Whereas a forged document is void, a document obtained by undue influence or misrepresentation is voidable. That means that it remains effective unless and until it is set aside. As explained in **CHAPTER 24**, the Tribunal has all the jurisdiction of the High Court to rectify or set aside a document which effects a registrable disposition of a registered estate or charge or is a contract to make such a disposition or effects a transfer of an interest which is the subject of a notice in the register: see LRA 2003, s 108, as amended.

A party who challenges the validity of a document as a forgery may also wish to consider whether to make an application to the Tribunal under LRA 2003, s 108, as amended to set the document aside. When this happens both matters can be case managed and heard together.

The reader is referred to **CHAPTER 10** for a consideration of expert evidence. For directions for expert evidence, see **FORM** 77 and **FORM** 78 in **APPENDIX 14**.

PRESCRIPTIVE EASEMENTS

22.13 Only the express grant of an easement requires to be completed by registration before it will operate at law. Prescriptive easements become legal interests without the need for registration.

Provision is made for registered proprietors claiming the benefit of a prescriptive easement to apply for it to be registered as appurtenant to the estate: see LRR 2003, r 73A(1)(b) and (3), as inserted.

The application must be made in prescribed Form AP1 (see **Form 12** in **appendix 13**). The application must be supported by evidence, which may consist of or include a statement of truth in prescribed Form ST4 (see **Form 27** and **Form 28** in **appendix 13**). For an objection and reply, see **Form 29** and **Form 30** in **appendix 13**. For statements of case where the dispute has been referred to the Tribunal, see **Form 63** and **Form 64** in **appendix 13**.

The law of prescription is notoriously complex and there are three bases upon which a case can be put:

- common law;
- lost modern grant;
- the Prescription Act 1832.

Each has its difficulties. The common law presumption requires proof of user since 1189. Lost grant has been described by Lush J as a 'revolting fiction': see *Angus & Co v Dalton* (1877) 3QBD 85, 94. The 1832 Act has been described by the Law Reform Committee as 'one of the worst drafted Acts on the Statute Book'. For details of the substantive law reference should be made to a real property textbook or a specialist work such as Gale on Easements.

Practitioners should note that there is an important distinction between claims based on lost modern grant and the 1832 Act. Where there is no user as of right for the whole of the 20 year period next before the action is brought, the claim under the 1832 Act will fail. The period of enjoyment under the 1832 Act is required to be next before some suit or action in which the claim is brought into question.

In *Wilkin & Sons Ltd v Agricultural Facilities Ltd* (Reference/2011/420) (2012), unreported the Adjudicator said that there would appear to be four possible interpretations of 'some suit or action' where the Adjudicator (now the Tribunal) is considering a claim based on the 1832 Act:

- the making of an application to Land Registry for the registration of a right of way is not 'some suit or action';
- the 'suit or action' is the date of the making of the application to Land Registry;
- the 'suit or action' is the date when notice of an objection is given; or
- the 'suit or action' is the date when the dispute is referred to the Adjudicator (now the Tribunal).

The Adjudicator held that the date of the making of the application to Land Registry is the date of the 'suit or action' in which the claim is brought into question. The Tribunal re-affirmed this decision in *Russo and Gleaves v Clarke* (Reference/2012/600/668) (2014), unreported.

Delay between the user ceasing to be of right and the commencement of proceedings (for these purposes the original application to Land Registry will be treated as the bringing of the action) is not fatal to a lost modern grant claim, provided there has been 20 years' user as of right at some time. It is therefore advisable, if there is any suggestion that the user has ceased to be as of right before the original application was made, to make it clear in the statement of case that the claim is based on both lost modern grant and the 1832 Act: see *Smith v Brudenell-Bruce* [2002] 2 P&CR 51.

The witness statements in a prescriptive easement case should be drafted with care and in detail. The activities relied upon, such as walking along a path, should be described carefully and chronologically. Broad sweeping assertions, such as, 'For 20 years I have walked along the path without force, openly and without permission' should be avoided.

In *Winterburn v Bennett* (Reference/2013/81) (2013), unreported the Applicant had applied to Land Registry for the registration of a prescriptive easement in certain terms. The judge found that a prescriptive easement had been established, but, on the facts, it was of a more restricted nature than claimed. He held that qualifying the easement sought to be registered, in its more restricted nature, formed part of his determination and was not the determination of a different matter to that referred to him by Land Registry. He had jurisdiction under Rule 40(3)(a) to attach a condition to his direction to the Registrar and such a condition would qualify the nature of the easement to be registered.

On the other hand, the Adjudicator has refused to direct that the entry in the register in respect of a prescriptive right of way should record the dimension of the opening. It is not the normal practice of the Registrar to record the precise dimension on the register, and the Adjudicator was not in a position to do so with the required degree of accuracy even if he had considered it appropriate, which he did not: see *Bloomfield v Bates* (Reference/2011/1181/1183) (2012), unreported.

Chapter 23

NETWORK ACCESS AGREEMENT APPEALS

Key topics in this Chapter

- Electronic conveyancing
- Network access agreements
- Termination of network access agreements
- The right to appeal to the Tribunal
- Procedure on appeals
- Costs
- Setting aside, reviews and appeals from the Tribunal

ELECTRONIC CONVEYANCING

23.1 The Registrar has set up an electronic conveyancing network. This network is authorised by LRA 2002, s 92(1), and is known as a land registry network ('the network'). LRA 2002, s 92, schedule 5 and the Land Registration (Network Access) Rules 2008, as amended in 2011, contain the detailed provisions relating to the network.

Electronic conveyancing will be operated through the network. There is power to make electronic conveyancing compulsory: see LRA 2002, s 93. At the time of writing, electronic conveyancing has become operational only in a modest way. The Land Registration (Electronic Conveyancing) Rules 2008 have introduced a limited number of electronic legal charges.

Land Registry announced in 2011 that, following a consultation, it was proposing to put the development of an e-transfer system on hold for the immediate future, and to delay implementation of the planned new electronic conveyancing rules until the return of a healthier financial climate and a more active property and mortgage market. This did not mean it was abandoning its work on electronic conveyancing and hoped to produce a more acceptable solution to present concerns, such as fraud, over the next few years.

NETWORK ACCESS AGREEMENTS

23.2 A person who is not a member of Land Registry only has access to the network under authority conferred by means of an agreement with the Registrar. Such an agreement is known as a "network access agreement" and may authorise access to the network for the communication, posting or retrieval of information, the making of changes to the register of title or cautions register, the issue of official search certificates, the issue of official copies and such other conveyancing purposes as the Registrar may think fit.

There are three types of network access agreement:

- a full network access agreement is a network access agreement which permits the subscriber to carry out network transactions;
- a read-only network access agreement is a network access agreement which only permits the subscriber to retrieve information on the network;
- a signature network access agreement, other than a full network access agreement, permits the subscriber to apply an electronic signature to a document and retrieve information on the network.

The Registrar does not have a discretion whether or not to enter into a network access agreement with a person. If the Applicant meets the criteria provided, the Registrar must enter into a network access agreement with him.

In relation to a read-only network access agreement or a signature network access agreement, the criteria are that the Applicant has informed the Registrar that he will accept the terms of the agreement and, if an individual, has attained the age of 18 years.

In relation to a full network access agreement, the criteria are more stringent. They include:

- the professional qualifications of the Applicant;
- the holding of adequate insurance;
- an ability to comply with the system and security requirements;
- an ability to meet the Registrar's fees and charges; and
- in the case of an Applicant where there are certain disciplinary concerns, that he is likely to comply with the agreement.

TERMINATION OF NETWORK ACCESS AGREEMENTS

23.3 The Registrar has power to terminate a network access agreement. In the case of all types of network access agreements, the Registrar may terminate all subsisting network access agreements if he is of the opinion that it is no longer practicable to operate the network. In the case of a full network access agreement, the Registrar may terminate a full network access agreement with immediate effect on one of several specified grounds. Alternatively, the Registrar may, on one of the same grounds, give the subscriber a notice of termination.

The specified grounds of termination are:

- the subscriber has ceased to be a person with whom the Registrar would be obliged to enter into an agreement;
- the subscriber has become insolvent;
- the subscriber is an individual who, in relation to any aspect of the use of the network, lacks capacity within the meaning of the Mental Capacity Act 2005;
- the practice of the subscriber has been the subject of an intervention;
- there has been a serious breach of the agreement;
- the subscriber has failed to comply with a default notice given to him by the Registrar (a default notice is a notice given by the Registrar to the subscriber specifying a minimum period of 10 days in which the subscriber is to take certain steps in respect of a breach of the agreement).

There are two categories of serious breach:

- an act or failure to act which, in the opinion of the Registrar, damages or threatens the security or integrity of the land registry network, information on that network, the register, or other information kept by the Registrar in electronic form;
- the subscriber giving a materially incorrect certificate to the Registrar in connection with a contract, disposition or application which has been or is being made using the network.

Where the Registrar terminates an agreement with immediate effect he must give the subscriber a written notice as soon as is practicable. Such notice must specify:

- each ground of termination relied upon;
- the facts which, in the opinion of the Registrar, justify each ground relied upon;
- why the Registrar considers termination with immediate effect is justified; and
- give notice of the right of appeal.

Where the Registrar gives the subscriber a notice of termination, the notice must, amongst other things, specify:

- when it will expire;
- each ground of termination relied upon;
- the facts which, in the opinion of the Registrar, justify each ground relied upon; and
- give notice of the right of appeal.

A subscriber served with a notice of termination may require it to be suspended pending an appeal. The Registrar may withdraw a notice of termination at any time before the agreement has terminated. Where termination has not been suspended, the agreement will terminate on the expiry of the notice of termination. Where termination has been suspended, the agreement will terminate on the expiry of the notice of termination or on the determination of the appeal and of any subsequent appeal, whichever occurs later.

THE RIGHT TO APPEAL TO THE TRIBUNAL

23.4 When electronic conveyancing becomes wider in its scope, the refusal to enter into a network access agreement or the termination of a network access agreement will be an extremely serious matter for the person concerned, who will not be able to carry out conveyancing work. It is therefore provided that a person who is aggrieved by a decision of the Registrar with respect to entry into, or termination of, a network access agreement may appeal against the decision to the Tribunal: see LRA 2002, s 108(1)(b) and s 92, schedule 5 para 4, as amended.

It is intended that such an appeal will be a full appeal and not simply a review of the Registrar's decision. The right to appeal is unconditional: permission to appeal is not required. On determining an appeal the Tribunal may give such directions as it considers appropriate to give effect to its determination.

PROCEDURE ON APPEALS

23.5 Prior to 1 July 2013 network access agreement appeals to the Adjudicator were governed by their own procedural code contained in the Network Access Appeal Rules 2008 ('NAAR 2008'). Since 1 July 2013, when the jurisdiction to hear these appeals was transferred to the Tribunal, the procedure is governed by the Rules 2013. NAAR 2008 have been repealed and thus consigned to history.

An appeal must be made by way of a written notice of application, signed, dated and sent or delivered to the Tribunal by the Applicant: see Rule 26(1). In a network access agreement appeal the Registrar is the Respondent: see Rule 1(3). For notices of application, see **Form 101** and **Form 103** in **appendix 15**.

Important points about a notice of application are:

- it must be provided to the Tribunal within 28 days after the date on which notice of the decision to which the appeal relates was sent to the Applicant: see Rule 27(2);
- it must state the name and address of the Applicant, the name and address of the Applicant's representative (if any), an address where documents for the Applicant may be sent or delivered, and the name and address of the Respondent (ie the Registrar): see Rules 26(2)(a)-(d);
- it must state the result the Applicant is seeking and the Applicant's reasons for making the application: see Rules 26(2)(h) and (i);
- it must include a statement that the Applicant believes that the facts stated in the application are true see Rule 26(2)(j);
- the Applicant must file with it a copy of the Registrar's decision forming the subject matter of the appeal and any statement of reasons for the Registrar's decision which the Applicant has or can reasonably obtain: see Rule 26(4).

When the Tribunal receives the notice of application, it must provide a copy of the application to the Registrar: see Rule 29(1). It must also provide to the Registrar a written notice informing the Registrar of the requirements relating to the service and contents of the response: see Rule 29(2).

The Registrar must, subject to any direction to the contrary, within 28 days after the date on which he was provided with a copy of the notice of application, send or deliver to the Tribunal a response: see Rule 30(3). For responses, see **Form 102** and **Form 104** in **appendix 15**.

Important points about a response are:

- it must state the name and address of the Registrar, the name and address of the Registrar's representative (if any) and an address where documents for the Registrar may be sent or delivered: see Rules 30(4)(a)-(c);
- it must state whether the Registrar opposes the application and, if so, any grounds for such opposition which are not contained in another document provided with the response: see Rule 30(4)(e);
- It must state whether the Registrar would be content for the case to be dealt with without a hearing if the Tribunal considers it appropriate: see Rule 30(4)(f).

The Registrar must provide with the response a copy of any written record of the decision appealed and any statement of reasons for that decision which the Applicant did not provide and the Registrar has or can reasonably obtain: see Rule 30(5).

The Registrar must send or deliver a copy of the response and any accompanying documents to the Applicant at the same time as it provides the response to the Tribunal: see Rule 30(6).

Prior to 1 July 2013, when network access agreement appeals to the Adjudicator were governed by their own procedural code contained in the NAAR 2008, specific rules were in place governing how that the appeal would be conducted. Since 1 July 2013, when the jurisdiction to hear these appeals was transferred to the Tribunal and the procedure is governed by the the Rules 2013, there is now no distinction between the way in which these appeals are case managed and heard and the way in which all other cases in the Tribunal are dealt with. Reference should therefore be made to the earlier chapters in the book.

COSTS

23.6 Since 1 July 2013 the Tribunal's power to make an award of costs in respect of network access agreement appeals is given by Rule 13(1)(c) and is the same power that applies to all other land registration cases in the Tribunal. The exercise of this power is dealt with in CHAPTER **19**.

SETTING ASIDE, REVIEWS AND APPEALS FROM THE TRIBUNAL

23.7 An appeal to the Upper Tribunal lies from the Tribunal's decision on a network access agreement appeal, but as this is a second appeal it is only possible on a point of law: see LRA 2002, s 111(2A), as amended. Such an appeal on a point of law is made pursuant to TCEA 2007, s 11. The procedure on such an appeal, including the need to obtain permission to appeal, is considered in CHAPTER **20**.

The Tribunal also has powers to set aside its decisions or to review them in certain circumstances. These powers apply to decisions in network access agreement appeals in the same way as they apply to decisions in references from the Registrar to the Tribunal, and are also considered in CHAPTER **20**.

Chapter 24

RECTIFICATION AND SETTING ASIDE OF DOCUMENTS

Key topics in this Chapter

JURISDICTION

24.1 The Tribunal has a free-standing independent jurisdiction, wholly separate from its jurisdiction to determine matters referred to it by the Registrar, to make any order which the High Court could make for the rectification or setting aside of certain documents connected with land registration: see LRA 2002, s 108(2), as amended. This is the only original jurisdiction of the Tribunal in a land registration case. An application for the rectification or setting aside of documents under this jurisdiction is referred to by the generic title of a rectification application. For the purposes of the Rules 2013 a rectification application means an application to rectify or set aside a document under LRA 2002, s 108(2), as amended: see Rule 1(3).

The Tribunal's jurisdiction to rectify or set aside a document is restricted to a document which:

- effects a qualifying disposition of a registered estate or charge: see LRA 2002, s 108(2)(a), as amended;
- is a contract to make such a disposition: see LRA 2002, s 108(2)(b), as amended; or
- effects the transfer of an interest which is the subject of a notice in the register: see LRA 2002, s 108(2)(c), as amended.

A qualifying disposition is either a registrable disposition (for example, a transfer of the freehold) or a disposition which creates an interest which may be the subject of a notice in the register (for example, an instrument creating a restrictive covenant): see LRA 2002, s 108(3).

EXAMPLE 1

A has the benefit of a right to graze on B's land. This profit à prendre is noted on the register of B's title but cannot be registered with its own title. A agrees to assign the benefit of the profit à prendre to C, but there is an error in the assignment which wrongly identifies the assignee as D. The Tribunal has jurisdiction to rectify the assignment under LRA 2002, s 108(2)(c), as amended.

The question has arisen as to whether a disposition giving rise to first registration is a qualifying disposition within the definition.

EXAMPLE 2

A agrees to sell his unregistered land to B. This triggers first registration and A executes a transfer in prescribed Form TR1. By mistake the transferee is named as C. Does the Tribunal have jurisdiction to rectify the mistake in the Form TR1?

There is as yet no High Court or Upper Tribunal authority on this point. It is suggested that on a strict construction of LRA 2002, s 108(2), as amended, the Tribunal does not have jurisdiction to rectify the Form TR1. Although the disposition is a registrable one, it is not the disposition of a registered estate. The estate is still unregistered at the time of the disposition.

However, this limitation on the power of the Tribunal is a curious one. It is difficult to see why the Tribunal should not have power to rectify or set aside a transfer triggering first registration. No explanation for this apparent lacuna in the Tribunal's powers appears from the commentary on the Land Registration Bill appearing in the Law Commission's 2001 Report "Land Registration for the Twenty-First Century: A Conveyancing Revolution."

RECTIFICATION OF DOCUMENTS

24.2 Rectification of a document is not to be confused with alteration or rectification of the register. If a party wishes to rectify the register, he must apply to the Registrar in prescribed Form AP1. He cannot apply directly to the Tribunal, which will only become involved if there is an objection to the application and the dispute is referred to it under LRA 2002, s 73(7), as amended. Equally, if a party wishes to rectify a document, he can apply to the court or to the Tribunal but the Registrar has no jurisdiction to rectify a document.

EXAMPLE 3

A agrees to sell commercial premises to B. The premises consist of a large shop registered under one title, and a small garage at the rear registered under a separate title. By mistake only the title number of the small garage is inserted in panel 2 in prescribed Form TR1. Land Registry registers B as the proprietor of the small garage only. A disappears. B asks Land Registry to alter the register to show B as the proprietor of the large shop.

Land Registry will refuse to do so as it has not made a mistake. The mistake is in the Form TR1 which Land Registry has no jurisdiction to correct. Before the register can be altered B will need to apply to the court or to the Tribunal for rectification of the Form TR1.

For examples of where the Adjudicator has rectified a document, see *Tingle v Crutchley* (Rectification/2008/0007) (2009), unreported and *Palace Gate Worldwide Ltd v Palacegate Agencies Ltd* (Rectification/2009/0007) (2010), unreported.

The Tribunal does not expect the jurisdiction to rectify a document to be used as a first resort where there has been poorly-conducted conveyancing. If land has been transferred to the wrong transferee, the conveyancer responsible should first seek to obtain a transfer back from that transferee to the transferor, and then complete a fresh transfer to the correct transferee.

The Tribunal has no freestanding jurisdiction to construe documents connected to registered land. But there is no reason in principle if a party applies to rectify a document why the Tribunal should not, in an appropriate case, make a finding that the document bears the meaning contended for, not as a result of rectification, but as a matter of construction; see *Kutchinsky v Ballymoney Hill Estates Ltd* (Rectification/2013/0005) (2014), unreported. This is known as correction by construction. There will then be a binding determination between the parties on the true meaning of the document.

SETTING ASIDE OF DOCUMENTS

24.3 This useful jurisdiction of the Tribunal is often overlooked. Again, the setting aside of a document is not to be confused with alteration or rectification of the register. If a party wishes to set aside a document, he can apply to the court or to the Tribunal but the Registrar has no jurisdiction to set aside a document.

The jurisdiction to set aside a document will arise if a party contends that a transfer has, for example, been induced by misrepresentation, fraud, duress or undue influence.

Sometimes an allegation that a document is voidable will arise in the course of a dispute which has already been referred by Land Registry to the Tribunal.

> **EXAMPLE 4**
>
> A applies to cancel a unilateral notice entered by B. The notice protects an option to purchase granted to B. A alleges that the option to purchase is void as it was entered into as a result of a common mistake. The dispute is referred to the Tribunal. It becomes apparent from A's statement of case that A is also alleging that she entered into the option agreement as a result of B's undue influence. B argues in his statement of case that whilst the Tribunal has jurisdiction to determine whether or not the option to purchase is void as a result of a common mistake, it has no jurisdiction to set aside the option agreement on the grounds of undue influence.
>
> A could make a free standing application to the Tribunal to set aside the option agreement. With sensible case management the application could be heard at the same time as the dispute referred by the Registrar. Alternatively, the Tribunal might treat A's statement of case as including an informal application to the Tribunal to exercise its power under LRA 2002, s 108(2), as amended, to set aside the document. The Tribunal might dispense with the formal requirements of Part 3 of the Rules 2013, discussed below, requiring a separate application. This would be on the basis that the rules are directory and not mandatory, in the light of the overriding objective to be found in Rule 3.

APPLICATIONS

24.4 Prior to 1 July 2013 the form and contents of a rectification application to the Adjudicator were governed by a separate procedural code contained in Part 3 of the AR 2003. Since 1 July 2013, when the jurisdiction to hear a rectification application was transferred to the Tribunal, the procedure is governed by the Rules 2013 and a rectification application is now treated in exactly the same way as any other application permitted to be made to the Tribunal. AR 2003 have been repealed and thus consigned to history.

A rectification application must be made by way of a written notice of application, signed, dated and sent or delivered to the Tribunal by the Applicant: see Rule 26(1). In a rectification application the party or parties making an objection to the application are the Respondents: see Rule 1(3). For notices of application in rectification cases, see **Form 105** and **Form 105** in **appendix 16**.

Important points about a notice of application are:

- it must state the name and address of the Applicant, the name and address of the Applicant's representative (if any), an address in England and Wales where documents for the Applicant may be sent or delivered, and the name and address of the person or persons against whom the order is sought: see Rules 26(2)(a)-(d) and PDLR para 2.1(a)-(d);

- it must state details of the remedy being sought including the precise form of any words to be inserted in any rectified document and the grounds of the application identifying all relevant facts and matters relied upon: see Rules 26(2)(h) and (i) and PDLR para 2.1(e)-(f);
- it must include a statement that the Applicant believes that the facts stated in the application are true see Rules 26(2)(j) and PDLR para 2.3.

PDLR para 2.2 provides that the notice of application must also contain a list of documents which:

- are important to the Applicant's case; or
- the Tribunal or any other party to the proceedings will require in order properly to understand the Applicant's case

and copies of such documents must accompany the notice of application.

A copy of the instrument intended to be rectified or set aside must also be included. It is also good practice to send to the Tribunal a copy of the proposed changes to any document which is to be rectified.

OBJECTIONS IN RESPONSE

24.5 When the Tribunal receives the notice of application, it must provide to the person against whom the order is sought and any other person who the Tribunal considers should be a party to the proceedings

- a copy of the application, and
- a notice specifying that if the person wishes to object, the person must send or deliver to the Tribunal an objection in response within 28 days of the date on which the person received the copy of the application provided by the Tribunal: see Rule 29(8).

> **EXAMPLE 5**
> In 2010 A, the freeholder, granted a short occupational lease of a shop to B at a rack rent. In 2011 A agreed to grant a long concurrent lease of the shop to C. The concurrent lease would entitle C to receive the rent from A. By mistake the concurrent lease did not state that it was subject to and with the benefit of the occupational lease. In 2012 A transfers the freehold to Z. Z now refuses to agree to the rectification of the concurrent lease. A applies to the Tribunal to rectify the concurrent lease. The Tribunal serves the application on both Z as the current freeholder and A as the other party to the document to be rectified.

For responses, see Forms 108-110 in APPENDIX **16**.

Important points about a response are:

- it must state the name and address of the Respondent, the name and address of the Respondent's representative (if any) and an address in England and Wales where documents for the Registrar may be sent or delivered: see PDLR para 4.1(a)-(c);
- it must state the Respondent's reasons for objecting to the rectification application: see Rule 30(1)(a);
- it must state all relevant facts and matters relied upon by the Respondent in support of his case see PDLR para 4.1(d);
- it must include a statement that the Respondent believes that the facts stated in the response are true: see PDLR para 4.2.

Rule 30(1)(b) and PDLR para 4.2 provide that the response must be accompanied by copies of any documents available to the Respondent which:

- are important to the Respondent's case; or
- the Tribunal or any other party to the proceedings will require in order properly to understand the Respondent's case.

and a list of all such documents.

However, if on receipt of the application the Tribunal considers that it does not have jurisdiction in relation to the proceedings (for example, the application is completely misconceived or relates only to a document dealing with unregistered land), and the Tribunal does not exercise its power under Rule 6(3)(n) to transfer the proceedings elsewhere, the Tribunal must strike the proceedings out: see Rule 9(2).

PROCEDURE

24.6 Although the notice of application and the response take the place of statements of case served in the case of a reference by the Registrar to the Tribunal, thereafter the procedure for preparing a rectification application for determination by the Tribunal, and for the determination itself, is exactly the same procedure as in the case of a reference to the Tribunal. This has been explained in earlier chapters. For an example of the Tribunal using its powers of summary disposal under Rule 9(3)(e) to strike out an application to set aside a legal charge, where the argument originating in a document posted on the internet was wholly without merit, see *Sinclair v Accord Mortgages Ltd* (Rectification/2013/0031) (2014), unreported.

THE EFFECT OF AN ORDER

24.7 The general law about the effect of an order of the High Court for the rectification or setting aside of a document applies to an order made by the Tribunal: see LRA 2002, s 108(4). This means that the order will be retrospective back to the date of the document: *Craddock Bros v Hunt* [1923] 2 Ch 136, 151.

A question that has arisen is whether on an application to rectify a document the Tribunal has power to direct the Registrar to alter the register.

EXAMPLE 5

A agrees to sell commercial premises to B. The premises consist of a large shop registered under one title, and a small garage at the rear registered under a separate title. By mistake only the title number of the small garage is inserted in panel 2 in prescribed Form TR1. Land Registry registers B as the proprietor of the small garage only. A disappears. B applies to the Tribunal for the rectification of the TR1 to include the title number of the large shop in panel 2.

The Tribunal finds that the title number of the large shop was omitted from panel 2 by mistake, and retrospectively rectifies the Form TR1. Does the Tribunal have the jurisdiction to direct the Registrar to alter the proprietorship register of the large shop to show B as the proprietor? Or does B have to make a separate application to Land Registry to alter the register?

In *Palace Gate Worldwide Ltd v Palacegate Agencies Ltd* (Rectification/2009/0007) (2010), unreported it was held that on an application to rectify a document the Adjudicator had no power to direct the Registrar to alter the register.

Accordingly, the substantive order made by the Tribunal in a rectification application will differ from that made following a reference. If the application for rectification is successful, the Tribunal will order the document to be rectified as appropriate, but no direction to the Registrar will be given. Accordingly, the successful party may need to apply to the Registrar for alteration of the register to reflect the rectification of the document.

COSTS

24.8 The Tribunal may award costs in a rectification application on the application of a party or of his own motion, in the same way as in any other land registration case: see Rule 13. This is considered in CHAPTER **19**.

SETTING ASIDE, REVIEWS AND APPEALS FROM THE TRIBUNAL

24.9 An appeal to the Upper Tribunal lies from the Tribunal's decision in a rectification application, either on a point of law pursuant to TCEA 2007, s 11 or on the facts pursuant to LRA 2002, s 111(1), as amended. The procedure on such appeals, including the need to obtain permission to appeal, is the same as on an appeal from the Tribunal's decision on a reference, and is considered in CHAPTER 20.

The Tribunal also has powers to set aside its decisions or to review them in certain circumstances. These powers apply to decisions in rectification applications in the same way as they apply to decisions in references from the Registrar to the Tribunal, and are also considered in CHAPTER 20.

LAND REGISTRATION ACT 2002

(2002 c 9)

PART 11
ADJUDICATION

107 . . .

. . .

NOTES

Amendment

Repealed by SI 2013/1036, art 6(1), Sch 1, Pt 3, paras 225, 227.
Date in force: 1 July 2013: see SI 2013/1036, art 1; for savings see art 6(3), Sch 3, paras 1–8 thereto.

108 Jurisdiction

(1) The [First-tier Tribunal] has the following functions—

(a) determining matters referred to [it] under section 73(7), and

(b) determining appeals under paragraph 4 of Schedule 5.

(2) Also, the [First-tier Tribunal] may, on application, make any order which the High Court could make for the rectification or setting aside of a document which—

(a) effects a qualifying disposition of a registered estate or charge,

(b) is a contract to make such a disposition, or

(c) effects a transfer of an interest which is the subject of a notice in the register.

(3) For the purposes of subsection (2)(a), a qualifying disposition is—

(a) a registrable disposition, or

(b) a disposition which creates an interest which may be the subject of a notice in the register.

(4) The general law about the effect of an order of the High Court for the rectification or setting aside of a document shall apply to an order under this section.

[(5) The Lord Chancellor may require the registrar to make payments towards expenses of the Lord Chancellor in support of the functions conferred on the First-tier Tribunal by this section.]

NOTES

Initial Commencement

To be appointed

To be appointed: see s 136(2).

Appointment

Appointment: 13 October 2003: see SI 2003/1725, art 2(1).

Extent

This section does not extend to Scotland: see s 136(3).

Amendment

Sub-s (1): words "First-tier Tribunal" in square brackets substituted by SI 2013/1036, art 6(1), Sch 1, Pt 3, paras 225, 228(a).

Date in force: 1 July 2013: see SI 2013/1036, art 1; for transitional provisions see art 6(3), Sch 3, paras 1–8 thereto.

Sub-s (1): in para (a) word "it" in square brackets substituted by SI 2013/1036, art 6(1), Sch 1, Pt 3, paras 225, 228(b).

Date in force: 1 July 2013: see SI 2013/1036, art 1; for transitional provisions see art 6(3), Sch 3, paras 1–8 thereto.

Sub-s (2): words "First-tier Tribunal" in square brackets substituted by SI 2013/1036, art 6(1), Sch 1, Pt 3, paras 225, 228(c).

Date in force: 1 July 2013: see SI 2013/1036, art 1; for transitional provisions see art 6(3), Sch 3, paras 1–8 thereto.

Sub-s (5): inserted by SI 2013/1036, art 6(1), Sch 1, Pt 3, paras 225, 228(d).

Date in force: 1 July 2013: see SI 2013/1036, art 1; for transitional provisions see art 6(3), Sch 3, paras 1–8 thereto.

109 . . .

. . .

NOTES

Amendment

Repealed by SI 2013/1036, art 6(1), Sch 1, Pt 3, paras 225, 229.

Date in force: 1 July 2013: see SI 2013/1036, art 1; for savings see art 6(3), Sch 3, paras 1–8 thereto.

110 Functions in relation to disputes

(1) In proceedings on a reference under section 73(7), the [First-tier Tribunal] may, instead of deciding a matter . . ., direct a party to the proceedings to commence proceedings within a specified time in the court for the purpose of obtaining the court's decision on the matter.

(2) [Tribunal Procedure Rules] may make provision about the reference under subsection (1) of matters to the court and may, in particular, make provision about—

(a) adjournment of the proceedings before the [First-tier Tribunal] pending the outcome of the proceedings before the court, and

(b) the powers of the [First-tier Tribunal] in the event of failure to comply with a direction under subsection (1).

(3) [Tribunal Procedure Rules] may make provision about the functions of the [First-tier Tribunal] in consequence of a decision on a reference under section 73(7) and may, in particular, make provision enabling the [First-tier Tribunal] to determine, or give directions about the determination of—

(a) the application to which the reference relates, or

(b) such other present or future application to the registrar as [Tribunal Procedure Rules] may provide.

(4) If, in the case of a reference under section 73(7) relating to an application under paragraph 1 of Schedule 6, the [First-tier Tribunal] determines that it would be unconscionable because of an equity by estoppel for the registered proprietor to seek to dispossess the applicant, but that the circumstances are not such that the applicant ought to be registered as proprietor, the [First-tier Tribunal]—

(a) must determine how the equity due to the applicant is to be satisfied, and

(b) may for that purpose make any order that the High Court could make in the exercise of its equitable jurisdiction.

NOTES

Initial Commencement

To be appointed

To be appointed: see s 136(2).

Appointment

Appointment: 13 October 2003: see SI 2003/1725, art 2(1).

Extent

This section does not extend to Scotland: see s 136(3).

Amendment

Sub-s (1): words "First-tier Tribunal" in square brackets substituted by SI 2013/1036, art 6(1), Sch 1, Pt 3, paras 225, 230(a).
Date in force: 1 July 2013: see SI 2013/1036, art 1; for transitional provisions see art 6(3), Sch 3, paras 1–8 thereto.
Sub-s (1): word omitted repealed by SI 2013/1036, art 6(1), Sch 1, Pt 3, paras 225, 230(a).
Date in force: 1 July 2013: see SI 2013/1036, art 1; for savings see art 6(3), Sch 3, paras 1–8 thereto.
Sub-s (2): words "Tribunal Procedure Rules" in square brackets substituted by SI 2013/1036, art 6(1), Sch 1, Pt 3, paras 225, 230(b)(i).
Date in force: 1 July 2013: see SI 2013/1036, art 1; for transitional provisions see art 6(3), Sch 3, paras 1–8 thereto.
Sub-s (2): in paras (a), (b) words "First-tier Tribunal" in square brackets substituted by SI 2013/1036, art 6(1), Sch 1, Pt 3, paras 225, 230(b)(ii).
Date in force: 1 July 2013: see SI 2013/1036, art 1; for transitional provisions see art 6(3), Sch 3, paras 1–8 thereto.
Sub-s (3): words "Tribunal Procedure Rules" in square brackets substituted by SI 2013/1036, art 6(1), Sch 1, Pt 3, paras 225, 230(c)(i).
Date in force: 1 July 2013: see SI 2013/1036, art 1; for transitional provisions see art 6(3), Sch 3, paras 1–8 thereto.
Sub-s (3): words "First-tier Tribunal" in square brackets in both places they occur substituted by SI 2013/1036, art 6(1), Sch 1, Pt 3, paras 225, 230(c)(ii).
Date in force: 1 July 2013: see SI 2013/1036, art 1; for transitional provisions see art 6(3), Sch 3, paras 1–8 thereto.
Sub-s (3): in para (b) words "Tribunal Procedure Rules" in square brackets substituted by SI 2013/1036, art 6(1), Sch 1, Pt 3, paras 225, 230(c)(iii).
Date in force: 1 July 2013: see SI 2013/1036, art 1; for transitional provisions see art 6(3), Sch 3, paras 1–8 thereto.
Sub-s (4): words "First-tier Tribunal" in square brackets in both places they occur substituted by SI 2013/1036, art 6(1), Sch 1, Pt 3, paras 225, 230(d).
Date in force: 1 July 2013: see SI 2013/1036, art 1; for transitional provisions see art 6(3), Sch 3, paras 1–8 thereto.

Subordinate Legislation

Tribunal Procedure (First-tier Tribunal) (Property Chamber) Rules 2013, SI 2013/1169.

111 Appeals

[(1) Subject to this section, a person aggrieved by a decision of the First-tier Tribunal under this Act may appeal to the Upper Tribunal.

(2) An appeal may not be brought under subsection (1) on a point of law (as to which see instead section 11 of the Tribunals, Courts and Enforcement Act 2007 (right of appeal to Upper Tribunal)).

(2A) An appeal may not be brought under subsection (1) in the case of a decision under paragraph 4 of Schedule 5 (but this does not prevent an appeal on a point of law under section 11 of the Tribunals, Courts and Enforcement Act 2007).

(2B) An appeal may not be brought under subsection (1) if the decision is set aside under section 9 of the Tribunals, Courts and Enforcement Act 2007 (review of decision of First-tier Tribunal).

(2C) An appeal may be brought under subsection (1) only if, on an application made by the person concerned, the First-tier Tribunal or Upper Tribunal has given its permission for the appeal to be brought.]

(3) If on an appeal under this section [or under section 11 of the Tribunals, Courts and Enforcement Act 2007] relating to an application under paragraph 1 of Schedule 6 the [Upper Tribunal] determines that it would be unconscionable because of an equity by estoppel for the registered proprietor to seek to dispossess the applicant, but that the circumstances are not such that the applicant ought to be registered as proprietor, the [Upper Tribunal] must determine how the equity due to the applicant is to be satisfied.

[(4) In any case where the Upper Tribunal is determining an appeal under subsection (1), section 12(2) to (4) of the Tribunals, Courts and Enforcement Act 2007 (proceedings on appeal to the Upper Tribunal) apply.]

NOTES

Initial Commencement

To be appointed

To be appointed: see s 136(2).

Appointment

Appointment: 13 October 2003: see SI 2003/1725, art 2(1).

Extent

This section does not extend to Scotland: see s 136(3).

Amendment

Sub-ss (1), (2), (2A)–(2C): substituted, for sub-ss (1), (2) as originally enacted, by SI 2013/1036, art 6(1), Sch 1, Pt 3, paras 225, 231(a).

Date in force: 1 July 2013: see SI 2013/1036, art 1; for transitional provisions see art 6(3), Sch 3, paras 1–8 thereto.

Sub-s (3): words "or under section 11 of the Tribunals, Courts and Enforcement Act 2007" in square brackets inserted by SI 2013/1036, art 6(1), Sch 1, Pt 3, paras 225, 231(b)(i).

Date in force: 1 July 2013: see SI 2013/1036, art 1; for transitional provisions see art 6(3), Sch 3, paras 1–8 thereto.

Sub-s (3): words "Upper Tribunal" in square brackets in both places they occur substituted by SI 2013/1036, art 6(1), Sch 1, Pt 3, paras 225, 231(b)(ii).

Date in force: 1 July 2013: see SI 2013/1036, art 1; for transitional provisions see art 6(3), Sch 3, paras 1–8 thereto.

Sub-s (4): inserted by SI 2013/1036, art 6(1), Sch 1, Pt 3, paras 225, 231(c).

Date in force: 1 July 2013: see SI 2013/1036, art 1; for transitional provisions see art 6(3), Sch 3, paras 1–8 thereto.

112 Enforcement of orders etc

A requirement of the [First-tier Tribunal] shall be enforceable as an order of the court.

NOTES

Initial Commencement

To be appointed

To be appointed: see s 136(2).

Appointment

Appointment: 13 October 2003: see SI 2003/1725, art 2(1).

Extent

This section does not extend to Scotland: see s 136(3).

Amendment

Words "First-tier Tribunal" in square brackets substituted by SI 2013/1036, art 6(1), Sch 1, Pt 3, paras 225, 232.

Date in force: 1 July 2013: see SI 2013/1036, art 1; for transitional provisions see art 6(3), Sch 3, paras 1–8 thereto.

113 . . .

. . .

NOTES

Amendment

Repealed by SI 2013/1036, art 6(1), Sch 1, Pt 3, paras 225, 233.

Date in force: 1 July 2013: see SI 2013/1036, art 1; for savings see art 6(3), Sch 3, paras 1–8 thereto.

114 . . .

. . .

NOTES

Amendment

Repealed by SI 2013/1036, art 6(1), Sch 1, Pt 3, paras 225, 234.
Date in force: 1 July 2013: see SI 2013/1036, art 1; for savings see art 6(3), Sch 3, paras 1–8 thereto.

Appendix 2

TRIBUNALS, COURTS AND ENFORCEMENT ACT 2007

2007 CHAPTER 15

PART 1
TRIBUNALS AND INQUIRIES

CHAPTER 2

FIRST-TIER TRIBUNAL AND UPPER TRIBUNAL
Review of decisions and appeals

9 Review of decision of First-tier Tribunal

(1) The First-tier Tribunal may review a decision made by it on a matter in a case, other than a decision that is an excluded decision for the purposes of section 11(1) (but see subsection (9)).

(2) The First-tier Tribunal's power under subsection (1) in relation to a decision is exercisable—

(a) of its own initiative, or

(b) on application by a person who for the purposes of section 11(2) has a right of appeal in respect of the decision.

(4) Where the First-tier Tribunal has under subsection (1) reviewed a decision, the First-tier Tribunal may in the light of the review do any of the following—

(a) correct accidental errors in the decision or in a record of the decision;

(b) amend reasons given for the decision;

(c) set the decision aside.

(5) Where under subsection (4)(c) the First-tier Tribunal sets a decision aside, the First-tier Tribunal must either—

(a) re-decide the matter concerned, or

(b) refer that matter to the Upper Tribunal.

(6) Where a matter is referred to the Upper Tribunal under subsection (5)(b), the Upper Tribunal must re-decide the matter.

(7) Where the Upper Tribunal is under subsection (6) re-deciding a matter, it may make any decision which the First-tier Tribunal could make if the First-tier Tribunal were re-deciding the matter.

(8) Where a tribunal is acting under subsection (5)(a) or (6), it may make such findings of fact as it considers appropriate.

(9) This section has effect as if a decision under subsection (4)(c) to set aside an earlier decision were not an excluded decision for the purposes of section 11(1), but the First-tier Tribunal's only power in the light of a review under subsection (1) of a decision under subsection (4)(c) is the power under subsection (4)(a).

(10) A decision of the First-tier Tribunal may not be reviewed under subsection (1) more than once, and once the First-tier Tribunal has decided that an earlier decision should not be reviewed under subsection (1) it may not then decide to review that earlier decision under that subsection.

NOTES

Initial Commencement

To be appointed

To be appointed: see s 148(5).

Appointment

Sub-ss (1), (2), (4)–(11): Appointment: 3 November 2008: see SI 2008/2696, art 5(a).

11 Right to appeal to Upper Tribunal

(1) For the purposes of subsection (2), the reference to a right of appeal is to a right to appeal to the Upper Tribunal on any point of law arising from a decision made by the First-tier Tribunal other than an excluded decision.

(2) Any party to a case has a right of appeal, subject to subsection (8).

(3) That right may be exercised only with permission (or, in Northern Ireland, leave).

(4) Permission (or leave) may be given by—

(a) the First-tier Tribunal, or

(b) the Upper Tribunal,

on an application by the party.

(5) For the purposes of subsection (1), an "excluded decision" is—

(d) a decision of the First-tier Tribunal under section 9—

(i) to review, or not to review, an earlier decision of the tribunal,

(ii) to take no action, or not to take any particular action, in the light of a review of an earlier decision of the tribunal,

(iii) to set aside an earlier decision of the tribunal, or

(iv) to refer, or not to refer, a matter to the Upper Tribunal,

(e) a decision of the First-tier Tribunal that is set aside under section 9 (including a decision set aside after proceedings on an appeal under this section have been begun), or

NOTES

Initial Commencement

To be appointed

To be appointed: see s 148(5).

Appointment

Sub-ss (1)–(4), (5)(a)–(e): Appointment: 3 November 2008: see SI 2008/2696, art 5(a).

Amendment

Sub-s (5): para (aa) inserted by the Crime and Security Act 2010, s 48(4), Sch 2, para 5.
Date in force: 8 April 2010: see the Crime and Security Act 2010, s 59(2)(b).

12 Proceedings on appeal to Upper Tribunal

(1) Subsection (2) applies if the Upper Tribunal, in deciding an appeal under section 11, finds that the making of the decision concerned involved the making of an error on a point of law.

(2) The Upper Tribunal—

(a) may (but need not) set aside the decision of the First-tier Tribunal, and

(b) if it does, must either—

(i) remit the case to the First-tier Tribunal with directions for its reconsideration, or

(ii) re-make the decision.

(3) In acting under subsection (2)(b)(i), the Upper Tribunal may also—

(a) direct that the members of the First-tier Tribunal who are chosen to reconsider the case are not to be the same as those who made the decision that has been set aside;

(b) give procedural directions in connection with the reconsideration of the case by the First-tier Tribunal.

(4) In acting under subsection (2)(b)(ii), the Upper Tribunal—

(a) may make any decision which the First-tier Tribunal could make if the First-tier Tribunal were re-making the decision, and

(b) may make such findings of fact as it considers appropriate.

NOTES

Initial Commencement

To be appointed

To be appointed: see s 148(5).

Appointment

Appointment: 3 November 2008: see SI 2008/2696, art 5(a).

13 Right to appeal to Court of Appeal etc

(1) For the purposes of subsection (2), the reference to a right of appeal is to a right to appeal to the relevant appellate court on any point of law arising from a decision made by the Upper Tribunal other than an excluded decision.

(2) Any party to a case has a right of appeal, subject to subsection (14).

(3) That right may be exercised only with permission (or, in Northern Ireland, leave).

(4) Permission (or leave) may be given by—

(a) the Upper Tribunal, or

(b) the relevant appellate court,

on an application by the party.

(5) An application may be made under subsection (4) to the relevant appellate court only if permission (or leave) has been refused by the Upper Tribunal.

(8) For the purposes of subsection (1), an "excluded decision" is—

(c) any decision of the Upper Tribunal on an application under section 11(4)(b) (application for permission or leave to appeal),

(d) a decision of the Upper Tribunal under section 10—

(i) to review, or not to review, an earlier decision of the tribunal,

(ii) to take no action, or not to take any particular action, in the light of a review of an earlier decision of the tribunal, or

(iii) to set aside an earlier decision of the tribunal,

(e) a decision of the Upper Tribunal that is set aside under section 10 (including a decision set aside after proceedings on an appeal under this section have been begun), or

NOTES

Initial Commencement

To be appointed

To be appointed: see s 148(5).

Appointment

Sub-ss (1)–(5), (7), (8)(a)–(e), (11)–(13): Appointment: 3 November 2008: see SI 2008/2696, art 5(a).

Appendix 3

CIVIL PROCEDURE RULES 1998

SI 1998 No 3132

[PART 54
[JUDICIAL REVIEW AND STATUTORY REVIEW]]

[Contents of this Part]

II . . .

[III . . .]]

NOTES

Amendment

Substituted (for Contents as inserted by SI 2000/2092, r 22, Schedule, Pt 54) by SI 2003/364, r 4, Schedule, Pt 1.

Date in force: 1 April 2003 (being the date on which the Nationality, Immigration and Asylum Act 2002, ss 81–117 came into force): see SI 2003/364, r 1 and SI 2003/754, art 2(1), Sch 1; for transitional provisions see SI 2003/754, art 3, and Sch 2, para 1(4A), (4B) (as amended by SI 2003/1339, art 4) and (5).

Entry relating to Section I: words from "Who may exercise" to "Rule 54.1A" in square brackets inserted by SI 2012/2208, rr 2, 9(a)(i).

Date in force: 1 October 2012: see SI 2012/2208, r 1.

Entry relating to Section I: words from "Judicial review of" to "Rule 54.7A" in square brackets inserted by SI 2012/2208, rr 2, 9(a)(ii).

Date in force: 1 October 2012: see SI 2012/2208, r 1.

Entries relating to Section II: revoked by SI 2007/3543, r 7(a).

Date in force: 6 April 2008: see SI 2007/3543, r 1(b).

Entries relating to Section III: inserted by SI 2005/352, r 3, Schedule, Pt I.

Date in force: 4 April 2005: see SI 2005/352, r 1; for transitional provisions see r 9 thereof.

Entries relating to Section III: revoked by SI 2009/3390, r 29(a)(i), (ii).

Date in force: 15 February 2010: see SI 2009/3390, r 1(4).

[SECTION I—JUDICIAL REVIEW]

NOTES

Amendment

Section heading: inserted by SI 2003/364, r 4, Schedule, Pt 1.

Date in force: 1 April 2003 (being the date on which the Nationality, Immigration and Asylum Act 2002, ss 81–117 came into force): see SI 2003/364, r 1 and SI 2003/754, art 2(1), Sch 1; for transitional provisions see SI 2003/754, art 3, and Sch 2, para 1(4A), (4B) (as amended by SI 2003/1339, art 4) and (5).

[Rule 54.1 Scope and interpretation]

[(1) [This Section of this Part] contains rules about judicial review.

(2) [In this Section]—

(a) a "claim for judicial review" means a claim to review the lawfulness of—

(i) an enactment; or

(ii) a decision, action or failure to act in relation to the exercise of a public function.

(b) . . .

(c) . . .

(d) . . .

(e) "the judicial review procedure" means the Part 8 procedure as modified by [this Section];

(f) "interested party" means any person (other than the claimant and defendant) who is directly affected by the claim; and

(g) "court" means the High Court, unless otherwise stated.

(Rule 8.1(6)(b) provides that a rule or practice direction may, in relation to a specified type of proceedings, disapply or modify any of the rules set out in Part 8 as they apply to those proceedings)]

NOTES

Amendment

Inserted by SI 2000/2092, r 22, Schedule.

Date in force: 2 October 2000: see SI 2000/2092, r 1.

Para (1): words "This section of this part" in square brackets substituted by SI 2003/364, r 5(a).

Date in force: 1 April 2003 (being the date on which the Nationality, Immigration and Asylum Act 2002, ss 81–117 came into force): see SI 2003/364, r 1 and SI 2003/754, art 2(1), Sch 1; for transitional provisions see SI 2003/754, art 3, and Sch 2, para 1(4A), (4B) (as amended by SI 2003/1339, art 4) and (5).

Para (2): words "In this Section" in square brackets substituted by SI 2003/364, r 5(b)(i).

Date in force: 1 April 2003 (being the date on which the Nationality, Immigration and Asylum Act 2002, ss 81–117 came into force): see SI 2003/364, r 1 and SI 2003/754, art 2(1), Sch 1; for transitional provisions see SI 2003/754, art 3, and Sch 2, para 1(4A), (4B) (as amended by SI 2003/1339, art 4) and (5).

Para (2): sub-paras (b)–(d) revoked by SI 2003/3361, r 12.

Date in force: 1 May 2004: see SI 2003/3361, r 1(d).

Para (2): in sub-para (e) words "this Section" in square brackets substituted by SI 2003/364, r 5(b)(ii).

Date in force: 1 April 2003 (being the date on which the Nationality, Immigration and Asylum Act 2002, ss 81–117 came into force): see SI 2003/364, r 1 and SI 2003/754, art 2(1), Sch 1; for transitional provisions see SI 2003/754, art 3, and Sch 2, para 1(4A), (4B) (as amended by SI 2003/1339, art 4) and (5).

[Rule 54.1A Who may exercise the powers of the High Court]

[(1) A court officer assigned to the Administrative Court office who is—

(a) a barrister; or

(b) a solicitor,

may exercise the jurisdiction of the High Court with regard to the matters set out in paragraph (2) with the consent of the President of the Queen's Bench Division.

(2) The matters referred to in paragraph (1) are—

(a) any matter incidental to any proceedings in the High Court;

(b) any other matter where there is no substantial dispute between the parties; and

(c) the dismissal of an appeal or application where a party has failed to comply with any order, rule or practice direction.

(3) A court officer may not decide an application for—

(a) permission to bring judicial review proceedings;

(b) an injunction;

(c) a stay of any proceedings, other than a temporary stay of any order or decision of the lower court over a period when the High Court is not sitting or cannot conveniently be convened, unless the parties seek a stay by consent.

(4) Decisions of a court officer may be made without a hearing.

(5) A party may request any decision of a court officer to be reviewed by a judge of the High Court.

(6) At the request of a party, a hearing will be held to reconsider a decision of a court officer, made without a hearing.

(7) A request under paragraph (5) or (6) must be filed within 7 days after the party is served with notice of the decision.]

NOTES

Amendment

Inserted by SI 2012/2208, rr 2, 9(b).

Date in force: 1 October 2012: see SI 2012/2208, r 1.

[Rule 54.2 When this [Section] must be used]

[The judicial review procedure must be used in a claim for judicial review where the claimant is seeking—

(a) a mandatory order;

(b) a prohibiting order;

(c) a quashing order; or

(d) an injunction under section 30 of the [Senior Courts Act 1981] (restraining a person from acting in any office in which he is not entitled to act).]

NOTES

Amendment

Inserted by SI 2000/2092, r 22, Schedule.
Date in force: 2 October 2000: see SI 2000/2092, r 1.
Provision heading: word "Section" in square brackets substituted by SI 2003/364, r 5(c).
Date in force: 1 April 2003 (being the date on which the Nationality, Immigration and Asylum Act 2002, ss 81–117 came into force): see SI 2003/364, r 1 and SI 2003/754, art 2(1), Sch 1; for transitional provisions see SI 2003/754, art 3, and Sch 2, para 1(4A), (4B) (as amended by SI 2003/1339, art 4) and (5).
In para (d) words "Senior Courts Act 1981" in square brackets substituted by the Constitutional Reform Act 2005, s 59(5), Sch 11, Pt 1, para 1(2).
Date in force: 1 October 2009: see SI 2009/1604, art 2(d).

[Rule 54.3 When this [Section] may be used]

[(1) The judicial review procedure may be used in a claim for judicial review where the claimant is seeking—

(a) a declaration; or

(b) an injunction(GL).

(Section 31(2) of the [Senior Courts Act 1981] sets out the circumstances in which the court may grant a declaration or injunction in a claim for judicial review)

(Where the claimant is seeking a declaration or injunction in addition to one of the remedies listed in rule 54.2, the judicial review procedure must be used)

(2) A claim for judicial review may include a claim for damages[, restitution or the recovery of a sum due] but may not seek [such a remedy] alone.

(Section 31(4) of the [Senior Courts Act 1981] sets out the circumstances in which the court may award damages[, restitution or the recovery of a sum due] on a claim for judicial review)]

NOTES

Amendment

Inserted by SI 2000/2092, r 22, Schedule.
Date in force: 2 October 2000: see SI 2000/2092, r 1.
Provision heading: word "Section" in square brackets substituted by SI 2003/364, r 5(c).
Date in force: 1 April 2003 (being the date on which the Nationality, Immigration and Asylum Act 2002, ss 81–117 came into force): see SI 2003/364, r 1 and SI 2003/754, art 2(1), Sch 1; for transitional provisions see SI 2003/754, art 3, and Sch 2, para 1(4A), (4B) (as amended by SI 2003/1339, art 4) and (5).
Para (1): words "Senior Courts Act 1981" in square brackets substituted by the Constitutional Reform Act 2005, s 59(5), Sch 11, Pt 1, para 1(2).
Date in force: 1 October 2009: see SI 2009/1604, art 2(d).
Para (2): words ", restitution or the recovery of a sum due" in square brackets in both places they occur inserted by SI 2003/3361, r 13(a)(i), (b).
Date in force: 1 May 2004: see SI 2003/3361, rule 1(d).
Para (2): words "such a remedy" in square brackets substituted by SI 2003/3361, r 13(b).
Date in force: 1 May 2004: see SI 2003/3361, rule 1(d).
Para (2): words "Senior Courts Act 1981" in square brackets substituted by the Constitutional Reform Act 2005, s 59(5), Sch 11, Pt 1, para 1(2).
Date in force: 1 October 2009: see SI 2009/1604, art 2(d).

[Rule 54.4 Permission required]

[The court's permission to proceed is required in a claim for judicial review whether started under this [Section] or transferred to the Administrative Court.]

NOTES

Amendment

Inserted by SI 2000/2092, r 22, Schedule.
Date in force: 2 October 2000: see SI 2000/2092, r 1.

Word "Section" in square brackets substituted by SI 2003/364, r 5(d).

Date in force: 1 April 2003 (being the date on which the Nationality, Immigration and Asylum Act 2002, ss 81–117 came into force): see SI 2003/364, r 1 and SI 2003/754, art 2(1), Sch 1; for transitional provisions see SI 2003/754, art 3, and Sch 2, para 1(4A), (4B) (as amended by SI 2003/1339, art 4) and (5).

[Rule 54.5 Time limit for filing claim form]

[[(A1) In this rule—

"the planning acts" has the same meaning as in section 336 of the Town and Country Planning Act 1990;

"decision governed by the Public Contracts Regulations 2006" means any decision the legality of which is or may be affected by a duty owed to an economic operator by virtue of regulation 47A of those Regulations (and for this purpose it does not matter that the claimant is not an economic operator); and

"economic operator" has the same meaning as in regulation 4 of the Public Contracts Regulations 2006.]

(1) The claim form must be filed—

(a) promptly; and

(b) in any event not later than 3 months after the grounds to make the claim first arose.

(2) The time [limits] in this rule may not be extended by agreement between the parties.

(3) This rule does not apply when any other enactment specifies a shorter time limit for making the claim for judicial review.

[(4) Paragraph (1) does not apply in the cases specified in paragraphs (5) and (6).

(5) Where the application for judicial review relates to a decision made by the Secretary of State or local planning authority under the planning acts, the claim form must be filed not later than six weeks after the grounds to make the claim first arose.

(6) Where the application for judicial review relates to a decision governed by the Public Contracts Regulations 2006, the claim form must be filed within the time within which an economic operator would have been required by regulation 47D(2) of those Regulations (and disregarding the rest of that regulation) to start any proceedings under those Regulations in respect of that decision.]]

NOTES

Amendment

Inserted by SI 2000/2092, r 22, Schedule.

Date in force: 2 October 2000: see SI 2000/2092, r 1.

Para (A1): inserted by SI 2013/1412, r 4(a)(i).

Date in force: 1 July 2013: see SI 2013/1412, r 1; for transitional provision see r 5(2) thereof.

Para (2): word "limits" in square brackets substituted by SI 2013/1412, r 4(a)(ii).

Date in force: 1 July 2013: see SI 2013/1412, r 1; for transitional provision see r 5(2) thereof.

Paras (4)–(6): inserted by SI 2013/1412, r 4(a)(iii).

Date in force: 1 July 2013: see SI 2013/1412, r 1; for transitional provision see r 5(2) thereof.

[Rule 54.6 Claim form]

[(1) In addition to the matters set out in rule 8.2 (contents of the claim form) the claimant must also state—

(a) the name and address of any person he considers to be an interested party;

(b) that he is requesting permission to proceed with a claim for judicial review; . . .

(c) any remedy (including any interim remedy) he is claiming[; and

(d) where appropriate, the grounds on which it is contended that the claim is an Aarhus Convention claim].

[(Rules 45.41 to 45.44 make provision about costs in Aarhus Convention claims.)]

(Part 25 sets out how to apply for an interim remedy)

(2) The claim form must be accompanied by the documents required by [Practice Direction 54A].]

NOTES

Amendment

Inserted by SI 2000/2092, r 22, Schedule.
Date in force: 2 October 2000: see SI 2000/2092, r 1.
Para (1): in sub-para (b) word omitted revoked by SI 2013/262, r 18(a).
Date in force: 1 April 2013: see SI 2013/262, r 2; for transitional provisions see r 22(8) thereof.
Para (1): sub-para (d) and word "; and" immediately preceding it inserted by virtue of SI 2013/262, r 18(b), (c).
Date in force: 1 April 2013: see SI 2013/262, r 2; for transitional provisions see r 22(8) thereof.
Para (1): words "(Rules 45.41 to 45.44 make provision about costs in Aarhus Convention claims.)" in square brackets inserted by SI 2013/262, r 18(c).
Date in force: 1 April 2013: see SI 2013/262, r 2; for transitional provisions see r 22(8) thereof.
Para (2): words "Practice Direction 54A" in square brackets substituted by SI 2009/3390, r 29(b).
Date in force: 6 April 2010: see SI 2009/3390, r 1(2).

[Rule 54.7 Service of claim form]

[The claim form must be served on—

(a) the defendant; and
(b) unless the court otherwise directs, any person the claimant considers to be an interested party,

within 7 days after the date of issue.]

NOTES

Amendment

Inserted by SI 2000/2092, r 22, Schedule.
Date in force: 2 October 2000: see SI 2000/2092, r 1.

[Rule 54.7A Judicial review of decisions of the Upper Tribunal]

[(1) This rule applies where an application is made, following refusal by the Upper Tribunal of permission to appeal against a decision of the First Tier Tribunal, for judicial review—

(a) of the decision of the Upper Tribunal refusing permission to appeal; or
(b) which relates to the decision of the First Tier Tribunal which was the subject of the application for permission to appeal.

(2) Where this rule applies—

(a) the application may not include any other claim, whether against the Upper Tribunal or not; and
(b) any such other claim must be the subject of a separate application.

(3) The claim form and the supporting documents required by paragraph (4) must be filed no later than 16 days after the date on which notice of the Upper Tribunal's decision was sent to the applicant.

(4) The supporting documents are—

(a) the decision of the Upper Tribunal to which the application relates, and any document giving reasons for the decision;
(b) the grounds of appeal to the Upper Tribunal and any documents which were sent with them;
(c) the decision of the First Tier Tribunal, the application to that Tribunal for permission to appeal and its reasons for refusing permission; and
(d) any other documents essential to the claim.

(5) The claim form and supporting documents must be served on the Upper Tribunal and any other interested party no later than 7 days after the date of issue.

(6) The Upper Tribunal and any person served with the claim form who wishes to take part in the proceedings for judicial review must, no later than 21 days after service of the claim form, file and serve on the applicant and any other party an acknowledgment of service in the relevant practice form.

(7) The court will give permission to proceed only if it considers—

- (a) that there is an arguable case, which has a reasonable prospect of success, that both the decision of the Upper Tribunal refusing permission to appeal and the decision of the First Tier Tribunal against which permission to appeal was sought are wrong in law; and
- (b) that either—
  - (i) the claim raises an important point of principle or practice; or
  - (ii) there is some other compelling reason to hear it.

(8) If the application for permission is refused on paper without an oral hearing, rule 54.12(3) (request for reconsideration at a hearing) does not apply.

(9) If permission to apply for judicial review is granted—

- (a) if the Upper Tribunal or any interested party wishes there to be a hearing of the substantive application, it must make its request for such a hearing no later than 14 days after service of the order granting permission; and
- (b) if no request for a hearing is made within that period, the court will make a final order quashing the refusal of permission without a further hearing.

(10) The power to make a final order under paragraph (9)(b) may be exercised by the Master of the Crown Office or a Master of the Administrative Court.]

NOTES

Amendment

Inserted by SI 2012/2208, rr 2, 9(c).
Date in force: 1 October 2012: see SI 2012/2208, r 1.

[Rule 54.8 Acknowledgement of service]

[(1) Any person served with the claim form who wishes to take part in the judicial review must file an acknowledgement of service in the relevant practice form in accordance with the following provisions of this rule.

(2) Any acknowledgement of service must be—

- (a) filed not more than 21 days after service of the claim form; and
- (b) served on—
  - (i) the claimant; and
  - (ii) subject to any direction under rule 54.7(b), any other person named in the claim form,

as soon as practicable and, in any event, not later than 7 days after it is filed.

(3) The time limits under this rule may not be extended by agreement between the parties.

(4) The acknowledgement of service—

- (a) must—
  - (i) where the person filing it intends to contest the claim, set out a summary of his grounds for doing so; and
  - (ii) state the name and address of any person the person filing it considers to be an interested party; and
- (b) may include or be accompanied by an application for directions.

(5) Rule 10.3(2) does not apply.]

NOTES

Amendment

Inserted by SI 2000/2092, r 22, Schedule.
Date in force: 2 October 2000: see SI 2000/2092, r 1.

[Rule 54.9 Failure to file acknowledgement of service]

[(1) Where a person served with the claim form has failed to file an acknowledgement of service in accordance with rule 54.8, he—

(a) may not take part in a hearing to decide whether permission should be given unless the court allows him to do so; but

(b) provided he complies with rule 54.14 or any other direction of the court regarding the filing and service of—

(i) detailed grounds for contesting the claim or supporting it on additional grounds; and

(ii) any written evidence,

may take part in the hearing of the judicial review.

(2) Where that person takes part in the hearing of the judicial review, the court may take his failure to file an acknowledgement of service into account when deciding what order to make about costs.

(3) Rule 8.4 does not apply.]

NOTES

Amendment

Inserted by SI 2000/2092, r 22, Schedule.
Date in force: 2 October 2000: see SI 2000/2092, r 1.

[Rule 54.10 Permission given]

[(1) Where permission to proceed is given the court may also give directions.]

[(2) Directions under paragraph (1) may include—

(a) a stay (GL) of proceedings to which the claim relates;

(b) directions requiring the proceedings to be heard by a Divisional Court.]

NOTES

Amendment

Inserted by SI 2000/2092, r 22, Schedule.
Date in force: 2 October 2000: see SI 2000/2092, r 1.
Para (2): substituted by SI 2010/2577, r 3.
Date in force: 20 October 2010: see SI 2010/2577, r 1(2).

[Rule 54.11 Service of order giving or refusing permission]

[The court will serve—

(a) the order giving or refusing permission; and

(b) any directions,

on—

(i) the claimant;

(ii) the defendant; and

(iii) any other person who filed an acknowledgement of service.]

NOTES

Amendment

Inserted by SI 2000/2092, r 22, Schedule.
Date in force: 2 October 2000: see SI 2000/2092, r 1.

[Rule 54.12 Permission decision without a hearing]

[(1) This rule applies where the court, without a hearing—

(a) refuses permission to proceed; or

(b) gives permission to proceed—
    (i) subject to conditions; or
    (ii) on certain grounds only.

(2) The court will serve its reasons for making the decision when it serves the order giving or refusing permission in accordance with rule 54.11.

(3) [Subject to paragraph (7), the] claimant may not appeal but may request the decision to be reconsidered at a hearing.

(4) A request under paragraph (3) must be filed within 7 days after service of the reasons under paragraph (2).

(5) The claimant, defendant and any other person who has filed an acknowledgement of service will be given at least 2 days' notice of the hearing date.

[(6) The court may give directions requiring the proceedings to be heard by a Divisional Court.]

[(7) Where the court refuses permission to proceed and records the fact that the application is totally without merit in accordance with rule 23.12, the claimant may not request that decision to be reconsidered at a hearing.]]

NOTES

Amendment

Inserted by SI 2000/2092, r 22, Schedule.
Date in force: 2 October 2000: see SI 2000/2092, r 1.
Para (3): words "Subject to paragraph (7), the" in square brackets substituted by SI 2013/1412, r 4(b)(i).
Date in force: 1 July 2013: see SI 2013/1412, r 1; for transitional provision see r 5(1) thereof.
Para (6): inserted by SI 2010/2577, r 4.
Date in force: 20 October 2010: see SI 2010/2577, r 1(2).
Para (7): inserted by SI 2013/1412, r 4(b)(ii).
Date in force: 1 July 2013: see SI 2013/1412, r 1; for transitional provision see r 5(1) thereof.

[Rule 54.13 Defendant etc may not apply to set aside(GL)]

[Neither the defendant nor any other person served with the claim form may apply to set aside(GL) an order giving permission to proceed.]

NOTES

Amendment

Inserted by SI 2000/2092, r 22, Schedule.
Date in force: 2 October 2000: see SI 2000/2092, r 1.

[Rule 54.14 Response]

[(1) A defendant and any other person served with the claim form who wishes to contest the claim or support it on additional grounds must file and serve—
    (a) detailed grounds for contesting the claim or supporting it on additional grounds; and
    (b) any written evidence,
within 35 days after service of the order giving permission.

(2) The following rules do not apply—
    (a) rule 8.5(3) and 8.5(4) (defendant to file and serve written evidence at the same time as acknowledgement of service); and
    (b) rule 8.5(5) and 8.5(6) (claimant to file and serve any reply within 14 days).]

NOTES

Amendment

Inserted by SI 2000/2092, r 22, Schedule.
Date in force: 2 October 2000: see SI 2000/2092, r 1.

[Rule 54.15 Where claimant seeks to rely on additional grounds]

[The court's permission is required if a claimant seeks to rely on grounds other than those for which he has been given permission to proceed.]

NOTES

Amendment

Inserted by SI 2000/2092, r 22, Schedule.
Date in force: 2 October 2000: see SI 2000/2092, r 1.

[Rule 54.16 Evidence]

[(1) Rule 8.6[(1)] does not apply.

(2) No written evidence may be relied on unless—

(a) it has been served in accordance with any—

(i) rule under this [Section]; or

(ii) direction of the court; or

(b) the court gives permission.]

NOTES

Amendment

Inserted by SI 2000/2092, r 22, Schedule.
Date in force: 2 October 2000: see SI 2000/2092, r 1.
Para (1): reference to "(1)" in square brackets inserted by SI 2002/2058, r 21.
Date in force: 2 December 2002: see SI 2002/2058, r 1(b).
Para (2): in sub-para (a)(i) word "Section" in square brackets substituted by SI 2003/364, r 5(d).
Date in force: 1 April 2003 (being the date on which the Nationality, Immigration and Asylum Act 2002, ss 81–117 came into force): see SI 2003/364, r 1 and SI 2003/754, art 2(1), Sch 1; for transitional provisions see SI 2003/754, art 3, and Sch 2, para 1(4A), (4B) (as amended by SI 2003/1339, art 4) and (5).

[Rule 54.17 Court's powers to hear any person]

[(1) Any person may apply for permission—

(a) to file evidence; or

(b) make representations at the hearing of the judicial review.

(2) An application under paragraph (1) should be made promptly.]

NOTES

Amendment

Inserted by SI 2000/2092, r 22, Schedule.
Date in force: 2 October 2000: see SI 2000/2092, r 1.

[Rule 54.18 Judicial review may be decided without a hearing]

[The court may decide the claim for judicial review without a hearing where all the parties agree.]

NOTES

Amendment

Inserted by SI 2000/2092, r 22, Schedule.
Date in force: 2 October 2000: see SI 2000/2092, r 1.

[Rule 54.19 Court's powers in respect of quashing orders]

[(1) This rule applies where the court makes a quashing order in respect of the decision to which the claim relates.

[(2) The court may—

(a)

(i) remit the matter to the decision-maker; and

(ii) direct it to reconsider the matter and reach a decision in accordance with the judgment of the court; or

(b) in so far as any enactment permits, substitute its own decision for the decision to which the claim relates.

(Section 31 of the Supreme Court Act 1981 enables the High Court, subject to certain conditions, to substitute its own decision for the decision in question.)]

(3) . . .]

NOTES

Amendment

Inserted by SI 2000/2092, r 22, Schedule.
Date in force: 2 October 2000: see SI 2000/2092, r 1.
Para (2): substituted by SI 2007/3543, r 7(b).
Date in force: 6 April 2008: see SI 2007/3543, r 1(b).
Para (3): revoked by SI 2007/3543, r 7(c).
Date in force: 6 April 2008: see SI 2007/3543, r 1(b).

[Rule 54.20 Transfer]

[The court may—

(a) order a claim to continue as if it had not been started under this [Section]; and

(b) where it does so, give directions about the future management of the claim.

(Part 30 (transfer) applies to transfers to and from the Administrative Court)]

NOTES

Amendment

Inserted by SI 2000/2092, r 22, Schedule.
Date in force: 2 October 2000: see SI 2000/2092, r 1.
In para (a) word "Section" in square brackets substituted by SI 2003/364, r 5(e).
Date in force: 1 April 2003 (being the date on which the Nationality, Immigration and Asylum Act 2002, ss 81–117 came into force): see SI 2003/364, r 1 and SI 2003/754, art 2(1), Sch 1; for transitional provisions see SI 2003/754, art 3, and Sch 2, para 1(4A), (4B) (as amended by SI 2003/1339, art 4) and (5).

[SECTION II—STATUTORY REVIEW UNDER THE NATIONALITY, IMMIGRATION AND ASYLUM ACT 2002]

NOTES

Amendment

Inserted by SI 2003/364, r 5(f), Schedule, Pt 2.
Date in force: 1 April 2003 (being the date on which the Nationality, Immigration and Asylum Act 2002, ss 81–117 came into force): see SI 2003/364, r 1 and SI 2003/754, art 2(1), Sch 1; for transitional provisions see SI 2003/754, art 3, and Sch 2, para 1(4A), (4B) (as amended by SI 2003/1339, art 4) and (5).
Cross-heading: revoked by SI 2007/3543, r 7(d)(i).
Date in force: 6 April 2008: see SI 2007/3543, r 1(b).

[Rule 54.21 . . .]

[. . .]

NOTES

Amendment

Inserted by SI 2003/364, r 5(f), Schedule, Pt 2.
Date in force: 1 April 2003 (being the date on which the Nationality, Immigration and Asylum Act 2002, ss 81–117 came into force): see SI 2003/364, r 1 and SI 2003/754, art 2(1), Sch 1; for transitional provisions see SI 2003/754, art 3, and Sch 2, para 1(4A), (4B) (as amended by SI 2003/1339, art 4) and (5).
Revoked by SI 2007/3543, r 7(d)(ii).
Date in force: 6 April 2008: see SI 2007/3543, r 1(b).

[Rule 54.22 . . .]

[. . .]

NOTES

Amendment

Inserted by SI 2003/364, r 5(f), Schedule, Pt 2.
Date in force: 1 April 2003 (being the date on which the Nationality, Immigration and Asylum Act 2002, ss 81–117 came into force): see SI 2003/364, r 1 and SI 2003/754, art 2(1), Sch 1; for transitional provisions see SI 2003/754, art 3, and Sch 2, para 1(4A), (4B) (as amended by SI 2003/1339, art 4) and (5).
Revoked by SI 2007/3543, r 7(d)(ii).
Date in force: 6 April 2008: see SI 2007/3543, r 1(b).

[Rule 54.23 . . .]

[. . .]

NOTES

Amendment

Inserted by SI 2003/364, r 5(f), Schedule, Pt 2.
Date in force: 1 April 2003 (being the date on which the Nationality, Immigration and Asylum Act 2002, ss 81–117 came into force): see SI 2003/364, r 1 and SI 2003/754, art 2(1), Sch 1; for transitional provisions see SI 2003/754, art 3, and Sch 2, para 1(4A), (4B) (as amended by SI 2003/1339, art 4) and (5).
Revoked by SI 2007/3543, r 7(d)(ii).
Date in force: 6 April 2008: see SI 2007/3543, r 1(b).

[Rule 54.24 . . .]

[. . .]

NOTES

Amendment

Inserted by SI 2003/364, r 5(f), Schedule, Pt 2.
Date in force: 1 April 2003 (being the date on which the Nationality, Immigration and Asylum Act 2002, ss 81–117 came into force): see SI 2003/364, r 1 and SI 2003/754, art 2(1), Sch 1; for transitional provisions see SI 2003/754, art 3, and Sch 2, para 1(4A), (4B) (as amended by SI 2003/1339, art 4) and (5).
Revoked by SI 2007/3543, r 7(d)(ii).
Date in force: 6 April 2008: see SI 2007/3543, r 1(b).

[Rule 54.25 . . .]

. . .

NOTES

Amendment

Revoked by SI 2007/3543, r 7(d)(ii).
Date in force: 6 April 2008: see SI 2007/3543, r 1(b).

[Rule 54.26 . . .]

[. . .]

NOTES

Amendment

Inserted by SI 2003/364, r 5(f), Schedule, Pt 2.
Date in force: 1 April 2003 (being the date on which the Nationality, Immigration and Asylum Act 2002, ss 81–117 came into force): see SI 2003/364, r 1 and SI 2003/754, art 2(1), Sch 1; for transitional provisions see SI 2003/754, art 3, and Sch 2, para 1(4A), (4B) (as amended by SI 2003/1339, art 4) and (5).
Revoked by SI 2007/3543, r 7(d)(ii).
Date in force: 6 April 2008: see SI 2007/3543, r 1(b).

[Rule 54.27 . . .]

. . .

NOTES

Amendment

Revoked by SI 2007/3543, r 7(d)(ii).
Date in force: 6 April 2008: see SI 2007/3543, r 1(b).

[SECTION III—APPLICATIONS FOR STATUTORY REVIEW UNDER SECTION 103A OF THE NATIONALITY, IMMIGRATION AND ASYLUM ACT 2002]

NOTES

Amendment

Inserted by SI 2005/352, r 7, Schedule, Pt II.
Date in force: 4 April 2005: see SI 2005/352, r 1; for transitional provisions see r 9 thereof.
Revoked by SI 2009/3390, r 29(c).
Date in force: 15 February 2010: see SI 2009/3390, r 1(4).

[54.28 . . .]

[. . .]

NOTES

Amendment

Inserted by SI 2005/352, r 7, Schedule, Pt II.
Date in force: 4 April 2005: see SI 2005/352, r 1; for transitional provisions see r 9 thereof.
Revoked by SI 2009/3390, r 29(c).
Date in force: 15 February 2010: see SI 2009/3390, r 1(4).

[54.28A . . .]

[. . .]

NOTES

Amendment

Inserted by SI 2005/3515, r 12(b).
Date in force: 6 April 2006: see SI 2005/3515, r 1.
Revoked by SI 2009/3390, r 29(c).
Date in force: 15 February 2010: see SI 2009/3390, r 1(4).

[54.28B . . .]

[. . .]

NOTES

Amendment

Inserted by SI 2005/3515, r 12(b).
Date in force: 6 April 2006: see SI 2005/3515, r 1.
Revoked by SI 2009/3390, r 29(c).
Date in force: 15 February 2010: see SI 2009/3390, r 1(4).

[54.29 . . .]

[. . .]

NOTES

Amendment

Inserted by SI 2005/352, r 7, Schedule, Pt II.
Date in force: 4 April 2005: see SI 2005/352, r 1; for transitional provisions see r 9 thereof.
Revoked by SI 2009/3390, r 29(c).
Date in force: 15 February 2010: see SI 2009/3390, r 1(4).

[54.30 . . .]

[. . .]

NOTES

Amendment

Inserted by SI 2005/352, r 7, Schedule, Pt II.
Date in force: 4 April 2005: see SI 2005/352, r 1; for transitional provisions see r 9 thereof.
Revoked by SI 2009/3390, r 29(c).
Date in force: 15 February 2010: see SI 2009/3390, r 1(4).

[54.31 . . .]

[. . .]

NOTES

Amendment

Inserted by SI 2005/352, r 7, Schedule, Pt II.
Date in force: 4 April 2005: see SI 2005/352, r 1; for transitional provisions see r 9 thereof.
Revoked by SI 2009/3390, r 29(c).
Date in force: 15 February 2010: see SI 2009/3390, r 1(4).

[54.32 . . .]

[. . .]

NOTES

Amendment

Inserted by SI 2005/352, r 7, Schedule, Pt II.
Date in force: 4 April 2005: see SI 2005/352, r 1; for transitional provisions see r 9 thereof.
Revoked by SI 2009/3390, r 29(c).
Date in force: 15 February 2010: see SI 2009/3390, r 1(4).

[54.33 . . .]

[. . .]

NOTES

Amendment

Inserted by SI 2005/352, r 7, Schedule, Pt II.
Date in force: 4 April 2005: see SI 2005/352, r 1; for transitional provisions see r 9 thereof.
Revoked by SI 2009/3390, r 29(c).
Date in force: 15 February 2010: see SI 2009/3390, r 1(4).

[54.34 . . .]

[. . .]

NOTES

Amendment

Inserted by SI 2005/352, r 7, Schedule, Pt II.
Date in force: 4 April 2005: see SI 2005/352, r 1; for transitional provisions see r 9 thereof.
Revoked by SI 2009/3390, r 29(c).
Date in force: 15 February 2010: see SI 2009/3390, r 1(4).

[54.35 . . .]

[. . .]

NOTES

Amendment

Inserted by SI 2005/352, r 7, Schedule, Pt II.
Date in force: 4 April 2005: see SI 2005/352, r 1; for transitional provisions see r 9 thereof.
Revoked by SI 2009/3390, r 29(c).

Date in force: 15 February 2010: see SI 2009/3390, r 1(4).

[Rule 54.36 . . .]

[. . .]

NOTES

Amendment

Inserted by SI 2006/1689, r 8(3).
Date in force: 2 October 2006: see SI 2006/1689, r 1.
Revoked by SI 2009/3390, r 29(c).
Date in force: 15 February 2010: see SI 2009/3390, r 1(4).

Appendix 4

PRE-ACTION PROTOCOL FOR JUDICIAL REVIEW

THIS PRE-ACTION PROTOCOL CAME INTO FORCE ON 4 MARCH 2002

Contents:

INTRODUCTION

This protocol applies to proceedings within England and Wales only. It does not affect the time limit specified by Rule 54.5(1) of the Civil Procedure Rules which requires that any claim form in an application for judicial review must be filed promptly and in any event not later than 3 months after the grounds to make the claim first arose or the shorter time limits specified by Rules 54.5(5) and (6) which set out that a claim form for certain planning judicial reviews must be filed within six weeks and a claim form for certain procurement judicial reviews must be filed within 30 days.

1 Judicial review allows people with a sufficient interest in a decision or action by a public body to ask a judge to review the lawfulness of:

- an enactment; or
- a decision, action or failure to act in relation to the exercise of a public function.

2 Judicial review may be used where there is no right of appeal or where all avenues of appeal have been exhausted.

Alternative Dispute Resolution

3.1 The parties should consider whether some form of alternative dispute resolution procedure would be more suitable than litigation, and if so, endeavour to agree which form to adopt. Both the Claimant and Defendant may be required by the Court to provide evidence that alternative means of resolving their dispute were considered. The Courts take the view that litigation should be a last resort, and that claims should not be issued prematurely when a settlement is still actively being explored. Parties are warned that if the protocol is not followed (including this paragraph) then the Court must have regard to such conduct when determining costs. However, parties should also note that a claim for judicial review "must be filed promptly and in any event not later than 3 months after the grounds to make the claim first arose".

3.2 It is not practicable in this protocol to address in detail how the parties might decide which method to adopt to resolve their particular dispute. However, summarised below are some of the options for resolving disputes without litigation:

- Discussion and negotiation.
- Ombudsmen – the Parliamentary and Health Service and the Local Government Ombudsmen have discretion to deal with complaints relating to maladministration. The British and Irish Ombudsman Association provide information about Ombudsman schemes and other complaint handling bodies and this is available from their website at http://www.bioa.org.uk. Parties may wish to note that the Ombudsmen are not able to look into a complaint once court action has been commenced.
- Early neutral evaluation by an independent third party (for example, a lawyer experienced in the field of administrative law or an individual experienced in the subject matter of the claim).
- Mediation - a form of facilitated negotiation assisted by an independent neutral party.

3.3 The Legal Services Commission has published a booklet on "Alternatives to Court", CLS Direct Information Leaflet 23 (http://www.clsdirect.org.uk), which lists a number of organisations that provide alternative dispute resolution services.

3.4 It is expressly recognised that no party can or should be forced to mediate or enter into any form of ADR.

4 **Judicial review may not be appropriate in every instance.**

Claimants are strongly advised to seek appropriate legal advice when considering such proceedings and, in particular, before adopting this protocol or making a claim. Although the Legal Services Commission will not normally grant full representation before a letter before claim has been sent and the proposed defendant given a reasonable time to respond, initial funding may be available, for eligible claimants, to cover the work necessary to write this. (See Annex C for more information).

5 This protocol sets out a code of good practice and contains the steps which parties should generally follow before making a claim for judicial review.

6 This protocol does not impose a greater obligation on a public body to disclose documents or give reasons for its decision than that already provided for in statute or common law. However, where the court considers that a public body should have provided relevant documents and/or information, particularly where this failure is a breach of a statutory or common law requirement, it may impose sanctions.

This protocol will not be appropriate where the defendant does not have the legal power to change the decision being challenged, for example decisions issued by tribunals such as the Asylum and Immigration Tribunal.

This protocol will not be appropriate in urgent cases, for example, when directions have been set, or are in force, for the claimant's removal from the UK, or where there is an urgent need for an interim order to compel a public body to act where it has unlawfully refused to do so (for example, the failure of a local housing authority to secure interim accommodation for a homeless claimant) a claim should be made immediately. A letter before claim will not stop the implementation of a disputed decision in all instances.

This protocol may not be appropriate in cases where one of the shorter time limits in Rules 54.5(5) or (6) applies. In those cases, the parties should still attempt to comply with this protocol but the court will not apply normal cost sanctions where the court is satisfied that it has not been possible to comply because of the shorter time limits.

7 All claimants will need to satisfy themselves whether they should follow the protocol,

depending upon the circumstances of his or her case. Where the use of the protocol is appropriate, the court will normally expect all parties to have complied with it and will take into account compliance or non-compliance when giving directions for case management of proceedings or when making orders for costs.[3] However, even in emergency cases, it is good practice to fax to the defendant the draft Claim Form which the claimant intends to issue. A claimant is also normally required to notify a defendant when an interim mandatory order is being sought.

The letter before claim

8 Before making a claim, the claimant should send a letter to the defendant. The purpose of this letter is to identify the issues in dispute and establish whether litigation can be avoided.

9 Claimants should normally use the suggested **standard format** for the letter outlined at Annex A.

10 The letter should contain **the date and details of the decision, act or omission being challenged and a clear summary of the facts** on which the claim is based. It should also contain the **details of any relevant information** that the claimant is seeking and an explanation of why this is considered relevant. If the claim is considered to be an Aarhus Convention claim, the letter should state this clearly and explain the reasons, since specific rules as to costs apply to such claims.

11 The letter should normally contain the **details of any interested parties** known to the claimant. They should be sent a copy of the letter before claim for information. **Claimants are strongly advised to seek appropriate legal advice when considering such proceedings and, in particular, before sending the letter before claim to other interested parties or making a claim.**

12 The claim should not normally be made until the proposed reply date given in the letter before claim has passed, unless the circumstances of the case require more immediate action to be taken.

The letter of response

13 Defendants should normally respond within 14 days using the **standard format** at Annex B. Failure to do so will be taken into account by the court and sanctions may be imposed unless there are good reasons.

14 Where it is not possible to reply within the proposed time limit the defendant should send an interim reply and propose a reasonable extension. Where an extension is sought, reasons should be given and, where required, additional information requested. **This will not affect the time limit for making a claim for judicial review** nor will it bind the claimant where he or she considers this to be unreasonable. However, where the court considers that a subsequent claim is made prematurely it may impose sanctions.

15 If the **claim is being conceded in full**, the reply should say so in clear and unambiguous terms.

16 If the **claim is being conceded in part or not being conceded at all**, the reply should say so in clear and unambiguous terms, and:

(a) where appropriate, contain a new decision, clearly identifying what aspects of the claim are being conceded and what are not, or, give a clear timescale within which the new decision will be issued;
(b) provide a fuller explanation for the decision, if considered appropriate to do so;
(c) address any points of dispute, or explain why they cannot be addressed;
(d) enclose any **relevant** documentation requested by the claimant, or explain why the documents are not being enclosed; and

(e) where appropriate, confirm whether or not they will oppose any application for an interim remedy.

If the letter before claim has stated that the claim is an Aarhus Convention claim but the defendant does not accept this, the reply should state this clearly and explain the reasons.

17 The response should be sent to **all interested parties** [7] identified by the claimant and contain details of any other parties who the defendant considers also have an interest.

ANNEX A
LETTER BEFORE CLAIM
SECTION 1. INFORMATION REQUIRED IN A LETTER BEFORE CLAIM

Proposed claim for judicial review

1 **To**

(Insert the name and address of the proposed defendant - see details in section 2)

2 **The claimant**

(Insert the title, first and last name and the address of the claimant)

3 **Reference details**

(When dealing with large organisations it is important to understand that the information relating to any particular individual's previous dealings with it may not be immediately available, therefore it is important to set out the relevant reference numbers for the matter in dispute and/or the identity of those within the public body who have been handling the particular matter in dispute - see details in section 3)

4 **The details of the matter being challenged**

(Set out clearly the matter being challenged, particularly if there has been more than one decision)

5 **The issue**

(Set out the date and details of the decision, or act or omission being challenged, a brief summary of the facts and why it is contented to be wrong)

6 **The details of the action that the defendant is expected to take**

(Set out the details of the remedy sought, including whether a review or any interim remedy are being requested)

7 **The details of the legal advisers, if any, dealing with this claim**

(Set out the name, address and reference details of any legal advisers dealing with the claim)

8 **The details of any interested parties**

(Set out the details of any interested parties and confirm that they have been sent a copy of this letter)

9 **The details of any information sought**

(Set out the details of any information that is sought. This may include a request for a fuller explanation of the reasons for the decision that is being challenged)

10 **The details of any documents that are considered relevant and necessary**

(Set out the details of any documentation or policy in respect of which the disclosure is sought and explain why these are relevant. If you rely on a statutory duty to disclose, this should be specified)

11 **The address for reply and service of court documents**

(Insert the address for the reply)

12 **Proposed reply date**

(The precise time will depend upon the circumstances of the individual case. However, although a shorter or longer time may be appropriate in a particular case, 14 days is a reasonable time to allow in most circumstances)

SECTION 2. ADDRESS FOR SENDING THE LETTER BEFORE CLAIM

Public bodies have requested that, for certain types of cases, in order to ensure a prompt response, letters before claim could be sent to specific addresses.

- **Where the claim concerns a decision in an Immigration, Asylum or Nationality case:**
  The claim may be sent electronically to the following UK Border Agency email address: mailto://UKBAPAP@UKBA.gsi.gov.uk
  Alternatively the claim may be sent by post to the following UK Border Agency postal address:

  Judicial Review Unit
  UK Border Agency
  Lunar House
  40 Wellesley Road
  Croydon CR9 2BY
- **Where the claim concerns a decision by the Legal Services Commission:**
  The address on the decision letter/notification;
  Legal Director

  Corporate Legal Team
  Legal Services Commission
  102 Petty France
  London SW1H 9AJ
- **Where the claim concerns a decision by a local authority:**
  — The address on the decision letter/notification; and
  — Their legal department[8]
- **Where the claim concerns a decision by a department or body for whom Treasury Solicitor acts <u>and Treasury Solicitor has already been involved in the case</u> a copy should also be sent, quoting the Treasury Solicitor's reference, to:**
  Treasury Solicitor

  One Kemble Street
  London WC2B 4TS

In all other circumstances, the letter should be sent to the address on the letter notifying the decision.

SECTION 3. SPECIFIC REFERENCE DETAILS REQUIRED

Public bodies have requested that the following information should be provided in order to ensure prompt response.

- **Where the claim concerns an Immigration, Asylum or Nationality case, dependent upon the nature of the case:**
  — The Home Office reference number

— The Port reference number
— The the Asylum and Immigration Tribunal reference number
— The National Asylum Support Service reference number

Or, if these are unavailable:

— The full name, nationality and date of birth of the claimant.

- **Where the claim concerns a decision by the Legal Services Commission:**
  — The certificate reference number.

ANNEX B
RESPONSE TO A LETTER BEFORE CLAIM

INFORMATION REQUIRED IN A RESPONSE TO A LETTER BEFORE CLAIM

Proposed claim for judicial review

1 **The claimant**

(Insert the title, first and last names and the address to which any reply should be sent)

2 **From**

(Insert the name and address of the defendant)

3 **Reference details**

(Set out the relevant reference numbers for the matter in dispute and the identity of those within the public body who have been handling the issue)

4 **The details of the matter being challenged**

(Set out details of the matter being challenged, providing a fuller explanation of the decision, where this is considered appropriate)

5 **Response to the proposed claim**

(Set out whether the issue in question is conceded in part, or in full, or will be contested. Where it is not proposed to disclose any information that has been requested, explain the reason for this. Where an interim reply is being sent and there is a realistic prospect of settlement, details should be included)

6 **Details of any other interested parties**

(Identify any other parties who you consider have an interest who have not already been sent a letter by the claimant)

7 **Address for further correspondence and service of court documents**

(Set out the address for any future correspondence on this matter)

ANNEX C
NOTES ON PUBLIC FUNDING FOR LEGAL COSTS IN JUDICIAL REVIEW

Public funding for legal costs in judicial review is available from legal professionals and advice agencies which have contracts with the Legal Services Commission as part of the Community Legal Service. Funding may be provided for:

- **Legal Help** to provide initial advice and assistance with any legal problem; or
- **Legal Representation** to allow you to be represented in court if you are taking or defending court proceedings. This is available in two forms:
  — **Investigative Help** is limited to funding to investigate the strength of the proposed claim. It includes the issue and conduct of proceedings only so

far as is necessary to obtain disclosure of relevant information or to protect the client's position in relation to any urgent hearing or time limit for the issue of proceedings. This includes the work necessary to write a **letter before claim** to the body potentially under challenge, setting out the grounds of challenge, and giving that body a reasonable opportunity, typically 14 days, in which to respond.

— **Full Representation** is provided to represent you in legal proceedings and includes litigation services, advocacy services, and all such help as is usually given by a person providing representation in proceedings, including steps preliminary or incidental to proceedings, and/or arriving at or giving affect to a compromise to avoid or bring to an end any proceedings. Except in emergency cases, a proper **letter before claim** must be sent and the other side must be given an opportunity to respond before *Full Representation* is granted.

Further information on the type(s) of help available and the criteria for receiving that help may be found in the Legal Service Manual Volume 3: "*The Funding Code*". This may be found on the Legal Services Commission website at: http://www.legalservices.c o.uk

A list of contracted firms and Advice Agencies may be found on the Community Legal Services website at: http://www.justask.org.uk

Appendix 5

LAND REGISTRATION (REFERRAL TO THE ADJUDICATOR TO HM LAND REGISTRY) RULES 2003

SI 2003 No 2114

1 Citation and commencement

These rules may be cited as the Land Registration (Referral to the Adjudicator to HM Land Registry) Rules 2003 and shall come into force on 13 October 2003.

NOTES

Initial Commencement

Specified date

Specified date: 13 October 2003: see above.

2 Interpretation

In these rules—

"the Act" means the Land Registration Act 2002;

"business day" means a day when the land registry is open to the public under rule 216 of the Land Registration Rules 2003;

"disputed application" means an application to the registrar under the Act to which an objection has been made;

"objection" means an objection made under section 73 of the Act;

"the parties" means the person who has made the disputed application and the person who has made an objection to that application.

NOTES

Initial Commencement

Specified date

Specified date: 13 October 2003: see r 1.

3 Procedure for referral to the [First-tier Tribunal]

(1) When the registrar is obliged to refer a matter to the [the First-tier Tribunal] under section 73(7) of the Act, he must as soon as practicable—

(a) prepare a case summary containing the information set out in paragraph (2),

(b) send a copy of the case summary to the parties,

(c) give the parties an opportunity to make comments on the contents of the case summary in the manner, to the address, and within the time specified by him, and

(d) inform the parties in writing that the case summary together with copies of the documents listed in it will be sent to the [the First-tier Tribunal] with the notice referred to in rule 5(2).

(2) The case summary must contain the following information—

(a) the names of the parties,

(b) the addresses of the parties,

(c) details of their legal or other representatives (if any),

(d) a summary of the core facts,

(e) details of the disputed application,

(f) details of the objection to that application,

(g) a list of any documents that will be copied to the [the First-tier Tribunal], and

(h) anything else that the registrar may consider to be appropriate.

(3) The registrar may amend the case summary as he considers appropriate having considered any written comments made to him by the parties under paragraph (1)(c).

NOTES

Initial Commencement

Specified date

Specified date: 13 October 2003: see r 1.

Amendment

Provision heading: words "First-tier Tribunal" in square brackets substituted by SI 2013/1036, art 6(2), Sch 2, Pt 3, paras 63, 64(a).

Date in force: 1 July 2013: see SI 2013/1036, art 1; for transitional provisions see art 6(3), Sch 3, paras 1–8 thereto.

Para (1): words "the First-tier Tribunal" in square brackets substituted by SI 2013/1036, art 6(2), Sch 2, Pt 3, paras 63, 64(b).

Date in force: 1 July 2013: see SI 2013/1036, art 1; for transitional provisions see art 6(3), Sch 3, paras 1–8 thereto.

Para (1): in sub-para (d) words "the First-tier Tribunal" in square brackets substituted by SI 2013/1036, art 6(2), Sch 2, Pt 3, paras 63, 64(b).

Date in force: 1 July 2013: see SI 2013/1036, art 1; for transitional provisions see art 6(3), Sch 3, paras 1–8 thereto.

Para (2): in sub-para (g) words "the First-tier Tribunal" in square brackets substituted by SI 2013/1036, art 6(2), Sch 2, Pt 3, paras 63, 64(c).

Date in force: 1 July 2013: see SI 2013/1036, art 1; for transitional provisions see art 6(3), Sch 3, paras 1–8 thereto.

4 Parties' addresses

(1) If the address of a party set out in the case summary does not comply with paragraph (2), that party must provide the registrar with one that does.

(2) An address complies with this paragraph if it—

(a) is a postal address in England and Wales, and

(b) is either that of the party or of his representative.

NOTES

Initial Commencement

Specified date

Specified date: 13 October 2003: see r 1.

5 Notice of referral to the [First-tier Tribunal]

(1) This rule applies—

(a) when the registrar has considered any written comments made by the parties under rule 3(1)(c), or

(b) if he has not received any comments from the parties within the time specified under rule 3(1)(c), on the expiry of that period, and

(c) when he has amended the case summary, if appropriate, under rule 3(3).

(2) The registrar must as soon as practicable—

(a) send to the [First-tier Tribunal a written notice, accompanied by the documents set out in paragraph (3), stating that the matter is referred to the First-tier Tribunal] under section 73(7) of the Act,

(b) inform the parties in writing that the matter has been referred to the [First-tier Tribunal], and

(c) send the parties a copy of the case summary prepared under rule 3 in the form sent to the [First-tier Tribunal].

(3) The notice sent to the [First-tier Tribunal] under paragraph (2)(a) must be accompanied by—

(a) the case summary prepared under rule 3 amended, if appropriate, by the registrar under rule 3(3), and

(b) copies of the documents listed in that case summary.

NOTES

Initial Commencement

Specified date

Specified date: 13 October 2003: see r 1.

Amendment

Provision heading: words "First-tier Tribunal" in square brackets substituted by SI 2013/1036, art 6(2), Sch 2, Pt 3, paras 63, 65(a).

Date in force: 1 July 2013: see SI 2013/1036, art 1; for transitional provisions see art 6(3), Sch 3, paras 1–8 thereto.

Para (2): in sub-para (a) words from "First-tier Tribunal" to "First-tier Tribunal" in square brackets substituted by SI 2013/1036, art 6(2), Sch 2, Pt 3, paras 63, 65(b).

Date in force: 1 July 2013: see SI 2013/1036, art 1; for transitional provisions see art 6(3), Sch 3, paras 1–8 thereto.

Para (2): in sub-para (b) words "First-tier Tribunal" in square brackets substituted by SI 2013/1036, art 6(2), Sch 2, Pt 3, paras 63, 65(c).

Date in force: 1 July 2013: see SI 2013/1036, art 1; for transitional provisions see art 6(3), Sch 3, paras 1–8 thereto.

Para (2): in sub-para (c) words "First-tier Tribunal" in square brackets substituted by SI 2013/1036, art 6(2), Sch 2, Pt 3, paras 63, 65(c).

Date in force: 1 July 2013: see SI 2013/1036, art 1; for transitional provisions see art 6(3), Sch 3, paras 1–8 thereto.

Para (3): words "First-tier Tribunal" in square brackets substituted by SI 2013/1036, art 6(2), Sch 2, Pt 3, paras 63, 65(d).

Date in force: 1 July 2013: see SI 2013/1036, art 1; for transitional provisions see art 6(3), Sch 3, paras 1–8 thereto.

6 Specified time periods

(1) For the purposes of rule 3(1)(c), the time specified by the registrar must not end before 12 noon on the fifteenth business day after the date on which the registrar sends the copy of the case summary to the relevant party under rule 3(1)(b) or such earlier time as the parties may agree.

(2) On and after the date specified in any notice given pursuant to rule 216(2) of the Land Registration Rules 2003, paragraph (1) shall have effect with the substitution of the words "eighteenth business day" for the words "fifteenth business day".

NOTES

Initial Commencement

Specified date

Specified date: 13 October 2003: see r 1.

Appendix 6

ADJUDICATOR TO HER MAJESTY'S LAND REGISTRY (PRACTICE AND PROCEDURE) RULES 2003 (AS AMENDED BY SI 2008/1731) [NOW REPEALED]

SI 2003 No 2171

1 Citation and Commencement
These Rules may be cited as the Adjudicator to Her Majesty's Land Registry (Practice and Procedure) Rules 2003 and shall come into force on 13th October 2003.

NOTES

Initial Commencement

Specified date

Specified date: 13 October 2003: see above.

PART 1
INTRODUCTION

2 Interpretation

(1) In these Rules—

"applicant" means the party whom the adjudicator designates as such under rule 5 or under rule 24, or the party who makes a rectification application;

["document" means anything in which information is recorded in any form, and an obligation in these Rules to provide or allow access to a document or a copy of a document for any purpose means, unless the adjudicator directs otherwise, an obligation to provide access to such document or copy in a legible form or in a form which can be readily made into a legible form;]

"hearing" means a sitting of the adjudicator for the purpose of enabling the adjudicator to reach or announce a substantive decision, but does not include a sitting of the adjudicator solely in the exercise of one or more of the following powers—

(a) to consider an application, representation or objection made in the interim part of the proceedings;

(b) to reach a substantive decision without an oral hearing; or

(c) to consider whether to grant permission to appeal a decision or to stay the implementation of a decision pending the outcome of an appeal;

"matter" means the subject of either a reference or a rectification application;

"office copy" means an official copy of a document held or issued by a public authority;

"original application" means the application originally made to the registrar that resulted in a reference;

"proceedings" means, except in the expression "court proceedings", the proceedings of the matter before the adjudicator but does not include any negotiations, communications or proceedings that occurred prior to the reference or rectification application;

"record of matters" means a record of references, rectification applications and certain other applications and decisions, kept in accordance with these Rules and in particular in accordance with rule 46;

"rectification application" means an application made to rectify or set aside a document under section 108(2) for determination of the matter by the adjudicator;

"reference" means a reference from the registrar to the adjudicator under section 73(7) for determination of the matter by the adjudicator;

"respondent" means the party or parties who the adjudicator designates as such under rule 5 or rule 24, or the party or parties making an objection to a rectification application;

["statement of truth" means—

(a) in the case of a witness statement, a statement signed by the maker of the statement that the maker of the statement believes that the facts stated in the witness statement are true; or

(b) in the case of other documents, a statement that the party by whom or on whose behalf the document is submitted believes the facts stated in the document are true, signed by either—

(i) the party by whom or on whose behalf the document is submitted; or

(ii) that party's authorised representative, in which case the statement of truth must state the name of the representative and the relationship of the representative to the party;]

"substantive decision" means a decision of the adjudicator on the matter or on any substantive issue that arises in it but does not include any direction in interim parts of the proceedings [, any order made under rule 8(4) or 9(4),] or any order as to costs or any order as to costs thrown away;

"substantive order" means an order or direction that records and gives effect to a substantive decision;

"the Act" means the Land Registration Act 2002 and a reference to a section by number alone is a reference to a section of the Act;

"witness statement" means a written statement . . . containing the evidence that the witness intends to give [and verified by a statement of truth]; and

"working day" means any day other than a Saturday or Sunday, Christmas Day, Good Friday or any other bank holiday.

(2) [For the purposes of these] Rules a person has a document . . . in his possession or control if—

(a) it is in his physical possession;

(b) he has a right to possession of it; or

(c) he has a right to inspect or take copies of it.

NOTES

Initial Commencement

Specified date

Specified date: 13 October 2003: see r 1.

Amendment

Para (1): definition "document" inserted by SI 2008/1731, rr 4, 5(a)(i).

Date in force: 25 July 2008: see SI 2008/1731, r 1; for transitional provisions see r 3(1), (2) thereof.

Para (1): definition "statement of truth" inserted by SI 2008/1731, rr 4, 5(a)(ii).

Date in force: 25 July 2008: see SI 2008/1731, r 1; for transitional provisions see r 3(1), (2) thereof.

Para (1): in definition "substantive decision" words ", any order made under rule 8(4) or 9(4)," in square brackets inserted by SI 2008/1731, rr 4, 5(a)(iii).

Date in force: 25 July 2008: see SI 2008/1731, r 1; for transitional provisions see r 3(1), (2) thereof.

Para (1): in definition "witness statement" words omitted revoked by SI 2008/1731, rr 4, 5(a)(iv)(aa).

Date in force: 25 July 2008: see SI 2008/1731, r 1; for transitional provisions see r 3(1), (2) thereof.

Para (1): in definition "witness statement" words "and verified by a statement of truth" in square brackets inserted by SI 2008/1731, rr 4, 5(a)(iv)(bb).

Date in force: 25 July 2008: see SI 2008/1731, r 1; for transitional provisions see r 3(1), (2) thereof.

Para (2): words "For the purposes of these" in square brackets substituted by SI 2008/1731, rr 4, 5(b)(i).

Date in force: 25 July 2008: see SI 2008/1731, r 1; for transitional provisions see r 3(1), (2) thereof.

Para (2): words omitted revoked by SI 2008/1731, 4, 5(b)(ii).

Date in force: 25 July 2008: see SI 2008/1731, r 1; for transitional provisions see r 3(1), (2) thereof.

3 The overriding objective

(1) The overriding objective of these Rules is to enable the adjudicator to deal with matters justly.

(2) Dealing with a matter justly includes, so far as is practicable—

- (a) ensuring that the parties are on an equal footing;
- (b) saving expense;
- (c) dealing with the matter in ways that are proportionate—
  - (i) to the value of the land or other interests involved;
  - (ii) to the importance of the matter;
  - (iii) to the complexity of the issues in the matter; and
  - (iv) to the financial position of each party; and
- (d) ensuring that the matter is dealt with expeditiously and fairly.

(3) The adjudicator must seek to give effect to the overriding objective when he—

- (a) exercises any power given to him by these Rules; or
- (b) interprets these Rules.

(4) The parties are required to help the adjudicator to further the overriding objective.

NOTES

Initial Commencement

Specified date

Specified date: 13 October 2003: see r 1.

PART 2
REFERENCES TO THE ADJUDICATOR

4 Scope of this Part

The rules in this Part apply to references.

NOTES

Initial Commencement

Specified date

Specified date: 13 October 2003: see r 1.

5 Notice of receipt by the adjudicator of a reference

Following receipt by the adjudicator of a reference, the adjudicator must—

- (a) enter the particulars of the reference in the record of matters; and

(b) serve on the parties notice in writing of—
   (i) the fact that the reference has been received by the adjudicator;
   (ii) the date when the adjudicator received the reference;
   (iii) the matter number allocated to the reference;
   (iv) the name and any known address and address for service of the parties to the proceedings; and
   (v) which party will be the applicant for the purposes of the proceedings and which party or parties will be the respondent.

NOTES

Initial Commencement

Specified date

Specified date: 13 October 2003: see r 1.

6 Direction to commence court proceedings under section 110(1)

Where the adjudicator intends to direct a party to commence court proceedings under section 110(1), the parties may make representations or objections but any representations or objections must be concerned with one or more of the following—

(a) whether the adjudicator should make such a direction;
(b) which party should be directed to commence court proceedings;
(c) the time within which court proceedings should commence; and
(d) the questions the court should determine.

NOTES

Initial Commencement

Specified date

Specified date: 13 October 2003: see r 1.

7 Notification to the adjudicator of court proceedings following a direction to commence court proceedings under section 110(1)

(1) In this Part—

"the date that the matter before the court is finally disposed of" means the earliest date by which the court proceedings relating to the matter or on the relevant part (including any court proceedings on or in consequence of an appeal) have been determined and any time for appealing or further appealing has expired;

"the relevant part" means the part of the matter in relation to which the adjudicator has directed a party under section 110(1) to commence court proceedings; and

"the final court order" means the order made by the court that records the court's final determination (on appeal or otherwise).

(2) A party who has been directed to commence court proceedings under section 110(1) must serve on the adjudicator—

(a) within 14 days of the commencement of the court proceedings, a written notice stating—
   (i) that court proceedings have been issued in accordance with directions given by the adjudicator;
   (ii) the date of issue of the court proceedings;
   (iii) the names and any known addresses of the parties to the court proceedings;
   (iv) the name of the court at which the court proceedings will be heard; and
   (v) the case number allocated to the court proceedings;
(b) within 14 days of the date of the court's decision on any application for an extension of time, a copy of that decision; and

(c) within 14 days of the date that the matter before the court is finally disposed of, a copy of the final court order.

NOTES

Initial Commencement

Specified date

Specified date: 13 October 2003: see r 1.

8 Adjournment of proceedings before the adjudicator following a direction to commence court proceedings on the whole of the matter under section 110(1)

(1) This rule applies where the adjudicator has directed a party under section 110(1) to commence court proceedings for the court's decision on the whole of the matter.

(2) Once he has received notice under rule 7(2)(a) that court proceedings have been issued, the adjudicator must adjourn all of the proceedings before him pending the outcome of the court proceedings.

(3) [Subject to paragraph (4), once the adjudicator] has received a copy of the final court order [in accordance with rule 7(2)(c)] and unless the court directs otherwise, the adjudicator must close the proceedings before him without making a substantive decision.

[(4) Before closing the proceedings in accordance with paragraph (3) the adjudicator may make an order either with or without a hearing and either with or without giving prior notice to the parties if—

(a) such order is necessary, in addition to the final court order, to implement the decision of the court; and

(b) the adjudicator would have had the power to make such order if the adjudicator had made a substantive decision in relation to the proceedings.]

NOTES

Initial Commencement

Specified date

Specified date: 13 October 2003: see r 1.

Amendment

Para (3): words "Subject to paragraph (4), once the adjudicator" in square brackets substituted by SI 2008/1731, rr 4, 6(a)(i).

Date in force: 25 July 2008: see SI 2008/1731, r 1; for transitional provisions see r 3(1), (2) thereof.

Para (3): words "in accordance with rule 7(2)(c)" in square brackets inserted by SI 2008/1731, rr 4, 6(a)(ii).

Date in force: 25 July 2008: see SI 2008/1731, r 1; for transitional provisions see r 3(1), (2) thereof.

Para (4): inserted by SI 2008/1731, rr 4, 6(b).

Date in force: 25 July 2008: see SI 2008/1731, r 1; for transitional provisions see r 3(1), (3) thereof.

9 Adjournment of proceedings before the adjudicator following a direction to commence court proceedings on part of the matter under section 110(1)

(1) This rule applies where the adjudicator has directed a party under section 110(1) to commence court proceedings for the court's decision on the relevant part.

[(2) Once the adjudicator has received notice under rule 7(2)(a) that court proceedings have been issued in relation to the relevant part, the adjudicator must adjourn the proceedings brought under these Rules in relation to that part, pending the outcome of the court proceedings.]

(3) [Subject to paragraph (4), once the adjudicator] has received a copy of the final court order on the relevant part [in accordance with rule 7(2)(c)] and unless the court

directs otherwise, the adjudicator must close the proceedings before him in relation to the relevant part without making a substantive decision on that relevant part.

[(3A) Before closing the proceedings in relation to the relevant part in accordance with paragraph (3) the adjudicator may make an order either with or without a hearing and either with or without giving prior notice to the parties if—

(a) such order is necessary, in addition to the final court order, to implement the decision of the court; and

(b) the adjudicator would have had the power to make such order if the adjudicator had made a substantive decision in relation to the relevant part.]

(4) The adjudicator may adjourn the proceedings in relation to any other part of the matter before him pending the outcome of the court proceedings.

(5) While the court proceedings are still ongoing, the party directed to commence court proceedings must notify the court of any substantive decision made by the adjudicator within 14 days of service on that party of the substantive decision.

NOTES

Initial Commencement

Specified date

Specified date: 13 October 2003: see r 1.

Amendment

Para (2): substituted by SI 2008/1731, rr 4, 7(a).
Date in force: 25 July 2008: see SI 2008/1731, r 1; for transitional provisions see r 3(1), (2) thereof.
Para (3): words "Subject to paragraph (4), once the adjudicator" in square brackets substituted by SI 2008/1731, rr 4, 7(b)(i).
Date in force: 25 July 2008: see SI 2008/1731, r 1; for transitional provisions see r 3(1), (2) thereof.
Para (3): words "in accordance with rule 7(2)(c)" in square brackets inserted by SI 2008/1731, rr 4, 7(b)(ii).
Date in force: 25 July 2008: see SI 2008/1731, r 1; for transitional provisions see r 3(1) , (2) thereof.
Para (3A): inserted by SI 2008/1731, rr 4, 7(c).
Date in force: 25 July 2008: see SI 2008/1731, r 1; for transitional provisions see r 3(1), (3) thereof.

10 Notification where court proceedings are commenced otherwise than following a direction to commence court proceedings under section 110(1)

Where a party commences or has commenced court proceedings otherwise than following a direction under section 110(1) and those court proceedings concern or relate to the matter before the adjudicator, that party must serve—

(a) on the adjudicator within 14 days of the commencement of the court proceedings or, if later, within 7 days of service on that party of notification of the reference under rule 5(b), a written notice stating—
    (i) that court proceedings have been issued;
    (ii) the way and the extent to which the court proceedings concern or relate to the matter before the adjudicator;
    (iii) the date of issue of the court proceedings;
    (iv) the names and any known addresses of the parties to the court proceedings;
    (v) the name of the court at which the court proceedings will be heard; and
    (vi) the case number allocated to the court proceedings;

(b) on the adjudicator within 14 days of the date that the matter before the court is finally disposed of, a copy of the final court order; and

(c) on the court within 14 days of service on that party of such a decision, a copy of any substantive decision made by the adjudicator on the matter.

NOTES

Initial Commencement

Specified date

Specified date: 13 October 2003: see r 1.

11 Adjournment of proceedings before the adjudicator where court proceedings are commenced otherwise than following a direction to commence court proceedings under section 110(1)

Where court proceedings are commenced otherwise than following a direction to commence court proceedings under section 110(1), the adjudicator may adjourn the whole or part of the proceedings before him pending the outcome of the court proceedings.

NOTES

Initial Commencement

Specified date

Specified date: 13 October 2003: see r 1.

12 Applicant's statement of case and documents

Unless otherwise directed by the adjudicator, the applicant must serve on the adjudicator and each of the other parties within 28 days of service of the notification of the reference under rule 5(b)—

(a) his statement of case which must be in accordance with rule 14; and

[(b) copies of any documents in the applicant's possession or control which—

(i) are central to the applicant's case; or

(ii) the adjudicator or any other party to the proceedings will require in order properly to understand the applicant's statement of case].

NOTES

Initial Commencement

Specified date

Specified date: 13 October 2003: see r 1.

Amendment

Para (b): substituted by SI 2008/1731, rr 4, 8.

Date in force: 25 July 2008: see SI 2008/1731, r 1; for transitional provisions see r 3(1), (2) thereof.

13 Respondent's statement of case and documents

The respondent must serve on the adjudicator and each of the other parties within 28 days of service of the applicant's statement of case—

(a) his statement of case which must be in accordance with rule 14; and

[(b) copies of any documents in the respondent's possession or control which—

(i) are central to the respondent's case; or

(ii) the adjudicator or any other party to the proceedings will require in order properly to understand the respondent's statement of case].

NOTES

Initial Commencement

Specified date

Specified date: 13 October 2003: see r 1.

Amendment

Para (b): substituted by SI 2008/1731, rr 4, 9.
Date in force: 25 July 2008: see SI 2008/1731, r 1; for transitional provisions see r 3(1), (2) thereof.

14 Statement of case

(1) Where under these Rules a party is required to provide a statement of case, that statement of case must be in writing[, be verified by a statement of truth and include]—

- (a) the name of the party and confirmation of the party's address for service;
- (b) the party's reasons for supporting or objecting to the original application;
- (c) the facts on which the party intends to rely in the proceedings; [and]
- (d) . . .
- (e) a list of witnesses that the party intends to call to give evidence in support of the party's case.

(2) If in relation to part only of the matter—

- (a) a party has been directed to commence or has commenced court proceedings; or
- (b) the adjudicator has adjourned proceedings before him,

the adjudicator may direct that the statement of case should contain the information specified in paragraphs (1)(b) to (1)(e) inclusive only in relation to the part of the matter that is not before the court for the court's decision or has not been adjourned before the adjudicator.

NOTES

Initial Commencement

Specified date

Specified date: 13 October 2003: see r 1.

Amendment

Para (1): words ", be verified by a statement of truth and include" in square brackets substituted by SI 2008/1731, rr 4, 10(a).
Date in force: 25 July 2008: see SI 2008/1731, r 1; for transitional provisions see r 3(1), (2) thereof.
Para (1): in sub-para (c) word "and" in square brackets inserted by SI 2008/1731, rr 4, 10(b).
Date in force: 25 July 2008: see SI 2008/1731, r 1; for transitional provisions see r 3(1), (2) thereof.
Para (1): sub-para (d) revoked by SI 2008/1731, rr 4, 10(c).
Date in force: 25 July 2008: see SI 2008/1731, r 1; for transitional provisions see r 3(1), (2) thereof.

PART 3
RECTIFICATION APPLICATION TO THE ADJUDICATOR TO RECTIFY OR SET ASIDE DOCUMENTS

15 Scope of this Part

The rules in this Part apply to rectification applications.

NOTES

Initial Commencement

Specified date

Specified date: 13 October 2003: see r 1.

16 Form and contents of a rectification application

(1) A rectification application must—

(a) be made in writing;

(b) be dated and [verified by a statement of truth];

(c) be addressed to the adjudicator;

(d) include the following information—

(i) the name and address of the person or persons against whom the order is sought;

(ii) details of the remedy being sought;

(iii) the grounds on which the rectification application is based;

(iv) . . .

(v) a list of witnesses that the party intends to call to give evidence in support of the rectification application; and

(vi) the applicant's name and address for service;

(e) include the following copies—

[(i) copies of any documents in the applicant's possession or control which—

(aa) are central to the applicant's case; or

(bb) the adjudicator or any other party to the proceedings will require in order properly to understand the rectification application; and]

(ii) a copy of the document to which the rectification application relates, or if a copy is not available, details of the document, which must include if available, its nature, its date, the parties to it and any version number or other similar identification number or code that it has; and

(f) be served on the adjudicator.

(2) Following receipt by the adjudicator of a rectification application, the adjudicator must enter the particulars of the rectification application in the record of matters.

(3) If, having considered the rectification application and made any enquiries he thinks necessary, the adjudicator is satisfied that it is groundless, he must reject the rectification application.

NOTES

Initial Commencement

Specified date

Specified date: 13 October 2003: see r 1.

Amendment

Para (1): in sub-para (b) words "verified by a statement of truth" in square brackets substituted by SI 2008/1731, rr 4, 11(a).

Date in force: 25 July 2008: see SI 2008/1731, r 1; for transitional provisions see r 3(1), (2) thereof.

Para (1): sub-para (d)(iv) revoked by SI 2008/1731, rr 4, 11(b).

Date in force: 25 July 2008: see SI 2008/1731, r 1; for transitional provisions see r 3(1), (2) thereof.

Para (1): sub-para (e)(i) substituted by SI 2008/1731, rr 4, 11(c).

Date in force: 25 July 2008: see SI 2008/1731, r 1; for transitional provisions see r 3(1), (2) thereof.

17 Notice of a rectification application

(1) This rule does not apply where the adjudicator has rejected a rectification application under rule 16(3).

(2) Where a rectification application has been received by the adjudicator, he must [either serve, or direct the applicant to] serve on the person against whom the order is

sought and on any other person who, in the opinion of the adjudicator, should be a party to the proceedings—

(a) written notice of the rectification application; and

(b) a copy of the rectification application.

(3) The . . . notice under paragraph (2)(a) [must specify] that if a party receiving the notice has any objection to the rectification application and that party wishes to lodge an objection, he must lodge his objection within 28 days of service of the notice under paragraph (2)(a).

NOTES

Initial Commencement

Specified date

Specified date: 13 October 2003: see r 1.

Amendment

Para (2): words "either serve, or direct the applicant to" in square brackets inserted by SI 2008/1731, rr 4, 12(a).
Date in force: 25 July 2008: see SI 2008/1731, r 1; for transitional provisions see r 3(1), (2) thereof.
Para (3): words omitted revoked by SI 2008/1731, rr 4, 12(b)(i).
Date in force: 25 July 2008: see SI 2008/1731, r 1; for transitional provisions see r 3(1), (2) thereof.
Para (3): words "must specify" in square brackets inserted by SI 2008/1731, rr 4, 12(b)(ii).
Date in force: 25 July 2008: see SI 2008/1731, r 1; for transitional provisions see r 3(1), (2) thereof.

18 Objection to a rectification application

A person lodges an objection under rule 17(3) if within 28 days of service of the notice under rule 17(2)(a) he serves—

(a) on the adjudicator—

[(i) a written statement addressed to the adjudicator, dated and verified by a statement of truth, setting out the grounds for the objection;]

(ii) . . .

[(iii) copies of any documents in the party's possession or control which—

(aa) are central to the party's case; or

(bb) the adjudicator or any other party to the proceedings will require in order properly to understand the party's written statement;]

(iv) a written list of witnesses that the party intends to call to give evidence in support of the objection; and

(v) written confirmation of his name and address for service; and

(b) on the other parties a copy of all the information and documents served on the adjudicator under sub-paragraph (a).

NOTES

Initial Commencement

Specified date

Specified date: 13 October 2003: see r 1.

Amendment

Para (a)(i) substituted by SI 2008/1731, rr 4, 13(a).
Date in force: 25 July 2008: see SI 2008/1731, r 1; for transitional provisions see r 3(1), (2) thereof.
Para (a)(ii) revoked by SI 2008/1731, rr 4, 13(b).
Date in force: 25 July 2008: see SI 2008/1731, r 1; for transitional provisions see r 3(1), (2) thereof.

Para (a)(iii) substituted by SI 2008/1731, rr 4, 13(c).

Date in force: 25 July 2008: see SI 2008/1731, r 1; for transitional provisions see r 3(1), (2) thereof.

PART 4
PREPARATION FOR DETERMINATION OF REFERENCES AND RECTIFICATION APPLICATIONS

19 Scope of this Part

This Part sets out the procedure for the preparation for the determination of references and rectification applications.

NOTES

Initial Commencement

Specified date

Specified date: 13 October 2003: see r 1.

[20 Directions]

[(1) The adjudicator may at any time, on the application of a party or otherwise, give directions to enable the parties to prepare for a hearing, or to assist the adjudicator to conduct the proceedings or determine any question in the proceedings with or without a hearing.

(2) Such directions may include, but are not limited to—

(a) a direction that the parties attend a case management conference or a pre-hearing review; and

(b) such other directions as are provided for in these Rules.]

NOTES

Amendment

Substituted by SI 2008/1731, rr 4, 14.

Date in force: 25 July 2008: see SI 2008/1731, r 1; for transitional provisions see r 3(1), (2) thereof.

21 Form of directions

(1) Any direction made by the adjudicator must be—

(a) in writing;

(b) dated; and

(c) except in the case of requirement notices under rule 28, served by him on—

(i) every party to the proceedings;

(ii) where the person who made the application, representation or objection that resulted in the direction was not a party, that person; and

(iii) where the direction requires the registrar to take action, the registrar.

(2) Directions containing a requirement must [, where appropriate,] include a statement of the possible consequences of failure to comply with the requirement within any time limit specified by these Rules, or imposed by the adjudicator.

(3) Directions requiring a party to provide or produce a document . . . may require the party to provide or produce it to the adjudicator or to another party or both.

NOTES

Initial Commencement

Specified date

Specified date: 13 October 2003: see r 1.

Amendment

Para (2): words ", where appropriate," in square brackets inserted by SI 2008/1731, rr 4, 15(a).

Date in force: 25 July 2008: see SI 2008/1731, r 1; for transitional provisions see r 3(1), (2) thereof.

Para (3): words omitted revoked by SI 2008/1731, rr 4, 15(b).

Date in force: 25 July 2008: see SI 2008/1731, r 1; for transitional provisions see r 3(1), (2) thereof.

22 Consolidating proceedings

Where a reference or rectification application is related to another reference or rectification application and in the opinion of the adjudicator it is appropriate or practicable to do so, the adjudicator may direct that any or all of those related references or rectification applications be dealt with together.

NOTES

Initial Commencement

Specified date

Specified date: 13 October 2003: see r 1.

23 Intention to appear

The adjudicator may give directions requiring a party to state whether that party intends to—

(a) attend or be represented at the hearing; and

(b) call witnesses.

NOTES

Initial Commencement

Specified date

Specified date: 13 October 2003: see r 1.

24 Addition and substitution of parties

(1) The adjudicator may give one or more of the following directions—

(a) that any person be added as a new party to the proceedings, if it appears to the adjudicator desirable for that person to be made a party;

(b) that any person cease to be a party to the proceedings, if it appears to the adjudicator that it is not desirable for that person to remain a party; and

(c) that a new party be substituted for an existing party, if—

(i) the existing party's interest or liability has passed to the new party; and

(ii) it appears to the adjudicator desirable to do this to enable him to resolve the whole or part of the matter or any question of dispute in the proceedings.

(2) If the adjudicator directs that a new party is to be added to the proceedings, the adjudicator must specify—

(a) whether the new party is added as an applicant or a respondent; and

(b) how the new party is to be referred to.

(3) Each new party must be given a single identification that should be in accordance with the order in which they joined the proceedings, for example "second applicant" or "second respondent".

(4) If the adjudicator directs that a new party is to be substituted for an existing party, the adjudicator must specify which party the new party is to substitute, for example "respondent" or "second applicant".

(5) The adjudicator must [either serve, or direct one or more of the existing parties to] serve on each new party a copy of each of the following—

(a) the applicant's statement of case and copy documents served on the adjudicator under rule 12 or the applicant's rectification application served on the adjudicator under rule 16(1); and

(b) the respondent's statement of case and copy documents served on the adjudicator under rule 13 or the documents and information served by the respondent on the adjudicator under rule 18(a).

(6) If the new party is added to or substituted for parties to proceedings on a reference, the new party must serve on the adjudicator and each of the other parties within 28 days of service on him of the documents specified in paragraph (5)—

(a) his statement of case which must be in accordance with rule 14; and

[(b) copies of any documents in the new party's possession or control which—

(i) are central to the new party's case; or

(ii) the adjudicator or any other party to the proceedings will require in order properly to understand the new party's statement of case].

(7) If the new party is added to or substituted for parties to proceedings on a rectification application, the new party must serve on the adjudicator and each of the other parties, within 28 days of service on him of the documents specified in paragraph (5)—

(a) if the new party is added or substituted as an applicant, his rectification application which must be in accordance with rule 16(1); or

(b) if the new party is added or substituted as a respondent, his objection to the rectification application which must be in accordance with rule 18(a).

(8) If a continuing party wishes to respond to the documents specified in paragraph (6) or (7), he may apply to the adjudicator for leave to do so.

(9) If the adjudicator grants the requested leave to respond, the adjudicator must require the party requesting leave to respond to serve a copy of his response on the adjudicator and all other parties.

(10) [When directing] the addition or substitution of parties [or at any time thereafter] and if it is necessary to do so, the adjudicator may give consequential directions, including for—

(a) the preparation and updating of a list of parties;

(b) the delivery and service of documents; and

(c) the waiver of the requirement to supply copies of documents [under paragraph (6)(b)] where copies have already been [served by or on the adjudicator and each of the other parties] in the course of the proceedings.

NOTES

Initial Commencement

Specified date

Specified date: 13 October 2003: see r 1.

Amendment

Para (5): words "either serve, or direct one or more of the existing parties to" in square brackets inserted by SI 2008/1731, rr 4, 16(a).

Date in force: 25 July 2008: see SI 2008/1731, r 1; for transitional provisions see r 3(1), (2) thereof.

Para (6): sub-para (b) substituted by SI 2008/1731, rr 4, 16(b).

Date in force: 25 July 2008: see SI 2008/1731, r 1; for transitional provisions see r 3(1), (2) thereof.

Para (10): words "When directing" in square brackets substituted by SI 2008/1731, rr 4, 16(c)(i).

Date in force: 25 July 2008: see SI 2008/1731, r 1; for transitional provisions see r 3(1), (2) thereof.

Para (10): words "or at any time thereafter" in square brackets inserted by SI 2008/1731, rr 4, 16(c)(ii).

Date in force: 25 July 2008: see SI 2008/1731, r 1; for transitional provisions see r 3(1) , (2) thereof.

Para (10): in sub-para (c) words "under paragraph (6)(b)" in square brackets substituted by SI 2008/1731, rr 4, 16(c)(iii)(aa).

Date in force: 25 July 2008: see SI 2008/1731, r 1; for transitional provisions see r 3(1), (2) thereof.

Para (10): in sub-para (c) words "served by or on the adjudicator and each of the other parties" in square brackets substituted by SI 2008/1731, rr 4, 16(c)(iii)(bb).

Date in force: 25 July 2008: see SI 2008/1731, r 1; for transitional provisions see r 3(1), (2) thereof.

25 Further information, supplementary statements and further responses to statements of case

The adjudicator may give directions requiring a party to provide one or more of the following—

(a) a statement of the facts in dispute or issues to be decided;

(b) a statement of the facts on which that party intends to rely and the allegations he intends to make;

(c) a summary of the arguments on which that party intends to rely; and

(d) such further information, responses to statements of case or supplementary statements as may reasonably be required for the determination of the whole or part of the matter or any question in dispute in the proceedings.

NOTES

Initial Commencement

Specified date

Specified date: 13 October 2003: see r 1.

26 Witness statements

The adjudicator may give directions requiring a party to provide a witness statement made by any witness on whose evidence that party intends to rely in the proceedings.

NOTES

Initial Commencement

Specified date

Specified date: 13 October 2003: see r 1.

27 Disclosure and inspection of documents

(1) Any document . . . supplied to the adjudicator or to a party under this rule or under rule 28 may only be used for the purpose of the proceedings in which it was disclosed.

[(2) Within 28 days after service of the respondent's statement of case under rule 13 or the lodging of an objection under rule 18, each party must—

(a) serve on the adjudicator and each of the other parties a list, which complies with rule 47, of all documents in that party's possession or control which—

(i) that party intends to rely upon in the proceedings;

(ii) adversely affect that party's own case;

(iii) adversely affect another party's case; or

(iv) support another party's case; and

(b) send to the adjudicator copies of all documents in the list served under sub-paragraph (a).

(3) Paragraph (4) applies to documents—

(a) referred to in a party's—

(i) statement of case;

(ii) rectification application under rule 16(1); or
(iii) written statement under rule 18(a)(i); or

(b) appearing on a list served by a party under paragraph (2).

(4) In addition to any other requirement in these rules to disclose or provide copies of documents, in relation to any document referred to in paragraph (3) each party must—

(a) permit any other party to inspect and take copies on reasonable notice and at a reasonable time and place; and
(b) provide a copy if requested by another party on payment by such other party of reasonable copying costs.

(5) Paragraphs (2), (3) and (4) are subject to any direction of the adjudicator to the contrary.

(6) The adjudicator may at any time give directions requiring a party to state whether that party has any particular document, or class of documents, in its possession or control and, if so, to comply with the requirements of paragraphs (2), (3) and (4) in relation to such documents as if one of the categories at paragraph (2)(a) applied to them.]

NOTES

Initial Commencement

Specified date

Specified date: 13 October 2003: see r 1.

Amendment

Para (1): words omitted revoked by SI 2008/1731, rr 4, 17(a).
Date in force: 25 July 2008: see SI 2008/1731, r 1; for transitional provisions see r 3(1), (2) thereof.

Paras (2)–(6): substituted, for para (2) as originally enacted, by SI 2008/1731, rr 4, 17(b).
Date in force: 25 July 2008: see SI 2008/1731, r 1; for transitional provisions see r 3(1), (2) thereof.

28 Requirement notices

(1) The adjudicator may, at any time, require the attendance of any person to give evidence or to produce any document . . . specified by the adjudicator which is in that person's possession or control.

(2) The adjudicator must make any such requirement in a requirement notice.

(3) The requirement notice must be in the form specified by the adjudicator provided that the requirement notice—

(a) is in writing;
(b) identifies the person who must comply with the requirement;
(c) identifies the matter to which the requirement relates;
(d) states the nature of the requirement being imposed by the adjudicator;
(e) specifies the time and place at which the adjudicator requires the person to attend and, if appropriate, produce any document . . .; and
(f) includes a statement of the possible consequences of failure to comply with the requirement notice.

(4) The party on whose behalf it is issued must serve the requirement notice.

(5) Subject to paragraph (6) a requirement notice will be binding only if, not less than 7 working days before the time that the person is required to attend—

(a) the requirement notice is served on that person; and
(b) except in the case where that person is a party to the proceedings, the necessary expenses of his attendance are offered and (unless he has refused the offer of payment of his expenses) paid to him.

(6) At any time before the time that the person is required to attend, that person and the party on whose behalf the requirement notice is issued may substitute a shorter period for the period of 7 working days specified in paragraph (5) by—

(a) agreeing in writing such shorter period; and
(b) before the time that the person is required to attend, serving a copy of that agreement on the adjudicator.

(7) Where a requirement has been imposed on a person under paragraph (1), that person may apply to the adjudicator for the requirement to be varied or set aside.

(8) Any application made under paragraph (7) must be made to the adjudicator before the time when the person is to comply with the requirement to which the application under paragraph (7) relates.

NOTES

Initial Commencement

Specified date

Specified date: 13 October 2003: see r 1.

Amendment

Para (1): words omitted revoked by SI 2008/1731, rr 4, 18.
Date in force: 25 July 2008: see SI 2008/1731, r 1; for transitional provisions see r 3(1), (2) thereof.
Para (3): in sub-para (e) words omitted revoked by SI 2008/1731, rr 4, 18.
Date in force: 25 July 2008: see SI 2008/1731, r 1; for transitional provisions see r 3(1), (2) thereof.

29 Estimate of length of hearing

The adjudicator may require the parties to provide an estimate of the length of the hearing.

NOTES

Initial Commencement

Specified date

Specified date: 13 October 2003: see r 1.

30 Site inspections

(1) In this rule—

"the appropriate party" is the party who is in occupation or has ownership or control of the property;

"the property" is the land or premises that the adjudicator wishes to inspect for the purposes of determining the whole or part of the matter; and

"a request for entry" is a written request from the adjudicator to the appropriate party, requesting permission for the adjudicator to enter onto and inspect the property and such a request may include a request to be accompanied by one or more of—

(a) another party;
(b) such number of the adjudicator's officers or staff as he considers necessary; and
(c) if a member of the [Administrative Justice and Tribunals Council] informs the adjudicator that he wishes to attend the inspection, that member.

(2) The adjudicator, at any time for the purpose of determining the whole or part of the matter, may serve a request for entry on an appropriate party.

(3) The request for entry must specify a time for the entry that, unless otherwise agreed in writing by the appropriate party, must be not earlier than 7 days after the date of service of the request for entry.

(4) The adjudicator must serve a copy of the request for entry on any party (other than the appropriate party) and any member of the [Administrative Justice and Tribunals Council] named in the request for entry and, if reasonably practicable to do so in the circumstances, must notify them of any change in the time specified.

(5) If the adjudicator makes a request for entry and the appropriate party withholds or refuses his consent to the whole or part of the request without reasonable excuse, the adjudicator may take such refusal into account when making his substantive decision.

(6) If a request for entry includes a request for a member of the [Administrative Justice and Tribunals Council] to accompany the adjudicator and the appropriate party consents to the presence of that member, then that member shall be entitled to attend the site inspection but must not take an active part in the inspection.

NOTES

Initial Commencement

Specified date

Specified date: 13 October 2003: see r 1.

Amendment

Para (1): in sub-para (c) words "Administrative Justice and Tribunals Council" in square brackets substituted by SI 2008/1731, rr 4, 19.

Date in force: 25 July 2008: see SI 2008/1731, r 1; for transitional provisions see r 3(1), (2) thereof.

Para (4): words "Administrative Justice and Tribunals Council" in square brackets substituted by SI 2008/1731, rr 4, 19.

Date in force: 25 July 2008: see SI 2008/1731, r 1; for transitional provisions see r 3(1), (2) thereof.

Para (6): words "Administrative Justice and Tribunals Council" in square brackets substituted by SI 2008/1731, rr 4, 19.

Date in force: 25 July 2008: see SI 2008/1731, r 1; for transitional provisions see r 3(1), (2) thereof.

31 Preliminary issues

(1) At any time and on the application of a party or of his own motion, the adjudicator may dispose of any matter or matters that are in dispute as a preliminary issue.

(2) If in the opinion of the adjudicator the decision on the preliminary issue will dispose of the whole of the matter then the decision on the preliminary issue must be—

- (a) made in accordance with the provisions in these Rules on substantive decisions; and
- (b) treated as a substantive decision.

NOTES

Initial Commencement

Specified date

Specified date: 13 October 2003: see r 1.

PART 5
HEARINGS AND SUBSTANTIVE DECISIONS

32 Scope of this Part

This Part sets out the procedure for determination of references and rectification applications, the format of substantive decisions and substantive orders and rules on costs.

NOTES

Initial Commencement

Specified date

Specified date: 13 October 2003: see r 1.

[32A Summary disposal]

[(1) The adjudicator may summarily dispose of the proceedings or any particular issue in the proceedings on an application by a party or of its own motion if—

(a) the adjudicator considers that the applicant or respondent has no real prospect of succeeding in the proceedings or on the issue; and

(b) there is no other compelling reason why the proceedings or issue should not be disposed of summarily.

(2) Except with the permission of the adjudicator, an applicant may not apply for summary disposal until the respondent has served a statement of case or lodged an objection (as appropriate), or the respondent's time to do so has expired.

(3) A respondent may apply for summary disposal at any time after the applicant has served a statement of case or rectification application (as appropriate), or (in the case of service of a statement of case) the applicant's time to do so has expired.

(4) Paragraph (5) applies where—

(a) a respondent applies for summary disposal before serving a statement of case or lodging an objection (as appropriate) and before the time to do so has expired; and

(b) that application does not result in the disposal of the entire proceedings.

(5) In the circumstances described in paragraph (4) the respondent's time for serving a statement of case or lodging an objection is extended to—

(a) 28 days after service on the respondent of the adjudicator's decision in relation to the application for summary disposal; or

(b) such other time as the adjudicator directs.

(6) An application for summary disposal must include a witness statement in support of the application. That witness statement must state that the party making the application—

(a) believes that the other party has no real prospect of succeeding on the proceedings or on the issue to which the application relates; and

(b) knows of no other reason why the disposal of the proceedings or issue should not be disposed of summarily.

(7) When serving a notice under rule 51(5) or (7), or directing the party making the application to serve a notice under rule 51(5), and such notice relates in whole or in part to summary disposal, the adjudicator must give directions for the service of evidence by the parties and for the determination of the issue of summary disposal.

(8) When the adjudicator determines the issue of summary disposal the adjudicator may make an order—

(a) disposing of the proceedings or of any issue; or

(b) dismissing the application for or intention to consider summary disposal.

(9) Where an order made under paragraph (8) does not dispose of the entire proceedings, the adjudicator must give case management directions as to the future conduct of the proceedings.]

NOTES

Amendment

Inserted by SI 2008/1731, rr 4, 20.

Date in force: 25 July 2008: see SI 2008/1731, r 1; for transitional provisions see r 3(1), (2) thereof.

33 Substantive decision without a hearing

(1) There is a presumption that a substantive decision is made following a hearing.

(2) Subject to paragraph (1), the adjudicator may make a substantive decision without a hearing if—

(a) he is satisfied that there is no important public interest consideration that requires a hearing in public; and

(b) unless paragraph (3) applies, he has served written notice on the parties in accordance with these Rules that he intends to make a substantive decision without a hearing or that he has received an application requesting that the substantive decision be made without a hearing and—
  (i) the parties agree to the substantive decision being made without a hearing; or
  (ii) the parties fail to object within the specified period for objection to the substantive decision being made without a hearing.

(3) The adjudicator is not required to serve notice under paragraph (2)(b) if all parties have requested the adjudicator to make the substantive decision without a hearing.

NOTES

Initial Commencement

Specified date

Specified date: 13 October 2003: see r 1.

34 Notice of hearing

(1) Where the adjudicator is to hold a hearing, he must serve written notice of his intention to hear on such parties as he considers necessary.

(2) The adjudicator must specify in the notice under paragraph (1), the date, time and location of the hearing.

(3) The adjudicator must serve the notice under paragraph (1)—
  (a) no later than 28 days before the hearing; or
  (b) before the expiry of such shorter notice period as agreed by all the parties on whom he intends to serve notice under paragraph (1).

NOTES

Initial Commencement

Specified date

Specified date: 13 October 2003: see r 1.

35 Representation at the hearing

(1) At the hearing a party may conduct his case himself or, subject to paragraph (2), be represented or assisted by any person, whether or not legally qualified.

(2) If, in any particular case, the adjudicator is satisfied that there is sufficient reason for doing so, he may refuse to permit a particular person to represent or assist a party at the hearing.

NOTES

Initial Commencement

Specified date

Specified date: 13 October 2003: see r 1.

36 Publication of hearings

The adjudicator must publish details of all listed hearings at the office of the adjudicator and, if different, the venue at which the hearing is to take place.

NOTES

Initial Commencement

Specified date

Specified date: 13 October 2003: see r 1.

37 . . .

. . .

NOTES

Amendment

Revoked by SI 2008/1731, rr 4, 21.

Date in force: 25 July 2008: see SI 2008/1731, r 1; for transitional provisions see r 3(1), (2) thereof.

38 Absence of parties

(1) If any party does not attend and is not represented at any hearing of which notice has been served on him in accordance with these Rules, the adjudicator—

(a) may proceed with the hearing and reach a substantive decision in that party's absence if—

(i) the adjudicator is not satisfied that any reasons given for the absence are justified;

(ii) the absent party consents; or

(iii) it would be unjust to adjourn the hearing; or

(b) must otherwise adjourn the hearing.

(2) Following a decision by the adjudicator under paragraph (1) to proceed with or adjourn the hearing, the adjudicator may make such consequential directions as he sees fit.

NOTES

Initial Commencement

Specified date

Specified date: 13 October 2003: see r 1.

39 Substantive decision of the adjudicator

(1) Where there is a hearing, the substantive decision of the adjudicator may be given orally at the end of the hearing or reserved.

(2) A substantive decision of the adjudicator, whether made at a hearing or without a hearing, must be recorded in a substantive order.

(3) The adjudicator may not vary or set aside a substantive decision.

NOTES

Initial Commencement

Specified date

Specified date: 13 October 2003: see r 1.

40 Substantive orders and written reasons

(1) A substantive order must—

(a) be in writing;

(b) be dated;

[(c) be sealed and state the name of the person making the order;]

(d) state the substantive decision that has been reached;

(e) state any steps that must be taken to give effect to that substantive decision; and

(f) [where appropriate,] state the possible consequences of a party's failure to comply with the substantive order within any specified time limits.

(2) The substantive order must be served by the adjudicator on—

(a) every party to the proceedings; and

(b) where the substantive order requires the registrar to take action, the registrar.

(3) A substantive order requiring a party to provide or produce a document . . . may require the party to provide or produce it to any or all of the adjudicator, the registrar or another party.

(4) Unless the adjudicator directs otherwise, the substantive order must be publicly available.

(5) Where the substantive order is publicly available, the adjudicator may provide copies of it to the public on request.

(6) The adjudicator must give in writing to all parties his reasons for—

(a) his substantive decision; and

(b) any steps that must be taken to give effect to that substantive decision.

(7) The adjudicator's reasons referred to in paragraph (6) need not be given in the substantive order.

NOTES

Initial Commencement

Specified date

Specified date: 13 October 2003: see r 1.

Amendment

Para (1): sub-para (c) substituted by SI 2008/1731, rr 4, 22(a).
Date in force: 25 July 2008: see SI 2008/1731, r 1; for transitional provisions see r 3(1), (2) thereof.

Para (1): in sub-para (f) words "where appropriate," in square brackets inserted by SI 2008/1731, rr 4, 22(b).
Date in force: 25 July 2008: see SI 2008/1731, r 1; for transitional provisions see r 3(1), (2) thereof.

Para (3): words omitted revoked by SI 2008/1731, rr 4, 22(c).
Date in force: 25 July 2008: see SI 2008/1731, r 1; for transitional provisions see r 3(1), (2) thereof.

41 Substantive orders on a reference that include requirements on the registrar

(1) Where the adjudicator has made a substantive decision on a reference, the substantive order giving effect to that substantive decision may include a requirement on the registrar to—

(a) give effect to the original application in whole or in part as if the objection to that original application had not been made; or

(b) cancel the original application in whole or in part.

(2) A requirement on the registrar under this rule may include—

(a) a condition that a specified entry be made on the register of any title affected; or

(b) a requirement to reject any future application of a specified kind by a named party to the proceedings—

(i) unconditionally; or

(ii) unless that party satisfies specified conditions.

NOTES

Initial Commencement

Specified date

Specified date: 13 October 2003: see r 1.

[41A Orders under rule 8(4) or 9(4)]

[An order made under rule 8(4) or 9(4) must—

(a) comply with the requirements of rule 40(1)(a), (b), (c) and (f), (2), (3), (4) and (5) as if it were a substantive order;

(b) identify the decision of the court which the order implements; and

(c) state the reasons why the order complies with rule 8(4)(a) or 9(4)(a).]

NOTES

Amendment

Inserted by SI 2008/1731, rr 4, 23.

Date in force: 25 July 2008: see SI 2008/1731, r 1; for transitional provisions see r 3(1), (2) thereof.

42 Costs

(1) In this rule—

(a) "all the circumstances" are all the circumstances of the proceedings and include—

[(i) the conduct of the parties—

(aa) in respect of proceedings commenced by a reference, during (but not prior to) the proceedings; or

(bb) in respect of proceedings commenced by a rectification application, before and during the proceedings;]

(ii) whether a party has succeeded on part of his case, even if he has not been wholly successful; and

(iii) any representations made to the adjudicator by the parties; and

(b) the conduct of the parties . . . includes—

(i) whether it was reasonable for a party to raise, pursue or contest a particular allegation or issue;

(ii) the manner in which a party has pursued or defended his case or a particular allegation or issue; and

(iii) whether a party who has succeeded in his case in whole or in part exaggerated his case.

(2) The adjudicator may, on the application of a party or of his own motion, make an order as to costs.

(3) In deciding what order as to costs (if any) to make, the adjudicator must have regard to all the circumstances.

[(4) An order as to costs may, without limitation—

(a) require a party to pay the whole or a part of the costs of another party and—

(i) specify a fixed sum or proportion to be paid; or

(ii) specify that costs from or until a certain date are to be paid;

(b) if the adjudicator considers it impracticable to make an order in respect of the relevant part of a party's costs under paragraph (a), specify that costs relating to a distinct part of the proceedings are to be paid;

(c) specify an amount to be paid on account before costs are agreed or assessed; or

(d) specify the time within which costs are to be paid.]

[(5) The adjudicator may—

(a) summarily assess the whole or a part of a party's costs; or

(b) specify that, if the parties are unable to reach agreement on an amount to be paid, the whole or a part of a party's costs be assessed in a specified manner.]

(6) [An order as to costs must be recorded in a costs order and] must—

(a) be in writing;

(b) be dated;

(c) be [sealed and state the name of the person making the order];

(d) state the order as to costs; and

(e) be served by the adjudicator on the parties.

(7) Where the costs are to be assessed by the adjudicator, he may assess the costs—

(a) on the standard basis; or

(b) on the indemnity basis,

but in either case the adjudicator will not allow costs that have been unreasonably incurred or are unreasonable in amount.

(8) The adjudicator must inform the parties of the basis on which he will be assessing the costs.

(9) Where the amount of the costs are to be assessed on the standard basis, the adjudicator must—

(a) only allow costs which are proportionate to the matters in issue; and

(b) resolve any doubt that he may have as to whether costs were reasonably incurred or reasonable and proportionate in favour of the paying party.

(10) In deciding whether costs assessed on the standard basis were either proportionately and reasonably incurred or proportionate and reasonable in amount, the adjudicator must have regard to all the circumstances.

[(11) Where costs are to be assessed on the indemnity basis, the adjudicator must resolve in favour of the receiving party any doubt as to the reasonableness of the incurring or the amount of the costs.]

(12) In deciding whether costs assessed on the indemnity basis were either reasonably incurred or reasonable in amount, the adjudicator must have regard to all the circumstances.

(13) Once the adjudicator has assessed the costs, he must serve on the parties written notice—

(a) of the amount which must be paid;

(b) by whom and to whom the amount must be paid; and

(c) if appropriate, the time by when the amount must be paid.

NOTES

Initial Commencement

Specified date

Specified date: 13 October 2003: see r 1.

Amendment

Para (1): sub-para (a)(i) substituted by SI 2008/1731, rr 4, 24(a).

Date in force: 25 July 2008: see SI 2008/1731, r 1; for transitional provisions see r 3(1), (2) thereof.

Para (1): in sub-para (b) words omitted revoked by SI 2008/1731, rr 4, 24(b).

Date in force: 25 July 2008: see SI 2008/1731, r 1; for transitional provisions see r 3(1), (2) thereof.

Para (4): substituted by SI 2008/1731, rr 4, 24(c).

Date in force: 25 July 2008: see SI 2008/1731, r 1; for transitional provisions see r 3(1), (2) thereof.

Para (5): substituted by SI 2008/1731, rr 4, 24(d).

Date in force: 25 July 2008: see SI 2008/1731, r 1; for transitional provisions see r 3(1), (2) thereof.

Para (6): words "An order as to costs must be recorded in a costs order and" in square brackets substituted by SI 2008/1731, rr 4, 24(e)(i).

Date in force: 25 July 2008: see SI 2008/1731, r 1; for transitional provisions see r 3(1), (2) thereof.

Para (6): in sub-para (c) words "sealed and state the name of the person making the order" in square brackets substituted by SI 2008/1731, rr 4, 24(e)(ii).

Date in force: 25 July 2008: see SI 2008/1731, r 1; for transitional provisions see r 3(1), (2) thereof.

Para (11): substituted by SI 2008/1731, rr 4, 24(f).

Date in force: 25 July 2008: see SI 2008/1731, r 1; for transitional provisions see r 3(1), (2) thereof.

43 Costs thrown away

(1) In this rule—

"costs thrown away" means costs of the proceedings resulting from any neglect or delay of the legal representative during (but not prior to) the proceedings and which—

(a) have been incurred by a party; or

(b) have been—

(i) paid by a party to another party; or

(ii) awarded to a party,

under an order made under rule 42;

"an order as to costs thrown away" means an order requiring the legal representative concerned to meet the whole or part of the costs thrown away; and

"the legal representative" means the legally qualified representative of a party.

(2) The adjudicator may, on the application of a party or otherwise, make an order as to costs thrown away provided the adjudicator is satisfied that—

(a) a party has incurred costs of the proceedings unnecessarily as a result of the neglect or delay of the legal representative; and

(b) it is just in all the circumstances for the legal representative to compensate the party who has incurred or paid the costs thrown away, for the whole or part of those costs.

(3) If the adjudicator has received an application for or proposes to make an order as to costs thrown away, he may give directions to the parties and the legal representative about the procedure to be followed to ensure that the issues are dealt with in a way that is fair and as simple and summary as the circumstances permit.

(4) An order as to costs thrown away may—

(a) specify the amount of costs to be paid by the legal representative; and

(b) if the adjudicator considers it appropriate, specify the time within which the costs are to be paid.

(5) An order as to costs thrown away must be recorded in a costs thrown away order.

(6) A costs thrown away order must—

(a) be in writing;

(b) be dated;

(c) be [sealed and state the name of the person making the order];

(d) state the order as to costs thrown away; and

(e) be served by the adjudicator on the parties and the legal representative.

NOTES

Initial Commencement

Specified date

Specified date: 13 October 2003: see r 1.

Amendment

Para (6): in sub-para (c) words "sealed and state the name of the person making the order" in square brackets substituted by SI 2008/1731, rr 4, 25.

Date in force: 25 July 2008: see SI 2008/1731, r 1; for transitional provisions see r 3(1), (2) thereof.

PART 6
APPEALS FROM ADJUDICATOR

44 Scope of this Part

This Part contains provisions in relation to appeals to the High Court of decisions by the adjudicator and includes provisions about the adjudicator staying implementation of his decision pending the outcome of an appeal.

NOTES

Initial Commencement

Specified date

Specified date: 13 October 2003: see r 1.

45 Appeals to the High Court

(1) Where a party is granted permission to appeal, the adjudicator may, of his own motion or on the application of a party, stay the implementation of the whole or part of his decision pending the outcome of the appeal.

(2) A party who wishes to apply to the adjudicator to stay the implementation of the whole or part of a decision pending the outcome of the appeal must make such an application to the adjudicator at the same time that he applies to the adjudicator for permission to appeal.

(3) Where a party applies under paragraph (2) to the adjudicator to stay implementation of the whole or part of a decision, that party must at the same time provide reasons for the application.

(4) Before reaching a decision as to whether to grant permission to appeal a decision or to stay implementation of a decision, the adjudicator must allow the parties the opportunity to make representations or objections.

(5) The adjudicator must serve written notice on the parties of any decision that he makes as to whether to grant permission to appeal or to stay the implementation of the whole or part of his decision pending the outcome of the appeal.

(6) Where the adjudicator's decision to grant permission to appeal or to stay implementation of a decision relates to a decision contained in a substantive order, the adjudicator must serve on the registrar a copy of the notice under paragraph (5).

(7) The notice under paragraph (5) must—

- (a) be in writing;
- (b) be dated;
- (c) specify the decision made by the adjudicator;
- (d) include the adjudicator's reasons for his decision; and
- (e) be [sealed and state the name of the person making the order].

NOTES

Initial Commencement

Specified date

Specified date: 13 October 2003: see r 1.

Amendment

Para (7): in sub-para (e) words "sealed and state the name of the person making the order" in square brackets substituted by SI 2008/1731, rr 4, 26.

Date in force: 25 July 2008: see SI 2008/1731, r 1; for transitional provisions see r 3(1), (2) thereof.

PART 7
GENERAL

46 Record of matters

(1) The adjudicator must keep at his principal office a record of matters that records the particulars of all—

- (a) references;
- (b) rectification applications;
- (c) substantive decisions; and
- (d) all applications and decisions made under rule 45.

(2) Subject to paragraph (3), the record of matters must be open to the inspection of any person without charge at all reasonable hours on working days.

(3) Where the adjudicator is satisfied that it is just and reasonable to do so, the adjudicator may exclude from inspection any information contained in the record of matters.

(4) Depending on all the circumstances, it may be just and reasonable for the adjudicator to exclude from inspection any information contained in the record of matters if it is in the interest of morals, public order, national security, juveniles or the protection of the private lives of the parties to the proceedings, or where the adjudicator considers that publicity would prejudice the interests of justice.

NOTES

Initial Commencement

Specified date

Specified date: 13 October 2003: see r 1.

47 List of documents and documents

(1) For the purposes of these Rules, a list of documents must be in writing and [, subject to paragraph (1A),] must contain the following information where available in relation to each document—

- (a) a brief description of the nature of the document;
- (b) . . .
- (c) whether the document is an original, a copy certified to be a true copy of the original, an office copy or another type of copy;
- (d) the date of the document;
- (e) the document parties or the original author and recipient of the document; and
- (f) the version number or similar identification number or code of the document.

[(1A) If a large number of documents fall into a particular class, that class of documents may be listed in accordance with paragraph (1) as if it were an individual document.

(1B) If a class of documents is listed in accordance with paragraph (1A), the description of the class of documents must be sufficiently clear and precise to enable any party receiving the list to identify—

- (a) the nature of the contents of each document included within that class of documents; and
- (b) whether any particular document which exists is included within that class of documents.]

(2) Unless the adjudicator otherwise permits, where a document provided for the purposes of the proceedings is or contains a coloured map, plan or drawing, any copy provided of that map, plan or drawing must be in the same colours as the map, plan or drawing of which it is a copy (so for example, where a plan shows the boundary of a property in red, a copy of the plan must also show the boundary in red).

NOTES

Initial Commencement

Specified date

Specified date: 13 October 2003: see r 1.

Amendment

Para (1): words ", subject to paragraph (1A)," in square brackets inserted by SI 2008/1731, rr 4, 27(a)(i).

Date in force: 25 July 2008: see SI 2008/1731, r 1; for transitional provisions see r 3(1), (2) thereof.

Para (1): sub-para (b) revoked by SI 2008/1731, rr 4, 27(a)(ii).

Date in force: 25 July 2008: see SI 2008/1731, r 1; for transitional provisions see r 3(1), (2) thereof.

Paras (1A), (1B): inserted by SI 2008/1731, rr 4, 27(b).
Date in force: 25 July 2008: see SI 2008/1731, r 1; for transitional provisions see r 3(1), (2) thereof.

48 Evidence

(1) The adjudicator may require any witness to give evidence on oath or affirmation and for that purpose there may be administered an oath or affirmation in due form.

(2) No person may be compelled to give any evidence or produce any document . . . that that person could not be compelled to give or produce on a trial of an action in a court of law in England and Wales.

NOTES

Initial Commencement

Specified date

Specified date: 13 October 2003: see r 1.

Amendment

Para (2): words omitted revoked by SI 2008/1731, rr 4, 28.
Date in force: 25 July 2008: see SI 2008/1731, r 1; for transitional provisions see r 3(1), (2) thereof.

49 Expert evidence

No party may call an expert, or submit an expert's report as evidence, without the adjudicator's permission.

NOTES

Initial Commencement

Specified date

Specified date: 13 October 2003: see r 1.

50 Service of documents

(1) A party's address for service must be a postal address in England and Wales.

(2) The address for service in paragraph (1) must be either that of the party or of the party's representative who has been appointed as his representative for the purposes of the proceedings.

(3) A party's address for service remains that party's address for service for the purposes of these Rules unless and until he serves on the adjudicator and the other parties notice of a different address for service.

(4) Any document to be served on or delivered to any person (other than the adjudicator) under these Rules may only be served—

- (a) by first class post to his postal address given as his address for service;
- (b) by leaving it at his address for service;
- (c) . . . by document exchange;
- (d) subject to paragraph (6), by fax;
- (e) subject to paragraph (7), by email; or
- (f) where no address for service has been given, by post to or leaving it at his registered office, principal place of business, head or main office or last known address, as appropriate.

(5) . . .

(6) A document may be served by fax on any person other than the adjudicator, to a fax number at the address for service for that person if, in advance, the recipient has informed the adjudicator and all parties in writing—

- (a) that the recipient is willing to accept service by fax; and
- (b) of the fax number to which the documents should be sent.

(7) A document may be served by email on any person other than the adjudicator, if, in advance, the recipient has informed the adjudicator and all parties in writing—

(a) that the recipient is willing to accept service by email;
(b) of the email address to which documents should be sent, which shall be deemed to be at the recipient's address for service; and
(c) if the recipient wishes to so specify, the format in which documents must be sent.

(8) Any document addressed to the adjudicator must be sent—
(a) by first class post to an address specified by the adjudicator; or
(b) by such other method as the adjudicator may specify, including document exchange, fax or email.

(9) Where under paragraph (8)(b) the adjudicator specifies another method of service, the adjudicator may—
(a) specify that that method may be used generally or only in relation to a certain document or documents;
(b) specify that the specified method is no longer available or substitute that specified method with another specified method; and
(c) make such directions in relation to the use of the specified method as he deems appropriate.

(10) Any document served on an unincorporated body may be sent to its secretary, manager or similar officer duly authorised to accept such service.

(11) Any document which is served in accordance with this rule shall be regarded as having been served on the day shown in the table below—

Method of service	*Day of service*
Leaving it at a postal address within England and Wales	The working day after it was left.
Document exchange within England and Wales	The second working day after it was left at the document exchange.
Fax	The working day after it was transmitted.
Email	The working day after it was transmitted.

(12) The adjudicator may direct that service under these Rules of any document may be dispensed with and in those circumstances may make such consequential directions as he deems appropriate.

NOTES

Initial Commencement

Specified date

Specified date: 13 October 2003: see r 1.

Amendment

Para (4): in sub-para (c) words omitted revoked by SI 2008/1731, rr 4, 29(a).
Date in force: 25 July 2008: see SI 2008/1731, r 1; for transitional provisions see r 3(1), (2) thereof.
Para (5): revoked by SI 2008/1731, rr 4, 29(b).
Date in force: 25 July 2008: see SI 2008/1731, r 1; for transitional provisions see r 3(1), (2) thereof.

51 Applications, actions by the adjudicator of his own motion, notification, representations and objections

(1) This rule does not apply to Part 3 and rule 45.

(2) An application to the adjudicator must—
(a) be in writing;

(b) state the name of the person applying or on whose behalf the application is made;

(c) be addressed to the adjudicator;

(d) state the nature of the application;

(e) state the reason or reasons for the application; and

(f) if any of the parties or persons who would be affected by the application consent to it, either—

(i) be signed by all the parties or persons who consent or their duly authorised representatives; or

(ii) have attached to it a copy of their written consent.

(3) The adjudicator may dispense with any or all of the requirements under paragraph (2)—

(a) in relation to an application made to the adjudicator at a time when all persons who would be affected by the application are present before the adjudicator; or

(b) if the adjudicator otherwise considers it appropriate or practicable to do so.

(4) For the purposes of paragraph (2)(f), the written consent referred to in that paragraph may be in the form of a letter, fax or email.

(5) If an application is not consented to by all persons who will be affected by the application then, subject to paragraph (10), the adjudicator must [either serve, or direct the party making the application to] serve written notice on persons who have not consented to the application but who would be affected by it [, and any such direction to the party making the application must include the information to be included in the notice under paragraph (6)(d)].

(6) [The] notice under paragraph (5) . . . must state—

(a) that the application has been made;

(b) details of the application;

(c) that the person has a right to make written objections to or representations about the application; and

(d) the period within which such objections or representations must be lodged with the adjudicator.

(7) If the adjudicator intends to act of his own motion under these Rules then, subject to paragraph (10), he must serve written notice of his intention on all persons who will be affected by the action.

(8) In the notice under paragraph (7) the adjudicator must state—

(a) that the adjudicator intends to take action of his own motion;

(b) the action the adjudicator intends to take;

(c) that a person has a right to make written objections or representations to the action that the adjudicator intends to take; and

(d) the period within which such objections or representations must be lodged with the adjudicator.

(9) A person lodges an objection or representation if within the specified period he serves—

(a) on the adjudicator a written statement setting out the grounds for his objection or representation; and

(b) on all the other persons who will be affected by the action a copy of the written statement served on the adjudicator under sub-paragraph (a).

(10) The adjudicator shall not be required to [serve, or direct the applicant to] serve notice under paragraphs (5) and (7) if, in the circumstances, he does not consider it appropriate or practicable to do so.

[(11) Paragraph (10) does not apply to notices—

(a) under paragraphs (5) or (7) which relate to a proposal that the adjudicator exercise the power under rule 32A(1); or

(b) required to be served by rule 33.]

NOTES

Initial Commencement

Specified date

Specified date: 13 October 2003: see r 1.

Amendment

Para (5): words "either serve, or direct the party making the application to" in square brackets inserted by SI 2008/1731, rr 4, 30(a)(i).

Date in force: 25 July 2008: see SI 2008/1731, r 1; for transitional provisions see r 3(1), (2) thereof.

Para (5): words from ", and any such" to "under paragraph (6)(d)" in square brackets inserted by SI 2008/1731, rr 4, 30(a)(ii).

Date in force: 25 July 2008: see SI 2008/1731, r 1; for transitional provisions see r 3(1), (2) thereof.

Para (6): word "The" in square brackets substituted by SI 2008/1731, rr 4, 30(b)(i).

Date in force: 25 July 2008: see SI 2008/1731, r 1; for transitional provisions see r 3(1), (2) thereof.

Para (6): words omitted revoked by SI 2008/1731, rr 4, 30(b)(ii).

Date in force: 25 July 2008: see SI 2008/1731, r 1; for transitional provisions see r 3(1), (2) thereof.

Para (10): words "serve, or direct the applicant to" in square brackets inserted by SI 2008/1731, rr 4, 30(c).

Date in force: 25 July 2008: see SI 2008/1731, r 1; for transitional provisions see r 3(1), (2) thereof.

Para (11): substituted by SI 2008/1731, rr 4, 30(d).

Date in force: 25 July 2008: see SI 2008/1731, r 1; for transitional provisions see r 3(1), (2) thereof.

52 Consideration by the adjudicator of applications (including applications for directions), representations and objections

(1) In relation to any application, representation or objection made to the adjudicator, unless—

(a) the adjudicator is satisfied that it is frivolous or vexatious; or

(b) it is received by the adjudicator after the expiry of any time limit specified for making that application, representation or objection,

the adjudicator must consider all applications, representations or objections made to him.

(2) If an application, representation or objection is received by the adjudicator after the expiry of any time limit specified for making it, the adjudicator may consider the application, representation or objection, but he is not bound to do so.

(3) In considering any application, representation or objection, the adjudicator must make all enquiries he thinks necessary and must, if required by these Rules or if he considers it necessary, give the person making the application, representation or objection and the parties or other persons who will be affected by it the opportunity to appear before him or to submit written representations.

(4) The adjudicator may decide to accept or reject an application, representation or objection in whole or in part.

(5) Following his consideration of any applications, representations or objections that are made to him, the adjudicator must notify the person who made the application, representation or objection and the parties and any other persons who will be affected by it, of his decision in accordance with these Rules.

NOTES

Initial Commencement

Specified date

Specified date: 13 October 2003: see r 1.

53 Adjournment

In addition to the powers and obligations to adjourn proceedings contained in Part 2 and rule 38, the adjudicator may adjourn the whole or part of the proceedings when and to the extent that he feels it reasonable to do so.

NOTES

Initial Commencement

Specified date

Specified date: 13 October 2003: see r 1.

54 Power to vary or set aside directions

Subject to these Rules, the adjudicator may at any time, on the application of a party or otherwise, vary or set aside directions made under these Rules.

NOTES

Initial Commencement

Specified date

Specified date: 13 October 2003: see r 1.

55 Failure to comply with a direction

(1) Where a party has failed to comply with a direction given by the adjudicator (including a direction to commence court proceedings under section 110(1)) the adjudicator may impose a sanction on the defaulting party—

(a) on the application of any other party; or

(b) of his own motion.

(2) Where the defaulting party was the person who made (or has been substituted for or added to the party who made) the original application, the sanction may include requiring the registrar to cancel the original application in whole or in part.

(3) Where the defaulting party was a person who objected to (or has been substituted for or added to the party who objected to) the original application, the sanction may include requiring the registrar to give effect to the original application in whole or in part as if the objection had not been made.

(4) A sanction that includes either of the requirements on the registrar under paragraph (2) or (3) shall be treated as the substantive decision on that matter.

(5) If the sanction does not include either of the requirements on the registrar under paragraph (2) or (3), the adjudicator must serve written notice on the parties of his decision as to what if any sanctions are imposed, and he may make consequential directions.

NOTES

Initial Commencement

Specified date

Specified date: 13 October 2003: see r 1.

56 Errors of procedure

Where, before the adjudicator has made his final substantive order in relation to a matter, there has been an error of procedure such as a failure to comply with a rule—

(a) the error does not invalidate any step taken in the proceedings, unless the adjudicator so orders; and

(b) the adjudicator may make an order or take any other step that he considers appropriate to remedy the error.

NOTES

Initial Commencement

Specified date

Specified date: 13 October 2003: see r 1.

57 Accidental slips or omissions

The adjudicator may at any time amend an order or direction to correct a clerical error or other accidental slip or omission.

NOTES

Initial Commencement

Specified date

Specified date: 13 October 2003: see r 1.

58 Time and place

If the adjudicator deems it appropriate to do so, he may alter—

(a) any time limit specified in these Rules;

(b) any time limit set by the adjudicator; or

(c) the date, time or location appointed for a hearing or for any other appearance of the parties before him.

NOTES

Initial Commencement

Specified date

Specified date: 13 October 2003: see r 1.

59 Calculation of time

(1) Where a period of time for doing an act is specified by these Rules or by a direction of the adjudicator, that period is to be calculated—

(a) excluding the day on which the period begins; and

(b) unless otherwise specified, by reference to calendar days.

(2) Where the time specified by these Rules or by a direction of the adjudicator for doing an act ends on a day which is not a working day, that act is done in time if it is done on the next working day.

NOTES

Initial Commencement

Specified date

Specified date: 13 October 2003: see r 1.

60 Representation of parties

(1) If a party who was previously unrepresented appoints a representative or, having been represented, appoints a replacement representative, that party must, as soon as reasonably practicable following the appointment, notify the adjudicator and the other parties in writing—

(a) of the fact that he has appointed a representative or replacement representative;

(b) the name and contact details of the representative or replacement representative;

(c) whether the representative or replacement representative has been authorised by the party to accept service of documents; and

(d) if the representative or replacement representative has been authorised to accept service, the address for service.

(2) If a party who was previously represented ceases to be represented, that party must, as soon as reasonably practicable following the ending of his representation, notify the adjudicator and the other parties in writing—

(a) of the fact that he is no longer represented; and

(b) where the party's address for service had previously been the address of the representative, the party's new address for service.

NOTES

Initial Commencement

Specified date

Specified date: 13 October 2003: see r 1.

61 Independence of adjudicator's staff

When undertaking a non-administrative function of the adjudicator on the adjudicator's authorisation, a member of the adjudicator's staff is not subject to the direction of the Lord Chancellor or any other person or body.

NOTES

Initial Commencement

Specified date

Specified date: 13 October 2003: see r 1.

FIRST-TIER TRIBUNAL AND UPPER TRIBUNAL (CHAMBERS) (AMENDMENT) ORDER 2013

SI 2013 No 1187

Citation and commencement

1
This Order may be cited as the First-tier Tribunal and Upper Tribunal (Chambers) (Amendment) Order 2013 and comes into force on 1st July 2013.

NOTES

Initial Commencement

Specified date

Specified date: 1 July 2013: see above.

Amendments to the First-tier Tribunal and Upper Tribunal (Chambers) Order 2010

2
The First-tier Tribunal and Upper Tribunal (Chambers) Order 2010 is amended as follows.

NOTES

Initial Commencement

Specified date

Specified date: 1 July 2013: see art 1.

3
In article 2 (First-tier Tribunal Chambers), after paragraph (c), insert—
"(cc) the Property Chamber;"

NOTES

Initial Commencement

Specified date

Specified date: 1 July 2013: see art 1.

4
After article 5 (functions of the Immigration and Asylum Chamber of the First-tier Tribunal), insert—

"5A Functions of the Property Chamber
To the Property Chamber are allocated all functions conferred on the First-tier Tribunal relating to—

(a) a reference by the Chief Land Registrar and any other application, matter or appeal under the Land Registration Act 2002;
(b) proceedings under any of the enactments referred to in section 6A(2) of the Agriculture (Miscellaneous Provisions) Act 1954 or the Hill Farming Act 1946;
(c) housing etc, under the Housing Act 2004;
(d) leasehold property;
(e) residential property;
(f) rents;
(g) the right to buy;
(h) applications and appeals under the Mobile Homes Act 1983."

NOTES

Initial Commencement

Specified date

Specified date: 1 July 2013: see art 1.

5

In article 10 (functions of the Administrative Appeals Chamber), in paragraph (e) after "allocated to" insert "the Lands Chamber by article 12(cc) or to".

NOTES

Initial Commencement

Specified date

Specified date: 1 July 2013: see art 1.

6

In article 12 (functions of the Lands Chamber)—

(a) for paragraph (a)(ii) substitute—

"(ii) appeals from decisions of—

(aa) the First-tier Tribunal made in the Property Chamber other than appeals allocated to the Tax and Chancery Chamber by article 13(h);

(ab) leasehold valuation tribunals in Wales, residential property tribunals in Wales, rent assessment committees in Wales, the Agricultural Land Tribunal in Wales or the Valuation Tribunal for Wales;

(ac) the Valuation Tribunal for England;"

(b) after paragraph (c), insert—

"(cc) any case which may be transferred under Tribunal Procedure Rules to the Upper Tribunal from the Property Chamber of the First-tier Tribunal in relation to functions listed in article 5A(c) to (h);".

NOTES

Initial Commencement

Specified date

Specified date: 1 July 2013: see art 1.

7

In article 13 (functions of the Tax and Chancery Chamber), after paragraph (g) insert a semi-colon and—

"(h) an appeal against a decision of the First-tier Tribunal made in the Property Chamber in a case mentioned in article 5A(a)."

NOTES

Initial Commencement

Specified date

Specified date: 1 July 2013: see art 1.

Appendix 8

TRANSFER OF TRIBUNAL FUNCTIONS ORDER 2013

SI 2013 No 1036

Transfer of functions and abolition of tribunals

4

(1) The functions of the Adjudicator to Her Majesty's Land Registry are transferred to the First-tier Tribunal.

(2) The Adjudicator to Her Majesty's Land Registry is abolished.

NOTES

Initial Commencement

Specified date

Specified date: 1 July 2013: see art 1.

Transfer of persons into the First-tier Tribunal and the Upper Tribunal

5

A person who, immediately before 1st July 2013, holds an office listed in column (1) of the following table is to hold the office or offices listed in the corresponding entry in column (2) of the table.

Office held	*Office to be held*
Adjudicator to Her Majesty's Land Registry	Transferred-in judge of the First-tier Tribunal and deputy judge of the Upper Tribunal
Member of the Adjudicator's staff who is authorised by the Adjudicator to carry out functions of the Adjudicator which are not of an administrative character	Transferred-in judge of the First-tier Tribunal

NOTES

Initial Commencement

Specified date

Specified date: 1 July 2013: see art 1.

Consequential, transitional and saving provisions

6

(1) Schedule 1 contains consequential amendments and repeals to primary legislation as a consequence of the transfers of functions effected by this Order.

(2) Schedule 2 contains consequential amendments and revocations to secondary legislation as a consequence of the transfers of functions effected by this Order.

(3) Schedule 3 contains transitional and saving provisions.

NOTES

Initial Commencement

Specified date

Specified date: 1 July 2013: see art 1.

SCHEDULE 1

CONSEQUENTIAL PROVISIONS—PRIMARY LEGISLATION

Article 6(1)

PART 3
PROVISIONS CONSEQUENTIAL UPON TRANSFER OF FUNCTIONS FROM AND ABOLITION OF THE ADJUDICATOR TO HER MAJESTY'S LAND REGISTRY

Land Registration Act 2002

225

The Land Registration Act 2002 is amended as follows.

226

In section 73(7) (objections), for "adjudicator", substitute "First-tier Tribunal".

227

Omit section 107 (the adjudicator).

228

In section 108 (jurisdiction)—

(a) in subsection (1), for "adjudicator", substitute "First-tier Tribunal";

(b) in paragraph (a) of subsection (1), for "him" substitute "it";

(c) in subsection (2), for "adjudicator" substitute "First-tier Tribunal";

(d) after subsection (4) insert—

"(5) The Lord Chancellor may require the registrar to make payments towards expenses of the Lord Chancellor in support of the functions conferred on the First-tier Tribunal by this section."

229

Omit section 109 (procedure).

230

In section 110 (functions in relation to disputes)—

(a) in subsection (1), for "adjudicator", substitute "First-tier Tribunal" and omit "himself";

(b) in subsection (2)—

(i) for "Rules" substitute "Tribunal Procedure Rules";

(ii) in paragraphs (a) and (b), for "adjudicator", in both places, substitute "First-tier Tribunal";

(c) in subsection (3)—

(i) for "Rules", substitute "Tribunal Procedure Rules";

(ii) for "adjudicator", in both places, substitute "First-tier Tribunal";

(iii) for "the rules", substitute "Tribunal Procedure Rules";

(d) in subsection (4), for "adjudicator", in both places, substitute "First-tier Tribunal".

231

In section 111 (appeals)—

(a) For subsections (1) and (2), substitute—

"(1) Subject to this section, a person aggrieved by a decision of the First-tier Tribunal under this Act may appeal to the Upper Tribunal.

(2) An appeal may not be brought under subsection (1) on a point of law (as to which see instead section 11 of the Tribunals, Courts and Enforcement Act 2007 (right of appeal to Upper Tribunal)).

(2A) An appeal may not be brought under subsection (1) in the case of a decision under paragraph 4 of Schedule 5 (but this does not prevent an appeal on a point of law under section 11 of the Tribunals, Courts and Enforcement Act 2007).

(2B) An appeal may not be brought under subsection (1) if the decision is set aside under section 9 of the Tribunals, Courts and Enforcement Act 2007 (review of decision of First-tier Tribunal).

(2C) An appeal may be brought under subsection (1) only if, on an application made by the person concerned, the First-tier Tribunal or Upper Tribunal has given its permission for the appeal to be brought.";

(b) in subsection (3)—

  (i) after "under this section" insert "or under section 11 of the Tribunals, Courts and Enforcement Act 2007";

  (ii) for "court" in both places, substitute "Upper Tribunal";

(c) after subsection (3) insert—

"(4) In any case where the Upper Tribunal is determining an appeal under subsection (1), section 12(2) to (4) of the Tribunals, Courts and Enforcement Act 2007 (proceedings on appeal to the Upper Tribunal) apply."

232

In section 112 (enforcement of orders etc) for "adjudicator" substitute "First-tier Tribunal".

233

Omit section 113 (fees).

234

Omit section 114 (supplementary).

235

In section 128 (rules, regulations and orders)—

(a) in subsection (4)(b), for "Part 11 or section 121", substitute "section 121, or";

(b) omit subsection (4)(c).

236

In section 132 (general interpretation), in subsection (1), omit the entry relating to the adjudicator.

237

In Schedule 5, in paragraph 4 (land registry network: appeals)—

(a) in sub-paragraph (1), for "adjudicator" substitute "First-tier Tribunal";

(b) in sub-paragraph (2)—

  (i) for "adjudicator" substitute "First-tier Tribunal";

  (ii) for "he" substitute "the tribunal";

  (iii) for "his" substitute "its".

(c) omit sub-paragraph (3).

238

Omit Schedule 9 (which makes further provision about the adjudicator).

NOTES

Initial Commencement

Specified date

Specified date: 1 July 2013: see art 1.

SCHEDULE 2

CONSEQUENTIAL PROVISIONS—SECONDARY LEGISLATION

Article 6(2)

PART 3
PROVISIONS CONSEQUENTIAL UPON TRANSFER OF FUNCTIONS FROM AND ABOLITION OF THE ADJUDICATOR TO HER MAJESTY'S LAND REGISTRY

The Land Registration (Referral to the Adjudicator to HM Land Registry) Rules 2003

63

The Land Registration (Referral to the Adjudicator to HM Land Registry) Rules 2003 are amended as follows.

64

In rule 3 (procedure for referral to the adjudicator)—

(a) in the heading, for "adjudicator" substitute "First-tier Tribunal";

(b) in paragraph (1), in both places, for "adjudicator" substitute "the First-tier Tribunal";

(c) in paragraph (2)(g), for "adjudicator" substitute "First-tier Tribunal".

65

In rule 5 (notice of referral to the adjudicator)—

(a) in the heading, for "adjudicator" substitute "First-tier Tribunal";

(b) in paragraph (2)(a), for the words from "adjudicator" to "referred to him" substitute "First-tier Tribunal a written notice, accompanied by the documents set out in paragraph (3), stating that the matter is referred to the First-tier Tribunal";

(c) in paragraph (2)(b) and (c), for "adjudicator" in both places, substitute "First-tier Tribunal";

(d) in paragraph (3), for "adjudicator" substitute "First-tier Tribunal".

The Adjudicator to Her Majesty's Land Registry (Practice and Procedure) Rules 2003

66

The Adjudicator to Her Majesty's Land Registry (Practice and Procedure) Rules 2003 are revoked.

The Land Registration (Acting Adjudicator) Regulations 2003

67

The Land Registration (Acting Adjudicator) Regulations 2003 are revoked.

The Network Access Appeal Rules 2008

70

The Network Access Appeal Rules 2008 are revoked.

The Adjudicator to Her Majesty's Land Registry (Practice and Procedure) (Amendment) Rules 2008

71

The Adjudicator to Her Majesty's Land Registry (Practice and Procedure) (Amendment) Rules 2008 are revoked.

The Land Registration (Network Access) Rules 2008

72

The Land Registration (Network Access) Rules 2008 are amended as follows.

73

In rule 8 (termination after notice)—

(a) in paragraph (6), for "adjudicator", in both places, substitute "First-tier Tribunal";

(b) in paragraph (8)(e), for "adjudicator or the High Court", substitute "First-tier Tribunal or the Upper Tribunal".

74

In rule 10 (suspension of termination pending appeal)—

(a) in paragraph (1), for "adjudicator" substitute "First-tier Tribunal";

(b) in paragraph (2)(b), for "adjudicator" substitute "First-tier Tribunal";

(c) in paragraph (7)(e), for "adjudicator or the High Court", substitute "First-tier Tribunal or the Upper Tribunal".

NOTES

Initial Commencement

Specified date

Specified date: 1 July 2013: see art 1.

SCHEDULE 3

TRANSITIONAL AND SAVING PROVISIONS

Article 6(3)

1

Any proceedings before an old tribunal which are pending immediately before 1st July 2013 shall continue on and after that date as proceedings before the First-tier Tribunal.

2

Any case in the process of being referred to an old tribunal on 1st July 2013 shall continue on or after that date as a case being referred to the First-tier Tribunal.

3

(1) The following sub-paragraphs apply where proceedings are continued in the First-tier Tribunal by virtue of paragraph 1.

(2) Where a hearing began before 1st July 2013 but was not completed by that date, the First-tier Tribunal must be comprised for the continuation of that hearing of the person or persons who began it.

(3) The First-tier Tribunal may give any direction to ensure that proceedings are dealt with fairly and, in particular, may—

(a) apply any provision in procedural rules which applied to the proceedings before 1st July 2013; or

(b) disapply provisions of Tribunal Procedure Rules.

(4) In sub-paragraph (3) "procedural rules" means provision (whether called rules or not) regulating practice or procedure before an old tribunal.

(5) Any decision (whether or not called a decision) or direction or order given or made in proceedings which is in force immediately before 1st July 2013 remains in force on and after that date as if it were a decision, direction or order of the First-tier Tribunal.

(6) A time period which has started to run before 1st July 2013 and which has not expired shall continue to apply.

(7) An order for costs may only be made if, and to the extent that, an order could have been made before 1st July 2013.

4

Where an appeal lies to the High Court from any decision made by an old tribunal before 1st July 2013, that right of appeal has not been exercised, and the time to exercise that right of appeal has not expired before 1st July 2013—

(a) section 11 of the Tribunals, Courts and Enforcement Act 2007 (right to appeal to Upper Tribunal),

(b) section 111 of the Land Registration Act 2002 as amended by this Order, where the old tribunal is the Adjudicator to Her Majesty's Land Registry,

shall apply as if the decision were a decision made on or after 1st July 2013 by the First-tier Tribunal, and any reference to an old tribunal in an enactment relating to such an appeal, express or otherwise, is to be taken as a reference to the First-tier Tribunal.

7

Staff appointed to an old tribunal before 1st July 2013, apart from those transferring in as members of the First-tier Tribunal, are to be treated on and after that date, for the purpose of any enactment, as if they had been appointed by the Lord Chancellor under section 40(1) of the Tribunals, Courts and Enforcement Act 2007 (tribunal staff and services).

8

For the purposes of this Schedule, "an old tribunal" means—

(f) the Adjudicator to Her Majesty's Land Registry.

NOTES

Initial Commencement

Specified date

Specified date: 1 July 2013: see art 1.

Appendix 9

TRIBUNAL PROCEDURE (FIRST-TIER TRIBUNAL) (PROPERTY CHAMBER) RULES 2013 (AS AMENDED BY SI 2014/2128)

SI 2013 No 1169

PART 1
INTRODUCTION

1 Citation, commencement and interpretation

(1) These Rules may be cited as the Tribunal Procedure (First-tier Tribunal) (Property Chamber) Rules 2013 and come into force on 1st July 2013.

(2) These Rules apply to proceedings before the Property Chamber of the First-tier Tribunal.

(3) In these Rules—

"the 1983 Act" means the Mobile Homes Act 1983;

"the 1986 Act" means the Agricultural Holdings Act 1986;

"the 1991 Act" means the Land Drainage Act 1991;

"the 2002 LR Act" means the Land Registration Act 2002;

"the 2004 Act" means the Housing Act 2004;

"the 2007 Act" means the Tribunals, Courts and Enforcement Act 2007.

"agricultural land and drainage case" means any case in respect of which the Tribunal has jurisdiction conferred—

(a) by or under any enactment specified in section 6A(2) of the Agriculture (Miscellaneous Provisions) Act 1954; or

(b) by the Hill Farming Act 1946;

"applicant" means—

(a) the person who commences Tribunal proceedings, whether by making an appeal, an application, an objection or otherwise;

(b) where an issue in proceedings before a court is transferred by order of the court to the Tribunal, the claimant or applicant in those proceedings;

(c) where proceedings before another tribunal are transferred to the Tribunal, the claimant or applicant in those proceedings;

(d) in a land registration case, the party which the Tribunal has specified as applicant under rule 28(3)(c);

(e) a person who is added or substituted as an applicant under rule 10;

and "application" bears a corresponding meaning;

"designated applicant" in relation to agricultural land and drainage cases means a person who is validly designated by the deceased in the deceased's will in accordance with section 39(4) of the 1986 Act;

"document" means anything in which information is recorded in any form, and an obligation under these Rules or any practice direction or direction to provide or allow access to a document or a copy of a document for any purpose means, unless the Tribunal directs otherwise, an obligation to provide or allow access to such document or copy in a legible form or in a form which can be readily made into a legible form;

"hearing" means an oral hearing and includes a hearing conducted in whole or in part by video link, telephone or other means of instantaneous two-way electronic communication;

"holding" means land (including a ditch) in respect of which an application under the 1986 Act is made;

"IMO authorisation application" means an application for authorisation to make an interim management order under section 102(4) or (7) of the 2004 Act, and "IMO" bears a corresponding meaning;

"interested person"—

(a) in relation to an agricultural land and drainage case under section 39 of the 1986 Act, includes—
  (i) any other applicant under that section or any other person eligible to be such an applicant;
  (ii) any personal representative of the deceased tenant, any person eligible to apply to be the personal representative of the deceased tenant or any person administering the estate of the deceased tenant;

(b) in relation to a residential property case, means—
  (i) a person other than the applicant who would have been entitled under the 2004 Act or the Housing Act 1985 to make the application;
  (ii) a person to whom notice of the application must be given in accordance with the following provisions of the 2004 Act—
    (aa) paragraph 11(2) of Schedule 1; or
    (bb) paragraph 14(2) of Schedule 3;
  (iii) a person to whom the Tribunal must give the opportunity of being heard in accordance with the following provisions—
    (aa) section 34(4) of the 2004 Act; or
    (bb) section 317(2) of the Housing Act 1985;
  (iv) except in relation to an application made under the 1983 Act, the local housing authority, where it is not a party to the application;
  (v) the person to whom the occupier wants to sell or gift a mobile home under [paragraph 7B or 8B] of Chapter 2 of Part 1 of Schedule 1 to the 1983 Act;
  (vi) a qualifying residents' association;

"land registration case" means a case in respect of which the Tribunal has jurisdiction under the 2002 LR Act;

"leasehold case" means a case in respect of which the Tribunal has jurisdiction under any of the enactments specified in section 176A(2) of the Commonhold and Leasehold Reform Act 2002;

"official expert" means a person who for agricultural, drainage or similar expertise is engaged by the Secretary of State to report or act on behalf of the Secretary of State in connection with an application in an agricultural land case;

"original application" means the application originally made to the registrar under the 2002 LR Act that resulted in a reference;

"party" means a person who is, or if the proceedings have been concluded, a person who was, an applicant or respondent when the Tribunal finally disposed of all issues in the proceedings;

"practice direction" means a direction given under section 23 of the 2007 Act;

"qualifying residents' association" means an association that meets the requirements set out in Part 1 of Schedule 1 to the 1983 Act;

"rectification application" means an application to rectify or set aside a document under section 108(2) of the 2002 LR Act;

"registrar" means the Chief Land Registrar;

"residential property case" means a case in respect of which the Tribunal has jurisdiction conferred by or under [the Caravan Sites and Control of Development Act 1960,] the 1983 Act, the Housing Act 1985 or the 2004 Act;

"respondent" means—

(a) in an appeal against a decision, direction or order, the person who made the decision, direction or order appealed against;

(b) a person against whom an applicant otherwise brings proceedings;

(c) in a case referred to the Tribunal by a rent officer who has registered a rent under the Rent Act 1977, the landlord or the tenant, as the case may be, who has not objected to the rent which has been registered;

(d) where an issue in proceedings before a court is transferred by order of the court to the Tribunal, the person who was the defendant or respondent in the court proceedings;

(e) in relation to residential property cases or leasehold cases listed in a Schedule to a practice direction, the person or persons, or one of the persons, identified as the respondent in the relevant Schedule to the practice direction;

(f) in a land registration case—

(i) in a reference by the registrar, the party or parties which the Tribunal has specified as respondent under rule 28(3)(c);

(ii) in proceedings under section 108(2) of the 2002 LR Act, the party or parties making an objection to a rectification application;

(iii) in an appeal under paragraph 4 of Schedule 5 to the 2002 LR Act, the registrar;

(g) a person added or substituted as a respondent under rule 10;

"Tribunal" means the First-tier Tribunal.

NOTES

Initial Commencement

Specified date

Specified date: 1 July 2013: see para (1) above.

Amendment

Para (3): in definition "interested person" in para (b)(v) words "paragraph 7B or 8B" in square brackets substituted by SI 2014/2128, rr 29, 30(a).

Date in force: 1 September 2014: see SI 2014/2128, r 1(a).

Para (3): in definition "residential property case" words "the Caravan Sites and Control of Development Act 1960," in square brackets inserted by SI 2014/2128, rr 29, 30(b).

Date in force: 1 September 2014: see SI 2014/2128, r 1(a).

2 Rules not overriding enactments

Nothing in these Rules overrides any specific provision that is contained in an enactment which confers jurisdiction on the Tribunal.

NOTES

Initial Commencement

Specified date

Specified date: 1 July 2013: see r 1(1).

3 Overriding objective and parties' obligation to co-operate with the Tribunal

(1) The overriding objective of these Rules is to enable the Tribunal to deal with cases fairly and justly.

(2) Dealing with a case fairly and justly includes—

- (a) dealing with the case in ways which are proportionate to the importance of the case, the complexity of the issues, the anticipated costs and the resources of the parties and of the Tribunal;
- (b) avoiding unnecessary formality and seeking flexibility in the proceedings;
- (c) ensuring, so far as practicable, that the parties are able to participate fully in the proceedings;
- (d) using any special expertise of the Tribunal effectively; and
- (e) avoiding delay, so far as compatible with proper consideration of the issues.

(3) The Tribunal must seek to give effect to the overriding objective when it—

- (a) exercises any power under these Rules; or
- (b) interprets any rule or practice direction.

(4) Parties must—

- (a) help the Tribunal to further the overriding objective; and
- (b) co-operate with the Tribunal generally.

NOTES

Initial Commencement

Specified date

Specified date: 1 July 2013: see r 1(1).

4 Alternative dispute resolution and arbitration

(1) The Tribunal should seek, where appropriate—

- (a) to bring to the attention of the parties the availability of any appropriate alternative procedure for the resolution of the dispute; and
- (b) if the parties wish, and provided that it is compatible with the overriding objective, to facilitate the use of the procedure.

(2) Part 1 of the Arbitration Act 1996 does not apply to proceedings before the Tribunal.

NOTES

Initial Commencement

Specified date

Specified date: 1 July 2013: see r 1(1).

PART 2
GENERAL POWERS AND PROVISIONS

5 Delegation to staff

(1) Staff appointed under section 40(1) of the 2007 Act (tribunal staff and services) may, with the approval of the Senior President of Tribunals, carry out functions of a judicial nature permitted or required to be done by the Tribunal.

(2) The approval referred to at paragraph (1) may apply generally to the carrying out of specified functions by members of staff of a specified description in specified circumstances.

(3) Within 14 days after the date that the Tribunal sends notice of a decision made by a member of staff pursuant to an approval under paragraph (1) to a party, that party may apply in writing to the Tribunal for that decision to be considered afresh by a judge.

NOTES

Initial Commencement

Specified date

Specified date: 1 July 2013: see r 1(1).

6 Case management powers

(1) Subject to the provisions of the 2007 Act and any other enactment, the Tribunal may regulate its own procedure.

(2) The Tribunal may give a direction in relation to the conduct or disposal of proceedings at any time, including a direction amending, suspending or setting aside an earlier direction.

(3) In particular, and without restricting the general powers in paragraphs (1) and (2), the Tribunal may—

- (a) extend or shorten the time for complying with any rule, practice direction or direction, even if the application for an extension is not made until after the time limit has expired;
- (b) consolidate or hear together two or more sets of proceedings or parts of proceedings raising common issues, or treat a case as a lead case (whether under rule 23 or otherwise);
- (c) permit or require a party to amend a document;
- (d) permit or require a party or another person to provide or produce documents, information or submissions to any or all of the following—
  - (i) the Tribunal;
  - (ii) a party;
  - (iii) in land registration cases, the registrar;
- (e) direct that enquiries be made of any person;
- (f) require a party to state whether that party intends to—
  - (i) attend,
  - (ii) be represented, or
  - (iii) call witnesses,

  at the hearing;
- (g) deal with an issue in the proceedings as a preliminary issue;
- (h) hold a hearing to consider any matter, including a case management issue;
- (i) decide the form of any hearing;
- (j) adjourn or postpone a hearing;
- (k) require a party to produce a bundle for a hearing;
- (l) require a party to provide an estimate of the length of the hearing;
- (m) stay proceedings;
- (n) transfer proceedings to another court or tribunal if that other court or tribunal has jurisdiction in relation to the proceedings and
  - (i) because of a change of circumstances since the proceedings were started, the Tribunal no longer has jurisdiction in relation to the proceedings; or
  - (ii) the Tribunal considers that the other court or tribunal is a more appropriate forum for the determination of the case;

(o) suspend the effect of its own decision pending the determination by the Tribunal or the Upper Tribunal of an application for permission to appeal against, and any appeal or review of, that decision.

NOTES

Initial Commencement

Specified date

Specified date: 1 July 2013: see r 1(1).

7 Procedure for applying for and giving directions

(1) The Tribunal may give a direction on the application of one or more of the parties or on its own initiative.

(2) An application for a direction may be made—

(a) by sending or delivering a written application to the Tribunal; or

(b) orally during the course of a hearing.

(3) An application for a direction must include the reason for making that application.

(4) Except with the permission of the Tribunal, if a written application for a direction is made without the consent of every party the applicant must provide—

(a) a copy of the proposed application to every other party before it is made; and

(b) confirmation to the Tribunal that the other parties have been notified that any objection they wish to make to the application must be provided in accordance with paragraph (5).

(5) A party who wishes to object to a written application that has been made to the Tribunal for a direction must send written notice of the objection to the Tribunal and the applicant for the direction.

(6) Unless the Tribunal considers that there is good reason not to do so, the Tribunal must send written notice of any direction made by the Tribunal to every party and to any other person affected by the direction.

(7) If a party or any other person sent notice under paragraph (6) of the direction made by the Tribunal wishes to challenge that direction, they may do so by applying for another direction which amends, suspends or sets aside the first direction.

NOTES

Initial Commencement

Specified date

Specified date: 1 July 2013: see r 1(1).

8 Failure to comply with rules, practice directions or Tribunal directions

(1) An irregularity resulting from a failure to comply with any provision of these Rules, a practice direction or a direction does not of itself render void the proceedings or any step taken in the proceedings.

(2) If a party has failed to comply with a requirement in these Rules, a practice direction or a direction, the Tribunal may take such action as the Tribunal considers just, which may include—

(a) waiving the requirement;

(b) requiring the failure to be remedied;

(c) exercising its power under rule 9 (striking out a party's case);

(d) exercising its power under paragraph (5); or

(e) barring or restricting a party's participation in the proceedings.

(3) In land registration cases, the action that the Tribunal may take includes—

(a) where the party who failed to comply was the person who made (or has been substituted for or added to the party who made) the original application, directing the registrar to cancel the original application in whole or in part;

(b) where the party who failed to comply was an objector to (or was substituted for or added as an objector to) the original application, directing the registrar to give effect to that application in whole or in part as if that objection had not been made.

(4) In land registration cases, the Tribunal must, if the action taken does not include either of the requirements referred to in paragraph (3), send written notice to the parties of the Tribunal's decision as to what action is taken (if any) and give any consequential directions.

(5) The Tribunal may refer to the Upper Tribunal, and ask the Upper Tribunal to exercise its power under section 25 of the 2007 Act in relation to, any failure by a person to comply with a requirement imposed by the Tribunal—

(a) to attend at any place for the purpose of giving evidence;

(b) otherwise to make themselves available to give evidence;

(c) to swear an oath in connection with the giving of evidence;

(d) to give evidence as a witness;

(e) to produce a document; or

(f) to facilitate the inspection of a document or any other thing (including any premises).

NOTES

Initial Commencement

Specified date

Specified date: 1 July 2013: see r 1(1).

9 Striking out a party's case

(1) The proceedings or case, or the appropriate part of them, will automatically be struck out if the applicant has failed to comply with a direction that stated that failure by the applicant to comply with the direction by a stated date would lead to the striking out of the proceedings or that part of them.

(2) The Tribunal must strike out the whole or a part of the proceedings or case if the Tribunal—

(a) does not have jurisdiction in relation to the proceedings or case or that part of them; and

(b) does not exercise any power under rule 6(3)(n)(i) (transfer to another court or tribunal) in relation to the proceedings or case or that part of them.

(3) The Tribunal may strike out the whole or a part of the proceedings or case if—

(a) the applicant has failed to comply with a direction which stated that failure by the applicant to comply with the direction could lead to the striking out of the proceedings or case or that part of it;

(b) the applicant has failed to co-operate with the Tribunal such that the Tribunal cannot deal with the proceedings fairly and justly;

(c) the proceedings or case are between the same parties and arise out of facts which are similar or substantially the same as those contained in a proceedings or case which has been decided by the Tribunal;

(d) the Tribunal considers the proceedings or case (or a part of them), or the manner in which they are being conducted, to be frivolous or vexatious or otherwise an abuse of the process of the Tribunal; or

(e) the Tribunal considers there is no reasonable prospect of the applicant's proceedings or case, or part of it, succeeding.

(4) The Tribunal may not strike out the whole or a part of the proceedings or case under paragraph (2) or paragraph (3)(b) to (e) without first giving the parties an opportunity to make representations in relation to the proposed striking out.

(5) If the proceedings or case, or part of them, have been struck out under paragraph (1) or (3)(a), the applicant may apply for the proceedings or case, or part of it, to be reinstated.

(6) An application under paragraph (5) must be made in writing and received by the Tribunal within 28 days after the date on which the Tribunal sent notification of the striking out to that party.

(7) This rule applies to a respondent as it applies to an applicant except that—

- (a) a reference to the striking out of the proceedings or case or part of them is to be read as a reference to the barring of the respondent from taking further part in the proceedings or part of them; and
- (b) a reference to an application for the reinstatement of proceedings or case or part of them which have been struck out is to be read as a reference to an application for the lifting of the bar on the respondent from taking further part in the proceedings, or part of them.

(8) If a respondent has been barred from taking further part in proceedings under this rule and that bar has not been lifted, the Tribunal need not consider any response or other submission made by that respondent, and may summarily determine any or all issues against that respondent.

NOTES

Initial Commencement

Specified date

Specified date: 1 July 2013: see r 1(1).

10 Addition, substitution and removal of parties

(1) The Tribunal may give a direction adding, substituting or removing a person as an applicant or a respondent.

(2) If the Tribunal gives a direction under paragraph (1) it may give such consequential directions as it considers appropriate.

(3) A person who is not a party may apply to the Tribunal to be added or substituted as a party.

NOTES

Initial Commencement

Specified date

Specified date: 1 July 2013: see r 1(1).

11 Fees: non-payment

(1) In any case where a fee is payable under an order made under section 42 of the 2007 Act (fees), the Tribunal must not proceed further with the case until the fee is paid.

(2) Where a fee remains unpaid for a period of 14 days after the date on which the fee is payable, the case, if not already started, must not be started.

(3) Where the case has started, it shall be deemed to be withdrawn 14 days after the date on which the Tribunal sends or delivers to the party liable to make payment a written notification that the fee has not been paid.

NOTES

Initial Commencement

Specified date

Specified date: 1 July 2013: see r 1(1).

12 Security for costs

(1) In a land registration case, a respondent may apply for security for the respondent's costs of the proceedings in the Tribunal.

(2) Paragraph (1) does not apply where the Tribunal has directed a party under section 110(1) of the 2002 LR Act to commence court proceedings for the court's decision on the whole or part of a matter.

(3) An application for security for costs must be supported by written evidence and copies of the application and supporting evidence must be provided by the respondent to the applicant in the proceedings.

(4) The Tribunal may make an order for security for costs if it is satisfied that—

- (a) one or more of the conditions subject to which security for costs might be ordered in proceedings in a court to which the Civil Procedure Rules 1998 apply exists;
- (b) it is just to make such an order; and
- (c) the applicant in the proceedings has the ability to comply with the order.

(5) Where the Tribunal decides to order security for costs, it must—

- (a) determine the amount of security; and
- (b) direct the manner in which, and the time within which, the security must be given.

NOTES

Initial Commencement

Specified date

Specified date: 1 July 2013: see r 1(1).

13 Orders for costs, reimbursement of fees and interest on costs

(1) The Tribunal may make an order in respect of costs only—

- (a) under section 29(4) of the 2007 Act (wasted costs) and the costs incurred in applying for such costs;
- (b) if a person has acted unreasonably in bringing, defending or conducting proceedings in—
  - (i) an agricultural land and drainage case,
  - (ii) a residential property case, or
  - (iii) a leasehold case; or
- (c) in a land registration case.

(2) The Tribunal may make an order requiring a party to reimburse to any other party the whole or part of the amount of any fee paid by the other party which has not been remitted by the Lord Chancellor.

(3) The Tribunal may make an order under this rule on an application or on its own initiative.

(4) A person making an application for an order for costs—

- (a) must, unless the application is made orally at a hearing, send or deliver an application to the Tribunal and to the person against whom the order is sought to be made; and
- (b) may send or deliver together with the application a schedule of the costs claimed in sufficient detail to allow summary assessment of such costs by the Tribunal.

(5) An application for an order for costs may be made at any time during the proceedings but must be made within 28 days after the date on which the Tribunal sends—

- (a) a decision notice recording the decision which finally disposes of all issues in the proceedings; or

(b) notice of consent to a withdrawal under rule 22 (withdrawal) which ends the proceedings.

(6) The Tribunal may not make an order for costs against a person (the "paying person") without first giving that person an opportunity to make representations.

(7) The amount of costs to be paid under an order under this rule may be determined by—

(a) summary assessment by the Tribunal;

(b) agreement of a specified sum by the paying person and the person entitled to receive the costs (the "receiving person");

(c) detailed assessment of the whole or a specified part of the costs (including the costs of the assessment) incurred by the receiving person by the Tribunal or, if it so directs, on an application to a county court; and such assessment is to be on the standard basis or, if specified in the costs order, on the indemnity basis.

(8) The Civil Procedure Rules 1998, section 74 (interest on judgment debts, etc) of the County Courts Act 1984 and the County Court (Interest on Judgment Debts) Order 1991 shall apply, with necessary modifications, to a detailed assessment carried out under paragraph (7)(c) as if the proceedings in the Tribunal had been proceedings in a court to which the Civil Procedure Rules 1998 apply.

(9) The Tribunal may order an amount to be paid on account before the costs or expenses are assessed.

NOTES

Initial Commencement

Specified date

Specified date: 1 July 2013: see r 1(1).

14 Representatives

(1) A party may appoint a representative (whether legally qualified or not) to represent that party in the proceedings.

(2) If a party appoints a representative, that party must send or deliver to the Tribunal and to each other party written notice of the representative's name and address.

(3) Anything permitted or required to be done by or provided to a party under these Rules, a practice direction or a direction may be done by or provided to the representative of that party except—

(a) signing a witness statement; or

(b) sending or delivering a notice under paragraph (2), if the representative is not a person who, for the purposes of the Legal Services Act 2007, is an authorised person in relation to an activity which constitutes the exercise of a right of audience or the conduct of litigation within the meaning of that Act.

(4) A person who receives due notice of the appointment of a representative—

(a) must thereafter provide to the representative any document which is required to be sent to the represented party, and need not provide that document to the represented party; and

(b) may assume that the representative is and remains authorised until receiving written notification to the contrary and an alternative address for communications from the representative or the represented party.

(5) At a hearing a party may be accompanied by another person whose name and address has not been notified under paragraph (2) but who, with the permission of the Tribunal, may act as a representative or otherwise assist in presenting the party's case at the hearing.

(6) Paragraphs (2) to (4) do not apply to a person who accompanies a party under paragraph (5).

NOTES

Initial Commencement

Specified date

Specified date: 1 July 2013: see r 1(1).

15 Calculating time

(1) An act required by these Rules, a practice direction or a direction to be done on or by a particular day must be done before 5pm on that day.

(2) If the time specified by these Rules, a practice direction or a direction for doing any act ends on a day other than a working day, the act is done in time if it is done on the next working day.

(3) In this rule "working day" means any day except a Saturday or Sunday, Christmas Day, Good Friday or a bank holiday under section 1 of the Banking and Financial Dealings Act 1971.

NOTES

Initial Commencement

Specified date

Specified date: 1 July 2013: see r 1(1).

16 Provision of documents

(1) Any document to be provided under these Rules, a practice direction or a direction must be—

- (a) sent by prepaid post or by document exchange, or delivered by hand to the address specified in paragraph (5);
- (b) sent by fax to the number specified for the proceedings;
- (c) as regards any document sent or delivered to or by the Tribunal, by such other method as the Tribunal may permit; or
- (d) as regards any document to be sent or delivered by a method other than one provided for by sub-paragraphs (a), (b) or (c) or another paragraph in this rule, by such other method as the recipient may permit.

(2) The Tribunal may provide any document (including any notice or summons or other information) under these Rules by—

- (a) itself sending or delivering the document; or
- (b) requiring a party to do so.

(3) In any case to which section 39, 41 or 53 of the 1986 Act applies, the applicant, not the Tribunal, must send or deliver a copy of the application and accompanying documents to the landlord of the agricultural holding to which the application relates and to any other person known to the applicant to be interested in the outcome of the application.

(4) If the Tribunal permits or directs documents to be provided to it by email, any requirement in these Rules for a signature on a document may be satisfied by a typed instead of a handwritten signature.

(5) Subject to paragraph (6), the address for the purposes of paragraph (1)(a) is—

- (a) in the case of the Tribunal, the address of the office of the Tribunal;
- (b) in the case of an incorporated company or other body registered in the United Kingdom, the address of the registered or principal office of the company or body or any alternative address notified by that company or body to the Tribunal and all other parties for the purposes of provision of documents;

(c) in the case of any other person, body or authority, the usual or last known address of that person, body or authority.

(6) The Tribunal and each party may assume that the address provided by a party or its representative or, in a reference, by the registrar is and remains the address to which documents should be sent or delivered until receiving written notification to the contrary and an alternative address for communications.

(7) Subject to paragraph (8), if a party provides a fax number, email address or other details for the electronic transmission of documents to them, that party must accept delivery of documents by that method.

(8) If a party informs the Tribunal and all other parties that a particular form of communication, other than pre-paid post or delivery by hand, should not be used to provide documents to that party, that form of communication must not be used.

(9) If the Tribunal or a party sends a document to another party or to the Tribunal by email or any other electronic means of communication, the recipient may request that the sender provide a hard copy of the document to the recipient. The recipient must make such a request as soon as reasonably practicable after receiving the document electronically.

(10) Unless the Tribunal otherwise permits, where a document is provided for the purposes of the proceedings is or contains a map, plan, drawing or photograph, any copy provided of that map, plan or drawing must be in the same colours as the map, plan, drawing or photograph of which it is a copy, and in agricultural land and drainage cases, maps of any holding or land must be to a scale of 1:10,000 or larger.

(11) The Tribunal may waive a requirement under these Rules to send or deliver a notice or other document to a person or make an order for provision by alternative method (whether by advertisement in a newspaper or otherwise) as the Tribunal may think fit if that person—

(a) cannot be found after all diligent enquiries have been made;

(b) has died and has no personal representative;

(c) is out of the United Kingdom; or

(d) for any other reason a notice or other document cannot readily be sent or delivered to that person in accordance with these Rules.

(12) Where an enactment requires evidence that a party has supplied any person with a document, that party may satisfy the requirement by providing a certificate signed by the party confirming that the document was provided in accordance with the requirements of this rule.

NOTES

Initial Commencement

Specified date

Specified date: 1 July 2013: see r 1(1).

17 Prevention of disclosure or publication of documents and information

(1) The Tribunal may make an order prohibiting the disclosure or publication of—

(a) specified documents or information relating to the proceedings; or

(b) any matter likely to lead members of the public to identify any person whom the Tribunal considers should not be identified.

(2) The Tribunal may give a direction prohibiting the disclosure of a document or information to a person if—

(a) the Tribunal is satisfied that such disclosure would be likely to cause that person or some other person serious harm; and

(b) the Tribunal is satisfied, having regard to the interests of justice, that it is proportionate to give such a direction.

(3) If a party (the first party) considers that the Tribunal should give a direction under paragraph (2) prohibiting the disclosure of a document or information to another party (the second party), the first party must—

- (a) exclude the relevant document or information from any documents that will be provided to the second party; and
- (b) provide to the Tribunal the excluded document or information, and the reason for its exclusion, so that the Tribunal may decide whether the document or information should be disclosed to the second party or should be the subject of a direction under paragraph (2).

(4) The Tribunal may give a direction that certain documents or information must or may be disclosed to the Tribunal on the basis that the Tribunal will not disclose such documents or information to other persons, or specified other persons.

(5) A party making an application for a direction under paragraph (4) may withhold the relevant documents or information from other persons, or the specified other persons, until the Tribunal has made a decision on the application.

(6) Unless the Tribunal considers that there is good reason not to do so, the Tribunal must send notice that a party has made an application for a direction under paragraph (4) to each other party.

(7) In a case involving matters relating to national security, the Tribunal must ensure that information is not disclosed contrary to the interests of national security.

(8) The Tribunal must conduct proceedings and record its decision and reasons appropriately so as not to undermine the effect of an order made under paragraph (1), a direction given under paragraph (2) or (4) or the duty imposed by paragraph (7).

NOTES

Initial Commencement

Specified date

Specified date: 1 July 2013: see r 1(1).

18 Disclosure, evidence and submissions

(1) Without restriction on the general powers in rule 6(1) and (2) (case management powers), the Tribunal may give directions as to—

- (a) the exchange between parties of lists of documents which are relevant to the application, or relevant to particular issues, and the inspection of such documents;
- (b) the provision by parties of statements of agreed matters;
- (c) issues on which it requires evidence or submissions;
- (d) the nature of the evidence or submissions it requires;
- (e) whether the parties are permitted or required to provide expert evidence, and if so whether the parties must jointly appoint a single expert to provide such evidence;
- (f) any limit on the number of witnesses whose evidence a party may put forward, whether in relation to a particular issue or generally;
- (g) the manner in which any evidence or submissions are to be provided, which may include a direction for them to be given—
  - (i) orally at a hearing; or
  - (ii) by written submissions or witness statement; and
- (h) the time at which any evidence or submissions are to be provided.

(2) Instead of giving directions under paragraph (1)(a), the Tribunal may provide for the disclosure and inspection of documents to any extent which it considers relevant to the issues in dispute, including—

- (a) taking all reasonable steps to ensure that each of the parties is given a copy of any document which has been received from any other party or former party; or

(b) supplying the parties with a copy of any document which embodies the results of any relevant enquiries made by or for the Tribunal for the purposes of the proceedings.

(3) A party to whom a document has been disclosed may use the document only for the purpose of the proceedings in which it is disclosed except where—

(a) the document has been read to or by the Tribunal, or referred to, at a hearing which has been held in public;

(b) the Tribunal gives permission; or

(c) the party who disclosed the document and the person to whom the document belongs agree.

(4) The Tribunal may make an order restricting or prohibiting the use of a document which has been disclosed, even where the document has been read to or by the Tribunal, or referred to, at a hearing which has been held in public.

(5) An application for such an order may be made—

(a) by a party; or

(b) by any person to whom the document belongs.

(6) The Tribunal may—

(a) admit evidence whether or not it—

(i) would be admissible in a civil trial in England and Wales; or

(ii) was available to a previous decision maker; or

(b) exclude evidence that would otherwise be admissible where—

(i) the evidence was not provided within the time allowed by a direction or a practice direction;

(ii) the evidence was otherwise provided in a manner that did not comply with a direction or a practice direction; or

(iii) it would otherwise be unfair to admit the evidence.

(7) The Tribunal may consent to a witness giving, or require any witness to give, evidence on oath, and may administer an oath for that purpose.

(8) A party cannot be directed to produce any document which a party could not be compelled to produce on the trial of an action in a court of law.

(9) On receipt of written notice from the Tribunal of an application under the 1991 Act, the Secretary of State must provide the Tribunal with a report on the matters to which the application relates.

NOTES

Initial Commencement

Specified date

Specified date: 1 July 2013: see r 1(1).

19 Expert evidence

(1) It is the duty of an expert to help the Tribunal on matters within the expert's expertise and this duty overrides any obligation to the person from whom the expert has received instructions or by whom the expert is paid.

(2) No party may adduce expert evidence without the permission of the Tribunal.

(3) Expert evidence is to be given in a written report unless the Tribunal directs otherwise.

(4) Subject to paragraph (6), each party must provide a copy of the written report of any expert witness to the Tribunal and each other party at least 7 days before—

(a) the date of the hearing; or

(b) the date notified upon which the issue to which the expert evidence relates will be determined without a hearing.

(5) A written report of an expert must—

(a) contain a statement that the expert understands the duty in paragraph (1) and has complied with it;

(b) contain the words "I believe that the facts stated in this report are true and that the opinions expressed are correct";

(c) be addressed to the Tribunal;

(d) include details of the expert's qualifications and relevant experience;

(e) contain a summary of the instructions the expert has received for the making of the report; and

(f) be signed by the expert.

(6) The Tribunal may direct that—

(a) the expert's evidence must be limited to such matters as the Tribunal directs;

(b) the expert must attend a hearing to give oral evidence; or

(c) the parties must jointly instruct the expert.

NOTES

Initial Commencement

Specified date

Specified date: 1 July 2013: see r 1(1).

20 Summoning of witnesses and orders to answer questions or produce documents

(1) On the application of a party or on its own initiative, the Tribunal may—

(a) by summons require any person to attend as a witness at a hearing at the time and place specified in the summons; or

(b) order any person to answer any questions or produce any documents in that person's pos-session or control which relate to any issue in the proceedings.

(2) A summons under paragraph (1)(a) must—

(a) give the person required to attend not less than 14 days' notice of the hearing or such shorter period as the Tribunal may direct; and

(b) where the person is not a party, make provision for the person's necessary expenses of attendance to be paid, and state who is to pay them.

(3) No person may be compelled to give any evidence or produce any document that the person could not be compelled to give or produce on a trial of an action in a court of law.

(4) A summons or order under this rule must—

(a) state that the person on whom the requirement is imposed may apply to the Tribunal to vary or set aside the summons or order, if they have not had an opportunity to object to it; and

(b) state the consequences of failure to comply with the summons or order.

NOTES

Initial Commencement

Specified date

Specified date: 1 July 2013: see r 1(1).

21 Site inspections

(1) Subject to paragraph (2), the Tribunal may inspect—

(a) the land, property or premises which is the subject of the application;

(b) any other land, property or premises inspection of which may assist the Tribunal in determining the application;

(c) the locality of the land, property or premises.

(2) The making of and attendance at an inspection is subject to the Tribunal obtaining all appropriate consents to its request for entry.
(3) The Tribunal must give reasonable written notice of the date and time proposed for the inspection.
(4) The Tribunal may include in its request for entry a request to be accompanied by one or more of—
- (a) the parties (and any party's representative);
- (b) in an agricultural land and drainage case, the official expert;
- (c) if the Tribunal considers necessary—
  - (i) any party's witness;
  - (ii) one or more members of the Tribunal's staff;
- (d) any other person, if the Tribunal considers it appropriate.

(5) In an agricultural land and drainage case, the condition of consent referred to in paragraph (2) does not apply, but the exercise of the right of entry under this paragraph or paragraph (6) is subject to the Tribunal making a direction requiring the person who is the owner or occupier to permit entry to the land, property or premises.
(6) In an agricultural land and drainage case, the Tribunal may direct any person who owns or occupies any land or premises which are relevant to the proceedings to permit the official expert to enter and inspect the land or premises for the purposes for which the official expert was appointed.
(7) Every direction under paragraph (5) or (6) must, unless the occupier was present when the direction was made, contain a statement that the occupier may apply to the Tribunal to vary or set aside the direction.
(8) Where a direction has been made under paragraph (5) or (6), the occupier of the land, property or premises must be given at least 7 days' notice of any inspection.
(9) Rule 19 also applies to the report and evidence of the official expert.

NOTES

Initial Commencement

Specified date

Specified date: 1 July 2013: see r 1(1).

22 Withdrawal

(1) Subject to paragraph (2), a party may give notice of the withdrawal of its case, or any part of it—
- (a) orally at a hearing; or
- (b) by sending or delivering to the Tribunal a written notice of withdrawal.

(2) A written notice of withdrawal must—
- (a) be signed and dated;
- (b) identify the case or part of the case which is withdrawn;
- (c) state whether any part of the case, and if so what, remains to be determined;
- (d) confirm that a copy of the notice of the withdrawal has been provided to all other parties and state the date on which this was done;
- (e) include the written consent of any of the other parties who have consented to the withdrawal.

(3) Notice of withdrawal will not take effect unless the Tribunal consents to the withdrawal.
(4) The Tribunal may make such directions or impose such conditions on withdrawal as it considers appropriate.
(5) A party which has withdrawn its case may apply to the Tribunal for the case to be reinstated.

(6) An application under paragraph (5) must be made in writing and be received by the Tribunal within 28 days after—

(a) the date of the hearing at which the case was withdrawn orally under paragraph (1)(a); or

(b) the date on which the Tribunal received the notice under paragraph (1)(b).

(7) The Tribunal must notify each party in writing of a withdrawal under this rule.

(8) Any party may, within 28 days after the date of receipt of notification by the Tribunal under paragraph (7), apply for a case, or part of a case, which has been withdrawn under this rule to be re-instated.

NOTES

Initial Commencement

Specified date

Specified date: 1 July 2013: see r 1(1).

23 Lead cases

(1) This rule applies if—

(a) two or more cases have been started before the Tribunal;

(b) in each such case the Tribunal has not made a decision disposing of the proceedings; and

(c) the cases give rise to common or related issues.

(2) The Tribunal may direct that one or more such cases be specified as a lead case, and stay the other cases ("the related cases").

(3) The Tribunal must send a copy of any direction given under paragraph (2) to each party in a lead case and in the related cases.

(4) A party in a related case referred to in paragraph (3) may apply for the related case to be substituted as the lead case (or added as a lead case) within 28 days after the date of receipt of notification from the Tribunal of a direction made under paragraph (2).

(5) Where the Tribunal makes a decision in a lead case or cases in respect of the common or related issues—

(a) the Tribunal must send a copy of the decision to each party in each of the related cases; and

(b) subject to paragraph (6), the decision will be binding on each of those parties in relation to the common or related issues.

(6) Within 28 days after the date on which the Tribunal sent a copy of the decision to a party under paragraph (5)(a), that party may apply in writing for a direction that the decision is not binding on the parties to a particular related case.

(7) The Tribunal must give directions in respect of cases which are stayed under paragraph (2), providing for the disposal of or further directions in those cases.

(8) If a lead case is withdrawn before the Tribunal makes a decision in respect of the common or related issues, the Tribunal must give directions as to—

(a) whether another case or other cases are to be specified as a lead case or lead cases; and

(b) whether any direction affecting the related cases should be set aside or amended.

NOTES

Initial Commencement

Specified date

Specified date: 1 July 2013: see r 1(1).

24 Subsequent applications related to lead case

(1) This rule applies where a decision has been given in a lead case in accordance with rule 23 and a subsequent application is made which includes any of the common or related issues.

(2) The Tribunal may send written notice to the parties to the subsequent application of—

- (a) the matters which it appears to the Tribunal are the common or related issues in the subsequent application and the previously decided lead case;
- (b) the decision recorded in respect of the common or related issues in the lead case;
- (c) the Tribunal's proposal to record its decision on the common or related issues in the subsequent application in materially identical terms to the decision in the lead case;
- (d) the date (being not less than 21 days after the date that the notice was sent) by which any objection to this proposal must be received by the Tribunal; and
- (e) a requirement that any objection must include the grounds on which it is made.

(3) Where no objection is received on or before the date specified in the notice—

- (a) the Tribunal need not determine the matters mentioned in paragraph (2)(a); and
- (b) the decision of the Tribunal in respect of the common or related issues in the lead case must be recorded as the decision of the Tribunal in respect of the common or related issues in the subsequent application.

(4) Where an objection is delivered to the Tribunal's proposal on or before the date specified in the notice the Tribunal must determine the application in accordance with the other provisions of these Rules.

NOTES

Initial Commencement

Specified date

Specified date: 1 July 2013: see r 1(1).

25 Transfer of case to the Upper Tribunal

(1) The Tribunal may refer a case to the President of the Property Chamber with a request that the case be considered for transfer to the Upper Tribunal.

(2) If a case has been referred under paragraph (1), the President of the Property Chamber may, with the concurrence of the President of the Lands Chamber, direct that the case be transferred to and determined by the Upper Tribunal.

(3) The President of the Property Chamber may only direct a transfer under paragraph (2) if the President of the Property Chamber considers that the issues in dispute are likely to be further appealed to the Upper Tribunal and—

- (a) will require lengthy or complex evidence or a lengthy hearing; or
- (b) involve a complex or important principle or issue; or
- (c) involve a large financial sum.

(4) This rule does not apply to a land registration case or an agricultural land and drainage case.

NOTES

Initial Commencement

Specified date

Specified date: 1 July 2013: see r 1(1).

PART 3
WRITTEN DOCUMENTATION, TIME LIMITS ETC

26 Starting proceedings

(1) An applicant must start proceedings before the Tribunal by sending or delivering to the Tribunal a notice of application.

(2) Such an application must be signed and dated and, unless a practice direction makes different provision, include—

- (a) the name and address of the applicant;
- (b) the name and address of the applicant's representative (if any);
- (c) an address where documents for the applicant may be sent or delivered;
- (d) the name and address of each respondent;
- (e) the address of the premises or property to which the application relates;
- (f) the applicant's connection with the premises or property;
- (g) the name and address of any landlord or tenant of the premises to which the application relates;
- (h) the result the applicant is seeking;
- (i) the applicant's reasons for making the application;
- (j) a statement that the applicant believes that the facts stated in the application are true;
- (k) the name and address of every person who appears to the applicant to be an interested person, with reasons for that person's interest;
- (l) in agricultural land and drainage cases, a description of all the land or holding to which the application relates;
- (m) in agricultural land and drainage cases relating to succession under section 39, 41 or 53 of the 1986 Act—
  - (i) confirmation that the applicant has given prior written notice of the application to the landlord of the holding and has brought the application to the notice of other persons interested in the outcome of the application; and
  - (ii) the names and addresses of each person to whom the applicant has provided such notice;
- (n) all further information or documents required by a practice direction.

(3) Where an application is made to which a paragraph in a practice direction relating to residential property cases or leasehold cases applies, it must be accompanied by the particulars and documents specified in the relevant paragraph.

(4) In proceedings to appeal a decision to the Tribunal, the application must be accompanied by a copy of any written record of that decision and any statement of reasons for that decision that the applicant has or can reasonably obtain.

(5) The applicant must provide with the notice of application any fee payable to the Tribunal.

(6) This rule does not apply to the extent that rule 28 applies.

(7) This rule does not apply where a form is prescribed for the purposes of starting proceedings in the Tribunal under Part V of the Rent Act 1977 (rents under restricted contracts) or Part 1 of the Housing Act 1988 (assured tenancies, shorthold and non-shorthold).

NOTES

Initial Commencement

Specified date

Specified date: 1 July 2013: see r 1(1).

27 Time limits

(1) This rule applies where no time limit for starting proceedings is prescribed by or under another enactment.

(2) Where the notice of application relates to a right to appeal from any decision (including any notice, order or licence), the applicant must provide the notice of application to the Tribunal within 28 days after the date on which notice of the decision to which the appeal relates was sent to the applicant.

(3) In a land registration case to which rule 28(3)(c) applies (references by the registrar), the person directed to be the applicant must provide the statement of case to the Tribunal within 28 days after the date on which written notice of receipt by the Tribunal of the reference by the registrar was sent to the applicant.

(4) In an agricultural land and drainage case—

(a) a notice of application under section 67(5) of the 1986 Act (compensation for long-term improvements: consent needed) must be made within 28 days after the date on which notice in writing of the Tribunal's decision approving the carrying out of the improvement was sent to the landlord;

(b) in proceedings under section 26(1) or 28(2) of the 1986 Act (restriction on operation of notices to quit) for the Tribunal's consent to the operation of a notice to quit, made by a landlord after service on the landlord by the tenant of a counter-notice, the notice of application must be made within two months after the date of service of the counter-notice;

(c) where, at the expiry of the period specified in section 39(1) of the 1986 Act (application for tenancy of holding), only one application under that section in respect of the holding has been made, any application by the landlord under section 44(1) of that Act (opportunity for landlord to seek Tribunal's consent to serve notice to quit) must be made before the expiry of two months after the end of that period;

(d) where, at the expiry of the period specified in section 39(1) of the 1986 Act (application for tenancy of holding), more than one application under section 39 of the 1986 Act has been made, any application by the landlord under section 44(1) of that Act must be made before the expiry of two months after the Tribunal notifies the landlord that the number of applications under section 39 of the 1986 Act is reduced to one.

NOTES

Initial Commencement

Specified date

Specified date: 1 July 2013: see r 1(1).

28 Referred and transferred cases

(1) This rule applies where a matter is referred, sent or transferred to the Tribunal by—

(a) a rent officer under paragraph 6 of Schedule 11 to the Rent Act 1977;

(b) the registrar under section 73(7) of the 2002 LR Act;

(c) another tribunal, or

(d) a court.

(2) The requirement to start proceedings in accordance with rule 26(1) does not apply.

(3) Upon receipt of a matter to which this rule relates, the Tribunal must provide to the parties written notice specifying—

(a) the date when the Tribunal received the matter;

(b) the names and any known addresses of the parties to the proceedings; and

(c) in a case referred by the registrar, which party or parties will be the applicant or applicants for the purposes of the proceedings and which party or parties will be the respondent or respondents.

(4) Each party whom the Tribunal directs in accordance with paragraph (3)(c) to act as an applicant for the purposes of the Tribunal proceedings, must send or deliver to the Tribunal a statement of case—

(a) containing any information referred to in rule 26(2) which the Tribunal requires;

(b) stating the applicant's reasons for supporting or objecting to the original application to the registrar;

(c) accompanied by copies of any documents available to the applicant which—

(i) are important to the applicant's case; or

(ii) the Tribunal or any other party to the proceedings will require in order properly to understand the applicant's case.

(5) Where a matter has been transferred by a court, the Tribunal may require any party to provide it with a copy of the court order by which the matter was transferred.

NOTES

Initial Commencement

Specified date

Specified date: 1 July 2013: see r 1(1).

29 Notice to respondents, interested persons and other persons

(1) When the Tribunal receives a notice of application in accordance with rule 26(1) or a statement of case in accordance with rule 28(4), the Tribunal must provide a copy of the application and any accompanying documents to the respondent.

(2) The Tribunal must also provide to the respondent a written notice informing the respondent of the requirements of rule 30.

(3) On being notified of the name and address of an interested person, the Tribunal must provide that person with a copy of the application and any accompanying documents.

(4) On receipt of an application relating to service charges, administration charges or estate charges the Tribunal must provide notice of the application to—

(a) the secretary of any recognised tenants' association within the meaning of section 29 of the Landlord and Tenant Act 1985 identified in the application; and

(b) any person whose name and address is known to the Tribunal whom the Tribunal considers is likely to be significantly affected by the application.

(5) In paragraph (4), "an application relating to service charges, administration charges or estate charges" means an application made under—

(a) section 20ZA or section 27A of or paragraph 8 of the Schedule to the Landlord and Tenant Act 1985; or

(b) section 159 of or paragraph 3 of Schedule 11 to the Commonhold and Leasehold Reform Act 2002.

(6) The Tribunal may give notice of the application to any other person it considers appropriate.

(7) Any notice given under paragraph (4) or (6)—

(a) must state that a person may apply to the Tribunal to be joined as a party to the proceedings; and

(b) may be given by publication of the notice in two newspapers (at least one of which should be a freely distributed newspaper) circulating in the locality in which the premises to which the application relates are situated.

(8) Where a rectification application under section 108(2) of the 2002 LR Act has been received by the Tribunal, the Tribunal must provide the person against whom the order is sought and any other person who the Tribunal considers should be a party to the proceedings, with—

(a) a copy of the application, and

(b) a notice specifying that if the person wishes to object, the person must send or deliver to the Tribunal an objection in response within 28 days of the date on which the person received the copy of the application provided by the Tribunal.

(9) The requirement to provide documents referred to in paragraph (1) does not apply where the Tribunal is satisfied that the circumstances to which rule 9(2)(a) (no Tribunal jurisdiction) applies exist.

(10) The requirement under paragraph (3) to provide the notice of application to an interested person does not apply in cases to which section 39, 41 or section 53 of the 1986 Act applies (succession cases); see instead rule 16(3).

NOTES

Initial Commencement

Specified date

Specified date: 1 July 2013: see r 1(1).

30 The response

(1) In circumstances to which rule 28(1)(b) or 29(8) (certain land registration cases) apply, the respondent's response must—

(a) state the respondent's reasons for supporting or objecting to the original application or for objecting to the rectification application (as the case may be);

(b) be accompanied by copies of any documents available to the respondent which—

(i) are important to the respondent's case; or

(ii) the Tribunal or any other party to the proceedings will require in order properly to understand the respondent's case; and

(c) in circumstances to which rule 28(1)(b) applies, be the respondent's statement of case and sent or delivered to the Tribunal within such time as the Tribunal may direct.

(2) In an appeal, paragraphs (3) to (6) apply.

(3) The respondent must, unless a practice direction or direction makes different relevant provision, within 28 days after the date on which the respondent was provided with a copy of the notice of application, send or deliver to the Tribunal a response.

(4) The response must state—

(a) the name and address of the respondent;

(b) the name and address of the respondent's representative (if any);

(c) an address where documents for the respondent may be sent or delivered;

(d) where not included in the application, the name and address of every person who appears to the respondent to be an interested person, with reasons for that person's interest;

(e) whether the respondent opposes the application and, if so, any grounds for such opposition which are not contained in another document provided with the response;

(f) whether the respondent would be content for the case to be dealt with without a hearing if the Tribunal considers it appropriate; and
(g) any further information or documents required by a practice direction or direction.

(5) The respondent must provide with the response a copy of any written record of the decision appealed and any statement of reasons for that decision that the applicant did not provide and the respondent has or can reasonably obtain.

(6) The respondent must send or deliver a copy of the response and any accompanying documents to each other party at the same time as it provides the response to the Tribunal.

NOTES

Initial Commencement

Specified date

Specified date: 1 July 2013: see r 1(1).

PART 4
HEARINGS

31 Decision with or without a hearing

(1) Subject to the remainder of this rule, the Tribunal must hold a hearing before making a decision which disposes of proceedings.

(2) The Tribunal need not hold a hearing if consent to proceeding without a hearing has been given by—
(a) each party; and
(b) each other person who has been sent a notification as being entitled, invited or permitted to attend the hearing.

(3) For the purposes of paragraph (2) a party or other person shall be taken to have consented if—
(a) the Tribunal has given that party or other person not less than 28 days' notice of its intention to dispose of the proceedings without a hearing, and
(b) no objection has been received from that party or other person within that time,

except that the Tribunal may regard such a party or other person as having consented upon shorter notice in urgent or exceptional circumstances.

(4) The Tribunal may in any event dispose of proceedings without a hearing under rule 9 (striking out a party's case) or under rule 39(4) (implementation of court order in land registration cases).

NOTES

Initial Commencement

Specified date

Specified date: 1 July 2013: see r 1(1).

32 Notice of hearings

(1) The Tribunal must give each party reasonable notice of the time and place of the hearing (including any adjourned or postponed hearing) and any changes to the time and place of the hearing.

(2) The notice period for a hearing to consider disposal of the proceedings must be no less than 14 days, except that the Tribunal may give shorter notice—
(a) with the parties' consent; or
(b) in urgent or exceptional circumstances.

NOTES

Initial Commencement

Specified date

Specified date: 1 July 2013: see r 1(1).

33 Public and private hearings

(1) Subject to the following paragraphs, all hearings must be held in public.

(2) The Tribunal may give a direction that a hearing, or part of it, is to be held in private.

(3) Where a hearing, or part of it, is to be held in private, the Tribunal may determine who is permitted to attend the hearing or part of it.

(4) The Tribunal may admit persons to a hearing under paragraph (3) on such terms and conditions as it considers appropriate.

(5) The Tribunal may give a direction excluding from any hearing, or part of it—

(a) any person whose conduct the Tribunal considers is disrupting or is likely to disrupt the hearing;

(b) any person whose presence the Tribunal considers is likely to prevent another person from giving evidence or making submissions freely;

(c) any person who the Tribunal considers should be excluded in order to give effect to the requirement at rule 17(8) (prevention of disclosure or publication of documents and information); or

(d) any person where the purpose of the hearing would be defeated by the attendance of that person.

(6) The Tribunal may give a direction excluding a witness from a hearing until that witness gives evidence.

NOTES

Initial Commencement

Specified date

Specified date: 1 July 2013: see r 1(1).

34 Hearings in a party's absence

If a party fails to attend a hearing the Tribunal may proceed with the hearing if the Tribunal—

(a) is satisfied that the party has been notified of the hearing or that reasonable steps have been taken to notify the party of the hearing; and

(b) considers that it is in the interests of justice to proceed with the hearing.

NOTES

Initial Commencement

Specified date

Specified date: 1 July 2013: see r 1(1).

35 Consent orders

(1) The Tribunal may, at the request of the parties but only if it considers it appropriate, make a consent order disposing of the proceedings and making such other appropriate provision as the parties have agreed.

(2) Notwithstanding any other provision of these Rules, the Tribunal need not hold a hearing before making an order under paragraph (1) or provide reasons for the order.

NOTES

Initial Commencement

Specified date

Specified date: 1 July 2013: see r 1(1).

36 Decisions

(1) The Tribunal may give a decision orally at a hearing.

(2) Subject to rule 17(8) (prevention of disclosure or publication of documents and information), the Tribunal must provide to each party as soon as reasonably practicable after making a decision (other than a decision under Part 6) which finally disposes of all issues in the proceedings or of a preliminary issue dealt with following a direction under rule 6(3)(g)—

- (a) a decision notice stating the Tribunal's decision;
- (b) written reasons for the decision or, in cases relating to rents, notification of the right to request written reasons under paragraph (4); and
- (c) notification of any right of appeal against the decision and the time within which, and manner in which, such right of appeal may be exercised.

(3) The Tribunal may provide written reasons for any decision to which paragraph (2) does not apply.

(4) Where a party is notified under paragraph (2)(b) of the right to request written reasons any such request must be made not later than 1 month from the date the Tribunal sends to the party the decision notice and notification of any right of appeal.

NOTES

Initial Commencement

Specified date

Specified date: 1 July 2013: see r 1(1).

PART 5
SPECIAL PROCEDURES

CHAPTER 1

LAND REGISTRATION CASES: REQUIREMENTS RELATING TO COURT PROCEEDINGS, REGISTRAR ETC

37 Consideration of direction to commence court proceedings under section 110(1) of the 2002 LR Act

Before the Tribunal decides to direct a party to commence court proceedings under section 110(1) of the 2002 LR Act, the parties may make representations as to—

- (a) whether the Tribunal should make such a direction;
- (b) which party should be directed to commence court proceedings;
- (c) the time within which court proceedings must commence; and
- (d) the questions the court should determine.

NOTES

Initial Commencement

Specified date

Specified date: 1 July 2013: see r 1(1).

38 Notification relevant to related court proceedings

(1) This rule applies where a party—

(a) is directed to commence court proceedings by the Tribunal under section 110(1); or
(b) commences, or has commenced, court proceedings which concern or relate to the matter before the Tribunal.

(2) The party referred to in paragraph (1) must provide to the Tribunal and all other parties—

(a) written notice stating—
  (i) that court proceedings have been issued;
  (ii) the date of issue of the court proceedings;
  (iii) the names and any known addresses of the parties to the court proceedings;
  (iv) the name of the court at which the court proceedings are pending;
  (v) the case number allocated to the court proceedings; and
  (vi) the way and the extent to which the court proceedings concern or relate to the matter before the Tribunal;
(b) within 14 days after the date of any decision on any application for an extension of time, a copy of that decision; and
(c) within 14 days after the date on which the matter before the court is finally disposed of, a copy of the final court order.

(3) Where the party has been directed to commence proceedings under section 110(1), the written notice to which paragraph (2)(a) refers must be provided within 14 days after the date of issue of the court proceedings.

(4) Where the party commences or has commenced court proceedings otherwise than in consequence of a direction made by the Tribunal, the written notice to which paragraph (2)(a) refers must be provided within 14 days after the date of commencement of the court proceedings or, if later, within 7 days after the date of provision of the written notice in accordance with rule 28(3) that the matter has been received by the Tribunal.

(5) In this rule—

"the date on which the matter before the court is finally disposed of" means the earliest date on which the court proceedings relating to the matter (including any court proceedings on or in consequence of an appeal) have been determined and any time for appealing or further appealing has expired.

(6) In this rule and in rule 39—

"the final court order" means the order made by the court that records the court's final determination (on appeal or otherwise).

NOTES

Initial Commencement

Specified date

Specified date: 1 July 2013: see r 1(1).

39 Stay of Tribunal proceedings following a direction relating to the whole or part of a matter

(1) This rule applies where the Tribunal has directed a party under section 110(1) of the 2002 LR Act to commence court proceedings for the court's decision on the whole or part of a matter.

(2) Upon receipt by the Tribunal of notice under rule 38(2)(a) that court proceedings have been issued, the Tribunal proceedings, or the relevant part of those proceedings, are automatically stayed pending the final court order.

(3) Subject to sub-paragraph (4) and any question of costs, once the Tribunal has received a copy of the final court order in accordance with rule 38(2)(c), unless the court directs otherwise, the Tribunal proceedings, or the part of the matter, are to be regarded as stayed.

(4) The Tribunal may make a decision, including lifting a stay under this rule, either with or without a hearing and either with or without giving prior notice to the parties if—

(a) such a decision is necessary, in addition to the final court order, to implement the final court order; and

(b) the Tribunal would have had the power to make such a decision if the Tribunal had made a decision in relation to the proceedings.

(5) Where the stay referred to in paragraph (2) relates only to part of the matter, the Tribunal may stay the proceedings in relation to any other part of the matter before the Tribunal pending the final court order.

(6) While the court proceedings are still pending, the party directed to commence court proceedings must notify the court of any decision made by the Tribunal within 14 days after the date on which it receives the Tribunal decision.

NOTES

Initial Commencement

Specified date

Specified date: 1 July 2013: see r 1(1).

40 Requirements directed to the registrar

(1) The Tribunal must send written notice to the registrar of any direction which requires the registrar to take action.

(2) Where the Tribunal has made a decision, that decision may include a direction to the registrar to—

(a) give effect to the original application in whole or in part as if the objection to that original application had not been made; or

(b) cancel the original application in whole or in part.

(3) A direction to the registrar under paragraph (2) must be in writing, must be sent or delivered to the registrar and may include—

(a) a condition that a specified entry be made on the register of any title affected; or

(b) a direction to reject any future application of a specified kind by a named party to the proceedings—

(i) unconditionally; or

(ii) unless that party satisfies specified conditions.

NOTES

Initial Commencement

Specified date

Specified date: 1 July 2013: see r 1(1).

CHAPTER 2

Agricultural Land and Drainage Cases Relating to Succession

41 Succession cases

(1) This rule applies to an application made under section 39 or section 53 of the 1986 Act.

(2) In proceedings under section 39, an applicant who opposes or intends to oppose any other application under that section may include in their own notice of application, or in a separate response, the following additional information—

(a) the reasons why they oppose or intend to oppose that other application;

(b) a statement whether they dispute that applicant's claim to be a designated applicant and, if so, why;

(c) a claim to be a more suitable applicant than any other and, if so, why;

(d) a statement whether or not the applicant has agreed with one or more other applicants or intending applicants to request the landlord's consent to a direction entitling them to a joint tenancy of the holding or might be willing to do so.

(3) If the landlord does not respond to an application within the time allowed, the landlord is not entitled to dispute any matter alleged in the application but—

(a) in the case of an application under section 39 or section 53, the landlord is entitled to give the landlord's views on the suitability of the applicant; and

(b) in the case of an application under section 39, the landlord may make an application under section 44 of the 1986 Act for consent to the operation of a notice to quit.

NOTES

Initial Commencement

Specified date

Specified date: 1 July 2013: see r 1(1).

42 Procedure at hearing in case of multiple applicants where designation is claimed

(1) In proceedings under section 39 of the 1986 Act, the Tribunal must (in such sequence as the Tribunal considers appropriate) at a hearing consider and determine the validity of each applicant's claim, if any, to be a designated applicant, giving all other parties and all other applicants for succession the opportunity to be heard.

(2) If the Tribunal determines that any such claim is valid, the Tribunal must then hear that applicant's application as if that applicant were the only applicant and, if the Tribunal determines that the applicant is a suitable person to become the tenant of the holding, the Tribunal must dismiss all other applications under section 39 of the 1986 Act in respect of the same holding.

(3) If the Tribunal determines that the designated applicant is not a suitable person to become a tenant of the holding, the Tribunal must dismiss the application.

NOTES

Initial Commencement

Specified date

Specified date: 1 July 2013: see r 1(1).

43 Multiple applications under the 1986 Act where there is no designated applicant

(1) The Tribunal must, subject to any direction by the Tribunal to the contrary, consider any issue of eligibility or suitability by applying the 1986 Act in the following sequence—

(a) any question arising under section 41(3) of the 1986 Act (treatment as eligible person);

(b) any question of eligibility under section 39(2) of the 1986 Act, as applied by section 39(3) of that Act;

(c) any question of suitability under section 39(2) of the 1986 Act, as applied by section 39(3) of that Act;

(d) any exercise of discretion under section 39(9) of the 1986 Act (direction for joint tenancy);

(e) any question of relative suitability under section 39(6) of the 1986 Act;

(f) any question arising under section 39(10) of the 1986 Act (tenancy of part of holding);

(g) any question arising under section 44 of the 1986 Act (consent to operation of notice to quit).

(2) Before giving a direction under section 39(9) of the 1986 Act, the Tribunal must—

- (a) ask the landlord if the landlord consents to the giving of a direction; and
- (b) consider any representations made by other suitable applicants.

(3) The landlord will be deemed not to consent to the giving of a direction under section 39(9) of the 1986 Act if the landlord does not respond to the Tribunal within the period specified by the Tribunal.

(4) Before giving a direction under section 39(10) of the 1986 Act, the Tribunal must ask each applicant whether that applicant agrees to such a direction being given.

NOTES

Initial Commencement

Specified date

Specified date: 1 July 2013: see r 1(1).

CHAPTER 3

Residential Property Cases: Urgent Cases, Interim Orders, etc

44 Urgent IMO authorisation applications

(1) This rule applies when a local housing authority makes an urgent IMO authorisation application.

(2) If it appears to the Tribunal, on the basis of information accompanying the application that the exceptional circumstances mentioned in paragraph (3) exist, it must order that an urgent hearing be held and must follow the procedure set out in rule 46.

(3) The exceptional circumstances are that—

- (a) there is an immediate threat to the health and safety of the occupiers of the house or to persons occupying or having an estate or interest in any premises in the vicinity of the house; and
- (b) by making the IMO as soon as possible (together where applicable with such other measures as the local housing authority intends to take) the local housing authority will be able to take immediate appropriate steps to arrest or significantly reduce the threat.

NOTES

Initial Commencement

Specified date

Specified date: 1 July 2013: see r 1(1).

45 . . .

. . .

NOTES

Amendment

Revoked by SI 2014/2128, rr 29, 31.
Date in force: 1 September 2014: see SI 2014/2128, r 1(a).

46 Procedure in urgent cases

(1) In cases to which this rule applies, the Tribunal must as soon as practicable notify the parties and each interested person whose name and address have been notified to it—

- (a) that the application is to be dealt with as a matter of urgency;
- (b) why it appears to the Tribunal that the exceptional circumstances exist;
- (c) of any requirement to be satisfied by a party before the hearing; and

(d) the date on which the hearing will be held.

(2) The date of the hearing must be not more than 10 days after the date that notification of the hearing is sent.

(3) At the hearing the Tribunal may, if it is not satisfied that the exceptional circumstances exist, adjourn the hearing and give such directions as it considers appropriate.

NOTES

Initial Commencement

Specified date

Specified date: 1 July 2013: see r 1(1).

47 Interim orders

(1) This rule applies where an enactment relating to a residential property case allows the Tribunal to make an interim order—

(a) suspending, in whole or in part, the effect of any decision, notice, order or licence which is the subject matter of proceedings before it; or

(b) for the time being granting any remedy which it would have had power to grant in its final decision.

(2) The Tribunal must provide notice of the order to each party as soon as reasonably practicable after making an interim order and, except in the case of an order made with the consent of all parties, giving reasons for the order.

(3) A party may request that the interim order be varied or set aside, if the Tribunal has made an interim order without first giving the parties the opportunity to make representations.

(4) Any such request may be made—

(a) orally at a hearing;

(b) in writing; or

(c) by such other means as the Tribunal may permit.

(5) This rule does not apply to an application for an urgent IMO authorisation . . ..

NOTES

Initial Commencement

Specified date

Specified date: 1 July 2013: see r 1(1).

Amendment

Para (5): words omitted revoked by SI 2014/2128, rr 29, 32.
Date in force: 1 September 2014: see SI 2014/2128, r 1(a).

48 Detrimental effect of mobile homes on the amenity of the site applications

(1) This rule applies if a site owner applies for a determination under paragraph 5A(2)(a) of Chapter 2, or paragraph 6(1)(a) of Chapter 4, of Part 1 of Schedule 1 to the 1983 Act that, having regard to its condition, the mobile home is having a detrimental effect on the amenity of the site.

(2) If, at a hearing, it appears to the Tribunal that the mobile home is having a detrimental effect on the amenity of the site, but that if certain repairs to the mobile home were carried out, the mobile home would cease to have such a detrimental effect, it must—

(a) inform the site owner and the occupier of the repairs which should be carried out;

(b) invite both the occupier of the mobile home and the site owner to provide information in relation to those repairs as to—

(i) the time needed to carry them out; and

(ii) the cost of carrying them out; and

(c) invite the occupier of the mobile home to indicate whether or not the occupier would be willing to carry out those repairs.

(3) The Tribunal, having regard to information given under paragraph (2)(b) and (c) must either—

(a) make a determination under paragraph 5A(2)(a) of Chapter 2, or paragraph 6(1)(a) of Chapter 4, of Part 1 of Schedule 1 to the 1983 Act; or

(b) if paragraph 5A(4) of Chapter 2, or paragraph 6(2) of Chapter 4, of Part 1 of that Schedule applies, make an interim order requiring the occupier of the mobile home to carry out such repairs within such time as the Tribunal considers reasonable.

(4) Upon making an interim order under paragraph (3)(b), the Tribunal must adjourn the hearing and set a further hearing date for within 7 days from the date by which the specified repairs must be carried out.

(5) The Tribunal must request each of the site owner and the occupier to state, no later than 4 days before the date of the further hearing, whether (in their opinion) the specified repairs have been completed.

(6) When setting a further hearing date under paragraph (4), the Tribunal must—

(a) give the parties not less than 14 days' notice of the hearing date; and

(b) invite both the site owner and the occupier to indicate, no later than 4 days before the date of the hearing, whether in their opinion the repairs described in the order have been completed.

(7) At the further hearing—

(a) if the Tribunal has received notification from each of the occupier and the site owner that the repairs ordered under paragraph (3)(b) have been completed, it must dismiss the application;

(b) if the Tribunal has not received such notification it must request the parties present to make representations as to the extent of repairs left to be carried out and the time needed to carry them out; and

(c) having considered any such representations, it must either make a further interim order under paragraph (3)(b) or make a determination under paragraph 5A(2)(a) of Chapter 2, or paragraph 6(1)(a) of Chapter 4, of Part 1 of Schedule 1 to the 1983 Act.

(8) If, before the date of the further hearing, the Tribunal is satisfied that the repairs have been completed, the Tribunal may dispense with the need for a further hearing and may dismiss the application.

NOTES

Initial Commencement

Specified date

Specified date: 1 July 2013: see r 1(1).

PART 6
CORRECTING, SETTING ASIDE, REVIEWING AND APPEALING TRIBUNAL DECISIONS

49 Interpretation

In this Part—

"appeal" means the exercise of a right of appeal from the Tribunal—

(a) on a point of law under section 11 of the 2007 Act;

(b) on a point other than a point of law where such a right of appeal is conferred—

(i) by any enactment in relation to a residential property case or a leasehold case;

(ii) by section 111(1) of the 2002 LR Act in relation to a land registration case;

"review" means the review of a decision by the Tribunal under section 9 of the 2007 Act.

NOTES

Initial Commencement

Specified date

Specified date: 1 July 2013: see r 1(1).

50 Clerical mistakes and accidental slips or omissions

The Tribunal may at any time correct any clerical mistake or other accidental slip or omission in a decision, direction or any document produced by it, by—

(a) sending notification of the amended decision or direction, or a copy of the amended document, to each party; and

(b) making any necessary amendment to any information published in relation to the decision, direction or document.

NOTES

Initial Commencement

Specified date

Specified date: 1 July 2013: see r 1(1).

51 Setting aside a decision which disposes of proceedings

(1) The Tribunal may set aside a decision which disposes of proceedings, or part of such a decision, and re-make the decision or the relevant part of it, if—

(a) the Tribunal considers that it is in the interests of justice to do so; and

(b) one or more of the conditions in paragraph (2) are satisfied.

(2) The conditions are—

(a) a document relating to the proceedings was not sent to, or was not received at an appropriate time by, a party or a party's representative;

(b) a document relating to the proceedings was not sent to or was not received by the Tribunal at an appropriate time;

(c) a party, or a party's representative, was not present at a hearing related to the proceedings; or

(d) there has been some other procedural irregularity in the proceedings.

(3) A party applying for a decision, or part of a decision, to be set aside under paragraph (1) must make a written application to the Tribunal so that it is received—

(a) within 28 days after the date on which the Tribunal sent notice of the decision to the party; or

(b) if later, within 28 days after the date on which the Tribunal sent notice of the reasons for the decision to the party.

NOTES

Initial Commencement

Specified date

Specified date: 1 July 2013: see r 1(1).

52 Application for permission to appeal

(1) A person seeking permission to appeal must make a written application to the Tribunal for permission to appeal.

(2) An application under paragraph (1) must be sent or delivered to the Tribunal so that it is received within 28 days after the latest of the dates that the Tribunal sends to the person making the application—

(a) written reasons for the decision;
(b) notification of amended reasons for, or correction of, the decision following a review; or
(c) notification that an application for the decision to be set aside has been unsuccessful.

(3) The date in paragraph (2)(c) applies only if the application for the decision to be set aside was made within the time stipulated in rule 51 or any extension of that time granted by the Tribunal.

(4) If the person seeking permission to appeal sends or delivers the application to the Tribunal later than the time required by paragraph (2) or by any extension of time under rule 6(3)(a) (power to extend time)—

(a) the application must include a request for an extension of time and the reason why the application was not received in time; and
(b) unless the Tribunal extends time for the application under rule 6(3)(a) (power to extend time) the Tribunal must not admit the application.

(5) An application under paragraph (1) must—

(a) identify the decision of the Tribunal to which it relates;
(b) state the grounds of appeal; and
(c) state the result the party making the application is seeking.

NOTES

Initial Commencement

Specified date

Specified date: 1 July 2013: see r 1(1).

53 Tribunal's consideration of application for permission to appeal

(1) On receiving an application for permission to appeal the Tribunal must first consider, taking into account the overriding objective in rule 3, whether to review the decision in accordance with rule 55 (review of a decision).

(2) If the Tribunal decides not to review the decision, or reviews the decision and decides to take no action in relation to the decision, or part of it, the Tribunal must consider whether to give permission to appeal in relation to the decision or that part of it.

(3) The Tribunal must send a record of its decision to the parties as soon as practicable.

(4) If the Tribunal refuses permission to appeal it must send with the record of its decision—

(a) a statement of its reasons for such refusal; and
(b) notification of the right to make an application to the Upper Tribunal for permission to appeal and the time within which, and the method by which, such application must be made.

(5) The Tribunal may give permission to appeal on limited grounds, but must comply with paragraph (4) in relation to any grounds on which it has refused permission.

NOTES

Initial Commencement

Specified date

Specified date: 1 July 2013: see r 1(1).

54 Stay pending appeal to the Upper Tribunal

(1) A party who wishes to apply to the Tribunal to stay the implementation of the whole or part of a decision pending the outcome of the appeal must make such an application to the Tribunal at the same time as the party applies to the Tribunal for permission to appeal.

(2) The party applying for a stay under paragraph (1) must provide reasons for the application and provide notice of the application to the other parties.
(3) Before reaching a decision to stay implementation of the whole or part of a decision, the Tribunal must allow the parties the opportunity to make representations or objections.
(4) The Tribunal must notify the parties of any decision that the Tribunal makes as to granting a stay of the implementation of the whole or part of the Tribunal's decision.
(5) In a land registration case, where the Tribunal's decision to stay implementation of a decision relates to a decision disposing of the proceedings, the Tribunal must provide to the registrar a copy of the notice under paragraph (4).
(6) The notice under paragraph (4) must—
- (a) be in writing;
- (b) be dated;
- (c) specify the decision made by the Tribunal; and
- (d) include the Tribunal's reasons for the decision.

NOTES

Initial Commencement

Specified date

Specified date: 1 July 2013: see r 1(1).

55 Review of a decision

(1) The Tribunal may only undertake a review of a decision—
- (a) pursuant to rule 53 (review on an application for permission to appeal); and
- (b) if it is satisfied that a ground of appeal is likely to be successful.

(2) The Tribunal must notify the parties in writing of the outcome of any review, and of any right of appeal in relation to the outcome.
(3) If the Tribunal takes any action in relation to a decision following a review without first giving every party an opportunity to make representations, the notice under paragraph (2) must state that any party that did not have an opportunity to make representations may apply for such action to be set aside and for the decision to be reviewed again.

NOTES

Initial Commencement

Specified date

Specified date: 1 July 2013: see r 1(1).

56 Power to treat an application about a decision as a different type of application

The Tribunal may treat an application for a decision to be corrected or set aside or for permission to appeal against that decision, as an application for any other one of those things.

NOTES

Initial Commencement

Specified date

Specified date: 1 July 2013: see r 1(1).

TRIBUNAL PROCEDURE (UPPER TRIBUNAL) RULES 2008

SI 2008 No 2698

PART 3
[PROCEDURE FOR CASES IN] THE UPPER TRIBUNAL

NOTES

Amendment

Part heading: words "Procedure for Cases in" in square brackets substituted by SI 2009/274, rr 3, 13.

Date in force: 1 April 2009: see SI 2009/274, r 1.

21 Application to the Upper Tribunal for permission to appeal

(1) . . .

(2) A person may apply to the Upper Tribunal for permission to appeal to the Upper Tribunal against a decision of another tribunal only if—

(a) they have made an application for permission to appeal to the tribunal which made the decision challenged; and

(b) that application has been refused or has not been admitted [or has been granted only on limited grounds].

(3) An application for permission to appeal must be made in writing and received by the Upper Tribunal no later than—

(b) otherwise, a month after the date on which the tribunal that made the decision under challenge sent notice of its refusal of permission to appeal, or refusal to admit the application for permission to appeal, to the appellant.

(4) The application must state—

(a) the name and address of the appellant;

(b) the name and address of the representative (if any) of the appellant;

(c) an address where documents for the appellant may be sent or delivered;

(d) details (including the full reference) of the decision challenged;

(e) the grounds on which the appellant relies; and

(f) whether the appellant wants the application to be dealt with at a hearing.

(5) The appellant must provide with the application a copy of—

(a) any written record of the decision being challenged;

(b) any separate written statement of reasons for that decision; and

(c) if the application is for permission to appeal against a decision of another tribunal, the notice of refusal of permission to appeal, or notice of refusal to admit the application for permission to appeal, from that other tribunal.

(6) If the appellant provides the application to the Upper Tribunal later than the time required by paragraph (3) or by an extension of time allowed under rule 5(3)(a) (power to extend time)—

(a) the application must include a request for an extension of time and the reason why the application was not provided in time; and

(b) unless the Upper Tribunal extends time for the application under rule 5(3)(a) (power to extend time) the Upper Tribunal must not admit the application.

(7) If the appellant makes an application to the Upper Tribunal for permission to appeal against the decision of another tribunal, and that other tribunal refused to admit the appellant's application for permission to appeal because the application for permission or for a written statement of reasons was not made in time—

(a) the application to the Upper Tribunal for permission to appeal must include the reason why the application to the other tribunal for permission to appeal or for a written statement of reasons, as the case may be, was not made in time; and

(b) the Upper Tribunal must only admit the application if the Upper Tribunal considers that it is in the interests of justice for it to do so.

[(8) In this rule, a reference to notice of a refusal of permission to appeal is to be taken to include a reference to notice of a grant of permission to appeal on limited grounds.]

NOTES

Initial Commencement

Specified date

Specified date: 3 November 2008: see r 1(1).

Amendment

Para (1): revoked by SI 2009/1975, rr 7, 15.
Date in force: 1 September 2009: see SI 2009/1975, r 1.
Para (2): in sub-para (b) words "or has been granted only on limited grounds" in square brackets inserted by SI 2014/514, rr 2, 7(a).
Date in force: 6 April 2014: see SI 2014/514, r 1.
Para (8): inserted by SI 2014/514, rr 2, 7(b).
Date in force: 6 April 2014: see SI 2014/514, r 1.

22 Decision in relation to permission to appeal

(1) [Subject to rule 40A,] If the Upper Tribunal refuses permission to appeal [or refuses to admit a late application for permission], it must send written notice of the refusal and of the reasons for the refusal to the appellant.

(2) If the Upper Tribunal gives permission to appeal—

(a) the Upper Tribunal must send written notice of the permission, and of the reasons for any limitations or conditions on such permission, to each party;

(b) subject to any direction by the Upper Tribunal, the application for permission to appeal stands as the notice of appeal and the Upper Tribunal must send to each respondent a copy of the application for permission to appeal and any documents provided with it by the appellant; and

(c) the Upper Tribunal may, with the consent of the appellant and each respondent, determine the appeal without obtaining any further response.

[(3) Paragraph (4) applies where the Upper Tribunal, without a hearing, determines an application for permission to appeal—

(a) against a decision of—

[(iib) the Property Chamber of the First-tier Tribunal;]

(4) In the circumstances set out at paragraph (3) the appellant may apply for the decision to be reconsidered at a hearing if the Upper Tribunal—

(a) refuses permission to appeal [or refuses to admit a late application for permission]; or

(b) gives permission to appeal on limited grounds or subject to conditions.

(5) An application under paragraph (4) must be made in writing and received by the Upper Tribunal within 14 days after the date on which the Upper Tribunal sent written notice of its decision regarding the application to the appellant.

NOTES

Initial Commencement

Specified date

Specified date: 3 November 2008: see r 1(1).

Amendment

Para (1): words "Subject to rule 40A," in square brackets inserted by SI 2014/1505, rr 2, 3.
Date in force: 30 June 2014: see SI 2014/1505, r 1.

Para (1): words "or refuses to admit a late application for permission" in square brackets inserted by SI 2014/514, rr 2, 8(a).
Date in force: 6 April 2014: see SI 2014/514, r 1.

Para (3): substituted by SI 2009/274, rr 3, 14.
Date in force: 1 April 2009: see SI 2009/274, r 1.

Para (3): sub-para (a)(iib) inserted by SI 2014/514, rr 2, 8(b).
Date in force: 6 April 2014: see SI 2014/514, r 1.

Para (4): in sub-para (a) words "or refuses to admit a late application for permission" in square brackets inserted by SI 2014/514, rr 2, 8(c).
Date in force: 6 April 2014: see SI 2014/514, r 1.

23 Notice of appeal

[(1) This rule applies—

(b) if another tribunal has given permission for a party to appeal to the Upper Tribunal; or

(c) subject to any other direction by the Upper Tribunal, if the Upper Tribunal has given permission to appeal and has given a direction that the application for permission to appeal does not stand as the notice of appeal.

(2) The appellant must provide a notice of appeal to the Upper Tribunal so that it is received within 1 month after—

(a) the date that the tribunal that gave permission to appeal sent notice of such permission to the appellant; or

(3) The notice of appeal must include the information listed in rule 21(4)(a) to (e) (content of the application for permission to appeal) and, where the Upper Tribunal has given permission to appeal, the Upper Tribunal's case reference.

(4) If another tribunal has granted permission to appeal, the appellant must provide with the notice of appeal a copy of—

(a) any written record of the decision being challenged;

(b) any separate written statement of reasons for that decision; and

(c) the notice of permission to appeal.

(5) If the appellant provides the notice of appeal to the Upper Tribunal later than the time required by paragraph (2) or by an extension of time allowed under rule 5(3)(a) (power to extend time)—

(a) the notice of appeal must include a request for an extension of time and the reason why the notice was not provided in time; and

(b) unless the Upper Tribunal extends time for the notice of appeal under rule 5(3)(a) (power to extend time) the Upper Tribunal must not admit the notice of appeal.

[(6) When the Upper Tribunal receives the notice of appeal it must send a copy of the notice and any accompanying documents—

(a) to each respondent;

NOTES

Initial Commencement

Specified date

Specified date: 3 November 2008: see r 1(1).

Amendment

Paras (1), (2): substituted by SI 2009/1975, rr 7, 17(a).
Date in force: 1 September 2009: see SI 2009/1975, r 1.
Para (6): substituted by SI 2009/1975, rr 7, 17(b).
Date in force: 1 September 2009: see SI 2009/1975, r 1.

24 Response to the notice of appeal

(1A) Subject to any direction given by the Upper Tribunal, a respondent may provide a response to a notice of appeal.]

(2) Any response provided under paragraph [(1A)] must be in writing and must be sent or delivered to the Upper Tribunal so that it is received—

[(a) if an application for permission to appeal stands as the notice of appeal, no later than one month after the date on which the respondent was sent notice that permission to appeal had been granted;]

(b) in any other case, no later than 1 month after the date on which the Upper Tribunal sent a copy of the notice of appeal to the respondent.

(3) The response must state—

(a) the name and address of the respondent;

(b) the name and address of the representative (if any) of the respondent;

(c) an address where documents for the respondent may be sent or delivered;

(d) whether the respondent opposes the appeal;

(e) the grounds on which the respondent relies, including [(in the case of an appeal against the decision of another tribunal)] any grounds on which the respondent was unsuccessful in the proceedings which are the subject of the appeal, but intends to rely in the appeal; and

(f) whether the respondent wants the case to be dealt with at a hearing.

(4) If the respondent provides the response to the Upper Tribunal later than the time required by paragraph (2) or by an extension of time allowed under rule 5(3)(a) (power to extend time), the response must include a request for an extension of time and the reason why the [response] was not provided in time.

(5) When the Upper Tribunal receives the response it must send a copy of the response and any accompanying documents to the appellant and each other party.

NOTES

Initial Commencement

Specified date

Specified date: 3 November 2008: see r 1(1).

Amendment

Paras (1), (1A): substituted, for para (1) as originally enacted, by SI 2009/1975, rr 7, 18(a).
Date in force: 1 September 2009: see SI 2009/1975, r 1.
Para (2): reference to "(1A)" in square brackets substituted by SI 2010/43, rr 5, 9.
Date in force: 18 January 2010: see SI 2010/43, r 1.
Para (2): sub-para (a) substituted by SI 2010/44, rr 2, 15(a).
Date in force: 15 February 2010: see SI 2010/44, r 1.
Para (3): in sub-para (e) words "(in the case of an appeal against the decision of another tribunal)" in square brackets inserted by SI 2009/1975, rr 7, 18(c).
Date in force: 1 September 2009: see SI 2009/1975, r 1.

Para (4): word "response" in square brackets substituted by SI 2009/274, rr 3, 15.
Date in force: 1 April 2009: see SI 2009/274, r 1.

25 Appellant's reply

(1) Subject to any direction given by the Upper Tribunal, the appellant may provide a reply to any response provided under rule 24 (response to the notice of appeal).

(2) [Subject to paragraph (2A), any] reply provided under paragraph (1) must be in writing and must be sent or delivered to the Upper Tribunal so that it is received within one month after the date on which the Upper Tribunal sent a copy of the response to the appellant.

(3) When the Upper Tribunal receives the reply it must send a copy of the reply and any accompanying documents to each respondent.

NOTES

Initial Commencement

Specified date

Specified date: 3 November 2008: see r 1(1).

Amendment

Para (2): words "Subject to paragraph (2A), any" in square brackets substituted by SI 2010/44, rr 2, 16(a).
Date in force: 15 February 2010: see SI 2010/44, r 1.

Appendix 11

PRACTICE DIRECTIONS
PROPERTY CHAMBER, FIRST-TIER TRIBUNAL
LAND REGISTRATION

1. COMMENCEMENT, APPLICATION AND INTERPRETATION

1.1. These Practice Directions—

(a) apply to proceedings in land registration cases before the Property Chamber of the First-tier Tribunal;
(b) come into force on 30 July 2013;
(c) supplement the Rules and must be read in conjunction with them;
(d) are made by the Senior President of Tribunals with the agreement of the Lord Chancellor in the exercise of powers conferred by section 23 of the Tribunals, Courts and Enforcement Act 2007.

1.2. In these Practice Directions—

(a) "the Rules" means the Tribunal Procedure (First-tier Tribunal) (Property Chamber) Rules 2013;
(b) "Rule", followed by a number, means the rule bearing that number in the Rules.

2. NOTICES OF APPLICATION UNDER RULE 26

2.1 A notice of application for relief pursuant to section 108(2) of the 2002 LR Act (for the rectification or setting aside of a document) shall include the following information:

(a) the name and address of the applicant;
(b) the name and address of the applicant's representative (if any);
(c) an address (in England and Wales) where documents for the applicant may be delivered;
(d) the name and address of the person or persons against whom the order is sought;
(e) details of the remedy being sought including the precise form of any words to be inserted in any rectified document;
(f) the grounds of the application identifying all relevant facts and matters relied upon;

2.2 The notice of application shall contain a list of all documents which (i) are important to the applicant's case; or (ii) the Tribunal or any other party to the proceedings will require in order properly to understand the applicant's case and copies of such documents shall accompany the notice. A copy of the instrument intended to be rectified or set aside must be included.

2.3 The notice of application must include a statement that the applicant believes that the facts stated in it are true.

3. STATEMENTS OF CASE SERVED UNDER RULE 28

3.1 A statement of case served under Rule 28(4) must contain any information referred to in Rule 26(2) which the Tribunal requires.

3.2 By reference to Rule 26(2), the following information must be contained in such a statement of case:

(a) the name and address of the applicant (paragraph (2)(a));
(b) the name and address of the applicant's representative (if any) (paragraph (2)(b));
(c) an address (in England and Wales) where documents for the applicant may be delivered (paragraph (2)(c));

(d) a statement that the applicant believes that the facts stated in it are true (paragraph (2)(j));
(and by reference to paragraph (2)(n) of Rule 26)
(e) the applicant's reasons for supporting or objecting to the original application to the registrar identifying all relevant facts and matters relied upon; and
(f) a list of all copy documents provided under Rule 28(4)(c).

4. RESPONSES SERVED UNDER RULE 30

4.1 A response served under Rule 30 shall contain (in addition to the matters set out at sub-rules (1)(a) and (b) the following:

(a) the name and address of the respondent;
(b) the name and address of the respondent's representative (if any);
(c) an address (in England and Wales) where documents for the respondent may be delivered;
(d) all relevant facts and matters relied upon by the respondent in support of his case;
(e) a list of all copy documents provided under Rule 30(1)(b).

4.2 The response must include a statement that the respondent believes that the facts stated in it are true.

5. EXPERT EVIDENCE UNDER RULE 19

5.1 Time limits

Subject to Rule 19(6) and notwithstanding Rule 19(4), each party must provide to the Tribunal and to each other party a copy of the written report of any expert witness at such time or within such period as the Tribunal shall direct.

5.2 Costs of the expert witness

The Tribunal may limit the amount of a party's expert's fees and expenses that may be recovered from any other party.

6. SITE INSPECTIONS UNDER RULE 21

6.1 Where appropriate the Tribunal will seek to enter and inspect the land or property that is the subject of the proceedings, and, where practicable, any other land or properties referred to by the parties or their experts.

6.2 At such inspection, the Tribunal ordinarily will (unless otherwise agreed) be accompanied by each party and/or or his representative.

6.3 At such inspection no person should attempt to communicate with the Tribunal except in the hearing of the parties or their representatives.

6.4 The Tribunal may make an unaccompanied inspection without entering on private land.

6.5 The Tribunal may enter land or property only with the consent of the occupier. If the occupier is a party to the proceedings the Tribunal may take into account the withholding of consent to enter and inspect that party's land without reasonable excuse when making any decision or deciding any application for costs.

7. INFORMATION DURING COURT PROCEEDINGS

7.1 This paragraph applies where a party has commenced court proceedings which concern or relate to the matter before the Tribunal.

7.2 The party who has commenced such proceedings must provide in writing to the Tribunal such information as to the progress of the proceedings as the Tribunal shall request in writing.

7.3 Unless the Tribunal otherwise directs, the information requested shall be provided to the Tribunal within 14 days of the date of the request by the Tribunal.

8. STRIKING OUT A PARTY'S CASE UNDER RULE 9(3)(E) – "SUMMARY DISPOSAL"

8.1 Except with the permission of the Tribunal, an applicant may not apply for summary disposal under Rule 9(3)(e) until the respondent has served a response in accordance with Rule 30 or the respondent's time to do so has expired.

8.2 A respondent may apply for summary disposal under Rule 9(3)(e) at any time after the applicant has served a notice of application under Rule 26 or a statement of case under Rule 28, or (in the case of service of a statement of case) the applicant's time to do so has expired.

8.3 A party making a written application for summary disposal under Rule 9(3)(e) must comply with the provisions of Rule 7 and must in addition serve together with the copy of the application the witness statement in support.

8.4 Paragraph 8.5 applies where

(a) a respondent applies for summary disposal before serving a response and before the time to do so has expired; and
(b) that application does not result in the disposal of the entire proceedings.

8.5 In the circumstances described in paragraph 8.4 the respondent's time for serving a response is extended to

(a) 28 days after service on the respondent of the Tribunal's decision in relation to the application for summary disposal; or
(b) such other time as the Tribunal directs.

8.6 An application for summary disposal under Rule 9(3)(e) must be supported by a witness statement in support of the application. That witness statement must state that the party making the application believes that the other party has no real prospect of succeeding on the proceedings or on the issue to which the application relates.

8.7 The Tribunal may give such other directions for the service of evidence by the parties as it shall think fit.

8.8 When the Tribunal determines the issue of summary disposal under Rule 9(3)(e) the Tribunal may make an order

(a) disposing of the proceedings or of any issue; or
(b) dismissing the application for summary disposal.

8.9 Where an order made under paragraph 8.8 does not dispose of the entire proceedings, the Tribunal may give case management directions as to the future conduct of the proceedings.

8.10 The Tribunal may make an order of its own motion under Rule 9(3)(e) for striking out a party's case in accordance with such directions as it shall consider appropriate.

8.11 An order striking out the proceedings under Rule 9(1) or 9(3) in referred cases under Rule 28 shall take the form of an order directing the Chief Land Registrar either to cancel or to give effect to the original application as the case may be together with such other order as may be appropriate in the circumstances.

9. ORDERS FOR COSTS UNDER RULE 13

9.1. <u>The Tribunal's discretion as to costs</u>

(a) The Tribunal has discretion as to –

(i) whether costs are payable by one party to another;
(ii) the amount of those costs; and
(iii) when they are to be paid.

(b) If the Tribunal decides to make an order about costs –

- (i) ordinarily the unsuccessful party will be ordered to pay the costs of the successful party; but
- (iii) the Tribunal may make a different order.

(c) In deciding what order (if any) to make about costs, the Tribunal will have regard to all the circumstances, including –

- (i) the conduct of all the parties;
- (ii) whether a party has succeeded on part of its case, even if that party has not been wholly successful; and
- (iii) any admissible offer to settle made by a party which is drawn to the Tribunal's attention.

(d) The conduct of the parties includes –

- (i) conduct before, as well as during, the proceedings;
- (ii) whether it was reasonable for a party to raise, pursue or contest a particular allegation or issue;
- (iii) the manner in which a party has pursued or defended its case or a particular allegation or issue; and
- (iv) whether a party who has succeeded in the case, in whole or in part, exaggerated its case.

(e) The orders which the Tribunal may make include that a party must pay –

- (i) a proportion of another party's costs;
- (ii) a specified amount in respect of another party's costs;
- (iii) costs from or until a certain date only;
- (iv) costs relating to particular steps taken in the proceedings;
- (v) costs relating only to a distinct part of the proceedings.

9.2 Basis of assessment

(a) Where the Tribunal is to assess the amount of costs (whether by summary or detailed assessment) it will assess those costs –

- (i) on the standard basis; or
- (ii) on the indemnity basis

but the Tribunal will in neither case allow costs which have been unreasonably incurred or are unreasonable in amount.

(b) Where the Tribunal assesses the amount of costs on the standard basis, it will –

- (i) only allow costs which are proportionate to the matters in issue. Costs which are disproportionate in amount may be disallowed or reduced even if they were reasonably or necessarily incurred; and
- (ii) resolve any doubt which it may have as to whether costs were reasonably and proportionately incurred or were reasonable and proportionate in amount in favour of the paying party.

(Factors which the Tribunal may take into account are set out in paragraph 9.3 hereof)

(c) Where the Tribunal assesses the amount of costs on the indemnity basis, it will resolve any doubt which it may have as to whether costs were reasonably incurred or were reasonable in amount in favour of the receiving party.

(d) Where the Tribunal makes an order about costs without stating the basis on which the costs are to be assessed the costs will be assessed on the standard basis.

(e) Costs incurred are proportionate if they bear a reasonable relationship to

(i) the value of any asset in issue in the proceedings;
(ii) the complexity of the proceedings;
(iii) any additional work caused by the conduct of the paying party; and
(iv) any wider factors involved in the proceedings, such as reputation or public importance.

9.3 Factors to be taken into account in deciding the amount of costs

(a) Where the Tribunal assesses costs on the standard basis it will have regard to all the circumstances in deciding whether costs were –

(i) proportionately and reasonably incurred; or
(ii) proportionate and reasonable in amount.

(b) Where the Tribunal assesses costs on the indemnity basis it will have regard to all the circumstances in deciding whether costs were –

(i) unreasonably incurred; or
(ii) unreasonable in amount.

(c) In particular, the Tribunal will give effect to any orders which have already been made.
(d) The Tribunal will also have regard to the –

(i) conduct of all the parties, including in particular –
  (aa) conduct before, as well as during, the proceedings; and
  (bb) the efforts made, if any, before and during the proceedings in order to try to resolve the dispute;
(ii) amount or value of any money or property involved;
(iii) importance of the matter to all the parties;
(iv) particular complexity of the matter or the difficulty or novelty of the questions raised;
(v) skill, effort, specialised knowledge and responsibility involved;
(vi) time spent on the case;
(vii) place where and the circumstances in which work or any part of it was done.

9.4 The provisions of the Civil Procedure Rules relating to the detailed assessment of costs are modified to the extent set out in this Practice Direction or as the Tribunal shall from time to time direct.

SIR JEREMY SULLIVAN

SENIOR PRESIDENT OF TRIBUNALS

30 July 2013

Appendix 12

JUDICIAL REVIEW

JUDICIAL CLAIM FORM

Judicial Review
Claim Form

In the High Court of Justice
Administrative Court

Notes for guidance are available which explain how to complete the judicial review claim form. Please read them carefully before you complete the form.

For Court use only	
Administrative Court Reference No.	
Date filed	

Seal

Guidance Notes

SECTION 1 Details of the claimant(s) and defendant(s)

Claimant(s) name and address(es)

name

address

Telephone no. **Fax no.**

E-mail address

Claimant's or claimant's solicitors' address to which documents should be sent.

name

address

Telephone no. **Fax no.**

E-mail address

Claimant's Counsel's details

name

address

Telephone no. **Fax no.**

E-mail address

1st Defendant

name

Defendant's or (where known) Defendant's solicitors' address to which documents should be sent.

name

address

Telephone no. **Fax no.**

E-mail address

2nd Defendant

name

Defendant's or (where known) Defendant's solicitors' address to which documents should be sent.

name

address

Telephone no. **Fax no.**

E-mail address

SECTION 2 Details of other interested parties

Include name and address and, if appropriate, details of DX, telephone or fax numbers and e-mail

name	name
address	address
Telephone no. / Fax no.	Telephone no. / Fax no.
E-mail address	E-mail address

SECTION 3 Details of the decision to be judicially reviewed

Decision:

Date of decision:

Name and address of the court, tribunal, person or body who made the decision to be reviewed.

name	address

SECTION 4 Permission to proceed with a claim for judicial review

I am seeking permission to proceed with my claim for Judicial Review.

Is this application being made under the terms of Section 18 Practice Direction 54 (Challenging removal)? ☐ Yes ☐ No

Are you making any other applications? If Yes, complete Section 8. ☐ Yes ☐ No

Is the claimant in receipt of a Community Legal Service Fund (CLSF) certificate? ☐ Yes ☐ No

Are you claiming exceptional urgency, or do you need this application determined within a certain time scale? If Yes, complete Form N463 and file this with your application. ☐ Yes ☐ No

Have you complied with the pre-action protocol? If No, give reasons for non-compliance in the box below. ☐ Yes ☐ No

Have you issued this claim in the region with which you have the closest connection? (Give any additional reasons for wanting it to be dealt with in this region in the box below). If No, give reasons in the box below. ☐ Yes ☐ No

2 of 6

Does the claim include any issues arising from the Human Rights Act 1998?
If Yes, state the articles which you contend have been breached in the box below. ☐ Yes ☐ No

SECTION 5 Detailed statement of grounds

☐ set out below ☐ attached

SECTION 6 Aarhus Convention claim

I contend that this claim is an Aarhus Convention claim ☐ Yes ☐ No

If Yes, indicate in the following box if you do not wish the costs limits under CPR 45.43 to apply.

If you have indicated that the claim is an Aarhus claim set out the grounds below

SECTION 7 Details of remedy (including any interim remedy) being sought

SECTION 8 Other applications

I wish to make an application for:-

3 of 6

SECTION 9 Statement of facts relied on

Statement of Truth

The claimant believes that the facts stated in this claim form are true.

Full name

Name of claimant's solicitor's firm

Signed ______ Position or office held ______

Claimant's solicitor (if signing on behalf of firm or company)

4 of 6

SECTION 10 Supporting documents

If you do not have a document that you intend to use to support your claim, identify it, give the date when you expect it to be available and give reasons why it is not currently available in the box below.

Please tick the papers you are filing with this claim form and any you will be filing later.

☐ Statement of grounds	☐ included	☐ attached
☐ Statement of the facts relied on	☐ included	☐ attached
☐ Application to extend the time limit for filing the claim form	☐ included	☐ attached
☐ Application for directions	☐ included	☐ attached

☐ Any written evidence in support of the claim or application to extend time

☐ Where the claim for judicial review relates to a decision of a court or tribunal, an approved copy of the reasons for reaching that decision

☐ Copies of any documents on which the claimant proposes to rely

☐ A copy of the legal aid or CSLF certificate *(if legally represented)*

☐ Copies of any relevant statutory material

☐ A list of essential documents for advance reading by the court *(with page references to the passages relied upon)*

If Section 18 Practice Direction 54 applies, please tick the relevant box(es) below to indicate which papers you are filing with this claim form:

☐ a copy of the removal directions and the decision to which the application relates	☐ included	☐ attached
☐ a copy of the documents served with the removal directions including any documents which contains the Immigration and Nationality Directorate's factual summary of the case	☐ included	☐ attached
☐ a detailed statement of the grounds	☐ included	☐ attached

Reasons why you have not supplied a document and date when you expect it to be available:-

Signed ______________________ Claimant's solicitor ______________________

6 of 6

CERTIFICATE OF SERVICE

Certificate of service

Name of court	Claim No.
Name of Claimant	
Name of Defendant	

On what day did you serve? ☐☐/☐☐/☐☐☐☐

The date of service is ☐☐/☐☐/☐☐☐☐

What documents did you serve?
Please attach copies of the documents you have not already filed with the court.

On whom did you serve?
(If appropriate include their position e.g. partner, director).

How did you serve the documents?
(please tick the appropriate box)

☐ by first class post or other service which provides for delivery on the next business day

☐ by delivering to or leaving at a permitted place

☐ by personally handing it to or leaving it with (................time left, where document is other than a claim form) *(please specify)*

☐ by other means permitted by the court *(please specify)*

☐ by Document Exchange

☐ by fax machine (................time sent, where document is other than a claim form) *(you may want to enclose a copy of the transmission sheet)*

☐ by other electronic means (................time sent, where document is other than a claim form) *(please specify)*

Give the address where service effected, include fax or DX number, e-mail address or other electronic identification

Being the ☐ claimant's ☐ defendant's ☐ solicitor's ☐ litigation friend

☐ usual residence

☐ last known residence

☐ place of business

☐ principal place of business

☐ last known place of business

☐ last known principal place of business

☐ principal office of the partnership

☐ principal office of the corporation

☐ principal office of the company

☐ place of business of the partnership/company/ corporation within the jurisdiction with a connection to claim

☐ other *(please specify)*

I believe that the facts stated in this certificate are true.

Full name

Signed

(Claimant) (Defendant) ('s solicitor) ('s friend)

Position or office held

(If signing on behalf of firm or company)

Date ☐☐/☐☐/☐☐☐☐

N215 Certificate of service (09.11)

Rules relating to the service of documents are contained in Part 6 of the Civil Procedure Rules (www.justice.gov.uk) and you should refer to the rules for information.

Calculation of deemed day of service of a claim
A claim form served within the UK in accordance with Part 6 of the Civil Procedure rules is deemed to be served on the second business day after the claimant has completed the steps required by CPR 7.5(1).

Calculation of the deemed day of service of documents other than the claim form (CPR 6.26)

Method of service	**Deemed day of service**
First class post or other service which provides for delivery on the next business day	The second day after it was posted, left with, delivered to or collected by the relevant service provider provided that day is a business day; or if not, the next business day after that day
Document exchange	The second day after it was left with, delivered to or collected by the relevant service provider provided that day is a business day; or if not, the next business day after that day
Delivering the document to or leaving it at a permitted address	If it is delivered to or left at the permitted address on a business day before 4.30pm, on that day; or in any other case, on the next business day after that day
Fax	If the transmission of the fax is completed on a business day before 4.30pm, on that day; or in any other case, on the next business day after the day on which it was transmitted
Other electronic method	If the email or other electronic transmission is sent on a business day before 4.30pm, on that day; or in any other case, on the next business day after the day on which it was sent
Personal service	If the document is served personally before 4.30pm on a business day, it is served on that day; or in any other case, on the next business day after that day

In this context 'business day' means any day except Saturday, Sunday or a bank holiday; (under the Banking and Financial Dealings Act 1971 in the part of the UK where service is to take place) includes Good Friday and Christmas Day.

DETAILS OF CLAIM FORM for judicial review of refusal to grant possessory title

In The High Court Of Justice

Administrative Court

Section 1: Details of the Claimant(s) and Defendant(s)

Claimant: The Queen on the application of (1) A. B.

Defendant: The Chief Land Registrar

Section 4: Permission to proceed with claim for judicial review

Are you making any other applications? If Yes, complete Section 7.Is the claimant in receipt of a Community Legal Service Fund (CLSF)certificate?

Are you claiming exceptional urgency, or do you need this application determined within a certain time scale? If Yes, complete Form N463 and file this with your application.

Have you complied with the pre-action protocol? If No, give reasons for non-compliance in the box below.

Have you issued this claim in the region with which you have the closest connection? (Give any additional reasons for wanting it to be dealt with in this region in the box below). If No, give reasons in the box below.

Does the claim include any issues arising from the Human Rights Act 1998? If Yes, state the articles which you contend have been breached in the space below.

Yes:

The cancellation of the Claimant's application to register title to the Claimant's home engages Article 8 (right to respect for family life and home).

Section 5: Detailed statement of grounds

The Defendant's refusal to grant the application for possessory title of the property was unlawful.

The provisions of s.144 of the Legal Aid Sentencing and Punishment of Offenders Act 2012 ("LASPOA") has no effect on the provisions of Schedule 6 of the Land Registration Act 2002.

The Claimant's actions of factual possession, such as securing windows and doors, were not unlawful under s.144 of LASPOA and were sufficient to entitle the Claimant to be registered with possessory title to the property.

To avoid a breach of Article 8 ECHR or Article 1 of Protocol 1 to the EHCR s.144 LASPOA is to be read as not affecting applications to register title and/or not preventing "living in" a house amounting to adverse possession for the purposes of Schedule 6 to the Land Registration Act 2002.

Section 6: Details of remedy (including any interim remedy) being sought

1. A declaration that the Defendant's refusal of the Claimant's application to be registered with possessory title to the property was unlawful
2. A mandatory order that the Defendant do give effect to the application of the Claimant to be registered with register with possessory title to the property.
3. Costs.
4. Such other remedy as the Court deems fit.

Section 7: Other applications

I wish to make an application for:

Section 8: Statement of facts relied on

1 Blackacre, Toy Town is a dwelling house. Freehold title is registered at HM Land Registry under title number TT1234; the registered proprietor being XY.

In 2000 the Claimant entered the property and did work to it, including repairing the roof, clearing the garden and taking other steps to make it wind and watertight. Over subsequent years, the Claimant replaced ceilings and skirting boards, installed new central heating, rewired the property, plastered and painted the walls. The Claimant entered the property and occupied it without the consent of the registered proprietor.

On 30th January 2012 the Claimant moved into the property and started to live there.

On 20th November 2012 the Claimant applied to HM Land Registry under paragraph 1 of Schedule 6 to the Land Registration Act 2002 to register title to the property on the basis that he had been in possession of the property for a period of 10 years ending on the date of the application.

On 20th February 2013 the Defendant cancelled the Claimant's application on the basis that the Claimant could not rely on a period of possession after 1st September 2012 because, the Defendant asserted, the Claimant's possession from that date was a criminal offence under s.144 of LASPOA

Attached to the Claim Form are copies of all correspondence between the

Claimants and the Defendant, together with supporting documents.

BUNDLE OF DOCUMENTS[1]

In the High Court of Justice

Administrative Court

The Queen
on the application of
(1) A. B. Claimants
(2) B. C.
and
London Borough of Defendant
. . . .

Index To Claimant's Documents

	Page
List of essential reading	1
Claim Form	2–6
Statement of the First Claimant	7–12
Statement of the Second Claimant	13–20
Decision of the Defendant	21–23
Defendant's policy	24–34

1 The claimant must file 2 copies of a paginated and indexed bundle containing the documents required to accompany the judicial review claim form: CPR PD 54A para 5.9. For a list of the documents see CPR 54.6 and CPR PD 54A paras 5.6, 5.7, Administrative Court Notes for Guidance on applying for judicial review paras 7.2, 7.5 (April 2011). For claim form see Form 3, **ACF Vol 1 (2012 Issue)** ADMINISTRATIVE COURT [403]. See also Procedural Table 2, **ACF Vol 1 (2012 Issue)** ADMINISTRATIVE COURT [392] step 11.

LIST OF ESSENTIAL READING[1]

In The High Court Of Justice

Administrative Court

The Queen
on the application of
(1) A. B.
(2) B. C. Claimants
and
London Borough of . . . . Defendant

List Of Essential Reading

	Page
Claim Form	2–6
Decision of the Defendant	21-23
Defendant's policy, paragraphs 5-10	26-27

1 The judicial review claim form must be accompanied by a list of the essential documents that will need to be read by the court: CPR PD 54A para 5.7(6), Administrative Court Notes for Guidance on applying for judicial review para 7.5 (April 2011). For the claim form see Form 3, **ACF Vol 1 (2012 Issue)** ADMINISTRATIVE COURT [403]. See also Procedural Table 2, **ACF Vol 1 (2012 Issue)** ADMINISTRATIVE COURT [392] step 1.

Appendix 13

APPLICATIONS AND OBJECTIONS TO THE REGISTRAR

1: Adverse Possession

Form 1: Application for first registration of unregistered land

Form 2: Statement of truth in support of an application for registration based upon adverse possession

Form 3: Sample details in a statement of truth in support of an application for first registration of unregistered land

Form 4: Objection to first registration of unregistered land

Form 5: Reply to an objection to first registration of unregistered land

Form 6: Application to be registered as proprietor of registered land under schedule 6 to the Land Registration Act 2002

Form 7: Statutory declaration in support of a first application to be registered as proprietor under schedule 6 to the Land Registration Act 2002

Form 8: Statutory declaration in support of a second application to be registered as proprietor under schedule 6 to the Land Registration Act 2002

Form 9: Counter notice to the registrar in respect of a first application to be registered as proprietor under schedule 6 to the Land Registration Act 2002

Form 10: Objection to a first application to be registered as proprietor on the grounds that the conditions in paragraph 5 schedule 6 to the Land Registration Act 2002 are not met

Form 11: Sample details in a counter notice to the registrar objecting to a first application to be registered as proprietor on the grounds that applicant has not been in adverse possession for the requisite period

Form 12: Application to change the register

Form 13: Sample details in a statement of truth in support of an application to be registered as proprietor of registered land under the transitional provisions

Form 14: Objection to application to be registered as proprietor of registered land under the transitional provisions

2: Unilateral Notices

Form 15: Application to enter a unilateral notice

Form 16: Sample details in an application to enter a unilateral notice

Form 17: Application to cancel a unilateral notice

Form 18: Objection to the cancellation of a unilateral notice

Form 19: Reply to an objection to the cancellation of a unilateral notice

3: Cautions Against Dealings

Form 20: Application to cancel a caution against dealings

Form 21: Notice showing cause why a caution against dealings should not be cancelled

Form 22: Reply to a notice showing cause why a caution against dealings should not be cancelled

4: Restrictions

Form 23: Application to enter a restriction

Form 24: Sample details in an application to enter a restriction

Form 25: Objection to the entry of a restriction

Form 26: Reply to an objection to the entry of a restriction

5: Easements by Prescription

Form 27: Statement of truth in support of an application to register the benefit of an easement by prescription as an appurtenant right

Form 28: Sample details in a statement of truth in support of an application to register the benefit of an easement by prescription as an appurtenant right

Form 29: Objection to registration of the benefit of an easement by prescription as an appurtenant right

Form 30: Reply to an objection to registration of the benefit of an easement by prescription as an appurtenant right

6: Alteration of the Register to correct a Mistake

Form 31: Statutory declaration in support of an application to alter the register to correct a mistake (land incorrectly registered)

Form 32: Objection to alteration of the register to correct a mistake (land incorrectly registered)

Form 33: Reply to an objection to alteration of the register to correct a mistake (land incorrectly registered)

Form 34: Statutory declaration in support of an application to alter the register to correct a mistake (forgery)

Form 35: Objection to alteration of the register to correct a mistake (forgery)

1: ADVERSE POSSESSION

(1) Unregistered land

FORM 1: APPLICATION for first registration of unregistered land

Land Registry
Application for first registration

FR1

LAND REGISTRY USE ONLY
Record of fees paid
Particulars of under/over payments
Reference number Fees debited £

You must lodge the documents of title with this application; these must be listed on Form DL.

If you need more room than is provided for in a panel, and your software allows, you can expand any panel in the form. Alternatively use continuation sheet CS and attach it to this form.

Land Registry is unable to give legal advice, but you can find guidance on Land Registry applications (including our practice guides for conveyancers) at www.gov.uk/land-registry.

Conveyancer is a term used in this form. It is defined in rule 217A, Land Registration Rules 2003 and includes persons authorised under the Legal Services Act 2007 to provide reserved legal services relating to land registration and includes solicitors and licensed conveyancers.

Where there is more than one local authority serving an area, enter the one to which council tax or business rates are normally paid.

1 Local authority serving the property:

Choose Local authority

Insert address including postcode (if any) or other description of the property, for example 'land adjoining 2 Acacia Avenue'.

On registering a rentcharge, profit a prendre in gross or franchise, insert a description, for example 'Rentcharge (or as appropriate) over 2 Acacia Avenue'.

2 Property:

Place 'X' in the appropriate box. Only use the third option where the property has an address and is fenced on the ground.

Enter reference, for example 'edged red'.

Enter nature and date of document.

3 The extent of the land to be registered can be clearly identified on the current edition of the Ordnance Survey map from

☐ the attached plan and shown:

☐ the plan attached to the:

☐ the address shown in panel 2

Place 'X' in the appropriate box.

4 The class of title applied for is

☐ absolute freehold

☐ possessory freehold

☐ absolute leasehold

☐ good leasehold

☐ possessory leasehold

5 Application, priority and fees

To find out more about our fees visit www.gov.uk/government/collections/fees-land-registry-guides

Application in priority order	Price paid/Value (£)	Fees paid(£)
First registration of the freehold/leasehold estate		
Total fees (£)		

Place 'X' in the appropriate box.

Fee payment method

☐ cheque made payable to 'Land Registry'

The fee will be charged to the account specified in panel 7.

☐ direct debit, under an agreement with Land Registry

Page 1 of 6

Provide the full name(s) of the person(s) applying for first registration. Where a conveyancer lodges the application, this must be the name(s) of the client(s), not the conveyancer. Complete as appropriate where the applicant is a company. Also, for an overseas company, unless an arrangement with Land Registry exists, lodge either a certificate in Form 7 in Schedule 3 to the Land Registration Rules 2003 or a certified copy of the constitution in English or Welsh, or other evidence permitted by rule 183 of the Land Registration Rules 2003.	6 The applicant: For UK incorporated companies/LLPs Registered number of company or limited liability partnership including any prefix: For overseas companies (a) Territory of incorporation: (b) Registered number in the United Kingdom including any prefix:
This panel must always be completed. If you are paying by direct debit, this will be the account charged. This is the address to which we will normally send requisitions. However if you insert an email address, we will use this whenever possible.	7 This application is sent to Land Registry by Key number (if applicable): Name: Address or UK DX box number: Email address: Reference: Phone no: Fax no:
Place 'X' in the appropriate box. In this and panel 10, each proprietor may give up to three addresses for service, one of which must be a postal address whether or not in the UK (including the postcode, if any). The others can be any combination of a postal address, a UK DX box number or an electronic address.	8 The address(es) for service for each proprietor of the estate to be entered in the register is ☐ the address of the property (where this is a single postal address) ☐ the following address(es):
Where the applicant is more than one person, place 'X' in the appropriate box. Complete as necessary. The registrar will enter a Form A restriction in the register *unless*: - an 'X' is placed: - in the first box, or - in the third box and the details of the trust or of the trust instrument show that the applicants are to hold the property on trust for themselves alone as joint tenants, *or* - it is clear from completion of a form JO lodged with this application that the applicants are to hold the property on trust for themselves alone as joint tenants. Please refer to *Joint property ownership* and *practice guide 24: private trusts of land* for further guidance. These are both available on the GOV.UK website.	9 Where the applicant is more than one person ☐ they hold the property on trust for themselves as joint tenants ☐ they hold the property on trust for themselves as tenants in common in equal shares ☐ they hold the property on trust:

Page 2 of 6

Where a charge has an MD reference we will ignore an address given in this panel unless the charge is in favour of a United Kingdom bank and neither the charge form nor any agreement we have with the lender specifies an address for service.

For permitted addresses see note to panel 8.

Complete as appropriate where the proprietor of the charge is a company. Also, for an overseas company, unless an arrangement with Land Registry exists, lodge either a certificate in Form 7 in Schedule 3 to the Land Registration Rules 2003 or a certified copy of the constitution in English or Welsh, or other evidence permitted by rule 183 of the Land Registration Rules 2003.

10 Name and address(es) for service of the proprietor of any new charge to be entered in the register:

For UK incorporated companies/LLPs
Registered number of company or limited liability partnership including any prefix:

For overseas companies
(a) Territory of incorporation:

(b) Registered number in the United Kingdom including any prefix:

If this statement applies (i) place 'X' in the box and (ii) enclose Form DI.

Rule 28 of the Land Registration Rules 2003 sets out the disclosable overriding interests that you must tell us about.

11 Disclosable overriding interests

☐ Disclosable overriding interests affect the estate.

12 Certificate

The title is based on the title documents listed in Form DL which are all those under the control of the applicant.

Details of rights, interests and claims affecting the estate (other than non-disclosable interests falling within rule 28(2) of the Land Registration Rules 2003) known to the applicant are, where applicable, disclosed in the title documents and Form DI if accompanying this application.

Place 'X' in the appropriate box.

☐ The applicant knows of no other such rights, interests and claims. Only the applicant is in actual possession of the property or in receipt of the rent and profits from the property.

If applicable complete the second statement with details of the interest (s); for interests disclosed only by searches do not include those shown on local land charge searches. Certify any interests disclosed by searches that do not affect the estate being registered.

☐ The applicant knows only of the following additional such rights, interests and claims, including those of any person (other than the applicant) in actual possession of the property or in receipt of the rent and profits from the property:

If you do not place 'X' in the box we will assume that you have examined the applicant's title or are satisfied that it has been examined in the usual way.

13 Examination of title

☐ I/we have not fully examined the applicant's title to the estate, including any appurtenant rights, or satisfied myself/ourselves that it has been fully examined by a conveyancer in the usual way prior to this application.

Page 3 of 6

Full details of the evidence of identity that is required can be found in Practice Guide 67 and in 'Completing the evidence of identity panels on forms AP1, FR1, and DS2' both of which can be found on the GOV.UK website.

14 Confirmation of identity

When registering transfers, charges, leases and other dispositions of land, Land Registry relies on the steps that conveyancers take, where appropriate, to verify the identity of their clients. These checks reduce the risk of property fraud.

Where a person was not represented by a conveyancer, Land Registry requires 'evidence of identity' in respect of that person, except where the first alternative in panel 15(2) applies.

'Evidence of identity' is evidence provided in accordance with any current direction made by the Chief Land Registrar under section 100(4) of the Land Registration Act 2002 for the purpose of confirming a person's identity.

Place 'X' in the appropriate box.

Conveyancer is defined in rule 217A, Land Registration Rules 2003 and includes persons authorised under the Legal Services Act 2007 to provide reserved legal services relating to land registration and includes solicitors and licensed conveyancers.

If this application is to register a transfer, lease or charge, or to give effect to a discharge in Form DS1 or a release in Form DS3 complete one of the following

☐ I am a conveyancer, and I have completed panel 15

☐ I am not a conveyancer, and I have completed panel 16

15 Where the application is sent to Land Registry by a conveyancer

(1) Details of conveyancer acting

If you are sending an application to register a transfer, lease or charge, for each party to each disposition that is to be registered state in the table below the details of the conveyancer (if any) who represented them.

Where a party is not represented by a conveyancer you must also complete (2) below.

Place 'X' in the box in the second column if the person or firm who is sending the application to Land Registry represented that party in the transaction. Otherwise complete the details in the third column. If the party is not represented insert 'none' in the third column.

Name of transferor, landlord, transferee, tenant, borrower or lender		Conveyancer's name, address and reference
	☐	Reference:
	☐	Reference:
	☐	Reference:

Place 'X' in the appropriate box(es).

Insert the name of each unrepresented transferor, landlord, transferee, tenant, borrower or lender for whom you give this confirmation.

Evidence of identity is defined in panel 14. Full details of the evidence of identity that is required can be found in Practice Guide 67 available on the GOV.UK website.

(2) Evidence of identity

Where any transferor, landlord, transferee, tenant, borrower or lender listed in (1) was not represented by a conveyancer

☐ I confirm that I am satisfied that sufficient steps have been taken to verify the identity of

and that they are the transferor, landlord, transferee, tenant, borrower or lender listed in (1) (as appropriate)

☐ I enclose evidence of identity in respect of each unrepresented transferor, landlord, transferee, tenant, borrower or lender for whom I have not provided the confirmation above

16 Where the application is sent to Land Registry by someone who is not a conveyancer

(1) Details of conveyancer acting

If you are sending an application to register a transfer, lease or charge (ie a mortgage), for each party to each disposition that is to be registered, state in the table below the details of the conveyancer (if any) who represented them.

You must also complete (2) below.

If the party is not represented insert 'none' in the second column.

Name of transferor, landlord, transferee, tenant, borrower or lender		Conveyancer's name, address and reference
	☐	Reference:
	☐	Reference:
	☐	Reference:

Place 'X' in the appropriate box(es).

Evidence of identity is defined in panel 14. Full details of the evidence of identity that is required can be found in 'Completing the evidence of identity panels on forms AP1, FR1, and DS2' available on the GOV.UK website.

(2) Evidence of identity

☐ for each applicant named in panel 6 is enclosed

☐ for each unrepresented transferor, landlord, transferee, tenant, borrower or lender listed in (1) is enclosed

Page 5 of 6

If a conveyancer is acting for the applicant, that conveyancer must sign.

If no conveyancer is acting, the applicant (and if the applicant is more than one person then each of them) must sign.

17

Signature of conveyancer: ....

Date:

OR

Signature of applicant: ....

Date:

WARNING

If you dishonestly enter information or make a statement that you know is, or might be, untrue or misleading, and intend by doing so to make a gain for yourself or another person, or to cause loss or the risk of loss to another person, you may commit the offence of fraud under section 1 of the Fraud Act 2006, the maximum penalty for which is 10 years' imprisonment or an unlimited fine, or both.

Failure to complete this form with proper care may result in a loss of protection under the Land Registration Act 2002 if, as a result, a mistake is made in the register.

Under section 66 of the Land Registration Act 2002 most documents (including this form) kept by the registrar relating to an application to the registrar or referred to in the register are open to public inspection and copying. If you believe a document contains prejudicial information, you may apply for that part of the document to be made exempt using Form EX1, under rule 136 of the Land Registration Rules 2003.

Sign and Lock >

Page 6 of 6

FORM 2: STATEMENT OF TRUTH in support of an application for registration based upon adverse possession

Land Registry
Statement of truth in support of an application for registration based upon adverse possession

ST1

If you need more room than is provided for in a panel, and your software allows, you can expand any panel in the form. Alternatively use continuation sheet CS and attach it to this form.

If a joint statement is made by two or more persons, consequential amendments can be made to the text in the panels (for example, 'I' can be changed to 'we').

Land Registry is unable to give legal advice, but you can find guidance on Land Registry applications (including our practice guides for conveyancers) at www.gov.uk/land-registry.

Insert full name. Insert full address.	1 I: of: make this statement in support of an application to Land Registry for registration based upon adverse possession.
Place 'X' in one box only. This is for cases where the squatter is a company or firm, someone who has died, or is otherwise incapable of making the statement personally. Insert the name and address of the squatter. Insert reasons and describe the relationship of the person making the statement to the person on whose behalf it is made. Enclose any relevant documentation (for example, office copy grant of probate).	2 Status I am ☐ the person currently in adverse possession ☐ a person who was previously in adverse possession ☐ making this statement on behalf of: who is currently or was previously in adverse possession but who cannot make this statement for the following reasons:
Insert address including postcode (if any) or other description of the property, for example 'land adjoining 2 Acacia Avenue'. Place 'X' in the appropriate box(es) and complete the relevant statement. State reference, for example 'edged red'. Insert title number(s) if the land is already registered. If only part of a registered title is affected the affected land should be clearly identified on an attached plan or by means of an existing reference on the title plan.	3 Property: ☐ The land is clearly identified on the attached plan and shown: ☐ The land is currently registered under title number(s):

Insert the dates the adverse possession started and finished. Any 'gaps' must be specified if the period is not continuous. Only include the period of adverse possession by the person making this statement or on whose behalf it is made.	4 Period of adverse possession:
Insert details of the acts relied on as establishing the necessary factual possession and intention to possess. Include details of the use made of the land by the owner and others.	5 Acts of adverse possession:
Insert details of the extent, if any, to which the land has been and/or is enclosed by fences or other boundary features. Specify the nature of these features, who erected them and when, and by whom they have been maintained. If there is a gate, specify whether there is a lock for it and, if so, who has the key. If any previous boundary features have been removed, specify when, by whom and in what circumstances this was done.	6 Enclosure of the land:
Place 'X' in the appropriate box(es) and complete the statement if applicable.	7 Permission to possess The possession has been ☐ without the consent, licence or permission of anyone at any time
Insert details of, for example, any tenancy or licence under which possession has been enjoyed, including the date of its expiry or determination.	☐ by virtue of the following consent, licence or permission, which has expired or determined:
Insert details.	☐ by virtue of the following consent, licence or permission:
Insert name and address of any known freehold owner of the land or person thought to be the freehold owner (such as the person having the unregistered documentary title to the land or being the registered proprietor of registered land) and/or any tenants and/or mortgagees. If not known, please state this by inserting 'not known'. If the land is unregistered, copies of any title deeds or other relevant documentation should be lodged, if available.	8 Details of any known freehold owner of the land or person thought to be the freehold owner and related persons:

Insert details of any past or present contact with the freehold owner of the land or person thought to be the freehold owner and/or any tenants and/or mortgagees, including dates. If none, please state this by inserting 'none'. If there has been any dispute concerning the adverse possession, insert details, including dates. Attach copies of all available correspondence or other documents relating to the contact or dispute.

9 Contact with freehold owner of the land and related persons:

Insert details of such property. Where the title to this other property is registered, please quote the relevant title number(s) and provide copies of the relevant pre-registration title deeds. Where the title to this other property is unregistered, please confirm whether this is freehold or leasehold and provide copies of the relevant title deeds.

10 Other property owned during the period referred to in panel 4 by the person making this statement or the person on behalf of whom this statement is made:

Insert other relevant details, (if any).

11 Other relevant details

12 If the application is under paragraph 1 of Schedule 6 to the Land Registration Act 2002 AND you are the applicant

Place 'X' in the box against each of the statements being made, and complete one or both of the final statements if they are being made.

You must make the first three statements, otherwise your application may be cancelled.

☐ Paragraph 1(3) of Schedule 6 to the Land Registration Act 2002 does not apply

☐ I confirm that to the best of my knowledge the restriction on applications in paragraph 8 of Schedule 6 to the Land Registration Act 2002 does not apply

☐ I confirm that to the best of my knowledge the estate is not, and has not been during any of the period of claimed adverse possession, subject to a trust (other than one where the interest of each of the beneficiaries is an interest in possession)

☐ Should a person given notice under paragraph 2 of Schedule 6 to the Land Registration Act 2002 require the application to be dealt with under paragraph 5 of that Schedule, the facts supporting my reliance on one or more of the conditions set out in that paragraph are as follows:

Insert details of the facts.

☐ I am relying on paragraph 1(2) of Schedule 6 to the Land Registration Act 2002 and the facts supporting such reliance are as follows:

Insert details of the facts.

Place 'X' in the box against each of the statements being made, and complete the final statement. You must make all these statements, and complete the final statement, otherwise your application may be cancelled. Insert full details.	13 If the application is under paragraph 6 of Schedule 6 to the Land Registration Act 2002 AND you are the applicant ☐ Paragraph 6(2) of Schedule 6 to the Land Registration Act 2002 does not apply ☐ I confirm that to the best of my knowledge the restriction on applications in paragraph 8 of Schedule 6 to the Land Registration Act 2002 does not apply ☐ I confirm that to the best of my knowledge the estate is not, and has not been during any of the period of claimed adverse possession, subject to a trust (other than one where the interest of each of the beneficiaries is an interest in possession) ☐ The full details of the rejected application are as follows:
If the person making the statement is unable to sign it, this wording will need to be amended to comply with rule 215A(5) and (6) of the Land Registration Rules 2003. In addition, and in cases where the person making the statement is unable to read, there will need to be an appropriate certificate: see rule 215A(4) and (5). Where the application is being made under Schedule 6 and the person making this statement, or on whose behalf it is made, is the applicant, the statement must be made not more than one month before the date of the application.	14 I believe that the facts and matters contained in this statement are true Signature (of person(s) making this statement): Print full name: Date:

WARNING

If the application proceeds, notice of the application (accompanied by a copy of this statement of truth) may be sent by the Registrar to the owner of the land or any person thought to be the owner and/or any other person upon whom the Registrar considers it necessary or desirable to serve notice.

If you dishonestly enter information or make a statement that you know is, or might be, untrue or misleading, and intend by doing so to make a gain for yourself or another person, or to cause loss or the risk of loss to another person, you may commit the offence of fraud under section 1 of the Fraud Act 2006, the maximum penalty for which is 10 years' imprisonment or an unlimited fine, or both.

Failure to complete this form with proper care may result in a loss of protection under the Land Registration Act 2002 if, as a result, a mistake is made in the register.

Under section 66 of the Land Registration Act 2002 most documents (including this form) kept by the registrar relating to an application to the registrar or referred to in the register are open to public inspection and copying. If you believe a document contains prejudicial information, you may apply for that part of the document to be made exempt using Form EX1, under rule 136 of the Land Registration Rules 2003.

Sign and Lock >

FORM 3: SAMPLE DETAILS in a statement of truth in support of an application for first registration of unregistered land[1]

ACTS OF ADVERSE POSSESSION

(*to be inserted in panel 5 of the statement of truth*)

I erected a timber framed hut on the land in February 1997 in which I have stored my farm implements and carried out repairs to them. I have also kept cattle on the land. I have had exclusive use of the land and the hut since February 1997.

ACTS OF ENCLOSURE OF THE LAND

(*to be inserted in panel 6 of the statement of truth*)

I have maintained the fencing around the land, and put barbed wire on the top. In addition I have put padlocks on the gates to keep other people out, and kept the key for my own use.

1 See Form 2, above.

FORM 4: OBJECTION to first registration of unregistered land

Dear Sir,

Title Number: . . . .

Property: . . . .

Dated: . . . . 20 . . .

We, as solicitors for [B] of (*address*) ("the Objector") give notice to the Chief Land Registrar that we object to the pending application for the registration of [A] of (*address*) ("the Applicant") as proprietor with possessory title of the above mentioned land ("the disputed land"). Our grounds are as follows:

1. The Objector is the freehold owner of Whiteacre Farm at (*address*). It is unregistered land. The Land is situated in the north east corner of Whiteacre Farm and consists of 2 fields.
2. The Applicant asserts in his statement of truth that he has been in possession of the disputed land since February 1997. The Objector denies that. We have obtained a statement from [C], the Objector's immediate predecessor in title, that the Applicant first made use of the disputed land 7 years ago, shortly before it was conveyed to the Objector. Accordingly, the Applicant cannot show possession for 12 years.
3. The Applicant has only ever used the disputed land for the occasional grazing of his cattle. Such a use cannot amount to possession for the purposes of adverse possession.
4. The gates to the disputed land have never been secured and the fences around it are there to keep cattle in and not to keep people out. Accordingly, the Applicant has never demonstrated the necessary intention to possess.
5. The Applicant wrote to the Objector 5 years ago offering to buy the disputed land for £5,000. We enclose a copy of that letter which amounts to an acknowledgement of the Objector's title within Section 29(2)(a) of the Limitation Act 1980. Time began running afresh on that date.

Each of these reasons demonstrates that the Applicant's application for first registration of the disputed land must fail and we ask you not to accede to it.

Yours faithfully,

(Signature)

FORM 5: REPLY to an objection to first registration of unregistered land

Dear Sir,

Title Number: . . . .

Property: . . . .

Dated: . . . . 20 . . .

We, as solicitors for [A] of (*address*) ("the Applicant") reply as follows to the objection dated . . . . 20 . . . given on behalf of [B] (*address*) ("the Objector"):

1. It is accepted that the disputed land is situated in the north east corner of Whiteacre Farm and consists of 2 fields.

2. [C] is wrong when he says that the Applicant first made use of the disputed land 7 years ago, shortly before it was conveyed to the Objector. [C] was living in Argentina at the time and Whiteacre Farm was being managed for him. The Applicant can produce evidence from 2 former farm workers, [D] and [E], to prove the Applicant has been in possession of the disputed land for over 12 years.

3. It is denied that the Applicant has only ever used the disputed land for the occasional grazing of his cattle. We enclose photographs showing a timber framed hut erected by the Applicant over 12 years ago, in which he stores his farm implements and carries out repairs to them.

4. The gates to the disputed land have been padlocked as the enclosed photographs demonstrate. From time to time someone comes and cuts the chains which the padlocks secure. The Applicant suspects the Objector has been doing this. There is barbed wire on top of the fence.

5. The letter relied upon as amounting to an acknowledgment of the Objector's title within Section 29(2)(a) of the Limitation Act 1980 was a draft, never signed by the Applicant because he changed his mind. Time has not stopped running.

We consider the objections put forward by the Objector to be groundless and ask for the Applicant to be registered as proprietor with a possessory title of the disputed land

Yours faithfully,

(Signature)

(2) Registered Land

FORM 6: APPLICATION to be registered as proprietor of registered land under Schedule 6 to the Land Registration Act 2002

Land Registry

Application for registration of a person in adverse possession under Schedule 6 to the Land Registration Act 2002

ADV1

If you need more room than is provided for in a panel, and your software allows, you can expand any panel in the form. Alternatively use continuation sheet CS and attach it to this form.

Land Registry is unable to give legal advice, but you can find guidance on Land Registry applications (including our practice guides for conveyancers) at www.gov.uk/land-registry.

Conveyancer is a term used in this form. It is defined in rule 217A, Land Registration Rules 2003 and includes persons authorised under the Legal Services Act 2007 to provide reserved legal services relating to land registration and includes solicitors and licensed conveyancers.

LAND REGISTRY USE ONLY
Record of fees paid
Particulars of under/over payments
Reference number Fees debited £

Where there is more than one local authority serving an area, enter the one to which council tax or business rates are normally paid.

1 Local authority serving the property:
Choose Local Authority

2 Title number(s) of property:

Insert address including postcode (if any) or other description of the property, for example 'land adjoining 2 Acacia Avenue'.

3 Property:

Place 'X' in the appropriate box.

The application relates to

☐ the whole of the title(s)

☐ part of the title(s) as shown:

Give a brief description of the part affected, for example 'edged red on the plan to the statutory declaration dated ....'. The statutory declaration or statement of truth must exhibit a plan identifying clearly the extent of the part, unless one of the exceptions in rule 188 of the Land Registration Rules 2003 applies.

To find out more about our fees visit www.gov.uk/government/collections/fees-land-registry-guides

4 Application and fee

Application	Fee paid (£)
Registration of a person in adverse possession	

Place 'X' in the appropriate box.

Fee payment method

☐ cheque made payable to 'Land Registry'

The fee will be charged to the account specified in panel 8.

☐ direct debit, under an agreement with Land Registry

List the documents lodged with this form. Copy documents should be listed separately. If you supply a certified copy of an original document we will return the original; if a certified copy is not supplied, we may retain the original document and it may be destroyed.	5	Documents lodged with this form: 1. Statutory declaration/ Statement of truth
Provide the full name(s) of the person(s) applying to be registered. Where a conveyancer lodges the application, this must be the name(s) of the client(s), not the conveyancer. Complete as appropriate where the applicant is a company. Also, for an overseas company, unless an arrangement with Land Registry exists, lodge either a certificate in Form 7 in Schedule 3 to the Land Registration Rules 2003 or a certified copy of the constitution in English or Welsh, or other evidence permitted by rule 183 of the Land Registration Rules 2003.	6	The applicant: For UK incorporated companies/LLPs Registered number of company or limited liability partnership including any prefix: For overseas companies (a) Territory of incorporation: (b) Registered number in the United Kingdom including any prefix:
Each proprietor may give up to three addresses for service, one of which must be a postal address whether or not in the UK (including the postcode, if any). The others can be any combination of a postal address, a UK DX box number or an electronic address.	7	Applicant's intended address(es) for service (including postcode) for entry in the register:
This panel must always be completed. If you are paying by direct debit, this will be the account charged. This is the address to which we will normally send requisitions and return documents. However if you insert an email address, we will use this whenever possible.	8	This application is sent to Land Registry by Key number (if applicable): Name: Address or UK DX box number: Email address: Reference: Phone no: Fax no:
Where there is more than one applicant, place 'X' in the appropriate box. Complete as necessary. The registrar will enter a Form A restriction in the register *unless*: – an 'X' is placed: – in the first box, or – in the third box and the details of the trust or of the trust instrument show that the applicants are to hold the property on trust for themselves alone as joint tenants, *or* – it is clear from completion of a form JO lodged with this application that the applicants are to hold the property on trust for themselves alone as joint tenants. Please refer to *Joint property ownership* and *practice guide 24: private trusts of land* for further guidance. These are both available on the GOV.UK website.	9	Declaration of trust. The applicant is more than one person and ☐ they are to hold the property on trust for themselves as joint tenants ☐ they are to hold the property on trust for themselves as tenants in common in equal shares ☐ they are to hold the property on trust:

Place 'X' in the appropriate box.	10	This application is made under ☐ Paragraph 1 of Schedule 6 to the Land Registration Act 2002 ☐ Paragraph 6(1) of Schedule 6 to the Land Registration Act 2002
Please confirm which, if any, of these conditions the applicant intends to rely on, if a counter notice under paragraph 3 of Schedule 6 is lodged in response to the application.	11	If applying under Paragraph 1 of Schedule 6 to the Land Registration Act 2002 confirm which, if any, of the following conditions you intend to rely on ☐ Paragraph 5(2) of Schedule 6 ☐ Paragraph 5(3) of Schedule 6 ☐ Paragraph 5(4) of Schedule 6
If a conveyancer is acting for the applicant, that conveyancer must sign. If no conveyancer is acting, the applicant (and if more than one person then each of them) must sign.	12	Signature of applicant or their conveyancer: ------------------------------------ Date:

WARNING
If you dishonestly enter information or make a statement that you know is, or might be, untrue or misleading, and intend by doing so to make a gain for yourself or another person, or to cause loss or the risk of loss to another person, you may commit the offence of fraud under section 1 of the Fraud Act 2006, the maximum penalty for which is 10 years' imprisonment or an unlimited fine, or both.

Failure to complete this form with proper care may result in a loss of protection under the Land Registration Act 2002 if, as a result, a mistake is made in the register.

Under section 66 of the Land Registration Act 2002 most documents (including this form) kept by the registrar relating to an application to the registrar or referred to in the register are open to public inspection and copying. If you believe a document contains prejudicial information, you may apply for that part of the document to be made exempt using Form EX1, under rule 136 of the Land Registration Rules 2003.

FORM 7: STATUTORY DECLARATION in support of a first application to be registered as proprietor under Schedule 6 to the Land Registration Act 2002

I, [A], of (*address*) solemnly and sincerely declare as follows:

1. I am the registered proprietor of a semi-detached house at 6 Cherry Close, (*address*), which is registered at HM Land Registry under title number . . . . ("number 6"). I bought number 6 off plan from the developers, [C Ltd], 15 years ago

2. [B] is the registered proprietor of the adjoining house, 8 Cherry Close, which is registered at HM Land Registry under title number . . . . ("number 8"). He has owned number 8 for the last 12 years.

3. Both houses have large back gardens. I discovered 3 weeks ago that [C Ltd] had placed the rear boundary fence between number 6 and number 8 in the wrong place. Instead of running in a straight line from the rear party wall between the houses, it veers off at an angle cutting into the land behind number 8 and giving number 6 an extra triangle of land ("the disputed land"). At the bottom of the garden the disputed land is a metre wide.

4. For the last 15 years I have believed that I owned the disputed land. I did not think anything was odd as [C Ltd's] foreman told me that this had been intended.

5. I have used the disputed land as part of my rear garden for the last 15 years. I keep my collection of 46 garden gnomes on it.

6. I refer to a plan marked "**A.B.1**" which shows the extent of the disputed land.

7. I can confirm that I am not a defendant in proceedings which involve asserting a right to possession of the disputed land nor has judgment for possession of the disputed land been given against me in the last 2 years.

8. I can also confirm that [B] is not an enemy alien or detained in enemy territory. Nor is he unable because of mental disability to make decisions about issues of the kind to which this application gives rise or unable to communicate such decisions because of mental disability or physical impairment.

9. To the best of my knowledge the disputed land is not and has not been during the last 15 years subject to a trust.

10. My occupation of the disputed land has not been under a lease, tenancy or licence, or with the consent of any person.

And I make this solemn declaration conscientiously believing the same to be true by virtue of the Statutory Declarations Act 1835.

Signature of declarant

Declared at . . . .

this . . . . day of . . . . before me,

Signature . . . .

Name . . . .

Address . . . .

Qualification . . . .

FORM 8: STATUTORY DECLARATION in support of a second application to be registered as proprietor under Schedule 6 to the Land Registration Act 2002

I, [A], of (*address*) solemnly and sincerely declare as follows:

1. I am the registered proprietor of a semi-detached house at 6 Cherry Close, (*address*), which is registered at HM Land Registry under title number . . . . ("number 6"). I bought number 6 off plan from the developers, [C Ltd], 17 years ago.
2. [B] is the registered proprietor of the adjoining house, 8 Cherry Close, which is registered at HM Land Registry under title number . . . . ("number 8"). He has owned number 8 for the last 14 years.
3. Both houses have large back gardens. [C Ltd] had placed the rear boundary fence between number 6 and number 8 in the wrong place. Instead of running in a straight line from the rear party wall between the houses, it veers off at an angle cutting into the land behind number 8 and giving number 6 an extra triangle of land ("the disputed land"). At the bottom of the garden the disputed land is a metre wide.
4. I have used the disputed land as part of my rear garden for the last 17 years. I keep my collection of 46 garden gnomes on it.
5. I have made a previous application for registration as proprietor on the basis of my having been in adverse possession of the disputed land for 10 years. The application was rejected 2 years 3 months ago. The Adjudicator found I could not bring myself within any of the conditions set out in paragraph 5 of Schedule 6 of the Land Registration Act 2002. I refer to a bundle marked "**A.B.1**" containing the documents relevant to that application.
6. I refer to a plan marked "**A.B.2**" which shows the extent of the disputed land.
7. I can also confirm that [B] is not an enemy alien or detained in enemy territory. Nor is he unable because of mental disability to make decisions about issues of the kind to which this application gives rise or unable to communicate such decisions because of mental disability or physical impairment.
8. To the best of my knowledge the disputed land is not and has not been during the last 17 years subject to a trust.
9. Despite making my earlier application, [B] has taken no steps to recover possession of the disputed land. I can confirm that I am not a defendant in proceedings which involve asserting a right to possession of the disputed land, nor has judgment for possession of the disputed land been given against me in the last 2 years, nor have I been evicted from the disputed land pursuant to a judgment for possession.

10. My occupation of the disputed land has not been under a lease, tenancy or licence, or with the consent of any person.

And I make this solemn declaration conscientiously believing the same to be true by virtue of the Statutory Declarations Act 1835.

Signature of declarant

Declared at (*address*)

this . . . . day of . . . . before me,

(Signature)

Name . . . .

Address . . . .

Qualification . . . .

FORM 9: COUNTER NOTICE to the Registrar in respect of a first application to be registered as proprietor under Schedule 6 to the Land Registration Act 2002

Land Registry

Notice to the registrar in respect of an adverse possession application

NAP

If you need more room than is provided for in a panel, and your software allows, you can expand any panel in the form. Alternatively use continuation sheet CS and attach to this form.

	1.	Title number(s) of the property affected by the application
Insert address including postcode (if any) or other description of the property, for example 'land adjoining 2 Acacia Avenue'.	2.	Property
Enter the name(s) of the person(s) making the application for registration based on advesrse possession.	3.	The applicant:
Conveyancers should give their client's name followed by their own name and address for service.	4.	Your name and address
Place 'X' in the appropriate box(es). See Practice Guide 4 for further information.	5.	☐ I consent to the registration of the applicant(s) ☐ I require the registrar to deal with the application under paragraph 5 of Schedule 6 to the Land Registration Act 2002 ☐ I object to the registration on the grounds stated in panel 6

	6. Give details of the grounds of your objection:
If a conveyancer is acting for the person named in panel 4, that conveyancer must sign. If no conveyancer is acting, the person(s) mentioned in panel 4 must sign.	7. Signature of the person named in panel 4 or their conveyancer: ---------------------------------- Date:

WARNING
If you dishonestly enter information or make a statement that you know is, or might be, untrue or misleading, and intend by doing so to make a gain for yourself or another person, or to cause loss or the risk of loss to another person, you may commit the offence of fraud under section 1 of the Fraud Act 2006, the maximum penalty for which is 10 years' imprisonment or an unlimited fine, or both.

Failure to complete this form with the proper care may result in a loss of protection under the Land Registration Act 2002 if, as a result, a mistake is made in the register.

Under section 66 of the Land Registration Act 2002 most documents (including this form) kept by the registrar relating to an application to the registrar or referred to in the register are open to public inspection and copying. If you believe a document contains prejudicial information, you may apply for that part of the document to be made exempt using Form EX1, under rule 136 of the Land Registration Rules 2003.

FORM 10: OBJECTION to a first application to be registered as proprietor on the grounds that the conditions in paragraph 5 Schedule 6 to the Land Registration Act 2002 are not met

Dear Sir,

Title Number: . . . .

Property: . . . .

Dated: . . . . 20 . . .

We, as solicitors for [B] of (address) ("the Objector") give notice to the Chief Land Registrar that we object to the pending application for the registration of [A] of (address) ("the Applicant") as proprietor of the above mentioned land ("the disputed land"). Our grounds are as follows:

1. The Objector is the registered proprietor of number 8 and the neighbour of the Applicant, as stated in his statutory declaration.
2. The Objector accepts that the Applicant has been in possession of the disputed land since the Objector moved into number 8, which was 12 years ago. The Applicant has been in possession of the disputed land for over 10 years.
3. But the Objector has recently spoken to [D], the original owner of number 8, who sold it to the Objector 12 years ago. When [D] sold number 8 to the Objector the rear boundary fence between number 6 and number 8 was in a straight line. The disputed land was enclosed within the back garden of number 8 and not within the back garden of number 6, as it now is.
4. Accordingly, the Applicant must have moved the rear boundary fence at the time of the sale of number 8 by [D] to the Objector. The Objector was working abroad when he bought number 8 and let it out for a number of years. All the arrangements for the purchase and letting out were undertaken by agents. This is not a case of mistake at all. The Applicant cannot reasonably believe he owns the disputed land.

Accordingly, the conditions set out in paragraph 5 of Schedule 6 to the Land Registration Act 2002 are not satisfied and the Applicant's application must fail. We ask you not to accede to it.

Yours faithfully,

(Signature)

FORM 11: SAMPLE DETAILS in a counter notice to the Registrar[1] objecting to a first application to be registered as proprietor on the grounds that applicant has not been in adverse possession for the requisite period

Panel 6. Please give details of the grounds of your objection:

1. The Objector is the registered proprietor of number 8 and the neighbour of the Applicant, as stated in his statutory declaration.
2. The Objector accepts that the Applicant has been in possession of the disputed land since the Objector moved into number 8, which was 12 years ago. The Applicant has been in possession of the disputed land for over 10 years.
3. But the Applicant had permission to use the disputed land until 4 years ago. When the Objector moved into number 8, he discovered the Applicant did not drive and had no use for his garage. The Applicant told the Objector he needed extra space outdoors as his gnome collection was growing. The parties agreed that the Applicant could move the rear boundary fence and use the disputed land and, in return, the Objector could set up his train set in the Applicant's garage. That agreement was to last until either party gave 6 months' notice.
4. About 4 years ago the Applicant said he wanted his garage back as he had learned to drive and the Objector cleared the garage out for him. At the same time the Objector asked the Applicant to move the rear boundary fence back so the disputed land could be restored to number 8, but he has failed to do so.

[1] The objection may be made in panel 6 of prescribed Form NAP, for which see Form 9.

(3) Transitional Provisions

FORM 12: APPLICATION to change the register

Land Registry
Application to change the register

AP1

LAND REGISTRY USE ONLY
Record of fees paid
Particulars of under/over payments
Reference number Fees debited £

If you need more room than is provided for in a panel, and your software allows, you can expand any panel in the form. Alternatively use continuation sheet CS and attach it to this form.

Land Registry is unable to give legal advice, but you can find guidance on Land Registry applications (including our practice guides for conveyancers) at www.gov.uk/land-registry.

Conveyancer is a term used in this form. It is defined in rule 217A, Land Registration Rules 2003 and includes persons authorised under the Legal Services Act 2007 to provide reserved legal services relating to land registration and includes solicitors and licensed conveyancers.

Where there is more than one local authority serving an area, enter the one to which council tax or business rates are normally paid.

1 Local authority serving the property:
Choose Local Authority
Full postcode of property (if any):

Enter the title number of each title that requires an entry to be made in that register.

2 Title number(s) of the property:

Place 'X' in the appropriate box.

Give a brief description of the part affected, for example 'edged red on the plan to the transfer dated ....'.

3 The application affects
☐ the whole of the title(s)
☐ part of the title(s) as shown:

To find out more about our fees visit www.gov.uk/government/collections/fees-land-registry-guides

4 Application, priority and fees

Applications in priority order	Price paid/Value (£)	Fees paid (£)
	Total fees (£)	

Place 'X' in the appropriate box.

The fee will be charged to the account specified in panel 7.

Fee payment method
☐ cheque made payable to 'Land Registry'
☐ direct debit, under an agreement with Land Registry

Page 1 of 6

List the documents lodged with this form. We only need certified copies of deeds or documents you send to us with Land Registry application forms. Once we have made a copy of the documents you send to us, they will be destroyed, this applies to both originals and certified copies.

5 Documents lodged with this form:

Provide the full name(s) of the person(s) applying to change the register. Where a conveyancer lodges the application, this must be the name(s) of the client(s), not the conveyancer.

6 The applicant:

Complete as appropriate where the applicant is a company. Also, for an overseas company, unless an arrangement with Land Registry exists, lodge either a certificate in Form 7 in Schedule 3 to the Land Registration Rules 2003 or a certified copy of the constitution in English or Welsh, or other evidence permitted by rule 183 of the Land Registration Rules 2003.

For UK incorporated companies/LLPs
Registered number of company or limited liability partnership including any prefix:

For overseas companies
(a) Territory of incorporation:

(b) Registered number in the United Kingdom including any prefix:

This panel must always be completed.

If you are paying by direct debit, this will be the account charged.

7 This application is sent to Land Registry by

Key number (if applicable):

Name:

Address or UK DX box number:

This is the address to which we will normally send requisitions. However if you insert an email address, we will use this whenever possible.

Email address:

Reference:

Phone no: Fax no:

Complete this panel if you want us to notify someone else that we have completed this application.

8 Third party notification

Name:

Address or UK DX box number:

Email address:

Reference:

Place 'X' in the appropriate box.

In this and panel 10, each proprietor may give up to three addresses for service, one of which must be a postal address whether or not in the UK (including the postcode, if any). The others can be any combination of a postal address, a UK DX box number or an electronic address.

9 The address(es) for service for each proprietor of the registered estate(s) to be entered in the register is

☐ the address of the property (where this is a single postal address)

☐ the address(es) for service from the transfer/assent

☐ (for existing proprietors who are remaining in the register) the current address(es) for service in the register

☐ the following address(es):

Page 2 of 6

Where a charge has an MD reference we will ignore an address given in this panel unless the charge is in favour of a United Kingdom bank and neither the charge form nor any agreement we have with the lender specifies an address for service.

For permitted addresses see note to panel 9.

Complete as appropriate where the lender is a company. Also, for an overseas company, unless an arrangement with Land Registry exists, lodge either a certificate in Form 7 in Schedule 3 to the Land Registration Rules 2003 or a certified copy of the constitution in English or Welsh, or other evidence permitted by rule 183 of the Land Registration Rules 2003.

10 Name and address(es) for service of the proprietor of any new charge to be entered in the register:

For UK incorporated companies/LLPs

Registered number of company or limited liability partnership including any prefix:

For overseas companies

(a) Territory of incorporation:

(b) Registered number in the United Kingdom including any prefix:

If this statement applies (i) place 'X' in the box and (ii) enclose Form DI.

Section 27 of the Land Registration Act 2002 lists the registrable dispositions.

Rule 57 of the Land Registration Rules 2003 sets out the disclosable overriding interests that you must tell us about.

11 Disclosable overriding interests

☐ This application relates to a registrable disposition and disclosable overriding interests affect the registered estate.

Full details of the evidence of identity that is required can be found in Practice Guide 67 and in 'Completing the evidence of identity panels on forms AP1, FR1, and DS2' both of which can be found on the GOV.UK website.

12 Confirmation of identity

When registering transfers, charges, leases and other dispositions of land, or giving effect to a discharge or release of a registered charge, Land Registry relies on the steps that conveyancers take, where appropriate, to verify the identity of their clients. These checks reduce the risk of property fraud.

Where a person was not represented by a conveyancer, Land Registry requires 'evidence of identity' in respect of that person, except where the first alternative in panel 13(2) applies.

'Evidence of identity' is evidence provided in accordance with any current direction made by the Chief Land Registrar under section 100(4) of the Land Registration Act 2002 for the purpose of confirming a person's identity.

If this application is to register a transfer, lease or charge, or to give effect to a discharge in Form DS1 or a release in Form DS3 complete one of the following

Place 'X' in the appropriate box.

Conveyancer is defined in rule 217(1) of the Land Registration Rules 2003 and includes, among others, solicitor, licensed conveyancer and fellow of the Institute of Legal Executives.

☐ I am a conveyancer, and I have completed panel 13

☐ I am not a conveyancer, and I have completed panel 14

13 Where the application is sent to Land Registry by a conveyancer

(1) Details of conveyancer acting

If you are sending an application to register a transfer, lease or charge, for each party to each disposition that is to be registered state in the table below the details of the conveyancer (if any) who represented them.

Where a party is not represented by a conveyancer you must also complete (2) below.

Place 'X' in the box in the second column if the person or firm who is sending the application to Land Registry represented that party in the transaction. Otherwise complete the details in the third column. If the party is not represented insert 'none' in the third column.

Name of transferor, landlord, transferee, tenant, borrower or lender		Conveyancer's name, address and reference
	☐	Reference:
	☐	Reference:
	☐	Reference:

If you are sending an application to give effect to a discharge in Form DS1 or release in Form DS3 for each lender, state in the table below the details of the conveyancer (if any) who represented them.

Where a lender is not represented by a conveyancer you must also complete (2) below.

Place 'X' in the box in the second column if the person or firm who is sending the application to Land Registry represented that party in the transaction. Otherwise complete the details in the third column. If the party is not represented insert 'none' in the third column.

Name of lender		Conveyancer's name, address and reference
	☐	Reference:
	☐	Reference:

Page 4 of 6

Place 'X' in the appropriate box(es).

Insert the name of each unrepresented transferor, landlord, transferee, tenant, borrower or lender for whom you give this confirmation.

Evidence of identity is defined in panel 12. Full details of the evidence of identity that is required can be found in Practice Guide 67 available on the GOV.UK website.

(2) Evidence of identity

Where any transferor, landlord, transferee, tenant, borrower or lender listed in (1) was not represented by a conveyancer

☐ I confirm that I am satisfied that sufficient steps have been taken to verify the identity of

and that they are the registered proprietor or have the right to be registered as the registered proprietor

☐ I enclose evidence of identity in respect of each unrepresented transferor, landlord, transferee, tenant, borrower or lender for whom I have not provided the confirmation above

If the party is not represented insert 'none' in the second column.

14 Where the application is sent to Land Registry by someone who is not a conveyancer

(1) Details of conveyancer acting

If you are sending an application to register a transfer, lease or charge (ie a mortgage), for each party to each disposition that is to be registered, state in the table below the details of the conveyancer (if any) who represented them.

You must also complete (2) below.

Name of transferor, landlord, transferee, tenant, borrower or lender		Conveyancer's name, address and reference
	☐	Reference:
	☐	Reference:
	☐	Reference:

Page 5 of 6

If the party is not represented insert 'none' in the second column.

If you are sending an application to give effect to a discharge in Form DS1 or release in Form DS3, for each lender state in the table below the details of the conveyancer (if any) who represented them.

You must also complete (2) below.

Name of lender		Conveyancer's name, address and reference
	☐	Reference:
	☐	Reference:

Place 'X' in the appropriate box(es).

Evidence of identity is defined in panel 12. Full details of the evidence of identity that is required can be found in 'Completing the evidence of identity panels on forms AP1, FR1, and DS2' available on the GOV.UK website.

(2) Evidence of identity

☐ for each applicant named in panel 6 is enclosed

☐ for each unrepresented transferor, landlord, transferee, tenant, borrower or lender listed in (1) is enclosed

If a conveyancer is acting for the applicant, that conveyancer must sign.

If no conveyancer is acting, the applicant (and if the applicant is more than one person then each of them) must sign.

15

Signature of conveyancer: ....

Date:

OR

Signature of applicant: ....

Date:

WARNING

If you dishonestly enter information or make a statement that you know is, or might be, untrue or misleading, and intend by doing so to make a gain for yourself or another person, or to cause loss or the risk of loss to another person, you may commit the offence of fraud under section 1 of the Fraud Act 2006, the maximum penalty for which is 10 years' imprisonment or an unlimited fine, or both.

Failure to complete this form with proper care may result in a loss of protection under the Land Registration Act 2002 if, as a result, a mistake is made in the register.

Under section 66 of the Land Registration Act 2002 most documents (including this form) kept by the registrar relating to an application to the registrar or referred to in the register are open to public inspection and copying. If you believe a document contains prejudicial information, you may apply for that part of the document to be made exempt using Form EX1, under rule 136 of the Land Registration Rules 2003.

Sign and Lock >

FORM 13: SAMPLE DETAILS IN A STATEMENT OF TRUTH in support of an application to be registered as proprietor of registered land under the transitional provisions[1]

ACTS OF ADVERSE POSSESSION

(*to be inserted in panel 5 of the statement of truth*)

I erected a timber framed hut on the land in September 1989 in which I have stored my farm implements and carried out repairs to them. I have also kept cattle on the land. I have had exclusive use of the land and the hut since September 1989.

ACTS OF ENCLOSURE OF THE LAND

(*to be inserted in panel 6 of the statement of truth*)

I have maintained the fencing around the land, and put barbed wire on the top. In addition I have put padlocks on the gates to keep other people out and kept the key for my own use.

1 See Form 2.

FORM 14: OBJECTION to application to be registered as proprietor of registered land under the transitional provisions

Dear Sir,

Title Number: . . . .

Property: . . . .

Dated: . . . . 20 . . .

We, as solicitors for [B] of (*address*) ("the Objector") give notice to the Chief Land Registrar that we object to the pending application for the registration of [A] of (*address*) ("the Applicant") as proprietor of the above mentioned land ("the disputed land"). Our grounds are as follows:

1. The Objector is the registered proprietor of Whiteacre Farm at (*address*), which is registered at HM Land Registry under title number . . . . The disputed land is situated in the north east corner of Whiteacre Farm and consists of 2 fields.

2. The Applicant asserts in his statement of truth that he has been in possession of the disputed land for 14 years immediately prior to 13 October 2003. The Objector denies that. We have obtained a statement from [C], the Objector's immediate predecessor in title, that the Applicant first made use of the disputed land 7 years ago, shortly before it was transferred to the Objector. Accordingly, the Applicant cannot show 12 years' possession prior to 13 October 2003.

Accordingly, the Applicant's application for first registration of the disputed land must fail and we ask you not to accede to it.

Yours faithfully,

(Signature)

2: UNILATERAL NOTICE

FORM 15: APPLICATION to enter a unilateral notice

Land Registry
Application to enter a unilateral notice

UN1

To enter an agreed notice use Form AN1. To enter a notice to protect home rights use Form HR1.

If you need more room than is provided for in a panel, and your software allows, you can expand any panel in the form. Alternatively use continuation sheet CS and attach it to this form.

Land Registry is unable to give legal advice, but you can find guidance on Land Registry applications (including our practice guides for conveyancers) at www.gov.uk/land-registry.

Conveyancer is a term used in this form. It is defined in rule 217A, Land Registration Rules 2003 and includes persons authorised under the Legal Services Act 2007 to provide reserved legal services relating to land registration and includes solicitors and licensed conveyancers.

LAND REGISTRY USE ONLY
Record of fees paid
Particulars of under/over payments
Reference number Fees debited £

Where there is more than one local authority serving an area, enter the one to which council tax or business rates are normally paid.

1 Local authority serving the property:

Choose Local Authority

2 Title number(s) of the property:

Insert address including postcode (if any) or other description of the property, for example 'land adjoining 2 Acacia Avenue'.

3 Property:

The interest to be protected by the unilateral notice affects

Place 'X' in the appropriate box and complete as necessary.

- ☐ the whole of the registered estate
- ☐ part of the registered estate as shown:

Give a brief description of the part affected, for example 'edged red on the attached plan'.

Complete details of charge if appropriate.

- ☐ the registered charge dated in favour of:

4 Application and fee

To find out more about our fees visit www.gov.uk/government/collections/fees-land-registry-guides

Application	Fee paid (£)
Entry of unilateral notice	

Fee payment method

Place 'X' in the appropriate box.

The fee will be charged to the account specified in panel 7.

- ☐ cheque made payable to 'Land Registry'
- ☐ direct debit, under an agreement with Land Registry

The applicant's statement in panel 11 or a conveyancer's certificate in panel 12 is sufficient. Supporting documents are not required but if you choose to enclose them list them here. If this application is accompanied by either Form AP1 or FR1 please only complete the corresponding panel on Form AP1 or DL (if used). Original documents are only required if your application is a first registration, we will return the originals if a certified copy is supplied. If your application is not a first registration then we only need certified copies of deeds or documents you send to us with Land Registry application forms. Once we have made a copy of the documents you send to us, they will be destroyed, this applies to both originals and certified copies.	5 Documents lodged with this form:
Provide the full name(s) of the person(s) applying for entry of the notice. Where a conveyancer lodges the application, this must be the name(s) of the client(s), not the conveyancer. Complete as appropriate where the applicant is a company.	6 The applicant: For UK incorporated companies/LLPs Registered number of company or limited liability partnership including any prefix: For overseas companies (a) Territory of incorporation: (b) Registered number in the United Kingdom including any prefix:
This panel must always be completed. If you are paying by direct debit, this will be the account charged. This is the address to which we will normally send requisitions. However if you insert an email address, we will use this whenever possible. Where an application is lodged by e-DRS all documents and correspondence will be dealt with electronically.	7 This application is sent to Land Registry by Key number (if applicable): Name: Address or UK DX box number: Email address: Reference: Phone no: Fax no:
Each applicant may give up to three addresses for service, one of which must be a postal address whether or not in the UK (including the postcode, if any). The others can be any combination of a postal address, a UK DX box number or an electronic address.	8 Address(es) for service of each applicant. The address(es) will be entered in the register and used for correspondence and the service of notice:
	9 The applicant as beneficiary applies for the entry of a unilateral notice against the title(s) referred to in panel 2

Complete this panel and either panel 11 or panel 12.

Place 'X' in the appropriate box and complete as necessary. See practice guide 19 available on the GOV.UK website if you are unsure which option you need to select.

10 Entitlement to apply

The applicant has an interest in the property as set out in the statement in panel 11 or the conveyancer's certificate in panel 12 and

☐ The applicant has made the statement in panel 11

☐ The certificate in panel 12 has been completed by a conveyancer on behalf of the applicant

Set out the nature of the beneficiary's interest.

Complete this panel if a conveyancer is not lodging the application. If a conveyancer is lodging the application, the conveyancer may either complete panel 12 and leave this panel blank, or arrange for the applicant to complete this panel.

See the warnings at the end of this form.

11 The applicant is interested in the property described in panel 3 as:

The interest described above is neither a public right nor a customary right.

Signature of applicant: ....

Set out the nature of the beneficiary's interest.

Only complete this panel if a conveyancer is lodging the application.

See the warnings at the end of this form.

12 I certify that the applicant is interested in the property described in panel 3 as:

I certify that the interest described above is neither a public right nor a customary right.

Signature of conveyancer: ------------------------------

The conveyancer's full name is:

If a conveyancer is acting for the applicant, that conveyancer must sign. If no conveyancer is acting, the applicant (and if more than one person then each of them) must sign.

13

Signature of applicant
or their conveyancer: --------------------------------

Date:

WARNING
If you dishonestly enter information or make a statement that you know is, or might be, untrue or misleading, and intend by doing so to make a gain for yourself or another person, or to cause loss or the risk of loss to another person, you may commit the offence of fraud under section 1 of the Fraud Act 2006, the maximum penalty for which is 10 years' imprisonment or an unlimited fine, or both.

Failure to complete this form with proper care may result in a loss of protection under the Land Registration Act 2002 if, as a result, a mistake is made in the register.

Under section 66 of the Land Registration Act 2002 most documents (including this form) kept by the registrar relating to an application to the registrar or referred to in the register are open to public inspection and copying. If you believe a document contains prejudicial information, you may apply for that part of the document to be made exempt using Form EX1, under rule 136 of the Land Registration Rules 2003.

FORM 16: SAMPLE DETAILS in an application to enter a unilateral notice[1]

NATURE OF THE APPLICANT'S INTEREST IN THE PROPERTY

(*to be inserted in panel 11 of the application*)

I have the benefit of a restrictive covenant preventing the registered proprietor from developing the rear garden of the property, contained in a deed made between the registered proprietor and myself and dated . . . . 20 . . .

1 See Form 15.

FORM 17: APPLICATION to cancel a unilateral notice

Land Registry
Application for the cancellation of a unilateral notice by a person who is (or is entitled to be) the registered proprietor

UN4

A registered beneficiary of a unilateral notice (or his personal representative or trustee in bankruptcy) wishing to apply for the removal of the notice must use Form UN2.

If you need more room than is provided for in a panel, and your software allows, you can expand any panel in the form. Alternatively use continuation sheet CS and attach it to this form.

Land Registry is unable to give legal advice, but you can find guidance on Land Registry applications (including our practice guides for conveyancers) at www.gov.uk/land-registry.

Conveyancer is a term used in this form. It is defined in rule 217A, Land Registration Rules 2003 and includes persons authorised under the Legal Services Act 2007 to provide reserved legal services relating to land registration and includes solicitors and licensed conveyancers.

LAND REGISTRY USE ONLY
Record of fees paid
Particulars of under/over payments
Reference number Fees debited £

Where there is more than one local authority serving an area, enter the one to which council tax or business rates are normally paid.

1 Local authority serving the property:

Choose Local Authority

2 Title number(s) of the property:

Insert address including postcode (if any) or other description of the property, for example 'land adjoining 2 Acacia Avenue'.

3 Property:

4 The applicant applies to cancel

Place 'X' in the appropriate box.

☐ the unilateral notice

Give a brief description of the part affected, for example 'edged red on the attached plan'.

☐ the unilateral notice as to the part shown:

State date of notice (as set out in the register in brackets at the beginning of the notice) and the full names of each person entered in the register as the beneficiary or beneficiaries of the notice to be cancelled. If there is more than one notice registered by the same person(s) on the same day, please specify which one the application relates to.

registered on

in the name of the following beneficiary or beneficiaries:

Currently no fee is payable for cancellation of a unilateral notice.

5 Application and fee

Application	Fee paid (£)
Cancellation of a unilateral notice	

Fee payment method

☐ cheque made payable to 'Land Registry'

☐ direct debit, under an agreement with Land Registry

List the documents lodged with this form. If you are a conveyancer, you can certify that you hold evidence – please see panel 9. If you are not a conveyancer, you must enclose the evidence with this application. Land Registry may destroy documents after scanning. If this application is accompanied by Form AP1 please only complete the corresponding panel on Form AP1 or Form DL (if used). We only need certified copies of deeds or documents you send to us with Land Registry application forms. Once we have made a copy of the documents you send to us, they will be destroyed, this applies to both originals and certified copies.	6 Documents lodged with this form:
Provide the full name(s) of the person(s) applying for the cancellation of a unilateral notice. Where a conveyancer lodges the application, this must be the name(s) of the client(s), not the conveyancer.	7 The applicant:
This panel must always be completed. If you are paying by direct debit, this will be the account charged. This is the address to which we will normally send requisitions. However if you insert an email address, we will use this whenever possible. Where an application is lodged by e-DRS all documents and correspondence will be dealt with electronically.	8 This application is sent to Land Registry by Key number (if applicable): Name: Address or UK DX box number: Email address: Reference: Phone no: Fax no:
You must place 'X' in one box only in this panel. If you are a conveyancer the certificate is sufficient to comply with Land Registry's requirements. If no conveyancer is acting, you must enclose the evidence of the applicant's entitlement with this application. Land Registry may destroy documents after scanning. An applicant applying for themselves should select one of the first two options only. List any supporting documents in panel 6 or on Form AP1 or DL (if used).	9 Status of applicant ☐ The applicant is the registered proprietor of the estate/charge affected by the above unilateral notice. ☐ The applicant is the person entitled to be registered as the proprietor of the estate/charge affected by the above unilateral notice and evidence of that entitlement accompanies this application. ☐ I am the applicant's conveyancer and certify that I am satisfied that the applicant is entitled to be registered as the proprietor of the estate/charge to which the unilateral notice referred to in panel 4 relates.
If a conveyancer is acting for the applicant, that conveyancer must sign. If no conveyancer is acting, the applicant (and if more than one person then each of them) must sign.	10 Signature of applicant or their conveyancer: .... Date:

WARNING
If you dishonestly enter information or make a statement that you know is, or might be, untrue or misleading, and intend by doing so to make a gain for yourself or another person, or to cause loss or the risk of loss to another person, you may commit the offence of fraud under section 1 of the Fraud Act 2006, the maximum penalty for which is 10 years' imprisonment or an unlimited fine, or both.

Failure to complete this form with proper care may result in a loss of protection under the Land Registration Act 2002 if, as a result, a mistake is made in the register.

Under section 66 of the Land Registration Act 2002 most documents (including this form) kept by the registrar relating to an application to the registrar or referred to in the register are open to public inspection and copying. If you believe a document contains prejudicial information, you may apply for that part of the document to be made exempt using Form EX1, under rule 136 of the Land Registration Rules 2003.

FORM 18: OBJECTION to the cancellation of a unilateral notice

Dear Sir,

Title Number: . . . .

Property: . . . .

Dated: . . . . 20 . . .

We, as solicitors for [A] of (*address*) ("the Objector") give notice to the Chief Land Registrar that we object to the pending application by [B] of (*address*) ("the Applicant") to cancel the unilateral notice entered in relation to the above mentioned land ("the burdened property"). Our grounds are as follows:

1. The Applicant is the registered proprietor of the burdened property.
2. The Objector is the registered proprietor of the adjoining house at (*address*), which is registered at HM Land Registry under title number . . . . ("the benefited property").
3. By a deed dated . . . . the Applicant covenanted, on behalf of himself and his successors in title, with the Objector and his successors in title for the benefit of the benefited property, that he would not develop the rear garden of the burdened property. A copy of the deed is annexed hereto.
4. The restrictive covenant contained in the deed is a burden affecting the burdened property, which is properly protected by the entry of the unilateral notice.

The application to cancel the unilateral notice is accordingly opposed.

Yours faithfully,

(Signature)

FORM 19: REPLY to an objection to the cancellation of a unilateral notice

Dear Sir,

Title Number: . . . .

Property: . . . .

Dated: . . . . 20 . . .

We, as solicitors for [B] of (*address*) ("the Applicant") reply as follows to the objection dated . . . . 20 . . . given on behalf of [A] of (*address*) ("the Objector"):

1. It is agreed that on . . . . the parties entered into the deed annexed to the objection.
2. Some time after the deed was executed a developer, [C Ltd], expressed an interest in buying the rear garden of the burdened property in order to build a new house on it. The Objector initially refused to release the restrictive covenant, as he did not want the development to take place.
3. However, after discussions the parties entered into a deed of release dated . . . . whereby in consideration of the Objector releasing the restrictive covenant, the Applicant paid the Objector £50,000. A copy of the deed of release is annexed hereto.

In the circumstances, we ask that the unilateral notice be cancelled.

Yours faithfully,

(Signature)

3. CAUTION AGAINST DEALINGS

FORM 20: APPLICATION to cancel a caution against dealings

Land Registry
Application to cancel a caution against dealings

CCD

If the caution to be cancelled is a caution against first registration, you must use Form CCT. If the caution is being withdrawn by the cautioner, you must use Form WCT.

If you need more room than is provided for in a panel, and your software allows, you can expand any panel in the form. Alternatively use continuation sheet CS and attach it to this form.

Land Registry is unable to give legal advice, but you can find guidance on Land Registry applications (including our practice guides for conveyancers) at www.gov.uk/land-registry.

Conveyancer is a term used in this form. It is defined in rule 217A, Land Registration Rules 2003 and includes persons authorised under the Legal Services Act 2007 to provide reserved legal services relating to land registration and includes solicitors and licensed conveyancers.

LAND REGISTRY USE ONLY
Record of fees paid
Particulars of under/over payments
Reference number Fees debited £

Where there is more than one local authority serving an area, enter the one to which council tax or business rates are normally paid.

1 Local authority serving the property:

Choose Local Authority

2 Title number(s) of property:

Insert address including postcode (if any) or other description of the property, for example 'land adjoining 2 Acacia Avenue'.

3 Property:

Currently no fee is payable for the cancellation of a caution.

4 Application and fee

Application	Fee paid (£)
Application to cancel a caution against dealings	

Fee payment method

cheque made payable to 'Land Registry'

direct debit, under an agreement with Land Registry

Provide the full name(s) of the person(s) applying to cancel the caution against dealings. Where a conveyancer lodges the application, this must be the name(s) of the client(s), not the conveyancer.

Complete as appropriate where the applicant is a company.

5 The applicant:

For UK incorporated companies/LLPs
Registered number of company or limited liability partnership including any prefix:

For overseas companies
(a) Territory of incorporation:

(b) Registered number in the United Kingdom including any prefix:

This panel must always be completed. If you are paying by direct debit, this will be the account charged. This is the address to which we will normally send requisitions. However if you insert an email address, we will use this whenever possible.	6	This application is sent to Land Registry by Key number (if applicable): Name: Address or UK DX box number: Email address: Reference: Phone no: Fax no:
Insert the name of the cautioner as shown on the register and if there are two or more cautions in favour of the same cautioner, please identify the caution to which this application relates by including the date at the beginning of the caution entry and, if that date is the same as that of one of the other cautions, brief details of the caution.	7	The applicant applies for the caution identified below to be cancelled Caution in favour of: Date of caution entry, if appropriate:
Place 'X' in one box. List the documents lodged with this form.We only need certified copies of deeds or documents you send to us with Land Registry application forms. Once we have made a copy of the documents you send to us, they will be destroyed, this applies to both originals and certified copies.	8	Entitlement to apply The applicant is the proprietor of the registered estate/charge to which the caution relates The applicant is, or but for the existence of the caution would be, entitled to be registered as proprietor of the registered estate/charge, and evidence of such entitlement is enclosed as set out below:
If a conveyancer is acting for the applicant, that conveyancer must sign. If no conveyancer is acting, the applicant (and if more than one person then each of them) must sign.	9	Signature of applicant or their conveyancer: ------------------------------------ Date:

WARNING
If you dishonestly enter information or make a statement that you know is, or might be, untrue or misleading, and intend by doing so to make a gain for yourself or another person, or to cause loss or the risk of loss to another person, you may commit the offence of fraud under section 1 of the Fraud Act 2006, the maximum penalty for which is 10 years' imprisonment or an unlimited fine, or both.

Failure to complete this form with proper care may result in a loss of protection under the Land Registration Act 2002 if, as a result, a mistake is made in the register.

Under section 66 of the Land Registration Act 2002 most documents (including this form) kept by the registrar relating to an application to the registrar or referred to in the register are open to public inspection and copying. If you believe a document contains prejudicial information, you may apply for that part of the document to be made exempt using Form EX1, under rule 136 of the Land Registration Rules 2003.

FORM 21: NOTICE showing cause why a caution against dealings should not be cancelled

Dear Sir,

Title Number: . . . .

Property: . . . .

Dated: . . . . 20 . . .

We, as solicitors for [A] of (*address*) ("the Objector") give notice to the Chief Land Registrar that we object to the pending application by [B] of (*address*) ("the Applicant") to cancel the caution against dealings lodged in relation to the above mentioned land ("the property"). Our grounds are as follows:

1. The Applicant is the registered proprietor of the property, which is an established sea side hotel. The Objector is a younger man with whom the Applicant had a same sex relationship for over 20 years, terminating in 2002.
2. The parties first met when the Objector went to work at the property as a trainee chef.
3. The Objector was able and ambitious but was told by the Applicant that if he carried on working at the hotel in return for board and lodging, the Applicant would leave him the property in his will.
4. The Objector had wanted to better himself and gave up the prospect of owning his own restaurant or of receiving higher wages in reliance on this promise.
5. When the relationship ended in 2002 and the Objector moved out of the property, the Applicant told the Objector that he was leaving the property to charity. Following this the Objector lodged a caution against dealings to protect his interests.

The application to cancel the caution against dealings is accordingly opposed.

Yours faithfully,

(Signature)

FORM 22: REPLY to a notice showing cause why a caution against dealings should not be cancelled

Dear Sir,

Title Number: . . . .

Property: . . . .

Dated: . . . . 20 . . .

We, as solicitors for [B] of (*address*) ("the Applicant") reply as follows to the objection dated . . . . 20 . . . given on behalf of [A] of (*address*) ("the Objector"):

1. It is agreed that for many years the parties had a relationship and that the Objector lived at and sometimes assisted at the property.
2. The Applicant never promised the Objector that he would leave him the property. The Applicant has always made it clear that he was intending to leave the property to charity.
3. The Objector chose the security and companionship of a shared life with the Applicant in the property. He was nervous of setting up in business on his own and agreed to help out occasionally in return for board and lodging.
4. The Objector received substantial material benefit from this arrangement over the years and it is denied in all the circumstances that he has any claim in respect of the property.

In the circumstances, we ask that the caution against dealings be cancelled.

Yours faithfully,

(Signature)

4. RESTRICTIONS

FORM 23: APPLICATION to enter a restriction

Land Registry
Application to enter a restriction

RX1

If you need more room than is provided for in a panel, you can expand any panel in this form. Simply continue typing until complete, then click on another panel to expand the form.

Land Registry is unable to give legal advice but our website www.landregistry.gov.uk provides guidance on Land Registry applications. This includes public guides and practice guides (aimed at conveyancers) that can also be obtained from any Land Registry office.

See www.landregistry.gov.uk/contact-us/offices if you are unsure which Land Registry office to send this application to.

Conveyancer is a term used in this form. It is defined in rule 217A, Land Registration Rules 2003 and includes persons authorised under the Legal Services Act 2007 to provide reserved legal services relating to land registration and includes solicitors and licensed conveyancers.

LAND REGISTRY USE ONLY
Record of fees paid
Particulars of under/over payments
Reference number Fees debited £

Where there is more than one local authority serving an area, enter the one to which council tax or business rates are normally paid.

1 Local authority serving the property:

Choose Local authority

2 Title number(s) of the property:

Insert address including postcode (if any) or other description of the property, for example 'land adjoining 2 Acacia Avenue'.

3 Property:

Place 'X' in the appropriate box.

The restriction applied for is to affect

☐ the whole of the registered estate

Give a brief description of the part affected, for example 'edged red on the attached plan'.

☐ the part(s) of the registered estate as shown:

Complete details of charge if appropriate.

☐ the registered charge(s) dated in favour of:

See fees calculator at www.landregistry.gov.uk/professional/fees/fees-calculator

4 Application and fee

Application	Fee paid (£)
Entry of restriction	

Place 'X' in the appropriate box.

The fee will be charged to the account specified in panel 7.

Fee payment method

☐ cheque made payable to 'Land Registry'

☐ direct debit, under an agreement with Land Registry

List the documents lodged with this form. If this application is accompanied by either Form AP1 or FR1 please only complete the corresponding panel on Form AP1 or DL (if used). Copy documents should be listed separately. If you supply a certified copy of an original document we will return the original; if a certified copy is not supplied, we may retain the original document and it may be destroyed.	5 Documents lodged with this form:
Provide the full name(s) of the person(s) applying to enter the obligation in the register. Where a conveyancer lodges the application, this must be the name(s) of the client(s), not the conveyancer.	6 The applicant:
If you are paying by direct debit, this will be the account charged. This is the address to which we will normally send requisitions and return documents. However if you insert an email address, we will use this whenever possible.	7 This application is sent to Land Registry by Key number (if applicable): Name Address or UK DX box number: Email address: Reference: Phone no: Fax no:

You must place 'X' in only one box in this panel. See Practice Guide 19 if you are unsure which option you need to select.

8 The applicant is entitled to apply for a restriction because

(A) Applicant is the registered proprietor

☐ The applicant is the registered proprietor of the estate/charge referred to in panel 3

(B) Applicant is entitled to be registered as the proprietor

List any supporting documents in panel 5 or on Form AP1 or DL (if used).

☐ Evidence of that entitlement accompanies this application

☐ I am the applicant's conveyancer and certify that I am satisfied that the applicant is entitled to be registered as proprietor and that I hold the originals of the documents that contain evidence of the applicant's entitlement, or an application for registration of the applicant as proprietor is pending at Land Registry

(C) Application made with the consent of the registered proprietor

Panel 11 must be completed or a separate consent enclosed.

☐ The relevant consent accompanies this application

☐ I am the applicant's conveyancer and certify that I hold the relevant consent

(D) Application made with the consent of person entitled to be registered as proprietor

List any supporting documents in panel 5 or on Form AP1 or DL (if used). Panel 11 must be completed or a separate consent enclosed.

☐ The relevant consent and evidence of that entitlement accompany this application

☐ I am the applicant's conveyancer and I certify that the relevant consent accompanies this application.

I also certify that I am satisfied that the person consenting to this application is entitled to be registered as proprietor and that I hold the originals of the documents that contain evidence of that person's entitlement, or an application for registration of that person as proprietor is pending at Land Registry

☐ I am the applicant's conveyancer and I certify that I hold the relevant consent.

I also certify that I am satisfied that the person consenting to this application is entitled to be registered as proprietor and that I hold the originals of the documents that contain evidence of that person's entitlement, or an application for registration of that person as proprietor is pending at Land Registry

(E) Other evidence in support of applicant's claim

List any supporting documents in panel 5 or on Form AP1 or DL (if used).

None of the above statements applies but the applicant has the following sufficient interest in the making of the entry of the restriction applied for in panel 9

☐ The applicant has made the statement in panel 12

☐ I am the applicant's conveyancer and I certify as to the applicant's interest in panel 13

Set out in full the wording of the restriction required. For standard form restrictions, also insert the reference letter(s) of the form. For non-standard form restrictions delete the words in square brackets. Standard forms of restriction are set out in Schedule 4 to the Land Registration Rules 2003. Further guidance is contained in Practice Guide 19. You must set out the wording of the restriction in full, unless you are applying for a standard form of restriction that has no variable content. You must include the address(es) for service where a standard form of restriction requires an address to be included or where any other restriction requires a consent or certificate to be provided, or notice to be served on the restrictioner. Each restrictioner may give up to three addresses for service, one of which must be a postal address whether or not in the UK (including the postcode, if any). The others can be any combination of a postal address, a UK DX box number or an electronic address. If the restriction refers to a registered company or limited liability partnership incorporated anywhere in the United Kingdom include the registered number (including any prefix) immediately after the name of the company. For an overseas company include the territory of incorporation and if its particulars are registered at Companies House, state the registered number in England and Wales.	9	The applicant applies to enter a restriction [in standard form] against the estate/charge referred to in panel 3 in the following words:
If a conveyancer is acting for the applicant, that conveyancer must sign. If no conveyancer is acting, the applicant (and if more than one person then each of them) must sign. The conveyancer must sign if they have given one of the certificates referred to in panel 8.	10	Signature of applicant or their conveyancer: ____________________ Date:
See panel 8.	11	I/We consent to the entry of the restriction specified in panel 9 against the estate or charge referred to in panel 3. Print full name — Signature 1. — 1. 2. — 2. 3. — 3. 4. — 4.

Only complete this panel if you have completed option (E) in panel 8. If a conveyancer is lodging the application, the conveyancer may either complete panel 13 and leave this panel blank, or may arrange for the applicant to complete this panel. Set out the nature of the applicant's interest. Set out details of the circumstances in which the interest arose. List any supporting documents in panel 5 or on Form AP1 or DL (if used). See the warnings at the end of this form.	12	The applicant states that the applicant has a sufficient interest in the restriction being entered in the register. Nature of applicant's interest: Details of how the applicant's interest arose: Signature of applicant: ____________________
Only complete this panel if you have completed option (E) in panel 8 and a conveyancer is lodging the application. Set out the nature of the applicant's interest. Set out details of the circumstances in which the interest arose. List any supporting documents in panel 5 or on Form AP1 or DL (if used). See the warnings at the end of this form.	13	I certify that the applicant has a sufficient interest in the restriction being entered in the register. Nature of applicant's interest: Details of how the applicant's interest arose: Signature of conveyancer: ____________________ The conveyancer's full name is:

WARNING

If you dishonestly enter information or make a statement that you know is, or might be, untrue or misleading, and intend by doing so to make a gain for yourself or another person, or to cause loss or the risk of loss to another person, you may commit the offence of fraud under section 1 of the Fraud Act 2006, the maximum penalty for which is 10 years' imprisonment or an unlimited fine, or both.

Failure to complete this form with proper care may result in a loss of protection under the Land Registration Act 2002 if, as a result, a mistake is made in the register.

Under section 66 of the Land Registration Act 2002 most documents (including this form) kept by the registrar relating to an application to the registrar or referred to in the register are open to public inspection and copying. If you believe a document contains prejudicial information, you may apply for that part of the document to be made exempt using Form EX1, under rule 136 of the Land Registration Rules 2003.

FORM 24: SAMPLE DETAILS in an application to enter a restriction

NATURE OF THE APPLICANT'S INTEREST

(*to be inserted in panel 12 of the application*)

I have a beneficial interest in the property as a result of an implied, resulting or constructive trust and/or by virtue of proprietary estoppel.

DETAILS OF HOW THE APPLICANT'S INTEREST AROSE

(*to be inserted in panel 12 of the application*)

At the time that [B] purchased the property in his sole name, I was in a relationship with him. I lived in the property with him for 3 years until the relationship broke down. I contributed £5,000 towards the deposit of the property. This money was a gift from my parents. During the 3 years I lived at the property I paid the mortgage. I gave up an assured tenancy of my flat on the promise by [B] that I would own the property equally with him.

FORM 25: OBJECTION to the entry of a restriction

Dear Sir,

Title Number: . . . .

Property: . . . .

Dated: . . . . 20 . . .

We, as solicitors for [B] of (address) ("the Objector") give notice to the Chief Land Registrar that we object to the pending application by [A] of (address) ("the Applicant") to enter restrictions in Form A and II in the register in respect of the above mentioned property ("the property"). Our grounds are as follows:

1. The Objector is the sole registered proprietor of the property. The Objector and the Applicant lived together at the property for 3 years after it was purchased before their relationship broke down and the Applicant moved out.

2. It is denied that the Applicant has any beneficial interest in the property, whether arising from an express, implied, constructive or resulting trust or from any form of proprietary or other estoppel.

3. The Applicant makes various assertions in panel 12 of the Form RX1. Firstly, she says that she contributed to the deposit when the Objector purchased the property. The Objector denies this. A payment of £5,000 was made by the Applicant to the Objector at this time, but it had nothing to do with the property. It was the repayment of a loan the Objector had made to the Applicant some 6 months earlier enabling the Applicant to buy a second hand car.

4. The Applicant also asserts that she contributed to the mortgage repayments in respect of the property whilst she lived there. This is not true. The Applicant made a modest contribution to the household kitty, if and when she was in employment, but that money was only ever used to pay for food; all mortgage repayments were made by direct debit from the Objector's bank account.

5. The Applicant finally claims that just before the purchase of the property the Objector took the Applicant out for dinner and told her that if she gave up her assured tenancy and kept house for him in the property, it would be owned "fifty/fifty" each. The Objector denies this. He did take the Applicant out for a meal at the Rose & Crown shortly before the property was purchased, but there was no such conversation as alleged. The Objector's recollection is that he spent the evening trying to explain the offside rule to the Applicant.

6. The Objector now needs to sell the property as he is moving to New Zealand and the application is interfering with his ability to market the property.

For these reasons we oppose the Applicant's application and ask you not to accede to it.

Yours faithfully,

(Signature)

FORM 26: REPLY to an objection to the entry of a restriction

Dear Sir,

Title Number: . . . .

Property: . . . .

Dated: . . . . 20 . . .

We, as solicitors for [A] of (*address*) ("the Applicant") reply as follows to the objection dated . . . . 20 . . . given on behalf of [B] of (*address*) ("the Objector"):

1. The Applicant did contribute £5,000 to the deposit when the Objector purchased the property. The sum of £5,000 was a gift to the Applicant from her parents and was specifically given to the Applicant to assist her in the purchase of the property. We enclose a photocopy of a page from the Applicant's parents' building society passbook showing the relevant withdrawal.
2. The Applicant did not borrow £5,000 from the Objector to help her buy a car. The Applicant was given £600 by her parents towards the cost of the car and is paying the balance by means of a credit agreement.
3. The Applicant worked throughout the 3 years the parties lived together at the property and was the principal breadwinner. She was regularly employed as a receptionist at a solicitors' practice. On the other hand the Objector, who is a freelance writer, only sold the occasional piece and was largely dependent on the Applicant's earnings and savings. The mortgage was supposed to be paid by direct debit from the Objector's bank account, but usually there were insufficient funds in the account, and the Applicant had to pay the monthly instalments in cash. We enclose photocopies of her bank statements showing her earnings and her withdrawals of cash to pay the mortgage.
4. The Applicant maintains that she gave up her assured tenancy on the understanding that the property was to be owned equally.

We consider the objections put forward by the Objector to be without any merit and ask for the entry of restrictions in Form A and II in the register of the property.

Yours faithfully,

(Signature)

5: EASEMENT BY PRESCRIPTION

FORM 27: STATEMENT OF TRUTH in support of an application to register the benefit of an easement by prescription as an appurtenant right

Land Registry
Statement of truth in support of an application for registration and/or noting of a prescriptive easement

ST4

If you need more room than is provided for in a panel, and your software allows, you can expand any panel in the form. Alternatively use continuation sheet CS and attach it to this form.

If a joint statement is made by two or more persons, consequential amendments can be made to the text in the panels (for example, 'I' can be changed to 'we').

Land Registry is unable to give legal advice, but you can find guidance on Land Registry applications (including our practice guides for conveyancers) at www.gov.uk/land-registry.

Insert full name. Insert full address.	1 I: of: make this statement in support of an application to Land Registry for registration and/or noting of an easement based upon prescription.
Place 'X' in one box only. This is for cases where the legal owner is a company or firm, someone who has died, or is otherwise incapable of making the statement personally. Insert the name and address of the legal owner. Please specify and enclose any relevant documentation. See note above.	2 Status of person making this statement I am ☐ the legal owner of the benefiting land (other than as personal representative) ☐ making this statement on behalf of: who is currently or was previously the legal owner of the benefiting land but who cannot make this statement for the following reasons: ☐ Other:
Place 'X' in one box only. If applying for entry of a unilateral notice, do not use this form - please use form UN1 instead.	3 Type of application ☐ Registration of benefit of an easement – benefiting land is registered and burdened land is unregistered ☐ Registration of benefit of easement and entry of notice of burden – benefiting land is registered and burdened land is registered ☐ Entry of notice of burden of easement – burdened land is registered and benefiting land is unregistered
Insert details of date and circumstances in which the estate was acquired by the current legal owner or (where the current legal owner is a personal representative) by the deceased previous legal owner.	4 Title number(s) of the benefiting land (if registered):

Insert address including postcode (if any) or other description of the property, for example 'land adjoining 2 Acacia Avenue'. If the benefit of the easement is claimed in relation to unregistered land or part only of the land in the claimant's registered title(s), you must identify the benefiting land by attaching a plan showing the relevant land or (if appropriate) by referring to an existing reference on the title plan. Place 'X' in the appropriate box(es) and complete the first statement if appropriate. Enter reference, for example 'edged red'. If the benefiting land is unregistered, enclose any copy title deeds, if available.	5 Description of the benefiting land: ☐ The land is clearly identified on the attached plan and shown: ☐ The land is unregistered and is comprised in the copy title deeds enclosed
	6 Title number(s) of the burdened land (if registered):
Insert address including postcode (if any) or other description of the property, for example 'land adjoining 2 Acacia Avenue'. If the easement affects unregistered land or part only of the land in one or more registered titles, you must identify the burdened land by attaching a plan showing the relevant land or (if appropriate) by referring to an existing reference on the title plan. Place 'X' in the appropriate box(es) and complete the first statement if appropriate. Enter reference, for example 'edged red'. If the burdened land is unregistered, enclose any copy title deeds, if available.	7 Description of the burdened land: ☐ The land is clearly identified on the attached plan and shown: ☐ The land is unregistered and is comprised in the copy title deeds enclosed
Insert name and address of any known freehold owner of the land or person thought to be the freehold owner, such as the person having the unregistered documentary title to the land or being the registered proprietor of registered land, and/or any tenants and/or mortgagees. If not known, please state this by inserting 'not known'.	8 Identity of the freehold owner of the burdened land or person thought to be the owner and related persons:
Describe the easement claimed to have been acquired by prescription as it might be described in the register. For example, 'a right of way with or without vehicles for the benefit of [describe benefiting land] over [describe burdened land]'.	9 Easement claimed:

Insert details of the facts relied on to support the claim that an easement has been acquired by prescription.	10 Details of user:
Insert details of date and circumstances in which the user in panel 10 started and finished. Any 'gaps' must be specified if the period is not continuous.	11 Period of user:
Place 'X' in one box only and complete the relevant statement if appropriate. Insert details, including dates, and attach any available correspondence or other relevant documentation. If you place 'X' in the second box you are unlikely to establish a claim to the easement by prescription.	12 User without force, secrecy or permission I confirm that ☐ to the best of my knowledge and belief, the user has always been exercised without force, secrecy or permission ☐ the user has not always been exercised without force, secrecy or permission because:
Insert details of any past or present contact with the owner of the burdened land or person thought to be the owner and/or any tenants and/or mortgagees of that land, including dates. If none, please state this by inserting 'none'. If there has been any dispute concerning the claimed right, please provide details, including dates. Attach copies of all available correspondence or documents relating to the contact or dispute.	13 Contact with freehold owner of the burdened land and related persons:
Insert any other relevant details, (if any).	14 Other relevant details
If the person making the statement is unable to sign it, this wording will need to be amended to comply with rule 215A(5) and (6) of the Land Registration Rules 2003. In addition, and in cases where the person making the statement is unable to read, there will need to be an appropriate certificate: see rule 215A(4) and (5).	15 I believe that the facts and matters contained in this statement are true Signature (of person(s) making this statement): Print full name: Date:

WARNING

If the application proceeds, notice of the application (accompanied by a copy of this statement of truth) may be sent by the Registrar to the owner of the land or any person thought to be the owner and/or any other person upon whom the Registrar considers it necessary or desirable to serve notice.

If you dishonestly enter information or make a statement that you know is, or might be, untrue or misleading, and intend by doing so to make a gain for yourself or another person, or to cause loss or the risk of loss to another person, you may commit the offence of fraud under section 1 of the Fraud Act 2006, the maximum penalty for which is 10 years' imprisonment or an unlimited fine, or both.

Failure to complete this form with proper care may result in a loss of protection under the Land Registration Act 2002 if, as a result, a mistake is made in the register.

Under section 66 of the Land Registration Act 2002 most documents (including this form) kept by the registrar relating to an application to the registrar or referred to in the register are open to public inspection and copying. If you believe a document contains prejudicial information, you may apply for that part of the document to be made exempt using Form EX1, under rule 136 of the Land Registration Rules 2003.

Sign and Lock >

FORM 28: SAMPLE DETAILS in a statement of truth in support of an application to register the benefit of an easement by prescription as an appurtenant right[1]

EASEMENT CLAIMED

(*to be inserted in panel 9 of the statement of truth*)

A right of way on foot over (describe the burdened land).

DETAILS OF USER

(*to be inserted in panel 10 of the statement of truth*)

I have regularly walked across (*describe the burdened land*) to gain access between (*describe the land benefited*) and the main road.

1 See Form 27.

FORM 29: OBJECTION to registration of the benefit of an easement by prescription as an appurtenant right

Dear Sir,

Title Number: . . . .

Property: . . . .

Dated: . . . . 20 . . .

We, as solicitors for [B] of (*address*) ("the Objector") give notice to the Chief Land Registrar that we object to the pending application by [A] of (*address*) ("the Applicant") to register the benefit of an easement by prescription as an appurtenant right to the above mentioned land belonging to the Applicant ("the red land").

1. The Objector is the registered proprietor of the land adjoining the red land at (*address*), which is registered at HM Land Registry under title number . . . . ("the blue land").

2. The Applicant claims that for the last 24 years he has openly, without force and without the permission of the Objector, walked across the forecourt of the blue land to gain access from the red land to the main road. The route of the right of way claimed ("the route") is marked in brown on the plan enclosed, which also shows the extent of the red land and the blue land.

3. It is denied that the Applicant has acquired a right of way along the route.

4. It is certainly true that the Applicant started using the route 24 years ago. But at that time the Applicant and the Objector were good friends and the Objector recalls that the Applicant expressly asked for permission to use the route, which was readily given.

5. Unfortunately, about 10 years ago the Applicant and the Objector fell out. The Applicant alleged the Objector had behaved inappropriately at the Applicant's daughter's wedding. As a result of this the Objector told the Applicant to stay off the blue land in the future.

6. The Objector then erected a fence between the parties' properties, so that the Applicant could no longer gain access to the blue land and use the route. Part of the fence was later broken down (the Objector believes by the Applicant) and if the Applicant has continued to use the route it has only been because of the force he used to break down the fence.

For these reasons we oppose the Applicant's application and ask you not to accede to it.

Yours faithfully,

(Signature)

FORM 30: REPLY to an objection to registration of the benefit of an easement by prescription as an appurtenant right

Dear Sir,

Title Number: . . . .

Property: . . . .

Dated: . . . . 20 . . .

We, as solicitors for [A] of (*address*) ("the Applicant") reply as follows to the objection dated . . . . 20 . . . given on behalf of [B] of (*address*) ("the Objector"):

1. For the last 24 years the Applicant has openly, without force and without the permission of the Objector, walked across the forecourt of the blue land to gain access from the red land to the main road. The route is indeed as described in the objection, and it affords a considerable short cut to the Applicant whose property has no direct access to the main road but only to a side road.

2. The Applicant denies that he ever had any sort of permission to use the route from the Objector. The parties were not friendly. Indeed, for many years they hardly spoke after the Objector's wife complained about the Applicant burning autumn leaves. The Applicant recalls inviting the Objector to his daughter's wedding but denies that any incident occurred or that what is said to have happened is of any relevance to the application.

3. The Objector did put up a fence between the parties' properties, but it was erected in mid October 1987. Within a few hours the panel crossing the route was blown down in the great storm of that year and has never been replaced. The Applicant denies interfering with the fence in any way.

4. The Applicant maintains that he has acquired for the red land the benefit of a right of way by prescription over the blue land along the route, at common law, by lost modern grant and under the Prescription Act 1832.

5. In the circumstances, we invite you to register the benefit of this right of way as appurtenant to the red land.

Yours faithfully,

(Signature)

6: ALTERATION OF THE REGISTER TO CORRECT A MISTAKE

FORM 31: STATUTORY DECLARATION in support of an application to alter the register to correct a mistake (land incorrectly registered)

I, [A], of . . . . solemnly and sincerely declare as follows:

1. I am the registered proprietor of the land at (address), which is registered at HM Land Registry under title number . . . . ("the blue land"). The blue land is shown edged in blue on the plan annexed hereto.
2. [B] is the registered proprietor of the following land at (address), which is registered at HM Land Registry under title number . . . . :

   (1) the land shown edged in green on the plan annexed hereto ("the green land"), which lies immediately to the north of the blue land; and

   (2) the land shown edged in red on the plan annexed hereto ("the red land"), which lies immediately to the west of the green land.
3. The blue, green and red land was in common ownership until 2005 when it was still all unregistered land. In 2006 the then owner, [C], transferred only the red land to [B]. In 2007 [B] was registered as the first proprietor of the red land, but by mistake the title plan shows him to be registered as the proprietor of the green land as well.
4. In 2013 [C] transferred the green and blue land to me. In 2014 I was registered as the first proprietor of the blue land. HM Land Registry refused to register me as the proprietor of the green land on the basis that it already fell within [B]'s registered title.
5. I have a better paper title to the green land than [B] does.
6. I ask for the register to be altered under paragraph 5 (a) of Schedule 4 of the Land Registration Act 2002 by removing the green land from [B]'s title plan and including it within my title plan.

And I make this solemn declaration conscientiously believing the same to be true by virtue of the Statutory Declarations Act 1835.

(Signature of declarant)

Declared at . . . .

this . . . . day of . . . . before me,

(Signature) . . . .

Name . . . .

Address . . . .

Qualification . . . .

FORM 32: OBJECTION to alteration of the register to correct a mistake (land incorrectly registered)

Dear Sir,

Title Number: . . . . . .

Property: . . . .

Dated: . . . .

We, as solicitors for [B] of (*address*) ("the Objector") give notice to the Chief Land Registrar that we object to the pending application by [A] of (*address*) ("the Applicant") to alter the register by the removal of the green land from the Objector's registered title. Our grounds are as follows:

1. On the true construction of the transfer made between [C] and the Objector in 2006, [C] transferred to the Objector not only the red land, but the green land as well. Accordingly the Objector was correctly registered as the proprietor of both the red and green land and there is no mistake in the register.
2. Alternatively, if the 2006 transfer did not include green land, the Applicant's application amounts to one for rectification as defined byparagraph 1 of Schedule 4 of the Land Registration Act 2002 as any correction would prejudicially affect the Objector's title.
3. The Objector is a proprietor in possession of the green land – it consists of a small outhouse in which he stores his deck chairs. The Objector does not consent to the application.

For these reasons we oppose the Applicant's application and ask you not to accede to it.

Yours faithfully,

(Signature)

FORM 33: REPLY to an objection to alteration of the register to correct a mistake (land incorrectly registered)

Dear Sir,

Title Number: . . . . . .

Property: . . . .

Dated: . . . .

We, as solicitors for [A] of (*address*) ("the Applicant") reply as follows to the objection dated . . . . given on behalf of [B] of (*address*) ("the Objector"):

1. It is denied that the Objector is a proprietor in possession of the disputed land within paragraph 6 (2) of Schedule 4 of the Land Registration Act 2002. Although he does keep his deck chairs in the small outhouse on the green land, he only does so by virtue of permission given to him by the Applicant. In any event, the small outhouse is also used by the Applicant who stores his barbecue in it.
2. Alternatively, the Applicant contends that the Objector is not entitled to the protection given to a proprietor in possession.
3. This is not a case of rectification as the title plan only shows a general boundary: see Derbyshire County Council v Fallon [2007] 3 EGLR 44.
4. Alternatively, if this is a case of rectification, the Applicant relies upon the exception within paragraph 6 (2)(a) of Schedule 4 of the Land Registration Act 2002, namely that the Objector has by his lack of proper care caused or substantially contributed to the mistake which has been made by HM Land Registry in including the green land on his title plan and refusing to include it on the Applicant's title plan.
5. If the Objector's solicitors had carefully checked the title plan when it was sent to them after first registration it would have been quite apparent that the green land was not included within the 2006 transfer. They should immediately have asked HM Land Registry to have made the necessary correction.

Yours faithfully,

(Signature)

FORM 34: STATUTORY DECLARATION in support of an application to alter the register to correct a mistake (forgery)

I, [A], of . . . . solemnly and sincerely declare as follows:

1. In 2010 I bought a flat at (*address*) ("the flat") and was registered as the proprietor at HM Land Registry under title number . . . .
2. In 2012 I retired to Spain and left the flat occupied by my daughter, [B].
3. I did not give [B] a power of attorney and she had no authority whatsoever to deal with the flat.
4. I recently tried to raise some money on the security of the flat, and discovered to my amazement that the flat is now registered in [B]'s name.
5. I have been show a transfer in Form TR1 which purports to show that I transferred the flat to [B]. It is not my signature on the transfer and I have never heard of [C] who is supposed to have witnessed my signature.
6. I am very concerned that [B] is intending to use the flat as security for a loan she wishes to use for the purposes of her business.
7. I would ask for [B]'s name to be removed from the proprietorship register of the flat and for my name to be restored.

And I make this solemn declaration conscientiously believing the same to be true by virtue of the Statutory Declarations Act 1835.

(Signature)

Declared at . . . .

this . . . . . . day of . . . . before me,

(Signature)

Name . . . .

Address . . . .

Qualification . . . .

FORM 35: OBJECTION to alteration of the register to correct a mistake (forgery)

Dear Sir,

Title Number: . . . . . .

Property: . . . .

Dated: . . . .

We, as solicitors for [B] of (*address*) ("the Objector") give notice to the Chief Land Registrar that we object to the pending application by [A] of (*address*) ("the Applicant") to alter the register by the removal of the Objector's name from the proprietorship register of the flat.

Our instructions are that in 2012, at the time that she retired to Spain, the Applicant decided to give the flat to the Objector. She duly executed a transfer in Form TR1. The consideration was expressed to be natural love and affection. The Applicant's signature was witnessed by [C], who is a solicitors' receptionist.

Last year the Applicant was reconciled with her son by a first marriage, [D], who was furious that the flat had been transferred to the Objector. He had a violent argument with the Objector about this. We believe that the Applicant is being put under pressure by [D] and now regrets making the transfer. The allegation of forgery is wholly without foundation.

For these reasons we oppose the Applicant's application and ask you not to accede to it.

Yours faithfully,

(Signature)

Appendix 14

REFERENCES FROM LAND REGISTRY TO THE TRIBUNAL

1: Land Registry's Case Summary and Notice of Referral

Form 36: Case Summary on reference to the Tribunal

Form 37: Notice of Referral on reference to the Tribunal

2: The Tribunal's Notices and Directions concerning Court Proceedings

Form 38: Notice proposing party commences court proceedings (beneficial interest)

Form 39: Notice proposing party commences court proceedings (non-beneficial interest)

Form 40: Notice proposing adjournment after party has commenced court proceedings (non-directed) (beneficial interest)

Form 41: Notice proposing adjournment after party has commenced court proceedings (non-directed) (non-beneficial interest)

Form 42: Notice proposing adjournment after party has proposed commencing court proceedings (non-directed) (beneficial interest)

Form 43: Notice proposing adjournment after party has proposed commencing court proceedings (non-directed) (non-beneficial interest)

Form 44: Direction to party to commence court proceedings

Form 45: Letter staying the proceedings pending outcome of court proceedings (directed)

Form 46: Direction staying the proceedings pending outcome of court proceedings (non-directed)

Form 47: Order implementing the decision of the court

3: The Tribunal's Directions to serve Statements of Case

Form 48: Direction naming the parties and directing the Applicant to serve a statement of case.

Form 49: Direction naming the parties and directing the Respondent to serve a statement of case in response.

4: Statements of Case

Form 50: Statement of Case of the Applicant: adverse possession of unregistered land.

Form 51: Statement of Case in response of the Respondent: adverse possession of unregistered land.

Form 52: List of Documents

Form 53: Statement of Case of the Applicant: adverse possession of registered land under Schedule 6 to the Land Registration Act 2002

Form 54: Statement of Case in response of the Respondent: adverse possession of registered land under Schedule 6 to the Land Registration Act 2002

Form 55: Statement of Case of the Applicant: adverse possession of registered land under the transitional provisions

Form 56: Statement of Case in response of the Respondent: adverse possession of registered land under the transitional provisions

Form 57: Statement of Case of the Applicant (the beneficiary of a unilateral notice designated the Applicant by the Tribunal): cancellation of a unilateral notice relating to a restrictive covenant

Form 58: Statement of Case in response of the Respondent (the maker of the application to cancel a unilateral notice designated the Respondent by the Tribunal): cancellation of a unilateral notice relating to a restrictive covenant

Form 59: Statement of Case of the Applicant (the cautioner designated the Applicant by the Tribunal): cancellation of a caution against dealings relating to proprietary estoppel

Form 60: Statement of Case in response of the Respondent (the maker of the application to cancel a caution designated the Respondent by the Tribunal): cancellation of a caution against dealings relating to proprietary estoppel

Form 61: Statement of Case of the Applicant: entry of a restriction relating to a beneficial interest

Form 62: Statement of Case in response of the Respondent: entry of a restriction relating to a beneficial interest

Form 63: Statement of Case of the Applicant: entry of the benefit of an easement by prescription

Form 64: Statement of Case in response of the Respondent: entry of the benefit of an easement by prescription

Form 63: Statement of Case of the Applicant: entry of the benefit of an easement by prescription

Form 64: Statement of Case in response of the Respondent: entry of the benefit of an easement by prescription

Form 65: Statement of Case of the Applicant: alteration of the register to correct a mistake (land incorrectly registered)

Form 66: Statement of Case in response of the Respondent: alteration of the register to correct a mistake (land incorrectly registered)

Form 67: Statement of Case of the Applicant: alteration of the register to correct a mistake (forgery)

Form 68: Statement of Case in response of the Respondent: alteration of the register to correct a mistake (forgery)

5: Applications, Directions and Orders in the course of the Proceedings before the Tribunal

Form 69: Application for an extension of time

Form 70: Order granting an extension of time

Form 71: Application of the Respondent for summary disposal

Form 72: Witness Statement in support of an application for summary disposal

Form 73: Order for summary disposal

Form 74: Application for security for costs

Form 75: Witness Statement in support of an application for security for costs

Form 76: Order for security for costs

Form 77: Application for permission to adduce expert evidence

Form 78: Order for permission to adduce expert evidence

Form 79: Application for a summons to require a person to attend to as a witness

Form 80: Summons to require a person to attend as a witness

Form 81: Application for an order to produce documents

Form 82: Order to produce documents

Form 83: Letter proposing mediation

Form 84: Mediation Agreement

Form 85: Notice of withdrawal

Form 86: Order giving permission to withdraw

Form 87: Order with sanctions: breach *will* lead to the striking out of the proceedings

Form 88: Order with sanctions: breach *may* lead to the striking out of the proceedings

Form 89: General Directions

Form 90: Particulars required in connection with a hearing

Form 91: Order including a direction to the Registrar

Form 92: Order by consent

6: Costs Orders

Form 93: Order for costs following a summary assessment

Form 94: Direction for a detailed assessment of costs

7: Setting Aside, Reviews and Appeals

Form 95: Application to the Tribunal to set aside a decision

Form 96: Order of the Tribunal setting a decision aside

References From Land Registry to the Tribunal

Form 97: Application to the Tribunal to review a decision

Form 98: Application to the Tribunal for permission to appeal

Form 99: Application to the Upper Tribunal for permission to appeal

Form 100: Application to the Tribunal for a stay pending appeal

1: LAND REGISTRY'S CASE SUMMARY AND NOTICE OF REFERRAL

Form 36: Case Summary on reference to the Tribunal

HM LAND REGISTRY

CASE SUMMARY

This case summary accompanies a notice to the Land Registration division of the Property Chamber, First-tier Tribunal under rule 5 of the Land Registration (Referral to the Adjudicator to HM Land Registry) Rules 2003.[1]

Title number:	. . . . . .
Property:	Whiteacre Farm (*address*)
Applicant:	[A]
Applicant's address	(*address*)
Objector:	[B]
Objector's address:	(*address*)
Applicant's legal or other representative:	Rural & Co of (*address*)
Objector's legal or other representative:	Urban LLP of (*address*)
Summary of core facts:	The Objector has paper title to the whole of Whiteacre Farm, (*address*). Whiteacre Farm is unregistered land.
Details of application:	Date of Application: [31 December 2013].
	The Applicant has applied for first registration as proprietor with possessory title of 2 fields within Whiteacre Farm ("the disputed land"). The basis for the application is adverse possession.
Details of objection:	Date of objection: [1 April 2014].
	Notice of the application was served on the Objector. The Objector has objected to the application by letter dated [28 March 2014] on the grounds that the Applicant has not been in possession of the disputed land for 12 years, has not shown the necessary intention to possess and has acknowledged the Objector's title.
Anything else that the Registrar considers to be appropriate:	Nothing.
Copy documents attached:	1. Application in Form FR1 dated . . . . 20. . . . . . 2. Statement of truth of the Applicant dated . . . . 20. . . . . . . 3. Plan showing the disputed land edged red. 4. Notice served on the objector dated . . . . 20. . . . . . . 5. Letter from the Objector's solicitors to Land Registry dated . . . . 20. . . . . . . 6. Letter from the Applicant's solicitors to Land Registry dated . . . . 20. . . . . . .

Signed . . . . Land Registrar for and on behalf of the Chief Land Registrar

Dated . . . . 20. . . . . .

[1] Although the Tribunal replaced the Adjudicator on 1 July 2013, the title of the rules regulating the reference from Land Registry have not been renamed.

Form 37: Notice of Referral on reference to the Tribunal

Notice to parties of referral to the Land Registration division of the Property Chamber, First-tier Tribunal

Section 73 (7) Land Registration Act 2002

Important -This notice is not a circular. Please read it carefully. If you do not know what to do, you should consider taking legal advice.

Title number	. . . . . .
Property	Whiteacre Farm (*address*)
Applicant	[A]
Objector	[B]

Dear [A]

I am writing to you about the application and objection affecting the above title.

As it is not been possible to dispose of the objection by agreement the matter in dispute must now be referred to the Land Registration division of the Property Chamber, First-tier Tribunal in accordance with section 73(7) of the Land Registration Act 2002. This letter constitutes formal notice of the referral to the Land Registration division of the Property Chamber, First-tier Tribunal pursuant to rule 5 (2)(b) of the Land Registration (Referral to the Adjudicator to HM Land Registry) Rules 2003.[1] A copy of the case summary sent to the Land Registration division of the Property Chamber, First-tier Tribunal is enclosed.

I am sending copies of this letter and the Case Summary to your solicitor today.

The Land Registration division of the Property Chamber, First-tier Tribunal will contact you (or your solicitor or other representative, if appropriate) in due course.

In the meantime, should you need to contact the Land Registration division of the Property Chamber, First-tier Tribunal, the address is as follows:

The Land Registration division of the Property Chamber, First-tier Tribunal

3rd floor
10 Alfred Place
London WC1E 7LR

If you would like to discuss any points arising from its letter or in relation to Land Registry's future role in the dispute process, please contact . . . . . . who is the departmental lawyer dealing with the matter by telephone on . . . . . . or by email on . . . .

Yours sincerely

1 Although the Tribunal replaced the Adjudicator on 1 July 2013, the title of the rules regulating the reference from Land Registry have not been renamed.

2: THE TRIBUNAL'S NOTICES AND DIRECTIONS CONCERNING COURT PROCEEDINGS

Form 38: Notice proposing party commences court proceedings (beneficial interest)

Property Chamber
Land Registration
First-tier Tribunal
3rd Floor
10 Alfred Place
London WC1E 7LR

Tel:	020 7291 7250
Fax:	020 7291 7251
Goldfax:	0870 739 4134
DX:	DX305001 Tottenham Court Road 5
Email:	landregistration@hmcts.gsi.gov.uk
Website:	www.justice.gov.uk/tribunals

Smiths, Solicitors

1 Reservoir Street
Ashopton

DE99 0XX

Your Ref: GG/HH/123

Our Ref: REF/2013/0680

5 September 2014

Dear Sir/Madam,

ZYX98765

Bea Lowater vs. Mark Highwater

00 Howden Bank, Derwent

The Tribunal's services are free of charge. However, there is power to decide whether to make orders for costs in Tribunal proceedings. The general rule is that the losing party will pay the successful party's costs, as well as his own.

We have received notice of a reference of the above case on the 29 August 2014 from the Land Registry Birkenhead Office. The matter has been given the reference number REF/2013/0680. This reference number must be quoted on all documents and communications. Please find attached an explanatory leaflet and extracts from the Rules for your information.

The Tribunal has directed that you will be the **Applicant** in these proceedings. The Respondent's address for service is:

Jones, solicitors
2, Flood Street
Ashopton DE99 1YY

Notice proposing party commences court proceedings (beneficial interest)

The Tribunal intends to make a direction under section 110(1) of the Land Registration Act 2002 that one of the parties commence court proceedings. The Tribunal's jurisdiction to grant relief in cases involving a claim to a beneficial interest is limited. For example, there is no power to

- order the sale of a Property;
- order a payment of money (other than the costs of these proceedings); or
- deal with disputes over goods.

Please see the enclosed explanatory leaflet for further details.

You have 28 days from the date of this letter to make any representations as to

a) whether or not the Tribunal should make such a direction; and, if so,

b) which party should be directed to commence court proceedings;

c) the time within which court proceedings should commence; and

d) the questions the court should determine.

Yours faithfully,

John Smith

For the Tribunal

Form 39: Notice proposing party commences court proceedings (non-beneficial interest)

Property Chamber
Land Registration
First-tier Tribunal
3rd Floor
10 Alfred Place
London WC1E 7LR

Tel:	020 7291 7250
Fax:	020 7291 7251
Goldfax:	0870 739 4134
DX:	DX305001 Tottenham Court Road 5
Email:	landregistration@hmcts.gsi.gov.uk
Website:	www.justice.gov.uk/tribunals

Smiths, Solicitors

1 Reservoir Street
Ashopton

DE99 0XX

Your Ref: GG/HH/123

Our Ref: REF/2013/0680

5 September 2014

Dear Sir/Madam,

ZYX98765

Bea Lowater vs. Mark Highwater

00 Howden Bank, Derwent

The Tribunal's services are free of charge. However, there is power to decide whether to make orders for costs in Tribunal proceedings. The general rule is that the losing party will pay the successful party's costs, as well as his own.

We have received notice of a reference of the above case on 29 August 2014 from the Land Registry Birkenhead Office. The matter has been given the reference number REF/2013/0680. This reference number must be quoted on all documents and communications. Please find attached an explanatory leaflet and extracts from the Rules for your information.

The Tribunal has directed that you will be the **Applicant** in these proceedings. The Respondent's address for service is

Jones, solicitors
2, Flood Street
Ashopton DE99 1YY

Notice proposing party commences court proceedings (non-beneficial interest)

The Tribunal intends to make a direction under section 110(1) of the Land Registration Act 2002 to the effect that one of the parties commence court proceedings. The Tribunal's jurisdiction to grant relief in cases such as these is limited to:-

- deciding whether the disputed application referred to him by the Land Registry should be
- cancelled or
  - given effect to and
  - making any order for costs in respect of proceedings before it.

There is no power to deal with any other issue or grant any other remedies.

You have 28 days from the date of this letter to make representations or objections as to:

a) whether the Tribunal should make such a direction;

b) which party should be directed to commence court proceedings;

c) the time within which court proceedings should commence; and

d) the questions the court should determine.

Yours faithfully,

John Smith

For the Tribunal

Form 40: Notice proposing adjournment after party has commenced court proceedings (non-directed) (beneficial interest)

Property Chamber
Land Registration
First-tier Tribunal
3rd Floor
10 Alfred Place
London WC1E 7LR

Tel:	020 7291 7250
Fax:	020 7291 7251
Goldfax:	0870 739 4134
DX:	DX305001 Tottenham Court Road 5
Email:	landregistration@hmcts.gsi.gov.uk
Website:	www.justice.gov.uk/tribunals

Smiths, Solicitors

1 Reservoir Street
Ashopton

DE99 0XX

Your Ref: GG/HH/123

Our Ref: REF/2013/0680

5 September 2014

Dear Sir/Madam,

ZYX98765

Bea Lowater vs. Mark Highwater

00 Howden Bank, Derwent

The Tribunal's services are free of charge. However, there is power to decide whether to make orders for costs in Tribunal proceedings. The general rule is that the losing party will pay the successful party's costs, as well as his own.

We have received notice of a reference of the above case on 29 August 2014 from the Land Registry Birkenhead Office. The matter has been given the reference number REF/2013/0680. This reference number must be quoted on all documents and communications. Please find enclosed an explanatory leaflet and extracts from the Rules for your information and refer to our website for further guidance.

The Tribunal has named you as the **Applicant** in this matter. The other party's address for service is

Jones, solicitors
2, Flood Street
Ashopton DE99 1YY

The case summary provided by the Land Registry indicates that one of the parties has already commenced court proceedings covering the issues before the Tribunal. If so the Tribunal is minded to adjourn these proceedings to await the outcome of those court proceedings.

If court proceedings have already been issued, the party who issued them must serve a written notice on the Tribunal within 7 days of receiving this letter setting out the following information:

(i) confirmation that court proceedings have been issued

(ii) the date of issue of the court proceedings

(iii) the names and any known addresses of the parties to the court proceedings

(iv) the name of the court at which the court proceedings are pending

(v) the case number allocated to the court proceedings and

(vi) the way and extent to which the court proceedings concern or relate to the matter before the Tribunal.

Possible direction to commence court proceedings

Unless the above information is provided, the Tribunal may direct that one of the parties commences court proceedings.

The Tribunal's powers in cases involving a claim to a beneficial interest are limited. For example, there is no power to

- order the sale of a Property;
- order a payment of money (other than the costs of the Tribunal's proceedings); or
- deal with disputes over goods.

Please see the enclosed explanatory leaflet for further details.

You have 28 days from the date of this letter to make representations or objections as to

a) whether the Tribunal should make such a direction;

b) which party should be directed to commence court proceedings;

c) the time within which court proceedings should commence; and

d) the questions the court should determine.

We look forward to hearing from you.

Yours faithfully,

John Smith

For the Tribunal

Form 41: Notice proposing adjournment after party has commenced court proceedings (non-directed) (non-beneficial interest)

Property Chamber
Land Registration
First-tier Tribunal
3rd Floor
10 Alfred Place
London WC1E 7LR

Tel:	020 7291 7250
Fax:	020 7291 7251
Goldfax:	0870 739 4134
DX:	DX305001 Tottenham Court Road 5
Email:	landregistration@hmcts.gsi.gov.uk
Website:	www.justice.gov.uk/tribunals

Smiths, Solicitors

1 Reservoir Street
Ashopton

DE99 0XX

Your Ref: GG/HH/123

Our Ref: REF/2013/0680

5 September 2014

Dear Sir/Madam,

ZYX98765

Bea Lowater vs. Mark Highwater

00 Howden Bank, Derwent

The Tribunal's services are free of charge. However, there is power to decide whether to make orders for costs in Tribunal proceedings. The general rule is that the losing party will pay the successful party's costs, as well as his own.

We have received notice of a reference of the above case on 29 August 2014 from the Land Registry Birkenhead Office. The matter has been given the reference number REF/2013/0680. This reference number must be quoted on all documents and communications. Please find enclosed an explanatory leaflet and extracts from the Rules for your information.

The Tribunal has named you as the **Applicant** in this matter. The other party's address for service is

Jones, solicitors
2, Flood Street
Ashopton DE99 1YY

Possible adjournment

The case summary provided by the Land Registry indicates that one of the parties has already commenced court proceedings covering the issues before the Tribunal. If so the Tribunal is minded to adjourn these proceedings to await the outcome of those court proceedings.

If court proceedings have already been issued, the party who issued them must serve a written notice on the Tribunal within 7 days of receiving this letter setting out the following information:

(i) that court proceedings have been issued

(ii) the date of issue of the court proceedings

(iii) the names and any known addresses of the parties to the court proceedings

(iv) the name of the court at which the court proceedings are pending

(v) the case number allocated to the court proceedings and

(vi) the way and extent to which the court proceedings concern or relate to the matter before the Tribunal.

Possible direction to commence court proceedings

Unless the above information is provided, the Tribunal may direct that one of the parties commences court proceedings.

The Tribunal's powers in cases such as these are limited to (i) deciding whether the disputed application referred by the Land Registry should be cancelled or given effect to and (ii) making any order for costs in respect of the Tribunal's proceedings. There is no power to deal with any other issue or grant any other remedies.

Please see the enclosed explanatory leaflet for further details.

You have 28 days from the date of this letter to make representations or objections as to

a) whether the Tribunal should make such a direction;

b) which party should be directed to commence court proceedings;

c) the time within which court proceedings should commence; and

d) the questions the court should determine.

We look forward to hearing from you.

Yours faithfully,

John Smith

For the Tribunal

Form 42: Notice proposing adjournment after party has proposed commencing court proceedings (non-directed) (beneficial interest)

Property Chamber
Land Registration
First-tier Tribunal
3rd Floor
10 Alfred Place
London WC1E 7LR

Tel:	020 7291 7250
Fax:	020 7291 7251
Goldfax:	0870 739 4134
DX:	DX305001 Tottenham Court Road 5
Email:	landregistration@hmcts.gsi.gov.uk
Website:	www.justice.gov.uk/tribunals

Smiths, Solicitors

1 Reservoir Street
Ashopton

DE99 0XX

Your Ref: GG/HH/123

Our Ref: REF/2013/0680

5 September 2014

Dear Sir/Madam,

ZYX98765

Bea Lowater vs. Mark Highwater

00 Howden Bank, Derwent

The Tribunal's services are free of charge. However, there is power to decide whether to make orders for costs in Tribunal proceedings. The general rule is that the losing party will pay the successful party's costs, as well as his own.

We have received notice of a reference of the above case on 29 August 2014 from the Land Registry Birkenhead Office. The matter has been given the reference number REF/2013/0680. This reference number must be quoted on all documents and communications. Please find enclosed an explanatory leaflet and extracts from the Rules for your information.

The Tribunal has named you as the **Applicant** in this matter. The other party's address for service is

Jones, solicitors
2, Flood Street
Ashopton DE99 1YY

The case summary provided by the Land Registry indicates that one of the parties proposes to commence court proceedings which will cover the issues before the Tribunal. If so, and if court proceedings are imminent, the Tribunal would be minded to adjourn these proceedings to await the outcome of those court proceedings.

Please let us know by 3 October 2014 if you are intending to issue court proceedings and, if so, by what date.

If in fact court proceedings have already been issued, the party who issued them must serve a written notice on the Tribunal within 7 days of receiving this letter setting out the following information:

(i) confirmation that court proceedings have been issued

(ii) the date of issue of the court proceedings

(iii) the names and any known addresses of the parties to the court proceedings

(iv) the name of the court at which the court proceedings are pending

(v) the case number allocated to the court proceedings and

(vi) the way and extent to which the court proceedings concern or relate to the matter before the Tribunal.

Possible direction to commence court proceedings

Unless court proceedings have already been issued, the Tribunal may direct that one of the parties commences court proceedings.

The Tribunal's powers in cases involving a claim to a beneficial interest are limited. For example, there is no power to

- order the sale of a Property;
- order a payment of money (other than the costs of the Tribunal's proceedings); or
- deal with disputes over goods.

Please see the enclosed explanatory leaflet for further details.

You have 28 days from the date of this letter to make representations or objections as to

a) whether the Tribunal should make such a direction;

b) which party should be directed to commence court proceedings;

c) the time within which court proceedings should commence; and

d) the questions the court should determine.

We look forward to hearing from you.

Yours faithfully,

John Smith

For the Tribunal

Form 43: Notice proposing adjournment after party has proposed commencing court proceedings (non-directed) (non-beneficial interest)

Property Chamber
Land Registration
First-tier Tribunal
3rd Floor
10 Alfred Place
London WC1E 7LR

Tel:	020 7291 7250
Fax:	020 7291 7251
Goldfax:	0870 739 4134
DX:	DX305001 Tottenham Court Road 5
Email:	landregistration@hmcts.gsi.gov.uk
Website:	www.justice.gov.uk/tribunals

Smiths, Solicitors

1 Reservoir Street
Ashopton

DE99 0XX

Your Ref: GG/HH/123

Our Ref: REF/2013/0680

5 September 2014

Dear Sir/Madam,

ZYX98765

Bea Lowater vs. Mark Highwater

00 Howden Bank, Derwent

The Tribunal's services are free of charge. However, there is power to decide whether to make orders for costs in Tribunal proceedings. The general rule is that the losing party will pay the successful party's costs, as well as his own.

We have received notice of a reference of the above case on 29 August 2014 from the Land Registry Birkenhead Office. The matter has been given the reference number REF/2013/0680. This reference number must be quoted on all documents and communications. Please find enclosed an explanatory leaflet and extracts from the Rules for your information.

The Tribunal has named you as the **Applicant** in this matter. The other party's address for service is

Jones, solicitors
2, Flood Street
Ashopton DE99 1YY

Possible adjournment

The case summary provided by the Land Registry indicates that one of the parties has already commenced court proceedings covering the issues before the Tribunal. If so the Tribunal is minded to adjourn these proceedings to await the outcome of those court proceedings.

If court proceedings have already been issued, the party who issued them must serve a written notice on the Tribunal within 7 days of receiving this letter setting out the following information:

(i) that court proceedings have been issued

(ii) the date of issue of the court proceedings

(iii) the names and any known addresses of the parties to the court proceedings

(iv) the name of the court at which the court proceedings are pending

(v) the case number allocated to the court proceedings and

(vi) the way and extent to which the court proceedings concern or relate to the matter before the Tribunal.

Possible direction to commence court proceedings

Unless the above information is provided, the Tribunal may direct that one of the parties commences court proceedings.

The Tribunal's powers in cases such as these are limited to (i) deciding whether the disputed application referred by the Land Registry should be cancelled or given effect to and (ii) making any order for costs in respect of the Tribunal's proceedings. There is no power to deal with any other issue or grant any other remedies.

Please see the enclosed explanatory leaflet for further details.

You have 28 days from the date of this letter to make representations or objections as to

a) whether the Tribunal should make such a direction;

b) which party should be directed to commence court proceedings;

c) the time within which court proceedings should commence; and

d) the questions the court should determine.

We look forward to hearing from you.

Yours faithfully,

John Smith

For the Tribunal

Form 44: Direction to party to commence court proceedings

Property Chamber
Land Registration
First-tier Tribunal
3rd Floor
10 Alfred Place
London WC1E 7LR

Tel:	020 7291 7250
Fax:	020 7291 7251
Goldfax:	0870 739 4134
DX:	DX305001 Tottenham Court Road 5
Email:	landregistration@hmcts.gsi.gov.uk
Website:	www.justice.gov.uk/tribunals

Smiths, Solicitors

1 Reservoir Street
Ashopton

DE99 0XX

Your Ref: GG/HH/123

Our Ref: REF/2013/0680

27 March 2014

Dear Sir/Madam,

ZYX98765

Bea Lowater vs. Mark Highwater

00 Howden Bank, Derwent

The Tribunal has now considered the parties' representations/objections and has directed under section 110(1) of the Land Registration Act 2002 that the Applicant commences court proceedings on or before 21 April 2014. A copy of this direction is enclosed.

You are required to serve on the Tribunal within 14 days of the commencement of court proceedings a written notice containing the following information:-

(i) confirmation that court proceedings have been issued
(ii) the date of issue of the court proceedings
(iii) the names and any known addresses of the parties to the court proceedings
(iv) the name of the court at which the court proceedings are pending
(v) the case number allocated to the court proceedings and
(vi) the way and extent to which the court proceedings concern or relate to the matter before the Tribunal.

Failure to comply with these requirements may result in sanctions being imposed by the Tribunal.

Yours faithfully,

John Smith

For the Tribunal

Property Chamber
Land Registration
First-tier Tribunal

DIRECTION

Case Number:	**REF/2013/0680**
Title Number:	**ZYX98765**
Property:	**00 Howden Bank, Derwent**
Applicant:	**Bea Lowater**
Respondent:	**Mark Highwater**

IT IS ORDERED THAT the Applicant commence court proceedings on or before 5 p.m. on 21 April 2014.

The issue/s upon which the court should make its determination is/are as follows-

[ISSUE]

Dated this 27 March 2014

By Order of The Tribunal

Form 45: Letter Staying the proceedings pending outcome of court proceedings (directed)

Property Chamber
Land Registration
First-tier Tribunal
3rd Floor
10 Alfred Place
London WC1E 7LR

Tel:	020 7291 7250
Fax:	020 7291 7251
Goldfax:	0870 739 4134
DX:	DX305001 Tottenham Court Road 5
Email:	landregistration@hmcts.gsi.gov.uk
Website:	www.justice.gov.uk/tribunals

Smiths, Solicitors

1 Reservoir Street
Ashopton

DE99 0XX

Your Ref: GG/HH/123

Our Ref: REF/2013/0680

22 April 2014

Dear Sir/Madam,

ZYX98765

Bea Lowater vs. Mark Highwater

00 Howden Bank, Derwent

The Tribunal has now received the requisite notice that court proceedings have been issued in accordance with the direction dated 27 March 2014.

The Tribunal's proceedings are therefore automatically stayed pending the outcome of those court proceedings.

The party who commenced the court proceedings must serve a copy of the final court order on the Tribunal within 14 days of its being made.

Yours faithfully,

John Smith

For the Tribunal

Form 46: Direction staying the proceedings pending outcome of court proceedings (non-directed)

Property Chamber
Land Registration
First-tier Tribunal
3rd Floor
10 Alfred Place
London WC1E 7LR

Tel:	020 7291 7250
Fax:	020 7291 7251
Goldfax:	0870 739 4134
DX:	DX305001 Tottenham Court Road 5
Email:	landregistration@hmcts.gsi.gov.uk
Website:	www.justice.gov.uk/tribunals

Smiths, Solicitors

1 Reservoir Street
Ashopton

DE99 0XX

Your Ref: GG/HH/123

Our Ref: REF/2013/0680

27 March 2014

Dear Sir/Madam,

ZYX98765

Bea Lowater vs. Mark Highwater

00 Howden Bank, Derwent

Please find enclosed a copy of the directions made by the Tribunal in the above matter for your attention dated 27 March 2014.

Failure to comply with these requirements may result in sanctions being imposed by the Tribunal.

Yours faithfully,

John Smith

For the Tribunal

Property Chamber
Land Registration
First-tier Tribunal

DIRECTION

Case Number:	**REF/2013/0680**
Title Number:	**ZYX98765**
Property:	**00 Howden Bank, Derwent**
Applicant:	**Bea Lowater**
Respondent:	**Mark Highwater**

IT IS ORDERED THAT:

1. These proceedings be stayed pending the outcome of court proceedings commenced by the Applicant in the High Court, Chancery Division under case number HQ14Z0123456.

2. The Applicant must serve on the Tribunal within 14 days of the date that the matter before the court is finally disposed of, a copy of the final court order.

Dated this 27 March 2014

By Order of The Tribunal

Form 47: Order implementing the decision of the court

The Land Registration division of the Property Chamber, First-tier Tribunal orders the Chief Land Registrar as follows:

To give effect to the original application dated . . . . to register a restriction in the proprietorship register of the above property . . . .

This order is made following the declaration of the County Court sitting at . . . . in claim number . . . . . . dated . . . . that the Applicant has a beneficial interest in the above property, but the Court did not order a restriction to be entered in the proprietorship register of the above property.

3: THE TRIBUNAL'S DIRECTIONS TO SERVE STATEMENTS OF CASE

Form 48: Direction naming the parties and directing the Applicant to serve a statement of case

Property Chamber
Land Registration
First-tier Tribunal
3rd Floor
10 Alfred Place
London WC1E 7LR

Tel:	020 7291 7250
Fax:	020 7291 7251
Goldfax:	0870 739 4134
DX:	DX305001 Tottenham Court Road 5
Email:	landregistration@hmcts.gsi.gov.uk
Website:	www.justice.gov.uk/tribunals

Smiths, Solicitors

1 Reservoir Street
Ashopton

DE99 0XX

Your Ref: GG/HH/123

Our Ref: REF/2013/0680

5 September 2014

Dear Sir/Madam,

ZYX98765

Bea Lowater vs. Mark Highwater

00 Howden Bank, Derwent

The Tribunal's services are free of charge. However, there is power to decide whether to make orders for costs in Tribunal proceedings. The general rule is that the losing party will pay the successful party's costs, as well as his own.

We have received notice of a reference of the above case on the 13 August 2013 from the Land Registry Birkenhead Office. The matter has been given the reference number REF/2013/0680. This reference number must be quoted on all documents and communications. Please find attached an explanatory leaflet and extracts from the Rules for your information and refer to our website for further guidance.

The Tribunal has directed that you will be the **Applicant** in these proceedings.

As the Applicant you are required to serve on the **Tribunal and each of the other**

parties a Statement of Case by **5 p.m. on 5 October 2014.**

The Statement of Case must include:

(a) confirmation of your address for service

(b) the facts you intend to rely on in the proceedings

(c) a list of the documents available to you which

  (i) are important to your case and/or

  (ii) the Tribunal or any other party to the proceedings will require in order properly to understand your case

(d) copies of those documents

  and

(e) a signed Statement of Truth in the following terms: 'The Applicant believes that the facts contained in this Statement of Case are true'.

The address of the Respondent that we have on record for service is:

Jones, solicitors
2, Flood Street
Ashopton DE99 1YY

Once all parties have served their Statements of Case, the Tribunal will consider further directions. These will usually include disclosure of any further relevant documents and exchange of witness statements. Such directions will not normally be made before Statements of Case.

Please note that under rule 38 you must notify the Tribunal if a party commences court proceedings within 14 days of the court proceedings being issued.

Failure to comply with these requirements may result in sanctions being imposed by the Tribunal.

Please also note that the Tribunal's powers are limited. For example, the Tribunal cannot:-

- order the sale of a Property;
- order a payment of money (other than the costs of these proceedings); or
- deal with disputes over goods.

Please see the enclosed explanatory leaflet for further details.

Subject to judicial and court availability, it is expected that this case will be heard between [insert date] and [insert date].

Finally, you must copy to the Respondent(s) **all** letters and documents you send to us.

Yours faithfully,

John Smith

For the Tribunal

Form 49: Direction naming the parties and directing the Respondent to serve a statement of case in response

Property Chamber
Land Registration
First-tier Tribunal
3rd Floor
10 Alfred Place
London WC1E 7LR

Tel:	020 7291 7250
Fax:	020 7291 7251
Goldfax:	0870 739 4134
DX:	DX305001 Tottenham Court Road 5
Email:	landregistration@hmcts.gsi.gov.uk
Website:	www.justice.gov.uk/tribunals

Smiths, Solicitors

1 Reservoir Street
Ashopton

DE99 0XX

Your Ref: GG/HH/123

Our Ref: REF/2013/0680

5 September 2014

Dear Sir/Madam,

ZYX98765

Bea Lowater vs. Mark Highwater

00 Howden Bank, Derwent

The Tribunal's services are free of charge. However, there is power to decide whether to make orders for costs in Tribunal proceedings. The general rule is that the losing party will pay the successful party's costs, as well as his own.

We have received notice of a reference of the above case on the 13 August 2013 from the Land Registry Birkenhead Office. The matter has been given the reference number REF/2013/0680. This reference number must be quoted on all documents and communications. Please find attached an explanatory leaflet and extracts from the Rules for your information and refer to our website for further guidance.

The Tribunal has directed that you will be the **Respondent** in these proceedings.

As the **Respondent** you are required to serve on the **Tribunal and each of the other parties a Statement of Case in response to the Applicant's Statement of Case by 5pm 28 days after you receive the Applicant's Statement of Case.** The Applicant's Statement of Case is due on 20 August 2015.

The response must include:

(a) confirmation of your address for service

(b) the facts you intend to rely on in the proceedings

(c) a list of the documents available to you which

(i) are important to your case and/or

(ii) the Tribunal or any other party to the proceedings will require in order properly to understand your case

(d) copies of those documents

and

(e) a signed Statement of Truth in the following terms: 'The Respondent believes that the facts contained in this Statement of Case are true'.

The address of the Applicant that we have on record for service is:

Smiths, Solicitors
1 Reservoir Street
Ashopton DE99 0XX

Once all parties have served their Statements of Case and any responses have been served the Tribunal will consider further directions. These will usually include disclosure of any further relevant documents and exchange of witness statements. Such directions will not normally be made before Statements of Case.

Please note that under rule 38 you must notify the Tribunal if a party commences court proceedings within 14 days of the court proceedings being issued.

Failure to comply with these requirements may result in sanctions being imposed by the Tribunal.

Please also note that the Tribunal's powers are limited. For example, the Tribunal cannot:-

- order the sale of a Property;
- order a payment of money (other than the costs of these proceedings); or
- deal with disputes over goods.

Please see the enclosed explanatory leaflet for further details.

Subject to judicial and court availability, it is expected that this case will be heard between [insert date] and [insert date]

Finally, you must copy to the Applicant(s) **all** letters and documents you send to us.

Yours faithfully,

John Smith

For the Tribunal

4: STATEMENTS OF CASE

(1) Adverse Possession

Form 50: Statement of Case of the Applicant: adverse possession of unregistered land[1]

Case Reference: Ref/. . . . . .

Property Chamber

Land Registration

First-tier Tribunal

between:

Applicant	[A]
	and
Respondent	[B]

Applicant's Statement of Case

The property

1. This reference concerns the unregistered land consisting of 2 fields situated in the north east corner of Whiteacre Farm (*address*), shown coloured red on the plan annexed hereto ("the disputed land").

2. The Respondent is the paper title owner of the whole of Whiteacre Farm, shown edged in blue on the plan annexed hereto.

The reference

3. On . . . . the Applicant applied[2] to be registered as the first proprietor of the disputed land on the grounds that he had acquired title to it by having been in adverse possession ("the original application").

4. By a letter from his solicitors dated . . . . the Respondent objected[3] to the original application.

5. On . . . . the Chief Land Registrar referred[4] the dispute to the Tribunal.

Names and addresses

6. The Applicant's name is [A]. His address is (*address*).

7. The Applicant's solicitors are [Y]. Their address is (*address*).

8. The address where documents for the Applicant may be delivered is (*address*).

The Applicant's reasons for supporting the original application

9. The Applicant has been in adverse possession of the disputed land for over 12 years prior to the date of the original application. The Applicant has been in factual possession of the disputed land with the necessary intention to possess.

<u>The facts on which the Applicant intends to rely</u>

10. The Applicant went into possession of the disputed land on about . . . . , which is now over 12 years ago.

11. The Applicant relies upon the following acts of possession:

    (1) He has grazed cattle on the disputed land continuously for over 12 years.

    (2) He has maintained the fencing around the disputed land.

    (3) He has padlocked the gates to the disputed land and kept the key for his sole use.

    (4) He has placed barbed wire on top of the fencing.

    (5) He has erected a timber framed hut on the disputed land in which he stores his farm instruments and carries out repairs to them.

12. The Applicant will rely upon the photographs which are annexed hereto.

13. Throughout the time in which the Applicant has been in possession of the disputed land, he has excluded and has intended to exclude the whole world including the Respondent.

<u>The documents</u>

14. A list of documents[5] is annexed hereto.

Statement of Truth

I believe the facts stated in this statement of case are true.

(Signature)

Date . . . .

Served by . . . .

1 For the Respondent's statement of case in response, see Form 51.

2 See Forms 1, 2, 3.

3 See Form 4. For the reply, see Form 5.

4 For the case summary and notice of referral, see Forms 34, 35.

5 See Form 52.

Form 51: Statement of Case in response of the Respondent: adverse possession of unregistered land[1]

Case Reference: Ref/. . . . . .

Property Chamber

Land Registration

First-tier Tribunal

between:

Applicant	[A]
	and
Respondent	[B]

Respondent's Statement of Case

Names and addresses

1. The Respondent's name is [B]. His address is (*address*).
2. The Respondent's solicitors are [Z]. Their address is (*address*).
3. The address where documents for the Respondent may be delivered is (*address*).

The Respondent's reasons for opposing the original application

4. The Applicant has never been in adverse possession of the disputed land. The Applicant has not been in factual possession of the disputed land, nor has he had the necessary intention to possess. The Applicant has acknowledged the Respondent's title.

The facts on which the Respondent intends to rely

5. Dealing with the allegations made in paragraph 11 of the Applicant's statement of case in the same order:

    (1) The Applicant has not grazed cattle on the disputed land continuously for over 12 years. The Applicant only began to use the disputed land for keeping cattle some 7 years ago. This was shortly before the Respondent bought Whiteacre Farm, which includes the disputed land, from [C].

    (2) The Applicant has not maintained the fencing around the disputed land. It has remained in the same condition it has always been in. In any event, such fencing was to keep cattle in and not people out.

    (3) The gates to the disputed land have never been secured.

    (4) The barbed wire on top of the fencing was not placed there by the Applicant. It was put there by [C].

    (5) The timber framed hut is not on the disputed land but is on a wholly different part of Whiteacre Farm. It is therefore outside the scope of the present dispute.

6. Further, the Applicant wrote to the Respondent 5 years ago offering to buy the disputed land for £5,000. A copy of the letter is annexed hereto. The letter amounts to an acknowledgement of the Respondent's title within Section 29 (2)(a) of the Limitation Act 1980. Time began running afresh on that date.

The documents

7. A list of documents[2] is annexed hereto.

Statement of Truth

I believe the facts stated in this statement of case are true.

(Signature)

Date . . . .

Served by . . . .

1 For the Applicant's statement of case, see Form 50.

2 See Form 52.

Form 52: List of Documents

Case Reference: Ref/. . . . . .

Property Chamber

Land Registration

First-tier Tribunal

between:

Applicant	[A]
	and
Respondent	[B]

List of Documents

Description	Who has possession	Original or copy	Date of document	Parties to document

Form 53: Statement of Case of the Applicant: adverse possession of registered land under Schedule 6 to the Land Registration Act 2002[1]

Case Reference: Ref/. . . . . .

Property Chamber

Land Registration

First-tier Tribunal

between:

Applicant	[A]
	and
Respondent	[B]

Applicant's Statement of Case

<u>The property</u>

1. The Applicant is the registered proprietor of 6 Cherry Close, (*address*), which is registered at HM Land Registry under title number . . . . and is shown edged in red on the plan annexed hereto ("number 6").

2. The Respondent is the registered proprietor of the adjoining property, 8 Cherry Close, which is registered at HM Land Registry under title number . . . . and is shown edged in blue on the plan annexed hereto ("number 8").

3. This reference concerns a triangular piece of land situated within the registered title of number 8 and which is shown hatched in green on the plan annexed hereto ("the disputed land").

<u>The reference</u>

4. On . . . . the Applicant applied[2] to be registered as the proprietor of the disputed land on the grounds that he had acquired title to it by having been in adverse possession for 10 years and that he satisfied the condition set out in paragraph 5 (4) of Schedule 6 to the Land Registration Act 2002 ("the original application").

5. By a counter notice[3] dated . . . . ("the counter notice") the Respondent required the Registrar to deal with the application under paragraph 5 to Schedule 6 of the Land Registration Act 2002.

6. By a letter from his solicitors dated . . . . [**or** in panel 6 of the counter notice] the Respondent objected[4] to the original application on the grounds that none of the conditions set out in paragraph 5 (4) of Schedule 6 to the Land Registration Act 2002 was met **and/or** on the grounds that the Applicant has not been in adverse possession for the requisite period.

7. On . . . . the Chief Land Registrar referred the dispute to the Tribunal.

<u>Names and addresses</u>

8. The Applicant's name is [A]. His address is (*address*).

9. The Applicant's solicitors are [Y]. Their address is (*address*).

10. The address where documents for the Applicant may be delivered is (*address*).

The Applicant's reasons for supporting the original application

11. The Applicant has been in adverse possession of the disputed land for over 10 years prior to the date of the original application. The Applicant has been in factual possession of the land with the necessary intention to possess.

12. The Applicant also satisfies the condition set out in paragraph 5 (4) of Schedule 6 to the Land Registration Act 2002.

The facts on which the Applicant intends to rely

13. The Applicant went into possession of the disputed land at the same time as he moved into number 6, which is now over 10 years ago.

14. The Applicant relies upon the following acts of possession:

(1) He has kept it fenced on two sides and has treated it as part of his large back garden for over 10 years.

(2) He has maintained the grass on the disputed land and has used it for displaying his collection of 46 garden gnomes.

15. Throughout the time in which the Applicant has been in possession of the disputed land, he has excluded and has intended to exclude the whole world including the Respondent.

16. As to the condition set out in paragraph 5 (4) of Schedule 6 of the Land Registration Act 2002:

(1) The disputed land is adjacent to number 6.

(2) The exact line of the boundary between the disputed land and number 6 has never been fixed by Land Registry.

(3) For at least 10 years of the period of adverse possession ending on the date of the original application, the Applicant reasonably believed that the disputed land belonged to him. When he bought number 6 from the developers, [C Ltd], 15 years ago the rear boundary fence was positioned so that the disputed land was included within the back garden of number 6. [C Ltd]'s foreman said this had been intended.

(4) Number 8 was registered more than one year prior to the date of the original application.

The documents

17. A list of documents[5] is annexed hereto.

Statement of Truth

I believe the facts stated in this statement of case are true.

(Signature)

Date . . . .

Served by . . . .

1 For the Respondent's statement of case in response, see Form 54.

2 See Forms 6, 7.

3 See Form 9.

4 See Forms 10, 11.

5 See Form 52.

Form 54: Statement of Case in response of the Respondent: adverse possession of registered land under Schedule 6 to the Land Registration Act 2002[1]

Case Reference: Ref/. . . . . .

Property Chamber

Land Registration

First-tier Tribunal

between:

Applicant	[A]
	and
Respondent	[B]

Respondent's Statement of Case

Names and addresses

1. The Respondent's name is [B]. His address is (*address*).
2. The Respondent's solicitors are [Z]. Their address is (*address*).
3. The address where documents for the Respondent may be delivered is (*address*).

The Respondent's reasons for opposing the original application

Where the Respondent does not dispute the Applicant has been in adverse possession for the requisite period:

4. The Respondent admits that the Applicant has been in adverse possession of the disputed land for over 10 years prior to the original application.

Where the Respondent disputes the Applicant has been in adverse possession for the requisite period:

4. The Applicant has not been in adverse possession of the disputed land for 10 years prior to the original application. Until 4 years ago the Applicant had the Respondent's permission to use the disputed land.

Where the Respondent disputes the conditions in paragraph 5 are met

5. The Respondent denies that any one of the conditions in paragraph 5 of Schedule 6 to the Land Registration Act 2002 is met.

The facts on which the Respondent intends to rely

Where the Respondent disputes the Applicant has been in adverse possession for the requisite period:

6. When the Respondent moved into number 8, 12 years ago, the parties agreed that the Applicant could move the rear boundary fence and use the disputed land and, in return, the Respondent could have the use of Applicant's garage. That agreement was to last until either party gave 6 months' notice.

7. About 4 years ago the Applicant said he wanted his garage back and the Respondent vacated it. At the same time the Respondent asked the Applicant to move the rear boundary fence back so the disputed land could be restored to number 8, but he has failed to do so.

Where the respondent disputes the conditions in paragraph 5 are met

8. When [C Ltd] originally sold number 6 and number 8, the disputed land was within the back garden of number 8 and not within the back garden of number 6.

9. When [D], the original owner of number 8, sold it to the Respondent 12 years ago, the disputed land was still within the back garden of number 8 and not within the back garden of number 6.

10. At the time of the sale of number 8 by [D] to the Respondent, the Applicant moved the rear boundary fence between number 6 and number 8, thereby incorporating the disputed land within number 6. The Respondent was abroad at the time and did not appreciate what had happened.

11. Accordingly, the Applicant cannot ever have reasonably believed he owned the disputed land.

The documents

12. A list of documents[2] is annexed hereto.

Statement of Truth

I believe the facts stated in this statement of case are true.

(Signature)

Date . . . .

Served by . . . .

1 For the Applicant's statement of case, see Form 53.

2 See Form 52.

Form 55: Statement Of Case of the Applicant: adverse possession of registered land under the transitional provisions[1]

Case Reference: Ref/. . . . . .

Property Chamber

Land Registration

First-tier Tribunal

between:

Applicant	[A]
	and
Respondent	[B]

Applicant's Statement of Case

The property

1. This reference concerns land consisting of 2 fields situated in the north east corner of Whiteacre Farm (*address*), shown coloured red on the plan annexed hereto ("the disputed land").

2. The Respondent is the registered proprietor of the whole of Whiteacre Farm, which is registered at HM Land Registry under title number . . . . and is shown edged in blue on the plan annexed hereto.

The reference

3. On . . . . the Applicant applied[2] to be registered as the proprietor of the disputed land on the grounds that he had acquired title to it by having been in adverse possession ("the original application").

4. By a letter from his solicitors dated . . . . the Respondent objected[3] to the original application.

5. On . . . . the Chief Land Registrar referred the dispute to the Tribunal.

Names and addresses

6. The Applicant's name is [A]. His address is (*address*).

7. The Applicant's solicitors are [Y]. Their address is (*address*).

8. The address where documents for the Applicant may be delivered is (*address*).

The Applicant's reasons for supporting the original application

9. The Applicant has been in adverse possession of the disputed land for over 12 years prior to 13 October 2003. The Applicant has been in factual possession of the disputed land with the necessary intention to possess. The Applicant relies upon the transitional provisions in paragraph 18 of Schedule 12 of the Land Registration Act 2002.

The facts on which the Applicant intends to rely

10. The Applicant went into possession of the disputed land on about . . . . , which was 12 years prior to 13 October 2003.

11. The Applicant relies upon the following acts of possession:

    (1) He has grazed cattle on the disputed land continuously for over 12 years.

    (2) He has maintained the fencing around the disputed land.

    (3) He has padlocked the gates to the disputed land and kept the key for his sole use.

    (4) He has placed barbed wire on top of the fencing.

    (5) He has erected a timber framed hut on the disputed land in which he carries out repairs to and stores his farm instruments.

12. The Applicant will rely upon the photographs which are annexed hereto.

13. Throughout the time in which the Applicant has been in possession of the disputed land, he has excluded and has intended to exclude the whole world including the Respondent.

The documents

14. A list of documents[4] is annexed hereto.

Statement of Truth

I believe the facts stated in this statement of case are true.

(Signature)

Date . . . .

Served by . . . .

1 For the Respondent's statement of case in response, see Form 56.

2 See Forms 12, 2, 13.

3 See Form 14.

4 See Form 52.

Form 56: Statement of Case in response of the Respondent: adverse possession of registered land under the transitional provisions[1]

Case Reference: Ref/. . . . . .

Property Chamber

Land Registration

First-tier Tribunal

between:

Applicant	[A]
	and
Respondent	[B]

Respondent's Statement of Case

Names and addresses

1. The Respondent's name is [B]. His address is (*address*).
2. The Respondent's solicitors are [Z]. Their address is (*address*).
3. The address where documents for the Respondent may be delivered is (*address*).

The Respondent's reasons for opposing the original application

4. The Applicant was not in adverse possession of the disputed land for a period of 12 years prior to 13 October 2003.

The facts on which the Respondent intends to rely

5. The Applicant only began to use the disputed land some 7 years ago. This was shortly before the Respondent bought Whiteacre Farm, which includes the disputed land, from [C].

The documents

6. A list of documents[2] is annexed hereto.

Statement of Truth

I believe the facts stated in this statement of case are true.

(Signature)

Date . . . .

Served by . . . .

1 For the Applicant's statement of case, see Form 55.

2 See Form 52.

(2) Unilateral Notices

Form 57: Statement of Case of the Applicant (the beneficiary of a unilateral notice designated the Applicant by the Tribunal): cancellation of a unilateral notice relating to a restrictive covenant[1]

Case Reference: Ref/. . . . . .

Property Chamber

Land Registration

First-tier Tribunal

between:

Applicant	[A]
	and
Respondent	[B]

Applicant's Statement of Case

The property

1. The Applicant is the registered proprietor of the house at *(address)*, which is registered at HM Land Registry under title . . . . ("the benefited property").

2. The Respondent is the registered proprietor of the adjoining house at *(address)*, which is registered at HM Land Registry under title . . . . ("the burdened property").

The reference

3. On . . . . the Respondent applied[2] to cancel a unilateral notice[3] entered by the Applicant on the register of title of the burdened property ("the original application"). The unilateral notice was entered to protect the priority of a restrictive covenant preventing the development of the rear garden of the burdened property granted by the Respondent to the Applicant by a deed dated . . . . ("the deed").

4. By a letter from his solicitors dated . . . . the Applicant objected[4] to the original application.

5. On . . . . the Chief Land Registrar referred the dispute to the Tribunal.

Names and addresses

6. The Applicant's name is [A]. His address is (*address*).

7. The Applicant's solicitors are [Y]. Their address is (*address*).

8. The address where documents for the Applicant may be delivered is (*address*).

The Applicant's reasons for opposing the original application

9. The Applicant has the benefit of the restrictive covenant granted by the deed and is entitled to protect its priority by entering a unilateral notice. There are accordingly no grounds for cancelling the unilateral notice.

The facts on which the Applicant intends to rely

10. By the deed the Respondent covenanted on behalf of himself and his successors in title with the Applicant and his successors in title that, for the benefit of the benefited property, he would not develop the rear garden of the burdened property. A copy of the deed is annexed hereto.

11. The Applicant is opposed to any development by the Respondent of the rear garden of the burdened land and is concerned that the Respondent proposes to sell the rear garden to a developer, [C Ltd].

The documents

12. A list of documents[5] is annexed hereto.

Statement of Truth

I believe the facts stated in this statement of case are true.

(Signature)

Date . . . .

Served by . . . .

1 For the Respondent's statement of case in response, see Form 58.

2 See Form 17.

3 See Forms 15, 16.

4 See Form 18. For the reply, see Form 19.

5 See Form 52.

Form 58: Statement of Case in response of the Respondent (the maker of the application to cancel a unilateral notice designated the Respondent by the Tribunal): cancellation of a unilateral notice relating to a restrictive covenant[1]

Case Reference: Ref/. . . . . .

Property Chamber

Land Registration

First-tier Tribunal

between:

Applicant	[A]
	and
Respondent	[B]

Respondent's Statement of Case

Names and addresses

1. The Respondent's name is [B]. His address is (*address*).
2. The Respondent's solicitors are [Z]. Their address is (*address*).
3. The address where documents for the Respondent may be delivered is (*address*).

The Respondent's reasons for supporting the original application

4. The Applicant no longer has the benefit of a restrictive covenant burdening the burdened land.

The facts on which the Respondent intends to rely

5. It is agreed that on . . . . the parties entered into the deed referred to in paragraph 3 of the Applicant's statement of case.
6. Some time after the deed was executed a developer, [C Ltd], expressed an interest in buying the rear garden of the burdened property in order to build a new house on it. The Applicant initially refused to release the restrictive covenant, as he did not want the development to take place.
7. However, after discussions the parties entered into a deed of release dated . . . . ("the deed of release") whereby in consideration of the Applicant releasing the restrictive covenant, the Respondent paid the Applicant £50,000. A copy of the deed of release is annexed hereto.

The documents

8. A list of documents[2] is annexed hereto.

Statement of Truth

I believe the facts stated in this statement of case are true.

(Signature)

Date . . . .

Served by . . . .

1 For the Applicant's statement of case, see Form 57.

2 See Form 52.

(3) Cautions against Dealings

Form 59: Statement Of Case of the Applicant (the cautioner designated the Applicant by the Tribunal): cancellation of a caution against dealings relating to a claim of proprietary estoppel[1]

Case Reference: Ref/. . . . . .

Property Chamber

Land Registration

First-tier Tribunal

between:

Applicant	[A]
	and
Respondent	[B]

Applicant's Statement of Case

The property

1. This reference concerns the freehold property known as (*address*), which is registered at HM Land Registry under title number . . . . ("the property").

2. The Respondent is the registered proprietor of the property.

The reference

3. On . . . . the Respondent applied[2] to cancel a caution against dealings lodged by the Applicant in respect of the property ("the original application"). The caution against dealings was entered to protect an interest in the property arising by virtue of proprietary estoppel.

4. By a letter from his solicitors dated . . . . the Applicant objected[3] to the original application.

5. On . . . . the Chief Land Registrar referred the dispute to the Tribunal.

Names and addresses

6. The Applicant's name is [A]. His address is (*address*).

7. The Applicant's solicitors are [Y]. Their address is (*address*).

8. The address where documents for the Applicant may be delivered is (*address*).

The Applicant's reasons for opposing the original application

9. The Applicant has an interest in the property arising by virtue of proprietary estoppel. There are accordingly no grounds for cancelling the caution against dealings.

The facts on which the Applicant intends to rely

10. The parties had a same sex relationship for over 20 years. The parties met when the Applicant, who is younger than the Respondent, went to work at the property as a trainee chef. The Applicant was able and ambitious but was told by the Respondent that if he carried on working at the property in return for board and lodging, the Respondent would leave him the property in his will.

11. The Applicant had wanted to better himself and gave up the prospect of owning his own restaurant or of receiving higher wages in reliance on this promise. When the relationship ended in 2002 and the Applicant moved out of the property, the Respondent told the Applicant that he was leaving the property to charity.

12. The Applicant's case is that:

(1) a representation was made to him;

(2) he has relied upon the representation;

(3) he has acted to his detriment to the knowledge of the Respondent;

(4) it would be unconscionable for the Respondent to renege on the promise;

(5) the minimum equity to do justice between the parties requires the Respondent to transfer his interest in the whole or part of the property to the Applicant.

The documents

13. A list of documents[4] is annexed hereto.

Statement of Truth

I believe the facts stated in this statement of case are true.

(Signature)

Date . . . .

Served by . . . .

1 For the Respondent's statement of case in response, see Form 60.

2 See Form 20.

3 See Form 21. For the reply, see Form 22.

4 See Form 52.

Form 60: Statement of Case in response of the Respondent (the maker of the application to cancel a caution designated the Respondent by the Tribunal): cancellation of a caution against dealings relating to a claim of proprietary estoppel[1]

Case Reference: Ref/. . . . . .

Property Chamber

Land Registration

First-tier Tribunal

between:

Applicant	[A]
	and
Respondent	[B]

Respondent's Statement of Case

Names and addresses

1. The Respondent's name is [B]. His address is (*address*).
2. The Respondent's solicitors are [Z]. Their address is (*address*).
3. The address where documents for the Respondent may be delivered is (*address*).

The Respondent's reasons for supporting the original application

4. The Applicant does not have an interest in the property either arising by virtue of proprietary estoppel or for any other reason.

The facts on which the Respondent intends to rely

5. The Respondent agrees that the parties had a relationship for 20 years, which began when the Applicant came to work at the property as a trainee chef. But the Respondent denies that he ever promised the Applicant that he would leave him the property or anything else in his will. The Respondent always made it clear that he was intending to leave the property to charity.
6. It is denied that the Applicant either had the desire or the ability to set up on his own or obtain promotion. The Applicant was nervous of setting up in business on his own and agreed to help out occasionally at the property in return for board and lodging. He chose the security and companionship of a shared life with the Respondent in the property.
7. In the circumstances there was no representation, no reliance and no detriment. On the contrary, the Applicant had the benefit of a home and very good lifestyle for 20 years paid for by the Respondent.

The documents

8. A list of documents[2] is annexed hereto.

Statement of Truth

I believe the facts stated in this statement of case are true.

(Signature)

Date . . . .

Served by . . . .

[1] For the Applicant's statement of case, see Form 59.

[2] See Form 52.

(4) Restrictions

Form 61: Statement Of Case of the Applicant: entry of a restriction relating to a beneficial interest[1]

Case Reference: Ref/. . . . . .

Property Chamber

Land Registration

First-tier Tribunal

between:

Applicant	[A]
	and
Respondent	[B]

Applicant's Statement of Case

<u>The property</u>

1. This reference concerns the freehold property known as (*address*), which is registered at HM Land Registry under title number . . . . ("the property").

2. The Respondent is the sole registered proprietor of the property.

<u>The reference</u>

3. On . . . . the Applicant applied[2] for the entry of restrictions in Form A and Form II in the register of the property on the grounds that she had a beneficial interest in the property ("the original application").

4. By a letter from his solicitors dated . . . . the Respondent objected[3] to the original application.

5. On . . . . the Chief Land Registrar referred the dispute to the Tribunal.

<u>Names and addresses</u>

6. The Applicant's name is [A]. Her address is (*address*).

7. The Applicant's solicitors are [Y]. Their address is (*address*).

8. The address where documents for the Applicant may be delivered is (*address*).

<u>The Applicant's reasons for supporting the original application</u>

9. It is accepted that the Applicant does not have a legal estate in the property.

10. The Applicant's case is that she has a beneficial interest in the property arising out an implied and/or resulting and/or constructive trust and/or by virtue of the doctrine of proprietary estoppel.

11. The Applicant will rely upon the case law regarding unmarried partners who have acquired property together (much of which is summarised in the decision of the Court of Appeal in *Oxley v Hiscock* [2004] EWCA Civ 546 and of the House of Lords in *Stack v Dowden* [2007] UKHL 17).

The facts on which the Applicant intends to rely

12. The parties are in their mid thirties and are both single. The Applicant is a receptionist at a solicitors' practice. The Respondent is a freelance writer.

13. In . . . . , the parties met and a relationship developed.

14. In . . . . , the parties decided to buy a home together and they jointly found and chose the property which was purchased on . . . . The parties moved into the property and lived together there until . . . . when the relationship broke down and the Applicant moved out.

15. The parties orally expressly agreed prior to its purchase that, if the Applicant gave up her assured tenancy of her maisonette and kept house for the Respondent, the property would be jointly owned between them in equal shares notwithstanding that it would be transferred into the sole name of the Respondent. This conversation took place over dinner on . . . . at the Rose & Crown, (*address*).

16. The purchase price of the property was £215,000. The Applicant paid £5,000 towards the deposit which was £21,500.

17. A substantial mortgage was taken out to help with the acquisition of the property. The Respondent was the sole mortgagor. However, whilst she was living at the property the Applicant contributed a large share of every monthly repayment by giving the relevant amount in cash to the Respondent, or by making payment herself in cash direct to the lender.

18. The Applicant made all the above payments and gave up the assured tenancy of her maisonette in the belief that she was a joint owner of the property and because she held that belief. This belief was based on the express discussions with the Respondent at the time of purchase.

19. The Applicant has heard that the Respondent is attempting to sell the property as he is proposing to emigrate.

The documents

20. A list of documents[4] is annexed hereto.

Statement of Truth

I believe the facts stated in this statement of case are true.

(Signature)

Date . . . .

Served by . . . .

1 For the Respondent's statement of case in response, see Form 62.

2 See Forms 23, 24.

[3] See Form 25. For the reply, see Form 26.

[4] See Form 52.

Form 62: Statement of Case in response of the Respondent: entry of a restriction relating to a beneficial interest[1]

Case Reference: Ref/. . . . . .

Property Chamber

Land Registration

First-tier Tribunal

between:

Applicant	[A]
	and
Respondent	[B]

Respondent's Statement of Case

Names and addresses

1. The Respondent's name is [B]. His address is (*address*).
2. The Respondent's solicitors are [Z]. Their address is (*address*).
3. The address where documents for the Respondent may be delivered is (*address*).

The Respondent's reasons for opposing the original application

4. The Applicant does not have a beneficial interest in the property.

The facts on which the Respondent intends to rely

5. Save as is set out below, the facts in paragraphs 12–14 of the Applicant's statement of case are admitted.
6. The Respondent did not make any agreement with the Applicant whereby she would have any beneficial interest in the property, as is asserted in paragraphs 14 and 15 of the Applicant's statement of case. The parties never discussed the ownership of the property.
7. As to paragraph 16 of the Applicant's statement of case, it is agreed that the purchase price of the property was £215,000 and the deposit was £21,500, but the Applicant did not contribute £5,000 or any sum towards the deposit. The Applicant did pay the Respondent £5,000, but this was the repayment of a loan made to the Applicant by the Respondent some 6 months earlier. The loan had been made to enable the Applicant to buy a car.
8. The Applicant never contributed to the repayment of the mortgage as asserted in paragraph 17 of the Applicant's statement of case. The Applicant was not in employment all the time. When she was in employment she made a modest contribution to the household kitty. The money contributed by the Applicant was only ever used for purchasing food.
9. The mortgage repayments were made by direct debit payments from the Respondent's bank account.

10. The facts set out in Paragraph 18 of the Applicant's statement of case are denied.

11. As to paragraph 19 of the Applicant's statement of case, the Respondent does have plans to emigrate and wishes to sell the property. The application for a restriction is preventing the Respondent from doing this.

The documents

12. A list of documents[2] is annexed hereto.

Statement of Truth

I believe the facts stated in this statement of case are true.

(Signature)

Date . . . .

Served by . . . .

[1] For the Applicant's statement of case, see Form 61.

[2] See Form 52.

(5) Easements by Prescription

Form 63: Statement of Case of the Applicant: entry of the benefit of an easement by prescription[1]

Case Reference: Ref/. . . . . .

Property Chamber

Land Registration

First-tier Tribunal

between:

Applicant	[A]
	and
Respondent	[B]

Applicant's Statement of Case

The property

1. The Applicant is the registered proprietor of the house at *(address)*, which is registered at HM Land Registry under title . . . . and is shown edged in red on the plan annexed hereto ("the red land").

2. The Respondent is the registered proprietor of the adjoining house at *(address)*, which is registered at HM Land Registry under title . . . . and is shown edged in blue on the plan annexed hereto ("the blue land").

The reference

3. On . . . . the Applicant applied[2] to register the benefit of a right of way for the red land over the blue land ("the original application"). The route of the right of way ("the right of way") is shown marked in brown on the plan annexed hereto.

4. By a letter from his solicitors dated . . . . the Respondent objected[3] to the original application.

5. On . . . . the Chief Land Registrar referred the dispute to the Tribunal.

Names and addresses

6. The Applicant's name is [A]. His address is (*address*).

7. The Applicant's solicitors are [Y]. Their address is (*address*).

8. The address where documents for the Applicant may be delivered is (*address*).

The Applicant's reasons for supporting the original application

9. The Applicant, as freeholder owner of the red land, has acquired the right of way by prescription for the benefit of the red land over the blue land.

10. The Applicant relies upon prescription at common law, the doctrine of lost modern grant and the Prescription Act 1832.

The facts on which the Applicant intends to rely

11. For the last 24 years the Applicant has openly, without force and without the permission of the Respondent, walked along the route to gain access from the red land to the main road. The route affords a considerable short cut to the Applicant, as the red land has no direct access to the main road but only to a side road.

12. The Applicant has never had any form of permission, oral or in writing, from the Respondent to use the route.

13. Although the Respondent did put up a fence between the red land and the blue land in mid October 1987, within a few hours the panel crossing the route was blown down in the great storm of that year and has never been replaced. The Applicant has had uninterrupted access to the main road along the route over the whole of the last 24 years.

14. Throughout this period the Applicant's use of the route has been apparent to the Respondent and his family.

The documents

15. A list of documents[4] is annexed hereto.

Statement of Truth

I believe the facts stated in this statement of case are true.

(Signature)

Date . . . .

Served by . . . .

1 For the Respondent's statement of case in response, see Form 64.

2 See Forms 12, 27, 28.

3 See Form 29. For the reply, see Form 30.

4 See Form 52.

Form 64: Statement Of Case in response of the Respondent: entry of the benefit of an easement by prescription[1]

Case Reference: Ref/. . . . . .

Property Chamber

Land Registration

First-tier Tribunal

between:

Applicant	[A]
	and
Respondent	[B]

Respondent's Statement of Case

Names and addresses

1. The Respondent's name is [B]. His address is (*address*).
2. The Respondent's solicitors are [Z]. Their address is (*address*).
3. The address where documents for the Respondent may be delivered is (*address*).

The Respondent's reasons for opposing the original application

4. The Applicant has not acquired any right of way for the benefit of the red land over the blue land.

The facts on which the Respondent intends to rely

5. The Respondent agrees that the red land does not have any direct access to the main road as stated in paragraph 11 of the Applicant's statement of case, and it is also agreed that for 24 years the Applicant has used the route. However, the Respondent says that this use was originally with permission and subsequently has been by force. Accordingly, 2 of the essential elements of prescription are missing.
6. The Respondent gave the Applicant express oral permission to use the route prior to the Applicant starting to use it, and that permission continued up until about 10 years ago.
7. About 10 years ago the Respondent withdrew his permission and erected a fence along the boundary between the red land and the blue land.
8. Subsequently, the fence panel along the route was broken down and any access through the fence has been as a result of the force used to break down the fence.

The documents

9. A list of documents[2] is annexed hereto.

Statement of Truth

I believe the facts stated in this statement of case are true.

(Signature)

Date . . . .

Served by . . . .

[1] For the Applicant's statement of case, see Form 63.

[2] See Form 52.

(6) Alteration of the Register to correct a Mistake

Form 65: Statement Of Case of the Applicant: alteration of the register to correct a mistake (land incorrectly registered)[1]

Case Reference: Ref/. . . . . .

Property Chamber

Land Registration

First-tier Tribunal

between:

Applicant	[A]
	and
Respondent	[B]

Applicant's Statement of Case

The property

1. The Applicant is the registered proprietor of the land at *(address)*, which is registered at HM Land Registry under title number . . . . ("the blue land"). The blue land is shown edged in blue on the plan annexed hereto.

2. The Respondent is the registered proprietor of the following land at *(address)*, which is registered at HM Land Registry under title number . . . . :

   (1) the land shown edged in green on the plan annexed hereto ("the green land"), which lies immediately to the north of the blue land; and

   (2) the land shown edged in red on the plan annexed hereto ("the red land"), which lies immediately to the west of the green land.

The reference

3. On . . . . the Applicant applied[2] to alter the register by removing the green land from the Respondent's title number . . . . . . and including it within the Applicant's title number . . . . . . ("the original application").

4. By a letter from his solicitors dated . . . . the Respondent objected[3] to the original application.

5. On . . . . the Chief Land Registrar referred the dispute to the Tribunal.

Names and addresses

6. The Applicant's name is [A]. His address is (*address*).

7. The Applicant's solicitors are [Y]. Their address is (*address*).

8. The address where documents for the Applicant may be delivered is (*address*).

The Applicant's reasons for supporting the original application

9. The Applicant has a better paper title to the green land than the Respondent does. The title plan to the Respondent's registered title includes the green land by mistake.

The facts on which the Applicant intends to rely

10. The blue, green and red land was in common ownership until 2005 when it was still all unregistered land.

11. In 2006 the then owner, [C], transferred only the red land to the Respondent.

12. In 2007 the Respondent was registered as the first proprietor of the red land, but by mistake the title plan shows him to be registered as the proprietor of the green land as well.

13. In 2013 [C] transferred the green and blue land to the Applicant.

14. In 2014 the Applicant was registered as the first proprietor of the blue land. HM Land Registry refused to register the Applicant as the proprietor of the green land on the basis that it already fell within the Respondent's registered title.

15. The Applicant asks for the register to be altered under paragraph 5 (a) of Schedule 4 of the Land Registration Act 2002 by removing the green land from the Respondent's title plan and including it within the Applicant's title plan.

16. The alteration does not amount to rectification as defined by paragraph 1 of Schedule 4 of the Land Registration Act 2002 as the title plan only shows a general boundary: Derbyshire County Council v Fallon [2007] 3 EGLR 44.

17. Alternatively, if the alteration amounts to rectification, the Applicant says as follows.

18. It is denied that the Respondent is a proprietor in possession. Any use made by the Respondent of the green land is with the permission of the Applicant and is a shared use.

19. If, which is denied, the Respondent is a proprietor in possession, he has contributed by his lack of proper care to the mistake, within paragraph 6 (2)(a) of Schedule 4 of the Land Registration Act 2002. . . . .

    Particulars

    If the Respondent's solicitors had carefully checked the title plan when it was sent to them after first registration it would have been quite apparent that the green land was not included within the 2006 transfer. They should immediately have asked HM Land Registry to have made the necessary correction.

20. The lack of proper care, particularised in paragraph 19 above, caused or materially contributed to the mistake which has been made by HM Land Registry in including the green land on the Respondent's title plan, and refusing to include it on the Applicant's title plan.

The documents

21. A list of documents[4] is annexed hereto.

Statement of Truth

I believe the facts stated in this statement of case are true.

(Signature)

Date . . . .

Served by . . . .

1 For the Respondent's statement of case in response, see Form 66.

2 See Forms 12, 31.

3 See Form 32. For the reply, see Form 33.

4 See Form 52.

Form 66: Statement Of Case in response of the Respondent: alteration of the register to correct a mistake (land incorrectly registered)[1]

Case Reference: Ref/. . . . . .

Property Chamber

Land Registration

First-tier Tribunal

between:

Applicant	[A]
	and
Respondent	[B]

Respondent's Statement of Case

Names and addresses

1. The Respondent's name is [B]. His address is (*address*).
2. The Respondent's solicitors are [Z]. Their address is (*address*).
3. The address where documents for the Respondent may be delivered is (*address*).

The Respondent's reasons for opposing the original application

4. It is denied that the Applicant has a paper title to the green land.
5. If, which is denied, the Applicant has a paper title to the green land it is denied this is a case of alteration only. It is a case of rectification as defined by paragraph 1 of Schedule 4 of the Land Registration Act 2002.
6. The Respondent is a proprietor in possession of the disputed land, and does not consent to the original application.
7. The Respondent not has caused or materially contributed by any lack of proper care to the mistake.
8. There are also exceptional circumstances which justify not making any alteration to the register.

The facts on which the Respondent intends to rely

9. On the true construction of the transfer made between [C] and the Respondent in 2006, [C] transferred to the Respondent not only the red land, but the green land as well. Accordingly the Respondent was correctly registered as the proprietor of both the red and green land and there is no mistake in the register.
10. Alternatively, if which is denied, the 2006 transfer did not include green land, the Applicant's application amounts to one for rectification as defined by paragraph 1 of Schedule 4 of the Land Registration Act 2002 as any correction would prejudicially affect the Respondent's title.

11. The Respondent is a proprietor in possession of the green land – it consists of a small outhouse in which he stores his deck chairs. The Respondent does not consent to the application.

12. It is denied that any failure by the Respondent's solicitors to check the Respondent's title plan on first registration of the red and green land (which is denied) could have caused or materially contributed to the alleged mistake.

13. The Applicant has stood by while the Respondent has developed the red land as a guesthouse. It is essential for the purposes of the business that the Respondent retains the use of the small outhouse in which to store the deckchairs which are a popular feature with his guests. There is no room for them on the red land. The Respondent has also incurred expenditure in redecorating and restoring the small outhouse.

The documents

10. A list of documents[2] is annexed hereto.

Statement of Truth

I believe the facts stated in this statement of case are true.

(Signature)

Date . . . .

Served by . . . .

1 For the Applicant's statement of case, see Form 65.

2 See Form 52.

Form 67: Statement of Case of the Applicant: alteration of the register to correct a mistake (forgery)[1]

Case Reference: Ref/. . . . . .

Property Chamber

Land Registration

First-tier Tribunal

between:

Applicant	[A]
	and
Respondent	[B]

Applicant's Statement of Case

The property

1. These proceedings concern a flat at *(address)* ("the flat ") which is registered at HM Land Registry under title number . . . .
2. On . . . . 2010 the Applicant was registered as the proprietor of the flat.
3. On . . . . 2013 the Respondent was registered as the proprietor of the flat in place of the Applicant.

The reference

4. On . . . . the Applicant applied[2] to alter the register by removing the Respondent's name from the proprietorship register of the flat and restoring the Applicant's name as the proprietor of the flat ("the original application").
5. By a letter from her solicitors dated . . . . the Respondent objected[3] to the original application.
6. On . . . . the Chief Land Registrar referred the dispute to the Tribunal.

Names and addresses

7. The Applicant's name is [A]. His address is (*address*).
8. The Applicant's solicitors are [Y]. Their address is (*address*).
9. The address where documents for the Applicant may be delivered is (*address*).

The Applicant's reasons for supporting the original application

10. The Applicant has never transferred the flat to the Respondent or anyone else. The purported transfer in Form TR1 dated . . . . 2012 relied upon by the Respondent ("the transfer") is a forgery.

The facts on which the Applicant intends to rely

11. In 2010 the Applicant bought the flat with her own money. She was duly registered as the sole legal proprietor. The flat was not bought with the assistance of a mortgage loan and the flat was unencumbered.

12. In 2012 the Applicant retired to Spain and left the flat occupied by the Respondent, who is the Applicant's daughter.

13. The Applicant has not given the Respondent or any other person a power of attorney or any authority whatsoever to deal with the flat.

14. In 2014 the Applicant tried to raise some money on security of the flat, but discovered to her surprise that the flat is now registered in the Respondent's name.

15. The Applicant made enquiries of HM Land Registry and was shown a copy of the transfer which purported to show that the Applicant had transferred the flat to the Respondent in consideration of her natural love and affection. The Applicant's signature on the transfer was purportedly witnessed by [C] who is unknown to the Applicant.

16. A copy of the transfer is annexed to this statement of case.

17. The Applicant has obtained a report by Dr Panesar, a forensic handwriting expert, whose opinion is that the signature purportedly of the Applicant on the transfer has been traced from other documents.

18. A copy of Dr Panesar's report is annexed to this statement of case. An application will be made to rely upon it pursuant to rule 19 of the Tribunal Procedure (First–tier Tribunal) (Property Chamber) Rules 2013.

The documents

19. A list of documents[4] is annexed hereto.

Statement of Truth

I believe the facts stated in this statement of case are true.

(Signature)

Date . . . .

Served by . . . .

1 For the Respondent's statement of case in response, see Form 68.

2 See Forms 12, 34.

3 See Form 35.

4 See Form 52.

Form 68: Statement of Case in response of the Respondent: alteration of the register to correct a mistake (forgery)[1]

Case Reference: Ref/. . . . . .

Property Chamber

Land Registration

First-tier Tribunal

between:

Applicant	[A]
	and
Respondent	[B]

Respondent's Statement of Case

Names and addresses

1. The Respondent's name is [B]. Her address is (*address*).
2. The Respondent's solicitors are [Z]. Their address is (*address*).
3. The address where documents for the Respondent may be delivered is (*address*).

The Respondent's reasons for opposing the original application

4. It is denied that the Respondent forged the transfer.

The facts on which the Respondent intends to rely

5. In 2012, the Applicant told the Respondent that she was going to live in Spain and that she wished to transfer the flat to the Respondent so that the Respondent would have the immediate benefit of it. The Applicant said that she had originally intended to leave the flat to the Respondent in her will, but now that she was not going to be living in it herself she had decided it would be more sensible to transfer it to the Respondent.
6. The Applicant has one other child, [D], apart from the Respondent. [D] is the Respondent's half-brother. In 2012 the Applicant was estranged from [D].
7. On . . . . 2012 the Applicant and the Respondent attended at the offices of [Q] Solicitors. In the presence of the receptionist [C], who witnessed the Applicant's signature, the Applicant executed the transfer.
8. The Applicant has obtained a report by Mr Swann, a forensic handwriting expert, whose opinion is that the signature of the Applicant on the transfer is, on the balance of probabilities, a true signature of the Applicant.
9. A copy of Mr Swann's report is annexed to this statement of case. An application will be made to rely upon it pursuant to rule 19 of the Tribunal Procedure (First–tier Tribunal) (Property Chamber) Rules 2013.
10. During 2013 [D] visited the Applicant in Spain and they were reconciled. On . . . . 2013 [D] visited the Respondent unannounced at the flat.

He was very upset that the flat had been transferred to the Respondent and said to the Respondent that if the flat was not transferred back to the Applicant the Respondent's "legs would be broken".

11. A list of documents[2] is annexed hereto.

Statement of Truth

I believe the facts stated in this statement of case are true.

(Signature)

Date . . . .

Served by . . . .

1 For the Applicant's statement of case, see Form 67.

2 See Form 52

5: APPLICATIONS, DIRECTIONS AND ORDERS IN THE COURSE OF THE PROCEEDINGS BEFORE THE TRIBUNAL

Form 69: Application for an extension of time

(Applicant's solicitors address)

Property Chamber

Land Registration

First-tier Tribunal

Case Reference: Ref/. . . . . .

We apply on behalf of [A], the Applicant, for an extension of time in which to serve the statement of case. We would ask for a further 14 days, terminating at 4.0pm on . . . . The reasons for this request are as follows *(state grounds)*. We have sent a copy of this letter to the solicitors for [B], the Respondent, and we have notified them that any objection they wish to make to this application must be provided in writing to the Tribunal.

Yours etc

Form 70: Order granting an extension of time

Upon reading the letter of the Applicant's solicitors dated . . . . and the letter of the Respondent's solicitors dated . . . .

IT IS ORDERED THAT the time for the service of the Applicant's statement of case is extended to 4.0pm on . . . .

Form 71: Application of the Respondent for summary disposal

(Respondent's solicitors address)

Property Chamber

Land Registration

First-tier Tribunal

Case Reference: Ref/. . . . . .

We apply on behalf of [B], the Respondent, to strike out the Applicant's proceedings by way of summary disposal on the grounds that there is no reasonable prospect of the proceedings succeeding. We refer to the witness statement of the Respondent in support of the application served herewith. We confirm that we have served the Applicant's solicitors with a copy of this application and the witness statement, and we have notified them that any objection they wish to make to this application must be provided in writing to the Tribunal.

Yours etc

Form 72: Witness Statement in support of an application for summary disposal

(1) Respondent

(2) [B]

(3) 1st

(4) "[B]1"

(5) [Date]

Case Reference: Ref/. . . . .

Property Chamber

Land Registration

First-tier Tribunal

between:

Applicant	[A]
	and
Respondent	[B]

I, [B] of *(address)*, farmer, will say as follows:

1. I am the Respondent and make this witness statement in support of my application for a summary disposal of these proceedings.
2. These proceedings concern an application by the Applicant for the first registration of unregistered land owned by me on the grounds that he has acquired title to the land by adverse possession.
3. This witness statement is made from facts within my own knowledge.
4. I refer to a letter written to me by the Applicant dated . . . . , offering to buy the land in dispute from me for £5,000, marked "[B]1". The letter amounts to an acknowledgement of my title within Section 29 (2)(a) of the Limitation Act 1980. Time began running afresh on that date, which is within the last 5 years.
5. The letter was written in my presence, and handed to me by the Applicant.
6. I believe that the Applicant has no real prospect of succeeding on the proceedings.
7. Accordingly, I ask the Tribunal to direct the Chief Land Registrar to cancel the Applicant's application be registered as the proprietor of the land in dispute.

Statement of Truth

I believe the facts stated in this witness statement are true.

(Signature)

Date . . . .

Served by . . . .

Form 73: Order for summary disposal

UPON READING:

1. The letter of the Respondent's solicitors dated . . . . and the witness statement of the Respondent dated . . . .

2. The witness statement of the Applicant dated . . . .

AND UPON the Tribunal finding that the Applicant has no real prospect of succeeding on the proceedings

The Land Registration division of the Property Chamber, First-tier Tribunal orders the Chief Land Registrar to cancel the original application dated . . . . for first registration of . . . .

Form 74: Application for security for costs

(Respondent's solicitors address)

Property Chamber

Land Registration

First-tier Tribunal

Case Reference: Ref/. . . . . .

We apply on behalf of [B], the Respondent, for security for costs in these proceedings on the grounds that:

(1) The Applicant is resident out of the jurisdiction, but not resident in a Brussels Contracting State, a State bound by the Lugano Convention or a Regulation State, as defined in section 1(3) of the Civil Jurisdiction and Judgments Act 1982.

(2) It is just to make such an order.

(3) The Applicant has the ability to comply with the order.

We refer to the witness statement of the Respondent in support of the application served herewith. We confirm that we have served the Applicant's solicitors with a copy of this application and the witness statement, and we have notified them that any objection they wish to make to this application must be provided in writing to the Tribunal.

Yours etc

Form 75: Witness Statement in support of an application for security for costs

(1) Respondent

(2) [B]

(3) 1st

(4) "[B]1", "[B]2"

(5) [Date]

Case Reference: Ref/. . . . . .

Property Chamber

Land Registration

First-tier Tribunal

between:

Applicant	[A]
	and
Respondent	[B]

I, [B] of *(address)*, a company director, will say as follows:

1. I am the Respondent and make this witness statement in support of my application that the Applicant the ordered to give security for costs in these proceedings.
2. This witness statement is made from facts within my own knowledge.
3. These proceedings concern an application by the Applicant to be reinstated as the proprietor of the above-mentioned house in place myself, on the grounds that I have been registered as the proprietor by mistake.
4. The Applicant claims that a fraudster impersonated him and sold the house to me. I deny this and, in any event, I am a proprietor in possession.
5. The Applicant has for many years lived in Somalia, and after he moved there he failed to notify HM Land Registry of his change of address.
6. I am not aware of any assets that the Applicant owns within the jurisdiction, and I do not believe that he has any assets within the jurisdiction.
7. I am very concerned that if the Applicant fails to succeed in these proceedings I am unlikely to be able to recover any of my costs.
8. My solicitors requested security in a letter dated . . . . addressed to the Applicant's solicitors but the request has been refused. Is now produced and shown to me marked "[B]1" a bundle comprising the relevant correspondence passing between the parties' respective solicitors.
9. There is now produced and shown to me marked "[B]2" a detailed and itemised account prepared by my solicitors of the costs, including counsel's fees which (1) have been incurred up to the date of the request for security and (2) which it is estimated will be incurred in the future conduct of these proceedings on my behalf.

10. The Applicant is the vice president of a large shipping corporation and I have no reason to doubt that he has the ability to comply with the order I seek.

11. Accordingly, I ask the Tribunal to order the Applicant to give security for my costs of these proceedings in the sum of £. . . . .

Statement of Truth

I believe the facts stated in this witness statement are true.

(Signature)

Date . . . .

Served by . . . .

Form 76: Order for security for costs

UPON READING:

1. The letter of the Respondent's solicitors dated . . . . and the witness statement of the Respondent dated . . . .
2. The witness statement of the Applicant dated . . . .

IT IS ORDERED THAT the Applicant gives security for the Respondent's costs of these proceedings in the sum of £. . . . . . . by lodging with the Respondent's solicitors a banker's draft by 4.0pm on . . . .

Form 77: Application for permission to adduce expert evidence

(Applicant's solicitors address)

Property Chamber

Land Registration

First-tier Tribunal

Case Reference: Ref/. . . . . .

We apply on behalf of [A], the Applicant, for permission to adduce expert forensic handwriting evidence in support of the Applicant's case in these proceedings. It will be seen from the statements of case which have been served that the issue in these proceedings is whether or not the Applicant's signature on the transfer in Form TR1 dated . . . . and relied upon by the Respondent is forged or not.

We propose to instruct Dr Panesar and would invite the Tribunal to provide directions and a timetable for the exchange of reports with any expert instructed by the Respondent.

We have sent a copy of this letter to the solicitors for [B], the Respondent, and we have notified them that any objection they wish to make to this application must be provided in writing to the Tribunal.

Yours etc

Form 78: Order for permission to adduce expert evidence

Case Reference: Ref/. . . . . .

Property Chamber

Land Registration

First-tier Tribunal

between:

Applicant	[A]
	and
Respondent	[B]

[SINGLE EXPERT]

1. Evidence as to whether [the signature on the TR1 dated . . . . is that of [A] or not shall be given by the report of a single forensic handwriting expert, instructed jointly by the parties.
2. The Applicant shall advise the Tribunal in writing by 4.0pm on . . . . whether or not the single expert has been instructed.
3. If the parties are unable to agree by that date who the single expert is to be and about the payment of his or her fees any party may apply for further directions.
4. Unless the parties agree in writing or the Tribunal orders otherwise, the fees and expenses of the single expert shall be paid to him or her by the parties equally.
5. The parties shall give agreed instructions or, failing agreement as to the terms of the instructions, each party shall give his instructions to each single expert by 4.0pm on . . . .
6. The report of the single expert in each field shall be filed by 4.00pm on . . . .
7. The question of whether the evidence of the single expert be given at the hearing by written report or oral evidence of the expert shall be determined following the filing to the report.

[SEPARATE EXPERTS]

1. Each party has permission to adduce oral evidence of a forensic handwriting expert as to whether [the signature on the TR1 dated . . . . is that of [A] or not], limited to one expert per party.
2. The experts' reports shall be exchanged by . . . .
3. The experts shall hold a discussion before . . . . for the purpose of:

   (1) identifying the issues, if any, between them; and

(2) where possible, reaching agreement on those issues.

4. The experts shall by . . . . prepare and file a statement for the Tribunal showing:

(1) those issues on which they did agree; and

(2) those issues on which they disagree and a summary of their reasons for disagreeing.

Form 79: Application for a summons to require a person to attend to as a witness

(Applicant's solicitors address)

Property Chamber

Land Registration

First-tier Tribunal

Case Reference: Ref/. . . . . .

We apply on behalf of [A], the Applicant, for a summons to require DC Dixon of the Metropolitan Police to attend as a witness at the hearing of these proceedings at . . . . court on . . . . at 4.00pm. It will be seen from the statements of case which have been served that the issue in these proceedings is whether or not a fraudster known as "Bosh" impersonated the Applicant and sold the Applicant's house to [B], the Respondent.

DC Dixon is the investigating officer in the case and has been attempting to trace "Bosh" through Interpol. DC Dixon is willing to give evidence in these proceedings but requires me to obtain a summons compelling him to attend.

We have sent a copy of this letter to the solicitors for the Respondent and we have notified them that any objection they wish to make to this application must be provided in writing to the Tribunal.

Yours etc

Form 80: Summons to require a person to attend as a witness

Property chamber

Land registration

First-tier tribunal

Case Number:	**REF/2013/0680**
Title Number:	**ZYX98765**
Property:	**00 Howden Bank, Derwent**
Applicant:	**Bea Lowater**
Respondent:	**Mark Highwater**

WITNESS SUMMONS

TO **Philip Church** of **101, Bell Street, Chaddesden DE99 9ZZ**

TAKE NOTICE that you are required to attend at 10 Alfred Place, London WC1E 7LR

at **10:30 a.m.** on **21 August 2014**

and each following day of the hearing until you are no longer required for the following purpose(s)

- to give evidence in this matter

This Summons was issued on the application of the [Applicants/Respondents], whose address for service and reference is:-

Jones, solicitors
2, Flood Street
Ashopton DE99 1YY

Validity of this notice

This Witness Summons is only binding if, not less than 14 days before the date specified above (or any lesser period as the Tribunal may have expressly directed), it has been served on you and (unless you are already a party in these proceedings) the necessary expenses of your attendance are offered and (unless you refuse them) paid to you.

Varying or setting aside this Witness Summons

Unless the Tribunal has already given you an opportunity to object to it, you may apply to the Tribunal to vary or to set aside this notice. Any such application should be made in writing and sent to (i) the Tribunal at 10 Alfred Place, London WC1E 7LR (tel 020 7291 7250) DX305001 Tottenham Court Road 5 and (ii) the party who has had this notice issued **BEFORE** this time required for you comply with this Summons.

The application should state the reasons for which you require the variation or the setting aside of this Summons and include any relevant documents or other evidence in support (e.g., a doctor's report). The application should include a statement that "I [the Applicant *as appropriate*] believe[s] the facts stated in this application are true."

UNDER SECTION 112 OF THE LAND REGISTRATION ACT 2002, THIS SUMMONS IS ENFORCEABLE AS AN ORDER OF THE COURT. IF YOU DO NOT COMPLY WITH THIS SUMMONS:-

(A) **THE PARTY WHO ASKED FOR IT TO BE ISSUED MAY APPLY TO THE COURT AND THE COURT MAY FIND YOU TO BE GUILTY OF A CONTEMPT OF COURT AND [YOU] [ANY OF YOUR DIRECTORS as appropriate] MAY BE SENT TO PRISON OR FINED OR YOUR ASSETS MAY BE SEIZED. YOU MAY ALSO BE LIABLE TO PAY ANY WASTED COSTS THAT ARISE BECAUSE OF YOUR NON-COMPLIANCE OR**

(B) **THE TRIBUNAL MAY REFER THE MATTER TO THE UPPER TRIBUNAL TO CONSIDER EXERCISING ITS OWN POWERS OF ENFORCEMENT WHICH, UNDER SECTION 25 TRIBUNALS COURTS AND ENFORCEMENT ACT 2007, ARE THE SAME AS THOSE OF THE HIGH COURT IN THIS RESPECT.**

Dated this 24 July 2014

By Order of The Tribunal

Form 81: Application for an order to produce documents

(Applicant's solicitors address)

Property Chamber

Land Registration

First-tier Tribunal

Case Reference: Ref/. . . . . .

We apply on behalf of [A], the Applicant, for a summons to require Peter Jones, a partner in the firm of John Lewis & Co Solicitors to attend at . . . . court on . . . . at 4.00pm and to produce the conveyancing file of the purchase of *(address)* ("the flat") by [B], the Respondent, on . . . . It will be seen from the statements of case which have been served that the issue in these proceedings is whether or not the Applicant has a beneficial interest in the flat by way of a constructive trust.

The Respondent instructed Peter Jones to act on the purchase of the flat. The Applicant's case is that she attended a meeting between Peter Jones and the Respondent prior to the purchase of the flat when the Respondent said that the flat was to be jointly owned. Accordingly, the conveyancing file and any attendance notes to be found in it are of relevance. We have written to Peter Jones asking the site of the conveyancing file, but he has declined to release it without an order being made by the Tribunal.

We have sent a copy of this letter to the solicitors for the Respondent and we have notified them that any objection they wish to make to this application must be provided in writing to the Tribunal.

Yours etc

Form 82: Order to produce documents

Property Chamber
First-tier Tribunal
Land Registration

Case Number:	**REF/2013/0680**
Title Number:	**ZYX98765**
Property:	**00 Howden Bank, Derwent**
Applicant:	**Bea Lowater**
Respondent:	**Mark Highwater**

WITNESS SUMMONS

TO **Philip Church** of **101, Bell Street, Chaddesden DE99 9ZZ**

TAKE NOTICE that you are required to attend at 10 Alfred Place, London WC1E 7LR

at **10:30 a.m.** on **21 August 2014**

and each following day of the hearing until you are no longer required for the following purpose(s)

- to produce the following document if they are in your possession or control, namely
- LIST

This Summons was issued on the application of the [Applicants/Respondents], whose address for service and reference is:-

Jones, solicitors
2, Flood Street
Ashopton DE99 1YY

Validity of this notice

This Witness Summons is only binding if, not less than 14 days before the date specified above (or any lesser period as the Tribunal may have expressly directed), it has been served on you and (unless you are already a party in these proceedings) the necessary expenses of your attendance are offered and (unless you refuse them) paid to you.

Varying or setting aside this Witness Summons

Unless the Tribunal has already given you an opportunity to object to it, you may apply to the Tribunal to vary or to set aside this notice. Any such application should be made in writing and sent to (i) the Tribunal at 10 Alfred Place, London WC1E 7LR (tel 020 7291 7250) DX305001 Tottenham Court Road 5 and (ii) the party who has had this notice issued **BEFORE** this time required for you comply with this Summons.

The application should state the reasons for which you require the variation or the setting aside of this Summons and include any relevant documents or other evidence in support (e.g., a doctor's report). The application should include a statement that "I [the Applicant *as appropriate*] believe[s] the facts stated in this application are true."

UNDER SECTION 112 OF THE LAND REGISTRATION ACT 2002, THIS SUMMONS IS ENFORCEABLE AS AN ORDER OF THE COURT. IF YOU DO NOT COMPLY WITH THIS SUMMONS:-

(A) THE PARTY WHO ASKED FOR IT TO BE ISSUED MAY APPLY TO THE COURT AND THE COURT MAY FIND YOU TO BE GUILTY OF A CONTEMPT OF COURT AND [YOU] [ANY OF YOUR DIRECTORS as appropriate] MAY BE SENT TO PRISON OR FINED OR YOUR ASSETS MAY BE SEIZED. YOU MAY ALSO BE LIABLE TO PAY ANY WASTED COSTS THAT ARISE BECAUSE OF YOUR NON-COMPLIANCE OR

(B) THE TRIBUNAL MAY REFER THE MATTER TO THE UPPER TRIBUNAL TO CONSIDER EXERCISING ITS OWN POWERS OF ENFORCEMENT WHICH, UNDER SECTION 25 TRIBUNALS COURTS AND ENFORCEMENT ACT 2007, ARE THE SAME AS THOSE OF THE HIGH COURT IN THIS RESPECT.

Dated this 24 July 2014

By Order of The Tribunal

Form 83: Letter proposing mediation

Property Chamber
Land Registration
First-tier Tribunal
3rd Floor
10 Alfred Place
London WC1E 7LR

Tel:	020 7291 7250
Fax:	020 7291 7251
Goldfax:	0870 739 4134
DX:	DX305001 Tottenham Court Road 5
Email:	landregistration@hmcts.gsi.gov.uk
Website:	www.justice.gov.uk/tribunals

Smiths, Solicitors

1 Reservoir Street
Ashopton

DE99 0XX

Your Ref: GG/HH/123

Our Ref: REF/2013/0680

5 September 2014

Dear Sir/Madam,

ZYX98765

Bea Lowater vs. Mark Highwater

00 Howden Bank, Derwent

The Tribunal Judge has now reviewed the file and has come to the view that this is a case which is suitable for mediation

Mediation is a voluntary process, the aim of which is to assist the parties to find a resolution to the dispute without incurring further lengthy delays and expense. It can also allow the parties to reach agreement on issues upon which the Tribunal Judge cannot make a decision (for instance, agreeing to a sale of a property, or paying compensation.)

The Property Chamber: Land Registration has recently introduced a mediation scheme. All mediators are trained and have considerable experience in mediation. They are also all Tribunal Judges. The Tribunal will not charge a fee for this service. We enclose a leaflet providing further information.

If the mediation is successful, no further steps will be taken by the Tribunal, other than to notify the Land Registry of the outcome. This must include agreement on how the Land Registry is to dispose of the disputed application(s) referred to the Tribunal. If not successful your case will proceed to a hearing and the Tribunal Judge who acted as mediator will take no further part in your case. Anything discussed in the mediation will remain strictly confidential, unless the parties agree otherwise.

If you are interested in mediation, please contact the office within 14 calendar days of today's date (**insert date**) or complete the attached form. We aim to ensure that the mediation takes place within 6 weeks from now (**insert date**). You will be asked to sign a mediation agreement before or at the mediation session.

If, at this stage, you are not interested in the scheme, the Tribunal Judge will consider listing the case for a case management conference at which further directions for the case will be given. The case management conference will also give you an opportunity to raise any queries you may have regarding mediation.

Yours faithfully,

John Smith

Form 84: Mediation Agreement

Mediation Agreement

This agreement is made on. . . . .

Between. . . . . ('the parties')

1. The parties will attempt to settle the dispute referred pursuant to section 73(7) of the Land Registration Act 2002/the rectification application (as the case may be) ('the Dispute') by mediation ('the Mediation').

2. The Mediator for the dispute is selected by the Property Chamber Land Registration First-tier Tribunal.

The parties' role and duties

3. Each of the parties will prepare and send to the Mediator and the other parties

   3.1 a concise summary setting out its position in relation to the Dispute ('the case summary') and

   3.2 any documents to which the case summary refers and any others to which it may wish to refer at the Mediation

4. The case summary and documents shall be sent to the mediator not less than 10 days before the date of the Mediation.

5. Each party may give to the Mediator further information or documents which are not to be disclosed to other parties such documents to be clearly marked ' confidential to the Mediator'.

6. Each of the parties will if appropriate attend the Mediation with a person (the 'Authorised Person') who has authority to bind that party to any agreement reached as a result of the Mediation.

7. The Mediation is an informal process and there is no need for the parties to engage representatives, professional or otherwise. But the parties are free to be represented if they so wish by a lawyer, relative, friend or volunteer.

The Mediator's role and duties

8. The Mediator will:

   8.1 Attend a site meeting if requested to do so or if he or she considers it appropriate;

   8.2 Discuss the Mediation on the telephone with any of the parties preceding the Mediation if requested to do so or if he or she considers it appropriate;

   8.3 Read before the Mediation the case summary and all other documents sent to him or her and/or in the office file

   8.4 Chair, and determine the procedure for, the Mediation

   8.5 Assist the parties to try to settle the Dispute by exploring the issues, interests, needs and the concerns of the parties;

   8.6 Assist the parties in drawing up any written settlement agreement

9. Neither the Adjudicator's office nor the Mediator will offer legal advice or act as a legal advisor to any of the parties. *If all parties ask* the Mediator *may* consider expressing a view or assessment of the merits of the issues in the Dispute. This is not a legal opinion and will not influence the Judge who will hear the Dispute if the matter proceeds to a hearing or a Court if proceedings are instituted. It is a view or assessment of the issues and merits based on the information available to the Mediator at the time. It is not binding.

The mediation

10. The Mediation will take place at. . . . . on. . . . .

11. The Mediation may last up to 5 hours

12. No transcript or recording shall be made of the Mediation or any part of it.

13. Any settlement reached in the Mediation shall not be legally binding unless it has been reduced in writing and signed by or on behalf of the Parties.

14. The settlement shall include a resolution of the Dispute which will enable the Land Registry to cancel or give effect to (as the case may be) the application made to the Land Registry

15. Any of the parties may withdraw from the Mediation at any time.

16. The Mediation shall terminate when any of the following occur:

    16.1 any of the parties withdraws from the Mediation; or

    16.2 a written settlement agreement is signed; or

    16.3 the Mediator terminates the Mediation for any of the reasons set out in clause 17 below.

17. The Mediator may terminate the Mediation if:

    17.1 The Mediator comes to the view that continuing the Mediation is unlikely to result in a settlement

    17.2 Any of the parties is acting in breach of this agreement

    17.3 Any of the parties is, in the Mediator's opinion, acting in an unconscionable or criminal manner

    17.4 The Mediator considers that he/she may be committing an offence under the Proceeds of Crime Act 2002 by continuing the Mediation

    17.5 Any of the parties alleges that the Mediator is acting in breach of this agreement.

18. The Mediator is not required to give any reasons for terminating the Mediation.

Confidentiality

19. The parties attend the Mediation for the purpose of reaching a settlement. Everything said or disclosed by any party at the Mediation or by the Mediator shall be treated in confidence and shall not be used for any other purpose and shall not be admissible or disclosable in any current or future litigation or other proceedings whatsoever (including the Adjudication). This does not apply to any information which would apart from this clause be admissible or disclosable in such proceedings.

20. If any information is provided to the Mediator by any party prior to or during the mediation and that information is expressly or impliedly confidential the

mediator will not reveal such information to any other party without the consent of the party who provided the information.

21. Any notes taken by the Mediator during the Mediation will be destroyed immediately after if has finalised.

22. None of the parties shall call the Mediator as a witness in any litigation or other proceedings whatsoever arising from or in connection with the matters in issue at the Mediation.

Costs

23. The parties will each bear their own costs of the mediation subject to any agreement which may be reached at the Mediation.

Exclusion of liability

24. The Mediator shall not be liable to the parties for any act or omission during or in connection with the Mediation giving rise to any liability whatsoever.

Law and Jurisdiction

25. This agreement shall be governed by English law and the courts of England and Wales shall have exclusive jurisdiction to settle any claim, dispute or matter of difference which may arise out of or in connection with this agreement,

Signed

. . . .

The mediator

. . . .

Party A

. . . .

Party B

. . . .

Party C

. . . .

Form 85: Notice of withdrawal

(Applicant's solicitors address)

Property Chamber

Land Registration

First-tier Tribunal

Case Reference: Ref/. . . . . .

We act on behalf of [A], the Applicant, in these proceedings. We hereby give notice of the withdrawal of the Applicant's case in these proceedings and of his original application relating to a right of way claimed by prescription over the land of the Respondent ("the land")

The reason for the withdrawal is that the parties have come to terms. As part of the settlement the Respondent will grant an express right of way over the land for benefit of the Applicant's property. Accordingly, it is the whole of the Applicant's case which is being withdrawn.

We can confirm that a copy of this notice of the withdrawal was sent to the Respondent's solicitors by first class post on . . . . We enclose with this notice the written consent to the withdrawal given by the Respondent's solicitors.

Yours etc

Form 86: Order giving permission to withdraw

UPON READING the letter of the Respondent's solicitors dated . . . .

AND UPON the Tribunal consenting to the withdrawal

The Land Registration division of the Property Chamber, First-tier Tribunal orders the Chief Land Registrar to cancel the original application dated . . . . to register the benefit of a right of way by prescription for the benefit of title number . . . . . . over title number . . . .

Form 87: Order with sanctions: breach *will* lead to the striking out of the proceedings

Unless the Applicant serves their [enter the required submission] on the Tribunal and the Respondent on or before 5.00pm on . . . . , the Tribunal will require the Chief Land Registrar to cancel the original application.

This Order is made pursuant to the provisions of Rule 9(1) of the Tribunal Procedure (First-tier Tribunal) (Property Chamber) Rules 2013

Form 88: Order with sanctions: breach *may* lead to the striking out of the proceedings

Unless the Applicant serves their [enter the required submission] on the Tribunal and the Respondent on or before 5.00pm on . . . . , the Tribunal may require the Chief Land Registrar to cancel the original application.

This Order is made pursuant to the provisions of Rule 9(3)(a) of the Tribunal Procedure (First-tier Tribunal) (Property Chamber) Rules 2013

Form 89: General Directions

Property Chamber
Land Registration
First-tier Tribunal
3rd Floor
10 Alfred Place
London WC1E 7LR

Tel:	020 7291 7250
Fax:	020 7291 7251
Goldfax:	0870 739 4134
DX:	DX305001 Tottenham Court Road 5
Email:	landregistration@hmcts.gsi.gov.uk
Website:	www.justice.gov.uk/tribunals

Smiths, Solicitors

1 Reservoir Street
Ashopton

DE99 0XX

Your Ref: GG/HH/123

Our Ref: REF/2013/0680

5 September 2014

Dear Sir/Madam,

ZYX98765

Bea Lowater vs. Mark Highwater

00 Howden Bank, Derwent

Please find enclosed a copy of the further Directions of the Tribunal dated.

Also, to enable the Tribunal to make arrangements for the hearing, you are required to complete and return the enclosed form LRHRG by. A similar request is being made to the other party.

Please note that the case will then be listed having regard to such information as the parties have provided in response. It is unlikely that any extension of time will be given for returning form LRHRG.

At least 14 days notice of the hearing will usually be given.

Please note that after a hearing date is fixed, the Tribunal will not be willing to postpone or adjourn it, even with the consent of both parties, except for the most compelling reasons (such as illness of an essential participant supported by a medical certificate, or a hearing of a court of superior jurisdiction). Any postponement application must be supported by full grounds.

Yours faithfully,

John Smith

For the Tribunal

Property Chamber, Land Registration
First-tier Tribunal

Order

Case Number:	**REF/2013/0680**
Title Number:	**ZYX98765**
Property:	**00 Howden Bank, Derwent**
Applicant:	**Bea Lowater**
Respondent:	**Mark Highwater**
Date:	

IT IS ORDERED as follows:

1. Disclosure

(1) Each party must serve on (i) the Tribunal and (ii) the other party/ies by 26 September 2014:

(a) A list of all relevant documents in that party's possession or control which

(i) That party intends to rely on in the proceedings; or

(ii) Adversely affects that party's own case; or

(iii) Adversely affects another party's case or

(iv) Supports another party's case

and

(b) Copies of documents in that list

(2) The parties must bring the original documents to the hearing

(3) Evidence not submitted in accordance with paragraph (1) above will only be admitted with the permission of the Tribunal and following consultation with the other parties.

2. **Witness statements**

(1) Each party must, by

(a) file with the Tribunal and

(b) exchange with the other party/ies

the witness statements of any witness of fact upon whose evidence they propose to rely.

(2) Each witness statement must contain a statement of truth signed by the witness making the statement as follows:

"I believe that the facts stated in this witness statement are true."

(3) If any party intends to rely on their Statement of Case as evidence, that party must (unless they have already done so) submit a verification, signed by that party, of their Statement of Case in the following terms

"I believe that the facts and matters contained in this Statement of Case are true."

(4) Where a witness is called to give oral evidence, his or her witness statement shall stand as his or her evidence, subject to any cross-examination by the other party/ies, unless the Tribunal orders otherwise.

(5) The parties may not call any witness other than those in respect of whom a statement has been served without the prior permission of the Tribunal

3. Additional directions (if any)

4. Service on the Tribunal

Anything to be sent to the Tribunal must quote the case reference number and be sent to:

Property Chamber
Land Registration
First-tier Tribunal
3rd Floor, 10 Alfred Place
London WC1E 7LR
DX305001 Tottenham Court Road 5

PLEASE NOTE

A If you think you need further or different directions please write to the Tribunal setting out any points you wish to make. **You must also send a copy of your letter to the other party/ies and confirm to the Tribunal that you have done so.**

B No reminders will be sent for compliance with these directions. If you do not comply with the timescales given the matter may progress to a hearing on the basis of the documents already filed.

C Further guidance on the matters referred to in this direction can be found in the explanatory leaflet previously sent to you.

Form 90: Particulars required in connection with a hearing

Case Number: REF/2013/0680

Property chamber
First-tier tribunal
Land Registration Act 2002

Particulars Required in Connection with a Hearing

Title Number: **ZYX98765**
Property: **00 Howden Bank, Derwent**
Solicitor(s):

(1) Name of Counsel (if any) representing your Client

(2) Name of Solicitor who will attend the Hearing whether or not Counsel is briefed

(3) Name, address and occupation of any witnesses to be called on your Client's behalf

	Name and Address	Occupation
(1)		
(2)		
(3)		

[continue on a separate sheet if required]

Time estimate

(4) Can you now provide a time estimate in half days indicating how long you consider the Tribunal should allow for the hearing? You may give a minimum and maximum. If the duration of the case is underestimated there may have to be an adjournment, causing inconvenience to parties and to the Tribunal. If counsel are instructed they should advise on this.

Minimum estimate . . . .

Maximum estimate . . . .

Dates to avoid

(5) Please give dates to avoid between [insert trial window]. If there are specific dates when you, your solicitor, counsel or witnesses cannot attend a hearing you must inform the office of the Tribunal now, or a hearing date will be fixed without further reference to you. If, after returning this form but before the case is given a hearing date you become aware of more dates to avoid, you should inform this office in writing immediately

You should be prepared to explain the reasons for the unsuitability of any date; blanket exclusions of long periods will not be accepted.

. . . .

. . . .

. . . .

. . . .

. . . .

. . . .

. . . .

Contact details

(6) If you do not have a legal representative, please fill in below your up to date contact details. Please continue to update us with any subsequent changes, bearing in mind we may need to contact you at short notice

Telephone . . . .

Mobile . . . .

Emai . . . .

Fax . . . .

Print name . . . .

Venue

(7) Can the case be conveniently heard in London? If not, what venue would be best? The availability of Judiciary and court facilities in London will allow an earlier date for listing.

. . . .

. . . .

Site inspection

(8) Will an inspection of the land in question be required?

☐ YES
☐ NO

Access needs

(9) If you, your representative, or any of your witnesses have any special needs, e.g if they are disabled, and require a venue or court with suitable access/facilities, please state what they are in your reply and they will be taken into consideration.

. . . .

. . . .

. . . .

. . . .

Interpreters

(10) If you or any of your witnesses require interpreters please specify below

(i) the required language and

(ii) any specific dialect

. . . .

. . . .

Please Note:

1. The Tribunal expects you to reply promptly and fully to the above questions.
2. If you do not wish to proceed with the case you should apply for a stay of proceedings, giving grounds. In the absence of a stay, the Tribunal will fix a hearing and will expect you to be ready.
3. **Please note that after a hearing date is fixed, the Tribunal will not be willing to postpone or adjourn it, even with the consent of all parties, except for the most compelling reasons (such as illness of an essential participant supported by a medical certificate, or a hearing of a court of superior jurisdiction). Any postponement application must be supported by full grounds and supporting evidence if available.**
4. The parties must keep the Tribunal informed of any prospect of settlement or withdrawal of the case. If possible, the parties should notify this office of any settlement or withdrawal no later than 2 days before the hearing to enable arrangements to be made to cancel the hearing.
5. The Tribunal hearing is a judicial hearing to decide the dispute. The Tribunal's decision is legally binding on the parties. There is, however, a right of appeal, with permission, to the Tax and Chancery Chamber of the Upper Tribunal
6. The Tribunal Procedure (First-tier Tribunal) (Property Chamber) Rules 2013 apply. Information about the Rules and other important matters can be found in the explanatory leaflet previously sent to you.
7. The Tribunal has power at any stage to direct any party to commence court proceedings.
8. If at any time parties cease to have legal representation at any time, PLEASE notify this office with their telephone contact details, bearing in mind we may need to contact you urgently.

Print name ....

Signature ....

Confirmation of Address for service

....

....

....

Form 91: Order including a direction to the Registrar

Property Chamber
Land Registration
First-tier Tribunal
3rd Floor
10 Alfred Place
London WC1E 7LR

Tel:	020 7291 7250
Fax:	020 7291 7251
Goldfax:	0870 739 4134
DX:	DX305001 Tottenham Court Road 5
Email:	landregistration@hmcts.gsi.gov.uk
Website:	www.justice.gov.uk/tribunals

Land Registry Birkenhead Office
DX 24270 Birkenhead 4

Our Ref: REF/2013/0680
5 September 2014

Dear Sir/Madam,

ZYX98765

Bea Lowater vs. Mark Highwater

00 Howden Bank, Derwent

Please find enclosed a copy of the Decision Notice of the Tribunal dated,

Please note that the matter will be held in abeyance in this office until we receive confirmation from you that the matter has been dealt with.

Yours faithfully,

John Smith

For the Tribunal

REF/2013/0680
Property Chamber, Land Registration
First-tier Tribunal
Land Registration Act 2002

IN THE MATTER OF A REFERENCE FROM HM LAND REGISTRY

BETWEEN

Bea Lowater

APPLICANT(S)

and

Mark Highwater

RESPONDENT(S)

Property Address: 00 Howden Bank, Derwent

Title Number: ZYX98765

Made By: [Name] sitting as Tribunal Judge

ORDER

IT IS ORDERED as follows:

The Chief Land Registrar is to [cancel/give effect to] the original application dated to.

Dated this

By order of The Tribunal

Form 92: Order by consent

UPON reading the letter from the Applicant's solicitors dated . . . . and the letter from the Respondent's solicitors dated . . . .

AND UPON the parties having entered into a deed dated . . . . annexed hereto whereby the Respondent has granted to the Applicant of a right of way over the above mentioned land ("the land").

BY CONSENT

1. The Land Registration division of the Property Chamber, First-tier Tribunal orders the Chief Land Registrar as follows:
   (1) to cancel the original application dated . . . . to register the Applicant as the first proprietor of the land;
   (2) to register the benefit of a legal easement granted by the deed annexed hereto as appurtenant to the Applicant's title number . . . .
2. The Applicant is to pay the Respondent £5,000 costs by 4.0 pm . . . .

6: COSTS ORDERS

Form 93: Order for costs following a summary assessment

UPON READING the schedule of costs served by the Respondent's solicitors dated . . . . and the representations of the Applicant's solicitors dated . . . .

IT IS ORDERED THAT the Applicant pays the Respondent's costs of £. . . . . . . by 4.0pm on . . . .

Form 94: Direction for a detailed assessment of costs

Case Reference: Ref/. . . . . .

Property Chamber

Land Registration

First-tier Tribunal

between:

Applicant	[A]	
	and	
Respondent	[B]	

1. The Applicants must file and serve their detailed bill of costs by 4.0pm . . . .
2. The Respondents must serve points of dispute on the bill of costs within 21 days of the service of the bill.
3. If the Respondents fail to serve points of dispute in compliance with this order the applicants may by letter, and without further notice to the respondents, request a Tribunal judge to assess the Applicants' bill of costs as drawn.
4. The Applicants may file a request for a hearing date after points of dispute have been served, but no later than . . . .
5. If a request for a hearing date is filed the matter will be listed for hearing.
6. If the Applicants wish to serve a reply, they must do so before filing a request for a hearing date.

Form 95: Application to the Tribunal to set aside a decision

(Applicant's solicitors address)

Property Chamber

Land Registration

First-tier Tribunal

Case Reference: Ref/. . . . . .

We apply on behalf of [A], the Applicant, for the Tribunal to set aside the decision of Judge [X] dated . . . . in which he directed the Registrar to cancel the Applicant's original application. The Applicant was not present at the hearing and this was a principal reason why the Respondent succeeded. It is now known that the Applicant was taken seriously ill on his way to the hearing and was unable to pass on a message as to why he was unable to attend. His oral evidence is critical and it is considered to be in the interest of justice that the decision should be set aside.

We have sent a copy of this letter to the solicitors for [B], the Respondent, and we have notified them that any objection they wish to make to this application must be provided in writing to the Tribunal.

Yours etc

Form 96: Order of the Tribunal setting a decision aside

Upon reading the letter of the Applicant's solicitors dated . . . . and the letter of the Respondent's solicitors dated . . . .

IT IS ORDERED THAT the decision of Judge [X] dated . . . . , in which he directed the Registrar to cancel the Applicant's original application, be set aside.

Form 97: Application to the Tribunal to review a decision

(Applicant's solicitors address)

Property Chamber

Land Registration

First-tier Tribunal

Case Reference: Ref/. . . . . .

We apply on behalf of [A], the Applicant, for the Tribunal to review the decision of Judge [X] dated . . . . in which he directed the Registrar to cancel the Applicant's original application, and in the light of the review to set the decision aside and direct a rehearing.

The Applicant was not represented at the hearing and this was a principal reason why the Respondent succeeded. Had the Judge had his attention drawn to the decision of the House of Lords in JA Pye (Oxford) Ltd v Graham [2003] 1 AC 419 he would not have decided that the Applicant had to show an intention to own the land he was squatting on in order to be in legal possession of it.

We have sent a copy of this letter to the solicitors for [B], the Respondent, and we have notified them that any objection they wish to make to this application must be provided in writing to the Tribunal.

Yours etc

Form 98: Application to the Tribunal for permission to appeal

Case Reference: Ref/. . . . . .

Property Chamber

Land Registration

First-tier Tribunal

between:

Applicant	[A]
	and
Respondent	[B]

The Applicant applies for permission to appeal from the decision of the Tribunal dated . . . . on the grounds that (*specify the grounds of appeal, eg* (*on a point of law*) the Judge erred in law in that . . . . *or (on the facts)* the finding that . . . . was against the weight of the evidence).

The Applicant seeks an order that . . . .

Form 99: Application to the Upper Tribunal for permission to appeal

Case Reference: Ref/. . . . . .

Tax and Chancery Chamber

Upper Tribunal

between:

Applicant	[A]
	and
Respondent	[B]

The Applicant applies for permission to appeal from the decision of the Tribunal dated . . . . on the grounds that (*specify the grounds of appeal, eg* (*on a point of law*) the Judge erred in law in that . . . . *or (on the facts)* the finding that . . . . was against the weight of the evidence).

The Applicant seeks an order that . . . .

The Applicant's address is . . . .

The Applicant's representative is . . . . and his address where documents for the Applicant may be sent or delivered is . . . .

The Application wants the application dealt with at a hearing.

There is enclosed with this application:

- The order to Land Registry by the Tribunal being challenged.
- The judgment of the Tribunal judge.
- A copy of the notice of refusal of permission to appeal from the Tribunal.

Form 100: Application to the Tribunal for a stay pending appeal

Case Reference: Ref/. . . . . .

Property Chamber

Land Registration

First-tier Tribunal

between:

Applicant	[A]
	and
Respondent	[B]

The Applicant applies for a stay of the decision of the Tribunal dated . . . . because the proposed appeal stands a real prospect of success for the reasons set out in the grounds of appeal, and if a stay is not granted any appeal, if successful, would be rendered ineffectual because (*here set out why any successful appeal would be rendered ineffectual eg* if the Respondent is registered with title to the land in dispute he would be able to make a disposition of it prior to the hearing of the appeal).

Appendix 15

NETWORK ACCESS APPEALS FROM LAND REGISTRY TO THE TRIBUNAL

Form 101: Notice of Application to appeal against a refusal to enter into a network access agreement

Form 102: Response to an appeal against a refusal to enter into a network access agreement

Form 103: Notice of Application to appeal against the termination of a network access agreement

Form 104: Response to an appeal against the termination of a network access agreement

Form 101: Notice of Application to appeal against a refusal to enter into a network access agreement

Case Reference: Appeal/. . . . .

Property Chamber

Land Registration

First-tier Tribunal

On appeal from the Chief Land Registrar

between:

Applicant	[A]
	and
Respondent	The Chief Land Registrar

Notice of Application

The appeal

1. The Applicant appeals against the decision of the Chief Land Registrar dated . . . . refusing the Applicant entry into a full network access agreement.

Names and addresses

2. The Applicant's name is [A]. His address is (*address*).
3. The Applicant's solicitors are [Y]. Their address is (*address*).
4. The address where documents for the Applicant may be delivered is (*address*).
5. The Respondent is the Chief Land Registrar. His addresses is Land Registry, Croydon Office, Trafalgar House, 1 Bedford Park Croydon CR0 2AQ.

The result the Applicant is seeking

6. The Applicant asks for the Chief Land Registrar to be directed to enter into a full network access agreement with the Applicant.

The Applicant's reasons for making the application

7. The grounds upon which the appeal should be granted in the Applicant's favour are as follows: *(set out the grounds of appeal eg)* The Chief Land Registrar was wrong to hold that the Applicant did not hold a policy of indemnity insurance which complies with the indemnity rules applicable to him. The Applicant does hold such a policy.

Statement of Truth

I believe the facts stated in this notice of application are true.

(Signature)

Date . . . .

Served by . . . .

Form 102: Response to an appeal against a refusal to enter into a network access agreement

Case Reference: Appeal/. . . . .

Property Chamber

Land Registration

First-tier Tribunal

On appeal from the Chief Land Registrar

between:

Applicant	[A]
	and
Respondent	The Chief Land Registrar

Response

Names and addresses

1. The Respondent's name is the Chief Land Registrar. His address is Land Registry, Croydon Office, Trafalgar House, 1 Bedford Park Croydon CR0 2AQ.
2. The Respondent's solicitors are [Z]. Their address is (*address*).
3. The address where documents for the Respondent may be delivered is (*address*).

The grounds on which the Respondent opposes the application

4. The grounds on which the Respondent opposes the application are as follows: *(set out the grounds eg)* The Applicant does not hold a policy of indemnity insurance which complies with the indemnity rules applicable to him. The policy relied upon has lapsed.

Statement of Truth

I believe the facts stated in this response are true.

(Signature)

Date . . . .

Served by . . . .

Form 103: Notice of Application to appeal against the termination of a network access agreement

Case Reference: Appeal/. . . . .

Property Chamber

Land Registration

First-tier Tribunal

On appeal from the Chief Land Registrar

between:

Applicant	[A]
	and
Respondent	The Chief Land Registrar

Notice of Application

The appeal

1. The Applicant appeals against the decision of the Chief Land Registrar dated . . . . terminating the full network access agreement entered into with the Applicant.

Names and addresses

2. The Applicant's name is [A]. His address is (*address*).
3. The Applicant's solicitors are [Y]. Their address is (*address*).
4. The address where documents for the Applicant may be delivered is (*address*).
5. The Respondent is the Chief Land Registrar. His addresses is Land Registry, Croydon Office, Trafalgar House, 1 Bedford Park Croydon CR0 2AQ.

The result the Applicant is seeking

6. The Applicant asks for the Chief Land Registrar to be directed not to terminate the full network access agreement entered into with the Applicant *(or)* to re-instate the full network access agreement entered into with the Applicant.

The Applicant's reasons for making the application

7. The grounds upon which the appeal should be granted in the Applicant's favour are as follows: *(set out the grounds of appeal eg)* The Chief Land Registrar was wrong to hold that there had been a serious breach of the agreement *(state reasons)*.

Statement of Truth

I believe the facts stated in this notice of application are true.

(Signature)

Date . . . .

Served by . . . .

Form 104: Response to an appeal against the termination of a network access agreement

Case Reference: Appeal/. . . . .

Property Chamber

Land Registration

First-tier Tribunal

On appeal from the Chief Land Registrar

between:

Applicant	[A]
	and
Respondent	The Chief Land Registrar

Response

Names and addresses

1. The Respondent's name is the Chief Land Registrar. His address is Land Registry, Croydon Office, Trafalgar House, 1 Bedford Park Croydon CRO 2AQ.
2. The Respondent's solicitors are [Z]. Their address is (*address*).
3. The address where documents for the Respondent may be delivered is (*address*).

The grounds on which the Respondent opposes the application

4. The grounds on which the Respondent opposes the application are as follows: (*set out the grounds eg*) The Applicant had committed a serious breach of the agreement (*state reasons*).

Statement of Truth

I believe the facts stated in this response are true.

(Signature)

Date . . . .

Served by . . . .

Appendix 16

RECTIFICATION AND SETTING ASIDE OF DOCUMENTS BY THE TRIBUNAL

Form 105: Notice of Application to rectify or set aside a document

Form 106: Sample Details in a notice of application to rectify a document

Form 107: Sample Details in a notice of application to set aside a document

Form 108: Response to an application to rectify or set aside a document

Form 109: Sample Details in a response to an application to rectify a document

Form 110: Sample Details in response to an application to set aside a document

Form 105: Notice of Application to rectify or set aside a document

Part 1 – Details of Applicant

Please fill in the contact details of the person making the application

Name	
Address	
Postcode	
Work phone no.	
Home phone no.	
Mobile phone no.	
Fax	
Email	

Part 2 – Details of Applicant's Solicitor or other representative

If applicable, please fill in the details of the applicant's solicitor

Name	
Address	
Postcode	
Phone no.	
Fax	
Email	

In the case of a lay representative (i.e. someone who is not a qualified solicitor or barrister), the Applicant's signature is required below to authorise the lay representative to act on their behalf.

Signature		Date	

Part 3 – Details of person(s) against whom an order is sought

Please enter the contact details of the person(s) against whom you are seeking an order

Name	
Address	
Postcode	
Work phone no.	
Home phone no.	
Mobile phone no.	
Fax	
Email	

Part 4 – Details of application

Please enter the details of the application, including the Land Registry Title Number.

Description/ address	
Title number	
Remedy sought	

Grounds on which application is based	

Part 5 – List of documents

Please list the documents in your possession or control which –

- are central to your case, or
- the Tribunal or any other party to the proceedings will require in order properly to understand the rectification application.

Description	Original/Copy	Date of document	Parties	Document number

[Please continue on a separate sheet if necessary]

Part 6 – List of witnesses

Please list any witnesses that you intend to call to give evidence to support your application.

Part 7 – Copy documents to include with your application

You are required to include the following with your application:

- A copy of each of the documents you have listed in Part 5
- A copy of the document to which this application relates

Part 8 – Statement of Truth

The application must be verified by a statement of truth before it can be accepted.

I believe/the Applicant believes that the facts stated in this application are true.

Signed: Date:

I am the ☐ Applicant

☐ Applicant's Representative

and my relationship to the Applicant is

Part 9 – Where to send this form

Please return the completed form and copy documents to:

HM Courts & Tribunals
Property Chamber
Land Registration Division
3rd Floor
10 Alfred Place
London WC1E 7LR

Form 106: Sample Details in a notice of application to rectify a document

DETAILS OF APPLICATION

(to be inserted in Part 4 of the application)

Remedy sought	Rectification of a transfer in Form TR1 dated . . . . made between [A] and [B] so that in panel 2 the words "and title number ABC123456" are inserted after the words "Title number ABC987654".
Grounds on which Application is Based	1. By an agreement in writing dated . . . . made between [A] and [B], [A] agreed to sell and [B] agreed to buy [A]'s premises at . . . . , which were registered under two separate title numbers, ABC123456 and ABC987654. 2. By mistake, title number ABC123456 was omitted from panel 2 in the Form TR1 executed by [A] and [B] on . . . . 3. On . . . . [B] was registered as proprietor of title number ABC987654, but [A] remains registered as proprietor of title number ABC123456. 4. [A] has refused a request made after the mistake was discovered to execute a separate transfer of title number ABC123456, and Land Registry will not alter the proprietorship register of title number ABC123456 unless and until the Form TR1 is rectified.

Form 107: Sample Details in a notice of application to set aside a document

DETAILS OF APPLICATION

(to be inserted in Part 4 of the application)

Remedy sought	The setting aside of a transfer of (*address*) ("the house") registered at HM Land Registry under title number . . . . in Form TR1 dated . . . . and made between [A] and [B].
Grounds on which Application is Based	1. [A] is now aged 87 and is [B]'s father.
	2. Following the death of [A]'s wife and [B]'s mother, [A] moved from the house to live with [B] and his family.
	3. [A] became totally dependent on [B] and his family for his care and financial advice.
	4. In 2013 [B] told [A] that he should transfer the house to [B], or he would not be able to remain living with [B] and his family. The house represented the entire capital assets owned by [A]. By transferring the house [A] has been left in a very vulnerable position.
	5. [A] has another child with whom he has good relations and to whom he had hoped to leave part of his estate.
	6. [A] receive no independent legal advice before making the transfer
	7. [A] wishes to set aside the transfer on the grounds of undue influence.

Form 108: Response to an application to rectify or set aside a document

Part 1 – Details of Respondent

Please fill in the contact details of the person making the objection

Name	
Address	
Postcode	
Work phone no.	
Home phone no.	
Mobile phone no.	
Fax	
Email	

Part 2 – Details of Respondent's Solicitor or other representative

If applicable, please fill in the details of the respondent's solicitor or other representative

Name	
Address	
Postcode	
Phone no.	
Fax	
Email	

In the case of a lay representative (i.e. someone who is not a qualified solicitor or barrister), the Respondent's signature is required below to authorise the lay representative to act on their behalf.

Signature		Date	

Part 3 – Grounds for the respondent's objection

Please enter the grounds for the objection

Part 4 – List of documents

Please list the documents in your possession or control which –

- are central to your case, or
- the tribunal or any other party to the proceedings will require in order properly to your grounds of objection.

Description	Original/Copy	Date of document	Parties	Document number

[Please continue on a separate sheet if necessary]

Part 5 – List of witnesses

Please list any witnesses that you intend to call to give evidence to support your objection.

Part 6 – Copy documents to include with your objection

You must:

- Include a copy of each of the documents you have listed in Part 4 of this form; and
- Serve on the other party/ies a copy of all the information and documents served on the Tribunal

Part 7 – Statement of Truth

The objection must be verified by a statement of truth before it can be accepted.

I believe/the Respondent believes that the facts stated in this application are true.

Signed: Date:

I am the ☐ Respondent

☐ Respondent's Representative

and my relationship to the Respondent is

Part 9 – Where to send this form

Please return the completed form and copy documents to:

HM Courts & Tribunals
Property Chamber
Land Registration Division
3rd Floor
10 Alfred Place
London WC1E 7LR

Form 109: Sample Details in a response to an application to rectify a document

GROUNDS FOR THE OBJECTION

(to be inserted in Part 4 of the objection)

Grounds on which Objection is Based	1. It is admitted that by an agreement in writing dated . . . . made between [A] and [B], [A] agreed to sell and [B] agreed to buy [A]'s premises at . . . . , which were registered under two separate title numbers, ABC123456 and ABC987654. 2. However, it was subsequently agreed on . . . . that since [B] could not raise the entire purchase price, there would only be transferred to [B] that part of the premises registered under title number ABC987654 and the purchase price would be reduced accordingly. 3. It is for this reason that no reference was made to title number ABC123456 in panel 2 in the Form TR1 executed by [A] and [B] on . . . . 4. It is admitted that [A] has refused a request made after the transfer was executed to execute a separate transfer of title number ABC123456. This is because there has been no mistake.

Form 110: Sample Details in response to an application to set aside a document

Grounds on which Objection is Based	1. It is admitted that [A] transferred the house to [B].
	2. It is denied that the transfer was induced by undue influence.
	3. [A] chose to live with [B] and his family. He made the transfer because he wanted to help with the cost of building the extension in which he lived. He felt very secure and well looked after by [B] and his family. In particular, he wanted to benefit his grandchildren.
	4. [A] was at the time of the transfer completely estranged from his other child, who failed to attend her mother's funeral without any good excuse, and who has a number of convictions for drug offences.
	5. [A] is of sound mind and was completely clear in wanting to benefit [B] and his family when he made the transfer.

Appendix 17

COURT PROCEEDINGS

Form 111: Claim Form: vacation of a unilateral notice

Form 112: Particulars of Claim: vacation of a unilateral notice

Form 113: Application Notice for summary vacation of a unilateral notice

Form 114: Witness Statement supporting an application for summary vacation of a unilateral notice

Form 115: Order for summary vacation of a unilateral notice

Form 116: Claim Form for an indemnity

Form 117: Particulars of Claim: claim for an indemnity

Form 118: Defence to claim for an indemnity pleading lack of proper care

Form 111: Claim Form: vacation of a unilateral notice

(Royal Arms)
Claim Form

In the High Court of Justice
Chancery Division
[District Registry]
Claim No HC . . . . . .
Issue date . . . . 20 . . . . . .

Claimant [A]
(address)
and
Defendant [B]
(address)

Brief Details of Claim

The Claimant's claim is for:

1. The vacation of a unilateral notice entered by the Defendant on . . . . 20. . . . . . on the charges register of title number . . . . . . (which is the title number of the property known as Whiteacre, ...) under the inherent jurisdiction of the court and/or Paragraph 2 of Schedule 4 of the Land Registration Act 2002.
2. Further or other relief.
3. Costs.

(Signature of legal representative)

Value £. . . . . . .

Defendant's name and address

Amount claimed £. . . . . . .

Court fee £. . . . . . .

Solicitor's costs £. . . . . . .

Total amount £. . . . . . .

Does, or will, your claim include any issues under the Human Rights Act 1998? Yes/No

Particulars of Claim

[Attached/To follow]

Statement of truth

[I believe *or* The Claimant believes] that the facts stated in this Claim Form are true.

Full name . . . .

[Name of the Claimant's Solicitor's Firm]

(Signature)

(claimant or claimant's solicitors)

[Position or office held . . . . *(if signing on behalf of firm or company)*]

Claimant's or Claimant's solicitor's address to which documents or payments should be sent if different from above including (if appropriate) details of DX, fax or e-mail.

The Court Office at . . . . is open between 10 am and 4.[00] pm Monday to Friday. When corresponding with the Court, please address forms or letters to the Court manager and quote the claim number.

Form 112: Particulars of Claim: vacation of a unilateral notice

In the High Court of Justice
Chancery Division
[District Registry]
Claim No HC . . . . . .

Claimant	[A]
	and
Defendant	[B]

Particulars of Claim

1. The Claimant is the sole freehold proprietor of Whiteacre,. . . . . , registered at HM Land Registry under title number. . . . . . ("the property").
2. By an agreement in writing dated . . . . 20. . . . . . ("the agreement"), a copy of which is attached, the Claimant agreed to sell the property to the Defendant for the sum of £. . . . .
3. The Defendant paid the Claimant a deposit of £. . . . .
4. Subsequently, the Defendant repudiated the agreement and the Claimant forfeited the deposit.
5. The Defendant denies that he repudiated the agreement but no longer wishes to complete and claims to have a purchaser's lien on the property for the return of the deposit.
6. On . . . . 20. . . . . . , the Defendant caused a unilateral notice to be entered in the charges register of the property ("the unilateral notice") in reliance upon the alleged purchaser's lien.
7. The Claimant now wishes to sell the property.

And the Claimant claims:

(1) under the inherent jurisdiction of the court and/or Paragraph 2 of Schedule 4 of the Land Registration Act 2002:

(i) an order that the Defendant forthwith obtain the removal of the unilateral notice; alternatively

(ii) an order that the unilateral notice be vacated;

(2) further or other relief;

(3) costs.

(Signature of legal representative)

Dated . . . . 20. . . . . .

Statement of truth

[I believe *or* The Claimant believes] that the facts stated in these Particulars of Claim are true.

Full name . . . .

[Name of the Claimant's Solicitor's Firm]

(Signature)

(claimant or claimant's solicitors)

[Position or office held . . . . *(if signing on behalf of firm or company)*]

Address for delivery of documents

(*name and address of claimant's solicitors or as the case may be*)

Form 113: Application Notice for summary vacation of a unilateral notice

In the High Court of Justice
Chancery Division
[District Registry]
Claim No HC . . . . . .
Dated . . . . 20 . . . . . .

Claimant	A. B.	
	and	
Defendant	C. D.	

Application Notice

1. (*Insert name or, if a solicitor, the name of firm*).
2. I am the [Claimant *or* Defendant *or* Solicitor *or as the case may be*].

   [(*If solicitor*): I represent . . . .]
3. I am asking the court to make the following order that the Defendant forthwith obtain the removal of the unilateral notice referred to in the claim form alternatively an order that the unilateral notice referred to in the claim form be vacated

Because

1. the Defendant is not entitled to the benefit of the unilateral notice referred to in the claim form.
2. the Claimant wishes to sell the property referred to in the claim form and deposit part of the net proceeds of sale in a joint account pending resolution of any issue relating to the purchaser's lien claimed by the Defendant or further order.
3. I have [not] attached a draft of the order I am applying for.
4. I wish to have this application dealt with [at a hearing *or* without a hearing *or* at a telephone hearing].
5. The time estimate is . . . . The time estimate is [not] agreed by all parties.
6. The details of any fixed trial date or period are . . . .
7. This hearing should be dealt with by a (*level of judge*).
8. The parties to be served are . . . .
9. I will be relying on [the attached witness statement *or* the statement of case *or* the evidence set out in the box below (*if necessary, continue on separate sheet*)].

Statement of truth

[I believe *or* The Applicant believes] that the facts stated in this section (and any continuation sheets) are true.

Signed . . . .

(*Applicant or applicant's solicitor or litigation friend*)

Full name . . . .

Name of Applicant's solicitor's firm . . . .

Position or office held (*if signing on behalf of firm or company*)

11. Signed . . . . (*applicant or applicant's solicitor or litigation friend*)

    Dated . . . . 20. . . . . .

    Position or office held . . . . (*if signing on behalf of firm or company*)

    Applicant's address to which documents about this application should be sent . . . .

    (*If applicable*) Phone no. . . . . . .

    Fax no. . . . . . .

    DX no. . . . . . .

    Ref no. . . . . . .

    E-mail address . . . .

Form 114: Witness Statement supporting an application for summary vacation of a unilateral notice

Claimant: (*initials and surname*): 1st: [A], 2: . . . . 20 . . . . . .

In the High Court of Justice
Chancery Division
[District Registry]
Claim No HC . . . . . .

Claimant	[A]
	and
Defendant	[B]

Witness Statement of [a]

I, [A] of *(state residence or workplace and occupation, or if none, description)*, the Claimant say as follows:

1. I am registered at HM Land Registry as the freehold proprietor of Whiteacre, ... ("the property") under title number . . . . I refer to official copy entries of the title marked "[A]1".

2. The Defendant has caused a unilateral notice to be entered in the charges register of the property ("the unilateral notice"). I make this witness statement in support of my application to vacate the unilateral notice. I make this witness statement from my own knowledge.

3. The property is a substantial commercial unit from which I carried on my wholesale business for many years. The Defendant was my senior manager.

4. Last year I decided to retire. Originally I had hoped to sell the business, including the property, as a going concern to the Defendant. We exchanged contracts and he paid a deposit of £. . . . .

5. Unfortunately, the Defendant's finance then fell through and he was unable to complete. I did not seek to enforce completion of the sale of the property but we both acknowledged that the contract had been repudiated and I kept the deposit. I refer to a bundle marked "[A]2" containing correspondence between our respective solicitors last year confirming this.

6. I could not find a buyer for the business as a going concern, so I wound the business down. I put the property up for sale with vacant possession.

7. The Defendant then asked me for the return of his deposit. I said this was not possible. The next thing I knew was that he had applied for the entry of a unilateral notice on the basis that he had a purchaser's lien.

8. I have found a purchaser for the property. The market is now falling. The business no longer functions and the property is empty. Substantial expenses are being incurred in respect of security and other outgoings. It is desirable that the property is sold as soon as possible.

9. Unless the unilateral notice is now vacated a sale will be prevented from taking place.

10.

I will undertake to pay a sum of £. . . . . out of the net proceeds of sale of the property into a joint account in the name of the parties' respective solicitors to abide the determination of any issue as to the return of the deposit, or until further order.

Statement of Truth

I believe that the facts stated in this Witness Statement are true.

Full name . . . .

(Signature)

Form 115: Order for summary vacation of a unilateral notice

In the High Court of Justice
Chancery Division
[District Registry]
Claim No HC . . . . . .

Before the Honourable
Mr Justice . . . .

Dated . . . . 20 . . . . . .

Claimant [A]
and
Defendant [B]

Order

Upon the application of [A] dated . . . .

and upon reading the written evidence filed

and upon hearing Counsel for the Claimant and for the Defendant

and upon the Claimant undertaking by his counsel to pay a sum of £. . . . . . . out of the net proceeds of sale of Whiteacre, ... (registered at HM Land Registry under title number . . . . . .) into a joint account in the name of the parties' respective solicitors to abide the determination of any issue as to the return of the Defendant's deposit

it is ordered:

1. that the unilateral notice registered for the benefit of the Defendant in the charges register of title number . . . . . . be vacated forthwith
2. that the Defendant pays the costs of the application assessed in the sum of £. . . . . . .

Form 116: Claim Form for an indemnity

(*Royal Arms*)
Claim Form

In the High Court of Justice
Chancery Division
[District Registry]
Claim No HC . . . . . .
Issue date . . . . 20 . . . . . .

Claimant [A]
(address)
and
Defendant [B]
(address)

Brief Details of Claim

The Claimant's claim is for:

1. A declaration pursuant to paragraph 7 of Schedule 8 of the Land Registration Act 2002 that he is entitled to an indemnity under Schedule 8 Land Registration Act 2002.
2. The determination of the amount of such indemnity.
3. Further or other relief.
4. An order that the costs and expenses reasonably incurred by the Claimant in relation to this matter may be provided for.

(Signature of legal representative)

Value £. . . . . . .

Defendant's name and address

Amount claimed £. . . . . . .

Court fee £. . . . . . .

Solicitor's costs £. . . . . . .

Total amount £. . . . . . .

Does, or will, your claim include any issues under the Human Rights Act 1998? Yes/No

Particulars of Claim

[Attached/To follow]

Statement of Truth

[I believe *or* The Claimant believes] that the facts stated in this Claim Form are true.

Full name . . . .

[Name of the Claimant's Solicitor's Firm]

(Signature)

(claimant or claimant's solicitors)

[Position or office held . . . . *(if signing on behalf of firm or company)*]

Claimant's or Claimant's solicitor's address to which documents or payments should be sent if different from above including (if appropriate) details of DX, fax or e-mail.

The Court Office at . . . . is open between 10 am and 4.[00] pm Monday to Friday. When corresponding with the Court, please address forms or letters to the Court manager and quote the claim number.

Form 117: Particulars of Claim: claim for an indemnity

[In the High Court of Justice
Chancery Division
[District Registry]
Claim No HC . . . . . .
or
In the County Court at
. . . .]
Claim No . . . . . .
Issue date . . . . . . 20. . . . . .

Claimant [A]
(address)
and
Defendant Chief Land Registrar

Particulars of Claim

1. In . . . . 20. . . . . . the Claimant wished to purchase Greenacre, ... ("the property") as an investment. Upon the advice of his then solicitor, [C], the purchase was made through the medium of an offshore company, [D] Ltd, which was registered as the proprietor of the property under title number . . . . The shares and directorship were in nominees for the Claimant.

2. Subsequently, and without the knowledge of the Claimant, [B] fraudulently allowed [D] Ltd to be struck off and incorporated a new company in the same name. That company then sold the property to [E], an innocent third party.

3. When [D] Ltd was struck off its assets vested in the Crown as bona vacantia. By a deed dated . . . . 20. . . . . . the Crown assigned its rights in the property to the Claimant.

4. As a result of the matters set out above an error or omission has occurred in the register but the register cannot be rectified.

5. The Claimant is accordingly entitled to be indemnified by the Defendant against the loss suffered pursuant to paragraph 1 (1)(b) of Schedule 8 of the Land Registration Act 2002.

6. The amount of the loss is as follows (*particularise the loss*).

And the claimant claims

(1) A declaration pursuant to paragraph 7 of Schedule 8 of the Land Registration Act 2002 that he is entitled to an indemnity under of Schedule 8 of the Land Registration Act 2002.

(2) The determination of the amount of such indemnity.

(3) Further or other relief.

(4) An order that the costs and expenses reasonably incurred by the Claimant in relation to this matter may be provided for.

(Signature of legal representative)

Statement of Truth

[I believe *or* The Claimant believes] that the facts stated in these Particulars of Claim are true.

Full name . . . .

[Name of the Claimant's Solicitor's Firm]

(Signature)

(claimant or claimant's solicitors)

[Position or office held . . . . *(if signing on behalf of firm or company)*]

Claimant's or Claimant's solicitor's address to which documents or payments should be sent if different from above including (if appropriate) details of DX, fax or e-mail.

Address for delivery of documents

(*name and address of claimant's solicitors or as the case may be*)

Form 118: Defence to claim for an indemnity pleading lack of proper care

In the High Court of Justice
Chancery Division
[District Registry]
Claim No HC . . . . . .
or
in the County Court at . . . .]
Claim No . . . . . .
Issue date . . . . 20 . . . . . .

Claimant [A]
and
Defendant Chief Land Registrar

Defence

1. Paragraphs 1–4 of the Particulars of Claim are admitted.

2. As to paragraphs 5 and 6 of the Particulars of Claim, any loss suffered by the Claimant (the amount of which the Defendant is unable to admit or deny and which the Claimant is required to prove) was caused wholly or partly as a result of his own lack of proper care.

Particulars

2.1. failing to pay any or any sufficient attention to the operation of [D] Ltd prior to its dissolution;

2.2. failing to pay any or any sufficient attention to the management of the property;

2.3. failing to act promptly once he had knowledge of the fraudulent dissolution of [D] Ltd, which knowledge predated the subsequent transfer of the property to [E].

3. Accordingly, pursuant to paragraph 5 of Schedule 8 of the Land Registration Act 2002, no indemnity is payable to the Claimant, alternatively any indemnity is to be reduced to such extent as is fair having regard to his share in the responsibility for the loss.

4. In the premises, the Claimant is not entitled to the relief claimed or any relief.

(Signature of legal representative)

Dated . . . . 20. . . . . .

Statement of Truth

[I believe *or* The Defendant believes] that the facts stated in this Defence are true.

Full name . . . .

[Name of the Defendant's Solicitor's Firm]

(Signature)

(defendant or defendant's solicitors)

[Position or office held . . . . *(if signing on behalf of firm or company)*]

Address for receiving documents

(name and address of defendant's solicitors or as the case may be).

Appendix 18

PROCEDURAL TABLE

No	Steps to be taken before the Land Registration division of the Property Chamber of the First-tier Tribunal ("the Tribunal")	Form No	The Tribunal Rules of Procedure[1] or Practice Direction[2]	The former comparableALR Rules of Procedure[3]
	A. Reference from the Registrar			
1	The Tribunal receives a reference from the Registrar and sends the parties written notice of the date when the Tribunal received the matter, the names and any known addresses of the parties to the proceedings, and which party or parties will be the Applicant or Applicants for the purposes of the proceedings and which party or parties will be the Respondent or Respondents.	38, 39, 40, 41, 42, 43, 48, 49[4]	r 28(3)	r 5(b)
	A.1. Court proceedings			
2	*If the Tribunal considers it appropriate to direct one of the parties to commence court proceedings:*			
	The Tribunal sends the parties notice inviting representations or objections to a proposed direction to commence court proceedings.	38, 39	r 37	r 6
3	Parties send the Tribunal representations or objections to a proposed direction to commence court proceedings. *Time: Within 28 days of service of the direction by the Tribunal.*			
4	*If the Tribunal decides to direct court proceedings:*			
	The Tribunal sends to the relevant party a direction to commence court proceedings.	44		
5	The relevant party sends the Tribunal notice that court proceedings have been commenced with further prescribed information. *Time: Within 14 days of the commencement of the court proceedings.*		r 38(2)(a) PD 7.1-7.3 r 38(3)	r 7(2)(a)
6	The Tribunal notifies the parties that the proceedings before it are automatically stayed pending the outcome of the court proceedings.	45	r 39(2)	r 8(2)
7	The relevant party sends the Tribunal a copy of the final order in the court proceedings.		r 38(2)(c)	r 7(2)(c)

No	Steps to be taken before the Land Registration division of the Property Chamber of the First-tier Tribunal ("the Tribunal")	Form No	The Tribunal Rules of Procedure[1] or Practice Direction[2]	The former comparableALR Rules of Procedure[3]
	Time: Within 14 days of the date that the matter before the court is finally disposed of.			
8	The Tribunal proceedings are to be regarded as stayed subject to the question of costs unless the court directs otherwise, or unless an order is necessary, in addition to the final court order, to implement the decision of the court.	47	r 39(3), (4)	r 8(3), (4)
9	*If one of the parties has already commenced or does commence court proceedings:*			
	The relevant party sends the Tribunal notice that court proceedings have been commenced with further prescribed information. *Time: Within 14 days of the commencement of the court proceedings or, if later, within 7 days of service on that party of notification of the receipt of the reference by the Tribunal.*		r 38(2)(a) PD 7.1-7.3 r 38(4)	r 10(a)
10	The Tribunal sends the parties notice inviting representations or objections to a proposed stay of the whole or part of the proceedings before it pending the outcome of the court proceedings.	40, 41, 42, 43	r 6(3)(m)	r 11
11	*If the Tribunal decides to stay the whole or part of the proceedings before it pending the outcome of the court proceedings.*			
	The Tribunal sends to the parties a direction staying the whole or part of the proceedings before it pending the outcome of the court proceedings.	46		
12	The relevant party sends the Tribunal a copy of the final order in the court proceedings. *Time: Within 14 days of the date that the matter before the court is finally disposed of.*		r 38(2)(c)	r 10(b)
	A.2. Jurisdiction retained by the Tribunal			
13	*If the Tribunal does not direct a party to commence court proceedings:*			

No	Steps to be taken before the Land Registration division of the Property Chamber of the First-tier Tribunal ("the Tribunal")	Form No	The Tribunal Rules of Procedure[1] or Practice Direction[2]	The former comparableALR Rules of Procedure[3]
	The Tribunal sends the parties a direction to serve their statements of case on the Tribunal and on the other parties[5], accompanied by copies of any documents which are important to that party's case or which the Tribunal or any other party will require in order properly to understand that party's case, and a list of those documents.	48, 49	rr 28(4), 30(1)	r 12
14	Applicant serves statement of case on the Tribunal and the other parties, accompanied by copies of any documents which are important to his case or which the Tribunal or any other party will require in order properly to understand his case, and a list of those documents. *Time: Within 28 days of service of the direction by the Tribunal.*	50, 53, 55, 57, 59, 61, 63, 65, 67 52	r 28(4) PD 3.1-3.2 r 27(3)	rr 12, 14, 47
15	Respondent serves statement of case on the Tribunal and the other parties, accompanied by copies of any documents which are important to his case or which the Tribunal or any other party will require in order properly to understand his case, and a list of those documents. *Time: Within 28 days of service of the Applicant's statement of case.*	51, 54, 56, 58, 60, 62, 64, 66, 68	r 30(1) PD 4.1-4.2 r 30(1)(c)	rr 13, 14, 47
	B. Application to rectify or set aside a document			
16	Applicant sends the Tribunal a notice of application containing the prescribed information, accompanied by copies of any documents which are important to his case or which the Tribunal or any other party will require in order properly to understand his case, a list of those documents, and a copy of the instrument to be rectified or set aside.	105, 106, 107	r 26(1), (2) PD 2.1-2.3	r 16(1)
17	The Tribunal provides a copy of the application and any accompanying documents to the Respondent.		r 29(1), (8)	r 17(2)
18	Respondent sends the Tribunal a response containing the prescribed information, accompanied by copies of any documents which are important to his case or which the Tribunal or any other party will require in order properly to understand his case, and a list of those documents.	108, 109, 110	r 30(3), (4)	r 18

No	Steps to be taken before the Land Registration division of the Property Chamber of the First-tier Tribunal ("the Tribunal")	Form No	The Tribunal Rules of Procedure[1] or Practice Direction[2]	The former comparableALR Rules of Procedure[3]
	Time: Within 28 days of service of the Applicant's application.		r 29(8)	
	C. Interim directions and applications			
19	*If the Tribunal considers the matter suitable for mediation.*			
	The Tribunal sends out a letter proposing mediation, and, where appropriate, a mediation agreement. *Time: After both parties have served their statements of case (or in the case of an application to rectify or set aside a document) after the Respondent has served a response.*	83, 84		
20	*If the Tribunal does not consider the matter suitable for mediation.*			
	The Tribunal sends the parties general directions providing for the exchange of witness statements, documentary evidence, lists of issues, chronologies and skeleton arguments, and the preparation of trial bundles. *Time: After both parties have served their statements of case.*	89	rr 6(3)(d), (3)(k), 18(1)(g)(ii), (2)	rr 20, 26, 27
21	The Tribunal sends the parties notice requiring listing information. *Time: After both parties have served their statements of case.*	90	r 6(3)(f), (3)(l)	
22	Parties send the Tribunal listing information. *Time: Within 42 days of service of the notice by the Tribunal.*	90		
23	The Tribunal may either on the application of a party or on its own accord make directions including, but not limited to, the following:		r 6(2)	r 22
	(1) consolidation;		r 6(3)(b)	r 22
	(2) intention to appear and call witnesses;		r 6(3)(f)	r 23
	(3) addition and substitution of parties;		r 10	r 24
	(4) further information;		r 6(3)(d)	r 25
	(5) provision of witness statements;		r 18(1)(g)	r 26
	(6) disclosure and inspection of documents;		r 18(1)(a), (2)	r 27
	(7) requirement to attend to give evidence or produce a document;	79, 80, 81, 82	r 20	r 28
	(8) time estimates;		r 6(3)(l)	r 29
	(9) site inspections;		r 21 PD 6.1-6.5	r 30
	(10) preliminary issues;		r 6(3)(g)	r 31

No	Steps to be taken before the Land Registration division of the Property Chamber of the First-tier Tribunal ("the Tribunal")	Form No	The Tribunal Rules of Procedure[1] or Practice Direction[2]	The former comparableALR Rules of Procedure[3]
	(11) adjournment or postponement of a hearing;		r 6(3)(j)	r 53
	(12) stay of proceedings;		r 6(3)(m)	r 53
	(13) amendment, suspension or setting aside of directions;		r 6(2)	rr 50, 54
	(14) extensions or shortening of time;	69, 70	r 6(3)(a)	r 58
	(15) expert evidence;	77, 78	rr 18(1)(e), 19 PD 5.1-5.2	r 49
	(16) summary disposal;	71, 72, 73	r 9(3)(e), (7) PD 8.1-8.11	r 32A
	(17) amendment of documents;		r 6(3)(c)	
	(18) holding a case management hearing;		r 6(3)(h)	
	(19) transferring proceedings to another court if that other court has jurisdiction in relation to the proceedings, and the court is the more appropriate forum;		r 6(3)(n)	
	(20) automatically striking out the proceedings or the appropriate part of them (in the case of an Applicant) or barring the Respondent from taking further part in the proceedings (in the case of a Respondent) for failure to comply with a direction that stated that failure would lead to such a sanction;	87	r 9(1), (7)	
	(21) striking out the proceedings if the Tribunal does not have jurisdiction;		r 9(2)	
	(22) striking out the proceedings or the appropriate part of them (in the case of an Applicant) or barring the Respondent from taking further part in the proceedings (in the case of a Respondent):			
	(i) for failure to comply with a direction that stated that failure could lead to such a sanction;	88	r 9(3)(a)	
	(ii) for failure to co-operate with the Tribunal such that the Tribunal cannot deal with the proceedings fairly and justly;		r 9(3)(b)	
	(iii) if the proceedings are between the same parties and arise out of facts which are similar or substantially the same as those contained in proceedings which have been decided by the Tribunal;		r 9(3)(c)	

No	Steps to be taken before the Land Registration division of the Property Chamber of the First-tier Tribunal ("the Tribunal")	Form No	The Tribunal Rules of Procedure[1] or Practice Direction[2]	The former comparableALR Rules of Procedure[3]
	(iv) if the proceedings are or are being conducted in a manner which is frivolous, vexatious or an abuse of the process of the Tribunal.		r 9(3)(d)	
	(23) security for costs;	74, 75, 76	r 12	
	(24) permission to withdraw;	85, 86	r 22	
	(25) lead cases.		r 23	
24	*If the Tribunal imposes a sanction where a party has failed to comply with a direction:*			
	Where the defaulting party made the original application, the Tribunal may direct the Registrar to cancel the original application;		r 8(3)(a)	r 55(2)
	Where the defaulting party objected to the original application, the Tribunal may direct the Registrar to give effect to the original application.		r 8(3)(b)	r 55(3)
	D. Decision without a hearing			
25	*If the Tribunal:* *(i) has given each party not less than 28 days' notice of its intention to dispose of the proceedings without a hearing and no objection has been received; or* *(ii) wishes to strike out the Applicant's case or debar the Respondent from taking further part in the proceedings pursuant to r 9(2) or (3); or* *(iii) wishes to make a decision implementing a court order pursuant to r 39(4):*		r 31(2), (3) r 31(4) r 31(4)	r 33
	The Tribunal provides to the parties as soon as reasonably practicable after making the decision: (i) a decision notice stating the Tribunal's decision, which may include a direction to the Registrar: (a) to give effect to the original application in whole or in part, as if the objection to that original application had not been made; or (b) to cancel the original application in whole or in part; (c) including a condition that a specified entry be made on the register of any title affected;	91	r 36(2)(a) r 40(2)(a) r 40(2)(b) r 40(3)(a)	rr 39(2), 40

No	Steps to be taken before the Land Registration division of the Property Chamber of the First-tier Tribunal ("the Tribunal")	Form No	The Tribunal Rules of Procedure[1] or Practice Direction[2]	The former comparableALR Rules of Procedure[3]
	(d) to reject any future application of a specified kind by a party to the proceedings, either unconditionally or unless that party satisfies specified conditions;		r 40(3)(b)	
	(ii) written reasons for the decision;		r 36(2)(b)	
	(iii) notification of any right of appeal against the decision and the time within which, and manner in which, such right of appeal may be exercised.		r 36(2)(c)	
	E. Decision with a hearing			
26	The Tribunal sends parties notice of the date, time and location of the hearing. *Time: Not later than 14 days before the hearing, unless with the parties' consent or in urgent or exceptional circumstances.*		r 32	r 34
27	Applicant (unless Respondent has been ordered to do so) sends to the Tribunal and other parties copy of the trial bundle. *Time: Not later than 14 days before the hearing.*			
28	Parties send to the Tribunal and exchange copies of lists of issues, chronologies, skeleton arguments and authorities. *Time: Not later than 7 days before the hearing.*			
29	At the hearing, which is in public[6], each party gives evidence, calls witnesses, questions witnesses and addresses the Tribunal. A party may conduct his case himself or be represented by counsel, solicitor, or a representative who is not legally qualified but who has been appointed to represent that party and whose name and address has been delivered in writing to the Tribunal and each other party.		r 14(1), (2)	r 35
	Alternatively, a party may be accompanied by another person whose name and address has not been notified, but who, with the permission of the Tribunal, may act as a representative or otherwise assist in presenting the party's case at the hearing.		r 14 (5)	
30	*If a party fails to appear or be represented:*			
	The Tribunal may proceed with the hearing if:		r 34	r 38

No	Steps to be taken before the Land Registration division of the Property Chamber of the First-tier Tribunal ("the Tribunal")	Form No	The Tribunal Rules of Procedure[1] or Practice Direction[2]	The former comparableALR Rules of Procedure[3]
	(i) it is satisfied that the party has been notified of the hearing or that reasonable steps have been taken to notify the party of the hearing; and (ii) considers that it is in the interests of justice to proceed with the hearing.			
31	The Tribunal decides case and gives substantive decision either orally or (usually) reserves substantive decision for later date.		r 36(1)	r 39(1)
32	The Tribunal provides to the parties as soon as reasonably practicable after making the decision:			rr 39(2), 40
	(i) a decision notice stating the Tribunal's decision, which may include a direction to the Registrar:	91	r 36(2)(a)	
	(a) to give effect to the original application in whole or in part, as if the objection to that original application had not been made; or		r 40(2)(a)	
	(b) to cancel the original application in whole or in part;		r 40(2)(b)	
	(c) including a condition that a specified entry be made on the register of any title affected;		r 40(3)(a)	
	(d) to reject any future application of a specified kind by a party to the proceedings, either unconditionally or unless that party satisfies specified conditions;		r 40(3)(b)	
	(ii) written reasons for the decision;		r 36(2)(b)	
	(iii) notification of any right of appeal against the decision and the time within which, and manner in which, such right of appeal may be exercised.		r 36(2)(c)	
	F. Costs			
33	The Tribunal sends to parties notice inviting them to make submissions on costs and, if it is to be a summary assessment, to submit schedule of costs and objections.		r 13(1)(c) PD 9.1	
34	Receiving party sends to the Tribunal and paying party submissions on costs and schedule of costs.		r 13(4)	
	Time: Within 28 days after the date on which the Tribunal sends a decision notice recording the decision which finally disposes of all issues in the proceedings or notice of consent to a withdrawal under r 22, which ends the proceedings.		r 13(5)	

No	Steps to be taken before the Land Registration division of the Property Chamber of the First-tier Tribunal ("the Tribunal")	Form No	The Tribunal Rules of Procedure[1] or Practice Direction[2]	The former comparableALR Rules of Procedure[3]
35	Paying party sends to the Tribunal and receiving party submissions on costs and objections. *Time: Within 14 days of service of the receiving party's submissions and schedule of costs.*		r 13(6)	
36	If it is to be a summary assessment, the Tribunal assesses costs and sends to the parties a written costs order.	93	r 13(7)(a) PD 9.2-9.3	r 42(5), (6)
37	If it is to be a detailed assessment, receiving party sends to the Tribunal and paying party detailed bill of costs. *Time: Within 21 days of direction for a detailed assessment.*	94	r 13(7)(c), (8) PD 9.2-9.4	
38	Paying party sends to the Tribunal and receiving party points of dispute. *Time: Within 21 days of the service of the bill.*	94		
39	If the paying party fails to serve points of dispute, the receiving party may by letter, and without further notice, request the Tribunal to assess the receiving party's bill of costs as drawn.	94		
40	If the receiving party wishes to serve a reply, he must do so before filing a request for a hearing date.	94		
41	The receiving party files a request for a hearing date after points of dispute have been served.	94		
42	If a request for a hearing date is filed the matter will be reserved to a judge who is also a deputy costs judge who will decide whether or not to hold an oral hearing.			
43	The Tribunal carries out a detailed assessment and sends to the parties a written costs order.			
	G. Setting aside, reviews and appeals			
44	A party may apply to set aside a decision on the grounds that it is in the interests of justice to do so, and there has been a procedural irregularity. *Time: Within 28 days after the date on which the Tribunal sent to the party notice of the decision, or notice of the reasons for the decision, if later.*	95, 96	r 51(1), (2) r 51(3)	
45	A person aggrieved by a decision of the Tribunal may appeal to the Tax and Chancery Chamber of the Upper Tribunal.[7]			

No	Steps to be taken before the Land Registration division of the Property Chamber of the First-tier Tribunal ("the Tribunal")	Form No	The Tribunal Rules of Procedure[1] or Practice Direction[2]	The former comparableALR Rules of Procedure[3]
46	A party wishing to appeal to the Tax and Chancery Chamber of the Upper Tribunal must obtain permission to appeal.[8] An application must be made in the first instance to the Tribunal and, if unsuccessful, to the Tax and Chancery Chamber of the Upper Tribunal.	98, 99	rr 52, 53	r 45(4)
47	On receiving an application for permission to appeal the Tribunal must first consider whether to review the decision.	97	rr 53, 55	
48	A party who wishes to apply to the Tribunal for a stay pending an appeal must apply at the same time as applying for permission to appeal.	100	r 54(1)	r 45(2)

1 The Tribunal Rules of Procedure are contained in The Tribunal Procedure (First-tier Tribunal) (Property Chamber) Rules 2013.

2 Practice Directions Property Chamber, First-tier Tribunal Land Registration approved by Sir Jeremy Sullivan on 30 July 2013.

3 The former rules of the Adjudicator to HM Land Registry, which were contained in the Adjudicator to HM Land Registry (Practice and Procedure) Rules 2003 and amended by the Adjudicator to HM Land Registry (Practice and Procedure) (Amendment) Rules 2008, are set out for comparison purposes.

4 The exact wording of the form will depend on whether (1) jurisdiction is being retained, or (2) court proceedings are contemplated by the Tribunal or one of the parties, or (3) court proceedings are already in existence.

5 Although r 29(1) requires the Tribunal to provide a copy of the Applicant's statement of case to the Respondent, the Tribunal is entitled under rule 16(2)(b) to require the Applicant to discharge that duty on its behalf. The Respondent must serve his statement of case on both the Tribunal and the Applicant: r 30(6).

6 Hearings are in public, except where the Tribunal directs that the hearing is to be held in private: r 33(1), (2).

7 The right to appeal on the facts is given by the Land Registration Act 2002, s 111 (1), as amended. The right to appeal on a point of law is given by the Tribunals, Courts and Enforcement Act 2007, s 11(1), (2).

8 Land Registration Act 2002, s 111 (2C), as amended. Tribunals, Courts and Enforcement Act 2007, s 11(1), (2).

Index

All references are to paragraph numbers.